HUME'S EPISTEMOLOGY
AND METAPHYSICS

"This is an excellent book. Dicker concentrates squarely on Hume's central arguments, usefully assessing them as contributions to contemporary philosophical debates. He also pays scrupulous attention to the texts, taking account of recent Hume scholarship but remaining attentive to the needs of inexperienced students."

Professor Gary Iseminger
Carleton College

Many of the current philosophical problems over meaning, knowledge, causality, and sense perception can be traced to David Hume's writings in his *Treatise of Human Nature* and *Enquiry Concerning Human Understanding.*

Hume's Epistemology and Metaphysics: An Introduction provides a clear, concise, and accessible guide to the key themes in Hume's philosophy. Issues discussed include Hume's argument that there can be no purely rational demonstration of anything's existence, so that God cannot be proven to exist; that all our scientific knowledge rests on inferences from past experiences that cannot be rationally justified; and that we cannot talk of causality apart from natural science. Georges Dicker reveals the contemporary significance of these problems by clearly and sharply analyzing Hume's reasoning. Throughout, Hume's arguments are also placed against a historical background providing us with essential insight into his criticisms of rationalism and his central place as a founder of empiricism.

Key features of the book also include discussion of Kant's responses to Hume and consideration of more recent responses to Hume's philosophy, allowing the full significance of his thought for contemporary philosophy to emerge.

Accessible to anyone coming to Hume's philosophy for the first time, *Hume's Epistemology and Metaphysics: An Introduction* provides an ideal guide to the main themes in his writing.

Georges Dicker is Professor of Philosophy and Chair of the Philosophy Department at the State University of New York College at Brockport. He is author of *Descartes: An Analytical and Historical Introduction* (1993), *Perceptual Knowledge: An Analytical and Historical Study* (1980), and *Dewey's Theory of Knowing* (1976).

HUME'S EPISTEMOLOGY AND METAPHYSICS

An Introduction

Georges Dicker

London and New York

First published 1998
by Routledge
11 New Fetter Lane, London EC4P 4EE

Simultaneously published in the USA and Canada
by Routledge
29 West 35th Street, New York, NY 10001

Typeset in Baskerville by J&L Composition Ltd, Filey, North Yorkshire
Printed and bound in Great Britain by
Creative Print and Design (Wales), Ebbw Vale

British Library Cataloguing in Publication Data
A catalogue record for this book is available from the British Library

Library of Congress Cataloging in Publication Data
Dicker, Georges, 1942–
Hume's epistemology and metaphysics: an introduction/
Georges Dicker.
p.   cm.
Includes bibliographical references and index.
ISBN 0–415–16318–8 (hb: alk. paper) (paper: alk. paper)
1. Hume, David, 1711–1776 – Contributions in theory of knowledge.
2. Hume, David, 1711–1776 – Contributions in metaphysics.
3. Knowledge, Theory of – History – 18th century.
4. Metaphysics – History – 18th century.
I. Title.
B1499.K7D53   1998
192–dc21   97–34891
CIP

ISBN 0–415–16318–8 (hbk)
ISBN 0–415–16319–6 (pbk)

To Marjorie

CONTENTS

Preface	ix
Acknowledgments	xi
Note on References and Abbreviations	xii

Introduction   1

1 Hume's theory of meaning and its implications   **5**

1 Hume's theory of impressions and ideas and meaning-empiricism 5
2 Application of Hume's test for meaning to "substance" and "self" 15
3 An alternative to the substance theory 21
4 Critique of Hume's bundle theory of the self 31

2 Hume's theory of knowledge (I): "Hume's Fork"   **35**

1 Introduction 35
2 "Relations of ideas" and "matters of fact" 35
3 A modernized version of Hume's Fork 41
4 A critique of the modernized "Fork" 49
5 Hume's denials concerning matters of fact 55

3 Hume's theory of knowledge (II): causal reasoning and the problem of induction   **61**

1 Introduction 61
2 Hume's critique of causal reasoning 62
3 The problem of induction 73
4 Hume's psychological explanation of induction 89
5 Need induction be justified? 91

4 Hume's theory of causality   99

1 Introduction 99
2 Necessary connection 100
3 Hume's analysis of causation 110
4 The regularity theory: some objections and replies 116

5 Hume's critique of the causal principle   133

1 Introduction 133
2 Why the causal principle is neither self-evident nor demonstrable 134
3 Stroud's critique of Hume's argument 140
4 Kant's "answer" to Hume 143

6 The belief in the existence of body   154

1 Introduction 154
2 Three assumptions behind Hume's account 154
3 The general nature of Hume's account 161
4 The nature and origin of the belief in the existence of body 163
5 The "vulgar system" and the "philosophical system" 174
6 A criticism of Hume's account 178
7 A contemporary perspective on Hume's account 183
8 A Kantian response to scepticism regarding the senses 190

Notes   195
Bibliography   207
Index   211

PREFACE

The purpose of this book is to present and assess David Hume's most influential contributions to epistemology and metaphysics in a manner that does not presuppose familiarity with Hume on the reader's part and yet is sufficiently deep and rigorous to interest more advanced students of his thought. Hume's influence on contemporary epistemology and metaphysics is second to none; probably no other philosopher of the "modern" period continues to have as much influence on the views actually held by contemporary analytic philosophers as does David Hume. Hume is famous, for example, for arguing that meaningful words must have an empirical reference, so that "substance underlying all of a thing's perceivable qualities" and "immaterial soul" lack meaning; that there can be no purely rational demonstration of anything's existence, so that God cannot be proved to exist; that all of our knowledge of scientific laws rests on inferences from experience that are not susceptible of any rational justification; that every claim of the type "A caused B" involves at least one law of nature, so that it is nonsense to talk of cause and effect or causal explanation outside the context of natural science; that the principle that every beginning of existence must have a cause of existence cannot be known *a priori*; that our belief in objects existing independently of our perceptions of them is highly problematic. Such Humean tenets continue to define the broad parameters of much contemporary philosophy, and must be reckoned with by any thinker who wishes to go outside them.

Hume offers his arguments on these and related matters in several key sections of his *A Treatise of Human Nature*, first published in 1739–40, and *An Enquiry Concerning Human Understanding*, published in 1748; those sections are doubtless the Humean texts most frequently encountered by students. One of the chief aims of this book is to analyze and evaluate the arguments contained in those sections, while providing some of the historical background against which they are to be understood. This is worth doing not only because of the intrinsic interest and powerful influence of Hume's arguments, but also because of Hume's manner of exposition. Each work is written in such a way that the reader may be hard pressed to break down Hume's arguments into steps – to analyze them in ways commended by the methods of present-day analytical philosophy. In the youthful *Treatise*, Hume's style is tortuous and complex; in the mature *Enquiry*, it is so elegant and graceful that the hard muscle and sinews of Hume's thinking may not be apparent. Throughout this book, therefore, one of my chief aims is to present Hume's arguments in a manner which is both sufficiently rigorous to bring out their power and yet sufficiently perspicuous to be accessible to non-specialists in the field. I attempt also to provide informed and reasoned assessments of these arguments; in so doing I discuss some Kantian and several contemporary responses to Hume.

I should also indicate what this book does not attempt to do. The field of Hume studies is today one of the most active in philosophical scholarship, and in the past two decades there have appeared several excellent books proposing new interpretations of Hume's overall system of thought. Some major controversies have emerged: for example whether Hume should be seen as an empiricist and sceptic or as a constructive naturalist. Some novel proposals have been made: for example that Hume believed in objective necessary connections between causes and effects. Although I allude to some of these rival interpretations, that is not my main focus in this book. Rather, this book attempts to explain and assess what I take to be Hume's most *influential* ideas in epistemology and metaphysics. For, perhaps more than any other philosopher of the great age of philosophy that comprised the seventeenth and eighteenth centuries, Hume is a "contemporary" philosopher: his epistemological and metaphysical ideas continue to permeate the current philosophical landscape. It is fitting, then, that an introduction to his epistemology and metaphysics not only guides the reader through the key texts where these ideas are expounded, but also treats them as a living part of ongoing philosophical inquiry.

G. D.
Brockport, New York
July 1997

ACKNOWLEDGMENTS

I am grateful to several anonymous readers for detailed comments on earlier drafts of this book, which led me to make very significant revisions. I am grateful also to the students in my distance-learning Hume–Kant seminar, taught in spring 1997 at SUNY Brockport and transmitted via interactive television to SUNY Cortland and SUNY Fredonia, and to my friend Professor Kenneth G. Lucey, who did me the honor of auditing the course at Fredonia, for comments that led me to clarify several passages. I am solely responsible, of course, for whatever shortcomings remain.

I thank Robert J. McLean, Dean of the School of Letters and Sciences at SUNY Brockport, for support of a course release that enabled me to work on revisions of the manuscript during the Spring 1997 semester.

I am deeply grateful to my companion and colleague Marjorie Stewart for her encouragement and support in all aspects of this book's production.

All quotations of David Hume are from the following editions:

A Treatise of Human Nature, ed. L. A. Selby-Bigge and P. H. Nidditch, Oxford: Oxford University Press, 2nd edn, 1978.

Enquiries Concerning Human Understanding and Concerning the Principles of Morals, ed. L. A. Selby-Bigge and P. H. Nidditch, Oxford: Oxford University Press, 3rd edn, 1975.

All quotations of these two works are included by permission of Oxford University Press. I am grateful to Oxford University Press for permission to reprint this material.

Chapter 2 is based, in part, on my article, "Hume's Fork Revisited," *History of Philosophy Quarterly* 8(4): 327–42. I am grateful to the Editor of *HPQ* for permission to use this material.

NOTE ON REFERENCES
AND ABBREVIATIONS

References to the works of David Hume are given in parentheses in the text; references to other authors' works are given according to the Harvard System (author's surname followed by the year of publication of the text cited, and page number(s). Full bibliographical information is given in the Bibliography.

In the references to and extracts from Hume's *A Treatise of Human Nature*, I have cited the 1978 edition, published by Oxford University Press, and edited by L. A. Selby-Bigge and P. H. Nidditch. References to this work are abbreviated as "T" and are given by page number; for example the reference "(T:188)" is to page 188 of the *Treatise*. Occasionally the citation may be "T:*Abstract*" or simply "*Abstract*," to indicate that the reference is to Hume's *Abstract* of the *Treatise*, which is printed on pages 645–62 of the Selby-Bigge–Nidditch edition.

In the references to and extracts from Hume's *An Enquiry Concerning Human Understanding*, I have cited three editions: the 1975 (Oxford University Press) edition, edited by Selby-Bigge and Nidditch; the 1993 (Hackett Publishing Company) edition, edited by Eric Steinberg; and the 1988 (Open Court Publishing Company) edition, edited by Anthony Flew. The quotations follow the Selby-Bigge–P. H. Nidditch edition; the punctuation and spelling in the other editions may occasionally vary from it. The references to the *Enquiry* cite all three of these editions. The Selby-Bigge–Nidditch edition is cited as "E"; the Steinberg edition is cited as "S"; the Flew edition is cited as "F". For example, the reference "(E:25; S:15; F:71)" is to page 25 in the Selby-Bigge–P. H. Nidditch edition; and the passage cited or quoted may also be found on page 15 of the Steinberg edition and on page 71 of the Flew edition.

The Steinberg and the Flew editions of the *Enquiry* also include Hume's *Abstract of A Treatise of Human Nature*, and the Flew edition includes Section 3 of Book I part iii (on "Why a cause is always necessary") of the *Treatise* as well. Accordingly, when citing the *Abstract* or that section of the *Treatise*, references to these editions are given as well, using "S" followed by the page number for Steinberg and "F" followed by the page number for Flew.

INTRODUCTION

David Hume (1711–76) is chronologically the last, and generally regarded as the most powerful, of the three greatest British Empiricist philosophers, John Locke, George Berkeley, and David Hume. To introduce Hume's philosophy, a brief survey is made of some of the main intellectual currents that influenced his thought.

First, Hume reacted *against* the metaphysical systems of the Rationalist philosophers, the most important of whom are Descartes, Spinoza, and Leibniz. Each of these thinkers started from certain self-evident principles and attempted to deduce from these principles a complete system of knowledge. Following this method, however, they arrived at radically different conclusions. Thus Descartes, starting from his famous "I am thinking, therefore I exist" and a small number of other principles that he found to be self-evident – such as the principle that a cause must contain as much perfection as its effect, and the principle that whatever things we can conceive clearly and distinctly to exist separately from each other can really exist separately from each other – tried to demonstrate that God exists and that the universe God created consists of two completely different kinds of substance: minds, which are totally nonphysical and whose only properties are their thoughts or conscious states; and matter, which is totally incapable of thought or consciousness, and whose defining property is extension (i.e. three-dimensionality). But Spinoza, starting from various "axioms," "definitions," and "postulates" that he took to be self-evident, arrived at the conclusion that the whole universe consists of only one infinite substance which is both conscious and three-dimensional, which may be called either "God" or "Nature" depending on one's point of view, and of which individual persons and things are only finite aspects or "modes." Finally Leibniz, starting from several principles with names like the "Principle of Sufficient Reason," the "Principle of Perfection," and "the Identity of Indiscernibles," arrived at the conclusion that the universe consists of an infinite number of nonmaterial substances, called "monads," which are differentiated only by the perceptions they have, and that extension is not a real property of those monads but one that they only appear to have.

What characterized each of these Rationalist philosophers, then, was this: they speculated boldly and confidently about the ultimate nature of reality, and their confidence in the conclusions they reached stemmed from their conviction that those conclusions were rigorously deduced from self-evident premises. Hume, however, saw that by following essentially the same method of deducing conclusions from supposedly self-evident premises these mighty thinkers had arrived at drastically different, mutually incompatible, results. His reaction, as we shall see later, was to criticize the theory of knowledge that underlies the Rationalists' method, and to propose a very different theory of knowledge to replace it.

A second, more positive, influence on Hume was Isaac Newton, the founder of classical physics whom Hume admired and even revered. Newton did not develop his physics by arguing deductively from supposedly self-evident premises. Rather, he confined himself to hypotheses that could be experimentally tested, thereby shedding enormous light on the workings of nature. Hume, as we shall see, sought to adapt Newton's experimental method to his own inquiries.

A third influence on Hume was John Locke, the founder of the British Empiricist school. Three aspects of Locke's thought are especially relevant. The first is what we may call Locke's "epistemological turn." This is the view that before tackling big questions about the nature of reality – such as the existence and nature of God, or the basic properties of matter, or the immortality of the soul – we need to investigate the human mind with a view to ascertaining both its powers and its limitations, so that we are enabled to determine what we may realistically hope to know. The second influential aspect is what Locke called the "Way of Ideas." This is the view, derived mainly from Descartes, that what each human knows best and with certainty is his or her own conscious states or "ideas," and that all the rest of one's knowledge must in some fashion be based upon these ideas. Thus, for example, at this moment you presumably know that there are several physical objects close to you, such as the book you are reading, the desk or table at which you may be sitting, the windows and walls of the room in which you are, and so forth. According to the way-of-ideas doctrine, this knowledge must be based on certain conscious states you are in, such as visual experiences of color and shape and tactile sensations of hardness or solidity. Furthermore, since you could have similar experiences in a vivid dream or hallucination, the manner in which your knowledge is based on those conscious states is problematic and indeed calls for an explanation or even for a theory. The third aspect is Locke's famous denial of innate ideas. Briefly, an innate idea would be one that had not been acquired or extrapolated from any experience one had, because the idea was somehow possessed by or built into the mind from birth. Hume, as we shall see, agrees with Locke that all of our ideas must originate in experience.

As we shall see later, there were still other intellectual currents that influenced Hume's thinking, notably philosophical scepticism.[1] But against the background of the three factors just surveyed, it is possible to describe in general terms Hume's basic "agenda" or program.[2] Hume sought to adapt the experimental method of Newton to the investigation of the powers and principles of the human mind launched by Locke. Here I have said "adapt" rather than "adopt," because Hume did not think that physical experiments could be performed on the mind. Rather, he thought that the mind's workings are accessible to introspection, and that by careful introspective study of one's own conscious states, one would be able to discover general principles that apply to those states; much as by carefully studying the operations of physical objects Newton had discovered general principles applying to them, such as the laws of motion and gravitation. The result of this essentially introspective study of the mind was to be a truly empirical science of human nature. Hume would then use the findings of this new science of human nature, negatively, to criticize the overly ambitious theories of rationalist metaphysicians. He would also use his findings, positively, to offer his own accounts of the origin of certain basic human beliefs: for example, the belief in causal connections between events; the belief in the existence of objects independently of our perceptions of them; and the belief in the existence of a continuing mind or self.

Hume's first philosophical work was his *A Treatise of Human Nature*, an enormous book of over 600 pages that he published anonymously when he was only 28 years old, after several years of intense labor that left him drained and in ill health. Probably because of its difficult style, great length, and revolutionary content, the *Treatise* was initially a failure. As Hume put it in his brief autobiography "My own Life" (1993: 351–6): "Never literary attempt was more unfortunate than my *Treatise of Human Nature*. It fell dead-born from the press, without reaching such distinction as even to excite a murmur among the zealots" (p. 352).

Hume recovered from his disappointment, and wrote two further works in which he presented many of the *Treatise*'s themes in a more accessible literary manner: *An Enquiry Concerning Human Understanding* and *An Enquiry Concerning the Principles of Morals*. Although the two *Enquiries* were better received than had been the *Treatise*, Hume's fame during his own lifetime was based primarily on his non-philosophical writings. These include a six-volume history of England and several political and literary essays. Hume's last philosophical work was his *Dialogues Concerning Natural Religion*, a classic critique of arguments for the existence of God that was published only after his death.

Our focus will be primarily on certain key sections of *An Enquiry Concerning Human Understanding* (hereafter called simply "the *Enquiry*") and of Book I of the *Treatise*. Occasionally I shall refer also to a short work called *An Abstract of a Book Lately Published, Entitled, A Treatise of Human Nature, &c* (hereafter called simply "*Abstract*"). This is actually a book review of the *Treatise*, written anonymously by Hume himself, which contains clear brief expositions of several of the points on which our attention will focus.

3

1

HUME'S THEORY OF MEANING
AND ITS IMPLICATIONS

1 Hume's theory of impressions and ideas and meaning-empiricism

Both the *Treatise* and the *Enquiry* open, after introductory sections, with almost identically titled chapters: "Of the Origin of our Ideas" and "Of the Origin of Ideas", respectively. As the titles indicate, the purpose of these sections is to explain how we acquire our ideas. Hume's basic thesis, which is a cornerstone of his empiricism and which had already been enunciated by Locke in his *Essay Concerning Human Understanding*, is that we acquire all of our ideas from experience, where "experience" is taken as including both sense perception and the introspective awareness of our own states of mind. From this starting point, Hume will ultimately derive momentous consequences.

In setting forth his basic thesis, Hume uses three special terms: "perception," "impression," and "idea." By a *perception*, Hume means any conscious state whatsoever. Hume divides perceptions into two classes: impressions and ideas. By an *impression*, he means any experience, such as a visual experience, an auditory experience, or a pain. Hume further subdivides impressions into two classes: sense experiences, such as visual, tactual, auditory, gustatory, olfactory, and kinesthetic experiences; and "inner" or introspectible experiences, such as joy, sadness, anger, and desire. In the *Enquiry*, he refers to impressions of the first kind as "outward sentiments" or "outward sensations" and to impressions of the second kind as "inward sentiments" or "inner sensations" (E:19, 22; S:11, 13; F:65, 67). In the *Treatise*, on the other hand, he uses a more technical terminology that is borrowed in part from Locke: he calls impressions of the first kind "impressions of sensation" and impressions of the second kind "impressions of reflection" (T:7). Here the term "reflection" does not mean that such impressions are more abstract or intellectual than are impressions of sensation, but rather that one becomes aware of them by introspection – by a kind of reflection on one's own state of mind. By an *idea*, Hume means any conscious state other than an impression. Ideas include especially concepts, but also mental images, such as those that occur when one imagines something or, sometimes, when one remembers something. In the *Treatise*, Hume also observes that the introspectible experiences, or impressions of reflection, are often caused by ideas; for example, an idea of pain may cause an impression of fear, or an idea of pleasure may cause an impression of desire (T:8).

The distinction between "impressions" and "ideas" probably seems fairly obvious to you. Hume himself thought it quite unproblematic, saying that "it requires no nice discernment or metaphysical head to mark the distinction between them" (E:18; S:10; F:63). Before seeing how Hume uses these terms in formulating his basic thesis, however, we need to take note of an ambiguity in his account of the difference between impressions of sensation and ideas. Hume's main or "official" way of distinguishing between impressions and ideas is to say that impressions are lively, vivid, or "forcible," whereas ideas are "faint" or "dull." But Hume adds immediately that a person whose mind is "disordered by disease or madness" may have ideas that are "altogether indistinguishable" from his or her impressions (E:17; S:10; F:63). Hume's point here is that people who are insane, or suffering from psychotic delusions or hallucinations, may have ideas which are every bit as vivid or lively as their impressions of sensation. Now in saying this, Hume is tacitly appealing to a criterion for distinguishing between impressions of sensation and ideas other than vivacity, because he still calls a deranged person's vivid hallucinations "ideas;" but their vividness would force him to classify them as impressions, if vividness or vivacity were the operative criterion for distinguishing between impressions and ideas. What other criterion, then, is Hume appealing to? As Jonathan Bennett has pointed out (1971: 224–5), he is appealing to the criterion of *objectivity*, according to which impressions of sensation are experiences had when people really perceive physical objects; whereas hallucinations, no matter how vivid they may be, are only ideas. There are several other places where Hume does this: in the *Abstract*, he says that "when we . . . have the images of external objects conveyed by our senses, the perception of the mind is . . . an *impression*," and he equates the claim that "our [visual] ideas [of sensation] . . . are derived from impressions" with the claim that "we can never think of anything which we have not seen without [outside] us" (T:647; S:128; F:31); in the text of the *Treatise* proper, he contrasts "that idea of red, which we form in the dark," with "that impression, which strikes our eyes in sun-shine" (T:3); in the *Enquiry*, he introduces the term "impression" by listing "perceptions, when we hear, or see, or feel" among the examples of what he will mean by that term (E:18; S:10; F:64). In these passages, from which we have quoted only short excerpts, Hume *also* characterizes impressions as being our "more lively" or "strong" perceptions, but the fact remains that he equates impressions of sensation with those had when we are really perceiving physical objects or, in Bennett's language, having "experience of the objective realm" (1971: 224–5). Thus, Hume has two different and incompatible criteria for distinguishing between impressions of sensation and ideas: his official criterion of "force and vivacity," and the implicit and unacknowledged criterion of objectivity.

The probable explanation of this ambiguity stems from a factor that we mentioned (but postponed describing) in the Introduction, when surveying the intellectual currents that influenced Hume: namely, his preoccupation with philosophical scepticism. Scepticism, a philosophical position that dates back to ancient Greece and has proponents to this very day, calls into question the possibility of knowledge. It does so by using certain arguments that are designed to show that our cognitive faculties and powers – our senses, reasoning ability, and memory – are not reliable enough to enable us to distinguish securely between truth and error, appearance and reality, well-grounded belief and mere opinion. The type of scepticism that is directly relevant to Hume's conflicting criteria for distinguishing between impressions and ideas is scepticism about the reliability of the senses. Such scepticism was a major force in Hume's day, and was advocated by one of Hume's favorite writers, Pierre Bayle. But to understand it, we should refer to Descartes, one of its most famous and powerful sources.

Descartes himself was no sceptic; indeed, he attempted to refute scepticism. But in preparing the way for his refutation, he first presented the case *for* scepticism so as to be in a better position to demolish that case. Indeed, his strategy was to radicalize the case for scepticism – to make it more sweeping and powerful than the sceptics themselves had done – and then to refute the radicalized sceptical arguments so as to abolish scepticism once and for all. Descartes begins modestly enough, by pointing out that our senses are sometimes deceptive, as when we misperceive an object's shape or size.[1] Of course, he then notes, this hardly shows that our senses are never trustworthy, since such errors typically occur because the object is far away or seen through a fog or the like. But why can't we rely on our senses when the conditions of observation are favorable, for example, when viewing a nearby object in good light? Descartes answers with two different sceptical arguments. First, he argues, as had other philosophers before him, that even our very best sense perceptions – those that occur under the most favorable conditions of observation – can be duplicated in vivid dreams. In other words, some dreams are so life-like, so vivid, that we are completely taken in by them and so cannot reliably distinguish them from our best waking perceptions. Second, he introduces an argument that no one before him had used and that is now commonly regarded as his most important sceptical argument. This is the argument that perhaps, for all we can tell, all of our sense experiences are produced by a source completely different from that which we think is responsible. We think, of course, that our visual, tactile, auditory, gustatory, and olfactory experiences are produced when physical objects stimulate our sense-receptor organs – our eyes, skin, ears, taste buds, noses. But what if, instead, they are caused in some radically different way; say by God himself, or perhaps by some powerful and evil demon bent on deceiving us? At first, this argument may seem utterly bizarre, perhaps even laughable. But on reflection it tends to "grow on" one. For, after all, a very powerful and intelligent being such as God, or some evil counterpart of God, presumably could generate in humans a perfectly undetectable hallucination of an entire physical world. All that this being would have to do is to cause us to have sense experiences that are vivid and that fall into orderly coherent patterns, so that we could, for example, correctly and consistently predict future experiences on the basis of present ones. How can we possibly know that this is not the way our experiences are in fact produced, since by hypothesis the experiences themselves would be exactly the same if they were so produced?

Descartes thought that he could refute this "deceiver argument." He attempted to refute it by offering proofs that there exists a benevolent God who would not deceive his creatures about the causes of their sense experiences. But Descartes' proofs of God's existence convinced few philosophers, so that his presentation of the problem of scepticism has endured while his attempt to solve it has not. Other philosophers have attempted to provide more effective responses to scepticism. John Locke, for example, attempts to solve Descartes' problem without appealing to God, by means of a quasi-scientific argument to the effect that the best explanation of the order and coherence of our sense experiences is that they are produced by a world of physical objects interacting with each other and with our sensory organs in regular, lawful ways. But Locke's successor in the British Empiricist tradition, Bishop Berkeley, argued powerfully that nothing Locke said successfully rules out other possible explanations of the order and coherence of our sense experiences. He then proceeded to argue that the experiences are indeed caused by God himself; except that Berkeley saw nothing sceptical about this view, because he combined it with the extraordinary thesis that matter does not really exist, and that what we call physical objects really are nothing but orderly groups of sensations or ideas caused by God!

Hume fully appreciated the force of Descartes' sceptical arguments, and he agreed with Berkeley's criticisms of Locke. But Hume could not accept Berkeley's own cure for scepticism, and indeed regarded Berkeley as just another sceptic. Accordingly, Hume adopted a thoroughgoing scepticism concerning the senses: he maintained that our belief in a material world, though it is a belief that we cannot avoid having, is not susceptible to any rational justification.[2] In the *Treatise*, he says that our impressions of sensations arise "from unknown causes" (T:7). So, Hume tries to find a criterion for distinguishing impressions of sensation from ideas that does not depend on knowing whether any of the impressions are caused by physical things – a purely immanent or phenomenological criterion that can be applied simply by using introspection. The criterion he comes up with is vivacity or liveliness; and this he adopts as his official way of distinguishing between impressions and ideas.

However, when Hume is not actually discussing the problem of perception, he tends not to keep in mind his scepticism concerning the senses. For example, as we shall see in Chapters 3 and 4, Hume's discussions of cause-and-effect reasoning, and of the nature of the cause-effect relationship itself, are among his most important contributions to philosophy. But as we shall also see, his discussion of those topics is written from a point of view that just takes for granted our knowledge through perception of physical objects and events; while discussing causal reasoning and causality, his deep interest in these topics simply overrides his sceptical doubts about the senses. This is not necessarily an inconsistency on Hume's part; for he can be interpreted as asking the questions: *if* we had knowledge of physical objects and events, then what would be the correct accounts of causal reasoning about them and of causal relationships among them? In any case, it is fortunate that Hume does abstract from or put to one side his scepticism about the senses while discussing causal reasoning and causality, because it is doubtful that he could have made his seminal claims about these topics if he had consistently stuck to such a sceptical stance, allowing himself to speak about impressions and ideas only and never about physical objects.

Now another place where Hume does not (or, at any rate, not always) bear this scepticism in mind is in presenting his theory of impressions and ideas. This is why he allows himself to appeal to objectivity as a criterion for distinguishing impressions of sensation from ideas. But, in this instance again, the resulting ambiguity, while potentially confusing, turns out not to be damaging. For, as we shall see, the importance of Hume's theory of impressions and ideas lies chiefly in the way he uses the theory to criticize certain conceptions taken for granted by his philosophical predecessors, such as the conception of substance, and his use of the theory does not depend on which of the two criteria is used to distinguish between impressions and ideas.

Accordingly, let us grant Hume his distinction between impressions and ideas, without worrying further about the ambiguity just discussed. We can then set forth Hume's basic principle about the relationship between impressions and ideas, which is his main opening thesis in both the *Enquiry* and the *Treatise*. This principle, which we will call the "principle of empiricism," can be put as follows: every idea is either

(a) derived from a corresponding impression, or
(b) composed of simpler ideas, each of which is derived from a corresponding impression.

Here "derived from" means, roughly, *copied from* and "corresponding" means *resembling*. An example of an idea falling under (a) would be that of some specific shade of red, say crimson. Hume would say that this idea is derived from a corresponding impression – an experience in which crimson itself is presented. An example of an idea falling under (b) might be the idea of a centaur. For, suppose a person has never seen a centaur (since there are none), nor ever had a vivid hallucination of one (so as to guarantee that the person has never had an impression of a centaur, whichever criterion we use for distinguishing impressions from ideas). Still, that person can have an idea of a centaur. For this idea can be broken down into two simpler components, such as the idea of a human being's head and torso and the idea of a horse's trunk and limbs. So, provided the person has had impressions of people's heads and torsos and of horses' trunks and limbs (impressions that can be obtained simply by seeing people and seeing horses), he or she can have the idea of a centaur. For then the person can have the ideas of a human head and torso and of a horse's trunk and limbs, and can combine these ideas to form the idea of a centaur. In a similar way, a person can have innumerable ideas that have no exact counterparts among impressions, provided that those ideas can be analyzed into component ideas all of which do have counterparts among the impressions. As examples of such ideas, Hume mentions those of a golden mountain and a virtuous horse.

Given the importance that Hume attaches to his principle of empiricism, his defense of the principle is surprisingly brief and also vulnerable to attack. First, he simply challenges the reader to find a counterexample to the principle; that is, to find an idea – any idea – that is not derived from impressions in either manner (a) or manner (b). Second, he claims that if a person's sensory organs are defective, so that the person cannot obtain the impressions of sensation normally generated when those organs are stimulated, then he or she cannot have the corresponding ideas: "A blind man can form no notion of colours; a deaf man of sounds" (E:20; S:12; F:65).

At first, these two points may seem quite persuasive; but on further reflection both become quite problematic. To begin with the first point, it is somewhat surprising that Hume himself, shortly after challenging the reader to find an idea which is not derived from any impression, describes a case that meets this very challenge! This is his famous case of the "missing shade of blue." Hume asks us to imagine a person who has seen every shade of blue from the darkest to the lightest, except for just one intermediate shade. Hume then asks whether this person could conjure up imaginatively the idea of that "missing" shade of blue, despite never having had an impression of it. Hume answers, plausibly enough, that the person could conjure up or visualize the missing shade. Notice that this case is a direct and convincing counterexample to Hume's own principle. For the idea of the missing shade of blue is by hypothesis not derived from any corresponding impression; nor can it be broken down into simpler ideas each of which is derived from a corresponding impression, because it is not composed of parts. Rather, the idea of any shade of blue is uniform, uncompounded, or simple; so that, unlike the idea of a centaur, it cannot be divided up into component ideas, each of which might be derived from different impressions. Furthermore, it seems that other examples of the same sort can easily be given, involving shades of other colors and perhaps also sounds. Yet, Hume dismisses the example as unimportant, saying that "it does not merit, that for it alone we should alter our general maxim" (E II:21; S:13; F:66; T I i 1:6). This is certainly puzzling: how can Hume maintain his principle, even though he knows that there is a clear counterexample to it?

Hume's second point – about defective sensory organs – also runs into difficulty. To see why, consider a hypothetical case. Suppose that instead of becoming deaf in his later years, Beethoven had been deaf from birth, and so had never had any impressions of sound. What could Hume say if our congenitally deaf Beethoven assured him that he knew very well what sound was, and presented him with the scores of his nine symphonies, thirty-two piano sonatas, etc., as evidence? It looks very much as if, in the face of such evidence, Hume would have to admit that his principle was false. Here you may be inclined to defend Hume by saying that the case of a congenitally deaf Beethoven does not really count against Hume's principle, because it is just an imaginary example. In order to show that Hume's principle is false, one must show that there really is a person who has ideas without having had the corresponding impressions.

The trouble with this possible defense of Hume, however, is that it does not square with the way he himself treats his principle, for it treats the principle as a falsifiable empirical or a posteriori thesis, whereas Hume treats it as an unfalsifiable a priori thesis. To explain this point, we need to define the terminology used. An empirical or a posteriori statement is one that can be known only by experience; for example, the statements that snow is white, or that water boils at 212°F at sea level, or that thunder follows lightning. An a priori statement is one that can be known just by thinking; for example, the statements that $1 + 2 = 3$, or that nobody is his or her own mother, or that if X is to the left of Y, then Y is to the right of X. We shall meet this basic distinction again, and discuss it in more depth, in the next chapter. For the present, we need to note only one more point about it. This is that empirical generalizations, which are statements of the form "All As are Bs," are always falsifiable; meaning that one can always conceive of some experience or observation that would show such a statement to be false. For instance, finding a patch of purple snow would show that the statement *all snow is white* is false; finding some water that failed to boil when heated to 212°F at sea level would falsify (show to be false) the statement *all water boils at 212°F at sea level*, and so forth. (Incidentally, notice that calling a statement *falsifiable* is, of course, not the same as calling it false: it means that some possible experience *could* conceivably show the statement to be false, not that the statement actually is false; so that many statements of whose truth we are quite certain are nevertheless falsifiable.) By contrast, no a priori statement is falsifiable. We cannot conceive, for example, of any experience that would show *1 + 2 = 3* to be false. For suppose that we try to do so: imagine, for example, inserting two marbles through a small opening to a box already containing one marble, and that on opening the box you find only two marbles therein. Would that falsify the arithmetical statement *1 + 2 = 3*? Or would it show that $1 + 2 = 2$? Surely not. At best, it would show that one marble had somehow exited the box while you were not looking. Failing some such natural explanation, it might even show that one of the marbles had somehow dematerialized; but it would not show *1 + 2 = 3* to be false.

To return to Hume's principle. We saw that this principle can be challenged by the hypothetical case of a congenitally deaf Beethoven. We said that a possible reply to that case is that it is merely imaginary, and that Hume's principle can be refuted only by a real case. Now this possible reply obviously assumes that the principle is falsifiable, and therefore also that it is an empirical generalization to the effect that all ideas are, as a matter of ascertainable fact, derived from corresponding impressions or else are composed of simpler ideas each of which is so derived. But although Hume sometimes writes (especially in *Treatise* Book I, part i, Section 1) as if his principle were an empirical hypothesis, we shall see that he does not treat it that way. For every time a case arises where people claim to have an idea for which Hume can find no impression or impressions (as in the cases of the ideas of substance and of self, to be discussed in the following part), he concludes that people do not really have the idea in question (and usually proposes some substitute idea that can be derived from impressions). He does not consider seriously the possibility that his principle might instead be false; even when, as in his "Appendix" to the *Treatise* (T:633–6), he sees that it has led him to a view of the self that he himself finds untenable. Thus, despite the fact that Hume sometimes speaks as if his principle were a falsifiable empirical generalization, in practice he treats it rather as an a priori truth. But then his appeal to empirical evidence to support the principle – for instance, to the fact that people with defective sensory-organs lack the corresponding ideas – is irrelevant and misleading, since the principle is not really based on empirical evidence. Furthermore, it is not at all clear how a generalization about the origin of our ideas *could* be known a priori.

In what follows, we shall propose a way of interpreting Hume's principle that solves the difficulty raised by the missing shade of blue and the difficulty raised by the congenitally deaf Beethoven scenario. Let us begin by considering the final paragraph of the second section of the *Enquiry*. For this paragraph sets Hume's principle in a certain light, in which the cases of the missing shade of blue and of a congenitally deaf Beethoven no longer cause trouble for the principle. The paragraph reads as follows:

> Here, therefore, is a proposition, which not only seems, in itself, simple and intelligible; but, if a proper use were made of it, might render every dispute equally intelligible, and banish all that jargon, which has so long taken possession of metaphysical reasonings, and drawn disgrace upon them. All ideas, especially abstract ones, are naturally faint and obscure: the mind has but a slender hold of them: they are apt to be confounded with other resembling ideas; and when we have often employed any term, though without a distinct meaning, we are apt to imagine it has a determinate idea annexed to it. On the contrary, all impressions, that is, all sensations, either outward or inward, are strong and vivid: the limits between them are more exactly determined: nor is it easy to fall into any error or mistake with regard to them. When we entertain, therefore, any suspicion that a philosophical term is employed without any meaning or idea (as is but too frequent), we need but enquire, *from what impression is that supposed idea derived*? And if it be impossible to assign any, this will serve to confirm our suspicion.
>
> (E:22; S:13; F:67; see also *Abstract* in: T:649; S:129; F:32)

In this passage, Hume introduces a topic that he has not previously mentioned: the topic of meaning. He alludes to "jargon" (meaningless verbiage, gibberish), and implies that certain disputes are unintelligible. He twice mentions the possibility of a term being employed without any meaning, and tells us how to guard against this. Indeed, what Hume does in this paragraph is to derive from his principle of empiricism a test for meaning. This test can be put as follows:

If T is a general, classificatory, or descriptive term that supposedly has an idea, *I*, as its meaning, but there is no impression(s) from which *I* is derived, then T does not stand for any idea and is therefore meaningless.

The last two sentences of the passage quoted foreshadow the way in which Hume will apply this test. He will apply it to three philosophical terms that are central in the work of nearly all his predecessors: the terms "substance," "self," and "cause." Indeed, as we shall see, some of Hume's chief contributions to philosophy arise when he subjects these three terms to his test for meaning.

Today, the importance of Hume's principle of empiricism is generally taken to lie primarily in the test for meaning that he derived from it. Indeed, recent Empiricist philosophers (who still look to Hume as their philosophical progenitor) are not generally satisfied with Hume's formulation of the principle of empiricism. For Hume's principle is, as we have seen, a genetic principle – one about the origin or genesis of our ideas. As such, it runs into the difficulties that we have noted: the problem that a person might, for all we know, have ideas that did not originate in any impressions (e.g. our congenitally deaf Beethoven's ideas of sound), and the problem that a person who had received impressions of all but a few shades of a color could surely visualize the shade(s) that he or she had never experienced (e.g. the missing shade of blue). Furthermore, it seems implausible to maintain that whether or not a term has a meaning depends on whether a given person, or several persons, have had impressions answering to (the idea associated with) that term. On the other hand, it is not implausible to maintain that whether or not a descriptive term has a meaning depends on whether something that *could* be experienced would answer to that term (or at least to other terms by which it was defined).

Accordingly, most contemporary Empiricists would recast Hume's entire position as one whose concern is about meaning. Thus, they would recast his principle of empiricism along the following lines, suggested by H. H. Price:

> Every meaningful general term T is definable either: (a′) ostensively, i.e. by indicating something that can be encountered in experience and saying: "that is an instance of what I mean by 'T'", or (b′) by means of other terms that are themselves definable in manner (a′).
>
> (Price 1965: 6)

There is a very close parallel between this "Empiricist view of meaning" (as we may call it), and Hume's principle of empiricism. For, notice that we can very plausibly use the same example, "crimson," to illustrate (a′) that we used to illustrate (a), and the same example, "centaur," to illustrate (b′) that we used to illustrate (b). Furthermore, from the Empiricist view of meaning, we can derive a modernized version of Hume's test for meaning: if T is a general or classificatory or descriptive term, but T cannot be defined either in manner (a′) or in manner (b′), then T is a meaningless term.

13

The main difference between Hume's principle of empiricism and test for meaning and their modern counterparts is this: in Hume's formulations, considerations of meaning are intertwined with a psychological, genetic thesis about the origin of our ideas – about how we *learn* meanings. The modern formulations, by contrast, are purely principles about what it is for a term to *have* meaning. As suggested above, this gives the modern formulations an advantage: they do not face the difficulties that afflict Hume's own position. Consider first the case of the missing shade of blue. As we have seen, this case is a clear counterexample to Hume's formulation of the principle of empiricism. But it is not a counterexample to the Empiricist view of meaning. For that view requires only that some observable or experienceable item *would answer* to the term for that shade of blue. It does not require anyone to have actually seen that shade. It requires only that the term's meaning *could* be defined ostensively or, as Price (1965: 7) put it, that the term be "cashable" in experience. A similar point solves the difficulty raised by the case of a congenitally deaf Beethoven. If Hume's thesis about the relation between impressions and ideas is construed along the lines suggested by the Empiricist view of meaning, then it requires only that every idea could be *exemplified* by an impression (or be composed of simpler ideas that could be exemplified by impressions), not that it be derived from an impression. But if someone had ideas that were not *derived* from any impressions, it would not follow that those ideas could not be *exemplified* by impressions, that they could not be "cashed" in experience. Even if Beethoven had really been congenitally deaf and despite this still had ideas of sounds, it would not follow that those ideas could not be exemplified by impressions. On the contrary, they could be exemplified by impressions of sound, despite Beethoven's never having had such impressions. Those ideas would still be "cashable" in experience, even though they had not *originated* in experience. To put the point differently: even if Beethoven had been congenitally deaf and nonetheless had ideas of sounds, it would not follow that nothing in any experience he could have had, had he not been congenitally deaf, would have answered to those ideas. On the contrary, auditory impressions, which he then could have had, would have answered to his ideas of sound.

Following Bennett (1971: 225–30), let us call the modernized versions of Hume's principle of empiricism and test for meaning "meaning-empiricism." Meaning-empiricism, as we have just seen, avoids the problems that we raised for Hume's own formulations.[3] Does this mean that we should accept meaning-empiricism? Not necessarily; for it may be that there are terms which are meaningful, but do not satisfy the Empiricist conditions for meaning. Hume himself, as we mentioned, examines three terms that his predecessors took to be not only meaningful, but also central to our thinking: "substance," "self," and "cause." In the next part, we shall consider what he says about substance and self, leaving "cause" aside until we have set out his related views about causal reasoning. At the end, we should be in a better position to assess meaning-empiricism.

2 Application of Hume's test for meaning to "substance" and "self"

In this part, we shall apply the Empiricist test for meaning to "substance" and "self." In order to prepare the ground, however, we need to recount how the notions of substance and self were understood by the philosophers whose views Hume was criticizing.

The notion of *substance* is the centerpiece of a view that we shall call the "substance theory." The substance theory, which can be traced back at least to Aristotle and which was upheld by most medieval thinkers and by the Rationalists of the seventeenth and eighteenth centuries, is essentially an attempt to answer the philosophical question: "What is a thing?" There are two competing answers to this question: the bundle theory and the substance theory. According to the bundle theory, which was favored by Empiricist philosophers like Berkeley, Hume himself, and (in the twentieth century) Bertrand Russell, a thing is nothing but a collection of coexisting properties. For example, a tomato is nothing but roundness, redness, squashiness, juiciness, and so on, existing together at a certain place and time. According to the substance theory, however, a thing is composed of more than just its properties: it is composed of those properties *plus* an underlying substance to which all the properties belong.[4] Thus the tomato, on this view, is composed only in part of the properties just mentioned; for it is also composed of an underlying substance to which all those properties belong and in which they are said to "inhere." As a very rough analogy, think of a pin-cushion with pins stuck in it: the pins are analogous to the properties, the pin-cushion to the substance.

On the standard seventeenth- and eighteenth-century view stemming largely from Descartes, there are two different kinds of substance. One is matter or material substance, whose basic properties are shape, size, and solidity.[5] The other is mind or mental substance, whose *only* properties are conscious states. Furthermore, according to this view, which is called "substance dualism," "Cartesian dualism," or sometimes simply "dualism," a person or self is identified with his or her mind or mental substance.

The principal rationale for the substance theory is provided by what is called the "argument from change." This argument is implicit in a very famous passage in the *Second Meditation*, where Descartes describes what happens to a piece of wax, freshly taken from a beehive, when that wax is put near a fire. As the wax is heated, its properties change: its hardness is replaced by a soft, gooey texture, its lumpish form by an elongated shape, its brown color by a translucid tint, its fragrant aroma by a smoky smell. Even its capacity to make a noise when struck with a finger is lost. Yet, one and the same piece of wax still exists despite all these changes. Why is that? Why isn't it the case, instead, that the wax ceases to exist and that another and new object begins to exist? The answer, according to the argument from change, is that although the properties of the wax have changed, the underlying substance has not: one and the same substance existed throughout the process of change and still exists now.

15

This is an important argument, so let us formulate it carefully. To do this, we need to make a distinction between properties of two kinds: determinate properties and determinable properties. A determinate property is one that is absolutely specific, whereas a determinable property is one that is not absolutely specific. Take for example the property of being elliptical, or ellipticalness. This is a determinable property, not a determinate one, because there are many different elliptical shapes: thick ones, thin ones, in-between ones, and so forth. A determinate property, by contrast, must be absolutely specific. Only an elliptical shape satisfying a particular mathematical equation (ellipticity) would be a determinate property. Color is another example of a determinable property, since there are many different colors. Even particular colors like red, blue and yellow are determinable rather than determinate properties, because there are many shades of each of those colors. Only absolutely specific shades would be determinate properties, even if we do not have names for each such shade.

Having distinguished between determinate and determinable properties, we can now state the argument from change accurately:

(1) We can distinguish between (a) all of a thing's determinate properties changing without the thing's ceasing to exist and (b) a thing's ceasing to exist.
(2) We can distinguish between (a) and (b) only if a thing is composed, in addition to its properties, of a permanent underlying substance.

∴ A thing is composed, in addition to its properties, of a permanent, underlying substance.

To grasp this argument, think again of Descartes' example of the melting wax. The example can be understood as raising a challenge: namely, what justifies us in taking the melting wax to be a case of (a) rather than a case of (b) – that is, in thinking that the wax, all the determinate properties of which have changed, has not therefore ceased to exist? Premiss (2) says, in effect, that the only way to answer this challenge is to admit that the wax is composed of something *more* than just its properties, of something permanent to which those properties belong. The conclusion is simply a statement of the substance theory itself, so that the argument as a whole purports to prove that this theory is correct.

You may be wondering why the term "determinate" is needed in premiss (1). The answer has to do with the nature of change. We say, of course, that when a thing alters, its properties or characteristics have changed. But what does this mean? Not that the properties *themselves* have changed, because a property itself can never change: red, for example, is just red, and to say that it had changed would really mean that it had been *replaced* by another property, say by the property blue. Thus, to say that a thing's properties have changed is to say that it has lost certain properties and acquired others. Suppose, then, that the word "determinate" were left out of premiss (1). Then the premiss would say that a thing could lose all of its properties, *including its determinable properties*, without ceasing to exist. But this would be false, for a thing's determinable properties include shape and size – not this or that specific shape and size, but just having some shape and size or other, or having what Descartes called "extension" – and a (physical) thing cannot lose all shape and size whatsoever without thereby also ceasing to exist. Thus, the term "determinate" must be included in premiss (1) for that premiss to have a chance of being true.

You may now ask: why then isn't the word "determinate" also included in premiss (2)? The answer is that to preserve the argument's validity, the conclusion would then also have to include that word, and so would have to read: "A thing is composed, in addition to its determinate properties, of a permanent underlying substance." But this is false, for it means that a thing is composed *only* of its determinate properties and its underlying substance. But a determinate property cannot possibly be present unless a corresponding determinable property is also present; for example, squareness cannot be present unless shape is present. Thus, in order for the argument's conclusion to stand a chance of being true, the word "determinate" must not be included in premiss (2).

The argument from change can also be applied to the non-physical, purely mental, thing that most seventeenth- and eighteenth-century philosophers took a human mind to be. Thus Descartes wrote:

> [T]he human mind is a pure substance. For even if all the accidents of the mind change, so that it has different objects of the understanding and different desires and sensations, it does not on that account become a different mind.
>
> (1984: 10)

Here the term "accidents" refers to properties of a certain kind – namely, accidental properties. Accidental properties are those that a thing may have but need not have in order to be what it is, such as a certain triangle's property of being green. Accidental properties contrast with essential properties, which are those that a thing must have in order to be what it is, like the triangle's property of being three-sided. Descartes' phrase, "different objects of the understanding and different desires and sensations," here refers to a mind's specific, determinate conscious states. Thus, Descartes identifies the accidental properties of a mind with its determinate, conscious states. But if a mind's accidental properties are determinate conscious states, then those properties are also determinate properties. Therefore, the argument of the passage could be summarized: "A human mind is a substance, because even if all its determinate properties change, it is still the same mind." This is simply the argument from change applied to the mind rather than to a physical thing like the wax.

Although the substance theory was upheld by most major philosophers of Hume's day, it is not without its problems. Before looking at Hume's own specific objection to the theory, it will be useful to state briefly the central difficulty faced by the theory. This is that substance is unperceivable. Imagine, for example, that you wanted to see the substance of a piece of wood. So you obtain a carpenter's plane and shave off a thin layer of wood. What do you then see? Well, you see a new set of properties – a slightly diminished size, a slightly altered shape, a slightly different shade of color. It is obvious that planing away still more layers of wood will not get you any closer to seeing the piece of wood's underlying substance. No matter how many layers you plane away, you will see only more properties – until, at last, all the wood is gone. What this type of thought experiment reveals is that substance is just not something that can be perceived: nothing one could do would even count as perceiving substance.[6] Substance is, as philosophers say, unperceivable *in principle*. For this reason, some philosophers of the seventeenth and eighteenth centuries became increasingly suspicious of the notion of substance; and many contemporary philosophers reject "substance" altogether.

Against the background of the substance theory and the fundamental difficulty that it faces, we are ready to see how Hume applies his test for meaning to "substance" and to "self." In order to keep our discussion anchored to Hume's texts, we shall use his own formulation of the test: from what impression(s) are the ideas of substance and of self derived? It should always be remembered, however, that this question could be reformulated in terms of modern meaning-empiricism: can the terms "substance" and "self" be defined ostensively, by indicating something in experience that would answer to them?

In the following paragraph from a section of the *Treatise* (T:16) entitled "Of Modes and Substances," Hume applies his test for meaning to the notion of substance:

> I wou'd fain ask those philosophers, who found so much of their reasonings on the distinction of substance and accident, and imagine we have clear ideas of each, whether the idea of *substance* be deriv'd from the impressions of sensation or reflexion? If it be convey'd to us by our senses, I ask, which of them; and after what manner? If it be perceiv'd by the eyes, it must be a colour; if by the ears, a sound; if by the palate, a taste; and so of the other senses. But I believe none will assert, that substance is either a colour, or sound, or taste. The idea of substance must therefore be derived from an impression of reflexion, if it really exist. But the impressions of reflexion resolve themselves into our passions and emotions; none of which can possibly represent a substance. We have therefore no idea of substance, distinct from that of a collection of particular qualities, nor have we any other meaning when we talk or reason concerning it.

Hume's point, of course, is that "substance" fails to pass his test for meaning. For in order for this term to have meaning for us, we must have an idea of substance. Now, argues Hume, if we have an idea of substance, then that idea must be derived either from an impression of sensation or an impression of reflection. So, using the strategy that we shall see him use again for "self" and for "cause," Hume challenges philosophers who rely on the notion of substance to specify the impression from which it is derived. If it is derived from an impression of sensation, then substance must be something we perceive through our senses, for instance, as a color or a sound or a taste. But substance cannot possibly be a color or a sound or a taste, since these are supposed to be qualities *of* substances. So, the idea of substance is not derived from any impression of sensation. If, on the other hand, it is derived from an impression of reflection, then substance must be something we are aware of by introspection – some conscious state such as an emotion or a feeling. But no such introspectible conscious states can possibly be equated with a substance, since they are supposed to be properties of a (mental) substance. Therefore, Hume concludes, we have no idea of substance, and the term "substance" is meaningless. In the final sentence of the passage, Hume concludes that we have no choice but to opt for the bundle theory: a thing is just a bundle of properties (a "collection of particular qualities").

Put in terms of modern meaning-empiricism, Hume's argument would go as follows. We cannot find anything in our experience, whether through sense perception or introspection, that answers to the term "substance." For substance is supposed to be something that has, supports, or underlies all of a thing's observable properties, but that is not itself perceivable. If it were perceivable, it would not be a substance but only a property. Substance itself is unperceivable in principle. Therefore, the term "substance" fails to pass the modernized Empiricist test for meaning and is, accordingly, meaningless.

As we have said, seventeenth- and eighteenth-century philosophers commonly held, following Descartes, that there is such a thing as a purely mental substance – one that has no physical properties like shape or size, but whose only properties are its conscious states. It might perhaps be thought, then, that even if Hume has shown that we have no idea of material or physical substance, we still have an idea of mental substance. Indeed, one major philosopher who strenuously rejected the notion of material substance, Bishop Berkeley, nevertheless retained and even glorified the notion of mental substance.[7] But Hume, with ruthless consistency, applies his test for meaning to this notion as well. He does this in a section of the *Treatise* called "Of personal identity." In that section, Hume applies his test to the notion of *self*. But the notion of self that he has in mind is obviously that of a mental substance, mind, or soul; so that he is in effect applying his test to the notion of mental substance used by Descartes and most other seventeenth- and eighteenth-century philosophers. Here is part of what Hume says:

> There are some philosophers, who imagine we are every moment intimately conscious of what we call our SELF; that we feel its existence and its continuance in existence; and are certain, beyond the evidence of a demonstration, both of its perfect identity and simplicity . . . .
> Unluckily all these positive assertions are contrary to that very experience, which is pleaded for them, nor have we any idea of self, after the manner it is here explain'd. For, from what impression cou'd this idea be

deriv'd? This question 'tis impossible to answer without a manifest contradiction and absurdity; and yet 'tis a question, which must necessarily be
answer'd, if we wou'd have the idea of self pass for clear and intelligible.
It must be some one impression that gives rise to every real idea. But self
or person is not any one impression, but that to which our several
impressions and ideas are suppos'd to have a reference. If any impression
gives rise to the idea of self, that impression must continue invariably the
same, thro' the whole course of our lives; since self is suppos'd to exist
after that manner. But there is no impression constant and invariable.
Pain and pleasure, grief and joy, passions and sensations succeed each
other, and never all exist at the same time. It cannot, therefore, be from
any of these impressions, or from any other, that the idea of self is deriv'd;
and consequently there is no such idea . . . .

I may venture to affirm . . . that [a mind is] nothing but a bundle or
collection of different perceptions, which succeed each other with an
inconceivable rapidity, and are in perpetual flux and movement. Our
eyes cannot turn in their sockets without varying our perceptions. Our
thought is still more variable than our sight . . . The mind is a kind of
theatre, where several perceptions successively make their appearance;
pass, re-pass, glide away, and mingle in an infinite variety of postures and
situations . . . . The comparison of the theatre must not mislead us. They
are the perceptions only, that constitute the mind; nor have we the most
distant notion of the place, where these scenes are represented, or of the
materials, of which it is compos'd.

(T:251–3)

In the second paragraph of the passage just quoted, Hume makes two points. One
is that if one tries to pinpoint the impression from which the idea of one's own
mind or self is derived, one simply does not find it. All one finds, instead, is a
constantly shifting vista of sense impressions, feelings, images, etc. One does not
find, in addition to these, any single enduring unchanging impression that one
could identify as one's own self or mind. In other words, if one tries to spot one's
own self or mind by introspection, one just cannot find it. As Hume puts it (T:252):

For my part, when I enter most intimately into what I call *myself*, I always
stumble on some particular perception or other, of heat or cold, light or
shade, love or hatred, pain or pleasure. I never can catch *myself* at any
time without a perception, and can never observe anything but the
perception . . . . If any one, upon serious and unprejudic'd reflexion,
thinks he has a different notion of *himself*, I must confess I can reason no
longer with him.

Hume's other point is that it is not even *possible* for there to be an impression of
self. For "self or person is not any one impression, but that to which our several

impressions and ideas are supposed to have a reference." What Hume is saying can be put this way. To try to spot one's self by introspection is to try to introspect the very subject of consciousness – the subject which is conscious *of* all the objects that one is aware of. But this is like trying to see the point *from which* one sees everything. The attempt is bound to fail, for that point cannot be seen; it is the one point which can never be in one's visual field. Thus, not only is there no impression of the self; there cannot be one. It follows from each of these two points, together with Hume's test for meaning, that the notion of a self, understood as a mental substance or mind that has various conscious states as its properties, is meaningless. It is just as empty as is the notion of a material substance that has various qualities as its properties.

In the last of the paragraphs quoted above, Hume draws his conclusion. The only tenable view of the mind or self is in terms of a bundle theory: the mind is "a bundle or collection of different perceptions . . . . They are the successive perceptions only, that constitute the mind." A mind, then, is nothing but a succession of conscious states.

When Hume's test for meaning is applied to the notion of a material substance, it yields the result that the notion is meaningless and that a thing can be only a bundle of properties. Likewise, when the test is applied to the notion of a mental substance, it yields the result that this notion is meaningless and that a mind can be only a bundle of conscious states. Meaning-empiricism leaves no room at all for the notion of substance as distinct from its properties, whether it be a material substance or a mind. In the next two parts, we shall consider whether these results are philosophically acceptable.

3 An alternative to the substance theory

Meaning-empiricism implies that the substance theory should be rejected. We have seen, however, that the substance theory rests on an argument, namely the argument from change. If we wish to reject the substance theory, therefore, we must be prepared to refute that argument. One cannot both accept an argument for a theory and reject that very theory. The time has come, therefore, for us to evaluate the argument from change. The argument, you will recall, goes like this:

(1) We can distinguish between (a) all of a thing's determinate properties changing without the thing's ceasing to exist, and (b) a thing's ceasing to exist.
(2) We can distinguish between (a) and (b) only if a thing is composed, in addition to its properties, of a permanent underlying substance.

∴ A thing is composed, in addition to its properties, of a permanent underlying substance.

Premiss (1) might be challenged, in the following way. Can we really distinguish between *all* of a thing's determinate properties changing without the thing ceasing to exist, and the thing ceasing to exist? In order for a thing to continue existing, must it not retain at least some of its determinate properties – if only a single one? And isn't this condition, in fact, satisfied in the case of Descartes' piece of wax? For although all of the wax's observable properties have changed, does not the wax still retain a determinate chemical composition – or perhaps a determinate atomic structure – by virtue of which it continues to exist despite the change in the properties that can be observed with the unaided senses?

Although this line of attack certainly has some force, and would be endorsed by those contemporary philosophers who call themselves "scientific realists," there are other contemporary philosophers who would oppose it. For suppose, as is quite conceivable, chemists or atomic physicists discovered that when wax is melted, its color, shape, consistency, and other observable properties are not the only ones that change. Rather, its chemical composition and/or atomic structure are *also* altered (perhaps only very slightly so). Would we then have to agree that the piece of wax Descartes describes ceases to exist when it is melted? Opponents of scientific realism would answer that we would not – at least not merely on the strength of what we have supposed so far, namely, that both the wax's more obvious properties and its "scientific" properties have altered. They would hold that if, by cooling and moulding the melted stuff, we could easily get it back to its previous shape, size, texture, and consistency, and do such things as use it for a candle or as a water repellent, then it would still be wax, even if its atomic or chemical structure had altered. If this is right, then what accounts for the wax continuing to exist when melted is not that it retains "scientific" properties like its chemical composition or its atomic structure; those could change, as well as the more obvious properties of shape, size, hardness, color, odor, and so on. So, the opponent of scientific realism would say, premiss (1) withstands the challenge that was raised against it.

A committed scientific realist, however, would probably not be impressed by this line of thought, but would insist that a thing simply cannot continue to be wax if it loses the atomic or chemical structure of wax. Rather than dismissing this view as false, accordingly, we shall maintain that if scientific realism is correct, then premiss (1) of the argument from change need only be qualified, along the following lines:

(1a) We can distinguish between (a) all of a thing's determinate properties *except* for scientific properties P changing without the thing's ceasing to exist, and (b) a thing's ceasing to exist.

Here "scientific properties P" denotes whatever determinate scientific property or properties the scientific realist holds that a thing must retain in order to continue existing. As I will argue, however, there is good reason to think that even if (1) is false, then at least this qualified version of (1) is true.

What I have to say about (1a), however, will be clearer if first we critically examine the *second* premiss of the argument from change, to which we therefore now turn our attention. One might challenge the "only if" in premiss (2), that is, the very strong claim that we can distinguish between (a) all of a thing's determinate properties changing without the thing's ceasing to exist and (b) the thing's ceasing to exist, in *only one* way – i.e. *only if* the substance theory is true. The best way to make good such a challenge, of course, would be to provide an alternative account of how this distinction can be made – an account that does not involve substance. For premiss (2) operates as a kind of challenge: how can we justify saying that a thing, all of whose determinate properties have changed, has not itself ceased to exist *unless* we postulate an underlying substance that has not changed? Clearly if an Empiricist can give an alternative account of the distinction between (a) and (b), then this challenge will have been met.

As a preliminary to offering such an account, we will raise an objection to premiss (2). This is that "substance" is actually quite incapable of explaining our ability to distinguish (a) from (b). For how do we actually make this distinction? The answer, surely, is that we make it on the basis of the changes that we observe. Speaking very roughly, if the changes we observe in a thing are not too radical, then we say that it has changed its properties without losing its identity; whereas if the changes we observe are more radical, then we say that the thing has lost its identity or, which amounts to the same thing, that it has ceased to exist. Notice, then, that when we actually determine whether a thing has merely undergone a change of properties or has ceased to exist, "substance" plays no role: it is simply irrelevant. Furthermore, "substance" *could not* help; it is *useless*. For how could an unperceivable substance possibly help us to make a distinction that we make on the basis of what we observe? It would seem, then, that we have already found good reason to doubt premiss (2) of the argument from change.

In order to give an alternative account of how (a) is distinguished from (b), an Empiricist needs to offer an account of what it is for a thing to retain its identity while undergoing change, or of "identity through change." In other words, the Empiricist needs to answer the following question: what is required for a thing to continue to be the same thing, during a period of time in which it changes? For if one can specify such a requirement, then one can hold that whether we have a case of (a) or of (b) turns on whether that requirement is satisfied.

Hume himself had a response to this question, but we shall not try to defend it. For basically, Hume's response was to reject the question, on the grounds that in order for a thing to retain its identity, it *cannot change at all*. So, for example, if a few planks in a ship's hull were replaced, it would no longer be the same ship; or if one new bolt were added to your car, it would no longer be the same car. Hume bases this surprising view on an exceedingly narrow definition of identity through time, according to which such identity means that a thing is not only "uninterrupted," but also "invariable" or unchanging (T:235; see also T:201–2). He says therefore that when we ascribe identity to something that has changed, we are simply mistaken. He adds, however, that there are certain features of things that induce us to make this mistake: namely, their changing only in small ways or in proportionally small ways, or gradually, or their having parts that serve a unified function (a "common end or purpose"), or parts that are interdependent and serve such a function, or their having temporal stages that exhibit qualitative sameness or "specific identity" (as opposed to numerical identity), or their being by nature changeable. These features, he says, persuade us to mistake what is really a succession of related things for one and the same thing, because the act of mind by which we consider such a succession of related things closely resembles or feels very like the act of mind by which we consider an uninterrupted and unchanging thing (T:6, 255–8). Some recent philosophers would say that the very features Hume mentions are in fact those that *justify* us in ascribing to things identity through change, rather than, as he thought, features that *mislead* us into ascribing identity to things that are really diverse. Seen in this way, Hume's discussion is illuminating, because the features he insightfully locates are indisputably relevant to our ordinary judgments of identity.[8]

Despite Hume's insightfulness, however, his narrow definition of identity prevents him from taking seriously the question of what is required for a thing to retain its identity even though it has changed. Rather than expounding Hume's view in more detail, therefore, we shall sketch out an answer, suggested by Locke (1975) in Chapter 27 (titled "Of Identity and Diversity") of Book II of his *Essay Concerning Human Understanding*, and favored by many empirically minded contemporary philosophers. This is the view that the fundamental requirement for identity through change is *spatiotemporal continuity.*

The requirement of spatiotemporal continuity is best introduced negatively, by considering a case in which it would be violated. Here, then, is such a case. Suppose that on a table at the front end of a room, there is a large, heavy object – say a marble statue of George Washington. Next, suppose that this statue ceases to occupy its place on the table and that, some time afterwards, a statue exactly like it begins to occupy a place at the back end of the room. Furthermore, imagine (this requires indulging in a bit of science fiction) that the statue did not occupy a series of contiguous places between the front of the room and the back of the room; nor did it somehow get transformed into energy and occupy such a series of places in that form, before rematerializing as a marble statue when it reached the back of the room. Rather, what happened is simply that the statue ceased to occupy its place at the front of the room, and later a statue exactly like it began to occupy a place at the back of the room. Now consider this question: was the statue at the front of the room the same statue as the one at back of the room? Here it is important to understand what this question is asking. It is not asking whether the statue at the front of the room was *qualitatively* the same as the one at the back. By hypothesis, it was the same: we just said that the statue in the back was "exactly like" the one in the front; meaning that it had the same weight, color, shape, size, workmanship, etc. So, it was qualitatively the same – it had exactly the same qualities or properties – as the one at the front. The question is, rather, whether the statue at the front of the room and the one at the back of the room were *numerically* the same: was there just one statue which existed at the earlier time and also at the later time, or were there two statues, one at the earlier time and another at the later time? (Was the situation like that of one person at two different times, or like that of identical twins? Was the statue at the front of the room the *same one* as the statue at the back, or only the *same as* the one at the back?) It should be clear, perhaps after a bit of reflection, that the answer is that the statue at the back of the room and the one at the front of the room were not numerically identical. They were qualitatively identical, but numerically distinct (like the twins). The statue at the front of the room was the same *as* the one at the back, but it was not the same *one* as the one at the back. The reason is that between the time the statue at the front of the room ceased to occupy its place and the one at the back began to occupy its place, there was an interruption or break in spatiotemporal continuity. The statue at the front of the room was not spatiotemporally continuous with the one at the back, as it would have been if, for example, someone had carried it from one place to the other.

At this point, you may feel like raising the following objection. "The case of the 'vanishing statue' just presented is a science-fiction case; it couldn't really happen. So, how can it be relevant to our question?" The answer is that in considering conceptual questions, such as the question of what is required for a thing to retain its identity through time, unrealistic cases are sometimes indispensable. To see this, let us return to Descartes' case of the melting wax. In most cases in which a thing's properties change without the thing losing its identity, what happens is that only a few of its determinate properties change. For example, a leaf changes color, or develops a hole, or falls from a tree. In such cases, we have no trouble determining that the leaf is still the same leaf: it just hasn't changed enough for the question even to arise of whether it has ceased to exist. On the other hand, in cases where a thing changes so much that it does lose its identity, what generally happens is that the properties change quite drastically. For example, a piece of paper is burned until it is just a pile of ashes. In that case, we have no trouble determining that the paper has been destroyed: it has changed in ways that prevent it from continuing to exist as a piece of paper. Descartes' case of the wax, however, sits uneasily between those two clear cases. On the one hand, it is like the burning paper example in that the wax's determinate properties have changed drastically. On the other hand, it is like the leaf case in that the wax does not get destroyed.

So, in order to get clear on what is required for a thing to retain its identity through change, we can ask: what more would have to happen in order for the wax to be destroyed? Well, we know that if it changed in still other ways – if it underwent certain chemical reactions that broke it down into separate elements – it would be destroyed. But is there anything else that could conceivably happen, besides such a chemical change or some other dramatic change in the wax's properties, that would make the wax cease to exist? If we can specify something else, then we will have unearthed a condition of identity through change other than any condition pertaining to the loss and gain of properties. Well then: suppose that the wax had ceased to occupy its place, and that a puddle of melted wax, or even a piece of unmelted wax exactly like it, had begun to occupy a different place, in the same way as our "vanishing statue." *Of course* this doesn't really happen: we are in the realm of science fiction again. But suppose it did happen. It is, after all,

25

perfectly conceivable; it is a logical possibility. Then, would we not admit that the original piece of wax had ceased to exist, and that another piece of wax had begun to exist? It seems clear enough that we would. But then this shows that spatio-temporal continuity is one of our requirements for identity through change.

Indeed, this requirement appears to be fundamental. For suppose that scientific realists are right, and that a thing cannot retain its identity if it loses certain determinate "scientific" properties, like its atomic or chemical structure. In that case, as we saw, premiss (1) of the argument from change would have to be reformulated to say:

(1a) We can distinguish between (a) all of a thing's determinate properties, *except* for scientific properties P, changing without the thing's ceasing to exist, and (b) a thing's ceasing to exist.

Is (1a) true or false? The answer seems to be that (1a) is true; for if we suppose that a piece of wax ceased to occupy a certain place, p_1, and that one exactly like it later began to occupy another place, p_2 (in the same way as our "vanishing statue"), *and that the wax in both places had the chemical or atomic structure of wax*, it would still be true that the piece of wax that had occupied p_1 was numerically different from the one that occupied p_2: we would then have a case of (b) rather than a case only of (a), just because of the break in spatiotemporal continuity. Thus even if scientific realism is right, it does not follow that spatiotemporal continuity is not a necessary condition for identity through time. Rather, what follows is that keeping the same molecular or atomic structure is *also* a necessary condition of identity through time.

Having introduced the requirement of spatiotemporal continuity, let us formu-late it explicitly, and give a definition of spatiotemporal continuity itself. We can formulate the requirement as follows:

X at time t_1 is the same thing as Y at time t_2 only if X is spatiotemporally continuous with Y from t_1 to t_2.

Here both "X" and "Y" denote one specific object of a specific kind, such as the book you are holding now and the book that is in your knapsack later. In cases where both "X" and "Y" designate the very same thing considered at one moment of its existence, t_1 and t_2 will refer to the same time, and the condition of spatiotemporal continuity will be automatically satisfied in virtue of the fact that X and Y also occupy exactly the same place at that time. In cases like those which we are chiefly concerned with, where X is the same thing as Y despite having undergone change, t_1 and t_2 must of course refer to different times. X could be Descartes' unmelted lump of wax and Y the melted wax. The requirement then states that in order for the unmelted wax to be the same thing as the melted wax, the unmelted wax must be spatiotemporally continuous with the melted wax.

The definition of spatiotemporal continuity itself is more difficult to give. The basic notion is that of uninterrupted existence in space and time – a condition that was *not* met in our case of the "vanishing statue." But, while it seems easy enough to have an intuitive understanding of this notion, it is difficult to say precisely what the notion comes to. We shall now try to give an exact definition, but since this definition will have to be somewhat technical, the following four paragraphs may be skipped (or returned to later) without risk of losing the main thread of argument being developed.

Let us try the following definition where, again, "X" and "Y" stand for particular objects of specific kinds, but where "an X" or "a Y" stand for any objects of specific kinds:

D1: X is spatiotemporally continuous with Y from t_1 to t_2 = *df.*

(1) X occupies p_1 at t_1;
(2) Y occupies p_2 at t_2;
(3) either (i) p_1 is identical with p_2 and, from t_1 to t_2, either an X or a Y occupies p_2; or (ii) p_1 is not identical with p_2, but there is a series of contiguous places, $S_1 \ldots S_n$, such that (a) S_1 is contiguous with p_1 and S_n is contiguous with p_2, (b) at every time from t_1 to t_2 every contiguous member of $S_1 \ldots S_n$ is successively occupied by either an X or a Y.

Clause (3) is intended to cover two different possible situations: (i) that in which a thing changes while remaining stationary; and (ii) that in which a thing both changes and moves. Suppose for example that X is a particular lump of unmelted wax and Y is a particular lump of partially melted wax. Then there are two ways in which clause (3) can be satisfied. *Either* the place occupied by the unmelted wax is the same as the place occupied by the partially melted wax, and from t_1 to t_2 this place is always occupied by either unmelted wax or partially melted wax – in which case we have a stationary piece of melting (or perhaps alternately melting and solidifying) wax. *Or* there is a series of contiguous places between the place occupied by the unmelted wax and the place occupied by the partially melted wax, such that:

(a) the first member of the series is contiguous with the place occupied by the unmelted wax and the last member is contiguous with the place occupied by the partially melted wax;
(b) at all times from t_1 to t_2, every contiguous member of this series of places is successively occupied by either unmelted wax or partially melted wax – in which case we have a moving piece of melting (or perhaps alternately melting and solidifying) wax.

D1, however, will not quite do. For consider a case where a piece of wax gradually melts until it is completely liquid. We want the definition to let us say that the unmelted wax is spatiotemporally continuous with the completely melted wax (for otherwise, we will not be able to say, given that spatiotemporal continuity is a requirement for identity through change, that it is the same piece of wax). But it does not. For in such a case, clause (3) will not be satisfied, whether the wax remains stationary or moves. If it remains stationary, then there will be a time between t_1 and t_n when the place the wax occupies is occupied by neither unmelted nor totally melted wax, but by partially melted wax instead, so (3i) will not be satisfied. (Nor, of course, will (3ii) be satisfied, since it requires that X be at a different place at t_1 from Y at t_2, which cannot happen if the wax remains stationary.) If the wax moves, then between t_1 and t_2 there will be at least two contiguous members of $S_1 \ldots S_n$ such that they are not successively occupied by either unmelted or totally melted wax, but rather by unmelted wax and partially melted wax, or by (totally) melted wax and partially melted wax; so (3ii) will not be satisfied. (Nor, of course, will (3i) be satisfied, since it requires that X at t_1 be at the same place as Y at t_2, which cannot happen if the wax moves.)

To get around this difficulty, we must expand the definition as follows:

D2: X is spatiotemporally continuous with Y from t_1 to t_2 = *df*.

Either:

(1)   X occupies p_1 at t_1;
(2)   Y occupies p_2 at t_2;
(3)   either (i) p_1 is identical with p_2 and, from t_1 to t_2, either an X or a Y occupies p_2; or (ii) p_1 is not identical with p_2, but there is a series of contiguous places, $S_1 \ldots S_n$, such that (a) S_1 is contiguous with p_1 and S_n is contiguous with p_2, (b) at every time from t_1 to t_2 every contiguous member of $S_1 \ldots S_n$ is successively occupied by either an X or a Y.

Or

(4)   X is spatiotemporally continuous with Z_1 from t_1 to t^*, and Z_1 is spatiotemporally continuous with Y from t^* to t_2; or X is spatiotemporally continuous with Z_1 from t_1 to t^*, Z_1 is spatiotemporally continuous with Z_2 from t^* to t^{**}, and Z_2 is spatiotemporally continuous with Y from t^{**} to t_2; or X is spatiotemporally continuous with Z_1 from t_1 to t^*, Z_1 is spatiotemporally continuous with Z_2 from t^* to t^{**}, Z_2 is spatiotemporally continuous with Z_3 from t^{**} to t^{***}, and Z_3 is spatiotemporally continuous with Y from t^{***} to t_2; or . . . and so on.

More simply, the last clause says that X must be spatiotemporally continuous with something which is itself spatiotemporally continuous with Y, or with a member of a series each of whose members is spatiotemporally continuous with the next member, and whose last member is spatiotemporally continuous with Y. This covers the case of the gradually melting wax, because the unmelted wax is spatiotemporally continuous with the partially melted wax, which is spatiotemporally continuous with wax in a still more advanced state of melting, and so on. In other words, the totally unmelted wax is spatiotemporally continuous with a member of a series whose members are in progressively more advanced stages of melting, each of which is spatiotemporally continuous with the next, and the last of which is spatiotemporally continuous with the totally melted wax.

D2 is an example of a kind of definition called a *recursive* definition. For its *definiendum* (the term being defined) recurs within the *definiens* (the terms doing the defining). Thus the term, " — is spatiotemporally continuous with — from — to —," which is the one being defined, recurs in (4). The definition is not circular, however, because each occurrence of this term in (4) is completely defined in terms of the definiens's first disjunct, that is, in terms of clauses (1), (2), and (3).

The requirement of spatiotemporal continuity provides at least a partial answer to the challenge posed by the argument from change. For if that requirement is *not* satisfied, then we have a case of a thing ceasing to exist, rather than a case of a thing's properties changing. (Actually, for this claim to be true in all cases, the requirement must be slightly amended. The reason why, and the amendment needed, will be given at the very end of this part.) Notice also that the requirement of spatiotemporal continuity is an *empirical* requirement: we can determine by observation whether or not it is satisfied.

But can we also say that whenever the requirement is satisfied, then we have only a case of a thing's properties changing? No. For consider again the case of the paper that burns down to a heap of ashes. In that case, the requirement is satisfied: the piece of paper is spatiotemporally continuous with the heap of ashes. Yet, the paper has certainly lost its identity, or been destroyed. It would be easy to describe other similar cases. Such cases are important, for they show that although, if X is the same thing as Y, X is spatiotemporally continuous with Y, it is false that, if X is spatiotemporally continuous with Y, X is the same thing as Y. In other words, although X is the same thing as Y *only if* X is spatiotemporally continuous with Y, we cannot correctly say that X is the same thing as Y *if* (*just* because) X is spatiotemporally continuous with Y. Nor, therefore, can we say that X is the same thing as Y *if and only if* X is spatio-temporally continuous with Y. To put this point still another way: spatiotemporal continuity is a *necessary condition* for identity through change, but it is not also a *sufficient condition* for identity through change.

Then what conditions *are* sufficient? What, in addition to spatiotemporal continuity, would ensure that X is the same thing as Y? Our answer to this question – an answer that derives again from Locke's account of identity and diversity – may be a bit disappointing. It is that the conditions that are sufficient depend on the *sort* of thing we are talking about. For example, suppose that we are talking about a molecule of water. Then not only must it satisfy the continuity requirement, but it must retain exactly two atoms of hydrogen and one atom of oxygen; take away either the atom of oxygen or one of the atoms of hydrogen, and you have destroyed the molecule of water. On the other hand, suppose we are talking about a tree. Then not only must it satisfy the continuity requirement, but it must retain a certain configuration involving trunk, branches, etc. Except for spatiotemporal continuity, there is so to speak no exact "common measure" between the two cases. Again, it would be easy to give further examples illustrating the same point, and this shows that no specific sufficient condition of identity through change can be given that applies generally or across the board. What one can do, however, is to give a necessary condition (spatiotemporal continuity), and to indicate by examples how the conditions that are sufficient vary from one sort of object to another. From these examples, we can also extract certain features that are often relevant to a thing maintaining its identity through change, such as the features Hume identified: if the thing changes slowly, or in small ways, or in ways that preserve its function, etc. But we cannot say that any set of these features is sufficient in all cases; we cannot give a "recipe" that tells us what, beyond spatiotemporal continuity, always ensures that a thing preserves its identity.

If what we have said is correct, then there are three noteworthy consequences. First, the argument from change may now be rejected as unsound, since its second premiss is false. So, we are free to accept a bundle theory, on which a thing is a collection of property instances exhibiting spatiotemporal continuity, plus whatever other conditions are appropriate to the sort of thing that it is. Second, the substance theory commits a double error. For it purports to give a condition – retaining the same underlying substance – which is *both necessary and sufficient* for retaining an identity through change. But the condition is not necessary, and the attempt to give a sufficient condition is misconceived. Third, our discussion suggests that although we cannot give a condition for identity over time which is both necessary and sufficient, we can give at least the general form of such a condition; provided that we frame the question, not as "what is the general form of the necessary and sufficient conditions for X at t_1 to be the same thing as Y at t_2?", but rather as "what is the general form of the necessary and sufficient conditions for X at t_1 to be the same F as Y at t_2?" where F designates a kind or sort of thing. (For example, instead of asking for the necessary and sufficient conditions for the unmelted wax to be the same *thing* as the melted wax, we ask for the necessary and sufficient conditions for the unmelted wax to be the same *wax* as the melted wax.)

We can then answer our question as follows: X at t_1 is the same F as Y at t_2 if and only if:

Either

(1) X is spatiotemporally continuous with Y from t_1 to t_2; and
(2) X is a thing of kind F at t_1 and Y is a thing of kind F at t_2; and
(3a) for all times t_x and t_y between t_1 and t_2, there is no Z such that Z is spatiotemporally continuous with X or with Y from t_x to t_y and Z is not a thing of kind F.

Or

(3b) If X and Y are composed of parts, then a set of parts of X and of Y – such that, if those parts were assembled in a certain way, they would then constitute a thing of kind F – is such that each of its members satisfies conditions (1), (2), and (3a).

Clause (3b) is needed to cover cases of the sort: my watch is disassembled, the parts are sent for repair to different locations, and the watch is reassembled. Without clause (3b), we could not say that the reassembled watch is the same watch as the original one. But (3b) allows us to say that so long as the watch is composed of parts each of which individually meets conditions (1), (2), and (3a) – as would, for example, one of the watch's gears, just by virtue of exhibiting spatiotemporal continuity and being a *gear* from the time of disassembly to the time of reassembly – the reassembled watch is the same watch as the original. Finally, notice that such cases, involving disassembly, also show that the basic requirement of spatiotemporal continuity must be amended, as follows:

X at time t_1 is the same thing as Y at time t_2 only if either X is spatiotemporally continuous with Y from t_1 to t_2 or some part(s) of X are spatiotemporally continuous with some part(s) of Y from t_1 to t_2.

4 Critique of Hume's bundle theory of the self

The foregoing discussion has shown that the notion of substance, at least with respect to material things, need not be accepted. For it is possible to give an account of such things' identity through change without postulating an underlying permanent substance. So, the bundle theory (now elaborated as saying that a thing is a collection of instantiated properties exhibiting spatiotemporal continuity plus whatever other features are appropriate to the kind of thing it is) seems to be tenable and, given the objections to the substance theory that have been discussed, preferable to the substance theory. As we have seen, however, Hume also offers a bundle theory of the self or mind. Is such a theory tenable? Our thesis in this part will be that it is not.

One way to approach the issue would be to take a course parallel to that taken for material things. We could proceed by asking: what, other than mental substance, is required for a person to retain an identity over time and through change? This question, which is called "the problem of personal identity," has been discussed by both classical and contemporary philosophers. Hume, operating with his narrow definition of identity, held that personal identity is nothing but a fiction. Locke, in a classic and very influential treatment of the issue, tried to define personal identity purely in terms of memory (see Locke 1975: Book 2, Chap. 27). Today, some philosophers believe that a person retains personal identity as long as he or she retains the same body – or at least the same brain. Perhaps most contemporary philosophers think that both memory and the body must enter into an adequate account of personal identity.

Although the problem of personal identity is a fascinating one, we shall not delve into it, because to do so would require digressing at too great a length from our study of Hume.[9] Instead, we shall limit ourselves to advancing a single objection to Hume's bundle theory of the mind. In fairness to Hume, it should be noted that he may have been aware of the objection. For in his "Appendix" to the *Treatise* (T:633–6), he himself expressed dissatisfaction with his bundle theory of the self, and even retracted the theory. But he also declared himself unable to offer a better theory; for, as he acknowledged, the theory is the logical outcome of applying his test of meaning to the notion of mental substance – a test that Hume remained unable or unwilling to give up. Despite Hume's disavowal of his own bundle theory of the self, therefore, we need to see for ourselves what is wrong with the theory, and what the implications are for meaning-empiricism.

Our objection to the bundle theory may be called "the argument from the awareness of succession in time." Historically, it derives from Immanuel Kant's *Critique of Pure Reason* (1781), but this treatment is more directly inspired by the lucid presentation given by the twentieth-century English philosopher Charles A. Campbell (1962: 224–235). Suppose, to use Campbell's example, that you hear three successive strokes of a church bell.

Clearly, this is something that all of us with normal hearing can do: we can all hear the first stroke, and then hear the second stroke *as coming after the first*, and then the third stroke *as coming after the first two*. Indeed, this case is just a simple example of a basic fact about human awareness or consciousness: it is always successive or durational, and not just a momentary affair, like a spark. Admittedly, this fact does not appear to be a necessary feature of any consciousness whatsoever. A state of perpetually renewed amnesia is not logically impossible: there could be a person who at every moment forgot the preceding moment. Such a person would never have the experience of succession in time. He or she could not hear the strokes of the church bell as a succession – could not hear the second stroke as coming after the first, or the third as coming after the first and the second. For by the time this person heard the second stroke, the first stroke would have been forgotten, and by the time the person heard the third stroke, the second would have been forgotten. Nor could such a person hear a melody, or understand a sentence; he or she could have only the most primitive, momentary awareness – say a sensation of pain or of pleasure – which would be promptly forgotten forever. Such an impoverished awareness is no doubt possible; but happily it isn't the sort of awareness that we in fact have. Awareness is, for us, awareness of one state of things coming after another. Any theory of the self or the mind that is incompatible with this basic fact is untenable.

Is Hume's theory compatible with awareness of succession? According to the bundle theory, a mind or self is nothing but a series of perceptions. In terms of our example, these perceptions include each of the auditory perceptions of the bell, plus all the previous perceptions beginning with those had in infancy, and all the subsequent ones up until death. But there is no enduring mind or self, distinct from these perceptions. Does this allow for awareness of succession in time? Could a self or mind, as described by Hume, experience the second stroke as the successor of the first, and the third as the successor of the second?

To begin with, it is questionable whether Hume's theory even allows for aware-ness of each stroke *singly*. Recall that Hume holds that there cannot be any impression of the conscious subject, any more than there can be a visual impression of the point from which one sees. But if there cannot be an impression of the conscious subject, then there can be no idea of it either; so the notion ought to be rejected as meaningless. So Hume's principles commit him not only to a bundle-theory of the mind but, so to speak, to a "no-subject bundle theory." But if there is no conscious subject, then *who* or *what* is aware of each stroke of the bell? The answer, it would seem, is "no one." But then there is no awareness of the strokes, even singly; for awareness of X is a two-term relation which requires not just X, but also a conscious subject who is aware of X.

Suppose, however, that we amend Hume's theory, by supplying a conscious subject who is aware of each stroke of the bell. In other words, suppose that we change Hume's theory into a "subject bundle theory", or better put, a "bundle-of-subjects" theory, represented by the following diagram:

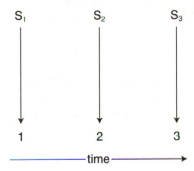

This allows for awareness of each stroke singly. But does it allow for awareness of them as successive? It does not. For if the strokes are to be heard as successive, then all of them must be heard by the same conscious subject, who must continue to exist at least from the beginning to the end of the succession. The situation must be as represented by this diagram:

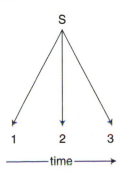

But on the "bundle-of-subjects" theory, the strokes are not heard by the same conscious subject; rather, each stroke is heard by a different conscious subject. Therefore, they are not heard as coming one after another. It is much as if our victim of perpetually renewed amnesia had been listening to the bell. The argument from the awareness of succession in time, then, is this. Awareness of succession in time requires a conscious subject who continues to exist at least from the beginning to the end of the succession; but, on Hume's theory, there is no such subject. Therefore, Hume's theory does not allow for awareness of succession in time.

As mentioned earlier, this argument derives from Kant's *Critique of Pure Reason* (in a famous and very difficult section called "The Transcendental Deduction of the Pure Concepts of the Understanding"). Later in the same work (in a section called the "Paralogisms of Pure Reason"), Kant cautions against drawing illegitimate conclusions from the argument. He points out, for example, that it does not follow that the conscious subject is an immaterial substance, or that it is indestructible, immortal, or anything of the sort. More basically, Kant points out that from this argument alone we cannot tell anything about the *nature* of the conscious subject. We can only know there must be such a subject, since that is a necessary condition of any awareness of succession in time. But our notion of this subject (to which Kant gives the imposing name "the transcendental unity of apperception") is devoid of any specific content: it is simply that which is successively aware of various items.

In somewhat the same spirit as Kant's, we should not draw illegitimate conclusions from the failure of Hume's bundle theory of the mind. In particular, we should not conclude that the Empiricist view of meaning that led to this bundle theory is completely mistaken; for an Empiricist could modify the view as follows. Instead of requiring that every meaningful descriptive term be either ostensively definable, or definable by means of terms that are themselves ostensively definable, the Empiricist could broaden the view to allow also that any term designating something which is a logically necessary condition of the sorts of experience that we have, is also meaningful. This would allow the term "conscious subject" and its cognates to be meaningful, without allowing the term "substance underlying a thing's observable properties" and its cognates to be meaningful. It would preserve the linkage of meaning to experience upon which meaning-empiricism insists.

HUME'S THEORY OF KNOWLEDGE (I)

"Hume's Fork"

1 Introduction

This chapter will discuss Hume's division of knowable propositions into two classes: "relations of ideas" and "matters of fact."[1] This division, which has come to be known as "Hume's Fork," is fundamental both to Hume's empiricism and to the twentieth-century empiricism that it inspired.[2] Hume presents it in the first two paragraphs of Section IV of the *Enquiry* (hereafter designated simply as "Section IV"). It sets the stage for the seminal critique of causal and inductive reasoning that occupies the rest of Section IV, which will be discussed in Chapter 3.

2 "Relations of ideas" and "matters of fact"

The first two paragraphs of Section IV of the *Enquiry* are as follows:

All the objects of human reason or enquiry may naturally be divided into two kinds, to wit, *Relations of Ideas*, and *Matters of Fact*. Of the first kind are the sciences of Geometry, Algebra, and Arithmetic; and, in short, every affirmation, which is either intuitively or demonstratively certain. *That the square of the hypothenuse is equal to the squares of the two sides*, is a proposition which expresses a relation between these figures. *That three times five is equal to the half of thirty*, expresses a relation between these numbers. Propositions of this kind are discoverable by the mere operation of thought, without dependence on what is anywhere existent in the universe. Though there never were a circle or triangle in nature, the truths, demonstrated by Euclid, would forever retain their certainty and evidence.

Matters of fact, which are the second objects of human reason, are not ascertained in the same manner; nor is our evidence of their truth, however great, of a like nature with the foregoing. The contrary of every matter of fact is still possible; because it can never imply a contradiction, and is conceived by the mind with the same facility and distinctness, as if ever so conformable to reality. *That the sun will not rise to-morrow* is no less intelligible a proposition, and implies no more contradiction, than the affirmation, *that it will rise*. We should in vain, therefore, attempt to demonstrate its falsehood. Were it demonstratively false, it would imply a contradiction, and could never be distinctly conceived by the mind.

What Hume is saying can be summarized as follows. There are only two kinds of knowable proposition: relations of ideas, and matters of fact. Relations of ideas have two characteristics: they are either "intuitively or demonstratively certain;" (C1) and they do not assert the existence of any non-abstract entities, such as physical objects or minds or physical or mental events or states (C2).[3] Matters of fact, on the other hand, have the following two contrasting characteristics: they do assert the existence of non-abstract entities (C3) and they are neither intuitively nor demonstratively certain (C4). Figure 2.1 expresses these contrasting characteristics.

Relations of ideas	Matters of fact
Are intuitively or demonstratively certain (C1)	Are neither intuitively nor demonstratively certain (C4)
Do not assert the existence of any non-abstract entities (C2)	Do assert the existence of non-abstract entities (C3)

Figure 2.1 Contrasting characteristics of relations of ideas and matters of fact

As we shall see shortly, (C3) requires a qualification: there is a class of propositions which Hume regards as expressing matters of fact even though those propositions do not assert the existence of anything. But before introducing this qualification, an explanation is required of the first three characteristics just mentioned, beginning with (C1) and going counter-clockwise through the above diagram.

Relations of ideas are intuitively or demonstrably certain (C1)

By a proposition which is "intuitively certain," we may understand Hume to mean one that we can know to be true just by understanding what it says; for example, *1 + 1 = 2* and *a triangle has three sides*. Notice that the proposition that *I am thinking*, whose certainty was emphasized by Descartes, is not intuitively certain in Hume's sense, even if we agree with Descartes that this proposition can be known with absolute certainty. For one does not know that this proposition is true just by understanding what it says; rather, one must not only understand the proposition, but also be introspectively aware of one's own thinking – of a certain psychological fact about oneself. An intuitively certain proposition, as Hume is here using the term, is one that we can know to be true *just* by understanding what it says; or, as some philosophers would put it, one that can be known "*ex terminis*" ("from the terms" or words in the proposition).[4] Accordingly, instead of continuing to use

Hume's term "intuitively certain," we shall henceforth say that such a proposition is *self-evident,* because the term "self-evident" nicely brings out the fact that such a proposition makes itself evident or provides the evidence for itself. By a proposition which is "demonstratively certain" we may understand Hume to mean one that follows logically from one or more self-evident propositions.[5] For convenience, we shall say that such a proposition is "demonstrable." Relations of ideas, then, are either self-evident or demonstrable.

Relations of ideas do not assert existence (C2)

In saying that relations of ideas do not assert the existence of any non-abstract entities, we are trying to state a key insight of Hume – that which he himself expresses by saying that these propositions are discoverable "without dependence on what is anywhere existent in the universe," and that "though there never were a circle or triangle in nature, the truths, demonstrated by Euclid, would forever retain their certainty and evidence." To grasp Hume's insight, consider his example of the Pythagorean theorem: "the square of the hypotenuse of a right triangle is equal to the squares of its other two sides." Suppose that no right triangles existed anywhere in the physical world, and that no one had ever even thought about a right triangle. Then the proposition that the square of the hypotenuse of a right triangle is equal to the squares of its sides *would still be true;* for in order for that proposition to be true, there do not actually have to be any right triangles (or even any triangles at all) in the world, nor need anyone ever have thought about a right triangle. The proposition only states a condition that would have to be satisfied by any right triangle that happened to exist or that anyone happened to think about; it just says that *if* X is a right triangle, then the square on X's hypotenuse must be equal to the squares on its sides. The basic point is this: propositions like the Pythagorean theorem, or that *three times five is equal to the half of thirty,* remain true regardless of what non-abstract entities exist or do not exist. But then it follows that the proposition does not assert the existence of any non-abstract entities. For if it did, then its truth would depend on whether certain non-abstract entities existed, and so it would not remain true even if those entities did not exist. A proposition that asserts the existence of X cannot remain true regardless of whether or not X exists. The argument:

p remains true regardless of whether X exists or not

∴ *p* does not assert the existence of X

is incontrovertibly valid. For brevity, we shall express Hume's point by saying that relations of ideas do not "assert existence." So, in what follows, the phrase "asserts existence" should always be understood simply as an abbreviation for "asserts the existence of some non-abstract entity."

37

Matters of fact do assert existence (C3)

In contrast to relations of ideas, propositions expressing matters of fact do – with one important exception, to be noted in a moment – assert existence. Admittedly, Hume does not explicitly state (C3) in the first two paragraphs of Section IV of the *Enquiry* (quoted above), where he presents his "Fork." Instead, the point about matters of fact that he emphasizes is that "the contrary of every matter of fact is still possible; because it can never imply a contradiction" (E:25; S:15; F:71). However, as we shall see, that point is nothing but a concise statement of Hume's fundamental argument for (C4)'s claim that no matter of fact is "demonstratively certain."[6] (C3), on the other hand, is required in order for (C2) – which, we have seen, Hume does explicitly state, if only briefly and somewhat allusively, in his remarks about mathematics in the first paragraph of Section IV – to be a characteristic that *differentiates* relations of ideas from matters of fact. Furthermore, there is ample textual support, in the rest of Section IV of the *Enquiry* and beyond, for holding that Hume regards (C3) as a defining characteristic of matters of fact: after his initial presentation of the "Fork" in the first two paragraphs of Section IV, he seldom uses the phrase "matter of fact" by itself. Instead, he often uses such phrases as: "*real existence* and matter of fact" (E:26–27; S:16–17; F:72–3); "matter of fact and *existence*" (E:35, E:156, 163–4; S:22, 107, 113; F:79, 187, 193); "matter of fact and *real existence*" (E:35; S:22, F:79); "matter of fact *or real existence*" (E:46; S:30, F:89); "*fact and existence*" (E:158; S:109; F:189; emphasis added). Consider also Hume's very first example of a matter of fact: "the sun will rise tomorrow." This proposition asserts the (future) occurrence of a physical event: the sun's rising tomorrow. And since the proposition cannot be true unless the sun exists, we may also say that the proposition asserts the existence of a physical object: the sun.

There is, however, one kind of proposition that Hume regards as expressing matters of fact even though it does not assert existence. This is any proposition that, taken together with a proposition(s) reporting what is observed at a given time t, or at a set of times $t_1, t_2, \ldots t_n$, implies the existence of some non-abstract entity which need not be observed at t, or at any of $t_1, t_2, \ldots t_n$. For example, consider a proposition in which Hume was very interested, namely the so-called "causal principle" or "causal maxim," which says that *every event has a cause.* Taken by itself, this proposition does not assert the existence of anything. But, taken together with a proposition reporting some observed event, it implies the existence of a cause of that event – whether or not that cause is also observed. We shall call propositions of this sort *bridging propositions*, since they allow one to infer the existence of something unobserved from something observed:

Every event has a cause (bridging proposition).
Event e was observed at t (observation).

∴ Event e had a cause, c (item that need not be observed).

Particular causal laws, and laws of nature in general, are bridging propositions. To take a simple example, from the proposition that water boils at 212 F° at sea level, together with the observation that a certain quantity of water is now boiling at sea level, one can infer the existence of a source of heat, whether or not that source is observed; so the law that water boils at 212 F° at sea level is a bridging proposition. As can be seen from our two examples, bridging propositions can have various degrees of generality. The principle that every event has a cause, ranging as it does over all events, past, present, and future, is much more general than the law about water or any other specific law of nature.

Another highly general bridging proposition in which Hume was especially interested (for reasons discussed in Chapter 3) is the so-called "principle of induction" or "principle of the uniformity of nature," i.e. the principle that "the future will resemble the past" or that "there is a conformity between the future and the past." That Hume considered this principle to be a matter of fact is clear from his *Abstract* of the *Treatise*, where he explicitly says: "All probable arguments are built on the supposition that there is this conformity betwixt the future and the past. . . . This conformity is a *matter of fact*". (T:651; S:131; F:34).

To see that the Principle of Induction is also a bridging proposition, suppose that we conjoin it with the following report of our observations: "Past flashes of lightning have always been followed by claps of thunder, and there is now a flash of lightning." Then, assuming that the "conformity" or "resemblance" Hume speaks of is understood, as he intends, to assert that events which in our past experience have always been paired will continue to be paired in the future, the principle of induction, conjoined with the proposition reporting our observations, implies that there will be a thunderclap. Thus:

The future will resemble the past (bridging proposition).
Past lightning flashes have been followed by thunderclaps,
and there is now a flash of lightning (observations made at $t_1, t_2, \ldots t_n$).

∴ There will be a thunderclap (the as yet unobserved event).

Hume's "matters of fact," then, include bridging propositions as well as propositions that actually assert existence, and his relations of ideas exclude them. For convenience, we shall say that bridging propositions "imply existence." So, in what follows, the phrase "implies existence" will always be an abbreviation for the longer expression, "does not assert existence, but does imply, in conjunction with a proposition(s) reporting what is observed at t, or at $t_1, t_2 \ldots t_n$, the existence of some non-abstract entity that need not be observed at t, or at any of $t_1, t_2 \ldots t_n$." Hume's "matters of fact," then, either assert or imply existence; his "relations of ideas" neither assert nor imply existence.

Using these abbreviations, together with the terms "self-evident" and "demonstrable" that we substituted for Hume's "intuitively certain" and "demonstratively certain," we can update Figure 2.1 and summarize his overall doctrine this way:

Relations of ideas	Matters of fact
Are self-evident or demonstrable (C1)	Are neither self-evident nor demonstrable (C4)
Do not assert or imply existence (C2)	Assert or imply existence (C3)

Figure 2.2 Matters of fact and relations of ideas: Hume's doctrine summarized

Matters of fact are neither self-evident nor demonstrable

We come at last to the key negative thesis of Hume's doctrine – that no proposition stating any matter of fact is either self-evident or demonstrable. This claim has sweeping implications for philosophy. For if Hume is right, then it follows that the only propositions that are either self-evident or demonstrable are those expressing "relations of ideas" – propositions that do not assert or imply existence. By contrast, no proposition that asserts or implies existence is either self-evident or demonstrable. Therefore, what Rationalist metaphysicians tried to do – to demonstrate the existence of various entities such as God, souls, substance, monads, or even the material world – is impossible. In the famous peroration of the *Enquiry,* Hume trumpets forth the sweeping implications of his "Fork:"

> When we run over libraries, persuaded of these principles, what havoc must we make? If we take in our hand any volume; of divinity or school metaphysics, for instance; let us ask, *Does it contain any abstract reasoning concerning quantity or number?* No. *Does it contain any experimental reasoning concerning matter of fact and existence?* No. Commit it then to the flames: for it can contain nothing but sophistry and illusion.
>
> (E:165; S:114; F:195)

What Hume's Fork denies, then, is nothing less than the possibility of using reason to demonstrate the existence of anything either natural or divine.

Here it might be objected that we are exaggerating the implications of Hume's doctrine, because not all the major arguments offered by Rationalist metaphysicians are demonstrations in Hume's sense. For example, Descartes' causal proofs of God's existence in his *Third Meditation,* as well as his proof of the physical world's existence in his *Sixth Meditation,* use premises describing his ideas of God and his ideas of sensible things, respectively, that are not self-evident in Hume's sense, but are supposed to be certain through introspection. However, those proofs also use bridging propositions (notably certain causal principles) which are not certain through introspection and which, if Hume is right, are neither self-evident nor demonstrable. So Hume's Fork does imply – assuming (as Descartes and virtually all other seventeenth- and eighteenth-century philosophers did assume, and as more than just a few contemporary philosophers also assume) that knowledge requires certainty, and that the only sources of certainty are introspection, self-evidence, and demonstration – that those arguments do not yield knowledge of their conclusions.

We shall need, therefore, to look carefully at Hume's rationale for (C4) – his key negative claim that no matter of fact is either self-evident or demonstrable. This will be done partly in the final of the present chapter, and partly in the next chapter. The purpose of the next two parts of this chapter, however, is to relate Hume's Fork to the well-known formulation of the more modern Empiricist position on knowledge due to Immanuel Kant. So, if you are interested in immediately considering Hume's rationale for (C4), or in focusing exclusively on the development of Hume's own theory of knowledge quite apart from Kant's formulation of the Humean position, then you may wish to go directly to the material in part 5 of the present chapter and in parts 1–4 of Chapter 3. (Except for some cautionary remarks in the third and fourth paragraphs of part 5 of the present chapter and in notes 18 and 19, this material does not presuppose anything in parts 3 and 4 of the present chapter, although part 5 of Chapter 3 does presuppose familiarity with some basic definitional points about "a priori"–"a posteriori" and "analytic"–"synthetic" that are explained at the beginning of the next part.)

3 A modernized version of Hume's Fork

As we have just seen, Hume's Fork poses a basic challenge to the ambitions of Rationalist metaphysicians. In our own century, however, this challenge usually has been formulated in a way rather different from Hume's. Instead of using Hume's concepts of relations of ideas and matters of fact, recent Empiricists have formulated Hume's challenge in the a priori–a posteriori, analytic–synthetic terminology introduced by Immanuel Kant. Their position, the modernized version to the extent that it is directly inspired by Hume's doctrine, can be formulated in this way:

MV *All knowable propositions are either analytic a priori or synthetic a posteriori.*

In this part, we shall discuss this modernized version of Hume's Fork. This will enable us to deepen our understanding of the issue between Rationalist and Empiricist traditions. It will also put us in a position to indicate some subtle differences between Hume's own empiricism and the contemporary empiricism it has inspired – differences that are commonly overlooked but that need to be noticed in order to assess Hume's position accurately.

Let us begin by going over Kant's terminology. Kant offers us two pairs of contrasting terms, "a priori" versus "a posteriori," and "analytic" versus "synthetic," that are used to classify statements or propositions along two different dimensions.

41

The a priori–a posteriori contrast classifies statements in terms of how they can be known; it is an epistemological contrast. The analytic–synthetic contrast classifies statements in terms of what makes them true or false; it is a semantic contrast. Let us look more closely at each of these two contrasts.

As we saw in Chapter 1, an a priori proposition is defined as one that is knowable just by thinking (e.g. "no one can be his or her own parent"), and an a posteriori proposition is defined as one that is knowable only by experience (e.g. "some people are over six feet tall"). To avoid possible misunderstanding, we should note here that "knowable just by thinking" does not mean "not knowable by experience;" for it is possible for an a priori proposition to be known by experience. For example, although mathematical statements are a priori, many of them are complex and so are known just by thinking only by those mathematicians who grasp their proofs, while other people may know them on the basis of experience – by hearing of their truth from mathematicians or reading that they are true in mathematics texts. Rather than meaning "not knowable by experience," then, the phrase "knowable just by thinking" means, roughly speaking, "knowable without experience." To see why this is still only roughly right, note that for us to know even a simple a priori statement like *1 + 1 = 2* or *no one can be his/her own parent* some experience is needed; namely, the experience required to learn the meanings of terms – of "1", "+", "2," "parent," etc. Thus, if "knowable just by thinking" meant "knowable without *any* experience whatsoever," then no statements would be a priori, because a statement cannot be known unless it is understood; but it cannot be understood unless its constituent terms are understood, and those terms cannot be understood (at least by human beings) unless their meanings have been learned through various sorts of experience. Thus, a more accurate interpretation of the phrase "knowable just by thinking" is this: "knowable without experience, except for the experience required to learn the meanings of terms."

By contrast, an a posteriori statement cannot be known in this way; for even after one fully understands (the meanings of the terms in) a statement like *some people are over six feet tall*, one may be completely in the dark as to whether the statement is true or false: only experience can determine this. Note, however, that the phrase "knowable only by experience" also requires a bit of clarification; for it does not mean, as one might think, "knowable just by experience." This is because at least some a posteriori statements require thinking as well as experience in order to be known; for example, our knowledge of scientific laws rests not only on observations but also on complex inferences or extrapolations from those observations.[7] Thus, instead of meaning "knowable just by experience," the phrase "knowable only by experience" means "not knowable without experience (other than or in addition to the experience needed to learn the meanings of terms)."

Although "a priori" and "a posteriori" are used to classify statements, they are essentially epistemological terms, pertaining to the *way* in which those statements are *known*. So, we shall follow the common practice of sometimes using these terms apart from reference to statements. For example, we shall sometimes speak simply of a priori knowledge, meaning knowledge had just by thinking; and of something being knowable a priori or in an a priori manner, meaning that it is knowable just by thinking. Of course, "knowable just by thinking" here does not exclude whatever experience may be needed to acquire the concepts presupposed by the knowledge in question.

Let us now turn to the analytic–synthetic contrast. To avoid misrepresenting the current philosophical landscape, we should first note that the analytic–synthetic distinction is by no means uncontroversial. Some contemporary philosophers, notably the influential American thinker W. V. O. Quine, question the tenability of the distinction; others defend the distinction.[8] Our purpose here, however, is to see how the distinction is commonly used to define the issue between Rationalists and Empiricists, and to see how that issue, so defined, relates to Hume's own "Fork." Therefore, we shall not enter into the controversy concerning the tenability of the analytic–synthetic distinction, but rather assume that the distinction is tenable and merely expound it as it would be usually understood by those who accept it.

An analytic statement is defined as one which is true solely in virtue of the meanings of its constituent terms.[9] A standard example is "all bachelors are unmarried men."[10] Notice that although this statement is not couched in the form of a definition – it does not start with "a bachelor is . . . " or "the term 'bachelor' means . . . " – it is actually a definition, since "bachelor" means just "unmarried man." This is why the statement is true solely in virtue of the meanings of its constituent terms. Definitions, then, are one type of analytic statement.

Another type of analytic statement consists of what we may call "conceptual truths." These are not definitions, but they are still true in virtue of meaning. An example is "something cannot be both round and square." Although not a definition of either "round" or "square," this statement is still true in virtue of those terms' meanings, or of the *concepts* "round" and "square;" for "round" is defined partly in terms of "having no angles," while "square" is defined in terms of "rectangular," which in turn is defined in terms of "having four angles."

The third and most fundamental type of analytic statement consists of statements that are true in virtue of their logical form. Two examples are: "either it is raining or it is not raining;" and "it is not both raining and not raining." To see why these two statements are true because of their logical forms, we can extract their respective forms, as follows:

Either p or not p.

Not (p and not p).

It is obvious that any statement having either of these forms, no matter what specific sentence one substitutes for "p," must be true. This is why the two statements about rain, as well as any other statements obtained by substituting a given statement for "p" in either form, can be said to be "true because of their

43

logical form." But why, you may ask, are such statements analytic? The answer is that, like definitions and conceptual truths, they are true solely in virtue of the meanings of their constituent terms. Specifically, our sample statements are true in virtue of the meanings of the terms "either–or," "not," and "and," – terms that give the statements their logical form and that, in the field of logic, are called "logical connectives."

There is an important relationship between analyticity (i.e. being an analytic statement) and contradiction: the negation (denial) of the truth of an analytic statement is always a contradiction, and conversely the negation of a contradiction is always an analytic statement. Thus, for example, the negation of "all bachelors are unmarried men" is "some bachelors are not unmarried men," which is a contradiction because "bachelor" means "unmarried man;" so that the negated statement says that some unmarried men are not unmarried men, which is a contradiction (since it means that some men are both unmarried and not unmarried). Conversely, the negation of "some bachelors are not unmarried men" is "all bachelors are unmarried men," which is analytic. Similar considerations apply to the other examples we have given. Thus, for instance, the negation of "either p or not p" is "neither p nor not p", meaning the same as "not p and (also) not not p," meaning simply "not p and p," which is of course a contradiction. Conversely, the negation of "not p and p" is "not (not p and p)," which is analytic.

To turn to the last of Kant's four terms, "synthetic": a synthetic statement is simply one whose truth or falsity does *not* depend solely on the meanings of its constituent terms. Three such statements are: "all bachelors are taxpayers;" "there are nine planets;" and "every event has a cause." None of these is true solely by virtue of its constituent terms, and each of them can be denied without embracing a contradiction. Notice how the first statement, "all bachelors are taxpayers," contrasts with "all bachelors are unmarried men." Notice also that the third statement could be turned into an analytic truth by substituting "effect" for "event." As Hume remarked, "every event has a cause" is to "every effect has a cause" as "every man is married" is to "every husband is married" (T:82; F:50).

Using the four Kantian terms that we have now defined, we can classify all possible knowable propositions. As a preliminary point, notice that since one cannot *know* a false proposition – since "S knows that p" entails that p is true – we can limit this classification to true propositions.[11] We could avoid this limitation by construing "knowable" to mean not just "knowably true," but "knowably true or knowably false," and by stipulating that "analytic" applies to any proposition that is true *or false* solely by virtue of meaning, that is, to (what are sometimes called) "analytically false" as well as to "analytically true" propositions. But there is no important advantage to be gained by these maneuvers; so we shall confine the classification to true propositions.

Now, no true proposition can be neither analytic nor synthetic: it must be one or the other – either true solely in virtue of meaning, or true not solely in virtue of meaning. Furthermore, no knowable proposition can be neither a priori nor a posteriori: every such proposition must be either knowable just by thinking (i.e. knowable without experience except for the experiences required to learn the meanings of its constituent terms), or else knowable only by experience (i.e. not knowable without experience in addition to the experiences required to learn the meanings of its constituent terms). Thus, every knowable proposition must be either analytic or synthetic and either a priori or a posteriori. Furthermore, it is clear that no proposition can be both analytic and synthetic or both a priori and a posteriori. Thus, going simply by the permutations allowed by Kant's four terms, there are just four possible classes of knowable propositions: analytic a priori; synthetic a priori; analytic a posteriori; and synthetic a posteriori. We can represent these four classes as shown in Figure 2.3.

	Analytic	Synthetic
A priori	1	2
A posteriori	3	4

Figure 2.3 The four classes of knowable propositions

We can now formulate the issue between the Rationalist and Empiricist schools in terms of these four classes of propositions, for we can use the classification to express both the points of agreement and the point of disagreement between the two schools. Rationalists and Empiricists agree on three points.

1   Both affirm that there are instances of classes 1 and 4. It is generally agreed, for example, that at least definitions and the principles of logic are analytic a priori; and that perceptual judgments and the laws of physics are synthetic a posteriori. In addition, many philosophers believe that mathematics consists of analytic a priori statements; and many would say that there are purely conceptual truths which are properly classified as analytic a priori.

2   Rationalists and Empiricists agree that there are no instances of class 3, and thus that all analytic propositions are a priori. This is because if a proposition is analytic – if it is true solely by virtue of the meanings of its constituent terms – then surely experience is not required to determine its truth: that can be known just by understanding what the proposition says.

3   Rationalists and Empiricists agree that although important, instances of class 1

are *not informative about reality.* Consider for example any particular instance of the statement-form "*p* or not *p*" – say the statement "either it is raining or it is not raining." This statement remains true no matter what the weather is like; so it does not convey any information about the weather conditions. The same point applies to any other analytic statement. The statement that all bachelors are unmarried men, for example, would remain true even if there were no bachelors or men or unmarried people, since its truth is guaranteed by the mere synonymy of the words "bachelor" and "unmarried man." Thus it remains true no matter what anyone's marital status is, and so does not convey information about anyone's marital status. Putting the point more grandly, analytic statements do not convey any information about reality, since they remain true no matter what reality is like. This point is rather similar to, though more general than, one of Hume's key points about his "relations of ideas." Relations of ideas, you will recall, do not assert the existence of any non-abstract entities, since they remain true no matter what non-abstract entities (e.g. physical or mental objects, states, or events) exist or do not exist. Similarly, the reason why analytic propositions do not describe or convey any information about reality is that they remain true no matter what reality is actually like.

What then is the disagreement between Rationalist and Empiricist philosophers? This: Rationalists affirm, while Empiricists deny, that there are instances of class 2 – synthetic a priori propositions. To properly understand this disagreement, it is important to be clear as to exactly what is meant by denying that there are synthetic a priori propositions. This denial does not mean that there are no propositions which are synthetic but non-empirical (i.e. synthetic but not a posteriori). Rather, it means that any such proposition would be *unknowable.* In what follows, we shall often say that according to empiricism, there are no synthetic a priori propositions. But this will not mean that no proposition is both synthetic and not knowable by experience, but rather than no proposition is both synthetic and knowable just by thinking. Thus, empiricism, as here understood, implies that any proposition that is synthetic but not knowable by experience, while still a genuine proposition, also would not be knowable just by thinking and so would be utterly unknowable (assuming there are no sources of knowledge other than thinking and experience). As we shall see below, some twentieth-century Empiricists – the Logical Positivists – went even further, and claimed that no genuine proposition can be both synthetic and non-empirical. But the weaker doctrine that any such proposition is unknowable, if correct, is strong enough to ruin the hopes of Rationalist metaphysicians.

To gain a better grasp of why Rationalists are committed to affirming, and Empiricists to denying, that there are synthetic a priori propositions, consider the following five propositions:

(a) There is a reason or explanation for every matter of fact whatsoever.
(b) Every event has a cause.

(c)   If there is a property, then there must be a substance to which it belongs.

(d)   Existence is a perfection.

(e)   If I can clearly and distinctly conceive of X as existing apart from Y, then X really can exist without Y, at least by God's power.

This is simply a sample list of propositions that have been upheld by Rationalists. For example, Descartes holds at least (b)–(e), and uses these propositions in constructing proofs of the existence of God and of his famous dualism of mind and body. As for (a), which is called "the principle of sufficient reason," it has been upheld by Leibniz (who coined the name), Spinoza, and many other thinkers.

Now let us ask: into which of the three available classes of propositions – analytic a priori, synthetic a priori, and synthetic a posteriori – do (a)–(e) fall? Well, it is clear that none of them is true solely in virtue of the meanings of its constituent terms; so they are not analytic a priori. Therefore, they are either synthetic a priori or synthetic a posteriori. But we can eliminate the latter possibility, for historical as well as philosophical reasons. The historical reason is simply that philosophers who rely on these propositions do not take them to be a posteriori (empirical). Descartes, for example, would certainly not say that (b), (c), (d) or (e) rest on experience. Rather, each of these is supposed to be a "clear and distinct" proposition which is either self-evident or deducible from self-evident propositions. As for (a), philosophers who uphold it have usually taken it to be self-evident to any rational mind.

The fact that philosophers have not taken (a)–(e) to be empirical, however, is not the only reason for denying that they are empirical; there are genuinely philosophical reasons. In the case of (c), (d), and (e), these are fairly obvious. Empirical evidence seems simply irrelevant to their truth or falsity; no *observation*, it seems, could possibly count as evidence for or against them: they are simply not the sort of propositions that could be either supported or disconfirmed by observation.

In the case of (a) and (b), matters are more complex. It would no doubt be possible to regard (a) and (b) as expressing an empirical proposition. But then those propositions could not play the role assigned to them in major Rationalist systems like those of Descartes, Spinoza, or Leibniz. For in those systems, (a) and (b) are typically used to establish the existence of things which in the nature of the case cannot be observed, notably God. God is taken, by philosophers who appeal to (a), to be the reason or explanation for the most all-encompassing of matters of fact, namely the existence of the universe itself. Or God is taken, by philosophers who appeal to (b), to be the unseen "first cause" of all other causes. However, if (a) and (b) are regarded as empirical propositions, then they cannot be used in such a manner. The reason for this can be explained as follows. Principles (a) and (b) have the same logical form as the statement "every substance has a solvent": just as that statement, as understood in modern logic, says "for every substance, there exists some solvent," so (a) says "for every matter of fact, there exists some explanation," and (b) says "for every event, there exists some cause." Now such statements, unlike simple empirical generalizations of the form "every A is a B," are not falsifiable: for example, failure to identify a solvent for a substance cannot be used to show that it has no solvent, because we might simply not have looked long enough or far enough for the solvent. However, since "every substance has a solvent" is an empirical statement, the failure to find a solvent for a substance would provide at least some evidence that it has no solvent: it would *disconfirm*, though it would not *falsify* (i.e. definitely refute), the statement that every substance has a solvent. Likewise, if (a) and (b) are construed as empirical propositions, then the fact that we cannot observe God's existence or creative activity provides some evidence against, or disconfirms, those propositions. But then they cannot reasonably be used as premises to argue for that very existence or activity. For, surely, if failure to observe *that p* is a disconfirmation of *q*, and we do fail to observe *that p*, then *q* cannot reasonably be used as a premiss supporting *p*. For example, if failure to observe any solvent for a substance of kind *k* disconfirms the proposition that every substance has a solvent, and we do fail to observe any solvent for substances of kind *k*, then the proposition that every substance has a solvent cannot reasonably be used as support for the claim that there is a solvent for substances of kind *k*. Rather than regarding (a) and (b) as empirical claims, then, a Rationalist would hold that failing to observe a reason for some matter of fact, or a cause for a certain event, are not observations that would disconfirm (a) or (b); for (a) and (b) were not based on observation in the first place.

The upshot of all this is that (a)–(e) are neither analytic a priori nor synthetic a posteriori. So, they must be synthetic a priori (assuming that they are knowable at all).

Why do Empiricists deny that there are such propositions? The reason is that such a proposition would be both informative about reality, and knowable just by thinking. But Empiricists are convinced that any proposition that purports to inform us about reality must be based on experience. They find it mysterious, even incredible, that a proposition could be both informative about reality and knowable just by thinking. So, they conclude that the only propositions that can be known just by thinking are analytic a priori propositions, which convey no information about reality, since their truth depends solely on the meanings of their constituent terms. By contrast, Rationalists believe that some genuinely informative propositions, like (a)–(e), can be known just by thinking – that reason is an autonomous source of knowledge about reality.

It was this claim about the power of human reason that led Immanuel Kant, the first philosopher to formulate the issue between rationalism and empiricism in the way just presented, to assign great importance to his famous question: "How are synthetic a priori judgments possible?" As Kant's way of putting this question shows, he believed that there are synthetic a priori propositions – which makes him, strictly speaking, a Rationalist. However, Kant also drew a distinction *within* the class of propositions that are synthetic but non-empirical (i.e. synthetic but not knowable by experience) – a distinction, roughly speaking, between those that *apply* to experience (though they are not *based* on experience) and those that do not apply to experience. He then argued, against empiricism, that there are synthetic a priori propositions of the first sort, and, against rationalism, that there are no synthetic a priori propositions of the second sort. So Kant's own position, which is called "the Critical Philosophy," is neither purely Rationalist nor purely Empiricist.

In our own century, some Empiricists, known as the "Logical Positivists," went even further in their condemnation of synthetic a priori propositions than does the modernized version of Hume's "Fork". Instead of saying that any proposition which is both synthetic and non-empirical is unknowable, they maintained that, strictly speaking, there are no such propositions. They held that the sentences that *seem* to express such propositions, and which Rationalists hold to express synthetic a priori propositions, are literally meaningless. Such sentences are grammatically well-formed but senseless combinations of words – gibberish akin to "green pains listen chemically." To support this radical doctrine, the Logical Positivists invoked their notorious "verifiability criterion of meaning." This doctrine stated that every meaningful sentence must express either an analytic proposition or a proposition which is verifiable or testable by some empirical procedure.

Today this radical version of empiricism, which was at the forefront of philosophy in the 1930s and 1940s, is defunct. One reason for this is that the Logical Positivists were never able to explain clearly what they meant by "empirically verifiable." Every attempt they made to do so had the unwelcome result either that sentences that were supposedly unverifiable, for example theological sentences turned out to be verifiable after all, or that certain scientific sentences whose meaningfulness the Positivists were anxious to preserve (e.g. sentences in physics about unobservable particles) turned out to be unverifiable and so meaningless. Another reason for the demise of logical positivism was that philosophers soon realized that the verifiability criterion of meaning *itself* is neither analytic nor empirically verifiable; so that the criterion is, in a quite radical sense, self-refuting: it excludes itself from the class of meaningful sentences, i.e. it implies its own meaninglessness. As we shall see in part 4, an analogous difficulty afflicts the modernized version of Hume's "Fork" that we have been considering.

4 A critique of the modernized "Fork"

If the modernized version of Hume's "Fork" is sound, then an argument can easily be constructed to show that the propositions typically upheld by Rationalists are unknowable. This "anti-Rationalist argument" starts from the modernized fork (MV hereafter) itself and goes as follows:

MV: All knowable propositions are either analytic a priori or synthetic a posteriori. Propositions typically upheld by Rationalists, such as (a)–(e) (discussed in the previous part), are neither analytic a priori nor synthetic a posteriori.

∴ Propositions typically upheld by Rationalists are unknowable.

This part will offer a critique of this argument. The critique will focus on the leading principle of the argument, MV itself, and will argue that MV is a self-refuting principle, in a sense of "self-refuting" to be explained presently. Then we will examine the implications of this critique for the original version of Hume's Fork in terms of "relations of ideas" and "matters of fact."

Suppose that we ask the following question: is MV *itself* analytic a priori or synthetic a posteriori? If it is neither, the anti-Rationalist argument is ruined. For then the Rationalist can give the following counter-argument, which we will call the "anti-Empiricist rebuttal":

(A) If MV is knowable, then MV is either analytic a priori or synthetic a posteriori. (deduced from MV itself)
(B) MV is neither analytic a priori nor synthetic a posteriori.

(C) ∴ MV is unknowable.

The upshot is that if MV of Hume's Fork is true, then it is unknowable![12]

An analogy may help to clarify the logic of the situation. Consider statement (D): "All knowable statements are less than five words in length." Clearly, (D) is such that if (D) is true, then – since (D) itself is more than five words long – it cannot be known. We might say that (D) is an "epistemologically self-refuting" statement – one that, if true, is unknowable. Likewise, according to the above argument, MV is such that, if it is true, then – since MV itself is neither analytic a priori nor synthetic a posteriori – it cannot be known.

Since a proponent of MV is logically committed to premiss (A) in virtue of accepting MV itself, the only way she could refute the anti-Empiricist rebuttal would be to refute premiss (B), by showing either that MV is analytic a priori or that it is synthetic a posteriori. I will now argue that neither of these alternatives is tenable.

Let us consider, first, whether MV is analytic. It is certainly not an obviously analytic truth, like "all bachelors are unmarried" or "triangles are three-sided." It might be suggested, however, that it is an unobviously analytic truth – that it follows logically from statements that are themselves obviously analytic. Whether this is so depends on whether there exists a valid argument for MV, each premiss of which is obviously analytic.

Can one construct such an argument? There is reason to think that Empiricists would subscribe to the following argument, in which "p" ranges over all noncontradictory propositions.[13]

(1) If p is not true solely by virtue of meanings, then p is true or false by virtue of some feature of reality.
(2) If p is true or false by virtue of some feature of reality, then p is not knowable just by thinking.

From these two premisses, it follows that:

(3) If p is not true solely by virtue of meanings, then p is not knowable just by thinking.

From (3), it follows that:

(4) If p is knowable just by thinking, then p is true solely by virtue of meanings.

But, by the definition of an a priori proposition as one that is knowable just by thinking, and of an analytic proposition as one that is true solely by virtue of the meanings of its constituent terms, (4) says the same thing as:

(5) If p is a priori, then p is analytic.

Of course, (5) itself would already rule out synthetic propositions from the class of a priori propositions. So, if the argument as so far developed shows that (5) is analytic, then Empiricists are already vindicated: they need not establish MV's analyticity in order to secure their position. Nevertheless, it is worth noting that MV can be derived from (5), with the help of three further premisses. Those premisses are:

(6) If p is analytic, then p is a priori.
(7) If p is knowable, then either p is a priori or p is empirical.
(8) Either p is analytic or p is synthetic.

MV can now be deduced from (5)–(8), as follows:

(9) p is a priori if and only if p is analytic (from (5) & (6)).
(10) If p is knowable, then p is either analytic or synthetic (from (8)).
(11) If p is knowable, then p is either analytic a priori or synthetic and empirical (from (7), (9), & (10)).[14]

But (11) is logically equivalent to MV; so the derivation of MV is now complete.

But does the derivation show that MV is an unobviously analytic truth? It does so only if each of the five premisses (1), (2), (6), (7), and (8) is obviously analytic. Philosophers who accept the analytic–synthetic and a priori–a posteriori distinctions would presumably hold that (1), (6), (7), and (8) are conceptual truths that can be grasped by anyone who understands the terms involved. Since the analytic–synthetic and a priori–a posteriori distinctions themselves are not at issue here, let us grant, at least for the sake of the argument, that those premisses are obviously analytic. This leaves only one premiss to examine: premiss (2).

Is (2) obviously analytic? This question virtually answers itself: far from being obviously analytic, (2) is synthetic. For surely (2) is not a proposition that is true solely by virtue of the meanings of its constituent terms (or whose denial is self-contradictory). Rather, it expresses a substantive thesis. For the idea behind (2) is this: when a proposition is true or false because of some feature of reality – when its truth or falsity depends on what reality is like – then that proposition conveys some information (or misinformation) about reality: it makes a claim about reality;

but when a proposition makes a claim about reality, then it cannot be known by mere thinking. That, of course, is what Empiricists believe: they hold that when a proposition makes a claim about reality, then it can be known only by experience – that reason (rational thinking) is not an independent source of knowledge about reality. Notice that this does not mean just that thinking alone cannot establish the *existence* of certain things, like God. It means also that thinking alone cannot show that things known to exist by experience, such as persons, have certain general features, such as being only material, or only mental, or both material and mental. Now whether this view about the limitations of human reason is correct or incorrect, it certainly does not appear to be an analytic truth. We may conclude, then, that the above argument fails to show that MV is unobviously analytic.

Accordingly, let us next consider whether MV could be synthetic a posteriori. If it is, then, since it says that all knowable statements are analytic a priori or synthetic a posteriori, it would have the logical form of a simple empirical generalization, like "all crows are black."[15] But as we have seen, simple empirical generalizations (unlike generalizations of the kind "every substance has a solvent," which say that the items generalized about are related to some existing item, or involve what logic calls "mixed quantification") must be empirically falsifiable. It must be possible to describe some observation that would show such a statement to be false. Now, how could one show that MV is false? Well, one would have to show that some synthetic proposition(s) are a priori. There are only two ways in which this could be done. One would be to give some abstract argument showing that there are synthetic a priori propositions. But to give such an argument is obviously not to describe any *observation* that would falsify MV. The other way would be to discover the truth of, or actually come to know, some synthetic a priori proposition. Suppose that such a proposition, which we may call "p," did come to be known by a person, S. Could S's knowing that p empirically falsify MV? Clearly, the mere fact of S's knowing p just by thinking could not by itself empirically falsify MV, for it would then be a case of a priori knowledge and so not an observation. However, it might be argued that S's knowing p could empirically falsify MV, in either of two different ways:

(1) S might come to know p just by thinking and also come to know *that she had thus come to know p*, and this second-level knowledge of a synthetic proposition known a priori would itself be an observation that falsified MV; or
(2) S might know empirically, perhaps via a testimonial chain that S had good reason to trust, that someone else (perhaps an expert on the matter in question) knew p just by thinking, and this "second-hand" knowledge that there was a synthetic proposition known a priori would, again, be an observation that falsified MV.

Neither of these, however, constitutes empirical falsification in the relevant sense. For both of them appeal to observations that S can make only if S herself, or someone else, has come to know that p in a non-observational or a priori way. But for a proposition to be falsifiable in the sense that would show it to be an empirical proposition, it must not be the case that some proposition which must be known in order to make the falsifying observation must itself be known a priori. The falsifying observation must not be parasitic, so to speak, on some item of a priori knowledge. Otherwise, it would be possible to use the falsifiability test to "show" that many a priori propositions are really empirical ones. For consider a proposition that can be known a priori to be false, such as $2 + 3 = 6$. Suppose that either (i) S knows a priori that $2 + 3 \neq 6$, and observes that she knows this a priori, or (ii) for some reason S is unable to do any arithmetic, but comes to know that $2 + 3 \neq 6$ on the basis of testimony. Suppose we regard these observations as empirically falsifying $2 + 3 = 6$. Then $2 + 3 = 6$ must be regarded as an empirical falsehood. Furthermore, since the denial of an empirical statement must itself be empirical, $2 + 3 \neq 6$ must be regarded as an empirical statement. Surely, this is absurd: neither (i) nor (ii) shows that $2 + 3 = 6$ is a merely empirical falsehood, or that $2 + 3 \neq 6$ is an empirical statement. Likewise, neither (1) nor (2) above would show that MV is an empirical statement. We may conclude that MV is not an empirical proposition.

Our conclusion concerning MV, then, is that it is an epistemologically self-refuting proposition. (The same conclusion holds for the simpler (5): it too is synthetic but non-empirical, and so unknowable if true.) Therefore, MV cannot be used to show that there are no synthetic a priori propositions, or that propositions like (a)–(e) are unknowable. Note, however, that it does *not* follow from this that there *are* any synthetic a priori propositions, or that propositions like (a)–(e) are knowable. Whether this is so is a question that our critique of MV leaves open. Furthermore, an Empiricist can still argue that certain specific synthetic propositions are not a priori, or that certain types of synthetic proposition are not a priori. For instance, the Empiricist can still argue that no proposition that asserts or implies existence is a priori. As we shall see in the next part and in Chapter 3, this is in effect what Hume does.

Before concluding this part, however, one important question remains. The modernized fork, we have argued, is self-refuting. But what about Hume's own "Fork" – that all knowable propositions are either relations of ideas or matters of fact? Is it self-refuting too? Interestingly enough, the answer to this question is "no." For although it is sometimes uncritically assumed that Hume's relations of ideas are exactly the same as analytic a priori propositions and that his matters of fact are exactly the same as synthetic a posteriori propositions, there are in fact subtle differences between Hume's own Fork and MV. The most important difference is this: the class of propositions that according to Hume's doctrine can be known only by experience is *narrower* than the class of propositions that can be known only by experience according to MV. Concomitantly, the class of propositions that can be known a priori is potentially wider on Hume's doctrine than on MV. The reason for this difference is that Hume's "matters of fact," as we have seen, include only propositions *that assert or imply existence*. Now it is plausible to hold (at least if the ontological argument for God's existence is assumed to be unsound) that all propositions which assert existence are synthetic – that no non-abstract entities exist "by definition."[16] It seems safe to say also that propositions which imply existence, like *every event has a cause* and *there is a reason or explanation for every matter of fact whatsoever*, are synthetic. However, the converse does not hold: not all synthetic propositions assert or imply existence. On the contrary, there are some that do not, for instance "there are no three-winged birds." Hume's own Fork, unlike MV, leaves open the possibility that some of these synthetic propositions may be knowable a priori. One such proposition may well be Hume's Fork itself – the proposition that all knowable propositions are either relations of ideas or matters of fact. For this proposition obviously does not assert or imply the existence of anything. Hume's Fork would then itself have to fall into the class of relations of ideas, since all of his matters of fact do assert or imply existence, and relations of ideas comprise the only other class of knowable propositions. But, while this result may surprise those who assume that Hume's relations of ideas are exactly the same as analytic propositions, it does seem acceptable. For although all analytic propositions are relations of ideas, the converse need not hold. Hume's relations of ideas do not have to be analytic: they need only be knowable a priori and not assert or imply existence.

One may well feel that despite the differences between MV and Hume's own Fork, it should be possible to formulate Hume's Fork in Kant's terminology. This is indeed the case; the formulation, which we shall call MV1, would go as follows:

All knowable propositions are either:

(a)   analytic a priori; or
(b)   synthetic a priori propositions that do not assert or imply existence; or
(c)   synthetic a posteriori propositions that assert or imply existence.

Hume's "relations of ideas" are (a) and (b); his "matters of fact" are (c). Since MV1 itself falls into class (b), MV1, unlike MV, is not self-refuting.

MV1, however, reveals also (as the example concerning three-winged birds may have already suggested) that there is a class of synthetic a posteriori propositions that obviously do not assert or imply existence; namely, negative existentials like *there are no three-winged birds* and *there are no people with IQs of 300*. Indeed, such propositions *deny* the existence of certain non-abstract entities or, as we may say for short, "deny existence." In order for Hume's Fork to allow such propositions to be knowable, they would have to be included among the matters of fact. Hume's own examples of matters of fact are invariably propositions that assert or imply existence; he neither mentions nor gives examples of propositions that deny existence. But such propositions comfortably fit his descriptive phrase "matter of fact and real existence" and its cognates, and so may presumably be included, together with those which assert or imply existence, among the matters of fact. Such a widening of the class of matters of fact is certainly consistent with the spirit of Hume's doctrine; for it does not enlarge the class of propositions that can be known a priori beyond what he would have allowed. It only points to a class of a posteriori propositions that he does not explicitly discuss, due perhaps to an overriding interest in the question of how we know propositions that assert or imply existence.

It seems, then, that the most defensible formulation of Hume's Fork in Kant's terminology is MV2:

All knowable propositions are either:

(a) analytic a priori; or
(b) synthetic a priori propositions that do not assert or imply existence; or
(c′) synthetic a posteriori propositions that assert, imply, or deny existence.

The "relations of ideas" would be (a) and (b); the "matters of fact" would be (c′). Possibly, there are negative existential propositions concerning non-abstract entities that are synthetic and non-empirical, though it is hard to think of an example. But if there are any such propositions, then (b) should be expanded to read "synthetic a priori propositions that do not assert, imply, or deny existence."

The Empiricist position expressed by MV2, unlike MV1, cannot be refuted by pointing out that there are synthetic a posteriori propositions that deny existence. And whether MV2 is correct or incorrect, it is in any case not self-refuting; for MV2 itself falls into class (b). We may conclude that unlike the self-refuting MV and the overly restrictive MV1, MV2, which is equivalent to Hume's own Fork (now understood as including empirical negative existentials in the class of matters of fact), represents a position that is both self-consistent and not obviously incorrect. Its correctness or incorrectness will be explored in the next part and in Chapter 3.

5 Hume's denials concerning matters of fact

In this section, we shall analyze part of Hume's case for his key negative doctrine that no matter of fact is either self-evident or demonstrable. In order to maintain a close connection with Hume's text, our discussion will proceed in terms of his own terminology rather than Kant's; though, as the discussion of MV1 and MV2 has shown, it could be recast in Kant's terminology.

Hume's full defense of his negative doctrine in the *Enquiry* is really the burden of the whole of Section IV: it involves his entire critique of "all reasonings concerning matter of fact."[17] His central argument for holding that no proposition that asserts existence is demonstrable, in particular, stems directly from his critique of causal reasoning in paragraphs 3–13 of Section IV, part I. And his argument for holding that no proposition that implies existence, or "bridging proposition," is demonstrable, is given in the course of his critique of inductive reasoning in Section IV, part II. These texts will be analyzed in Chapter 3. Nevertheless, going just on what Hume says in the first two paragraphs of Section IV, it is possible to discern:

(1) his reason for saying that no matter of fact is self-evident;
(2) his general line of argument for saying that no "bridging" matter of fact proposition is demonstrable;
(3) the key logical point which underlies both that line of argument and his critique of causal reasoning.

Let us look at these three points now. Why does Hume hold that no matter of fact is self-evident? In the second paragraph of Section IV, Hume writes:

> The contrary of every matter of fact is still possible; because it can never imply a contradiction. . . . *That the sun will not rise to-morrow* . . . implies no more contradiction, than the affirmation *that it will rise.* We should in vain, therefore, attempt to demonstrate its falsehood. Were it demonstratively false, it would imply a contradiction . . .

The words "every matter of fact" suggest that Hume's reason for holding that no matter of fact is self-evident is the same as his reason for holding that none is demonstrable, and that this reason is that there is no matter of fact proposition whose denial implies a contradiction. However, we shall resist this interpretation, for the following reason: the proposed reason for denying that any matter of fact is self-evident would be a dangerous one for Hume to use; indeed its use would be self-defeating. For it would require holding that all self-evident propositions owe their status to the self-contradictoriness of their denials and are, therefore, analytic. A proposition whose denial is self-contradictory is always analytic. It would follow that all demonstrable propositions are also analytic, since analyticity is hereditary with respect to entailment – because if P entails Q and P is analytic, then Q is analytic, too. So all relations of ideas, being either self-evident or demonstrable, would be analytic. But this would make Hume's own Fork – his thesis that all knowable propositions are either relations of ideas or matters of fact – vulnerable to the same self-refutational objection that was raised against MV in the previous section; for which class of knowable propositions would his Fork itself fall into? For reasons like those given for the non-analyticity of MV, Hume's thesis is not analytic. So, his Fork could not be a relation of ideas, if these are all analytic. Could it then be a matter of fact? No: for it neither asserts, implies, nor denies existence. The upshot is that if Hume's reason for holding that matters of fact cannot be self-evident is that their denials are never self-contradictory, then his Fork is neither a relation of ideas nor a matter of fact and, therefore, it implies its own unknowability.

It is worth noting also that the view that Hume's reason for denying that any matters of fact are self-evident is the noncontradictory status of their denials is at best only weakly supported by the texts. For although there are many passages where Hume gives noncontradictoriness of the denial as the reason why matters of fact are not demonstrable, an examination of those passages provides little evidence that this is also his considered reason for holding that they are not self-evident. For example, in the passage just quoted, Hume's focus, despite the word "every," is clearly on what can and cannot be *demonstrated*.[18]

What then is Hume's reason for denying the self-evidential status of matters of fact? The best argument that can be extracted from what he says, I suggest, is this:

(1)   If p states a matter of fact, then p asserts or implies existence.
(2)   If p asserts or implies existence, then p is not self-evident.

∴ (3) If p states a matter of fact, then p is not self-evident.

Although this argument is a simple one, it seems very powerful. Its first premiss is true by definition: it simply spells out what Hume means by a "matter of fact."[19] The second, and key premiss is very plausible. For, recall what a self-evident proposition is: a proposition that we can know to be true just by understanding what it says. On reflection, it seems that, with one possible exception, no proposition that asserts existence can be known in this way. Obviously, propositions like "rocks exist" or "horses exist" are not self-evident. It is true that some philosophers believe (though Hume himself did not believe) that numbers and/or other abstract entities (such as universals) exist, and that those same philosophers would say that the existence of such things is self-evident. But numbers and other abstract entities, even if they can be said really to exist, do not provide counterexamples to premiss (2), because "asserts existence" in (2) means "asserts the existence of some non-abstract entity."

Perhaps the most challenging possible counterexample to (2) is the proposition *I exist*. It can be plausibly argued that this proposition is self-evident – that anyone who understands it must also know it to be true. The argument turns on the special function of the pronoun "I," and runs:

(1)   If S understands "I exist," then S knows what "I" means.
(2)   If S knows what "I" means, then S knows that "I" denotes or calls attention to the speaker or thinker.
(3)   If S knows that "I" denotes or calls attention to the speaker or thinker, then S knows that "I exist" is always a true statement.

∴ (4) If S understands "I exist," then S knows that "I exist" is always a true statement.

If this is a sound argument, then it seems to show that "I exist" is self-evident. In that case, the argument purporting to show that no matter of fact is self-evident must be amended – by adding "unless p = 'I exist'" to premiss (2) and to the conclusion. And Hume's position regarding the self-evidential status of propositions that assert existence must be amended to say that, with the exception of the special proposition "I exist," no proposition that asserts existence is self-evident.

This modification, however, would not seriously damage or affect Hume's overall position.

What about the "bridging" propositions that imply existence? Reflection seems to show that these too are not self-evident. Consider for example the proposition *every event has a cause.* Can that proposition be known to be true just by understanding what it says? The answer seems to be that it cannot. One can understand what the proposition says, without coming to know that there are no *uncaused* events. Of course, the proposition *every effect has a cause* can be known to be true just by understanding what it says, since it is analytic. But that proposition, unlike *every event has a cause,* is not a bridging proposition. For remember that a bridging proposition "implies existence:" when combined with a proposition reporting some observation(s) made at a particular time or times, it enables us to infer the existence of something that need not be observed at that time or those times or at any time. Thus *every event has a cause* is a bridging proposition, because when combined with *event e was observed at time* t, it enables us to infer the existence of a cause of *e,* which we need not observe at *t* or at any other time. But *every effect has a cause* does not work in the same way. For we do not observe at *t* that something is an *effect,* as opposed to being just an *event,* unless we also observe its cause at *t* – in which case the cause is obviously not something that need not be observed at *t.* Furthermore, it seems clear that bridging propositions other than *every event has a cause,* whether they be particular causal laws or the highly general principle that the future will resemble the past, are also not known just by understanding what they say. The argument that we have attributed to Hume for his claim that no matter of fact is self-evident, then, seems to be a sound one.[20]

Turning now to the question of whether any matter of fact is demonstrable, we have already seen that the reason Hume gives for denying that matters of fact are demonstrable is that their denials never imply a contradiction. This reason works in a rather different way for each of Hume's two types of matters of fact – those that assert existence and the "bridging" propositions which imply existence. We are not yet in a position to see how it works for propositions that assert existence, since that part of Hume's argument is inseparable from his analysis of causal reasoning, which will be considered in Chapter 3. But still going only on what Hume says in the second paragraph of Section IV, we can elicit his general line of argument for holding that no "bridging" propositions are demonstrable. It rests on the following principle, hereafter referred to as "principle (P):"

If *p* is demonstrable, then there is a set of statements, *S,* such that (1) the members of *S* are self-evident, and (2) *not p,* together with *S,* entails a contradiction.

In the second paragraph of Section IV, Hume may be seen as applying principle (P) to a simple example. He says, in effect: "let *p* be the proposition *the sun will rise tomorrow.* Then there is no set *S* of self-evident propositions, such that *S* together with *not p* entails a contradiction. Therefore, *p* is not demonstrable."

Principle (P) itself is based on two points:

(i)   If p is demonstrable, then p follows logically from some self-evident statement(s).

(ii) If p follows logically from some statement(s), then affirming those statements while denying p entails a contradiction.

(i) follows directly from the definition of a demonstrable statement as one that logically follows from self-evident premises. (ii) is the point that lies behind Hume's statement: "The contrary of every matter of fact is still possible, because it can never imply a contradiction." Hume is here making a basic point of logic: it is always a contradiction to affirm the premises and to deny the conclusion of a valid argument.

Since (ii) is the key logical point behind principle (P), and since it will also play an important role in Hume's critique of causal reasoning, let us consider an example to illustrate it. Consider any valid argument, say an argument of the form called "disjunctive syllogism":

$$\frac{\begin{array}{c} P \text{ or } Q \\ \text{Not } Q \end{array}}{\therefore\ P}$$

What happens if one affirms the premises and denies the conclusion? Well, to deny the conclusion, P, is to affirm its negation, namely *not P*. Now since we are affirming both premises, we are also affirming the conjunction of *not P* with the second premiss, that is, we are also affirming *not P and not Q*. But this contradicts the other premiss, *P or Q*. Obviously, it is a contradiction to say that at least one of two statements is true ("*P or Q*"), and also to say that both of those statements are false ("*not P and not Q*"). The same thing always results if one affirms the premises and denies the conclusion of a valid argument – this always leads to a contradiction.

It should now be clear why principle (P) is true: it follows logically from (i) and (ii). For when p is demonstrable, p logically follows from some set, S, of self-evident statements; but when p follows logically from any statements, to affirm those statements while denying p entails a contradiction; therefore, affirming S while denying p must lead to a contradiction.

To illustrate principle (P) itself, we can use a simple arithmetical example of a proposition that satisfies the principle:

Let p = No number is both odd and even.

Then, where n is any number,

not p = n is odd and n is even.

But now there is a set, S, of self-evident statements which, together with *not p*, entails a contradiction. That set is the pair:

(S_1) If x is odd, then x is not divisible by 2.

(S_2) If x is even, then x is divisible by 2.

This set together with *not p* entails a contradiction, because it follows from *not p* both that

(a) n is odd,

and that

(b) n is even.

Further, it follows from (S_1) and (a) that

(c) n is not divisible by 2,

and it follows from (S_2) and (b) that

(d) n is divisible by 2.

But (c) and (d) contradict each other. The contradiction results because the argument from (S_1) and (S_2) to p is valid, so that a contradiction must result from affirming (S_1) and (S_2) and denying p. This is also a case where p is demonstrable in Hume's sense, since the statements from which p follows, namely (S_1) and (S_2), are both self-evident.

$$
\left[\begin{array}{c} (S_1) \\ (S_2) \\ \hline \therefore p \end{array} \right]
$$

Now, Hume's general line of argument for the claim that no "bridging" matter-of-fact proposition is demonstrable goes as follows. Let p be any statement that implies existence. Then there is *no* set, S, of self-evident statements, such that S together with *not p* entails a contradiction. Therefore, by principle (P), p is not demonstrable. In Chapter 3, we shall see how Hume uses principle (P) to show that certain specific bridging propositions are not demonstrable.

3

HUME'S THEORY OF
KNOWLEDGE (II)

Causal reasoning and the problem of induction

1 Introduction

Having drawn his basic distinction between relations of ideas and matters of fact in the first two paragraphs of Section IV of the *Enquiry*, Hume devotes the rest of the section to an examination of our knowledge of matters of fact. It is here that we find his full defense of his thesis that no matter of fact, whether it be one that asserts existence or one that implies existence, is demonstrable. However, Hume does not simply advance a straightforward argument for his thesis in respect of each of these two salient points. Rather, his case for each is embedded in a larger context which involves his seminal analysis of causal reasoning and his critique of induction. His overall argument has a clear sequential structure, which successively defends three main theses:

T1: Knowledge of matters of fact that is not based on present perception or on memory is always based on causal (i.e. cause-effect) relations.

T2: Causal relations are not knowable a priori, but only by inference from past experience.

T3: Inference from past experience cannot be rationally justified.

We shall see that Hume's argument for the claim that no proposition that asserts existence is demonstrable stems from T1 and especially T2, and that his argument for the claim that no proposition that implies existence (no "bridging" proposition) is demonstrable comes in the course of his defense of T3.

Section IV is divided into "part I" and "part II." Part I presents the case for theses T1 and T2; Part II presents the argument for T3. Today, this latter argument is known as "the problem of induction," because inference from past experience is now usually called "induction" or "inductive inference." (Hume seldom uses the term "induction.") The present discussion is organized as follows. Part I is analyzed in the following in section, and part II in the third section. In the fourth section, we shall look briefly at the psychological account of induction that

Hume gives in Section V, part I, of the *Enquiry*. In the final section, we shall discuss one contemporary response to the problem of induction.

2 Hume's critique of causal reasoning

Some of the factual knowledge a person has at any particular time is based on what she is perceiving at that time, and some on what she remembers having previously perceived. For example, your present knowledge that there is a book before you is based on what you now see, and your knowledge that you did or did not eat breakfast today is based on what you remember. Of course, a philosopher influenced by sceptical arguments concerning the senses and concerning memory would say that what you know on the basis of your current perceptions is only that you *seem* to see a book, and similarly that what you know on the basis of memory is that you seem to remember eating (or skipping) breakfast today. In other words, such a philosopher would narrow down the field of what we know by present perception and by personal recollection to certain psychological facts about ourselves, and claim that the rest of our factual knowledge (if any) must rest on some kind of inference from those facts. But everyone, whether or not they would agree in thus narrowing down knowledge based on present perception and personal recollection, would agree that at best only a small portion of what we usually take ourselves to know is based on present perception and personal recollection. For most of our factual knowledge concerns things that are too remote, either in space or in time, or both, for us to have knowledge about them by either present sense perception or personal recollection.

Now Hume's central question in part I of Section IV is: On what is such knowledge based? As he puts it in the topic sentence of the third paragraph:

> It may, therefore, be a subject worthy of curiosity, to enquire what is the nature of that evidence, which assures us of any real existence and matter of fact, beyond the present testimony of our senses, or the records of our memory.
>
> (E:26; S:16; F:72)

We may state Hume's question this way:

> *Q1*: When our knowledge of a matter of fact rests neither on present perception nor on memory, on what does it rest?

Hume's answer comes in the topic sentence of the next paragraph: "All reasonings concerning matter of fact seem to be founded on the relation of Cause and Effect. By means of that relation alone we can go beyond the evidence of our memory and senses" (E:26; S:16; F:72). Hume's answer to Q1, then, is the first of the three theses we identified above:

T1: Knowledge of matters of fact that is not based on present perception or on memory is always based on causal relations.

Unless one is careful about how one interprets the phrase "matter of fact," T1 may seem too sweeping. If, for example, one interprets "matter of fact" as meaning any synthetic proposition whatsoever, then it seems that some synthetic propositions not known by present perception or memory might be known without any reliance on causal relations. Propositions describing some very general structural features of reality – such as that reality is wholly material, or partly mental and partly material, or wholly mental – might be of this kind. Hume's Fork itself would be another case in point, since it is a synthetic proposition, but one that can hardly be based on causal considerations. However, let us take our clue from Hume's expression, "real existence and matter of fact," and continue to interpret his "matters of fact" as covering only propositions that assert or imply the existence of some non-abstract entity; notably, those that assert or imply the existence of some physical or mental entity or the occurrence of some physical or mental event. Then what Hume is saying is very plausible. For how, except by reasoning from effects to causes or causes to effects, could one know the existence or occurrence of something that one neither perceives nor remembers having perceived? And how can a proposition imply existence – be a bridging proposition that allows us to infer the existence of something unobserved from something observed – unless that proposition asserts some causal relationship between the observed item and the unobserved one?

It is important not to be misled here by the way knowledge is shared and transmitted, especially in our own day and age. We live in an age of rapid, massive dissemination of information. Today, much of our factual knowledge comes from sophisticated electronic media, not to mention more traditional sources like books, teachers, and parents. So Hume's claim that this knowledge is acquired by causal reasoning may seem, at first, quaint and hopelessly naive. But to dismiss it on these grounds would be an egregious error. For, in the first place, there is a sense in which knowledge acquired from the media, books, and other people does rest on causal relations. For how do we know that these sources are reliable? What assures us that there is any connection at all between what they say and how things really are? The answer, it seems, is that we assume a vast network of causal connections between how things are and how the media, books and other people represent them to be. Were there no such connections, the only way to acquire reliable information would be by one's own devices. In the second place, Hume is asking especially about the *original acquisition* of knowledge, rather than about the transmission of knowledge already acquired by someone else. But how can one acquire a *new* piece of factual knowledge, in cases where one cannot rely merely on present observation? (Obviously one could not then rely merely on memory, which allows us to store previously acquired knowledge but not to acquire new knowledge.) The only way, it would seem, is by reasoning from effects to causes, causes to effects, effects to other effects of the same cause, etc. In such cases, we simply have nothing to "go on" except causal relations. And since the transmission of knowledge from one person to another presupposes that someone originally acquired the knowledge on his or her own, Hume seems to have put his finger on an extremely important truth when he suggests that all knowledge of "real existence and matter of fact" not based on perception or memory is ultimately based on causal reasoning.

Granting then the enormous importance of causal relations for acquiring factual knowledge – so granting the plausibility of Hume's thesis T1 – we can turn to the question Hume raises in the next paragraph of his clearly structured discussion: "If we would satisfy ourselves, therefore, concerning the nature of that evidence, which assures us of matters of fact, we must enquire how we arrive at the knowledge of cause and effect" (E:27; S:17; F:73). In other words:

Q2: How do we acquire knowledge of causal relationships?

Unless we can answer this question, we will not understand the basis of the greater part of our factual knowledge.

Hume's answer comes in the topic sentence of the next paragraph:

> I shall venture to affirm, as a general proposition, which admits of no exception, that the knowledge of this relation is not, in any instance, attained by reasonings *a priori*; but arises entirely from experience, when we find, that any particular objects are constantly conjoined with each other.
>
> (E:27; S:17; F:73)

Hume's answer to Q2, then, is the second of the three theses identified above:

T2: Causal relations are not knowable a priori, but only by inference from past experience.

T2 is a vital component of Hume's theory of knowledge; for it virtually establishes his doctrine that propositions which assert existence are not demonstrable. For if knowledge of those propositions rests on causal relations, but causal relations are knowable only by experience, then clearly those propositions themselves are knowable only by experience and, consequently, cannot be demonstrated.

This argument from T2 to the undemonstrability of propositions asserting existence is important, so let us restate it in a complete and careful way (one that "factors-in" the consideration that our knowledge of *some* propositions which assert existence rests on perception or memory rather than on causal relations).

The argument's first premiss, which is actually based on T1, is:

(1) Knowledge of propositions that assert existence is based on perception, memory, or causal relations.

The crucial T2 enters the argument as its second premiss:

(2)   Causal relations are knowable only by inference from past experience.

This is just the second, affirmative, clause of T2 itself. It now follows from (1) and (2) that:

(3)   Knowledge of propositions that assert existence is based on perception, memory, or inference from past experience.

Furthermore, we may correctly assert that:

(4)   If knowledge of propositions that assert existence is based on perception, memory, or inference from past experience, then propositions that assert existence are not demonstrable.

This is because a demonstrable proposition is, by definition, one that can be deduced from self-evident premisses. But if a proposition can be known only by sense perception or memory or inference from past experience, then obviously it cannot be deduced from self-evident premisses; it has a basis completely different from any proposition that can be so deduced. In different terms, a proposition that must rest on perception or memory or inference from past experience is a posteriori; while a proposition that can be deduced from self-evident premisses is a priori. From (3) and (4), however, there follows the conclusion:

(5)   Propositions that assert existence are not demonstrable.

If Hume can successfully establish T2, then he will have shown thereby that one of his two classes of matter-of-fact propositions – namely those that "assert existence" – cannot be demonstrated. Accordingly, we shall now look closely at his defense of T2, which occupies the bulk of part I of Section IV and contains some of his most influential reasoning about causal relations.

Hume's first reason for holding T2 is this. If the cause (or the effect) is something new in our experience, then we cannot tell, just by examining it, what effect it will have (or what its cause was). For example, Adam could not have told, just by seeing that water is something liquid and transparent, that it could drown him; or by seeing that fire is bright and feeling its warmth, that it could destroy him upon a closer approach. This point, Hume notes, is easily admitted for cases where we remember that the cause was once something new in our experience: we admit, for example, that we could not have known, from seeing for the first time two contiguous marble slabs, that they would be hard to pull apart, but easy to slide apart. The point is admitted also for cases where the cause is something relatively rare or uncommon in our experience: who could tell just from looking at gunpowder that it would explode, or from looking at a U-shaped piece of metal that it would attract iron filings? Finally, the point is easily admitted for cases where the cause involves some intricate or hidden mechanism. We easily admit, for example, that merely looking at the innards of a watch (or a computer!) gives us no knowledge of what it can do. But,

65

Hume says, we do not so easily admit this point for cases concerning which we remember no time when the things involved were new to us, where those things are not at all rare but quite commonplace, and where they involve no intricate mechanism but are quite simple. In such cases, Hume says:

> We are apt to imagine that we could discover these effects by the mere operation of our reason, without experience. [For example,] we fancy, that were we brought on a sudden into this world, we could at first have inferred that one Billiard-ball would communicate motion to another upon impulse; and that we needed not to have waited for the event, in order to pronounce with certainty concerning it.
>
> (E:28; S:18; F:74)

But the truth of the matter, Hume declares, is that his point holds just as strongly for cases where the cause is familiar, commonplace, and simple. Take for instance his case of colliding billiard balls. This is as clear and obvious a case of cause-and-effect as one could desire: perfectly familiar, quite commonplace, and involving no hidden mechanisms. Perhaps for this reason (together with the fact that Hume loved to play billiards!), it is his favorite illustration of causation. Now, he points out, even in the case of billiard balls, we can see on reflection that if we had to predict the effect without relying on past experience, then any prediction would be as good as any other. We could predict equally well, among other possibilities, that both balls would come to rest, or that the struck ball would roll off in any one of indefinitely many different directions. As Hume puts it:

> [W]ere we required to pronounce concerning the effect . . . without consulting past observation; after what manner, I beseech you, must the mind proceed in this operation? It must invent or imagine some event, which it ascribes to the object as its effect; and it is plain that this invention must be entirely arbitrary.
>
> (E:29; S:18; F:75)

Hume does not confine himself to the point that we cannot predict effects (or "retrodict" causes) without relying on past experience. To support T2, he also attacks a certain conception of causality – one which underlies the view that causal relations can be known a priori, and which we shall call the "Rationalist conception of causality." Hume never explicitly formulates this conception or announces that he is attacking it, but both the conception itself and Hume's objections to it can be extracted from what he does say. The Rationalist conception of causality has three related parts:

(a) the effect is contained in the cause;
(b) there is a special "tie" or "connection" that binds the effect to the cause; and
(c) the cause–effect relationship is identical with, or perhaps a special case of, the

premiss–conclusion relationship in a valid deduction: causality is identical with, or a special case of, logical deducibility or entailment.

Let us look at each of these points before seeing why Hume objects to them.

Point (a) reflects a way of thinking about causality that can be traced back to Greek philosophy. Causality was conceived of on the model of conception and birth: the effect must be precontained within the cause, almost as the fetus is contained within the womb. The distinguished historian of ideas A. O. Lovejoy calls this idea the "preformationist assumption about causality," and describes it as follows:

> That "there cannot be more in the effect than there is in the cause" is one of the propositions that men have been readiest to accept as axiomatic; a cause, it has been supposed, does not "account" for its effect, unless the effect is a thing which the eye of reason could somehow discern in the cause, upon a sufficiently thorough analysis.
>
> (Lovejoy 1962: 286)

Descartes, for example, thinks of causality in this way; his main proof of God's existence, presented in his *Third Meditation*, begins with these words:

> Now it is manifest by the natural light that there must be at least as much reality in the efficient and total cause as in the effect of that cause. For where, I ask, could the effect get its reality from, if not from the cause? And how could the cause give it to the effect unless it possessed it?
>
> (Descartes 1984: 28)

Descartes' reasoning is this:

(1) The cause must contain the reality of its effect.
(2) There are degrees of reality.

∴ (3) There must be as much reality in the cause as in the effect.

Descartes' argument contains many further steps, which we need not consider here. The point to notice is simply that the opening premis of his argument is very close to (a). Descartes does not quite say that the cause must literally contain the effect; he says that the cause must contain the *reality of* the effect. But one, very natural, way to understand this rather unclear claim is to interpret it, as does Lovejoy, as saying that the cause itself must somehow contain the effect. Thus, Descartes' entire argument for God's existence – one of the most important arguments in his philosophy – rests on (a), or at least on something very close to (a).

Locke too, although he is considered to be the founder of classical empiricism, advances an argument for God's existence that relies on (a) or something very like it. Locke begins by arguing that something must have existed from all eternity, since otherwise what exists now would have been "produced by nothing." He then argues that this something cannot have been just the material universe itself, because

> [W]hatsoever is first of all things must necessarily contain in it and actually have, at least, all the perfections that can ever after exist; nor can it ever give to another any perfection that it hath not, either actually in itself or at least in a higher degree: it necessarily follows that the first eternal being cannot be matter.
>
> (Locke 1975: 624)

Locke's point is that since the "perfections" that now exist include thought and intelligence, the "first eternal being" must itself be a thinking, intelligent one. The basic assumption behind this reasoning is, again, that the cause must contain everything (all the "perfections") that it will ever produce.

Point (b) of the Rationalist conception of causality is not one that is usually articulated. Nor does Hume clarify exactly what the "tie" or "connection" between cause and effect is supposed to be. Perhaps this is because later, in Section VII of the *Enquiry*, he will apply his Empiricist test for meaning to this notion, with dramatic results that he does not wish to anticipate in Section IV. Nonetheless, it would seem that (b) has a place in even the most rudimentary, unreflective thinking about causes and effects. Most people would probably nod their heads in agreement if asked whether there is some "tie" or "connection" between cause and effect, and be shocked if this were questioned. Hume, as we shall see, is quite prepared to shock us here.

Point (c) of the Rationalist conception was probably accepted, at least implicitly, by many philosophers before Hume; one Rationalist philosopher who explicitly asserts it is Spinoza. In his major work, *Ethics Demonstrated in Geometrical Order*, Spinoza says:

> But I think I have shown clearly enough (see [Proposition] 16) that from God's supreme power, *or* infinite nature, infinitely many things in infinitely many modes, i.e., all things, have necessarily flowed, or always follow, by the same necessity and in the same way as from the nature of a triangle it follows, from eternity to eternity, that its three angles are equal to two right angles.
>
> (Spinoza 1985: 426)

Immediately after his initial proof of this proposition, he sets forth the following "Corollary" of the proposition:

> Cor. 1: From this it follows that God is the efficient cause of all things which can fall under an infinite intellect.
>
> (ibid.: 425)

Spinoza is saying that, from the proposition *everything follows logically from God's nature*, it follows as a first "corollary" that God is the *cause* of everything. What is the assumption behind his reasoning? It must be that causality is identical with, or at least a special case of, logical deducibility. Of course, if this is true, then by knowing the cause, one can know all of its effects just by thinking – by a priori reasoning – which is the heart of what Hume denies.

Hume attacks separately each part of the Rationalist conception of causality. Against (*a*), he argues that if the effect were contained in the cause, then it would be possible to find or discern the effect by a careful examination of the cause. But, he says:

> The mind can never possibly find the effect in the supposed cause, by the most accurate scrutiny and examination. For the effect is totally different from the cause, and consequently can never be discovered in it. Motion in the second Billiard-ball is a quite distinct event from motion in the first; nor is there anything in the one to suggest the smallest hint of the other. A stone or piece of metal raised into the air, and left without any support, immediately falls: but to consider the matter *a priori*, is there anything we discover in this situation which can beget the idea of a downward, rather than an upward, or any other motion, in the stone or metal? . . . . In a word, then, every effect is a distinct event from its cause. It could not, therefore, be discovered in the cause, and the first invention or conception of it, *a priori*, must be entirely arbitrary.
>
> (E:29–30; S:18–19; F:74–5)

Drawing on this passage, we can construct the following argument against (a); the notion that the effect is contained in the cause:

(1) If (a) were true, then we would be able to discern the effect in the cause.
(2) The effect is an event totally different from the cause.
(3) If the effect is an event totally different from the cause, then we cannot discern the effect in the cause.
(4) We cannot discern the effect in the cause (from (2) & (3)).
(5) (a) is not true (from (1) & (4)).

The key steps in this argument are (2) and (3). In (2), as in the passage just quoted, both the cause and the effect are described as being "*events*." This reflects an important insight of Hume: namely, that the true members of a cause–effect relationship are events, rather than objects. Often, our ordinary speech masks this fact; for example, we say that "the rock broke the window." Here it almost sounds as if the cause is one object (the rock), and the effect another (the broken window). But, of course, what really happened is that the rock hitting the window caused the window to break. Now *the rock hitting the window* and *the window breaking* are not objects or things; they are events or occurrences. Once this point is understood, the claim made in (3) becomes evident. For, given that a cause and its effect are two distinct events, it is false to say that we can discern or discover the effect in the cause; for example, that we can discern or discover the event of the window breaking in the event of the rock hitting the window, in the way that we could discern or discover chocolates in a box of chocolates, or the chocolates' caramel fillings in the chocolates. This is not because an event can never be part of or contained in another "larger" event: a battle could be part of a war (though the battle would not then be caused by the war, but rather by certain decisions made by the military commanders, movements of troops, and the like). Nor is it even because the effect is always future to the cause: there are cases of simultaneous causation, as when a man makes a footprint in the sand – here the placing of the foot in the sand (cause) occurs at the same moment as the formation of the footprint (effect). Rather, it just seems obvious on the face of it that an event which is the *effect* of another event (as opposed to being a part of it) cannot be discerned in the event that caused it, cannot be discovered just by examining or scrutinizing the cause-event, no matter how minutely. Therefore, by the argument given above, the effect cannot be contained in the cause.

Of course, there are cases of causality that may seem to fit the "containment" model, such as the case of conception and birth. But in such a case, it is true only in a general or rough sense that the mother "caused" the baby. No biologist studying the process of reproduction would describe what happened in such an inexact way. Rather, what happened is that a complex sequence of events involving the mother caused the event of the baby's birth, and it makes little if any sense to say that any of those events "contained" their effects. It would seem, then, that Hume is on strong ground in thinking that the "containment" view of causality is an erroneously mythological one.

Hume finds (b) no more plausible than (a). Against the "supposed tie or connexion between the cause and effect, which binds them together, and renders it impossible that any other effect could result from the operation of that cause" (E:29; S:18; F:74–75), he argues that it is perfectly conceivable that a cause might have some totally new and unexpected effect:

> When I see, for instance, a Billiard-ball moving in a straight line toward another; even suppose motion in the second ball should by accident be suggested to me, as the result of their contact or impulse; may I not conceive, that a hundred different events might as well follow from that cause? May not both these balls remain at absolute rest? May not the first ball return in a straight line, or leap off from the second in any line or direction? All these suppositions are consistent and conceivable. Why then should we give the preference to one, which is no more consistent or conceivable than the rest? All our reasonings *a priori* will never be able to show us any foundation for this preference.
>
> (E:29–30; S:18–19; F:75)

This is basically a challenge to Hume's reader: since we can conceive of any number of effects following from a given cause, what justification do we have for thinking that there is a special "tie or connexion" between the cause and the effect? In Section VII of the *Enquiry*, entitled "Of the Idea of Necessary Connexion," Hume will extend this challenge by asking whether the notion of such a connection even makes sense. Notice that the "supposed tie or connexion" between cause and effect that Hume is calling into question is what would enable us to reason *a priori* from the cause to the effect, and that its absence seems to leave such an inference absolutely groundless. As Hume puts it:

> And here it is constantly supposed that there is a connexion between the present fact and that which is inferred from it. Were there nothing to bind them together, the inference would be entirely precarious.
>
> (E:26–7; S:16; F:72)

Of course, if (c) were correct – if the causal relation were identical with, or were a special case of, logical entailment – then this alone would mean that such an inference is justified after all. Against (c), however, Hume uses the basic logical point which underlies his principle (P) (*see pp.* 58–60). Although that point can be extracted from Section IV (e.g. by putting together what Hume says in the second and the tenth paragraphs), it is most explicitly stated in this passage from Hume's *Abstract of A Treatise of Human Nature*:

> [N]o inference from cause to effect amounts to a demonstration. Of which there is this evident proof. The mind can always *conceive* any effect to follow from any cause, and indeed any event to follow upon another; whatever we *conceive* is possible, at least in a metaphysical sense; but wherever a demonstration takes place the contrary is impossible and implies a contradiction. There is no demonstration, therefore, for any conjunction of cause and effect.
>
> (T:650–1; S:130; F:34)

The key point here is that it is never a *contradiction* to deny that the effect will follow the cause, as would have to be the case if (c) were correct.

To see this more clearly, compare the following two arguments:

(I)

Either it is raining or it is snowing.
It is not snowing.
_____

∴ It is raining.

(II)

There is an A-event (a flash of lightning).
_____

∴ There will be a B-event (a clap of thunder).

(I) is, of course, a deductively valid argument; while (II) is an example of causal reasoning. Now to refute (c), Hume drives a wedge deep between these two types of argument. What is the difference between them? Well, suppose we try to accept the premisses and deny the conclusion of each argument.

To deny the conclusion of (I) is to affirm *It is not raining*. This, taken together with the argument's second premiss (which, by hypothesis, we are accepting as true), yields the affirmation *It is not raining and it is not snowing*. But this affirmation contradicts the argument's other premiss, *Either it is raining or it is snowing* (which we are by hypothesis also accepting as true). In other words, by accepting the argument's premisses and denying its conclusion, we are saying, "Either it is raining or it is snowing, but it is not snowing and it is not raining," which is a contradiction – an utterance of the form *p and not p* – since it says both that at least one of the two statements, "it is raining" and "it is snowing," is true, and also that both statements are false. The same thing always results (as already pointed out in part 5 of Chapter 2) from accepting the premisses and denying the conclusion of any valid deductive argument.

But now, suppose we try accepting the premiss and denying the conclusion of argument II. In other words, suppose we say, *There is an A-event* (lightning), *but there will not be a B-event* (thunder). In light of our past experience, this may be foolish – but it is *not* a contradiction! To say, "There is lightning, but there will be no thunder," is not to say anything of the form *p and not p*. Therefore, a causal argument like (II) is not deductively valid. This proves that, contrary to (c), the causal relationship is neither identical with, nor a special case of, logical entailment. Causal relations are fundamentally different from logical relations. This distinction is one of Hume's most important contributions to philosophy.

Here you might object, however, that there are cases where a report of the cause does entail a report of the effect. For example, "Oswald killed Kennedy" entails "Kennedy died." Hume's response would be that this example is a cheat; for the premiss "Oswald killed Kennedy" does not report just the cause: it already reports both the cause and the effect. If the premiss had been "Oswald shot Kennedy," then it would have reported only the cause. But that premiss does not entail that Kennedy died; since it would not be a contradiction to assert "Oswald shot Kennedy, but Kennedy did not die." Hume's point is that a premiss that reports or describes only the cause never entails a conclusion that describes the effect. For exactly the same reason, he would say that a premiss that reports or describes only the effect never entails a conclusion that describes the cause.

In order to complete the analysis of Hume's case for holding that causal relations are never knowable a priori, we must now call attention to one final point. Notice that argument II could easily be converted into a valid argument. We need add only another premiss, namely:

If there is an A-event, then there will be a B-event.

Adding this premiss would obviously convert argument II into a valid case of *Modus Ponens*. Indeed, it seems quite clear that this premiss *should* be added; for our reason for inferring thunder when we see lightning is precisely our belief in such a premiss. Does adding the premiss then rehabilitate the Rationalist idea that causal relations are knowable a priori – that from our knowledge of a cause, we can reason a priori to its effect? No, it does not. For the new premiss itself is not known a priori. Rather, it is based on past experience – on the observed fact that past A-events have been followed by B-events. Instead of rehabilitating the idea that causal relations are knowable a priori, then, the new premiss opens up a new question: what entitles us to infer that just because past A-events have been followed by B-events, future A-events will be followed by B-events? It is to precisely this question that Hume turns in part II of Section IV.

3 The problem of induction

In part II of Section IV, Hume advances his famous argument for the thesis (T3) that inference from past experience cannot be rationally justified. This argument is really a continuation of the case for T2; the argument of part II dovetails with the argument of part I. So, we shall begin our analysis of part II by summarizing the relevant points from part I.

In support of his denial that causal relations are knowable a priori (and in opposition to point (c) of the Rationalist conception of causality), Hume argued that from a premiss of the form

(1) There is an A-event (e.g. there is a flash of lightning)

we cannot validly deduce a conclusion of the form:

(2) There will be a B-event (a clap of thunder).

Furthermore, one cannot show that causal relations are knowable a priori by adding the premiss

(3) If there is an A-event, then there will be a B-event.

For although the argument from (3) and (1) to (2) is now logically valid, (3) is not known a priori. Rather, (3) is inferred from our experience of A-events being followed by B-events. It is to this inference from experience, accordingly, that Hume now turns his attention. Thus, part II begins with these words:

> But we have not yet attained any tolerable satisfaction with regard to the question first proposed. Each solution still gives rise to a new question as difficult as the foregoing, and leads us on to farther enquiries. When it is asked, *What is the nature of all our reasonings concerning matter of fact?* [roughly, Q1 posed on page 62] the proper answer seems to be, that they are founded on the relation of cause and effect [= T1]. When again it is

73

asked, *What is the foundation of all our reasonings and conclusions concerning that relation?* [= Q2] it may be replied in one word, Experience [= T2]. But if we still carry on our sifting humor, and ask, *What is the foundation of all conclusions* [e.g. (3), above] *from experience?* this implies a new question, which may be of more difficult solution and explication.

(E:32; S:20; F:77)

What exactly is the inference from experience that Hume is proposing to examine? Well, (3) is inferred, roughly speaking, from a premiss of the sort: (4) Past A-events have always been followed by B-events. This formulation is rough, because an accurate report of past experience would say only that *observed* A-events have been followed by B-events, and would have to be restricted even further so as to capture only those cases where the observer remained in a position to observe whether or not a B-event followed the A-event. It would have to say something more like this: "All A-events observed in conditions C, and in cases in which we observed also whether or not a B-event followed, were followed by B-events," where conditions C would vary with the type of events in question. But for simplicity's sake, let us regard the inference from experience that Hume proposes to examine as being the inference from (4) to (3).

Up to this point, then, Hume's analysis of a typical or model case of causal reasoning looks like this:

(4)   Past A-events have always been followed by B-events.

(3)   If there is an A-event, then there will be a B-event (from (4)).

(1)   There is an A-event – a flash of lightning.

(2)   There will be a B-event – a clap of thunder (from (3) & (1)).

Notice that the *numbering* of these statements corresponds to the order in which they would naturally enter into our reasoning: we begin with the observation of an A-event (1), and from this observation we predict a B-event (2); this prediction, however, is supported by our belief that if an A-event occurs then a B-event will follow (3), and that belief in turn is based on our knowledge that past A-events have been followed by B-events (4). Notice also that an alternative wording of (3) (one suggested by Hume's own manner of expression in part II of Section IV) would be: "Future A-events will be followed by B-events." We have used an "if-then" format for (3) in order to preserve the formal validity of the argument from (3) and (1) to (2), which the alternative wording would not do. An amended version of the alternative wording that would preserve formal validity, and which could serve just as well as our formulation of (3), would be: "Present and future A-events will be followed by B-events."

Hume's present question, as we have seen, concerns the inference from (4) to (3): is this inference from experience legitimate? What, so to speak, are its credentials?

His answer comes in these words: "I say then, that, even after we have experience of the operations of cause and effect, our conclusions from that experience are *not* founded on reasoning, or any process of the understanding" (E:32; S:21; F:77). Here Hume is announcing T3 – his famous thesis that inferences from past experience cannot be rationally justified.

Hume's manner of expressing T3 calls for some special comment. He expresses it in psychological language: instead of saying that conclusions from experience cannot be rationally justified, he says that they are not "founded on reasoning, or any process of the understanding." This may make it sound as though his point were merely the psychological one that conclusions from experience are not the product of a particular faculty of our minds and of its workings, namely the "understanding" and its "processes." Now, this is indeed part of Hume's point. For, as we shall see, Hume goes on to hold, in Section V of the *Enquiry*, that conclusions from experience are the product of a purely psychological principle of association which he calls "custom;" his claim in Section IV that such conclusions are not arrived at by "reasoning, or any process of the understanding," is meant to prepare the way for his view, propounded in Section V, that they are, instead, the product of "custom." That view itself is part and parcel of an elaborate psychological theory that is prominent in the *Treatise* but still present, albeit in a muted form, in the *Enquiry*. Furthermore, this psychological theory reflects one of Hume's chief ambitions, which was to give a comprehensive psychology or "science of MAN" (as he called it in the Introduction of the *Treatise*). He hoped that his psychology would add as much to our knowledge of human nature as Newton, for whom Hume had the greatest admiration and reverence, had added to our knowledge of the physical world; he hoped to be, so to speak, the Newton of psychology. This ambition helps to explain the title of Hume's first work: *A Treatise of Human Nature*.

Some recent scholars have emphasized this constructive, naturalistic side of Hume's thought, and de-emphasized its sceptical side. They believe that Hume was more interested in replacing Rationalist ways of thinking about knowledge with a new naturalistic epistemology than he was in defending scepticism.[1] Other, more "traditional," interpreters of Hume see him as essentially a sceptic.[2] We shall not try to do justice to this controversy about Hume's overall intentions; for this would require an extended discussion of the secondary literature.[3] Rather, we shall simply maintain that *at least part* of Hume's purpose in Section IV is to establish that inference from past experience cannot be rationally justified. For his overall argument, as we shall see, is that there is a principle on which all such inferences depend, but that this principle cannot be established or supported by any reasoning or argument. In the *Abstract* of the *Treatise*, Hume sums up the results of his examination of inference from past experience by saying that all such inferences rest on "a supposition . . . which can admit of no proof at all, and which we take for granted without any proof (T:652; S:131; F:34–5)." Thus, both the overall character of his argument and the language he uses to describe it imply that Hume is not totally unconcerned with the question of the rational justification of these inferences – at least part of his message is that such inferences cannot be rationally justified. In the final section of this chapter, I shall argue that, appearances to the contrary notwithstanding, this negative thesis does not imply that the inferences are *irrational* or *unreasonable* – a point which may reduce the motivation to deny that Hume is even addressing questions about rational justification. But be that as it may, we shall maintain that despite Hume's interest in describing the workings of the human mind, in Section IV part II he is not merely rejecting what he takes to be a mistaken view about how our minds work: he is also putting forward a normative epistemological claim, namely, his thesis, T3, that the inference from (4) to (3) cannot be rationally justified.

Hume's argument for T3 has the following general structure: first, he argues that the inference from (4) to (3) is not valid as it stands; second, he argues that the additional premiss which would make it valid cannot be established. This structure can be seen in the following passage:

> These two propositions are far from being the same: *I have found that such an object has always been attended* with such an effect [which is essentially the same as (4)], and *I foresee, that other objects, which are, in appearance, similar, will be attended with similar effects* [essentially the same as (3)]. I shall allow, if you please, that the one proposition may be justly inferred from the other: I know, in fact, that it always is inferred. But if you insist, that the inference is made by a chain of reasoning, I desire you to produce that reasoning. The connexion between these propositions is not intuitive. There is required a medium, which may enable the mind to draw such an inference, if indeed it be drawn by reasoning and argument. What that medium is, I must confess, passes my comprehension; and it is incumbent on those to produce it, who assert, that it really exists, and is the origin of all our conclusions concerning matter of fact.
>
> (E:34; S:22; F:78–9)

Hume's remark that (3) may be "justly inferred" from (4) is ironic. His real point is that there is no valid immediate (one-step) inference from (4) to (3); or, as he puts it, the connection between them is not "intuitive." For, obviously, it would be possible for (4) to be true and (3) to be false; it would not be a contradiction to affirm (4) and to deny (3). So, the only way to get from (4) to (3) would be by way of an additional premiss; or, as he puts it, a "medium" is required to get from one proposition to the other. In saying "what that medium is . . . passes my comprehension," Hume is not saying that he doesn't know what the additional premiss is. On the contrary, he will shortly produce it. His point, rather, is that this additional premiss cannot be established. We shall see presently what the premiss is and why Hume thinks it cannot be established.

First, we should pause to note that Hume often formulates the inference from experience in a different way. Instead of talking merely about something being followed by or "attended with" an effect, he talks about certain sensible qualities possessing certain "secret powers." For example, he points out that just because things possessing the sensible qualities of bread have had the "secret power" to nourish humans in the past, we infer that such things will have this power in the future. The inference he is criticizing, reformulated in these terms, would go like this:

(4a) Sensible qualities, Q, have had "secret powers," P, in the past.

∴ (3a) Q will have P in the future.

Hume does not really think that (4a) and (3a) are better formulations than are (4) and (3); on the contrary, he thinks they are worse. For they employ the very notion of a "power" that Hume will attack in Section VII of the *Enquiry*. This is why he adds the footnote to the sentence that introduces the talk of sensible qualities having "secret powers:" "The word, Power, is here used in a loose and popular sense. The more accurate explication of it would give additional evidence to this argument. See Sect. 7" (E:33*n*; S:21; F:78).

Nevertheless, it is important to appreciate that, as Hume points out, the inference from (4a) to (3a) suffers from exactly the same defect as that from (4) to (3): it is simply invalid. As Hume says, in a passage that closely parallels the passage quoted on page 76:

> When a man says, *I have found, in all past instances, such sensible qualities conjoined with such secret powers* [= (4a)]: And when he says, *Similar sensible qualities will always be conjoined with similar secret powers* [= (3a)], he is not guilty of a tautology, nor are these propositions in any respect the same. You say that the one proposition is an inference from the other. But you must confess that the inference is not intuitive; neither is it demonstrative: Of what nature is it, then?
>
> (E:37; S:24; F:81)

The upshot is that bringing in "secret powers," even if this notion were legitimate, would not salvage the inference from experience. For the fact that certain observed qualities have been joined to certain secret powers in the past would not prove that they will be joined to those powers in the future. Nor, we may add, does the fact that those powers have *operated* in the past prove that they will operate in the future.

Here you might object that Hume's talk of "secret" powers reflects the backward state of eighteenth-century science, and that the difficulty he is discussing disappears if one thinks in terms of modern science. But this would be to miss the force of Hume's point; for the inference remains invalid when put this way:

Microstructure S has had power P in the past.

∴ Microstructure S will have power P in the future.

Hume's critique of inference from experience, then, cuts deep; it does not depend on any limitations of the science of his day.

What is the additional premiss or "medium" that would validate the inference from (4) to (3)? Well, there are several possibilities. The simplest would be: "If past A-events have always been followed by B-events, then so will present and future A-events." But instead of this premiss, Hume identifies the most basic and general principle that could play the logical role required to be, as he expresses it, "the supposition, that the future will be conformable to the past" (E:35; S:23; F:80), or that "the future will resemble the past" (E:37; S:24; F:81). Hume is asserting, then, that the premiss that would justify the inference from (4) to (3), and all others like it, is this one:

(5) The future will resemble the past.

Admittedly (5), like (4), is a rough formulation. In order to deduce (3) from (4), it is not enough to add a vague principle saying that the future will "resemble" or "be conformable to" the past. For that wording allows that the future might not resemble the past closely enough for the inference to go through. Rather, one must interpret (5), quite stringently, as saying that the same patterns of relations between kinds of event – the same laws of nature – will hold in the future as have held in the past. Interpreted in this way, (5) is sometimes called "the principle of the uniformity of nature," and also the "principle of induction." Although the exact interpretation of (5) is a difficult matter that could be discussed at greater length, here we shall simply grant that from (5) – suitably interpreted – together with (4), (3) can be validly derived. At this point, then, Hume's analysis of causal reasoning looks like this:

(5)　The future will resemble the past.

(4)　Past A-events have always been followed by B-events.

(3)　If there is an A-event, then there will be a B-event (alternatively: Present and future A-events will be followed by B-events) (from (4) & (5)).

(1) There is an A-event (a flash of lightning).

(2) There will be a B-event (a clap of thunder) (from (1) & (3)).

The obvious next question is whether (5) itself can be safely accepted. Famously, Hume argued that it cannot. His argument is contained in the following passage:

> All reasonings may be divided into two kinds, namely, demonstrative reasoning, or that concerning relations of ideas, and moral [probability] reasoning, or that concerning matter of fact and existence. That there are no demonstrative arguments in the case seems evident; since it implies no contradiction that the course of nature may change, and that an object,

seemingly like those which we have experienced, may be attended with different or contrary effects. May I not clearly and distinctly conceive that a body, falling from the clouds, and which, in all other respects, resembles snow, has yet the taste of salt or feeling of fire? Is there any more intelligible proposition than to affirm, that all the trees will flourish in December and January, and decay in May and June? Now whatever is intelligible, and can be distinctly conceived, implies no contradiction, and can never be proved false by any demonstrative argument or abstract reasoning *a priori*.

If we be, therefore, engaged by arguments to put trust in past experience, and make it the standard of our future judgment, these arguments must be probable only, or such as regard matter of fact and real existence, according to the division above mentioned. But that there is no argument of this kind, must appear, if our explication of that species of reasoning be admitted as solid and satisfactory. We have said, that all arguments concerning existence are founded on the relation of cause and effect; that our knowledge of that relation is derived entirely from experience; and that all our experimental conclusions proceed upon the supposition, that the future will be conformable to the past. To endeavour, therefore, the proof of this last supposition by probable arguments, or arguments regarding existence, must be evidently going in a circle, and taking that for granted, which is the very point in question.

(E:35–6; S:22–3; F:79–80)

We can summarize this passage's overall argument this way:

Step (i)   There are only two possible ways of establishing a proposition by reasoning: demonstratively, by deductively valid reasoning from self-evident premises; or inductively, by inductively correct reasoning from rationally acceptable premises.

Step (ii)   The proposition (5) "The future will resemble the past" cannot be established demonstratively, because its denial does not imply a contradiction.

Step (iii)   (5) cannot be established inductively, because all inductive inferences are based on (5), thus rendering an inductive argument for (5) circular.

∴ (5) cannot be established at all.

In what follows, we shall discuss each step of this argument in sequence.

Step (i)

Let us begin with a terminological point. As the wording of (i) indicates, we shall use the term "inductively" to mean "by inductively correct reasoning," or by reasoning in which the premises of an argument render its conclusion probable or likely.[4] Likewise, the terms "inductive argument" and "inductive inference" will mean "inductively correct argument" and "inductively correct inference," "inductive" will mean "inductively correct," and "induction" will refer to inductively correct argumentation in general. This is a slight departure from one common use of those terms. Often, an "inductive argument" is defined as one whose premises *purport* or are *intended* or *claimed* to provide less than conclusive support for the conclusion. Correspondingly, a "deductive argument" is defined as one whose premises *purport* or are *intended* or *claimed* to provide conclusive support for the conclusion. Although these definitions are common ones and are practical up to a point, on reflection they are problematic. To see why, consider a couple of examples. A standard example of a "deductive argument" is this:

All humans are mortal.
Socrates is human.
_____

∴ Socrates is mortal.

A typical example of an "inductive argument" is this:

Most adult humans are over four feet tall.
John is an adult human.
_____

∴ John is over four feet tall.

Now suppose that someone gives the first argument, but misguidedly *intends* or *claims* that the premises provide less than conclusive support for the conclusion, and that someone gives the second argument but misguidedly *intends* or *claims* that the premises provide conclusive, watertight support for the conclusion. Then it seems that, by the common definitions just mentioned, the first person's argument ought to be classified as an "inductive argument," and the second person's argument as a "deductive argument." But people who use those definitions would not accept this result: they would insist that no matter who gives these arguments, and regardless of anyone's intentions, the first argument should be classified as deductive and the second as inductive. Now although it may well be possible to amend the common definitions so as to justify this insistence, this seems by no means an easy task. We can avoid this difficulty by analyzing Hume's position in terms of two types of *logically correct* argument – deductively valid arguments and inductively correct arguments – rather than simply as two types of argument. This is why, throughout the rest of this chapter, we shall use "induction" as a label for inductively correct reasoning, "inductive argument" as short for "inductively correct argument," and "inductively" as short for "by inductively correct reasoning."

In light of this terminological point, it might now seem that step (i) ought to be formulated more simply, as follows:

(i′) There are only two kinds of correct reasoning: demonstrative reasoning, and inductively correct reasoning from rationally acceptable premisses.

This formulation would make it look as if Hume's argument starts simply from the division of all logically correct arguments or reasonings into two kinds, as his opening sentence admittedly suggests. Nevertheless, such a formulation would be a poor one. For logically correct arguments do not divide up into demonstrative arguments and inductively correct arguments from rationally acceptable premisses. Rather, they divide up simply into deductively valid arguments and inductively correct arguments. Thus, (i′) would be a confused and improper way of saying this:

(i″) There are only two kinds of correct reasoning: deductively valid reasoning and inductively correct reasoning.

But (i″), while now a correct statement, would not serve Hume's purpose. For he needs to start from a premiss that divides arguments *that can actually be used to establish a thesis* – such as (5), that the future will resemble the past – into two classes. But for that purpose, it will not do to start merely from the standard division of all logically correct arguments into deductively valid and inductively correct arguments. For the mere fact that an argument is deductively valid or inductively correct does not by itself mean that it can be used to establish any thesis. Whether it can also do that depends on whether the *premisses* of the argument are acceptable. Hume shows his awareness of this point by calling one of his two kinds of reasoning "demonstrative", since such reasoning must not only be deductively valid, but must proceed from self-evident premisses. Our own formulation of his opening premiss as (i) rather than (i″) is intended to allow for the same point, and to do so without the confusion involved in (i′). Of course, the phrase "rationally acceptable premisses" in (i) is vague. However, since Hume is going to argue that (5) cannot be established by *any* inductively correct argument (no matter how credible its premisses), we need not try to eliminate this vagueness.

It might now be objected, however, that (i) is false, because there are ways of arguing for a proposition other than the two allowed by (i).[5] Suppose that a proposition, q, is validly deduced from a proposition, p, but that p is not self-evident. Then the argument from p to q is not demonstrative in Hume's sense, since p is not self-evident; nor is it merely inductive, since q follows deductively from p. Hume does not consider this objection, but it seems that he could have answered it as follows. What is the basis of p? If p is itself deduced from a self-evident proposition(s), then the *complete* argument for q – the argument from those self-evident propositions to p to q – is demonstrative after all. If p is not deduced from self-evident premisses, then there are four possible cases to consider.

First, p might be inductively supported by some self-evident proposition(s). Then, in accordance with the principle that an argument can only be as a strong as its weakest link, the argument from those propositions to p to q should be classified as *inductive*.

Second, p might be inductively supported by propositions that, while not self-evident in Hume's sense, are known by introspection – propositions like "I seem to see a cat" or "I seem to remember seeing a cat." Then, in accordance with the same principle, the argument from those propositions to p to q should be classified as *inductive*.

Third, p could be based, either deductively or inductively, on propositions that are neither self-evident in Hume's sense nor knowable by introspection, such as observations of one's physical surroundings ("I see a cat") or memories ("I saw a cat yesterday"). Then matters become more complicated, but, briefly put, come to this. Insofar as Hume accepts the "way of ideas" doctrine that any statement about the physical world must ultimately rest on introspective reports, and inasmuch as statements about the physical world cannot be simply deduced from such reports but would have to be somehow inferred from them, the argument from introspective reports to p to q would again have to be classified as *inductive*. Alternatively, insofar as Hume holds the sceptical view that statements about the physical world must be inferred from introspective reports but that such an inference cannot succeed, the result would be that neither p nor q can be established at all.

Fourth, the final possible case is where p follows deductively from some statement(s) known by introspection. Terminologically, this would be the most awkward case for Hume, because the argument from those statements to p is then not demonstrative, since introspective reports are not self-evident in Hume's sense; but nor is it inductive, since p follows deductively from the introspective reports. But perhaps Hume could deal with this case by qualifying (i) as follows: the "proposition" in question must not be one that could be known merely by introspection. This qualification would get around the troublesome fourth case, because it seems clear that the only propositions that follow deductively from those that can be known by introspection are other propositions that could be known by introspection; thus, "I seem to see an animal" follows from "I seem to see a cat," but the former no less than the latter can be known by mere introspection. We shall henceforth assume, then, that the term "proposition" in (i) excludes propositions knowable by mere introspection.

Step (ii)

Hume's reason for denying that (5) is demonstrable is the by-now familiar consideration that its denial does not imply a contradiction. As he says:

> May I not clearly and distinctly conceive that a body, falling from the clouds, and which in all other respects, resembles snow, has yet the taste of salt or feeling of fire? Is there any more intelligible proposition than to affirm, that all the trees will flourish in December and January, and decay

in May and June? Now, whatever is intelligible, and can be distinctly conceived, implies no contradiction, and can never be proved false by any demonstrative argument or abstract reasoning *a priori*.

(E:35; S:22; F:79)

In order to analyze this reasoning, we need to recall "principle (P)" which, we saw, underlies Hume's case for saying that no "bridging" matter-of-fact proposition is demonstrable:

(P) If *p* is demonstrable, then there is a set of statements, S, such that (1) all the members of S are self-evident, and (2) *not p*, together with S, entails a contradiction.[6]

Early in Section IV Hume pointed out, in effect, that when *p* = *the sun will rise tomorrow*, the condition laid down by this principle is not satisfied; so *the sun will rise tomorrow* cannot be demonstrated. Now, he is asserting that when *p* is the highly general principle that the future will resemble the past, this condition is still not satisfied; therefore this general principle cannot be demonstrated either. In other words, Hume is saying that (5) cannot be demonstrated, because there is *no* set, S, of statements such that, first, all the members of S are self-evident, and second, *not (5)* together with S entails a contradiction. Putting it differently, he is saying that we cannot, in the following argument, correctly supply any statement(s) to substitute for "S":

not (5): The future will not resemble the past & S (S = some set of self-evident statements).

∴ contradiction

It is very difficult to disagree with Hume about this. For *what* self-evident statement(s), together with "the future will not resemble the past," entail a contradiction? If there were any such self-evident statements, then it seems that we ought to be able to specify them. For self-evident statements are especially obvious ones, whose truth we can know just by understanding them. Further, the range of relevant statements here is vanishingly small: although there are indefinitely many self-evident statements, such as simple arithmetical truths and obvious analytic truths, they seem logically quite unrelated to proposition (5) or its negation. But it seems clear that we cannot specify any self-evident statements that, together with not (5), entail a contradiction. It seems safe to conclude, then, that there are none, and therefore that (5) is not demonstrable.

The reasoning that Hume uses to show that (5) is not demonstrable has an importance that goes even beyond its role as support for T3; for it is this reasoning that enables him, finally, to complete the defense of his "Fork." To complete that defense, it will be recalled, Hume needed to establish the negative claim we called (C4), that no matter of fact whatsoever, whether it be one that asserts existence or whether it be a "bridging proposition" that implies existence, is either self-evident or demonstrable (see Chapter 2 part 5). We have already seen Hume's reasons for holding that no matter of fact of either type is self-evident, and his reasons for saying that no matter of fact which asserts existence is demonstrable; but we still have not fully seen why no bridging proposition is demonstrable.[7] We have just seen, however, why one important bridging proposition, namely (5), is not demonstrable. Now the reason why no other bridging proposition is demonstrable is exactly the same: Hume's argument showing that (5) is not demonstrable can be generalized to embrace other bridging propositions.

To see this, consider a more general atemporal analogue of (5): roughly, a principle to the effect that the unobserved resembles the observed. On reflection, it seems clear that this principle does not satisfy principle (P), any more than does (5); for again, there appears to be no set, S, of self-evident propositions which, together with "the unobserved does not resemble the observed," entails a contradiction. Indeed, Hume's focus on past-to-future bridging may well be an expository device – a convenient and dramatic way of focusing on *any* principle that would warrant an inference from the observed to the unobserved, whether the unobserved item be past, present, or future. It also seems obvious that no *less* general analogue of (5) – no proposition to the effect that if certain specific kinds of event have been paired in the past, then they will continue to be paired in the future – satisfies principle (P). Finally, in the *Treatise*, Hume argues powerfully that still another bridging principle – the principle that every event must have a cause (or, as Hume puts it, that "every beginning of existence must have a cause of existence") – does not satisfy principle (P). (T:78–82; F:47–50) It seems very doubtful, therefore, that any bridging principle satisfies principle (P). So, at this point Hume seems finally to have established his doctrine that no matter of fact whatsoever is demonstrable.

Step (iii)

Hume's reason for denying that (5) can be established inductively constitutes the heart of the classic "problem of induction," for whose discovery Hume is famous. The passage of the *Enquiry* in which Hume posed the problem was quoted earlier in this chapter, but calls for restatement here:

> [A]ll our experimental conclusions proceed upon the supposition that the future will be conformable to the past. To endeavour, therefore, the proof of this last supposition by probable arguments . . . must be evidently going in a circle, and taking that for granted, which is the very point in question.
>
> (E:35–6; S:23; F:80)

Hume makes the same point again a little later:

> To say [that the argument for (5)] is experimental, is begging the question. For all inferences from experience suppose, as their founda-

tion, that the future will resemble the past . . . . If there be any suspicion, that the course of nature may change, and that the past may be no rule for the future, all experience becomes useless, and can give rise to no inference or conclusion. It is impossible, therefore, that any arguments from experience can prove this resemblance of the past to the future; since all these arguments are founded on the supposition of that resemblance.

(E:37–8; S:24; F:81)

He makes the same point again in the *Abstract* of the *Treatise*:

[W]e could not so much as prove by any *probable* arguments, that the future must be conformable to the past. All probable arguments are built on the supposition, that there is this conformity betwixt the future and the past, and therefore can never prove it. This conformity is a *matter of fact*, and if it must be proved, will admit of no proof but from experience. But our experience in the past can be proof of nothing for the future, but upon a supposition, that there is a resemblance betwixt them. This, therefore, is a point, which can admit of no proof at all, and which we take for granted without any proof.

(T:651–2; S:130–1; F:34–5)

In all these passages, Hume is rehearsing the point, made in step (iii) of his argument, as to why (5) cannot be established: (5) cannot be established inductively because all inductive inferences presuppose (5) as their foundation, thus rendering any inductive argument for (5) circular or question-begging.

To grasp Hume's charge of circularity, we should first ask: what would an inductive argument for (5) look like?[8] The easiest way to answer this question is to forget Hume for a moment and simply to ask yourself: "why do I believe that the future will resemble the past?" There is only one possible answer: *because it always has*! The inductive argument for (5), then, must be this:

(6)   The future has always resembled the past.

∴ (5) The future will resemble the past.

Now, an inductive argument is one the premises of which show only that the conclusion is probable, rather than establishing it conclusively. Further, such arguments typically involve reasoning to unobserved cases from a sample of observed cases. The argument from (6) to (5), then, has the hallmarks of an inductive argument: the premiss renders the conclusion only probable (albeit highly probable), and the argument goes from the observed past to the as-yet unobserved future. Bertrand Russell, in *The Problems of Philosophy* (1912: 65), formulates the argument in a way that nicely captures its inductive character:

(6R) Past futures have resembled the past.

∴ (5R) Future futures will resemble the past.

The argument that Hume rejects as circular or question-begging, then, is the argument from (6) to (5), or from (6R) to (5R). Now, in one sense, Hume's charge of circularity is very puzzling. For what is a circular argument? In the straightforward logical sense, it is an argument that uses its conclusion as a premiss. In the most extreme case, it is an argument with the logical form:

$$p$$
$$\therefore p$$

In less extreme cases, it is an argument of the form *q & p; therefore p*; or *q & p & r; therefore p*, etc. But all such arguments are *deductively valid*! For obviously, if *p* is true as a premiss, *p* must be true as the conclusion, since the premiss and the conclusion are one and the same statement. A circular argument, then, is automatically a deductively valid argument. But an inductively correct argument cannot be deductively valid: its premises never entail its conclusion.[9] It follows that *it is impossible for an inductively correct argument to be circular or question-begging*, at least in the straightforward logical sense. Therefore, the argument from (6) to (5) is not circular in that sense, and Hume would be wrong to say that it is. But nobody thinks that Hume here has committed such a gross, elementary mistake. What, then, does Hume mean when he charges that the argument is "going in a circle" and "begging the question"?

The answer is as follows. The *purpose* of establishing (5) was to *justify all inductive inferences* like the inference from (4), Past A-events have always been followed by B-events, to (3), If there is an A-event, then there will be a B-event. But the inference from (6) to (5) is itself an inductive inference: it is just like the inference from (4) to (3), except for being more general in its scope. So the circularity consists in *using induction in order to justify the use of induction*. Hume's point is not that the inference from (6) to (5) is circular as it stands, or is circular outside the context of his search for a justification of induction. Looked at in that manner, the argument from (6) to (5) is a perfectly respectable inductive argument; indeed (6) is the only possible reason for believing (5). But anyone who uses this argument for the purpose of justifying induction is indeed begging the question, or "taking that for granted which is the very point in question." For the argument is itself inductive.

Our exposition of Hume's critique of all "reasoning concerning matters of fact" in Section IV part II is now substantially complete. This exposition has been rather complex, so we shall conclude this part by summarizing it.

Hume's critique summarized

It is helpful to think of Hume's discussion as containing both his *analysis* of "all reasonings concerning matter of fact," and his *critique* of that reasoning. His analysis involves the six propositions that we have introduced successively into our exposition. Fully stated, it goes as follows:

(6) The future has always resembled the past. (Russell's alternative formulation: "Past futures have resembled the past.")

(5) The future will resemble the past. (Russell's alternative formulation: "Future futures will resemble the past.) [Derived inductively from (6).]

(4) Past A-events have always been followed by B-events.

(3) If there is an A-event, then there will be a B-event. (Alternatively: Present and future A-events will be followed by B-events.) [Derived from (4) & (5).]

(1) There is an A-event (e.g. a flash of lightning).

(2) There will be a B-event (e.g. a clap of thunder). [Derived from (1) & (3).]

Hume's *critique* of the above reasoning can be summarized virtually in sentence-outline form, as follows:

I. Causal relations are not knowable a priori, but knowable only by inference from past experience (= T2).

A. (1)
———
∴ (2)
    is invalid (= Hume's objection to point (c) of the Rationalist conception of causality).

B. (3)
   (1)
———
∴ (2)
    is valid, but (3) is inferred from past experience, that is, from (4).

II. Inferences from past experience (inductive inferences) cannot be rationally justified (= T3).

A. (4)
———
∴ (3)
    is invalid.

B. The inference remains invalid when formulated in terms of "secret powers:"

(4a) Sensible qualities, Q, have had "secret powers" P in the past.

∴ (3a) Sensible qualities, Q, will have "secret powers" P in the future.

C. The inference from (4) to (3) (or from (4a) to (3a)) becomes valid if (5) is added as a premiss, but (5) cannot be established.

1. There are only two ways of establishing a proposition by argument: demonstratively, by deductively valid reasoning from self-evident premisses; or inductively, by inductively correct reasoning from rationally acceptable premisses.

2. (5) cannot be established demonstratively, because its denial does not imply a contradiction.

Note: More fully, Hume's reasoning here can be put this way:

(a) If p is demonstrable, then p follows logically from some self-evident statement(s).

(b) If p follows from any statement(s), then affirming those statements while denying p entails a contradiction.[10]

(c) "Principle (P)": If p is demonstrable, then there is a set, S, of statements such that (1) all the members of S are self-evident, and (2) not p, together with S, entails a contradiction (from (a) & (b)).[11]

(d) (5) does not satisfy principle (P) – there is no set, S, of statements such that, first, all the members of S are self-evident and, second, *not (5)* together with S entails a contradiction.

(e) (5) is not demonstrable (from (c) & (d)).

This reasoning can be generalized to show that no bridging proposition is demonstrable, simply by replacing (d) with:

(d′) No bridging proposition satisfies principle (P) – for any bridging proposition p, there is no set, S, of statements such that, first, all the members of S are self-evident and, second, *not p*, together with S, entails a contradiction;

and replacing (e) with:

(e′) No bridging proposition is demonstrable.

3. (5) cannot be established inductively (i.e. from (6)), because all inductive inferences presuppose (5) "as their foundation," thus rendering an inductive argument for (5) circular.

Note: The inference from (6) to (5) is not circular in the straightforward logical sense: no inductive inference could be. Rather, it is circular because the purpose of establishing (5) was to justify all inductive inferences, like the one from (4) to (3). But the inference from (6) to (5) is itself an inductive inference, just like (though more general than) the one from (4) to (3). So the circularity consists in using induction in order to justify the use of induction.

Before offering an assessment of Hume's critique, we shall look briefly at the views Hume proposes, in part I of Section V, to replace those which he thinks he has discredited.

4 Hume's psychological explanation of induction

Although Hume is persuaded that inductive inferences cannot be rationally justified, he believes that they can be psychologically explained. It is to this topic that he turns in Section V of the *Enquiry*. That section's title, "Sceptical Solution of these Doubts," can be misleading; especially if one ignores the word "Sceptical." Hume has no intention of arguing that inductive reasoning can be rationally justified after all. Rather, he wants to give a psychological explanation of such reasoning.

You might well ask: why does Hume bother to give this psychological explanation? The general answer is that it fits into his program of giving a complete psychology or "science of man." But perhaps a more specific answer can also be given – one that may go a little way toward explaining why Hume wants to provide such a science in the first place. It is a fact that all sane human beings perform countless inductive inferences every day of their lives. Now suppose someone asked *why* humans make such inferences. One possible answer would be that these inferences are rationally justified. After all, if someone asked why humans accept arguments of the form *Modus Ponens*, one relevant answer would be that such arguments are rationally justified, simply because they are deductively valid. But as regards inductive inferences, this answer is not open to Hume; for he has argued that such inferences cannot be rationally justified. But, then, how does he explain the fact that we all make inductive inferences, and generally arrive at the same results when we do? This is the question Hume tries to answer in Section V, part I. Since he cannot answer it by saying that we make these inferences because they are supported by certain standards of rationality, he says that we make them because our minds are influenced by a psychological principle.

Hume calls this principle "custom" or "habit." By the term "custom," he does not mean some sort of sociological principle. Rather, he means a principle of psychological association. The principle may be put as follows:

> If the mind is presented with repeated cases where A is followed by B (e.g. lightning by thunder), it will come to expect B whenever A is presented.

Hume stresses that this is simply a psychological principle that has nothing to do with the rational or reasoning side of human nature. He stresses also that the sentiment of expecting B or anticipating B, which we experience when A is presented, is something quite definite and strong. In terms of his theory of impressions and ideas, it is a distinctive "impression of reflection." As we shall see in Chapter 4, this impression plays an important role in Hume's theory of causality.

Hume has argued that inductive inference cannot be rationally justified; it is the work of a psychological principle that operates independently of logical or rational considerations. Is he saying, therefore, that we should stop making inductive inferences? No, he is not, and it would be a mistake to read him in that way. For, in the first place, Hume does not think that humans have any choice here: we cannot help but form beliefs about the future on the basis of our past experience. As he puts it:

> [H]aving found, in many instances, that any two kinds of objects – flame and heat, snow and cold – have always been conjoined together; if flame or snow be presented anew to the senses, the mind is carried by custom to expect heat or cold, and to *believe* that such a quality does exist, and will discover itself upon a nearer approach. This belief is the necessary result of placing the mind in such circumstances. It is an operation of the soul, when we are so situated, as unavoidable as to feel the passion of love, when we receive benefits; or hatred, when we meet with injuries. All these operations are a species of natural instincts, which no reasoning or process of the thought and understanding is able either to produce or to prevent.
>
> (E:46–7; S:30; F:89–90)

In the second place, Hume freely admits – in fact, he insists – that we cannot engage in any goal-oriented action unless we rely on induction. For if we had no beliefs or expectations about future outcomes, we would have nothing to guide our actions. As he puts it:

> Custom, then, is the great guide of human life. It is that principle alone which renders our experience useful to us, and makes us expect, for the future, a similar train of events with those which have appeared in the past. Without the influence of custom, we should be entirely ignorant of every matter of fact beyond what is immediately present to the memory and senses. We should never know how to adjust means to ends, or to employ our natural powers in the production of any effect. There would be an end at once of all action, as well as of the chief part of speculation.
>
> (E:44–5; S:29; F:89)

Here Hume declares that all our actions are based on the assumption that the future will resemble the past. He says also that most of natural science ("the chief part of speculation") rests on the belief that the course of nature will not change.

His view, then, is that while this belief is indispensable both to purposive action and to scientific inquiry, it has no rational foundation. His overall position is therefore this:

1 Inductive reasoning cannot be rationally justified.
2 Inductive reasoning is instinctual, as well as indispensable to both goal-oriented action and scientific inquiry.

As thinkers (philosophers), we must recognize that our "reasonings concerning matters of fact" are not susceptible of any rational justification. But, as humans planning and acting in the world and inquiring into its workings, we cannot avoid relying on it.

5 Need induction be justified?

Hume, as we have seen, argues that inference from experience, or induction, cannot be rationally justified. In this part, we shall address a question that naturally arises concerning the implications of Hume's thesis: namely, does it entail that induction is not rational, or irrational? It may seem that the answer to this question must be yes. Furthermore, Hume is often interpreted as holding just such a deeply sceptical view of induction.[12] Although this is a complex matter of interpretation, to which we cannot do justice here, it should be noted that there is certainly reason to doubt that Hume does take such a view. First, as we have seen, he holds that induction is indispensable to purposive action and in science. Second, in some of his writings, such as the *Dialogues concerning Natural Religion*, he holds that some inferences from experience are *better* than others – a view that is obviously incompatible with rejecting all inductive inferences as equally irrational – a point well made by Millican (1985: 127–30). Nevertheless, it may seem that, whether or not Hume thinks he has shown induction to be irrational, his critique of induction shows that it is irrational. The question we shall discuss is whether this is really the case. Our thesis will be that it is not – that one can hold that induction cannot be rationally justified *without* holding that it is therefore irrational. In defending this thesis, we shall draw on an incisive discussion of the problem of induction by the Oxford philosopher P. F. Strawson, who is a leading exponent of the so-called "ordinary-language" school of philosophy that flourished at Oxford in the 1950s.

To set the stage for a presentation of Strawson's position, we need to make two preliminary points. The first is that, in order to show that Hume's critique of induction entails that induction is irrational, one must rely on a key assumption: namely, that an inductive inference is rational only if it can be supported by some justificatory argument. Simply put, one must assume that *induction is rational only if it can be justified*. (This formulation is not an expression of the truism that induction is rational only if induction is rational; rather, it is a short way of saying that induction is rational only if an argument can be given to justify induction.)

The second preliminary point is that once this key assumption is made, it easily generates scepticism about induction. This is because not just any justification will do: any successful justification of induction must fulfill certain requirements. One crucial requirement is that the justification must not itself rely, at any point, on the use of induction. For of course it would be circular to use induction in order to justify using induction. One cannot justify a species of argument by using that very species of argument. This means that the justification will have to be *deductive* in nature. Indeed, it seems that the justification could consist only in showing that every inductively correct argument can be converted into a deductively valid one.[13] For otherwise, we would be left with an unsupported inductive component – an "exposed" inductive step, so to speak – that was not backed up by any justificatory argument. Now such a deductive justification of induction is exactly the kind of justification that Hume considers. For, as we saw, he considers the possibility of justifying the inference from

(4) Past A-events have always been followed by B-events

to

(3) If there is an A-event, there will be a B-event (or: present and future A-events will continue to be followed by B-events)

by adding the premiss:

(5) The future will resemble the past.

But, as we saw, adding (5) to (4) converts the argument for (3) into a deductively valid one. However, this maneuver can justify the inference from (4) to (3) only if the new premiss, (5), is itself rationally justified. But we cannot justify (5) by giving an inductive argument for it – by inferring it from (6), the statement that the future always has resembled the past. For this would be to fall into circularity; we would be using induction to justify using induction. So, the only course left open is to show that (5) is either self-evident or demonstrable. But clearly (5) is not self-evident: one cannot know it to be true just by understanding what it says. Further, (5) is not demonstrable, since its denial does not imply a contradiction, which is to say, since (5) does not satisfy principle (P).

The upshot is that induction cannot be justified; this much Hume seems to have established. But when this conclusion is combined with the premiss that induction is rational only if it can be justified, the result is obviously scepticism. The way in which Hume's critique of induction is *supposed* to lead to inductive scepticism, then, can be summarized as follows:

(A) Induction is rational only if it can be justified (assumption).
(B) Induction cannot be justified (Hume's discovery).

∴ (C) Induction is not rational (inductive scepticism).

In order to see how this position can be criticized, notice that (C) is not the only possible conclusion or moral that can be drawn from (B). A different moral would be this: the assumption that induction is rational only if it can be justified is simply wrong. In other words, perhaps the correct response to the above argument would be to apply to it what we might call the "pivot principle." At bottom, a deductively valid argument gives us a choice: either accept the conclusion, or reject at least one premiss. The premisses have no special or privileged status; so, if the conclusion is sufficiently repugnant, we have the option of "pivoting" – of rejecting a premiss. Suppose, for example, that someone were to offer a deductively valid argument purporting to prove that time does not exist – that there is no such thing as time. Our response might be to say: "I know that I had breakfast *before* I had lunch today, so your conclusion that time does not exist is obviously false; therefore at least one of your premisses is false."[14] Why, then, should we not, in the same spirit, reject (A): why should we accept the assumption that induction needs to be justified? Perhaps induction is rational even though it cannot be justified.

For this response to inductive scepticism to be convincing, one needs to build a case against (A) that does not rest just on baldly denying (C). It is here that Strawson's discussion, in the final chapter of his book *An Introduction to Logical Theory* (1952: 248–63), can help us; for Strawson argues effectively that (A) is false. His basic argument is a simple one: relying on induction is part of what it *means* to be rational, therefore induction is rational even if it cannot be justified.

To support this argument's premiss, Strawson does two different things. First, he argues that "induction is rational (reasonable)" is an analytic truth. He writes:

> It is an analytic proposition that it is reasonable to have a degree of belief in a statement which is proportional to the strength of the evidence in its favour; and it is an analytic proposition . . . that, other things being equal, the evidence for a generalization is strong in proportion as the number of favourable instances, and the variety of circumstances in which they have been found, is great. So to ask whether it is reasonable to place reliance on inductive procedures is like asking whether it is reasonable to proportion the degree of one's convictions on the strength of the evidence. Doing this is what "being reasonable" means in such a context.
>
> (Strawson 1952: 256–7)

Strawson is here saying that both of the premisses of the following valid argument are analytically true, so that its conclusion too must be analytic:

(D) It is reasonable to have a degree of belief in p proportional to the strength of the evidence for p.

(E) The strength of the evidence for p is proportional to the number of favorable instances and the variety of circumstances in which those instances occurred.

∴ (F) It is reasonable to have a degree of belief in p proportional to the number of favorable instances and the variety of circumstances in which those instances occurred.

But (F) is just a way of saying that induction is reasonable or rational. So, anyone who questions (F) – who asks "is it reasonable to rely on induction?" – is thereby also questioning (D), and asking the absurd question: "is it reasonable to base one's beliefs on the evidence?"

It might be objected that in giving this argument, Strawson is himself offering a justification of induction. Of course, if any argument that has "induction is reasonable" or some equivalent claim as its conclusion automatically counts as a "justification of induction," then Strawson is indeed offering his own justification of induction. But this would be a strange way to use the label "justification of induction." For anyone who harbors sceptical doubts about induction would presumably question (E), or regard (E) as question-begging. For (E) says that there being a large number of favorable instances that have occurred in a variety of circumstances really provides *sound evidence* for *p*: (E) makes a *normative* claim to the effect that inductive evidence is *genuine* or *good* evidence for a proposition. But this is precisely what an inductive sceptic questions. So, the demand for a justification of induction surely *includes* a demand for an argument supporting (E). Strawson's basic point, however, is that (E) requires no justification, for it is no less an analytic truth than is (D). To bring out (E)'s analyticity, Strawson gives no argument. Rather, he simply reminds us (p. 256) of the way certain phrases are actually used:

> Consider the uses of the phrases "good grounds", "justification", "reasonable", &c. Often we say such things as "He has *every justification* for believing that *p*"; "I have *very good reasons* for believing it"; "There are *good grounds* for the view that *q*"; "There is *good evidence* that *r*". We often talk, in such ways as these, of justification, good grounds or reasons or evidence for certain beliefs. Suppose such a belief were one expressible in the form "Every case of *f* is a case of *g*". And suppose someone were asked what he meant by saying that he had good grounds or reasons for holding it. I think it would be felt to be a satisfactory answer if he replied: "Well, in all my wide and varied experience I've come across innumerable cases of *f* and never a case of *f* which wasn't a case of *g*". In saying this, he is clearly claiming to have *inductive* support, *inductive* evidence, of a certain kind, for his belief; and he is also giving a perfectly proper answer to the question, what he meant by saying that he had ample justification, good grounds, good reasons for his belief.

The second thing Strawson does to support the premiss that relying on induction is part of what it means to be rational is to argue that the question, "is induction a justified, or justifiable, procedure?" does not really make sense. He begins by pointing out that it makes perfectly good sense to ask whether *specific* beliefs and *specific* methods of arriving at beliefs are justified, because in asking such questions we are asking how well those beliefs and methods conform to inductive standards. For example, we know what it means to ask whether the belief that it will not snow in New York State this winter is a reasonable one, or whether the method of looking at tea leaves to predict this year's weather is a rational one. In both cases, we would be asking whether the belief or method is inductively justified: whether past experience supports the belief that it will not snow in New York this winter, or whether it supports the view that looking at tea leaves is a reliable method of forecasting the weather. But when we ask whether an inductive standard or norm itself, such as (E), is reasonable, it is no longer clear what the question means. The question, Strawson suggests, is like asking whether the law is legal. It makes sense to ask whether particular actions are legal. For then we are asking whether they conform to the law. It even makes sense to ask whether particular laws or statutes are legal. For then we are asking whether those laws conform to the highest law of the land (e.g. its Constitution). But it does not make sense to ask whether the highest law of the land is legal (e.g. whether the Constitution is constitutional). For since it is itself the ultimate legal standard, there is no legal standard that it could either conform to or violate. Likewise, when it comes to judging the reasonableness of factual beliefs about the unobserved, and of methods for arriving at such beliefs, induction is itself the ultimate standard or yardstick against which these methods and beliefs are measured. There is no higher standard available by which to assess the reasonableness of inductive standards themselves.

Strawson suspects that some readers will not find his two points convincing. For directly after making them, he says:

> It seems . . . that this way of showing the request for a general justifica-
> tion to be absurd is sometimes insufficient to allay the worry that pro-
> duces it. And to point out that "forming rational opinions about the
> unobserved on the evidence available" and "assessing the evidence by
> inductive standards" are phrases which describe the same thing, is more
> apt to produce irritation than relief. The point is felt to be "merely a
> verbal" one; and though the point of this protest is itself hard to see, it is
> clear that something more is required.
>
> (ibid.: 258)

In other words, some people might object that even if we ordinarily *call* inductive evidence "good" or "valid" evidence, and so *call* beliefs based on induction "reasonable" or "rational," and use inductive standards as a yardstick of reasonableness for particular beliefs and methods of inquiry, it does not follow that any of these practices really *are* reasonable or rational. To put it more simply: some people might grant the premiss that relying on induction is part of what it means – part of what *we* mean – by being rational, but refuse to allow that it follows from this mere linguistic fact that relying on induction really *is* rational.

As Strawson's remark that "the point of this protest is hard to see" indicates, he does not really accept this objection. He is prepared to argue from "ordinary language" – from the fact that we *correctly* call beliefs based on induction "reasonable" – to the claim that those beliefs really *are* reasonable. But instead of just insisting on this basic argument, he makes a further point, which may well be his deepest one. He suggests that the demand for a justification of induction is based on confusing two very different propositions:

(i)　[The universe is such that] induction will continue to be successful.

(ii)　Induction is rational (reasonable).

Proposition (i) is a very general prediction to the effect that induction will continue to yield a rich harvest of true specific predictions about matters of fact. It amounts to saying that the universe will continue to exhibit a sufficient degree of order and regularity for our inductive beliefs about specific matters of fact to be generally true. So, (i) is a *synthetic* proposition: since its truth or falsity turns on how things will be, (i) is not true solely by virtue of its meaning. Further, the only way (i) can be supported is by induction, although this is of course not to justify induction itself; since we would then be using induction. So, (i) is *a posteriori*: it can be known only on the basis of (past) experience. Finally, as Hume saw, (i) could conceivably turn out to be false: the course of nature conceivably could change. Indeed, it is conceivable that nature might become so chaotic that none of our predictions came out true anymore. It is conceivable even that our expectation that we would all perish in such a chaotic universe could turn out false, and that someone could survive to witness this new chaos, in which nothing foreseeable happens. So, (i) is a *contingent* proposition; it is not a necessary truth. In brief, (i) is synthetic, *a posteriori*, and contingent.

Proposition (ii), by contrast, is of a fundamentally different kind. It is analytic, *a priori*, and necessary. In order to show this, Strawson makes (p. 262) perhaps his cleverest point:

> The chaotic universe just envisaged . . . is not one in which induction would cease to be rational; it is simply one in which it would be impossible to form rational expectations to the effect that specific things would happen. It might be said that in such a universe it would at least be rational to refrain from forming specific expectations, to expect nothing but irregularities. Just so. But this is itself a higher-order induction: where irregularity is the rule, expect further irregularities. Learning not to count on things is as much learning an inductive lesson as learning what things to count on.

In other words: even in a chaotic universe, induction would not cease to be rational. For now it would be rational not to make any specific predictions; in other words, to predict just more chaos or irregularity. But this prediction would itself be based on induction!

The most important implication of the contrast between (i) and (ii) is this: (ii) does not depend on (i). Even if (i) became false, (ii) would still be true. This means that showing how (i) conceivably could become false (as Hume does) has no tendency at all to show that induction is not rational.

Let us apply this point directly to the question of whether Hume's critique of induction implies that induction is not rational. Those who believe that it does presumably hold that whether an inductive inference like that from (4) to (3) is rational depends on whether (5) – the principle that the future will resemble the past – can be established. Simply put, they hold that:

(G) (ii) depends on (5).

Now, notice that (i) – the statement that [the universe is such that] induction will continue to be successful – is very closely related to (5) – the statement that the future will resemble the past. The only difference between them is that (i) does, while (5) does not, explicitly say that induction has and will be used; since (5) asserts only the uniformity of nature, while (i) affirms also the occurrence of induction within this uniform nature. Accordingly, consider a slightly modified version of (i):

(ia) [The universe is such that] induction, if correctly used, will continue to be successful.

Then it seems safe to say that (5) is true just in case (ia) is true; in other words, that:

(H) (5) is true if and only if (ia) is true.

Those who think that Hume's position implies the irrationality of induction, then, are committed to the logical consequence of (G) and (H), namely:

(I) (ii) depends on (ia).

But surely (I) is false: just as Strawson's chaotic universe scenario shows that (ii) does not depend on (i), it likewise shows that (ii) does not depend on (ia). So, since (H) is true, (G) must be false. In other words, we may respond to inductive scepticism by reversing or applying the "pivot principle" to the argument from (G) and (H) to (I), as follows:

(Not-I) (ii) does not depend on (ia).
(H) (5) is true if and only if (ia) is true.

∴ (Not-G) (ii) does not depend on (5).

We may conclude, therefore, that in order for inductive inferences like that from (4) to (3) to be rational, it is not necessary to justify them by means of (5),

Therefore, even if we accept Hume's demonstration that it is impossible to justify induction, we need not accept the sceptical conclusion that induction is therefore irrational.[15] Instead, we can reasonably maintain that induction is rational, even though it cannot be justified.[16]

HUME'S THEORY OF CAUSALITY

1 Introduction

As we have seen, Hume was deeply interested in the relation of cause and effect. For he held that all factual beliefs, except those based on present perception and on memory, ultimately rest on causal relationships. In Section IV of the *Enquiry*, accordingly, he focused on the question of how we acquire and use causal knowledge, or at least (as those who interpret Hume as an inductive sceptic would say) causal beliefs. In Section VII, entitled "Of the Idea of Necessary Connexion," he returns to the topic of causality, but approaches it from a different point of view. His interest now is no longer primarily epistemological; he is no longer primarily concerned with our *knowledge* of causal relationships. Rather, his interest in Section VII is an analytical or definitional one: he wants to discover what causality is, quite apart from the question of how we know whether or what causal relationships exist in the world.

More specifically, he has two related purposes. First, he wants to explain the meaning of the terms "power," "force," "energy," "necessary connection," and the like. (In his discussion of the same topic in the *Treatise*, he mentions also the terms "efficacy," "agency," "necessity," "connection," and "productive quality.") He wants to understand such terms, because they are obviously implicated in the notion of causality: when a cause operates, it is commonly thought to do so because it then exercises power, force, or energy; it is also thought of as producing or necessitating its effect, which is in that sense necessarily connected with the cause. Second, Hume seeks to give what contemporary philosophers call an "analysis" of causation: a definition that specifies, in a noncircular manner, only and all of those statements that must be true for a causal relationship to obtain, or that give the necessary and sufficient conditions for the statement *X caused Y.*

Throughout Section VII, Hume is guided by the principle of empiricism that he advanced in Section II. Thus, immediately after introducing the topic of necessary connection, he reasserts that principle:

> It seems a proposition, which will not admit of much dispute, that all our
> ideas are nothing but copies of our impressions, or, in other words, that it

is impossible for us to *think* of anything, which we have not antecedently *felt*, either by our external or internal senses.

(E:62; S:41; F:102)

This serves as a strong reminder that everything Hume will say about necessary connection and its cognates will be governed by his principle of empiricism. This principle, accordingly, dictates the method Hume will follow in order "to fix, if possible, the precise meaning of these terms" (E:62; S:40; F:102): he will apply his empirical test for meaning to them. In other words, his chief question about "necessary connexion" and its cognates will be: *from what impression(s) is the idea of necessary connection derived*? As he says:

> To be fully acquainted, therefore, with the idea of power or necessary connexion, let us examine its impression; and in order to find the impression with greater certainty, let us search for it in all the sources, from which it may possibly be derived.

(E:63; S:41; F:103)

Having announced his method, Hume launches into a search for the impression(s) of necessary connection. This impression hunt occupies much the greater part of Section VII – all of part I, and the first half of part II. Not until the second half of part II does Hume give, in the space of a single paragraph, his famous analysis of causality. We shall examine his search for the impression of necessary connection in part 2, and his analysis of causality in the third and fourth parts of this chapter.

2 Necessary connection

When looking for an observable item – an "impression" – answering to the idea of necessary connection, the natural way to proceed is by scrutinizing any pair of events related as cause and effect. Now some of the clearest cases of cause and effect are those involving ordinary material objects, such as Hume's favorite case of colliding billiard balls. It is with such cases, accordingly, that Hume begins his impression hunt. He asks us to consider two colliding billiard balls, and to reflect on the question: what do we actually observe in such a case? Well, we observe the cue ball rolling toward the object ball; we see the cue ball come into contact with the object ball, and we see the object ball roll away from the place where it was struck. No doubt, we also hear a noise when the balls come into contact. But do we see the cue ball exercising a power, or exerting a force, on the object ball? Do we see a connection or tie between the events involved – between the collision of the balls and the ensuing motion of the object ball? Do we even know what such a connection or tie would look like? To all these questions, Hume's answer is a resounding NO. Furthermore, since the case of the billiard balls is as clear, obvious, and typical a case of causation as one might like, Hume generalizes from it: he concludes that no individual case of causation involving only objects that we perceive by our senses yields any impression of necessary connection. As he puts it:

> When we look about us toward external objects, and consider the operation of causes, we are never able, in a single instance, to discover any power or necessary connexion; any quality, which binds the effect to the cause, and renders the one an infallible consequence of the other. We only find, that the one does actually, in fact, follow the other. The impulse of one billiard-ball is attended with motion in the second. This is the whole that appears to the *outward* senses.
>
> (E:63; S:41; F:103)

> In reality, there is no part of matter, that does ever, by its sensible qualities, discover any power or energy, or give us ground to imagine, that it could produce any thing, or be followed by any other object, which we could denominate its effect. Solidity, extension, motion; these qualities are all complete in themselves, and never point out any other event which may result from them. The scenes of the universe are constantly shifting, and one object follows another in an uninterrupted succession; but the power or force, which actuates the whole machine, is entirely concealed from us, and never discovers itself in any of the sensible qualities of body. We know that, in fact, heat is a constant attendant of flame; but what is the connexion between them, we have no room so much as to conjecture or imagine. It is impossible, therefore, that the idea of power can be derived from the contemplation of bodies, in single instances of their operation; because no bodies ever discover any power, which can be the original [origin] of this idea.
>
> (E:63–4; S:42; F:104)

Having argued that the idea of necessary connection cannot be derived from observing any individual event-pair in the physical world around us, Hume considers another possibility. Perhaps the idea of necessary connection is derived from introspection; specifically, from experiencing the operation of our own wills. In other words, perhaps one can detect, by introspection, a necessary connection between one's own will and its effects. Hume examines, at some length, two sub-possibilities: (1) that we can detect some necessary connection between our will and its effects when we perform voluntary bodily actions (such as raising an arm); and (2) that we can detect some necessary connection between the individual will (hereafter, the will) and its effects in deliberate thinking and/or imagining (e.g. when we conjure up a mental image). Hume argues against both of these possibilities, using three arguments against each of them. (He labels these arguments "*first*," "*Secondly*," and "*Thirdly*".)

We can summarize his arguments against (1) as follows. First, if we were aware of a necessary connection between the will and its effects in voluntary action, then we would understand how the mind interacts with the body. Since we do not grasp the "secret union of soul and body," it follows that we are not aware of any such connection. Second, if we could detect a power or force operating when we exercise the will in order to control our body, then we would understand exactly why we can voluntarily control some parts of our body (e.g. the legs and fingers) but not others (e.g. the liver and spleen). For then we would be aware of this force's presence in the former cases, and of its absence in the latter cases. But, says Hume, "we cannot assign any reason besides experience, for so remarkable a difference between one and the other" (E:65; S:43; F:105). All we know is that, in some cases, willing a certain bodily movement is followed by that movement; while in other cases, the movement does not occur no matter how intensely we may desire it. Third, science teaches us that the immediate effect of the will in voluntary movement is not the intended movement itself. Rather, it is an event of which we are wholly unaware and probably ignorant – presumably a brain event. (Although Hume himself does not here mention brain events, from our twentieth-century perspective it may be helpful to illustrate his point by reference to them.) This brain event in turn causes a series of neurological and physiological events, of which we are equally unaware, until at last the desired movement occurs. Now since we are unaware of the brain event, we are obviously also unaware of any necessary connection between it and the will. Again, all we are aware of is that willing a certain movement is followed by that movement. We are not aware of any necessary connection between volition and the brain event that initiates the sequence of neurological events, muscular contractions, etc., which ultimately leads to the desired movement.

We can summarize Hume's arguments against (2) as follows. First, when we deliberately conjure up an idea or image, we are of course conscious of that idea or image itself. But we have no understanding at all of the power by which we bring it to consciousness. Indeed, Hume suggests that such purely mental causation is even more mysterious than any so far considered, comparing it to God's creation of things *ex nihilo*, out of nothing:

> This is a real creation; a production of something out of nothing: which implies a power so great, that it may seem, at first sight, beyond the reach of any being, less than infinite.
>
> (E:68; S:45; F:108)

> Volition is surely an act of the mind, with which we are sufficiently acquainted. Reflect upon it. Consider it on all sides. Do you find anything in it like this creative power, by which it raises from nothing a new idea, and with a kind of *Fiat*, imitates the omnipotence of its Maker, if I may be allowed so to speak, who called forth into existence all the various scenes of nature? So far from being conscious of this energy in the will, it requires . . . experience . . . to convince us that such extraordinary effects do ever result from a simple act of volition.
>
> (E:69; S:45; F:108–9)

The upshot is, as before, that while we are conscious of the cause (e.g. willing or deciding to picture a triangle) and of the effect (the image of the triangle), we are not aware of any power or force by which the cause produces the effect. As Hume puts it: "We only feel the event, namely, the existence of an idea, consequent to a command of the will: but the manner, in which this operation is performed, the power, by which it is produced, is entirely beyond our comprehension" (E:68; S:45; F:108).

Hume's second and third arguments against (2) are variants of his second argument against (1). If we were aware of a necessary connection between the will and our thoughts, then we would be able to understand (i) why we have far less control over some of our thoughts (e.g. feelings like envy, anger, elation) than others (e.g. plans for tomorrow) and a rather limited control over them on the whole, and (ii) why we have more control over our thoughts at some times (e.g. when sober) than at other times (e.g. when intoxicated). But (second argument) we cannot "assign the ultimate reason of these boundaries, or show why the power is deficient in one case and not in another" (E:68; S:45; F:108); nor (third argument) can we "give any reason for these variations, except experience" (E:68; S:45; F:108). These two arguments cannot be refuted simply by giving psychological or biological explanations of our weak and/or variable control over our thoughts and emotions. For these explanations would surely appeal to "experience" – to empirical general- izations such as "when a man consumes alcohol, his control over his thoughts diminishes." But Hume's point is precisely that such explanations based on experi- ence are the *only* ones possible; whereas if we could detect a necessary connection between our will and our thoughts, then we could explain (i) and (ii) simply in terms of that connection itself, *without* referring to past experience or general- izations inferred from it.

There is a possible objection to Hume's arguments against (1) and (2) that we should consider. This is that in all these arguments Hume makes an unwarranted assumption. He assumes that in order to be aware *of* some connection between the will and its effects, we must also grasp or understand *how* this connection works. This assumption is very explicit, for example, in this passage from his third argument against (1): "[I]f the original power were felt, it must be known: Were it known, its effect must also be known; since all power is relative to its effect. And *vice-versa*, if the effect be not known, the power cannot be known nor felt." (E:66; S:44; F:106). Here Hume is saying that in order even to *feel* a power, one must "know" it, apparently in the sense of being able to foretell its effect without relying on past experience. In other words, he seems to be assuming that only a power or connection that would license a deductive inference from cause to effect or effect to cause – an inference of the sort he rejected in Section IV – could qualify as an impression of power or necessary connection. The same assumption was operative earlier, when he argued that we observe no necessary connection between cause and effect in the world around us:

> When we look about us toward external objects . . . we are never able, in
> a single instance, to discover any power or necessary connexion, any

quality which binds the effect to the cause, and renders the one an infallible consequence of the other.

(E:63; S:41; F:103; emphasis added)

Here again, Hume seems to be assuming that any power or necessary connection of which we might be aware must be one that makes the effect deducible from ("an infallible consequence" of) the cause. But this assumption is questionable. Suppose, for example, that you force yourself to hold up a heavy object, or to think about something difficult or unpleasant. It seems plausible to say that, in such a case, you are aware of a force or power – that you have, by introspection, an "impression" of power. Hume's only reason for denying this is that you do not understand how this power works, in the sense of knowing, apart from any previous experience, that the effect will occur. But this seems irrelevant: it does not show that you do not experience a feeling of power, force, or connection between your will and its effect. To say that it does show this would be to say that unless the power or force was actually "successful" in bringing about the effect, it did not even exist. But even if you *fail* to hold up the weight or to hold your attention on the unpleasant thought, do you not experience some feeling of (insufficient) force or power? And, if so, why isn't this an "impression" from which the idea of power can be derived?

Although this objection seems correct, it is not very damaging to Hume's basic position. For suppose that Hume simply conceded that we have an idea of power derived from an impression of power that we have when we exercise our wills. Could this idea be what we have in mind when we assert, for example, that one billiard ball exerts power or force on another, or that there is a necessary connection between the collision and the movement of billiard balls? Surely not. For a billiard ball is an unconscious, inanimate object; it cannot have an impression of power like the one we may have in voluntary action or deliberate thinking. The same is true of most of the objects that enter into causal relations: they are inanimate, material objects. Clearly, it would be wrong to model our understanding of a necessary connection between events involving these inanimate objects on human volition. But most of the causal relations we *want to understand* involve just such objects: causal relations between the will and its effects are only a tiny sub-class of all causal relations. So, with the possible exception of that sub-class, an idea of necessary connection derived from human volition cannot advance our understanding of causality. Furthermore, even if we do have some idea of a necessary connection between the will and its effects, this idea is not one that supports a deductive inference from cause to effect or from effect to cause.

It is worth noticing that, in at least one place, Hume does seem to concede that we have this limited idea of necessary connection, and to also point out that this does not seriously affect his overall position. He writes:

It may be pretended, that the resistance which we meet with in bodies, obliging us frequently to exert our force, and call up all our power, this gives the idea of force and power. It is this *nisus* or strong endeavour, of which we are conscious, that is the original impression from which this idea is copied.

(E:67*n*; S:44*n*; F:107)

Since Hume does not go on to deny that we do experience this "*nisus* or strong endeavour," he seems to be conceding that, in such an action as holding up a heavy weight, we do have some impression of force or power. But, in response, Hume says, among other things, that "We attribute power to . . . inanimate matter, which is not capable of this sentiment" (ibid.). This, of course, is the point we are insisting on: even if we do have an idea of power derived from human volition, this idea cannot help us to understand causation in inanimate objects. Hume then adds the revealing remark:

[T]his sentiment of an endeavour to overcome resistance has no known connexion with any event: What follows it we know by experience; but could not know it *a priori*. It must, however, be confessed, that the animal *nisus*, which we experience, though it can afford no accurate precise idea of power, enters very much into that vulgar, inaccurate idea, which is formed of it.

(ibid.)

This reveals once again Hume's assumption that any idea of power or necessary connection worth taking seriously must be such as to license a deductive inference from one event to another; otherwise the idea is not "accurate" or "precise" but only "vulgar" and "inaccurate." But the remark also betrays his realization that such an idea is, nevertheless, a genuine idea of power – an idea "which is formed of it."

Having found no impression from which to derive a suitable idea of necessary connection (one that at least would be applicable to causal relations between inanimate objects), Hume next launches a somewhat digressive polemic against philosophers who would try to base our understanding of necessary connection on the notion of acts of God. (Although he mentions no names, he seems to have in mind the Cartesian Occasionalists, especially Malebranche (1638–1715).)

To summarize this attack: Hume begins by asserting that ordinary people think that they actually see the forces operating in nature, except (only) in extraordinary cases that they cannot explain, like earthquakes, plague, and prodigies. In such cases, they attribute the causality to God's intervention. Philosophers, however, realize that

even in the most familiar events, the energy of the cause is as unintelligible as in the most unusual, and that we only learn by experience the frequent *Conjunction* of objects, without ever being able to comprehend any thing like *Connexion* between them.

(E:70; S:46; F:109)

105

Accordingly, philosophers go much further than do ordinary folk: they infer that the only real cause is always God. Events in the created world are at best only "occasions," that is, occurrences on the occasion of which God Himself causes the effects. This is Malebranche's completely general version of the Occasionalism according to which God causes *all* events and so serves as the causal intermediary between physical and mental events.

Needless to say, Hume rejects this view. Apart from eloquently expressing his scepticism about how we could ever know such a view to be true (E:72; S:47–8; F:111), he points out its uselessness for the purpose at hand: namely, the search for an impression of necessary connection.

> We are ignorant . . . of the manner in which bodies operate on each other: Their force or energy is entirely incomprehensible: But are we not equally ignorant of the manner or force by which a mind, even the supreme mind, operates either on itself or on body? Whence, I beseech you, do we acquire any idea of it? We have no sentiment or consciousness of this power in ourselves. We have no idea of the Supreme Being but what we learn from reflection on our own faculties. Were our ignorance, therefore, a good reason for rejecting any thing, we should be led into that principle of denying all energy in the Supreme Being as much in the grossest matter. We surely comprehend as little the operations of one as of the other.
>
> (E:72–3; S:48; F:111–12)

The upshot is that appealing to God's causality cannot increase our understanding of necessary connection beyond that which was attained by reflecting on human volition (which Hume, here again, declares to be nil, and which we have seen to be at least irrelevant to causation involving inanimate objects).

At the start of Section VII part II, Hume summarizes the results of his impression hunt. So far, these results have been totally negative: so long as we consider individual pairs of events – whether these be events involving the things we perceive outside us, or our own volitions and their effects – we find no (suitable) impression of necessary connection. As Hume puts it: "All events seem entirely loose and separate. One event follows another; but we never can observe any tie between them. They seem *conjoined*, but never *connected*" (E:74; S:49; F:113).

So, Hume declares, it looks as if we may be forced to conclude that the idea of power or necessary connection is simply nonexistent, and that these terms are therefore meaningless:

> And as we can have no idea of any thing which never appeared to our outward sense or inward sentiment, the necessary conclusion *seems* to be, that we have no idea of connexion or power at all, and that these words are absolutely without any meaning, when employed either in philosophical reasonings, or common life.
>
> (E:74; S:49; F:113)

At this point – just as it looks as if the search for necessary connection has ended in failure – Hume makes the key move in his entire discussion of causality. He asks: when do we first begin to infer, from the occurrence of one event, that some other event will occur? Do we make any such inference the first time that we perceive an event of any particular sort? Certainly not: as Hume has already argued at length, it is impossible, on perceiving an event that is new in our experience, for us to draw from it any inference to another event; the entire weight of his critique of causal reasoning lies behind this negative point. Rather, Hume says, it is only after we have observed that an event of a certain kind is always, in our experience, followed by an event of another kind, that we begin to infer, upon observing an event of the first kind, that an event of the second kind will follow. To use Hume's own famous term, it is only after we experience a *"constant conjunction"* between events – events of kind A always being followed, in our experience, by events of kind B – that we start to infer an event of kind B from observing an event of kind A. Only then do we begin to call one event the "cause" and the other the "effect;" only then do we begin to think that there is some necessary connection between the events. So, the idea of necessary connection must somehow arise from observing many similar pairs of events rather than any individual pairs: it arises from the experience of constant conjunction.

However, the introduction of constant conjunction seems at first not to help at all. For, obviously, if we do not observe a necessary connection between two events of a certain kind, then we do not observe such a connection merely by perceiving many more exactly similar pairs of events. There can be nothing in these similar pairs that was not in the first pair; otherwise they would not be exactly similar. What, then, can possibly be added by observing a multiplicity of similar event-pairs? Only this: a feeling of expectation or anticipation, whenever we perceive an event like the first member of the pair, that an event like the second member will follow. This feeling, which is something in our minds rather than in the events themselves, is the *only* new ingredient added by having the experience of constant conjunction. Therefore, Hume concludes, this feeling IS the impression of necessary connection! This striking thesis is also the point of contact between Hume's theory of causality and his psychological explanation of causal and inductive reasoning. For that explanation, you will recall, appeals to the psychological principle ("habit," "custom") that if the mind is presented with repeated cases in which A is followed by B, it will come to expect or anticipate B whenever it perceives A. Hume is now saying that this feeling of anticipation *is* the impression of necessary connection for which he has been searching. In the terminology of the *Treatise*, it is a definite "impression of reflection," just like joy, pain, or embarrassment.

But if necessary connection is merely a feeling in our minds, why do we think that we have a notion of some necessary connection between events themselves? To answer this question, Hume adds a final but very important point to his account of necessary connection. This is that we *project* our own feeling of expectation or anticipation outward into the observed events, and thereby mistakenly come to think that we are aware of a necessary connection between the events themselves.

107

As he puts it in the *Treatise* (where this point is made more emphatically than in the *Enquiry*):

> [T]he mind has a great propensity to spread itself on external objects. . . . This is the case, when we transfer the determination of the thought to external objects, and suppose any real intelligible connexion betwixt them; that being a quality, which can only belong to the mind that considers them.
>
> (T:167–8)

In the *Enquiry*, he puts the point this way: "[A]s we *feel* a customary connexion between the ideas, we transfer that feeling to the objects; as nothing is more natural than to apply to external bodies every internal sensation, which they occasion" (E:78*n*; S:52*n*; F:117). In fact, however, the only relation we observe between the events ("external objects," "external bodies") themselves is that of constant conjunction – the fact that events of the same kind as one of them are "constantly conjoined" in our experience with events of the same kind as the other. The upshot, as Hume puts it in the *Treatise*, is:

> Upon the whole, necessity is something, that exists in the mind, not in objects; nor is it possible for us ever to form the most distant idea of it, consider'd as a quality in bodies. Either we have no idea of necessity, or necessity is nothing but that determination of the thought to pass from causes to effects and from effects to causes, according to their experienc'd union.
>
> (T:165–6)

Before concluding this part, we should say something about a controversy that has emerged in recent Humean scholarship. Until quite recently, virtually all such scholars have taken Hume to have totally rejected the view that there are necessary connections between events. Against this standard interpretation, however, some writers have recently advanced an interpretation which Kenneth Winkler (1991: 541–79), a contemporary Hume scholar, aptly calls "the New Hume." According to proponents of this New Hume, Hume denied that humans *know* that there are necessary connections between events, but allowed that such connections may nevertheless exist.[1] Indeed, several of these proponents have gone so far as to assert that Hume himself actually believed that such connections exist, even though he admitted that neither he nor anyone else could know this to be the case.[2] As evidence for their interpretation, proponents point out that the *Treatise* and the *Enquiry* are rife with passages where Hume uses terms like "secret powers," "power," "the ultimate force and efficacy of nature," "the powers, by which bodies operate," "secret causes," "powers and principles on which the influence of . . . objects entirely depends," and the like, in ways that strongly suggest that he believes that causal powers do exist in objects, even though we cannot know or understand how they operate. The proponents of the New Hume argue also that Hume's "noncommittal" sceptical outlook would have prevented him from categorically denying that there are such powers; since this would have been to make a strong claim about reality that he could not really have known to be true (see especially Strawson 1989: 11–12, 94–101, 277).

In response to the New Hume proponents, scholars who defend the standard interpretation of Hume – who defend what Winkler calls "the Old Hume" – have proposed several ways of dealing with the passages in which Hume seems to be referring to "powers," "secret powers," "secret causes," etc. For example, it has been suggested that his use of such expressions is not genuinely referential; that, rather, it involves only "the use, for the sake of argument, of referential expressions favoured by a view that one is opposing" (Bottersill 1990: 205). It has been pointed out that Hume himself, in the footnote in Section IV of the *Enquiry* that we quoted earlier (see p. 77), says that his uses of the word "power" are to be taken in a "loose and popular sense" (cf. Winkler 1991: 545–6, 550). It has been suggested also that Hume's talk of secret powers and the like may really refer to minute mechanisms and structures rather than to hidden forces (ibid.: 547–50).

The textual issues between proponents of the New Hume and their critics are complex ones that could be settled only by a careful examination of numerous passages and their contexts – something we cannot undertake here. Rather, I shall emphasize only one point that seems to me to be crucial. This is that Hume's negative remarks about necessary connections between events and powers in objects, in the three places where he most directly and explicitly addresses this topic (Section VII of the *Enquiry*; Book I Part III Section XIV of the *Treatise*; and the *Abstract*), stem directly from his empiricist test for meaning – a test which Hume remained unwilling to give up even when it led him to consequences concerning the self that he found unacceptable. Thus, when Hume makes his negative remarks about necessary connection, he is not just saying that it is *false* that there are necessary connections between events, or that we have no way of knowing whether there are such connections. He is saying something much more radical: namely, that we do not even understand what such a necessary connection would be; so that, if we affirmed that there are such connections, we simply would not understand what we were saying. As Hume puts it in the *Abstract* of the *Treatise*:

> Upon the whole, then, either we have no idea at all of force and energy, and these words are altogether insignificant, or they can mean nothing but that determination of the thought, acquired by habit, to pass from the cause to its usual effect.
>
> (T:657; S:134; F:38)

And, again, in the *Enquiry*:

> [We] . . . cannot attain any . . . definition, which may point out that circumstance in the cause, which gives it a connexion with its effect. We

have no idea of this connexion, nor even any distinct notion of what it is we desire to know, when we endeavour a conception of it.

(E:77; S:51; F:116)

And this constancy [constant conjunction] forms the very essence of necessity, nor have we any other idea of it.

(E:96*n*; S:64*n*; F:132)

In these passages (and they are not the only ones of this kind: see e.g. T:165–6, quoted on p. 108; and T:168), Hume is saying that we simply do not have any idea or concept of a necessary connection between events. But if this is so, then contrary to what the proponents of the New Hume say, we cannot even really *believe* that there are such connections.[3] The closest we can come to such a belief is, as Hume says, to strongly expect that an effect will follow a cause, and to project onto or read into the events themselves this feeling of expectation. But this falls short of genuinely believing that there are necessary connections between the events themselves; for, as Winkler says, "we in no way *refer* to causation as it exists in objects (though we do refer to the objects) when we spread our internal impression of determination onto them" (p. 573).

However, it will be objected, if we cannot even believe that there are necessary connections between events, then neither can we meaningfully *deny* that there are such connections. So what does Hume's rejection of such connections amount to? Winkler offers a plausible answer to this question: he suggests (p. 560; see also pp. 543, 567) that Hume's position consists, not in denying that such connections exist, but rather "in a *refusal to affirm* the existence of [necessary connection between events], a refusal rooted in the belief that there is no notion of [necessary connection between events] to be affirmed or denied, or even entertained as a possibility."[4] As Winkler says a little later (p. 576): "Hume needn't say that there is no such thing as objective connection; it is enough for him to say that we cannot *in any way* conceive of it, and that as a result we cannot believe in it."

It is in this sense that I propose we understand Hume's rejection of necessary connection between events. For not only does this way of understanding Hume fit with the fact that his attack on the notion of necessary connection is deeply rooted in his meaning-empiricism, but it also harmonizes with his attempt to define the causal relation. For, as we shall see in the following part, the notion of a necessary connection between events has no place at all in Hume's definition of causality.

3 Hume's analysis of causation

Immediately after presenting his account of necessary connection, Hume offers us a definition of causation. Indeed, he offers two different definitions – a fact that has caused controversy as to how he should be interpreted. The first definition goes as follows:

Similar objects are always conjoined with similar. Of this we have experience. Suitably to this experience, therefore, we may define a cause to be *an object, followed by another, and where all the objects similar to the first are followed by objects similar to the second.*

(E:76; S:51; F:115)

The second definition goes this way:

The appearance of a cause always conveys the mind, by a customary transition, to the idea of the effect. Of this also we have experience. We may, therefore, suitably to this experience, form another definition of cause, and call it, *an object followed by another, and whose appearance always conveys the thought to that other.*

(E:77; S:51; F:116)

Hume illustrates both definitions with the same example:

We say, for instance, that the vibration of this string is the cause of this particular sound. But what do we mean by that affirmation? We either mean, *that this vibration is followed by this sound, and that all similar vibrations have been followed by similar sounds:* Or, *that this vibration is followed by this sound, and that, upon the appearance of the one the mind anticipates the senses, and forms immediately an idea of the other.* We may consider the relation of cause and effect in either of these two lights; but beyond these, we have no idea of it.

(E:77; S:51–2; F:116)

As scholars have pointed out, Hume's formulations are somewhat loose and ambiguous. One ambiguity is that Hume shifts back and forth between speaking of causes and effects as "objects" and as "events." In both definitions he speaks of them as "objects." But in the surrounding text (especially in the first three paragraphs of part II, where he makes his key claims about necessary connection), he repeatedly refers to them as "events." For example:

All events seem entirely loose and separate. One event follows another; but we never can observe any tie between them.

(E:74; S:49; F:113)

But when one particular species of events has always, in all instances, been conjoined with another, we make no longer any scruple of foretelling one upon the appearance of the other.

(E:74–5; S:50; F:114)

It appears, then, that this idea of a necessary connexion among events arises from a number of similar instances which occur of the constant conjunction of these events . . .

(E:75; S:50; F:114)

111

[A]fter a repetition of similar instances, the mind is carried by habit, upon the appearance of one event, to expect its usual attendant, and to believe that it will exist.

(E:75; S:50; F:114)

Altogether, the term "event(s)" occurs twelve times in the first three paragraphs of part II. This suggests that Hume's own position is that causes and effects are events rather than objects. On the other hand, the term "object" occurs five times in those paragraphs, and Hume does use it in formulating his two definitions. So, the matter cannot be settled on textual grounds alone. We have already seen (Chapter 3, section 2), however, that it is more accurate to regard causes and effects as events than as objects. We can speak of the objects themselves as causes only in a derivative sense, based on the consideration that events are generally changes in objects. For example, we can say that one billiard ball – a certain object – is "the cause" of motion in another, insofar as it is that ball which, by hitting the other, causes the motion. It is obvious, nevertheless, that the cause is not just the ball as such, but its collision with the other ball, which is an event. It is even more obvious that the effect is not the other ball itself, but rather that ball's movement following the collision, which is also an event. In what follows, therefore, we shall interpret Hume's definitions as pertaining to events rather than objects.

A second ambiguity arises from the generalization contained in the first definition. This generalization – that "all the objects [events] similar to the first, are followed by objects [events] similar to the second" – presumably refers to *all* such event-pairs, past, present, and future. But when Hume illustrates the definition with the example of the vibration and the sound, he formulates the corresponding generalization in the past tense: all similar vibrations, he says, "*have been followed by similar sounds.*" This refers only to past vibration–sound conjunctions. Now we have seen that for Hume, there is a major epistemological problem about how we can *know* that events which have been constantly conjoined in the past will be constantly conjoined in the future: this is none other than the problem of induction. Perhaps, then, it is Hume's scepticism about the possibility of justifying induction that lies behind his shift to the past tense in the example.

Nevertheless, we shall interpret the generalization contained in Hume's first definition as covering all cases – past, present, and future. There are two reasons for doing so. The first is a textual one. Hume states his first definition of causation on three other occasions – twice in the *Treatise* (T:170, 172) and once in the *Abstract* (T:649–50; S:129; F:33). It is true that on these occasions, he complicates matters somewhat. Instead of saying simply that the cause is "followed by" the effect, he breaks this statement down into two points: the cause is (a) *spatially contiguous* with and (b) *temporally prior* to the effect. This two-point interpretation of "followed by," which Hume presents in the *Treatise* but drops in the *Enquiry*, is problematic. For some causes, such as magnets attracting iron filings and heavenly bodies exercising gravitational "pull," at least seem to act at a distance: they are not spatially contiguous with their characteristical effects.[5] Further, some causes are simultaneous with their effects (e.g. stepping in sand and a footprint's formation) and thus are not temporally prior to their effects. Indeed, a few contemporary philosophers have even claimed that an effect could conceivably occur *before* its cause! We shall not pursue these points here (though simultaneity of cause and effect will come up again in part 4 in relation to causes as sufficient and necessary conditions). The point we wish to make, rather, is that on each of the other three occasions when Hume gives his first definition of causation (as well as in the *Enquiry* itself), he formulates the generalization that it contains as an absolute universal – one that covers all past, present, and future cases. Thus, it seems safe to assume that he does not intend to restrict the generalization only to past cases.

The other reason for interpreting the generalization as universal is philosophical rather than textual. One of the most important and influential ideas in Hume's theory of causality is that every particular cause-and-effect statement is implicitly a generalization. The statement that Louis XVI's decapitation *caused* his death, for example, is true only because decapitating a human being is *always* followed by death. If decapitating a human being were sometimes but not always followed by death, then it would not be true that decapitating Louis XVI *caused* his death. Rather, we would have to look for some other factor in the situation – one which *is* always followed by death – and say that *it* was the true cause of Louis's death. The statement that the decapitation did cause his death is true *because* the decapitation–death generalization is universal and without exception: it is a *law of nature*. Hume's idea, then, can also be put this way: every particular causal statement involves at least one law of nature. Now laws of nature do not hold just for past cases; they hold for all cases. Of course, if the problem of induction is taken to imply inductive scepticism, then it calls into question whether we can know that there are such laws. That is why inductive scepticism cuts deep: it concerns the very possibility of science, which seeks to discover laws of nature or scientific laws. The fact remains, however, that laws of nature are *supposed* to hold for all cases; otherwise they would not be laws. This is the fundamental reason for interpreting the generalization in Hume's first definition as covering not only past cases, but all present and future cases as well.

In line with the two interpretive points we have made – that both definitions pertain to events rather than objects, and that the generalization in the first definition pertains to all cases rather than only to past cases – we may formulate Hume's two definitions as follows, letting "E_1" and "E_2" stand for any two particular events that are related as cause and effect:

D1: E_1 causes E_2 $=df$

(1) E_1 is followed by E_2;
and
(2) all events similar to E_1 are followed by events similar to E_2.

D2: E_1 causes E_2 = *df*

(1) E_1 is followed by E_2;
and
(2a) observing an event similar to E_1 always leads us to expect an event similar to E_2.

The fact that Hume gives variant definitions of causation obviously calls for comment. Notice, first of all, that the definitions are different: a pair of events could satisfy *D1* without satisfying *D2*, and conversely a pair of events could satisfy *D2* without satisfying *D1*. Suppose for example that while events similar to E_1 are macroscopic ones that we frequently observe, events similar to E_2 are microscopic ones that science has not yet discovered. Then it could be true that events like E_1 are always followed by events like E_2, but false that events like E_1 always (or ever) lead us to expect events like E_2. In such a case, *D1*(2) would be satisfied, but *D2* (2a) would not be satisfied. Or suppose that we had been conditioned to expect rain after every solar eclipse, because, as it happened, each solar eclipse we knew of had been followed by rain. It could nonetheless be the case – in fact you and I know it is the case – that not every solar eclipse is followed by rain. So in such a situation, *D2*(2a) would be satisfied, but *D1*(2) would not. It is clear, then, that D1 and D2 are not equivalent. It is worth noting, however, that there is a relationship between them. The contemporary philosopher Barry Stroud, in his book *Hume*, helpfully describes this relationship as follows:

> The relation between them is something like this. Any events or objects observed to fulfil the conditions of the first "definition" are such that they will fulfil the conditions of the second "definition" also. That is to say that an observed constant conjunction between As and Bs establishes a "union in the imagination" such that the thought of an A naturally leads the mind to the thought of a B. That is just a fundamental, but contingent, principle of the human mind.
>
> (Stroud 1977: 90)

Otherwise put, Stroud's point is that any events that have been *observed* not to violate *D1*(2) will, because of the principle of association Hume has put forward, satisfy *D2*(2a).[6]

As previously mentioned, the nonequivalence of Hume's two definitions has led to controversy concerning his intentions. Some scholars have argued that only Hume's first definition represents his real view (see Robinson 1962). Some have argued that he has two different theories that can be integrated as one (Beauchamp and Rosenberg 1981). Stroud (1977: 89) holds that Hume never intended, strictly speaking, to give a definition of causation. Recently, Don Garrett (1997: 107–17) has argued that Hume's two definitions can be interpreted in such a way that they turn out to be equivalent, and that Hume accepts both of them.

We shall not delve into this debate. Rather, let us look into the implications of Hume's definitions for their own sake, without worrying further about his exact intentions. Specifically, let us ask this question: which of Hume's two definitions is a definition of causation as it occurs objectively in nature, regardless of whether there are any people or observers or sentient beings? The answer is obvious: only *D1*. For *D2* refers to observations, expectations, and the triggering of the latter by the former. But surely cause-and-effect relationships occur in nature independently of these things, and could have occurred even if there had never been any sentient beings capable of making observations or having expectations. To quote Stroud once again:

> [T]hings could fulfil the conditions of the first "definition" even if there were no minds at all, or if minds were very different from the way they actually are. The existence and precise nature of minds is irrelevant to the question whether members of one class of things are regularly followed by members of another class.
>
> (Stroud 1977: 90)

Let us take it, then, that *D1* is supposed to be the complete definition of causation, as it exists objectively in nature. *D2*, by contrast, makes only a contingent claim about *observed* cases of causation, as Stroud suggests. What are the implications? One of them, as we have already seen, is that every particular causal statement – every statement of the form "E_1 causes E_2" – implies that there is some law of nature linking events like E_1 and events like E_2. But there is another, and striking, implication. Notice that *D1* makes absolutely no reference to necessary connection or to necessity. The sole reference to necessary connection occurs, under another name, in *D2*; since necessary connection just *is* the feeling of expectation mentioned in *D2*. *D1*, by contrast, does not involve necessary connection. Instead, it involves only "constant conjunction" – one type of event being always accompanied or followed by another type of event. The essence of causation, then, is not necessary connection (which exists only in our minds), but constant conjunction. To put it differently, the essence of causation is not necessity, but *regular succession* or *regularity*.

An example should help to make this implication of *D1* more vivid. Think of a situation in which automobiles are being tested by the manufacturer for crash resistance. By signals from a radio transmitter, test cars are driven into a brick wall at various speeds, to determine the extent of damage that results. Imagine that a particular car is driven into the wall at 5 miles per hour. Imagine that upon impact the front bumper crumples. We may say, then, that *the impact of the car against the brick wall was followed by the crumpling of the car's bumper*. In other words, clause 1 of *D1* is satisfied. Now, what are we *adding* when we say that the impact *caused* the crumpling? According to *D1*, the only thing we are adding is that *all impacts of this kind are followed by crumplings of that kind* – a pure statement of regularity. We are *not* adding that the impact *necessitated* the crumpling, or that there was some necessary

115

connection between the two events. If we do say this, that is because we are projecting our own anticipation or expectation of the bumper's crumpling onto the events themselves – a mistake, as Hume has argued.

Finally, *D1* also has implications concerning the character of laws of nature. For, as we noted above, clause 2 of *D1* – the generalization that all events similar to E_1 are followed by events similar to E_2 – states the law of nature involved. But this generalization itself makes no reference to necessity: it is simply a universal exceptionless generalization. Thus, *D1* implies that laws of nature are only exceptionless but contingent regularities between kinds of events. They do not embody any element of necessity.

4 The regularity theory: some objections and replies

The analysis of causation given in Hume's first definition, and the view of laws of nature it embodies, are now commonly called the "regularity theory" of causality. There is a large and complex literature, both "pro" and "con," on the regularity theory. Indeed, this literature is only a part of a larger literature on a group of interrelated topics, including not only causation itself but also the nature of natural laws, the nature of events, scientific explanation, and others. We cannot possibly survey this literature here, nor even touch on all of the issues that it raises. Rather, we shall try only to bring out what makes the regularity theory appealing, and to defend it against a number of objections.

The main appeal of the regularity theory is probably this: it takes some of the mystery out of causality. For the notion of a necessary connection between events, of necessity *in nature* or *natural necessity*, is a puzzling and mysterious one. Hume's attempt to pinpoint something observable that would answer to this notion, whatever else may be said about it, serves at least to bring out the elusive character of such necessity. Compare it with logical necessity – with the necessity by which the conclusion q follows from the premises *if p, then q* and *p*. Although there are philosophical questions about the nature of logical necessity, there are several ways of getting a grasp of the notion. We can point out that it would be a contradiction to assert those premises and deny that conclusion. We can point out that there is no possible world in which both premises, p and *if p, then q*, are true and the conclusion, q, is false. We can point out that the statement, "{ *[If (if p, then q) and p], then q*}," is a truth of logic or a "tautology" – a statement that remains true no matter what combination of truth-values we assign to p and q individually. But none of these points carries over to causal relationships or laws of nature. It is never a contradiction, as Hume showed, to affirm that one event occurred but that another – distinct – event did not. There are possible worlds in which events that are conjoined in our world are disjoined, and in which different laws of nature obtain. The laws of nature are not truths of logic or tautologies. Thus, we cannot understand natural necessity in terms of logical necessity. When this (essentially Humean) insight is combined with Hume's point that nothing we can observe answers to the name of natural necessity, that notion seems mysterious and incomprehensible. By contrast, the notion of regularity seems clear, crisp, and unmysterious. We can observe regularities obtaining between events. We can use refined scientific methods to find the real regularities in nature, and to distinguish them from those suggested by superficial examination. Putting aside Hume's worries about induction, we can use those regularities to predict future events and to explain past events. So if causation and laws of nature are simply matters of regularity, our world is a little less mysterious than it would be if they embody some sort of non-logical, natural necessity.

But while the regularity theory is very appealing, it also faces difficult objections. In the subsections that follow, we shall discuss four of them.

The problem of similarity

In a number of writings, the contemporary American philosopher Richard Taylor attacks the regularity theory (e.g. 1967: 56–66; 1992: Chap. 10). In *Metaphysics* (1992); Taylor first offers the following test for the correctness of *D1*: in order for that definition to be correct, it must not be possible to describe any case where its *analysandum* or *definiendum* (the expression *to be* analyzed or defined, namely, "E_1 causes E_2") is true while its *analysans* or *definiens* (the defini*ng* expressions, namely, clauses 1 and 2 of *D1*) are false, or vice-versa. Taylor then argues that *D1* either fails the test or is circular. He focuses in on the question: what does "similar" mean in the definition? If it means "exactly similar" (i.e. similar in every respect, presumably including even spatial and temporal positioning), then the only event which is similar to E_1 is E_1 itself, and the only event which is similar to E_2 is E_2 itself (Taylor 1992: 92). But then if clause 1 of *D1* is satisfied – if E_1 is followed by E_2 – clause 2 is automatically satisfied as well. For since "similar" means "exactly similar," no other event can be similar to E_1, and likewise no other event can be similar to E_2: so, of course, all events similar to E_1 are followed by events similar to E_2! But this means that we can easily describe cases where both clauses 1 and 2 of *D1* are true while "E_1 causes E_2" is false (i.e. where the *analysans* is true but the *analysandum* is false). Any case where E_1 is followed by E_2, but E_1 does not cause E_2, will do. For example: I look at a red traffic light, and it turns green. The only event exactly similar to my act of looking at a red light is that very act itself, and the only event exactly similar to the event of the light turning green is that very event itself. So – assuming still that "similar" means "exactly similar" – all events similar to that act of looking are followed by events similar to that event of turning green. But it would be ridiculous to say that my looking at the red light causes it to turn green.

On the other hand, suppose that "similar" means "similar to a high degree." Then we can easily describe cases where the *analysandum* is true but the *analysans* is false. For example, suppose that striking a certain match (E_1) causes it to ignite (E_2). Then although clause 1 is satisfied – E_1 is followed by E_2 – clause 2 is not satisfied. For many events that are similar to a high degree to E_1, such as striking a damp match, or a dry match on too smooth a surface, are not followed by events similar in a high degree to E_2 (Taylor 1992: 92). So now we have a case where "E_1 causes E_2" is true, but where, due to the falsity of clause 2, the conjunction of clauses 1 and 2 is false – i.e. it is a case where the *analysandum* is true but the *analysans* is false.

It might be thought that the problem can be solved by letting "similar" mean "exactly similar except for space–time location." But on that interpretation of "similar," the match-striking case still shows that the *analysandum* might be true while the *analysans* was false. For a small variation occurring after an event "similar" to E_1 (striking the match), such as a light breeze arising, might result in the ignition or flaming up being a bit different from E_2 (the match's ignition); so that clause 2 of the *analysans* would be false: we would have a case where an event "exactly similar" to E_1 was *not* followed by an event "exactly similar" to E_2. Yet it would still be true that E_1 causes E_2.

Finally, suppose that we try to solve the difficulty by letting "similar" mean "similar in relevant respects." Then the analysis is spoiled; for what does "relevant respects" mean? Well, it can only mean "causally relevant respects" (Taylor 1992: 92). But this turns *D1* into a circular definition, for clause 2 now means:

(2b)   all events that in causally relevant respects are similar to E_1 are followed by events that in causally relevant respects are similar to E_2.

But this is, basically, to define causation in terms of itself. The upshot, then, is that *D1* is either incorrect or circular.

It must be admitted that Taylor's objection to *D1* is a powerful one. Nevertheless, the objection is not fatal to the regularity theory; for the objection hinges on the fact that Hume formulates the regularity – in clause 2 of *D1* – in terms of *similarity* or resemblance. But there is another way to formulate this regularity: namely, in terms of the kinds, classes, or species of event involved. In a passage quoted earlier, we saw that Barry Stroud does not hesitate to put Hume's view in this manner; he speaks of "members of one class of things [being] regularly followed by members of another class" (1977: 90). Indeed, Hume himself sometimes speaks in this way, as for example when he says:

> But when one particular *species of events* has always, in all instances, been conjoined with another, we make no longer any scruple of foretelling one upon the appearance of the other . . .
> (E:74–5; S:50; F:114; emphasis added)

> Let us try any other balls *of the same kind* in a like situation, and we shall always find that the impulse of the one produces motion in the other.
> (T *Abstract*:649; S:129; F:33; emphasis added)

Now if the generalization in *D1* is reformulated in terms of kinds or species or classes of event, then it must say that all events of one kind (species, class) are followed by events of another kind. Furthermore, *D1* as a whole must be modified, in order to bring it into line with this reformulation. The modified definition would go as follows:

D3: E_1 causes E_2 = *df.*

(1) E_1 is followed by E_2;
(2) all events of kind K1 are followed by events of kind K2;
(3) E_1 is of kind K1 and E_2 is of kind K2.

This definition may, of course, be vulnerable to other objections. But one thing seems clear: it is not vulnerable to Taylor's objection. For that objection hinges on the troublesome notion of similarity or resemblance – a notion that does not appear in *D3*.

There is a reason why Hume himself speaks mainly in terms of similarity between events rather than kinds of event: he is a nominalist. Nominalism is a theory about what it is for two or more things to have a common property. Roughly speaking, the theory says that things have a common property when they are similar – when they resemble each other. Furthermore, since every property defines a class or kind, nominalism is also a theory about what it is for two or more things to belong to the same class or to be of the same kind: again, the things are similar, or resemble each other. Now when Hume puts forward his regularity definition of causation, he does so within the framework of his nominalism. That is why he expresses the definition in terms of similarity. But in assessing the regularity theory, it seems only fair to separate it from the issue of nominalism. One question is whether it is possible to formulate a satisfactory definition of causation *purely* in terms of regular succession between events of certain kinds or species, without appealing to the notion of necessary connection. If the answer is yes, then the regularity theory is vindicated. Another question is whether nominalism is justifiable. If the answer is yes, then there seems no reason in principle why all statements referring to kinds or species of event could not be reformulated as statements referring only to resembling events – in which case Hume's combined regularity view of causation and nominalism would be vindicated too. But in assessing the regularity theory as such, it is necessary to separate it from the question of nominalism.

The trouble with Taylor's objection is that it depends precisely on not separating these issues. Taylor attacks the regularity theory by bringing out difficulties that stem only from Hume's nominalistic formulation of it. To see this, notice that nominalism itself could be attacked in much the same way as Taylor attacks *D1*. The nominalist holds that two things have a common property provided that they are similar. Now, Taylor could say: what does it mean for them to be similar? If it means that they are exactly similar, then they are not really two things but one. If it means that they are similar to a high degree, they might nonetheless not share a common property. If it means that they are similar in relevant respects, then the

119

theory is circular, because those "respects" can signify only the common property in question. To answer this objection, a nominalist would have to refine the theory in some way. Whether or not this can be successfully done is an interesting and controversial question in its own right. But this question is quite independent of whether causation can be defined in terms of regularity.

Causal laws versus accidental generalizations

Without doubt, the most common objection to the regularity theory is that it is incapable of distinguishing between two importantly different things: genuine causal relationships, and regular but non-causal relationships. As applied to *D3*, the objection is that we can easily describe cases where all three clauses of the *analysans* are satisfied, but E_1 does not cause E_2. For example, suppose that whenever the noon schoolbells ring in Washington, DC, students in New York City schools go to lunch. Suppose that Jefferson High is a school in Washington, DC, and that Dewey High is a school in New York City. On a given day, the noon schoolbell rings at Jefferson High, and the students at Dewey High troop off to lunch. Then it is true (i) that the bell's ringing at Jefferson High is followed by students going to lunch at Dewey High, (ii) that all events of the kind: noon schoolbells ringing in Washington, DC are followed by events of the kind: students going to lunch in New York City schools, and (iii) that the bell ringing at Jefferson High is an event of the kind: noon schoolbells ringing in Washington, DC, and students going to lunch at Dewey High is an event of the kind: students going to lunch in New York City schools. Yet it is clearly false that the bell ringing at Jefferson High causes students to go to lunch at Dewey High. Therefore, clauses 1, 2, and 3 of *D3*'s *analysans* are all satisfied, but E_1 does not cause E_2. So, *D3* must be incorrect.[7]

A regularity theorist would reply that the reason why E_1 does not cause E_2 in this example is quite obvious: the generalization stated in (ii) – that whenever noon schoolbells ring in Washington, DC, students in New York City schools go to lunch – is not a causal law or a law of nature. Rather, it is a true but accidental or coincidental generalization. In order for clause 2 of *D3*'s *analysans* to be satisfied, (ii) would have to cite a causal law, rather than just an accidental generalization.

This reply, however, leads directly to the question: how does the regularity theorist propose to distinguish between a causal law and an accidental generalization? This is a crucial question for the regularity theorist. For unless an answer is forthcoming, there is no way to save *D3* from the objection that its *analysandum* can be false while its *analysans* is true. As the contemporary British philosopher J. L. Mackie (1917–81), put the matter in his highly regarded *The Cement of the Universe*: "The problem . . . of distinguishing causal from accidental regularities, is the great difficulty for any regularity theory of causation" (1974: 196).

One way to make the distinction, of course, would be to say that a causal regularity always involves a necessary connection, while an accidental regularity does not. But this is precisely what a regularity theorist cannot say, without giving up the entire theory. The problem such a theorist faces, then, is to distinguish between a causal law and an accidental generalization *without* appealing to the notion of a necessary connection between a cause and its effect. To deepen our understanding of this problem, let us compare two statements: (a) Whenever a human being is beheaded, he or she dies. (b) Whenever John has eggs for breakfast, Mary has toast. We know, of course, that (a) is true, for it involves a law of nature. Suppose that (b) is also true. In other words, suppose it just happens to be true, throughout John and Mary's entire lives, that each time John eats eggs at breakfast, Mary eats toast. Both (a) and (b), then, are true and exceptionless generalizations. Yet, it is obvious that while (a) exemplifies a causal law, (b) is an accidental generalization. What is the difference between them?

One difference to which philosophers have called attention is this. Suppose that John is, happily enough, not beheaded. Then we can still be sure that (c) If John had been beheaded, he would have died. This statement is of a type called a *counterfactual conditional* or *contrary-to-fact conditional*. Such a statement says that if something which did not happen – something which is, so to speak, counter or contrary to the facts – *had* happened, then something else would have happened. Now an important feature of causal laws is that they allow us to infer various counterfactual conditionals. As it is usually put, causal laws "sustain" counter-factual conditionals. In the case at hand, (a) allows us to infer (c): it sustains (c). By contrast, a merely accidental generalization like (b) does not sustain any counter-factual conditional. To see this, suppose that on the morning of July 14, 2000 John does not have eggs for breakfast. Then we *cannot* infer from (b) that (d) If John had had eggs for breakfast on July 14, 2000 then Mary would have had toast. In other words, the fact that all occasions on which John has eggs for breakfast happen to be occasions on which Mary has toast does not enable us to infer that, if John had had eggs on a certain morning when he in fact did not, Mary would have had toast. On the other hand, the causal law that all occasions on which some person is beheaded are occasions on which that person dies does enable us to infer that, if John, who in fact was not beheaded, had been beheaded, then he would have died.

Now some philosophers argue that this difference shows that the problem faced by the regularity theory – that of distinguishing between causal laws and accidental generalizations without appealing to natural necessity – is insuperable. For it shows, they think, that (a) possesses a special necessity which (b) does not.

A regularity theorist, however, need not concede this point. For the theorist can point to a difference other than necessity between (a) and (b), by virtue of which (a) is a causal law but (b) is not. This is that (b), unlike (a), is not sufficiently general to sustain counterfactuals. For (b) refers to two *particular individuals*, John and Mary, and says that every occasion on which John has eggs for breakfast is an occasion on which Mary has toast. This provides no basis for saying that if, on a given occasion when John did not have eggs for breakfast, he had eaten eggs for breakfast, then Mary would have had toast. By contrast, (a) pertains to two *kinds* of event, and says that every event of kind K1 (beheading of a human) is followed by an event of kind K2 (death of that human). This *does* provide a basis for saying that if, on a given occasion when an event of kind K1 did not occur, an event of kind K1 had occurred, then an event of kind K2 would have occurred. It would seem, then, that what prevents (b) from sustaining counterfactuals, and so disqualifies it from being a causal law, is its reference to particular individuals. This harmonizes with something that we all know about laws of nature: laws of nature are not restricted to particular individuals. They pertain to kinds or types of event, regardless of particular circumstances of place and time. This is also why it cannot be a causal law that whenever noon schoolbells ring in Washington, DC, schools, students go to lunch in New York City schools. This generalization, in virtue of its reference to specific cities, fails to sustain counterfactuals, and is therefore disqualified from being a law of nature.

Although the requirement that a causal law cannot refer to particular individuals seems to dispose of the Washington–New York City case and the John–Mary case, there are examples of greater difficulty. Consider the following case, given by Richard Taylor (1992: 93–4). Suppose that we have a batch of 1,000 matches. Suppose that we decorate each of the matches with a special design, D, which is, say, a pattern of alternating red and green lines, around its stem. Suppose that in the entire history of the universe, no other match will ever be decorated with D. Finally, suppose that all of our D-decorated matches are struck against a piece of fresh sandpaper, and that all ignite. Then it is true that all strikings of D-decorated matches are followed by ignitions. Yet, this generalization is no law of nature; for it does not sustain the counterfactual claim that if some match, not from the original batch of 1,000, and so not decorated with D, had been decorated with D and struck against a fresh piece of sandpaper, it would have ignited. But why does it not sustain this counterfactual? The only reason that can be given, according to Taylor (1992: 94), is that there is no necessary connection between a match's having D and its igniting when struck, as there is, for instance, between its having a certain chemical composition and its igniting when struck.

In order to answer the objection, a regularity theorist must, again, be able to disqualify Taylor's generalization as a causal law without appealing to the notion of necessary connection. It may be tempting to suppose that this could be done in much the same way as before, by saying that the generalization does, after all, refer to certain specific matches. The fact that there are 1,000 of them, or that they do not have names like "John" or "New York City," does not prevent the generalization from referring illegitimately to certain individual things. Taylor, however, could reply that his reference to the 1,000 matches was made only in order to help us understand the example; no such reference is actually contained in the generalization at issue. For that generalization simply says that all D-decorated matches ignite when struck against fresh sandpaper. Unlike the Washington–New York City and John–Mary generalizations, it does not mention any individual things – it does not refer to the particular matches that happen to fall under it. Putting it in the terminology of D3, Taylor's generalization says only that all K1 events – events of the kind: striking of a D-decorated match against fresh sandpaper – are followed by K2 events – events of the kind: ignition of a D-decorated match. Since each of the 1,000 D-decorated matches that will ever exist does ignite when so struck, this generalization is perfectly true or exceptionless. Yet it is no law of nature, and the regularity theorist cannot tell us why.

The regularity theorist need not surrender. For ask yourself: would we really assert, in the case Taylor describes, that all K1 events are followed by K2 events? No. For to be in a position to assert that all K1 events are followed by K2 events, more is required than merely passive observation of a regularity between such events. We have to vary, in a controlled way, the conditions under which the events occur, to see whether K1 events are still followed by K2 events. As Kant put it:

> When Galileo caused balls, the weights of which he had himself pre-viously determined, to roll down an inclined plane; when Toricelli made the air carry a weight which he had calculated beforehand to be equal to that of a definite volume of water . . . or when Stahl changed metals into oxides, and oxides back into metal, by withdrawing something and then restoring it, a light broke upon all students of nature. They learned that reason has insight only into that which it produces after a plan of its own, and that it must not allow itself to be kept, as it were, in nature's leading-strings, but must itself show the way with principles of judgment based upon fixed laws, constraining nature to give answer to questions of reason's own determining. Accidental observations, made in obedience to no previously thought-out plan, can never be made to yield a necessary law, which alone reason is concerned to discover. Reason, holding in one hand its principles, according to which alone concordant appearances can be admitted as equivalent to laws, and in the other hand the experiment which it has devised in conformity with these principles, must approach nature in order to be taught by it. It must not, however, do so in the character of a pupil who listens to everything that the teacher chooses to say, but of an appointed judge who compels witnesses to answer questions which he has himself formulated.
>
> (Kant 1963: 20)

Apart from the phrase "a necessary law" (to which a regularity theorist would of course object) and the rationalistic-sounding references to "reason," this passage provides an eloquent antidote to Taylor's example. For the scenario his example suggests is the very antithesis of the scientific practices Kant describes: we have a batch of matches that have many properties besides D; we find that they all light when struck; and we conclude, in spite of the fact that we cannot control the variables involved, that it is D, rather than any of the other properties, which is always followed by ignition. Scientific laws are not established in such a manner.

The trouble is that Taylor sets up the case in such a way that no genuine testing of the generalization is possible. By hypothesis, no matches other than those we have ourselves decorated with D will ever, in the history of the universe, have D. This means that we cannot, for example, paint D on a wet match, or on a match

123

that has already been lit, so as to test the generalization that *all* D-decorated matches ignite when struck on fresh sandpaper. By hypothesis, we cannot perform the tests that any person with even a rudimentary understanding of scientific method knows are indispensable – tests which, in this case, would include putting D on matches not included in the original 1,000, giving them properties different from those of the one thousand (e.g. wetness), and striking them against fresh sandpaper. But since we cannot do this, it seems that instead of asserting that all K1 events are followed by K2 events, all we can reasonably say is: "So far, all K1 events have been followed by K2 events. But, unfortunately, we will never be able to know whether *all* K1 events are followed by K2 events. For all the D-decorated matches that we tested also had many other properties, such as being dry, not previously struck, etc. But since no other matches will ever have D, we will never know whether a match that has D but is wet, or has D but has been previously lit, ignites when struck. So, we will never know whether the regularity we observed between K1 and K2 events is a universal one." Suppose, on the other hand, that a generalization of the form "all K1 events are followed by K2 events" *is* scientifically tested and, as a result of such testing, held to be true – to be a law. Is there anything in this situation to indicate that the scientists have discovered something more than just an exceptionless regularity between K1 and K2 events? Must we say, for example, that they have found a *necessary* connection between such events? This seems in no way necessary; nor, as Hume has shown, is it at all clear what "necessary" means in this context.

The fundamental point can be put as follows. Consider the generalization:

(M)   All strikings of D-decorated matches are followed by ignition of D-decorated matches.

For this generalization to express a law of nature, it must not mean just that

(M')   All strikings of D-decorated matches that actually exist are followed by ignition of D-decorated matches.

Rather, it must mean that

(M″)   All strikings of D-decorated matches that actually exist are followed by, and all strikings of D-decorated matches that might have existed would be followed by, ignition of D-decorated matches.

But Taylor has described only a case where (M') obtains, not one where (M″) obtains. Further, if we were satisfied that (M″) was true, then we would be justified in regarding (M″) as a law of nature.[8]

Taylor might object that the counterfactual phrase ("that might have existed would be followed by") imports into (M″) the very notion of necessity that the regularity theory seeks to avoid. But the regularity theorist can reply that this is not at all obvious; for, if that phrase were replaced with the future-tense phrase "that will exist will be followed by," then it would not necessarily import the notion of a necessary connection between a cause and its effect. It would only express a prediction that the generalization will hold in the future, and is thus a genuinely exceptionless generalization. By the same token, there seems no reason to think that the counterfactual phrase, which the hypothesis that no other D-decorated matches will ever exist forces us to adopt, must import this notion of necessity.[9]

We conclude that, for all Taylor's example shows, the regularity theorist may be right in holding that the difference between an accidental generalization and a causal law is, at bottom, a matter of generality rather than necessity.

Causes as sufficient conditions and as necessary conditions

As we saw earlier, Hume states his first definition of causation this way: "[W]e may define a cause to be *an object, followed by another, and where all the objects similar to the first are followed by objects similar to the second*" (E:76; S:51; F:115). Immediately after giving this definition, however, Hume adds a very puzzling remark, which I did not include when first quoting the passage, and have simply ignored until now. He says: "Or, in other words, where, *if the first object had not been, the second never had existed*" (E:76; S:51; F:115). The reason this remark is puzzling is that, despite Hume's preface "in other words," it is not at all equivalent to the definition he has just given; nor is it even implied by that definition. This can be seen by looking at *D3*, which is modeled closely on Hume's own definition. Clauses 2 and 3 of *D3* imply that if E_1 occurs, then E_2 occurs. So, *D3* implies that when E_1 causes E_2, E_1 is a *sufficient condition* for E_2. Clauses 2 and 3 do not imply, however, that if E_1 does not occur, then E_2 does not occur. So, *D3* does not imply that when E_1 causes E_2, E_1 is a *necessary condition* of E_2. Yet, in his remark Hume seems to be saying that *D3* does carry this implication.

Hume makes this puzzling remark only once; so it might be tempting to dismiss it as just a careless slip. But the remark cannot be treated so lightly; for some contemporary philosophers would say that it betrays Hume's fleeting realization that his definition of causation leaves out something important. In other words, they would say that an adequate analysis of causation *should* imply that a cause is not just a sufficient condition for its effect, but also a necessary condition for its effect.[10] Consider, for example, the statement that striking a match causes it to ignite. On *D3*, this statement implies only that striking the match is sufficient for it to ignite – that if the match is struck, then it ignites. But does not the statement also imply that striking the match is necessary for it to ignite – that if the match is not struck, it will not ignite? Some contemporary philosophers, J. L. Mackie and Richard Taylor for example, would claim that it does. They would argue, furthermore, that although Hume's definition can be expanded so as to carry this implication, the expanded definition runs into serious difficulty. Let us consider how the expanded definition would go, what difficulties result, and how Hume (or a regularity theorist) might deal with them.

In order for *D3* to imply that a cause is a necessary condition for its effect, we would have to add the following statement to clause 2: "and all events of kind K2 are preceded by events of kind K1." The expanded clause would then read:

(2') All events of kind K1 are followed by events of kind K2, and all events of kind K2 are preceded by events of kind K1.

This statement, together with clause 3 of *D3*, implies not only that if E_1 occurs, then E_2 occurs, but also that if E_2 occurs, then E_1 occurs. So if 2' is substituted for 2 in *D3*, then *D3* implies that when E_1 causes E_2, E_1 is not only a sufficient condition for E_2, but also a necessary condition for E_2.

However, this expanded version of *D3* runs into the following difficulty. If E_1 is both sufficient and necessary for E_2, then E_2 is both sufficient and necessary for E_1. For the former says that (a) if E_1 occurs then E_2 occurs and if E_2 occurs then E_1 occurs, while the latter says that (b) if E_2 occurs then E_1 occurs and if E_1 occurs then E_2 occurs. But (a) and (b) say exactly the same thing; they differ only in word order. The consequence is that the relationship between E_1 and E_2 turns out to be perfectly symmetrical. But this is an absurd consequence. For we all know that the causal relation is an asymmetrical one – that, for example, striking the match causes it to ignite, but its igniting does not cause it to be struck. The upshot is that, when we expand *D3* so as to accommodate the idea that a cause is a necessary as well as a sufficient condition for its effect, we can no longer distinguish between cause and effect![11]

One way to deal with the difficulty would be to insist, as Hume does, that the cause must occur *before* the effect in time – that E_1 must be temporally prior to E_2. This would certainly restore the required asymmetry of the causal relation.

Unfortunately, however, this solution is not very satisfactory; for there are cases where cause and effect occur simultaneously. Kant cites a case where a ball is placed on a cushion and a hollow is formed, and earlier we mentioned the case of making a footprint in the sand; there are other cases as well. No doubt, not *all* causes are simultaneous with their effects; for, if they were, there would be no such thing as a causal chain or series some of whose members occur before the others. But it has to be admitted that some causes occur at the same time as their effects. (As mentioned earlier, some philosophers have even suggested that some causes occur after their effects!) Now the original – unexpanded – version of *D3*, despite the term "followed by," can be read so as to allow for simultaneous causes and effects, and so as to preserve the asymmetry of causation as well. For "followed by" can be interpreted to mean simply "accompanied by." In that case, clause 2 will mean that all events of kind K1 are accompanied by events of kind K2 – that a K1 event never occurs without a K2 event occurring. This allows that the K2 event may occur either after, or at the same time as, the K1 event (or even before it!). So, this reading of clause 2 allows for cases where cause and effect occur simultaneously. It also allows for the possibility that a K2 event occurs without a K1 event occurring. For it means only that all K1 events are accompanied by K2 events, which does not entail that all K2 events are accompanied by K1 events. So it leaves a sense in which K1 events are "followed by"

K2 events, but not vice-versa; it preserves the asymmetry of the causal relation. However, if clause 2 is expanded into 2′, then interpreting "followed by" as "accompanied by" no longer suffices to preserve causal asymmetry as well as allowing for cases of simultaneity. For 2′ now says both that all events of kind K1 are accompanied by events of kind K2 and that all events of kind K2 are accompanied by events of kind K1, thereby losing the asymmetry. (Of course, "preceded by" also must be read as "accompanied by" if 2′ is to cover cases of simultaneity.) Thus, trying to accommodate the idea that a cause is a necessary as well as a sufficient condition for its effect while allowing for cases where cause and effect occur simultaneously leaves us unable to distinguish causes from effects.

To deal with this difficulty more satisfactorily, let us begin by noting a potentially misleading feature of *D3* – one that I have so far ignored. As stated, *D3* suggests that causes are much simpler than they actually are. It suggests, for example, that striking a match is always followed by its igniting; so that striking the match is by itself sufficient for its igniting. But, of course, we know that this is not so. Striking a match is followed by its igniting only if certain background conditions obtain. For example, the match must be dry, there must be oxygen present, etc. John Stuart Mill (1806–73), who defended a more refined version of Hume's regularity theory, expressed the point thus:

> It is seldom, if ever, between a consequent and a single antecedent that this invariable sequence subsists. It is usually between a consequent and the sum of several antecedents; the concurrence of all of them being requisite to produce, that is, to be certain of being followed by, the consequent.
>
> (Mill 1973: 327)

Of course, we could read "event of kind K1" in *D3* as *including* all of these conditions or "antecedents." Indeed, there is a sense in which the oxygen and dryness are just as much "causes" of a match's ignition as is its being struck. For various reasons, we commonly select the striking of the match as "the cause" of its lighting, and regard the other parts of the total cause as background conditions. But these reasons have more to do with economy of language and our practical purposes than with the nature of causality. Nevertheless, if we wished to do justice to the distinction between causes and background conditions in *D3*, we could reformulate clause 2 as follows:

(2A) All events of kind K1 in conditions C are followed by events of kind K2.

Together with clause 3 (see page 119), this implies:

(A)   If E_1 occurs in conditions C, then E_2 occurs.

In other words, a cause is sufficient for its effect, provided that certain other conditions obtain.

Just as *D3* can misleadingly suggest that striking a match is by itself sufficient for its igniting, so the expanded version of *D3* – in which 2' is substituted for 2 – suggests that striking a match is always necessary for its igniting. But of course, this too is false. For there are many other possible causes of a match igniting: it might be brought in close contact with a burning match; it might be touched by a very hot piece of metal; it might be exposed to superheated air, etc. In general, a given effect can be produced in a variety of different ways. As Mill put it:

> It is not true, then, that one effect must be connected with only one cause, or assemblage of conditions; that each phenomenon can be produced only in one way. There are often several independent modes in which the same phenomenon could have originated. One fact may be the consequent in several invariable sequences; it may follow, with equal uniformity, any one of several antecedents, or collections of antecedents. Many causes may produce mechanical motion: many causes may produce some kinds of sensation: many causes may produce death. A given effect may really be produced by a certain cause, and yet be perfectly capable of being produced without it.
>
> (1973: 435)

This important point provides a solution to our difficulty. For it shows that the idea that a cause is a necessary condition for its effect is not wholly accurate. Rather, a cause is necessary for its effect only on the assumption that no other cause of that effect is operative. It is incorrect, for example, to hold that "striking the match caused it to ignite" implies that if the match had not been struck, it would not have ignited. Rather, this statement implies that if the match had not been struck *and nothing else had caused it to ignite*, then it would not have ignited (assuming that it would not have ignited without *some* cause). Now if one wishes to incorporate this idea into *D3*, then (2') will not serve. Instead, one must add:

(2″) All events of kind K1 are followed by events of kind K2 and all events of kind K2 are preceded by events of kind K1 or K3 or K4 or . . . K*n*.

Here, K3, K4 . . . K*n* refer to other kinds of event that are also always followed by events of kind K2. In terms of our example, they refer to such events as one match being brought into close proximity to a lighted match, or touched by a piece of hot metal, or exposed to superheated air. Now from 2″ and 3, we cannot deduce that if E_2 occurs, then E_1 occurs. Rather, we can only deduce that if E_2 occurs *and no event of kind K3, K4, or . . . Kn occurs*, then E_1 occurs. Therefore, the definition no longer implies that a cause is both sufficient and necessary for its effect. Rather, it implies that a cause is sufficient for its effect, and that it is necessary for its effect given the *nonoccurrence* of other conditions that would also have been sufficient for that same effect. The same point holds true if *D3* is formulated so as to incorporate the common-sense distinction between causes and background conditions. To capture this distinction, 2″ must be reformulated as:

(2A″) All events of kind K1 in conditions C are followed by events of kind K2, and all events of kind K2 are preceded by events of kind K1 in conditions C, or K3 in conditions C, or K4 in conditions C, or . . . Kn in conditions C.

Here, conditions C refer to the background conditions that must always obtain for an event of kind K2 to occur. In terms of our example, they refer to such things as the presence of oxygen, the dryness of the match, and the like. Now from 2A″ and D3, we cannot deduce:

(B) If E_2 occurs, then E_1 occurs in C.

Rather, we can deduce only:

(C) If E_2 occurs, and if no event of kind K3 occurs in C and no event of kind K4 occurs in C . . . and no event of kind Kn occurs in C, then E_1 occurs in C.

If the definition did imply both (A) and (B), this would mean that the occurrence of E_1 in C was both sufficient and necessary for the occurrence of E_2. The consequence, again, would be to represent the causal relation as symmetrical. But the combination of (A) and (C) does not have this consequence; it allows for the asymmetry that the causal relation requires.

However, it might now be objected that this asymmetry has been preserved only because the expanded definition is incomplete. To make it complete, one must add still another condition to D3, namely:

(4) E_2 is not preceded by an event of kind K3, or K4, or . . . Kn.

Once clause 4 is added to clauses 1, 2″, and 3, the asymmetry of the causal relation is once again denied. For 2″ and 3 imply that if E_1 occurs, then E_2 occurs; while 2″, 3, and 4 imply that if E_2 occurs, then E_1 occurs. So the complete, expanded version of D3 implies that E_1 is both sufficient and necessary for E_2 – thus making the relationship between E_1 and E_2 perfectly symmetrical. Furthermore, it does not help to reformulate 4 as:

(4A) E_2 is not preceded by an event of kind K3 in C, or an event of kind K4 in C, or . . . an event of kind Kn in C.

For 2A″, 3, and 4A imply (B), which, together with (A), again makes the relationship between E_1 in C and E_2 symmetrical.

The reply to this objection is that a regularity theorist can reasonably refuse to add 4 or 4A to the definition. For once either of these clauses is added, the definition is no longer an analysis of "E_1 causes E_2." Rather, it is an analysis of "E_1 causes E_2 and nothing else causes E_2," or "E_1 is the (only) cause of E_2." No doubt when we make ordinary causal judgments, we often assume that no other cause is operative – that the effect is not overdetermined. But this assumption should not be built into the definition of causation. For it is an additional assumption that people commonly make when they assert that E_1 causes E_2, and not a necessary condition for the truth of that assertion.

The common assumption that no other cause is operative may lie behind the puzzling remark of Hume with which we began this part. Hume, you will recall, seems mistakenly to equate "*all the objects similar to the first are followed by objects similar to the second*" with "*if the first object had not been, the second had never existed.*" But perhaps his thought is this: when we assert that E_1 caused E_2, this means that (a) E_1 was sufficient for E_2. However, we commonly make two additional assumptions: (b) that E_2 would not have occurred without *some* sufficient condition (other than itself); and (c) that there was no *other* sufficient condition for E_2 besides E_1. Now from (a), (b), and (c), it does follow that *if E_1 had not occurred, E_2 would not have occurred*; or, in Hume's words, that "*if the first object had not been, the second never had existed.*" Thus, we can understand why Hume might have thought that this remark was an appropriate way for him to paraphrase or gloss his definition of causation.

In order to avoid the difficulties we have explored in this part, however, we need to see that (c) does not have to be true in order for "E_1 caused E_2" to be true. Therefore, (c) should not be included in the definition or analysis of causation. It should be regarded, as suggested above, as an additional assumption that we generally make when we assert that E_1 caused E_2. As for (b), it would seem that any analysis of causation which says that a cause, or some member of a disjunction of possible causes, is a necessary condition for its effect, must hold that (b) is part of the meaning of "E_1 causes E_2." Thus, such analyses seem to imply that any event that was caused could not have occurred uncaused. Provided that this "could not" is not interpreted in the sense of logical impossibility, this implication may well be acceptable. But if the implication is unacceptable – a matter that we shall not try to settle – then it is open to the regularity theorist to jettison the idea that a cause (or some member of a disjunction of possible causes) is a necessary condition for its effect, by sticking with the unexpanded version of *D3* that uses 2 or 2A rather than 2″ or 2A″.

The problem of collateral effects

The final problem for the regularity theory that we shall consider is a simple yet perplexing one, which has been emphasized by J. L. Mackie and other contemporary philosophers. Consider a cause, C, with two collateral effects, E_1 and E_2, where E_1 precedes E_2. How can a regularity theorist avoid saying, falsely, that E_1 causes E_2? To make this problem clearer, we can use an example given by Bernard Berofsky (1983: 485), in a review of a recent book that offers a detailed defense of the regularity theory. Suppose that " . . . a fatal viral disease V produces a distinctive rash R . . . " In such a case, the virus causes both the rash and the death, but the rash does not cause the death. As Berofsky puts it, "the sequence V → Death is causal, whereas the sequence R → Death is not." The problem is: how can a regularity theorist avoid saying, falsely, that R causes the death?

A regularity theorist could reply as follows. The problem turns on the assumption that R is always followed by death. So, according to the regularity theory, it is a law of nature that *whenever* R occurs, death occurs; in which case R causes death. However, the example does not really show that whenever R occurs, death occurs. Rather, it shows only that whenever R occurs *and was preceded by* V, death occurs. But, as we emphasized in the previous part, a given effect can be caused in a variety of different ways. Thus, R could be induced by an experimental vaccine or a drug, or by exposure to some irritant. But then R would not be followed by death; so "whenever R occurs, death occurs" is not a law of nature after all.

A critic of the regularity theory could make two possible responses to this reply. One response would be to stipulate that if the rash is artificially induced or caused in any way other than by V, then it is not a rash of kind R. Now this would be to say that being accompanied by V is part of what it means to be a rash of kind R, so that from the fact that a rash is of kind R, it follows logically that it is accompanied by V. But in that case, there are two points that a regularity theorist can make. First, we cannot say that R is caused by V. For, as Hume showed, one cannot logically deduce that a given cause has occurred solely from knowledge of its effect, any more than one can logically deduce that a given effect will occur solely from knowledge of its cause. Second, if part of what it means to be a rash of kind R is to be accompanied by V, then there is no reason to deny that R is a cause of death. For we know that V is a cause of death, and V is now, by stipulation, a constituent element of R.

The critic's other possible response would be to reject the assumption that there are other ways to produce R. Although all the rashes that we know about can be caused in a variety of different ways, the critic could stipulate that R is a very special rash that occurs only in connection with V: it cannot be artificially induced or produced in any other way. Of course, V would then be both sufficient and necessary for R; so it might seem that the asymmetry needed for V to be the cause of R would be absent. However, the critic could also stipulate that V precedes R in time, thereby preserving the asymmetry.

The regularity theorist, however, could now reply that it is no longer clear that R is not a cause of death. If such a case occurred, we might say that both R and V were causes of death, or perhaps that the complex event V-and-R was a cause of death. Of course, it sounds odd to say that the rash is just as much a cause of death as is the virus. But this may be because in all cases of fatal viruses that we know about, only the virus itself is the cause of death. Symptoms such as rashes and the like, since they can also occur without the fatal virus, are not causes of death. Nor do they occupy the central place in a theory of disease that the viruses occupy. But if the situation described by the critic were actual – if R were necessary and sufficient for V and R-and-V were sufficient for death – then R would occupy just as central a place in the diagnosis and treatment of the particular disease involved as does V, and it seems that there would be no reason to exclude its consideration as a cause of death.

5

HUME'S CRITIQUE OF THE CAUSAL PRINCIPLE

1 Introduction

Virtually all of us accept the principle that every event has a cause, even if we do not always know what that cause is. The idea of an uncaused event – of something happening without any cause that explains why it happened – strikes us as somehow "irrational" or absurd. As for philosophers, many of them have not only accepted the truth of the principle that every event has a cause, but have assumed that this truth is knowable by any rational mind, in much the same way as a simple mathematical truth like *2 + 2 = 4* or a simple logical truth like *not both p and not-p*. In other words, many philosophers have assumed that the causal principle (as we shall call the principle that every event has a cause) is knowable a priori. Accordingly, they have often gone on to use this principle in order to "prove" important conclusions, notably the existence of God. The principle has been used in this way by, for example, Aquinas, Descartes, Locke, and Berkeley, to name just a few.

Contrary to what is sometimes thought, Hume also accepts the causal principle as a true proposition. In a discussion of "freedom" in the *Enquiry*, he writes: "it is universally allowed that nothing exists without a cause of its existence" (E:95; S:63–4; F:131). He does not demur from this principle, but instead goes on to argue that it is compatible with human freedom. And in one of his letters Hume says: "I never asserted so absurd a Proposition as *that anything might arise without a Cause* . . ." (Greig 1932: 187). What Hume does not accept, however, is the view that the causal principle is knowable a priori; or, in his terminology, that it is either "intuitively or demonstratively certain" (self-evident or demonstrable).[1] In other words, Hume agrees with most other philosophers that the causal principle is *true*, but he disagrees with philosophers who came before him about how it can be *known to be true*; for *they* held it to be a priori, whereas Hume argues, famously, that it is neither self-evident nor demonstrable. Instead, Hume maintains that the causal principle is merely an empirical generalization: "the opinion of the necessity of a cause to every new production . . . must necessarily arise from observation and experience" (T:82; F:50).

Already, in previous chapters, we have reconstructed and favorably evaluated Humean arguments showing that no bridging proposition is self-evident or demonstrable, and pointed out that those arguments apply to the causal principle.[2] Hume, however, offers also arguments designed specifically to show that the causal principle is neither self-evident nor demonstrable, and it is to those arguments that we turn in this chapter. Hume's arguments themselves are analyzed in part 2. In part 3 we shall examine one contemporary critique of Hume's arguments, and lastly we shall consider Immanuel Kant's famous attempt to "answer" Hume's arguments.

2 Why the causal principle is neither self-evident nor demonstrable

Hume's critique of the causal principle is given only in the *Treatise*, Book I, Part iii, Section 3, which is entitled, ironically, "Why a Cause Is Always Necessary." Hume begins this section (hereafter called simply "Section 3") by accurately remarking that the causal principle was

> commonly taken for granted in all reasonings, without any proof given or demanded. [For it was] suppos'd to be founded on intuition, and to be one of those maxims, which tho' they may be deny'd with the lips, 'tis impossible for men in their hearts really to doubt of.
>
> (T:79; F:47)

In the discussion that follows, Hume formulates the principle in a number of different ways. Two of these are that "*whatever begins to exist, must have a cause of existence*" (T:78) and that "*whatever has a beginning has also a cause of existence*" (T:79; F:47). Those formulations make it sound as if Hume were concerned only with the causes of things' existence; however, Hume speaks also of our inability to "demonstrate the necessity of a cause to every new existence, *or new modification of existence*" (T:79; F:47; emphasis added), thereby showing that his concern extends to the causes of any event whatsoever (see Penelhum 1992: 117). His arguments, however, are couched in terms of the causes of things' beginning to exist, and we shall reconstruct them in those terms in order to stay close to his text.

Hume argues first that the causal principle is not self-evident ("intuitively certain"). His argument turns on a theory about relations that appears in the *Treatise* (see Book I, part iii, Section 1) but is dropped in the *Enquiry*, where it is replaced by the fundamental distinction between relations of ideas and matters of fact. The *Treatise*'s theory implies that a self-evident proposition must owe its self-evidence to one of four possible relationships between its terms, which Hume calls "*resemblance, proportions in quantity and number, degrees of any quality, and contrariety*" (T:79; F:47). Thus, for example, the statement that "red is more like pink than like white" can be known just by understanding what it says, because anyone who understands it grasps that the resemblance relations it reports are just what it states them to be; and the statement "no object is both black and white all over" is self-evident because anyone who understands it grasps that "black" and "white" are contrary terms. Hume then concludes that the causal principle is not self-evident, since it does not turn on any one of the four relations just mentioned.

A full-scale evaluation of this argument would require asking whether the four relations Hume specifies are the only possible sources of self-evidence. That there are only these four seems doubtful: the statement "if I am thinking, then I exist," for example, is self-evident, but seems not to involve any of Hume's four relations. Perhaps Hume himself came to think that his argument was a weak one, since he drops the *Treatise*'s theory of relations in the *Enquiry*. Be that as it may, the argument's weakness seems hardly to matter. For on reflection, it seems sufficiently clear that the causal principle, regardless of which of Hume's formulations we focus on, is not a proposition that can be known to be true merely by understanding what it says.

Next, Hume offers, in Section 3's third paragraph, a highly condensed and complex argument, which, he says, "proves at once that [the causal principle] is neither intuitively nor demonstratively certain." Here is the entire paragraph:

> But here is an argument, which proves at once, that the foregoing proposition is neither intuitively nor demonstrably certain. We can never demonstrate the necessity of a cause to every new existence, or new modification of existence, without shewing at the same time the impossibility there is, that any thing can ever begin to exist without some productive principle; and where the latter proposition cannot be prov'd, we must despair of ever being able to prove the former. Now that the latter proposition is utterly incapable of a demonstrative proof, we may satisfy ourselves by considering, that as all distinct ideas are separable from each other, and as the ideas of cause and effect are evidently distinct, 'twill be easy for us to conceive any object to be non-existent this moment, and existent the next, without conjoining to it the distinct idea of a cause or productive principle. The separation, therefore, of the idea of a cause from that of a beginning of existence, is plainly possible for the imagination; and consequently the actual separation of these objects is so far possible, that it implies no contradiction or absurdity; and is therefore incapable of being refuted by any reasoning from mere ideas; without which 'tis impossible to demonstrate the necessity of a cause.
>
> (T:79–80; F:47–8)

Let us grant that the causal principle is not self-evident (i.e. not "intuitively certain"), and try to reconstruct the argument showing that it is not demonstrable (i.e. not "demonstratively certain"), by analyzing the above paragraph into slightly edited segments and considering each in turn.

The first segment goes this way:

> We can never demonstrate the necessity of a cause to every new existence, or new modification of existence, without shewing at the same time the

impossibility there is, that any thing can ever begin to exist without some productive principle; and where the latter proposition cannot be prov'd, we must despair of ever being able to prove the former. Now . . . the latter proposition is utterly incapable of a demonstrative proof.

Hume's reasoning here is very straightforward: we cannot prove that every beginning of existence must have a cause unless we can prove that a beginning of existence without a cause is impossible; but we cannot prove that a beginning of existence without a cause is impossible; *ergo*, we cannot prove that every beginning of existence must have a cause.

But why does Hume think that we cannot prove the impossibility of a beginning of existence without a cause? The answer begins in the next segment, where Hume undertakes to show why "the latter proposition [i.e. that a beginning of existence without a cause is impossible] is utterly incapable of a demonstrative proof" and which is, from a logical point of view, the real starting-point of the argument (I have inserted numbers to identify the steps of the reasoning):

[A]s (1) all distinct ideas are separable from each other, and as (2) the ideas of cause and effect are evidently distinct, (3) 'twill be easy for us to conceive any object to be non-existent this moment, and existent the next, without conjoining to it the distinct idea of a cause or productive principle.

Step (2) is carelessly stated; for Hume is trying to show in step (3) that we can conceive a beginning of existence (an object that is "non-existent this moment, and existent the next") without a cause of existence – that we can conceive a certain kind of *event* occurring without any cause; not that we can conceive an *effect* without a cause, which would be absurd. Correcting for this carelessness, then, we can formulate the first part of Hume's argument like this:

(1) All distinct ideas are separable from each other (premiss).
(2) The idea of a cause of existence is distinct from the idea of a beginning of existence (premiss).
(3) We can conceive of something beginning to exist without a cause (from (1) & (2)).

Hume states the third part of the argument in the final segment:

The separation, therefore, of the idea of a cause from that of a beginning of existence, is plainly possible for the imagination; and consequently the actual separation of these objects is so far possible, that it implies no contradiction or absurdity; and is therefore incapable of being refuted by any reasoning from mere ideas; without which 'tis impossible to demonstrate the necessity of a cause.

Here it would seem that the first clause (up to the semicolon) is merely a restatement of (3) – the claim that we can *conceive* a beginning of existence without a cause – despite the fact that Hume switches from talk about what we can conceive to talk about what is "possible for the imagination." He moves now from this claim to the further claim that there is no "contradiction or absurdity" in the notion of a causeless beginning of existence, and from that claim to his key claim that we cannot "refute" the possibility of such a beginning of existence. To make these inferences, however, two premisses that Hume leaves unstated are required: namely, a premiss to the effect that whatever we can conceive or "imagine" is free of contradiction, and a premiss to the effect that whatever is free of contradiction cannot be proved to be impossible. Thus, we can formulate this part of the argument as follows:

(4)   Nothing that we can conceive implies a contradiction (suppressed premiss).
(5)   "*X began to exist* and *X had no cause*" does not imply a contradiction (from (3) & (4)).
(6)   If *p* does not imply a contradiction, then we cannot demonstrate that *p* is impossible (suppressed premiss).
(7)   We cannot demonstrate that a beginning of existence without a cause of existence is impossible (from (5) & (6)).

Hume indicates that his argument is now substantially complete by closing the paragraph with the words, "without which 'tis impossible to demonstrate the necessity of a cause." This is just a reminder of the reasoning in the paragraph's first segment, which we can now enter into our reconstruction of the argument in its logically correct place, thereby also completing the reconstruction:

(8)   We can demonstrate that whatever has a beginning of existence must have a cause of existence only if we can demonstrate that a beginning of existence without a cause of existence is impossible (premiss).
(9)   We cannot demonstrate that whatever has a beginning of existence must have a cause of existence (from (7) & (8)).

Having given this complex argument, Hume goes on to confirm its result by refuting three attempts to prove the causal principle. The three attempted proofs and Hume's refutations of them are much simpler than is the argument just analyzed, but highly instructive nevertheless. Let us consider them.

The first attempt, which Hume attributes to Thomas Hobbes, is this:

All the points of time and place . . . in which we can suppose any object to begin to exist, are in themselves equal; and unless there be some cause, which is peculiar to one time and to one place, and which by that means determines and fixes its existence, it must remain in eternal suspense; and the object can never begin to be, for want of something to fix its beginning.
(T:80; F:48)

This argument is a syllogism that can be put this way:

(1) All beginnings of existence must be beginnings of existence at a particular place and time.
(2) All beginnings of existence at a particular place and time must have a cause.

∴(3) All beginnings of existence must have a cause.

The nerve of the argument is (2), which invokes the idea that there must be a cause for a thing beginning to exist at one particular place and time rather than another. But Hume responds by rejecting (2). He argues that if the denial of (3) is not "intuitively absurd" – that is, if (3) is not self-evident – then the denial of (2) is not "intuitively absurd" either – that is, (2) is not self-evident either. Thus, for example, if it is not intuitively absurd for a unicorn to begin to exist without any cause, then neither is it intuitively absurd for a unicorn to begin to exist at noon on January 1, 2000 in San Diego Zoo, rather than at midnight on January 2, 2000 in London Zoo, without any cause. Hume's point is basically that if (3) is regarded as needing a proof, then (2) must be regarded also as needing a proof; and so (2) cannot be used as an unsupported premiss in an argument for (3).

The second attempt, which Hume attributes to Samuel Clarke, goes this way: "Every thing . . . must have a cause; for if anything wanted a cause, *it* would produce *itself*; that is, exist before it existed; which is impossible" (T:80; F:48). This argument can be stated as follows:

(1) If a thing has no cause, then it must produce itself.
(2) If a thing produces itself, then it must exist before it exists.
(3) Nothing can exist before it exists.

∴ Everything must have a cause.

Notice that (1), as stated, is very confusing; for it seems to be saying that if a thing has no cause, then it does have a cause after all! (Namely, itself.) Hume's trenchant response is that the argument simply begs the question; for (1) can only be a confused way of saying that if a thing does not have some *other* thing for a cause, then it must have *itself* for cause – which is to assume the very point in question; namely, that everything must have a cause. As Hume puts it:

> [T]o say that anything is produc'd, or to express myself more properly, comes into being, without a cause, is not to affirm, that 'tis itself its own cause; but on the contrary in excluding all external causes, excludes *a fortiori* the thing itself, which is created. An object, that exists absolutely without any cause, certainly is not its own cause; and when you assert, that the one follows from the other, you suppose the very point in question, and take it for granted, that 'tis utterly impossible any thing

can ever begin to exist without a cause, but that upon the exclusion of one productive principle, we must still have recourse to another.

(T:81; F:49)

The third attempt, which Hume attributes to John Locke,[3] is this:

Whatever is produc'd without any cause, is produc'd by *nothing*, or in other words, has nothing for its cause. But nothing can never be a cause, no more than it can be something, or equal to two right angles. By the same intuition, that we perceive nothing not to be equal to two right angles, or not to be something, we perceive, that it can never be a cause; and consequently must perceive, that every object has a real cause of its existence.

(T:81; F:49)

The argument can be put like this:

(1) If X is produced without any cause, then X is produced by nothing (i.e. X has nothing for its cause).
(2) Nothing cannot be a cause (any more than it can be something, or can be equal to two right angles).

∴ Everything must have a cause.

Notice that, like the first premiss of Samuel Clarke's argument, (1) is stated in a confused manner; for it seems, again, to be saying that if X is produced without any cause, then it has a cause after all – namely, nothingness, or non-being. Hume responds that the argument begs the question in almost exactly the same way as does Clarke's argument; for its first premiss can only be a confused way of saying that if X does not have some *existing* thing for a cause, then it must have nothing (nothingness, non-being) for a cause – which again is to assume that X must have a cause.

Hume's criticisms of Clarke and Locke's arguments are very instructive. For they show that the statement *Maybe X has no cause* does not mean, as Locke thinks, (a) Maybe X is caused by nothing(ness) or non-being; or, as Clarke thinks, (b) Maybe X is its own cause. Rather, it means only (c) Maybe X is *without* any cause. So the absurdity of (a) and (b), which Hume does not dispute, does not show that (c) is absurd.

Hume's criticism of Locke's argument could be applied also to this simple attempt to demonstrate the causal principle, which might at first seem quite plausible:

(1) Something cannot come from nothing (*Ex nihilo, nihil fit*).

∴ (2) Everything must have a cause.

A person who has understood Hume's response to Locke's argument could point out that the premiss, (1), has two possible meanings:

(1a) Nothing(ness) or non-being cannot be a cause; that is, something cannot be caused by nothing(ness) or non-being.

(1b) Something cannot exist without any cause; in other words, something cannot lack a cause.

If we suppose that the premiss "Something cannot come from nothing" means (1a), then (1) is self-evident; but (1) does not entail (2). On the other hand, if we suppose that (1) means (1b), then (1) *does* entail (2); indeed (1) and (2) are then logically equivalent. But if (1) means (1b), then (1) is not self-evident. The result is that on either interpretation of its premiss, this argument fails to prove the causal principle.

3 Stroud's critique of Hume's argument

In his book *Hume*, Barry Stroud criticizes Hume's complex proof that the causal principle cannot be demonstrated. In this part, we shall argue that Stroud's objections do not refute Hume's argument.

It will be helpful to begin by reviewing the steps of Hume's argument:

(1) All distinct ideas are separable from each other (premiss).
(2) The idea of a cause of existence is a distinct idea from the idea of a beginning of existence (premiss).
(3) We can conceive of something beginning to exist without a cause (from (1) & (2)).
(4) Nothing that we can conceive implies a contradiction (suppressed premiss).
(5) "X began to exist and X had no cause" does not imply a contradiction (from (3) & (4)).
(6) If p does not imply a contradiction, then we cannot demonstrate that p is impossible (suppressed premiss).
(7) We cannot demonstrate that a beginning of existence without a cause of existence is impossible (from (5) & (6)).
(8) We can demonstrate that whatever has a beginning of existence must have a cause of existence only if we can demonstrate the impossibility of a beginning of existence without a cause of existence (premiss).
(9) We cannot demonstrate that whatever has a beginning of existence must have a cause of existence (from (7) & (8)).

Stroud (1977: 46–50) makes two objections to this argument: first, that Hume's justification for (7) is circular; second, that (4) is simply false. Let us consider the objections in turn.

To show that Hume's justification for (7) is circular, Stroud begins by asking: how does Hume know that (2) is true – that the idea of a cause of existence is an idea different or distinct from the idea of a beginning of existence? It might be answered, says Stroud, that we know this by seeing that a beginning of existence without a cause of existence doesn't imply a contradiction. But in that case, he objects, (5) is being used to support (2), and so (2) cannot be used to support (5) without arguing in a circle. Furthermore, now we need some other way to support (5). It will not do, of course, to say that (5) is known to be true because, for all we can know a priori, an uncaused beginning of existence *is* possible. For this would be to use (7) to support (5), in which case, Stroud says (p. 48), "Hume's 'argument' . . . would shrink to the mere assertion of the possibility of something's beginning to exist without a cause."

Stroud next considers a way in which it may be possible to show that (5) is true without appealing to (7). To show this, it is necessary to provide some way of deciding whether a statement is a contradiction. If we confine our attention to statements formulated in the constructed, artificial language of formal logic, it is not difficult to provide such a test: a statement is a contradiction if and only if it has the form "p and not-p." This is something that we can determine just by looking at the statement. But when we broaden our attention to statements in a natural language like English, we are not always able to tell whether a statement is a contradiction just by looking at it. The statement, "there is a husband who lacks a wife," for example, is not obviously of the form "p and not-p;" it seems rather to have the form "p and not-q."[4] Some philosophers would give the following test for deciding when a statement in a natural language is a contradiction: a statement S is a contradiction just in case, when we replace some term(s) in S with other terms that stand for the same idea, the resulting statement has the form "p and not-p." For example, "there is a husband who lacks a wife" *is* a contradiction, because once we replace "husband" with "man who has a wife," then we see that the statement says, "there is a man who has a wife and does not have a wife" – which has the form "p and not-p."[5] Now, it might be said that applying this test to "X began to exist and X had no cause" shows that this statement does not imply a contradiction. For we cannot substitute terms in this statement with other terms that have the same meaning and thereby obtain a statement of the form "p and not-p." And this is why "X began to exist and X had no cause" does not imply a contradiction – which is to say, why (5) is true.

As we might expect in light of Stroud's initial objection, however, he rejects the proposed test for deciding when a natural-language statement implies a contradiction. For the proposed test obviously "makes essential use of the notion of the 'same' or 'distinct' ideas" (Stroud 1977: 48). So it is circular to use the proposed test as the test for contradictoriness, since contradictoriness is itself the only test that has so far been offered for the notion of "same/distinct idea." In other words, (2) is again being used to support (5), despite the fact that the only support given for (2) has been (5). Stroud concludes that "Hume really has no non-circular argument on this point at all. He thinks he can start from the 'evident' distinctness of two ideas, but he never says how he can recognize that distinctness" (ibid.).

Despite Stroud's ingenuity, his contention is debatable. He has certainly shown that sameness/distinctness of ideas, conceivability, contradiction, and possibility are interdependent notions; much as W. V. O. Quine, whom Stroud cites as an inspiration for his objection, does with analyticity, sameness of meaning, and synonymy in his famous paper "Two Dogmas of Empiricism" (Quine 1953: 20–46). It is questionable, however, that there is a vicious circularity in using some of these notions to clarify the others. After all, the notions of "same" and "distinct" ideas are not totally obscure; and in the case at hand it might even be plausibly said that the idea of a *beginning* of existence is clearly distinct from that of a *cause* of existence (as indeed Hume seems to believe); so that one can argue from this distinctness to the conceivability of an uncaused beginning of existence and from thence to the latter's possibility, as Hume does when he goes from (2) to (3) to (5). But if someone wanted confirmation of the distinctness of these two ideas, we could reverse the argument, by pointing out that it is conceivable that a thing might spring into existence *ex nihilo*, or that this supposition implies no contradiction. Hume's case for (7) would be viciously circular only if none of (2) or (3) or (5) had any independent plausibility; but in fact each of them is independently plausible, and so steps (1)–(7) are better seen as exhibiting the interconnections between the notions involved than as a linear defense of (7).

Stroud's second objection to Hume's argument is that (4) – the premiss that nothing of which we can conceive implies a contradiction – is false. In other words, conceivability is not a decisive criterion of what does or does not imply a contradiction (or of what is or is not impossible). To show this, Stroud points out that Goldbach's conjecture – that every even number is the sum of two prime numbers – has never been proved or disproved. Yet the conjecture is either necessarily true (in which case its denial implies a contradiction and is impossible), or necessarily false (in which case its affirmation implies a contradiction and is impossible). Now, says Stroud (p. 50),

> it seems easy to conceive of Goldbach's Conjecture's being proved one day . . . But I can also conceive of its being disproved, of someone's proving its negation, perhaps by finding a very large even number that is not the sum of two primes. I can conceive of a computer's coming up with one tomorrow.

Therefore, I can conceive of something that implies a contradiction and is impossible. So, (4) is false.

This objection seems flawed, also. For Stroud's conceivability claims seem to mean only that one can imagine someone doing some calculations and announcing that they prove Goldbach's conjecture, or imagine a person or a computer identifying a very large even number and telling us that it is not the sum of two primes. But it is questionable that this amounts to conceiving of the truth or the falsity of Goldbach's conjecture itself. After all, one can imagine or "conceive" of a famous mathematician declaring that he has proved that $1 + 1 = 3$, or of a computer outputting that $1 + 1 = 3$; but it does not follow that one can conceive that $1 + 1 = 3$.

Finally, we should point out that even if Stroud's objections are thought to carry some weight against Hume's explicit argument, it is possible to give a simpler proof that the causal principle is not demonstrable, based on "principle (P)" (see Chapter 2 part 5, and Chapter 3 part 3). This simpler argument is the following:

(1) If p is demonstrable, then there is a set of statements, S, such that (i) all the members of S are self-evident, and (ii) not-p, together with S, entails a contradiction (principle (P)).

(2) There is no set of statements, S, such that (i) all the members of S are self-evident, and (ii) "X began to exist and X had no cause," together with S, entails a contradiction.

∴(3) "Whatever has a beginning of existence has a cause of existence" is not demonstrable.

Given Stroud's objections to the use of the notion of contradiction (outside the context of purely formal logic), it would be disingenuous to claim that he must accept this argument even if he rejects Hume's own explicit argument. But if we are willing to accept the notion of contradiction, then this essentially Humean argument seems very powerful.

4 Kant's "answer" to Hume

The most famous attempt to answer Hume's arguments against the demonstrability of the causal principle is that of Immanuel Kant. This "answer" is given in a section of his *Critique of Pure Reason* called the "Second Analogy of Experience" (hereafter referred to as "the second analogy"). Kant's discussion of the causal principle is embedded in a very difficult and complex theory of knowledge, and there is a vast literature on that theory as well as specifically on Kant's second analogy. Although we cannot possibly do justice to Kant's discussion, its importance and direct bearing on Hume's treatment of the causal principle warrant giving an account of it here.

Although Kant disagrees with Hume about the status of the causal principle, it is important to note at the outset some points of agreement between the two. First, Kant agrees with Hume that the causal principle is not true simply by virtue of conceptual relationships or meanings of words – that it is not, in the modern parlance developed by Kant himself, an analytic proposition, but rather a synthetic one. Second, Kant does not think any more than does Hume that the causal principle can be demonstrated by manipulating general concepts like existence, beginning of existence, event, cause, and so on. Rather, Kant tries to show that the principle can be proved through what he calls a "transcendental" argument. This is an argument according to which the truth of a certain principle (in this case the causal principle) is a necessary condition of experience. So Kant's argument for the causal principle is that unless that principle were true, we could not have the sort of experience that we do. In order to appreciate how such an argument works, it is crucial to know exactly how the term "experience" is to be understood. In his *Critique of Pure Reason*, Kant gives a number of transcendental arguments for a number of different principles, and the term "experience" seems not to mean exactly the same thing in all of those arguments. But in the argument of the second analogy, the kind of experience Kant has in mind is that of knowing by perception that an event has occurred. Kant, as we shall see, tries to show that unless the causal principle were true, we could never know by perception that any event had occurred.

According to Kant, the fact that the causal principle can be proved only by a transcendental argument has a very important consequence: namely, that the principle can be proved to hold only for *observable* events; it cannot be proved to hold for events that we could not possibly experience. This means that there is an additional similarity between Hume and Kant's views of the causal principle: namely, that it cannot be used to show that events which supposedly occur totally outside the field of our experience, such as the origin of the universe, must have a cause. Thus, even if the principle can be demonstrated, it cannot be used, in the way that Rationalist philosophers employed it, to establish the existence of God or other entities that could not fall within the scope of our experience.

Having mentioned some similarities between Hume and Kant's views of the causal principle, we shall henceforth focus on the differences. First, there is an important difference between the version of the causal principle that Hume says cannot be proved and the version Kant thinks he can establish. The version Hume considers is unrestricted: it would apply to any beginning of existence or "modification of existence" whatsoever; simply put, Hume's version says that *every event whatsoever* has a cause. Now the principle that Kant claims to prove in his second analogy is this: "Everything that happens, that is, begins to be, presupposes something on which it follows according to a rule" (Kant 1963: A189). The wording of this principle makes it sound very much like the principle that Hume says cannot be proved: "whatever has a beginning of existence has a cause of existence." Despite its wording, however, Kant's principle contains the restriction just mentioned: it applies only to *observable events*. In other words, Kant thinks that he can prove that every event that we could ever observe must have a cause, but not that every event, period, must have a cause. However, Hume's arguments imply that not even Kant's restricted version of the causal principle can be proved; so a chief difference between Hume and Kant is that Hume holds that no version of the causal principle can be demonstrated, whereas Kant argues that a version restricted to observable events can be demonstrated. By showing that the version of the causal principle which is restricted to observable events can be demonstrated, while maintaining that an unrestricted version, supposedly applying beyond the bounds of human experience, cannot be known to be true, Kant saw himself as defending the foundations of Newtonian physics, without lapsing into the Rationalist metaphysics that he rejected no less than Hume did. Finally, Kant's "transcendental" way of arguing for the causal principle implies another difference between his position and Hume's, which is well stated by William H. Brenner:

> Hume thought that the principle of causality was a generalization from our experience of events. But if Kant's argument is sound, then all perception of events, and consequently all generalization from experience, *presupposes* the principle of causality. Kant's answer to Hume . . . is that the principle of causality is *presupposed* by the perception of events, not *derived from* it.
>
> (1989: 128)

In order for Kant to give an argument in support of (even his restricted version of) the causal principle that can "answer" Hume, that argument must start from premisses Hume himself would accept. Now, as the Kant scholar Lewis White Beck has shown (1978: 130–5) in an effective analysis of Kant's strategy for answering Hume, Kant's argument in the second analogy does start from a point which is common ground for them both. This is that any knowledge we have of causal relationships must be based on induction: we know that A-events cause B-events only because, in all cases we have observed, A-events have been followed by B-events – because A-events and B-events have been constantly conjoined in our experience.[6] As Beck says:

> [Kant] is in complete agreement with Hume that our knowledge of causal connections between specific events is a posteriori not a priori, synthetic not analytic, inductive not logical, probable not certain. His methods for finding the cause of B are exactly those which Hume prescribed, and the chances of success in this venture, as estimated by Kant and Hume, are very much the same. Kant's first answer to Hume, then, is to agree with him, and to disagree with the rationalists who thought that logical insight into causal connections was possible.
>
> (Beck 1978: 134)

As Beck points out, however, the ability to infer that A-events cause B-events from observing that A-events have been regularly followed by B-events presupposes that we can identify or discriminate events perceptually, that is, that we can tell by observation that an event is occurring. For if we could not do this, then we could not establish the *premiss* of the inference – that *events* of a certain kind have been regularly followed by *events* of a certain other kind.

Now Kant's key insight in the second analogy is that there is an epistemological problem about how we are able perceptually to identify or discriminate events. Specifically, there is a problem about how we are able to distinguish events from enduring states of affairs; for, whether we are perceiving an event or an enduring state of affairs, our perceptions occur successively or serially in time. Kant illustrates this point with the examples of perceiving a ship moving downstream and of perceiving a house. The ship moving from an upstream position to one further downstream is an event. On the other hand, the existence of the various parts of the house – its front, sides, back, foundation, roof – is an enduring state of affairs. But, in both cases, our perceptions occur successively or serially in time. In the case of the ship, we see it first upstream and then downstream. In the case of the house, we see first one side and then another side, or first the foundation and then the roof, or first the roof and then the foundation. This shows that we cannot tell, merely from the fact that our perceptions occur serially or successively, that we are perceiving an event rather than an enduring state of affairs. In other words, observation alone provides no criterion by which we can distinguish the two. How, then, can we tell if we are perceiving an event or an enduring state of affairs? To quote Beck: "[Hume] never discussed this problem; no one before Kant even saw that it was a problem" (1978: 135). Kant's thesis in the second analogy is that this problem can be solved in only one way: namely, if we grant that every observable event has a cause, or, as Kant puts it, that "everything that happens, that is, begins to be, presupposes something on which it follows according to a rule." In other words, Kant contends that we can distinguish between events and enduring states of affairs, and so identify events, only if the causal principle is true of those events.

Beck gives a succinct summary of Kant's strategy, involving three propositions (the wording of which has been slightly modified):

H   From observing repeated pairs of similar events, we infer that events like the first members of the pairs are causes of events like the second.

P   Events can be distinguished from enduring states of affairs, even though our perceptions of both are successive or serial.

K   "Everything that happens, that is, begins to be, presupposes something on which it follows by rule" (ibid.: 135).

Proposition *H* is common ground between Hume and Kant: thus it is a premiss that Hume himself accepts and is in no way question-begging.[7] Proposition *K* is Kant's statement of the causal principle which Hume says cannot be demonstrated. Clearly *H* implies *P*: we cannot establish correlations between events unless we can distinguish events from enduring states of affairs. The task of the second analogy is to show that *P* in turn implies *K*. If that can be shown, it will follow that *H* implies *K*, and thus that the causal principle can be demonstrated from a premiss which Hume himself accepts (Beck 1978: 135).

In what follows, we shall consider two possible arguments for getting from *P* to *K*. The first is quite strongly suggested by the text of the second analogy, and has often been thought to be Kant's authentic argument. However, as P. F. Strawson shows in his influential book on Kant *The Bounds of Sense* (1966: 133–40), it is a fallacious argument. The second argument is also suggested by Kant's text, and seems more promising.

The first argument, which I call the "irreversibility" argument, is suggested by what Kant says when he compares the examples of the house and the ship. In the case of the house, the series of perceptions obtained by the observer may be said to be *reversible*. This is because, depending on the circumstances and on the way the observer chooses to view the house, the observer can see first the front of the house and then the back of the house, or first the back and then the front; likewise the observer can see first the left side and then the right side or first the right side and then the left side, and first the basement and then the roof or first the roof and then the basement. In other words, in whatever order the observer's perceptions occur, they could have occurred in the opposite or reverse order instead. Kant puts the point this way:

> In the . . . example of a house my perceptions could begin with the apprehension of the roof and end with the basement, or could begin from below and end above; and I could similarly apprehend the manifold of empirical intuition either from right to left or left to right. In the series of perceptions there was thus no determinate order specifying at what point I must begin in order to connect the manifold empirically.[8]
>
> (1963: A192–3)

In the case of the ship moving downstream, on the other hand, the series of perceptions may be said to be *irreversible*. Assuming that the ship is moving downstream, one's perceptions can occur in only one order: first one sees the ship upstream and then one sees it downstream; one cannot see it first downstream and then upstream. One's perceptions cannot occur in any order other than the one that corresponds to the ship's successive positions in the stream. As Kant puts it:

> But, as I also note, in an appearance which contains a happening (the preceding state of the perception we may entitle A, and the succeeding B) B can be apprehended only as following upon A; the perception of A cannot follow upon B but only precede it. For instance, I see a ship move down stream. My perception of its lower position follows upon the perception of its position higher up in the stream, and it is impossible that in the apprehension of this appearance the ship should first be perceived lower down in the stream and afterwards higher up. The order in which the perceptions succeed one another in apprehension is in this instance determined, and to this order apprehension is bound down.
>
> (1963: A192)

At the end of the same paragraph, Kant concludes that "in the perception of an event there is always a rule that makes the order in which the perceptions (in the apprehension of this appearance) follow upon one another a *necessary* order" (ibid.: A193).

It is chiefly from these passages that the irreversibility argument is drawn. Strawson in effect divides the argument into two stages. In the first stage, Kant is seen as pointing to a criterion by which our perceptions of an event can be distinguished from those of an enduring state of affairs, despite the perceptions of both being successive or serial. This criterion is the reversibility or irreversibility of the series of perceptions. Thus the criterion by which a series of perceptions is apprehended as of (or taken to be of) an enduring state of affairs is *reversibility*: the series could have been obtained in the reverse order from that in which it actually occurred, as in the case of the house. And the criterion by which a series of perceptions is apprehended as of (or taken to be of) an event is *irreversibility*: the series could not have been obtained in the reverse order from that in which it actually occurred, as in the case of the ship. In other words, perceptions are of an enduring state of affairs if and only if they are reversible; whereas perceptions are of an event if and only if they are irreversible.[9] In the second stage of the argument, Kant is seen to argue from the irreversibility of perceptions of an event to the truth of the causal principle: since our perceptions of events are irreversible, those events must be subsumed under causal laws.

In order to evaluate this well-known yet puzzling argument, we need to state it in a somewhat more formal way. From the first stage of the argument, in which the reversibility–irreversibility criterion is put forward, we can extract the following premiss:

(1)   Necessarily, if S perceives an event A–B, then S's perceptions occur in the order A, B.

Here "an event A–B" means an event or change whose first stage is A and whose second stage is B; so that in Kant's example of the moving ship, A would designate the ship's being upstream and B would designate the ship's being downstream. So (1) says that if S perceives an event, such as the ship moving from an upstream to a downstream position, then S's perceptions of the stages of the event must occur in the same temporal order as did the stages of the event: they are "irreversible." I have placed the term (modal operator) "necessarily" in front of the statement, so that it applies to (or "governs") the if–then relation expressed by the statement as a whole, in order to bring out a claim made by Strawson (1966: 136) which seems correct. This is that (1) is a conceptual or analytic truth. Strawson bases this claim on the two more basic claims, which also seem correct, that:

(a)   It is a conceptual truth about sense perception that our perceptions of an object are caused by that very object.
(b)   It is a conceptual truth about causation that an effect cannot precede its cause, but must occur at the same time as or after its cause.[10]

He notes that (1) follows from these two conceptual truths, and so is itself a conceptual truth, provided one stipulation is made. The stipulation is that there must not be any difference in the causal conditions of the two perceptions as a result of which the perception of A occurs after the perception of B. For otherwise, one can think of cases where the earlier stage of an event is perceived after the later stage. For example, one could see the ship in its upstream position after seeing it in its downstream position, if the light from its upstream position were delayed by being reflected back and forth several times between mirrors; or one might *hear* a whistle blast that the ship emitted upstream after *seeing* the ship downstream, simply because sound travels slower than light. (Notice that in such cases the conceptual truth that an effect cannot precede its cause is not violated, because both perceptions still occur after their own causes.) Strawson points out that such cases can be circumvented by stipulating that the perceptions of A and B must be equally direct and in the same sensory mode, or by stipulating that there can be no difference in the causal conditions of the perceptions such that the perception of A occurs after the perception of B. Provided such a stipulation is understood, Strawson seems right to maintain that (1) is an analytic or conceptual truth.

The second stage of the irreversibility argument moves from (1) to the conclusion that the causal principle is true. In terms of the formulation being constructed here, this is to say that it moves from (1) to the conclusion: (C) Necessarily, if A occurs, then B occurs. Here the point of the modal term "necessarily" is just to say that the transition from A to B is governed by whatever type of "necessity" characterizes causation; or, as Kant puts it, that B follows upon A "according to a rule." Of course, if the Humean regularity view of causation discussed in Chapter 4 is correct, then the "necessity" or "rule" in question reduces to a contingent but exceptionless regularity. But, for the moment, we shall talk heuristically in terms of causal necessity; in due course we shall see how what is said below obtains even when we think of causality purely in terms of regularity or of Hume's "constant conjunction."

It is obvious that (C) does not logically follow from (1) alone; another premiss is needed for (C) to be entailed. This premiss can only be:

(2) *If* necessarily when S perceives an event A–B, then S's perceptions occur in the order A, B, *then* necessarily if A occurs, B occurs.

Now if the argument from (1) and (2) to (C) is really Kant's argument, then Strawson is certainly right to say that Kant has committed "a *non-sequitur* of numbing grossness" (1966: 137). The problem is not that the argument as we have formulated it is logically invalid; for its form is:

(1) Necessarily (P ⊃ Q)
(2) [Necessarily (P ⊃ Q)] ⊃ necessarily (R ⊃ S)

   ∴(C) Necessarily (R ⊃ S)

which is a perfectly valid (modal) *Modus Ponens*. The "numbing non-sequitur" occurs, rather, within (2), in the transition from its complex antecedent to its consequent. For the antecedent says that when we are perceiving an event, our perceptions of the stages of the event necessarily occur in the same order as those stages themselves. But the consequent says that the stages of an event necessarily occur in a certain order. In other words, the premiss as a whole says that if the order of our perceptions of an event necessarily corresponds to the order of the stages of the event, then the stages of the event necessarily have a certain order. This is fallacious; for it involves, as Strawson shows, a double equivocation on the notion of necessity.

1   The *sense* of necessity is not the same in the antecedent as in the consequent. In the antecedent necessity refers to conceptual or analytic necessity, as we explained earlier; while in the consequent it refers to causal necessity (however that kind of necessity is understood).

2   The *application* of the notion of necessity is not the same in the antecedent as in the consequent. In the antecedent, what is asserted to be necessary is the correspondence between the temporal order of the stages of an event and the temporal order of our perceptions of those stages; while in the consequent the notion of necessity is applied to the relation between the stages of an event themselves.

Strawson aptly sums up the situation: "It is a very curious contortion indeed whereby a conceptual necessity based on the fact of a change is equated with the causal necessity of that very change" (1996: 138).

The fallacy can be brought out, as we said above, even if we think of causality purely in terms of regular succession rather than causal necessity. To assert that an event A–B has a cause is, then, to assert that there is a kind of event, E, such that events of kind E are regularly followed by events of the kind to which A–B belongs. Keeping this in mind, what (2) asserts is that if our perceptions of the sequence A–B must occur in the order A, B, then there is a kind of event E such that all events of that kind are followed by events of the kind to which A–B belongs. Clearly this is fallacious: from the fact that our perceptions of a sequence A–B must occur in the same order as the members of that sequence, one cannot conclude that there is a kind of event E such that sequences like A–B invariably follow upon events of kind E.

We have dwelt on the irreversibility argument at some length, because it is quite commonly thought to reflect Kant's own thinking in the second analogy. Since it is a fallacious argument, however, and because Kant's second analogy is a difficult text that lends itself to more than one interpretation, it is natural to wonder whether Kant has a better argument for the causal principle. Kant scholars have offered many reconstructions of his reasoning, and these in turn have been criticized by other scholars. We cannot survey this ongoing debate here. Rather, I shall conclude this chapter by presenting one reading of Kant's argument, from

Paul Guyer's book *Kant and the Claims of Knowledge* (1987: Chapter 10), which seems more faithful to Kant's text as well as more promising than others.[11] Guyer's discussion is complex and richly ramified; we shall present only the core of his interpretation.

The question Kant is raising in the second analogy could be put in this way: how can I know by observation that event E is occurring? If we think of an event as Kant does, as a transition from a state A to a state B, then this question can be put also as follows: how can I know by observation that a state A is followed in time by a state B? Now Kant's key point, that one's perceptions are successive or serial regardless of whether one is perceiving an event or an enduring state of affairs, means that I cannot know that A is followed in time by B just by knowing that my perception of A is followed by my perception of B, since perceptions of co-existing states of an enduring object would also occur successively, as happens when one views the different sides of a house. According to the irreversibility criterion, the way in which I am supposedly able to tell that A is followed by B in time is by knowing that my perceptions of A and B are irreversible – that they could not have occurred in the order B, A, rather than A, B. However, as Guyer rightly notes (1987: 256), I *cannot* really tell that A is followed in time by B by knowing that my perceptions of A and B are irreversible. For I can know that they are irreversible only if I *already* know that A and B are occurring in the order A, B. This relatively simple point seems to me to be Guyer's key insight. For, in the first place, it goes directly against the "irreversibility" reading of Kant's argument, by showing that reversibility–irreversibility could not really be the criteria we use for determining perceptually whether we are observing an event or an enduring state of affairs. But, even more importantly, Guyer's point seems to be just what Kant needs in order to make his argument work. For if I cannot tell that I am perceiving that A is followed by B either by knowing my perceptions of A and B are successive or by knowing they are irreversible, then how can I tell this? The only answer available seems to be: by knowing that state B follows state A according to a rule; that is, that the event constituted by the transition from A to B has some *cause*. Note also that the irreversibility of my perceptions of A and B is a *consequence* of the fact that B follows A according to a rule, rather than a criterion for deciding whether A was followed in time by B.

To convey the power of this interpretation, I quote two passages: first the passage from Kant that seems to best support it, and then a fairly long passage from Guyer that contains the core of his interpretation. The passage from Kant is this:

> Let us suppose that there is nothing antecedent to an event, upon which it must follow according to a rule. All succession of perception would then be only in the apprehension, that is, would be merely subjective, and would never enable us to determine objectively which perceptions are those that really precede and which are those that follow. We would then have only a play of representations, relating to no object . . . . I could not

then assert that the two states follow upon one another in the field of appearance [by "field of appearance," Kant here means the objects perceived, such as the moving ship or the house], but only that one apprehension follows upon the other . . . .

If, then, we experience that something happens, we in so doing always presuppose that something precedes it, on which it follows according to a rule. Otherwise I should not say of the object that it follows. For mere succession in my apprehension, if there be no rule determining the succession in relation to something that precedes, does not justify me in assuming any succession in the object. I render my subjective synthesis of apprehension objective only by reference to a rule in accordance with which the appearances [again, "appearances" here means the objects or events perceived], in their succession, that is, as they happen, are determined by the preceding state. The experience of an event (i.e. of anything as *happening*) is itself possible only on this assumption.

(1963: A194–5/B239–40)

And here is the passage from Guyer:

[T]he present problem is only that of distinguishing between an event occurring among represented states of affairs from the event of a change in representations [i.e. perceptions] themselves . . . . Thus, the significance of the irreversibility of a sequence of representations . . . is only that such a fact would be a *consequence* of the occurrence of an event in what is being perceived, which *could* be used as a *symptom* of the occurrence of an event *if* it were directly given to consciousness. But what Kant's underlying assumption means is precisely that such a modal fact about the sequence of perceptions is *not* given to consciousness by apprehension alone . . . . So Kant's idea is that no alternative remains but that the occurrence of an event be inferred by *adding* to the omnipresent succession of mere representations a *rule* from which it can be inferred that in the circumstances at hand *one state of affairs* could *only* succeed the other, and *therefore* also that one *representation* could only succeed the other . . . . Only from a rule which says that one of the represented states *must* succeed the other can it be inferred that it *does* succeed the other. For . . . though their succession *could* be inferred from the *necessary* sequence or irreversibility of the representations of them if such irreversibility *were* [directly given to consciousness] – since the irreversibility of their representations would be a genuine consequence of the represented states of affairs – the necessity of the sequence of representations is . . . *not* directly given to consciousness. So nothing remains but to invoke a rule from which it follows that one objective state can only succeed and not coexist with the other, from which it *also* follows . . . that the *representation* of the one state not only does but also only could succeed the representation of the other . . . . And

152

a rule which dictates that in a given situation one state of affairs must succeed another is just what Kant means by a causal law. Thus, judgments that events occur are possible only if the states of affairs which comprise them are linked by causal laws.

(Guyer 1987: 247–9)

The argument that Guyer finds in Kant's text may be summarized in this way:

(1)   We cannot know by observation that an event – a transition from a state A to a state B – is occurring by knowing that the perceptions of A and B occur in the order A, B, or by knowing that the perceptions of A and B are irreversible.[12]

(2)   If (1), then the only way we can know by perception that an event – a transition from a state A to a state B – is occurring, is by knowing that B follows A according to a rule; which is to say that the event has a cause.

(3)   If the only way we can know by perception that an event – a transition from a state A to a state B – is occurring, is by knowing that B follows A according to a rule (that the event has a cause), then any event such that we can know of its occurrence by perception must have a cause.

∴ (4) Any event such that we can know of its occurrence by perception must have a cause.

Notice that the conclusion of this argument does not mean that we can know by perception that an event is occurring only if *every* event has a cause. Rather, it means that we can know by perception that an event is occurring only if *that* event has a cause. Notice also that, even if this argument is sound, it does not show that it would be impossible for the world we inhabit not to be governed by causal laws, or impossible for events not to have causes. Rather, it shows only that in such a world we would be unable to know by perception that events were occurring. Thus, Kant's transcendental argument for the causal principle, even if it is sound, constitutes a qualified answer to Hume's critique of that principle, showing, to quote William Brenner (1989: 128) once again, that "the principle of causality is *presupposed* by the perception of events, not *derived from* it."[13]

6

THE BELIEF IN THE EXISTENCE
OF BODY

1 Introduction

The purpose of this chapter is to present and discuss Hume's views about our belief in the existence of material things, especially as he presents them in a famous section of the *Treatise* called "Of Scepticism with regard to the Senses." Concerning this section, Jonathan Bennett has written:

> It is extremely difficult, full of mistakes, and – taken as a whole – a total failure; yet its depth and scope and disciplined complexity make it one of the most instructive arguments in modern philosophy. One philosopher might be judged superior to another because he achieved something of which the other was altogether intellectually incapable. By that criterion Hume surpasses Locke and Berkeley – because, and only because, of this one section.
>
> (Bennett 1971: 313)

Taking Bennett's words as a cue, the discussion will try to clear up some of the difficulties one encounters when reading this section of the *Treatise*, indicating where I believe Hume makes mistakes, and trying to identify ways in which his discussion is nonetheless instructive.

2 Three assumptions behind Hume's account

Hume's entire account of what he calls the "belief in the existence of body" rests on three assumptions. In calling these "assumptions," I do not mean to say that Hume never gives reasons for them, but rather that the emphasis of his discussion falls more heavily on developing their implications than it does on justifying them – more on working *from* them as "givens" than on working *to* them as points to be established. In this part, accordingly, we shall expound the three assumptions without criticizing them; though in part 6 we shall critically discuss the first assumption.

The first and most basic assumption behind Hume's account of our belief in the existence of body is one which was a commonplace of seventeenth- and eighteenth-century philosophy and still has some defenders today. This is the view Berkeley expressed by saying that the things we perceive by our senses are nothing but our own "sensations or ideas." Put in Hume's terminology, this view is that the only things we perceive by our senses are our own perceptions, more specifically, our own impressions (of sensation). As can be seen from the following passages, Hume regards this view as virtually axiomatic:

> We may observe, that 'tis universally allowed by philosophers, and is besides pretty obvious of itself, that nothing is ever really present with the mind but its perceptions or impressions and ideas . . . nothing is ever present to the mind but perceptions . . .
>
> (T:67)

> [P]hilosophy informs us, that every thing, which appears to the mind, is nothing but a perception, and is . . . dependent on the mind . . .
>
> (T:193)

> [N]othing is ever really present to the mind, besides its own perceptions
> . . .
>
> (T:197)

> [T]he slightest philosophy . . . teaches us, that nothing can ever be present to the mind but an image or perception, and that the senses are only the inlets, through which these images are conveyed, without being able to produce any immediate intercourse between the mind and the object.
>
> (E:152; S:104; F:183)

> The most vulgar philosophy informs us, that no external object can make itself known to the mind immediately, and without the interposition of an image or perception. That table, which just now appears to me, is only a perception, and all its qualities are qualities of a perception.
>
> (T:239)

> The mind has never anything present to it but the perceptions, and cannot possibly reach any experience of their connexion with objects.
>
> (E:153; S:105; F:184)

This *first* key assumption may strike you as strange, especially if Hume is one of the first philosophers you are studying. It will help, therefore, to begin by describing in summary fashion the motivation for the assumption. Since our purpose here is to understand where Hume is "coming from" – to see things from his point of view – I will for the time being simply expound the motivation behind his key assumption, postponing critical discussion of it until part 6.

The grounds for Hume's assumption consist chiefly in – what is often called –

the "argument from illusion." This label is something of a misnomer, since it covers a number of arguments, not all of which pertain to "illusions" in any ordinary sense of the term. Let us briefly consider some of these arguments.

The first is the *argument from perceptual relativity*. This argument is itself really a family of arguments which have been known at least since Plato's day and whose offspring are legion in the philosophy of perception. Such arguments appeal to the consideration that the way things appear to us in perception depends on a host of conditions, other than just those things' properties, in order to support various philosophical conclusions about perception and its objects. Plato, for example, used arguments, particularly in the *Theatetus* (see 151D–186E), from perceptual relativity to show that perception is not knowledge; and Berkeley used them in his *Three Dialogues* to show that sensible qualities are nothing but sensations or ideas (Berkeley 1993a: 168–82 especially). In the version most directly relevant to Hume's first assumption, the argument is supposed to show that what we really perceive by our senses is not bodies themselves, but rather our own impressions, "perceptions," or "images." Hume himself offers the following brief statement of the argument:

> The table, which we see, seems to diminish, as we remove further from it: but the real table, which exists independent of us, suffers no alteration: it was, therefore, nothing but its image, which was present to the mind.
>
> (E:152; S:104; F:183)

In other words, when one looks at an ordinary object like a table, what one sees changes as one's distance from the table and one's angle of vision change. But the table itself does not change. So, Hume concludes, what one sees is not really the table, but only a visual image, or rather a series of different images – impressions of sense, "sensations or ideas;" or, to use the twentieth-century term, "sense-data."

A second argument is the *argument from the causal facts of perception*. When one's sense-receptors (one's eyes, ears, nose, etc.) are stimulated by an ordinary object, what one perceives depends causally on the sense-receptors one possesses and on the condition (i.e. functional capability) of those organs. For example, when the eyes of a human being and the eyes of a housefly are each stimulated by a lump of sugar, what the human and the fly respectively see is presumably very different, because the eyes of a human and the eyes of a fly are very different. Or when the eyes of a near-sighted person, those of a person with 20–20 vision, and those of a far-sighted person are stimulated by a United States' flag, what each sees is different, because of the different capabilities (condition) of their eyes. But the properties of the stimulus-objects – the lump of sugar and the flag – do not causally depend on the type or the condition of anyone's sense-receptors; they are utterly independent of such facts. So, again, it is inferred that what one sees is not the stimulus-object itself, but rather an image or percept the qualities of which depend, at least in part, on the perceiver's sense-receptors.

A third argument is the *argument from illusion* (where the term "illusion" now refers to genuine cases of illusion). Hume gives a version of this argument, in a passage that also adduces perceptual relativity and the causal facts of perception:

> 'Twill . . . be proper to observe a few of those experiments, which convince us, that our perceptions are not possest of any independent existence. When we press one eye with a finger, we immediately perceive all the objects to become double, and one half of them to be remov'd from their common and natural position. But as we do not attribute a continu'd existence to both these perceptions, and as they are both of the same nature, we clearly perceive, that all our perceptions are dependent on our organs, and the disposition of our nerves and animal spirits. This opinion is confirm'd by the seeming encrease and diminution of objects, according to their distance; by the apparent alterations in their figure; by the changes in their colour and other qualities from our sickness and distempers; and by an infinite number of other experiments of the same kind; from all which we learn, that our sensible perceptions are not possest of any distinct or independent existence.
>
> (T:210–11)

In other words, by pressing one eye with a finger, one can cause oneself to see everything double. But in such a case, at least half of the things one sees are merely mental images that depend for their very existence on being perceived. Furthermore, there is no special, tell-tale, qualitative difference between these images and the other half of the things seen to indicate that while the former are merely mental images, the latter are material things that exist whether or not they are being perceived. So it is inferred that all the things seen are just mental images. A rather similar argument, called the "argument from hallucination," can be constructed by appealing to the occurrence of hallucinations. Since, again, there is no special discernible difference between what is experienced in a vivid hallucination and in a case of normal perception to indicate that only in the hallucination do we perceive merely a mental image, it is inferred that we perceive merely a mental image in both cases.

Fourth, and finally, *epistemological arguments* also have provided an impetus for the view that we perceive only our own impressions or "sense-data." One such argument – perhaps the strongest – goes as follows. Whatever else perception may be, we take it to be a way of acquiring knowledge of its objects. We firmly believe that by perceiving an object, one can come to know both that it exists and that it has certain properties. However, there is good reason to think that any perceptual experience had when a physical object is stimulating one's sense-receptors can be exactly duplicated when there is no such object stimulating one's sense-receptors. Such a duplicate experience can be produced, for example, by directly stimulating the brain, or in a drug-induced hallucination, or in a naturally occurring hallucination, or in a vivid dream. Conceivably, it could even be produced by a deceiving God, or by an evil deceiver like the one postulated by Descartes.[1] Therefore, it is inferred, the objects whose existence and properties we come to know in perception cannot really be physical objects that stimulate our sense-receptors, since sensory experiences indistinguishable from those they would thereby cause could be caused also in these other ways. What then are these objects? The answer given is that they are our own impressions or sense-data – entities that we experience regardless of the way the experience is generated. Only so, it seems, can we defend our deeply held conviction that in sense perception we acquire knowledge of the existence, and of at least some of the properties, of the objects perceived. Of course, however, the impressions or sense-data whose existence and nature we come to know are themselves not physical objects. Rather, it is claimed, our knowledge of physical objects must be somehow inferred or derived from the impressions or sense-data.

This last point brings us to the *second* assumption behind Hume's account – one that he shares with Berkeley, though this time not with most other seventeenth- and eighteenth-century philosophers. This assumption is that from knowledge of our impressions, we cannot legitimately infer the existence of bodies existing outside our minds. Many philosophers of the Modern period, including notably Descartes and Locke, have held that our knowledge of the existence of material things – of the entire material world – is based on an inference or argument from the occurrence of our sensations, ideas, or impressions to the existence of material things. This inference, though construed quite differently by individual philosophers, is basically a causal one, going from effects (the sensations, ideas, or impressions) to their supposed causes (material things, bodies).[2] The inference is supposed to show, not only that the impressions are caused by bodies, but also that they resemble those bodies to a certain extent; so that they provide knowledge of bodies by being representations of those bodies. The overall position that results – we perceive only our own impressions (or sensations, or ideas), but can infer from them the existence of bodies which cause them and which they represent – is commonly called "the causal theory of perception" or "the representational theory of perception."

Berkeley powerfully criticized this theory by challenging its proponents to show why our impressions could not be produced, as Descartes himself had initially wondered, in some quite different way. Thus, Berkeley wrote:

> [W]hat reason can induce us to believe the existence of bodies without the mind, from what we perceive . . . ? I say it is granted on all hands (and what happens in dreams, phrensies, and the like, puts it beyond dispute) that it is possible we might be affected with all the ideas we have now, though no bodies existed without, resembling them. Hence it is evident the supposition of external bodies is not necessary for the producing our ideas: since it is granted they are produced sometimes, and might possibly be produced always in the same order we see them in at present, without their concurrence . . . . Suppose, what no one can deny possible, an intelligence, without the help of external bodies, to be affected with the same train of sensations or ideas that you are, imprinted

in the same order and with like vividness in his mind. I ask whether that intelligence hath not all the reason to believe the existence of corporeal substances, represented by his ideas, and exciting them in his mind, that you can possibly have for believing the same thing? Of this there can be no question; which one consideration is enough to make any reasonable person suspect the strength of whatever arguments he may think himself to have, for the existence of bodies without the mind.

(Berkeley 1993b: 95–6)

Berkeley, then, strongly maintains that the causal-representational theory of perception unwittingly leads to *scepticism*: since what it proposes as the only way to arrive at knowledge of bodies is an indefensible causal inference.

Hume fully endorses this Berkeleyan critique of the theory; indeed, he supplements it with his own original argument against the theory. This influential argument, which Hume gives in both the *Treatise* and the *Enquiry*, goes as follows:

The only existences, of which we are certain, are perceptions, which being immediately present to us by consciousness, command our strongest assent, and are the first foundation of all our conclusions. The only conclusion we can draw from the existence of one thing to that of another, is by means of the relation of cause and effect, which shews, that there is a connexion betwixt them, and that the existence of one is dependent on that of the other. The idea of this relation is deriv'd from past experience, by which we find, that two beings are constantly conjoin'd together, and are always present at once to the mind. But as no beings are ever present to the mind but perceptions; it follows that we may observe a conjunction or a relation of cause and effect between different perceptions, but can never observe it between perceptions and objects. 'Tis impossible, therefore, that from the existence or any of the qualities of the former, we can ever form any conclusion concerning the existence of the latter, or ever satisfy our reason in this particular.

(T:212)

It is a question of fact, whether the perceptions of the senses be produced by external objects, resembling them: how shall this question be determined? By experience surely; as all other questions of a like nature. But here experience is, and must be entirely silent. The mind has never anything present to it but the perceptions, and cannot possibly reach any experience of their connexion with objects. The supposition of such a connexion is, therefore, without any foundation in reasoning.

(E:153; S:105; F:184)

This argument stems directly from Hume's analysis of causal reasoning; it shows that when that analysis is combined with the view that we perceive only our own impressions, the result is that a causal inference from the impressions to the existence of bodies is completely worthless. Of course, Hume is committed by his critique of induction to the view that causal inferences cannot be rationally justified. Nevertheless, it is clear from many places in his writings that he regards reasoning from past experience as being more legitimate than, say, superstition or mere guesswork. Indeed, in the *Treatise*, he even includes a chapter, entitled "Rules by which to judge of causes and effects," offering eight rules that are hard to interpret otherwise than as criteria for distinguishing between "better" and "worse" causal inferences (T:Book I, part iii, Section 15). To what extent this is consistent with Hume's critique of induction, and to what extent it argues for a more "naturalistic" reading of Hume that de-emphasizes the negative aspect of his position, are controversial questions of interpretation that we have not tried to resolve (although we have argued that Hume's thesis according to which inductive inferences cannot be rationally justified does not commit him to the view that such inferences are not rational).[3] But the point to be made here is that, in the passages just quoted, Hume is arguing that the causal inference from impressions to objects, quite apart from what may be said about other causal inferences or causal reasoning in general, is *wholly worthless*: even if other causal inferences, such as those from past to future constant conjunctions, could be given a rational justification, the inference from impressions to objects would still be illegitimate. The reason why this is so can be stated as a simple argument:

(1) We can establish a causal relation between *A*s and *B*s only by observing that *A*s and *B*s have been constantly conjoined.
(2) We can observe that *A*s and *B*s have been constantly conjoined only if we can perceive *A*s and we can perceive *B*s.
(3) We can perceive impressions but we cannot perceive bodies.

∴ We cannot establish a causal relation between impressions and bodies.

The *third* assumption behind Hume's account is his rejection of Berkeley's positive theory of perception and its objects. Berkeley argued for the novel view, now known as "immaterialism," that matter does not exist, and that what people call "material objects" or "bodies" are really nothing but ordered groups of sensations or ideas. As he puts it:

> Thus, for example, a certain colour, taste, smell, figure and consistence having been observed to go together, are accounted one distinct thing, signified by the name *apple*. Other collections of ideas constitute a stone, a tree, a book, and the like sensible things.
>
> (Berkeley 1993b: 89)

One chief benefit of this theory, as Berkeley sees it, is that it eliminates the need for the indefensible causal inference from ideas to bodies, since bodies are themselves only groups of ideas. Thus, by reducing bodies to ideas, Berkeley takes himself to have disposed of scepticism about our knowledge of bodies; he sees his immaterialism as the best cure for scepticism. Hume, however, rejects Berkeley's reduction of bodies to ideas. His general attitude to Berkeley's views is encapsulated in the following passage:

> [M]ost of the writings of that very ingenious author form the best lessons of scepticism, which are to be found among the ancient or modern philosophers, Bayle not excepted. He professes . . . to have composed his book against sceptics. . . . But that all his arguments, though otherwise intended, are, in reality, merely sceptical, appears from this, *that they admit of no answer and produce no conviction.*
>
> (E:155n; S:106–7n 64; F:186)

It should now be clear that Hume is committed to a deep scepticism with respect to our knowledge of a material world. For he assumes that

(1) we perceive only our own impressions;
(2) any inference from those impressions to the existence of bodies causing the impressions is wholly illegitimate; and
(3) bodies are not merely groups of impressions.

These three assumptions imply that our belief in the existence of bodies is completely unfounded. Everything Hume says about this belief – and he has much more to say about it – needs to be understood against this sceptical background.

3 The general nature of Hume's account

Although Hume holds that our belief in the existence of bodies has no rational foundation, he holds also that humans have an irresistible propensity to believe that bodies exist. Indeed, this propensity is so powerful that, most of the time, we have no choice but to yield to it. It is only while we are actually engaged in philosophical reflection on the topic of sense perception that we can bring ourselves to suspend judgment regarding the existence of bodies. Even the sceptic, as soon as he or she ceases to focus on the arguments that show this belief to be without any rational foundation, falls back into the notion that the very things he or she perceives *are* bodies. This contrast between the results of reasoned reflection, on the one hand, and what we spontaneously and naturally believe, on the other hand, is part and parcel of Hume's naturalism, which has been so strongly emphasized by recent Hume scholars. In the section of the *Treatise* that we are examining (Book I, part iv, section 2), he expresses the contrast in these words:

> There is a great difference betwixt such opinions as we form after a calm and profound reflection, and such as we embrace by a kind of instinct or

161

natural impulse, on account of their suitableness and conformity to the mind. If these opinions become contrary, 'tis not difficult to foresee which of them will have the advantage. As long as our attention is bent on the subject, the philosophical and study'd principle may prevail; but the moment we relax our thoughts, nature will display herself, and draw us back to our former opinion.

(T:214)

So, near the end of the section, after going through a series of arguments designed to show that our belief in the existence of bodies is shot through with errors and has no rational justification, he concludes with these ironical words: "I . . . take it for granted, whatever may be the reader's opinion at this present moment, that an hour hence he will be persuaded there is both an external and internal world" (T:218).

Another way of putting Hume's point – that the conclusions of philosophical reflection are inevitably overshadowed by our natural propensity to believe in external objects – is this: although our belief in the existence of bodies cannot be the result of rational reflection, it is the product of certain psychological principles of human nature. In other words, the belief cannot be rationally justified, but it can be psychologically or naturalistically explained by an adequate "science of man." This is of course Hume's position, and it explains why he introduces the section as he does: "We may well ask, *What causes induce us to believe in the existence of body?* but 'tis vain to ask, *Whether there be body or not?* That is a point, which we must take for granted in all our reasonings" (T:187). Hume's point is that philosophy wastes its time when it asks whether bodies exist or not, because no amount of argument or reasoning can show that they exist, and our human nature compels us anyway to believe that they exist. Rather, the proper business of philosophy is to ask: what are the principles of human nature that make us believe that bodies exist? Accordingly, Hume announces that "the subject, then, of our present enquiry is concerning the *causes* which induce us to believe in the existence of body" (T:187–8).

Notice that this approach to the belief in body is closely parallel to Hume's treatment of induction and of personal identity. When Hume finds that induction cannot be rationally justified, he is not content with this negative conclusion. Rather, he goes on to give a psychological explanation – in terms of his principle of association of ideas – of inductive inferences. This explanation also provides the material for his account of the idea of necessary connection, as a projection into the phenomena we perceive of our feelings of expectation. As for personal identity, recall that Hume finds there is no impression of the self from which can be derived any idea of a continuing self persisting through time. Coupled with his strict view of identity as requiring no change and no interruption, this finding leads him to the conclusion that the self possesses no real identity through time. But again, Hume is not content to stop with this negative conclusion; instead, he goes on to offer an explanation, in terms of psychological principles, of why we nevertheless ascribe to

162

ourselves identity through time and change. Thus, Hume takes a similar approach with respect to induction, the belief in personal identity, and the belief in the existence of body. First he argues that these embody various errors and have no rational foundation; then he gives a psychological explanation of them. This approach, which is especially prominent in the *Treatise* but by no means absent from the *Enquiry*, reflects Hume's desire to explode rationalist ways of thinking and to replace them with his naturalistic science of human nature.

4 The nature and origin of the belief in the existence of body

Hume begins his inquiry into the causes of our belief in body by analyzing or breaking down this belief into two parts:

(1) the *continued* existence of the objects of the senses while they are not being perceived; and
(2) the existence of the objects of the senses *distinct* from (independently of) being perceived.

Hume means that our belief in the existence of bodies boils down to a belief in (1) and (2); that is to say, it consists in believing that the things we perceive by our senses *continue* to exist at times when we are not perceiving them, and that they exist *independently* of whether or not we are perceiving them. Thus, for example, your belief that Mount Everest exists consists in your believing that Mount Everest continues to exist when neither you nor anyone else is perceiving it, and that it exists regardless of whether anyone is perceiving it. Hume says that (1) and (2) are logically related. For if (1) is true – if sensible objects continue to exist while not being perceived – then (2) must be true also; that is, sensible objects must exist independently of being perceived. Hume also says that, conversely, if (2) is true, then (1) is true: he thinks that (1) and (2) are mutually entailing beliefs, and so stand or fall together. This, however, is questionable; for why could there not be momentary objects which, though they do not depend on being perceived for their existence, happen to exist only when they are perceived? If there could be such objects, then Hume is wrong to think that (2) – distinct or independent existence – entails (1) – continued existence. But this matters little to his discussion, which, as we shall see, requires only that (1) entail (2). Hume himself emphasizes this entailment when he says that "the opinion of the *continu'd* existence of body . . . is prior to that of its *distinct* existence, and produces that latter principle" (T:199), and that "'tis the opinion of a continu'd existence, which first takes place, and without much study or reflection draws the other along with it, wherever the mind follows its first and most natural tendency" (T:210).

Hume, nevertheless, devotes some space, at the beginning of his discussion, to the belief in the independent or "distinct" existence of the objects we perceive. He

163

first offers some arguments to show that this belief cannot arise from the *senses* themselves; let us look at two of these arguments.

The first argument is that our impressions themselves have no distinct existence; so the only way our senses could produce a belief in distinct existence would be if we perceived those impressions as images or representations of some other distinct objects. But, Hume says:

> That our senses offer not their impressions as the images of something *distinct*, or *independent*, and *external*, is evident; because they convey to us nothing but a single perception, and never give us the least intimation of any thing beyond. A single perception can never produce the idea of a double existence.
>
> (T:189)

The second argument is designed to defeat a possible explanation of how our impressions give rise to the belief in distinct existence, despite the fact that they are not perceived as images of distinct objects. This possible explanation is that the belief in distinct existence arises from the fact that we perceive impressions as external to our own bodies and hence as external to ourselves.[4] As Hume puts it:

> [O]ur own body evidently belongs to us; and as several impressions appear exterior to the body, we suppose them also exterior to ourselves. The paper, on which I write at present, is beyond my hand. The table is beyond the paper. The walls of my chamber are beyond the table. And in casting my eye towards the window, I perceive a great extent of fields and buildings beyond my chamber. From all this it may be infer'd, that no other faculty is requir'd, besides the senses, to convince us of the external existence of body.
>
> (T:190–1)

Hume rejects this explanation, for the following reason (among others):

> [P]roperly speaking, 'tis not our body we perceive, when we regard our limbs and members, but certain impressions, which enter by the senses, so that the ascribing a real and corporeal existence to these impressions, or to their objects, is an act of mind as difficult to explain, as that which we examine at present.
>
> (T:191)

In other words: since we do not really perceive our own bodies but only certain impressions of our own arms, hands, fingers, etc., the fact that we have impressions also of other things – of a paper, table, walls, and fields – does not amount to perceiving those items to be exterior to our bodies or to ourselves; it amounts only to perceiving an array of impressions that includes the impressions both of our own bodily parts and those of other things.[5] The explanation proposed of why we believe the latter to be exterior to ourselves could work only if we already had an explanation of why we believe the former to have a "distinct" existence – which is the very sort of explanation we are looking for and have not yet found.

Having argued that the belief in the independent or "distinct" existence of the objects of sense perception cannot arise from the senses themselves, Hume argues next that it cannot be based on reason. His argument is contained in the following passage:

> [P]hilosophy informs us, that every thing, which appears to the mind, is nothing but a perception, and is interrupted, and dependent on the mind; whereas the vulgar confound perceptions and objects; and attribute a distinct continu'd existence to the very things they feel and see. This sentiment, then, as it is entirely unreasonable, must proceed from some other faculty than the understanding. To which we may add, that as long as we take our perceptions and objects to be the same, we can never infer the existence of the one from that of the other, nor form any argument from the relation of cause and effect; which is the only one that can assure us of matter of fact. Even after we distinguish our perceptions from objects, 'twill appear presently, that we are still incapable of reasoning from the existence of the one to that of the other: So that upon the whole our reason neither does, nor is it possible it ever shou'd, upon any supposition, give us an assurance of the continu'd and distinct existence of body.
>
> (T:193)

Here Hume does not separate the issue of "distinct" existence from that of "continu'd" existence; he treats the two together. But insofar as the argument bears just on "distinct" existence, it seems to boil down to the simple reasoning that since it is so easily shown to be *false* that the objects of sense perception have such an existence – since the slightest philosophy "informs us" that they are "dependent on the mind" – it follows that any belief to the contrary must be "entirely unreasonable," and so not based on reason. To be sure, Hume also says that we cannot *both* identify perceptions and objects *and* regard the latter as causes of the former, but this point does nothing to support the claim that belief in distinct existence cannot be based on reason; rather it has force only against someone who would say that impressions are both the sole objects of perception and that they are caused by objects of perception – an absurd position that no philosopher would maintain. Hume also says that once we distinguish perceptions from objects, the causal inference from the perceptions to the existence of objects is illegitimate; but this point, though it foreshadows his argument against causal theories of perception, has no bearing on the question of whether the belief that *the very objects we perceive* have a "distinct" existence is based on reason. So Hume's argument that

165

this belief is not based on reason does seem to reduce to saying that the belief is so easily shown to be false that it cannot be reasonable.[6]

Hume, then, thinks he has shown that our belief in the "distinct" or independent existence of the objects of sense perception cannot arise either from the senses themselves or from reason. But what about our belief in the "continu'd" existence of these objects: what is its status, and how does it arise? This question brings us to the heart of Hume's discussion, most of which is directly addressed to explaining the belief that the objects of sense perception continue to exist when they are no longer being perceived. Further, if Hume can explain this belief, then he will also have explained the belief that these objects have a "distinct" existence – that they exist independently of perception – since, as we have seen, the former belief entails the latter.

For brevity's sake, we shall henceforth often call the belief that the objects of sense perception continue to exist when they are no longer being perceived the "belief in object-continuity." (Note, then, that the term "object," when it occurs within this phrase, will always refer to the very object which is perceived by the senses.) Now the central theme of Hume's discussion of our belief in object-continuity is that this belief is simply false, and that our firm acceptance of this falsehood is precisely what his psychological principles must explain. Let us consider first why Hume thinks the belief is false, and afterwards why he thinks we accept it despite its falsity.

In some places, Hume attacks the belief in object-continuity by attacking the belief in distinctness; he uses a *Modus Tollens* argument that goes this way (see T:210–11, 214):

(1) If the objects of sense perception continue to exist while not being perceived, then they exist independently of being perceived.
(2) The objects of sense perception do not exist independently of being perceived.

∴ The objects of sense perception do not continue to exist while not being perceived.

To support this argument's second premiss, Hume cites the "experiments, which convince us, that our perceptions are not possest of any independent existence," such as pressing one eye with a finger and seeing everything double – which, as we saw earlier, he regards as showing that we perceive only our own impressions.

Hume has, however, what he regards as a much more fundamental reason against the belief in object-continuity: namely, that this belief is just false on the face of it. This is because our perceptions are *obviously* discontinuous, "broken," or "interrupted." Consider, for example, your present visual impressions of the book you are reading. Those impressions are plainly discontinuous: they vanish each time you glance away from the book, and they cease to exist for the much longer periods of time during which you are asleep, or engaged in activities other than reading this book. This simple and obvious point, Hume thinks, plainly reveals the falsity of the belief in the "continu'd" existence of the objects of sense perception.

To grasp Hume's thinking here, it is crucial to understand that when he says our perceptions are interrupted or discontinuous, he is not saying merely that our perceivings, or acts of perception, or perceptual episodes, are discontinuous, which is of course true. Rather, he is claiming also that the *objects of* our perceptions – the things that we perceive – are discontinuous. For Hume simply does not distinguish between perceptual episodes and the objects perceived by them; his use of the terms "perceptions" and "impressions" to stand indifferently for both perceptual episodes and their objects is not just linguistic carelessness or sloppiness, but embodies a genuine failure to distinguish between them. The only form in which he recognizes a distinction between perception and its objects is that of the philosophical theory of the "double existence of perception and objects" advocated by Descartes, Locke and others – a theory that Hume strongly rejects. Except within the context of this theory, Hume sees no place for a distinction between perception and its objects.

Hume's denial of this distinction calls for an explanation, if only because the distinction is so elementary. Even ordinary, unsophisticated, common sense would distinguish between perceiving something, or the perception of something, and *what* is perceived: between seeing an apple and the apple which is seen; or between touching a cat and the cat which is touched; or between smelling a flower and the flower which is smelled, etc. Why then does Hume deny this elementary distinction? The reason, I suggest, lies in the basic governing assumption of his account of perception – his thesis that we perceive only our own "perceptions" or impressions. For impressions have exactly the same temporal characteristics, including notably the same duration, as perceptions, taken as perceptual episodes or acts of perceiving. So the thesis that we perceive only impressions implies that the objects of perception last no longer than the perceptions themselves. But in that case, the distinction between perceptions and objects collapses, at least for an Empiricist like Hume. For, as Kant shows, one key difference between perceptions and their objects is precisely their respective temporal properties: on viewing a house, one's perceptions of the front, sides, and back of the house are successive and may be interrupted, but the parts of the house are co-existent and exist continuously. Furthermore, from Hume's Empiricist point of view, it seems that this temporal difference is the *only* thing that could differentiate between perceptions and their objects, because any "act" of perception distinct from the object perceived would not be something of which we could have any impression: it would be, so to speak, diaphanous or "transparent." Thus Hume's acceptance of the philosophical view that we perceive only our own impressions seems to explain his otherwise puzzling denial of the elementary distinction between perceptions and objects. By the same token, it explains why it would be so foreign to Hume to distinguish, as Kant does, between the time-relations of perceptual episodes and those of their objects – to say that while the perceptual episodes are always successive, their objects may be co-existent; or that while the perceptions of the front of a house are interrupted during the time that the observer sees the back, and the perceptions of the back are interrupted during the time the observer sees the front, the very front and back of the house that the observer successively sees exist continuously. For Hume, by contrast, the fact that perceptual episodes are discontinuous entails that the objects of perception are discontinuous too.

The chief mistake which Hume accordingly thinks our belief in body involves – that of mistaking manifestly discontinuous items for continuous ones – is so gross that it cries out for an explanation. So, it is this very mistake that Hume's psychological principles are invoked to explain; the bulk of his discussion is an explanation of our (false) belief in the "continu'd" existence of the objects of the senses, or in object-continuity. But since the "continu'd" existence of objects entails their "distinct" existence, Hume thinks, as already mentioned, that if he can successfully explain our belief in the former, he will have explained also our belief in the latter.

Hume asks first whether the belief in object-continuity is based on the senses. He answers that it cannot be:

> [T]he SENSES . . . are incapable of giving rise to the notion of the *continu'd* existence of their objects, after they no longer appear to the senses. For that is a contradiction in terms, and supposes that the senses continue to operate, even after they have ceas'd all manner of operation.
>
> (T:188)

In other words, belief that the objects of sense perception continue to exist while they are not being perceived could arise from the senses only if we continued to perceive the objects at the very times when we do *not* perceive them; but we do not continue to perceive them at those times (that would be self-contradictory); therefore, this belief cannot arise from the senses. This argument seems quite decisive.

Hume considers next whether the belief in object-continuity is based on reason. In a passage that we have already quoted, he argues that it is not. Here is the key part of that passage:

> [P]hilosophy informs us, that every thing, which appears to the mind, is nothing but a perception, and is interrupted, and dependent on the mind; whereas the vulgar confound perceptions and objects; and attribute a distinct continu'd existence to the very things they feel and see. This sentiment, then, as it is entirely unreasonable, must proceed from some other faculty than the understanding . . . . [U]pon the whole our reason neither does, nor is it possible it ever shou'd, upon any supposition, give us an assurance of the continu'd and distinct existence of body.
>
> (T:193)

As noted earlier, this passage treats "continu'd" and "distinct" existence together; so it is, at least in part, a defense of Hume's claim that the belief in distinct existence is not based on reason, as we have already seen. But since Hume does not offer any further or separate reasons for denying also that belief in continued existence is based on reason, it seems that he regards the passage as sufficient to support *that* denial as well. As such, it seems to amount to the simple argument that since "every thing, which appears to the mind" is obviously "interrupted," the "sentiment" that what appears to the mind has a continued existence is therefore "entirely unreasonable," and so cannot be produced by our reason. Just as in the case of "distinctness," Hume's argument seems again to be that just because the belief in continuity is so easily shown to be *false*, it cannot be *reasonable*, and so cannot stem from the use of our reason.

If the belief in object-continuity does not arise from either the senses or the exercise of reason, then how does it arise? Hume's answer is that our impressions have two features – "constancy" and "coherence" – which cause us mistakenly to believe that the impressions themselves continue to exist between the times that we perceive them. Since this belief is not based on the senses or on reason, and since it amounts to positing something – the continued existence of the impressions – which is in fact untrue, and which is purely a product of our own human invention, Hume ascribes it to the faculty or power of *imagination*. His basic thesis is that the imagination, stimulated by the constancy and coherence of our impressions, naturally "fills in the gaps" between discontinuous impressions, thereby making us believe that they continue to exist between the times we perceive them. As he puts it, in an apt and striking image: "[T]he imagination, when set into any train of thinking, is apt to continue, even when its object fails it, and like a galley put into motion by the oars, carries on its course without any new impulse" (T:198).

To better understand Hume's basic thesis, we need to see what he means by "constancy" and "coherence." The reader is warned, however, that Hume's characterizations of these two features are careless, and need to be corrected in order to serve his purposes. Here is Hume's characterization of *constancy*:

> After a little examination, we shall find, that all those objects, to which we attribute a continu'd existence, have a peculiar *constancy*, which distinguishes them from the impressions, whose existence depends upon our perception. Those mountains, and houses, and trees, which lie at present under my eye, have always appear'd to me in the same order; and when I lose sight of them by shutting my eyes or turning my head, I soon after find them return upon me without the least alteration. My bed and table, my books and papers, present themselves in the same uniform manner, and change not upon account of any interruption in my seeing or perceiving them.
>
> (T:194–5)

And here is Hume's characterization of coherence:

> Bodies often change their positions and qualities, and after a little absence or interruption may become hardly knowable. But here 'tis

observable, that even in these changes they preserve a *coherence*, and have a regular dependence on each other; which is the foundation of a kind of reasoning from causation, and produces the opinion of their continu'd existence. When I return to my chamber after an hour's absence, I find not my fire in the same situation, in which I left it: But then I am accustom'd in other instances to see a like alteration produc'd in a like time, whether I am present or absent, near or remote. This coherence, therefore, in their changes is one of the characteristics of external objects, as well as their constancy.

(T:195)

In these passages, Hume's intention is to describe certain kinds of order, uniformity or recurrence in our *impressions*, which he calls "constancy" and "coherence." But instead of confining himself to impressions, he talks about "bodies" – physical things like mountains, houses, trees, books, papers, and his bed, table, and fire-place. Further, he even says that coherence and constancy are "characteristics of external objects" or "bodies," as opposed to features of impressions. This is careless, and Hume should not have done it. For his purpose is to explain, in terms of certain kinds of order or recurrence in our impressions, why we believe that there are physical things or bodies; so his explanation must not appeal to (our belief in) the existence of such things, but only to features of the impressions themselves – a point well made by such commentators as Bennett (1971: 323) and Stroud (1977: 100). One cannot explain *why* it is believed that there are Xs by appealing to the belief *that* there are Xs.

Mindful of this point, let us try to characterize constancy and coherence without assuming the existence of physical things. We may define constancy this way: to say that our impressions have constancy means that our experience presents us with discontinuous sets of impressions whose members exactly resemble each other. For example, on each occasion when Hume has the experience that he would call "looking at my bed and table, books and papers," he has a similar array of visual impressions. This resemblance, Hume thinks, causes the imagination to "fill in the gaps" between these occasions, by supposing that those visual impressions contin-ued to exist during the times he was no longer having such an experience. As for coherence, we may define it this way: to say that our impressions have coherence means that the temporal relations that we observe between members of an altering but continuous series of impressions are preserved between members of other altering continuous series composed of similar impressions, and also between members of discontinuous series of impressions that resemble members of those continuous series.

Here is an example, based on Hume's illustration. Suppose I have the experi-ence that I would call continuously viewing a slowly diminishing fire in my fire-place. Then, when I have another continuous visual experience whose constituent elements are the same, those elements occur with the same temporal relations as before: I do not, for example, first have impressions of a small fire, then of a medium-sized one, and finally of a large one; rather, I once again have impressions of a large fire, then a medium-sized one, then a small one. Also, when I have an experience that I would call discontinuously viewing such a fire – of seeing the fire in the fireplace, then leaving the area for an hour, and returning to see fire in the fireplace – the relations between the elements of that experience are the same as are the relations between the "matching" elements of the continuous experiences: for example, the impressions of the fire had at the end are impressions of a smaller fire than the impressions of the fire had at the beginning, not of one larger than, or as large as, the fire at the beginning. This coherence among our impressions, Hume thinks, also contributes to the belief in object-continuity; for example, to the belief that when I have impressions of a large fire in my fireplace, followed by no impressions of fire, followed by impressions of a small fire in my fireplace, a slowly-diminishing fire existed unperceived in between.

Hume discusses separately, and in great detail, how constancy and coherence each contribute to the belief in object-continuity. His general position is that coherence alone is "too weak to support so vast an edifice, as is [belief in] the continu'd existence of all external bodies" (T:198–9), and he places the greater weight on constancy. Let us accordingly focus here on constancy; we shall return to coherence in part 7 of this chapter.

To explain the role of constancy, Hume presents a four-part "system" that is supposed to show how the constancy of our impressions gives rise to the belief in their "continu'd existence." Without trying to cover or discuss all the complexities in his account, its salient points may be summarized in the following way.

The "first part of [Hume's] system" is just his account of identity, which was discussed in Chapter 1. It will be remembered that Hume's account is essentially an account of identity through time: it aims to say what is required for any thing to retain its identity, to remain the same thing, through a period of time. His view, you will recall, is a strict one: identity through time requires not only that there be no break or interruption in a thing's existence throughout the time in question, but also that the thing not change in any way during that time. This definition of identity is stated most explicitly in the section on personal identity, where Hume writes: "We have a distinct idea of an object, that remains invariable and unin-terrupted thro' a suppos'd variation of time; and this idea we call that of *identity* or *sameness*" (T:253). But the same notion of identity is operative in the section that we are now discussing, where Hume says:

> [T]he *principium individuationis*, or principle of identity . . . . [or] principle of individuation is nothing but the *invariableness* and *uninterruptedness* of any object, thro' a suppos'd variation of time, by which the mind can trace it in the different periods of its existence, without any break of the view . . .
> (T:199–201)

The "second part" of Hume's "system" turns on a common element as between identity (as he has defined it) and constancy, and invokes a psychological principle concerning the effects on our minds of resemblance. When an item that we may call "X" that exists at a time t_1 is identical with an item that we may call "Y" that exists at a time t_2, then of course, given Hume's notion of identity, the item called "X" must be exactly like the one called "Y;" for otherwise "X" and "Y" could not denote the same *unchanging* thing and so would each denote a different thing rather than a single thing. But likewise, when a set of impressions, I, had at a time t_1 bears the relation of constancy to another set of impressions, I', had at a time t_2, the impressions in I exactly resemble those in I'. Thus, we can say that I and I' satisfy one of the two conditions required for I and I' to be identical with each other: they are exactly alike. However, they do not satisfy the other condition required for identity, since there is an "interruption" or "gap" between them – a time between t_1 and t_2 when I and I' do not exist or occur. Were there no such interruption, we could say that I and I' were identical; in such a case, says Hume, "the interruption of our perceptions . . . is the only circumstance that is contrary to their identity" (T:209).

However, Hume also maintains that whenever A exactly resembles B, the human mind has a powerful propensity to think that A is identical with B (T:61). This is one of the psychological principles that Hume insists upon in his *Treatise*; it has for him much the same status as the principle that whenever A is regularly followed by B, we come to expect B whenever we perceive A. Hume explains the principle about resemblance by noting that observing an exact resemblance between A and B *feels like* observing an uninterrupted and unchanging object; or, as he puts it, "the act of the mind [involved] in surveying a succession of resembling objects [itself resembles] that [act of mind involved] in surveying an identical object" (T:205n). Hume thinks that this resemblance between the experience of perceiving a succession of resembling objects and the experience of perceiving a single unchanging object causes us to confuse those two different experiences and, therefore, to confuse also what they are experiences *of*. It is just this confusion between resembling but numerically distinct items, and a single unchanging item, that Hume ascribes to the imagination: the confusion is, according to him, the work of the imagination. But from the principle that whenever A exactly resembles B, we come to think that A is identical with B, together with the point that I and I' (sets of impressions related by "constancy") are exactly alike, it follows that in such a case we will believe that I and I' are identical! This belief is presumably Hume's system's "second part;" he describes it this way:

> [T]he constancy of our perceptions makes us ascribe to them a perfect numerical identity, tho' there be very long intervals betwixt their appearance, and they have only one of the essential qualities of identity, *viz. invariableness.*
>
> (T:202)

The upshot is that the constancy of our impressions generates a conflict or "contradiction" in our minds. On the one hand, the resemblance between impressions exhibiting constancy causes us to believe that they are identical. On the other hand, the interruptions or gaps between those impressions means that they cannot be identical. Now the "third part" of Hume's "system" is that we resolve this conflict by "feigning" or positing the existence of something that eliminates or fills the gaps between the interrupted impressions; we come to think of those impressions not only as exactly alike ("invariable") but also as continuous ("uninterrupted"). This allows us to think that the impressions meet both of the conditions required for identity, and are, therefore, identical. As Hume puts it:

> The smooth passage of the imagination along the ideas of the resembling perceptions makes us ascribe to them a perfect identity. The interrupted manner of their appearance makes us consider them as so many resembling, but still distinct beings, which appear after certain intervals. The perplexity arising from this contradiction produces a propension to unite these broken appearances by the fiction of a continu'd existence, which is the *third* part of the hypothesis I propos'd to explain.
>
> (T:205)

But of course, to posit or to "feign" the existence of something that eliminates the gaps between our impressions is to regard those impressions as continuing to exist while we are not perceiving them.

At this stage of his account, then, Hume has come very close to his goal of explaining the belief in body. To complete the account, however, he connects it, in the "fourth member of this system" (T:208), with a definition of *belief* that he had offered earlier in the *Treatise*: belief is "a lively idea related to or associated with a present impression" (T:96). This definition of belief is rooted in Hume's view of causal inference: when we have experienced a constant conjunction between A and B, and have a present impression of A, our expectation of B consists in "a lively idea" of B, and Hume calls such an idea a "belief." Hume is now saying that the belief in body also consists in a lively idea related to a present impression. This works as follows. "Our memory presents us with a vast number of instances of perceptions perfectly resembling each other, that return at different distances of time, and after considerable interruptions" (T:208).

The point here is that, since constancy consists in resemblances between sets of impressions that occur at different times, including past times, it can be recognized only by the use of memory. Putting it still differently, the material on which the imagination works when it causes us to consider resembling sets of impressions as identical consists at least partly of present memories of past impressions (along perhaps with present sense impressions that resemble the past ones). Now Hume regards those memories as themselves consisting of impressions rather than merely of ideas, because "ideas of memory . . . are equivalent to impressions" (T:82). This "equivalence" stems, presumably, from the fact that ideas of memory, unlike purely imaginary ideas, have the liveliness in terms of which Hume defines impressions. In any case, it is these present memory-impressions that trigger our propensity to regard past – remembered – sets of resembling impressions as identical. But this propensity is so strong that, when we posit or "feign" the continued existence of those impressions, this posit has the liveliness or vivacity that characterizes belief. And since this posit is triggered by our present memory-impressions, it counts as a "lively idea related to a present impression." Therefore, it amounts to a *belief*, namely belief in the continued existence of our impressions – which is the very belief that Hume wanted to explain. Here is Hume's own summary of the entire account:

> Our memory presents us with a vast number of instances of perceptions perfectly resembling each other, that return at different distances of time, and after considerable interruptions. This resemblance gives us a propension to consider these interrupted perceptions as the same; and also a propension to connect them by a continu'd existence, in order to justify this identity, and to avoid the contradiction, in which the interrupted appearance of these perceptions seems necessarily to involve us. Here then we have a propensity to feign the continu'd existence of all sensible objects; and as this propensity arises from some lively impressions of the memory, it bestows a vivacity on that fiction; or in other words, makes us believe the continu'd existence of body.
>
> (T:208–9)

5 The "vulgar system" and the "philosophical system"

In a nutshell, Hume's explanation of our belief in the existence of body is that the imagination, stimulated by the constancy (and coherence) of our impressions, causes us to ascribe to those very impressions a continued existence, despite the fact that they are really discontinuous, "interrupted," or "broken." We simply gloss over the fact that our impressions have a discontinuous existence, for the imagination causes us to confuse the impressions with continuously existing bodies. As Hume puts it: "The very image, which is present to the senses, is with us the real body; and 'tis to these interrupted images we ascribe a perfect identity" (T:205). And again:

> 'Tis certain, that almost all mankind, and even philosophers themselves, for the greatest part of their lives, take their perceptions to be their only objects, and suppose, that the very being, which is intimately present to the mind, is the real body or material existence. 'Tis also certain, that this very representation or object is suppos'd to have a continu'd uninterrupted being, and neither to be annihilated by our absence, nor to be brought into existence by our presence.
>
> (T:206–7)

Hume calls this view, which confuses discontinuous, interrupted or intermittent perceptions (specifically, impressions of sensation), with continuous, enduring or persisting bodies, "the vulgar system." Here the term "vulgar" does not signify the modern sense of *vulgarity*; rather, it signifies that the view in question is the ordinary common-sense view – the one that humans naturally and spontaneously accept, prior to any philosophical reflection.

Hume has no sooner expounded the vulgar system, however, than he proceeds to argue that it will not withstand rational scrutiny. To show this, he simply invokes the "experiments," described earlier, "which convince us, that our perceptions are not possest of any independent existence" (T:210). Pressing one's eye with a finger and seeing double, or seeing a table's perceived shape and size vary as we move nearer to or further from it, as well as "an infinite number of other experiments of the same kind," show that "the doctrine of the independent existence of our sensible perceptions is contrary to the plainest experience." And since, as we have seen, the continuous existence of these "sensible perceptions" (i.e. objects of sense perception) implies their independent existence – since they can have a continuous existence *only if* they have an independent existence – "this leads us back on our footsteps to perceive the error in attributing a continu'd existence to our perceptions" (T:210). But do we therefore give up our belief in the existence of body? Not at all. Instead, we introduce the philosophical theory of "the double existence of perceptions and objects." This theory, which is none other than the causal or representational theory of perception favored by Descartes, Locke and most of Hume's contemporaries, admits that our perceptions are "interrupted, and perishing, and different at every return." But, at the same time, it holds that these fleeting perceptions are caused by, and represent, independently existing bodies which are "uninterrupted, and [which] preserve a continu'd existence and identity" (T:211). Hume dubs this theory "the philosophical system."

To see the logic of the situation, consider the following three propositions:

(1) The objects of the senses are bodies.
(2) The objects of the senses have a continuous existence.
(3) Bodies have a continuous existence.

The *vulgar* system, or common sense, holds that all three propositions are true. Hume, however, insists that (2) is false, and that common sense fails to recognize (2)'s falsity. He gives the complicated theory expounded in part 4 to explain why the common person wrongly affirms (2). The *philosophical* system, by contrast, recognizes that (2) is false, and is accordingly faced with the threat of contradiction, since the negation of (2) – the proposition that the objects of the senses have a discontinuous existence – combined with (1) and (3), entails that the objects of the senses have both a continuous and a discontinuous existence. In order to avoid the contradiction, the philosophical system denies (1), by coming up with the theory of "the double existence of perceptions and objects." The philosophical system, then, affirms the following three propositions:

175

(1')   The objects of the senses are our own impressions of sensation.

not (2) The objects of the senses have a discontinuous existence.

(3)   Bodies have a continuous existence.

We already know Hume's verdict concerning the vulgar system: although it is the one that our human psychology impels us to accept, it is *false*, indeed grossly false; for proposition (2) is false, and it is only the workings of our imagination that cause us to affirm it.

What then of the philosophical system: is it any better off than the vulgar one? Hume's answer is a resounding "No;" indeed, he argues brilliantly that the philosophical system is even worse off than is the vulgar one. He announces this thesis in these words:

> But however philosophical this new system may be esteem'd, I assert 'tis only a palliative remedy, and that it contains all the difficulties of the vulgar system, with some others, that are peculiar to itself. There are no principles either of the understanding or fancy, which lead us directly to embrace this opinion of the double existence of perceptions and objects, nor can we arrive at it but by passing thro' the common hypothesis of the identity and continuance of our interrupted perceptions. Were we not first perswaded, that our perceptions are our only objects, and continue to exist even when they no longer make their appearance to the senses, we shou'd never be led to think, that our perceptions and objects are different, and that our objects alone preserve a continu'd existence. "The latter hypothesis has no primary recommendation either to reason or the imagination, but acquires all its influence on the imagination from the former."
>
> (T:211)

Hume is here announcing his objections to the philosophical system: first, it has no rational justification; second, it derives all of its plausibility from the vulgar system. We have already seen, in effect, why he holds that the philosophical system has no rational justification: the causal inference from perceptions to objects on which that system rests is completely worthless – as part 2 of this chapter made clear. So let us now consider why he holds the philosophical system to be completely dependent on the vulgar system.

Hume's reasoning goes as follows. At first, the philosopher – the person who reflects critically on his or her beliefs, considered before the critical reflection begins – believes like everyone else that the very objects he or she perceives *are* bodies. Upon reflection, however, the philosopher realizes that the mind-dependence of the objects of the senses, as well as the interrupted or intermittent existence that this mind-dependence entails, give the lie to this view. But, at the same time, the imagination continues to give the philosopher (in the complicated way that we outlined in part 4) an overpowering propensity to believe that the objects perceived have the continuous existence characteristic of bodies. The philosopher is thus in danger of falling into the contradiction of holding that the objects of the senses are both continuous and discontinuous. Finally, the philosopher avoids the contradiction by means of the following artifice: ascribe the interruptedness or discontinuity to perceptions, then postulate body and ascribe the continued existence to it. The contradiction is avoided by ascribing the opposed properties to different things. Thus is born the system of "the double existence of perceptions and objects," and with it the very distinction between perceptions and objects, in the only form that Hume recognizes. But this does not alter the fact that the postulation of body has no rational foundation; it derives all of its force from the imagination's propensity to ascribe a continuous existence to interrupted, discontinuous perceptions, except that the continued existence is now ascribed to unperceivable and unknowable bodies that are supposed to be distinct from the perceptions. The result is that the philosophical system derives all of its appeal from the vulgar system – a system which is not only false in its own right, but which actually *contradicts* the philosophical system (inasmuch as the vulgar system affirms, while the philosophical system denies, the continuous existence of our "perceptions")! Hume's eloquent account of this result is worth quoting:

> This philosophical system, therefore, is the monstrous offspring of two principles, which are contrary to each other, which are both at once embrac'd by the mind, and which are unable mutually to destroy each other. The imagination tells us, that our resembling perceptions have a continu'd and uninterrupted existence, and are not annihilated by their absence. Reflection tells us, that even our resembling perceptions are interrupted in their existence, and different from each other. The contradiction betwixt these opinions we elude by a new fiction, which is conformable to the hypotheses both of reflection and fancy, by ascribing these contrary qualities to different existences; the *interruption* to perceptions, and the *continuance* to objects. Nature is obstinate, and will not quit the field, however strongly attack'd by reason; and at the same time reason is so clear in the point, that there is no possibility of disguising her. Not being able to reconcile these two enemies, we endeavour to set ourselves at ease as much as possible, by successively granting to each whatever it demands, and by feigning a double existence, where each may find something, that has all the conditions it desires. Were we fully convinc'd, that our resembling perceptions are continu'd, and identical, and independent, we shou'd never run into this opinion of a double existence; since we shou'd find satisfaction in our first supposition, and wou'd not look beyond. Again, were we fully convinc'd, that our perceptions are dependent, and interrupted, and different, we shou'd be as little inclin'd to embrace the opinion of a double existence; since in that case we shou'd clearly perceive the error of our first supposition of a continu'd existence,

and wou'd never regard it any farther. 'Tis therefore from the intermediate situation of the mind, that this opinion arises, and from such adher-
ence to these contrary principles, as makes us seek some pretext to justify
our receiving both; which happily at last is found in the system of double
existence.

(T:215–6)

Hume's overall position with regard to the belief in the existence of body, then,
is profoundly sceptical. He has examined two versions of this belief: the vulgar
system on which our "perceptions" are continuous (uninterrupted) and identical
with bodies; and the philosophical system on which our "perceptions" are discontinuous (interrupted) and distinct from bodies. The vulgar system, though it is
supposed to be the one humans spontaneously and naturally accept, and to reflect
ordinary common sense, is simply false. As Hume puts it:

> 'Tis a gross illusion to suppose, that our resembling perceptions are
> numerically the same; and 'tis this illusion, which leads us into the
> opinion, that these perceptions are uninterrupted, and are still existent,
> even when they are not present to the senses. This is the case with our
> popular ["vulgar"] system.

(T:217)

As for the philosophical system, not only does it lack rational foundation, but it
contradicts the very system that it depends upon or "lives off:"

> And as to our philosophical one, 'tis . . . over-and-above loaded with this
> absurdity, that it at once denies and establishes the vulgar supposition.
> . . . What then can we look for from this confusion of groundless and
> extraordinary opinions but error and falsehood? And how can we justify
> to ourselves any belief we repose in them?

(T:217–8)

6 A criticism of Hume's account

The thesis that leads Hume to contend that common sense is mistaken in holding
that the objects of the senses have a continuous existence is, as we have seen, the
philosophical view that the objects of our perceptions are our own impressions. As
I have said, this thesis is the most basic of the three assumptions that govern
Hume's whole account of the belief in the existence of body, and it was widely
accepted by his contemporaries. Thus far, the thesis has not been examined
critically; we have confined ourselves to tracking its role in Hume's account.
The time has come, then, for us to examine this key thesis critically. Now there
is a huge philosophical literature on this topic; indeed, perhaps no other question
has been debated as intensively in twentieth-century philosophy of perception as

this one: *do we perceive material things, or do we perceive only impressions* (or, as these have been variously called, sensations, ideas, percepts, appearances, sensa, sense-data)? Until about the middle of this century, most philosophers believed that arguments such as those sketched at the beginning of this chapter force us to accept the latter view, which is now commonly called the "sense-datum theory." Since that time, however, the arguments for the sense-datum theory have been intensively criticized, and most (though not all) philosophers now reject both the arguments and the theory. We cannot canvass here all of the arguments for the sense-datum theory.[7] Rather, we shall return only to those arguments, surveyed in part 2 of this chapter, that Hume advances when he speaks of the "experiments, which convince us, that our perceptions are not possest of any independent existence:" namely, the argument from perceptual relativity and the argument from the illusion of seeing double; and, more briefly, to the epistemological argument that appeals to the many alternative ways of causing any perceptual experience. We shall argue that those arguments are faulty, and our objections to them will be, in content and spirit, characteristic of the objections that have led most contemporary philosophers to reject the sense-datum theory.

Here then, once again, is Hume's brief statement of the argument from *perceptual relativity*:

> The table, which we see, seems to diminish, as we remove farther from it; but the real table, which exists independent of us, suffers no alteration: it was, therefore, nothing but its image, which was present to the mind.
>
> (E:152; S:104; F:183)

One way to summarize this reasoning is as follows:

(1) When we look at an object from different distances and angles, what we see changes.
(2) When we look at an object from different distances and angles, the object itself does not change.

∴ (3) When we look at an object from different distances and angles, what we see is something other than the object itself – an impression, image, or sense-datum.

Stated in this fashion, the argument is logically valid, but are both its premisses true? Many philosophers today, including myself, would say that while premiss (2) is obviously true, (1) is simply false. What we see on looking at an object from different distances and angles does not *really* change; rather, it only *seems* to change. In other words, (1) ought to replaced with:

(1a) When we look at an object from different distances and angles, the object's size and shape *seem* to change.

Unlike (1), (1a) does not assert that there is a seen object that really changes when we look at an ordinary object under different conditions; it says only that the object itself seems (in one sense of "seems") to change – that its size and shape *look* different from different distances and angles.[8] Hume's own language suggests this way of putting it: he says that what we see "*seems* to diminish" as we move away from it, not that it *does* diminish. The introduction here of the little word "seems" makes all the difference. For, once (1a) is substituted for (1) in the argument, it is no longer valid: from (1a) and (2), all that follows is that the object itself *looks* or *seems* different from different distances and angles, which is exactly what we expect (what would be strange is if the object continued to look exactly the same from any distance and angle!), and from which it does not follow at all that the object we see from one distance and angle really is different from the object we see from another distance and angle. The upshot is that the argument is either valid but unsound – the case where premiss (1) is retained – or invalid – the case where (1a) is substituted for (1).[9]

Some contemporary philosophers have given an illuminating diagnosis of the basic error committed by the argument from perceptual relativity. The argument's proponents have assumed that if a premiss like (1a) is true, then a premiss like (1) must also be true. More basically, they have assumed that from a premiss of the form: (A) Person S perceives something that *seems* or *appears* F, there follows a conclusion of the form: (B) Person S perceives an appearance (impression, sense-datum) that really *is* F. Suppose for example that someone, say Mary, sees a coin that, to her, looks elliptical because of her angle of vision. Then there does seem to be an elliptical *something* in her visual field, and so philosophers have assumed that Mary sees an object which really is elliptical. But since the coin is round, the elliptical object that Mary supposedly sees cannot be the coin itself. What then is it? The answer, it seems, is that this object can only be an impression – a percept, "image," or sense-datum. If this mode of reasoning were valid, then from a premiss like (1a), which says that what we see under different conditions *seems* or *appears* different, one could always derive a premiss like (1), which says that what we see under different conditions really *is* different.

In fact, however, the assumption that a premiss of form (A) entails a conclusion of form (B) is wrong. This point has been especially well made by Roderick M. Chisholm, who is an influential contemporary epistemologist and philosopher of perception. Chisholm shows that there are many arguments with a form-(A) premiss and a form-(B) conclusion that are obviously invalid – that can obviously have a true premiss and a false conclusion. Two such arguments are:

John sees a dog which looks vicious and more than 10 years old.
___

∴ John sees an appearance (impression, sense-datum) which is vicious and over 10 years old.

Mary sees a man who appears tubercular.
___

∴ Mary sees an appearance (impression, sense-datum) which is tubercular.[10]

Chisholm calls any argument with a form-(A) premiss and a form-(B) conclusion a case of "the Sense-Datum Fallacy," on the grounds that all such arguments are invalid, and because there is no true premiss that can be added to make them valid.[11]

Notice that our objections to the argument from perceptual relativity can also be applied to the argument from the causal facts of perception. That argument could be summarized this way:

(1') When an object is perceived by means of different sense-receptors (e.g. the eyes of a human and those of a housefly, or the eyes of a near-sighted person and those of a person with 20-20 vision), what is perceived varies.

(2') When an object is perceived by means of different sense-receptors, the object itself does not vary.

∴ (3') When an object is perceived by means of different sense-receptors, what is perceived is something other than the object itself – it is an impression, image, or sense-datum.

In parallel with our criticisms of the argument from perceptual relativity, we can here say that premiss (1') is false. What is true is rather: (1a') When an object is perceived by means of different sense-receptors, what is perceived seems to vary. But from (1a') and (2'), (3') does not follow. So again, the argument either has a false premiss, or is invalid.

Let us turn next to Hume's argument from *the illusion of seeing double*; here, once more, is his presentation of it:

> When we press one eye with a finger, we immediately perceive all the objects to become double, and one half of them to be remov'd from their common and natural position. But as we do not attribute a continu'd existence to both these perceptions, and as they are both of the same nature, we clearly perceive, that all our perceptions are dependent on our organs, and the disposition of our nerves and animal spirits.
>
> (T:210–11)

We may reconstruct this argument somewhat informally, as follows:

(1) When we press one eye with a finger, we see two of every object that we previously saw.

(2) At least one member of every such pair of objects lacks a continuous and independent existence.

(3) Both members of every such pair of objects are of the same nature.

∴ (4) Both members of every such pair of objects lack a continuous and independent existence.

181

Although this argument may have a certain plausibility, it is vulnerable to at least two objections. One objection concerns premiss (1), which says that upon pressing one eye we really see *two* objects for every one that we saw before – that the number of objects now seen actually increases (it doubles). The objection is that this is to take the element of truth expressed in premiss (1) too literally. All that premiss (1) really commits us to is that upon pressing one eye, we *seem* to see a "twin" of every object that we previously saw. But *seeming to see* a new object is not the same thing as *actually seeing* a new object – as would happen if, say, the object had undergone mitosis or fission – and the argument simply confuses these two importantly different things.

The second objection is that even if we were to grant premiss (1), and so to grant also the talk in (2) and (3) of pairs of "objects" that are seen when pressing one eye with a finger, the argument would still be faulty; for there is no good reason to accept (3), the claim that both members of such a pair of objects are "of the same nature." For why could we not maintain, instead, that one of the two objects in such a pair – the one that is not "remov'd from [its] common and natural position" – is a body or material thing, while only the other is an impression or "perception"?

Hume himself gives no reason why we should not say this, but more recent proponents of the sense-datum theory would give one on his behalf. This is that there is no special, discernible, tell-tale difference between the two "objects" to indicate that the one is a body, while the other is a fleeting, mind-dependent, impression; therefore, they must both be of the same nature, just as (3) says.[12] Thus, since according to (2) at least one of them must be a fleeting and mind-dependent impression, both must be impressions, just as the conclusion states.

But this reason for saying that both "objects" are of the same nature is defective. For the fact that two things are visually alike – that we can see no discernible difference between them – does not at all prove that they are "of the same nature." A real tomato and a wax replica of a tomato may be visually indistinguishable, but that certainly does not show that they are the same in nature. As J. L. Austin put the point in his short but very influential book *Sense and Sensibilia* (1962: 50–2):

> If I am told that a lemon is generically different from a piece of soap, do I "expect" that no piece of soap could look just like a lemon? Why should I? . . . . Why on earth should it *not* be the case that, in some few instances, perceiving one sort of thing is exactly like perceiving another?

We may conclude that Hume's argument from the illusion of seeing double is unsound: its first premiss is false and, even if that premiss were accepted, there would be no reason to accept its third premiss.

In part 2 of this chapter it was said that certain *epistemological arguments* have motivated the view that we perceive impressions or sense-data rather than physical objects. One such argument, we saw, stems from the consideration that any perceptual experience obtained when a physical object is stimulating one's sense-receptors could be caused in other ways, including direct brain stimulation or even an "evil deceiver" like the one postulated by Descartes in his *First Meditation*. We said that because this possibility threatens our deep-seated conviction that perception is a source of knowledge, some philosophers have suggested that in perception we come to know at least the existence and nature of our own impressions (from which we then have to infer the existence of some physical object). While this argument (to which we shall return in the next part) is a powerful one, the point needs to be made here that the argument does not establish that we perceive (or "immediately perceive," as is usually said) impressions or sense-data. For it is possible to hold that in perception *something* other than the existence and nature of physical objects can be known *without* holding that this something must therefore be the existence and nature of some *other* kind of object. Rather, what is known in perception can be simply a fact about one's self – a fact that contemporary philosophers such as Chisholm propose to describe by saying that the self is "appeared to" in a certain fashion, or that the self "senses" in a certain fashion. This is a complex matter that we shall not pursue in more detail here; but the essential point is that the epistemological purpose of introducing "impressions" or "sense-data" into an account of perception – which is to allow that something can be known in every case of perception despite the fact that any perceptual experience can be caused in a variety of ways – can be secured without postulating such special objects of perception, by holding that in perception we gain knowledge of certain sensory states of the self (from which, it is argued, we can infer the existence of physical objects causing those states).[13]

7 A contemporary perspective on Hume's account

In light of the above criticisms of Hume's account, you might now conclude that there is little to be learned from it, other than the avoidance of certain errors, such as the "sense-datum fallacy." But, to draw this conclusion would be too hasty; for it would be to assume that the sceptic's problems with sense perception depend wholly on the doctrine that we perceive only impressions, or percepts, or sense-data. In fact, however, such an assumption would be wrong; for "scepticism with regard to the senses" can arise quite independently of that doctrine.[14] A concise statement of how such scepticism can be generated is given by Robert M. Adams:[15]

> [O]ne of the most important sceptical arguments in modern philosophy. . . is due to Descartes and is based on the idea of "a God who is able to do anything." "How do I know that he did not bring it about that there be no earth at all, no heavens, no extended thing, no figure, no size, no place, and yet all these things should seem to me to exist precisely as they appear to do now?" Descartes was no sceptic, and thought he could solve the problem by proving the existence and nondeceitfulness of God. Descartes's problem has proved more durable than his solution, however . . . .
>
> The problem remains. All our beliefs about the material world are based ultimately on sense experience. Yet it seems quite conceivable that

everything might seem to us exactly as it actually seems to us in sense perception even if there were no material world at all outside our minds. So how do we know there is a material world outside our minds?

The sceptical argument that Adams here rightly attributes to Descartes does not involve the view that we cannot perceive material things but only impressions or sense-data. Rather, the argument is designed to show that even if we can, or in fact do, perceive material things, we can never *know* that we do, because such knowledge must be based on our sense experiences (visual experiences, tactile experiences, auditory experiences, etc.); but it is perfectly conceivable that we could have the very same sense experiences that we do in fact have even if no material things existed: this could happen if God, or perhaps some other being, such as Descartes' "evil deceiver," were causing us to have all the experiences.

Hume himself would presumably have accepted this argument's sceptical conclusion, since he explicitly holds that the belief in body has no rational basis. He contents himself, as we have seen, with pointing to certain features of our sense experience – constancy and coherence – that are supposed to explain causally why we believe in body. Some contemporary philosophers, however, have tried to use Hume's ideas about how constancy and coherence give rise to the belief in body in a way that was not envisioned by Hume. These philosophers have tried to see constancy and coherence as features of sense experience that *justify* the belief in body, or, as Jonathan Bennett (1971: 313–53) puts it, that justify our use of "objectivity-concepts" (See also Ayer 1940: 243–63). It is presumably because Hume's discussion lends itself to this purpose that Bennett, in the passage we quoted at the beginning of this chapter, says that despite being "full of mistakes and – taken as a whole – a complete failure," Hume's treatment is "one of the most instructive arguments in modern philosophy" (1971: 311). Let us therefore consider in rather more detail this manner of reading Hume, using Bennett as our guide.

Bennett focuses on a passage in which Hume discusses the role of *coherence*. Hume writes:

> I am here seated in my chamber with my face to the fire; and all the objects, that strike my senses, are contained a few yards around me . . . . I hear on a sudden a noise as of a door turning upon its hinges; and after a little see a porter, who advances towards me. This gives rise to many new reflexions and reasonings. First, I have never observ'd, that this noise cou'd proceed from anything but the motion of a door; and therefore conclude, that the present phaenomenon is a contradiction to all past experience, unless the door, which I remember on t'other side of the chamber, is still in being . . . . But this is not all. I receive a letter, which upon opening it I perceive by the hand-writing and subscription to have come from a friend, who says he is two hundred leagues distant. 'Tis evident I can never account for this phaenomenon, conformable to my

experience in other instances, without spreading out in my mind the whole sea and continent between us, and supposing the effects and continu'd existence of posts and ferries, according to my memory and observation. To consider these phaenomena of the porter and letter in a certain light, they are contradictions to common experience, and may be regarded as objections to those maxims, which we form concerning the connexions of causes and effects. I am accustom'd to hear such a sound, and see such an object in motion at the same time. I have not receiv'd in this particular instance both these perceptions. These observations are contrary, unless I suppose that the door still remains, and that it was open'd without my perceiving it: And this supposition, which was at first entirely arbitrary and hypothetical, acquires a force and evidence by its being the only one, upon which I can reconcile these contradictions. There is scarce a moment in my life, wherein there is not a similar instance presented to me, and I have not occasion to suppose the continu'd existence of objects, in order to connect their past and present appearances, and give them such an union with each other, as I have found by experience to be suitable to their particular natures and circumstances. Here then I am naturally led to regard the world, as something real and durable, and as preserving its existence, even when it is no longer present to my perception.

(T:196–7)

Bennett sees Hume to be making two different points in this passage:

(1) Unless I admit that the door, sea, continent, post offices, and ferries, etc., continue to exist while I do not perceive them, my experiences as of now hearing a door, seeing a letter, etc., are "contradictions" of my past experience.

(2) Unless I admit that the door, sea, continent, post offices, and ferries, etc., continue to exist while I do not perceive them, I cannot "account" for my experiences as of now hearing a door, seeing a letter, etc., in a way that conforms to my past experience.

We can illustrate the first point this way: suppose that upon having the experience of seeing the letter, I deny that the sea, continent, post offices and ferries continued to exist while I was not perceiving them. Then Bennett reads Hume as saying that I must believe both that "I received a letter that was ferried last week by the postal services across the sea and continent" and that "the sea, continent, postal services and ferries did not exist during the past week" – which is self-contradictory. Bennett, however, rejects this point, on the ground that the contradiction can be generated only if I *already* accept the existence of such things as the sea, continent, post offices, and ferries: if all I know is that I am now having certain visual experiences as of receiving a letter, and that in the past I have had experiences as of seeing the sea, continent, posts and ferries, then there is no contradiction in

185

denying that any of these things continued to exist while I did not perceive them. As he puts it:

> The notion of "contradiction" has no place here unless I already accept a large body of theory: the proposition that I inhabit a world of objects, many hypotheses about their general behaviour, and some hypotheses of the form "I have perceptions of kind K only when in the presence of objects of kind K*".
>
> (Bennett 1971: 324)

This objection seems right. On the other hand, Bennett sees much more merit in Hume's second point: He writes (1971: 325):

> [W]e could take [Hume's talk of removing contradictions] to mean "explain, without contradicting my other experience". This would put Hume on firmer ground: spreading out the sea and the continent is no longer removing a contradiction but providing an explanation.

And, a little later (p. 330), Bennett even talks of [Hume's] "manifest success, in the 'door' passage, in showing that The Belief [in the existence of body, of material things] does have a certain kind of legitimacy."

Bennett's position here, in its general character, is a fairly standard one in the philosophy of perception. The basic idea is that our sense experiences present certain features – especially certain kinds of order and recurrence, such as Hume's constancy and coherence – that are best explained by the theory that the experiences are experiences of an objective world, in which bodies exist independently of those experiences and causally interact among themselves and with our perceptual organs in regular, law-like ways. Bennett puts this basic idea as follows:

> I have a conceptual framework which lets me connect my various sensory episodes to form a coherent whole: I bring the brute, disconnected facts of my sensory history under a *theory* in terms of which I can adduce some of these facts as explaining others, can predict further ones, and so on. This theory does its work only because, through it, statements about past perceptions can imply statements about present and future ones. Also, the theory is . . . so structured that through it certain perception-statements can imply the existence of objects when I do not perceive them.
>
> (1971: 325)

The manner in which Bennett spells out the details of this general position, however, is original and of considerable interest. Building on Hume's example of the door, Bennett illustrates the way in which the "theory" of independently existing objects enables me to "connect my various sensory episodes to form a coherent whole" – to adduce some of "the brute, disconnected facts of my sensory history . . . as explaining others, . . . [and as] predict[ing] further ones." He writes (p. 331):

> When I see a door, turn my head away, and then turn back and see it again, my two visual impressions are connected by the statement that each is the seeing of a door. For example, the judgement that the first is the seeing of a door supports the prediction that when I turn my head back I shall have the second visual impression.

Here the point is that by treating my first visual experience as the perception of a door – a real door that exists independently of my experience of it – I can use the experience to predict that when I turn my head back I shall again have a visual experience as of a door, and also to explain why I have this latter experience upon turning my head. If, on the other hand, I regarded the first experience as just a sensory episode in my psychic history, not connected to or caused by a door, then I could not use it in these ways. Thus, Bennett declares: "In ways like this I bring objectivity-concepts to bear upon impressions which I do have; and Hume should admit that such procedures are useful, and are broadly causal in nature" (p. 331).

Having in this way illustrated how the belief in *independently* existing objects explains how we can use some experiences to explain and predict other experiences, Bennett, in one of the most interesting moves in his discussion, goes on to argue that such a belief perforce commits one also to the belief in *continuously* existing objects. He first invites us (p. 332) to suppose that Hume would resist this transition: that he would try to admit the explanatory usefulness of independently existing objects but refuse to extend this admission to continuously existing ones:

> Hume might still say: "But the fact remains that the utility of 'perceived object' does not help me with my problem about the utility of 'unperceived object'. Even if it is helpful to be able to say 'I now see a door' both at t_1 and t_3, I have shown that it cannot be helpful to say 'There is now a door which I don't see' at t_2."

To this, Bennett responds:

> But the benefits of "perceived object" come through a theory of which "unperceived object" is an *integral* part: we cannot lop off statements asserting the existence of objects while unperceived, while retaining the "useful" objectivity-statements which classify some of our perceptions as perceptions of objects.
>
> (1971: 332)

This seems right; for suppose that, in the door example, I did *not* admit that the door continued to exist while I was looking away. Then my first visual experience would provide no basis for predicting or explaining the second; instead, I might as

187

well suppose that a door like the first one *miraculously* sprang into existence when I looked again, which would be as good as admitting that the belief in an independently existing door had *no* explanatory value after all. Bennett goes on (pp. 332–3) to illustrate this vital link between admitting independent objects and continuous ones in terms of Hume's "sea and continent" example:

> [T]he "sea and continent" are supposed to raise a problem for me only in respect of their existence when I don't perceive them; but the statement "There is a sea between us *now*" is connected, through my general world-theory and thus through the conceptual framework which is its bone, with statements about perceptions which I do have at some time or other – what I shall observe if I take a certain journey, what I heard my friend say when asked "What route will you take?" and so on. I have no way of linking these perceptions of mine which doesn't involve my agreeing that the sea is there right now . . . . I rest my case on the . . . thesis that the only way I can helpfully bring objectivity-concepts to bear on *my* impressions – or you on yours, or Hume on his – is through a theoretic structure which, together with the given experiential data, implies that objects sometimes exist while unperceived. The only ground *we* have for claiming sometimes to perceive objects are equally grounds for claiming that objects sometimes exist when we do not perceive them.[16]

We shall conclude this part by raising a question about Bennett's "explanation-providing" defense of the belief in body. Clearly enough, the defense works only if a good case has been made for the belief in the *independent* existence of the objects of perception; for only then can Bennett's chief point – that any grounds there are for saying that we perceive (independent) objects are grounds also for saying that those objects continue to exist unperceived – come into play. The question we shall raise is simply this: has Bennett made a good case for the belief in object-independence? Such a case, it seems, would have to address effectively the sceptical argument, described at the beginning of this part, which R. M. Adams traces to Descartes: it would have to give a good reason for saying that our perceptual experiences are produced not by some extremely powerful and intelligent agent bent on deceiving us but rather by a physical world. But the only reason Bennett provides is the one he describes rather blandly, in connection with the door example, by saying: "In ways like this I bring objectivity-concepts to bear upon impressions which I do have; and Hume should admit that such procedures are useful, and broadly causal in nature" (1971: 331).

But suppose that a determined sceptic were to respond to Bennett by saying:

> "I admit that one way in which I can use a present perception as of a door to predict another such perception, or use one perception of a door to explain another one, is by agreeing that a door exists independently of those perceptions and continues to exist in between the times of their

occurrence. But this is only one possible explanation; there are others. Another possible explanation is that God, or some evil deceiver, wants to make me believe falsely that doors and other material things exist, and so causes in me a set of orderly and systematic perceptual experiences such that I can predict those I will have on the basis of those I have had, and explain some perceptions by adducing other perceptions, and so forth."

Now there seems to be nothing in Bennett's account – at least nothing that he explicitly says – to explain, even to suggest, why such an alternative theory is less reasonable than the physical-world theory.

Furthermore, in at least one passage, Bennett seems to overlook the type of sceptical challenge that we have raised. Bennett writes (p. 325) that, in the light of his account:

> In a given sensory situation I may have to choose between (a) accepting that there is such an object [i.e. an object that exists when I do not perceive it], (b) relinquishing the theory and thus my only chance of explaining my sensory present, and (c) retaining the theory while denying that there is an object which I don't perceive – thus committing myself to a falsehood about my sensory past. This is the case where I must choose (a) if I am to "account for [my present perception]^{17} conformable to past experience": if I choose (b) I cannot "account for" the perception, and if I choose (c) my explanation will not be "conformable" to my past experience.

To illustrate: suppose that my "given sensory situation" is that I seem to see a door on turning my head back, or have an experience as of seeing a door on seeming to turn my head back, along with the memory of having had a similar experience (minus the head-turning experience) a moment ago. Then, according to Bennett, I have three choices: (a) I accept that I am seeing a door; (b) I give up the theory that doors and other objects exist independently of my perceptions of them; and (c) I retain this theory but deny that I am now seeing a door. Bennett would say that if I choose (b) I relinquish "my only chance of explaining my sensory present;" and that if I choose (c) my explanation of my present sensory situation, whatever it is, will not be the same as it was in other similar situations; which is why, if I wish to explain my present sensory situation, and to do so in a way that matches similar situations (and, otherwise, what sort of "explanation" would it be?), I must opt for (a). The trouble, however, lies with Bennett's claim that if I opt for (b) then I relinquish "my *only* chance of explaining my sensory present," and so "*cannot* 'account for' the perception [emphases added]." A determined sceptic will not grant this claim. Rather, such a sceptical philosopher will say that there are other possible theories, such as the theory of a universal deceiver, that can serve to explain my present sensory situation just as well as the physical-world theory. There seems to be nothing in Bennett's account that can effectively meet this classic sceptical challenge.^{18}

189

8 A Kantian response to scepticism regarding
the senses

In this final part, we shall consider briefly another, quite different, response to the sceptical challenge: that of Immanuel Kant in his *Critique of Pure Reason* (hereafter, "the *Critique*"). As previously mentioned, Kant's theory of knowledge is an enormously complex one that lends itself to many different interpretations; here we shall consider only one key idea in *one* way of reading Kant.

As was mentioned in Chapter 5, in the *Critique* Kant gives a number of "transcendental arguments" – arguments intended to show that we could not have the kind of experience we do, unless certain principles were true. Such arguments start from some fact about experience which is supposed to be incontrovertible and which even a sceptic would admit, and then try to show that this fact, when reflected upon, implies the truth of a principle(s) that the sceptic doubts. The most ambitious such argument offered by Kant, in a famous and very difficult section of the *Critique* called the "Transcendental Deduction of the Pure Concepts of the Understanding," can be interpreted as an attempt to show that a certain incontrovertible fact about human experience would not be possible unless we employed concepts of physical objects.

On the interpretation of Kant's transcendental deduction (as this argument is usually called) that we shall briefly consider, the incontrovertible fact of experience with which the argument begins is what we shall call the "unity of consciousness."[19] To see what this means, notice first that human consciousness at any given time is typically not consciousness of just one thing, but rather of *many* things. We are seldom if ever conscious of only one item – our experience would be very dull if we were – but of a diversity of items (which Kant called a "manifold of representations"). For example, when simply gazing into an ordinary furnished room, you are conscious not only of a door, but also of walls, a chair, a table, a bed, windows, a carpet, light fixtures, and so on. Now this simple fact requires something noteworthy; namely, that each of the items of which you are aware be presented to *one and the same* consciousness. If the chair were presented to one consciousness, the table to another, the bed to a third, and so on, then there would be no awareness of the furnished room, but only separate awarenesses of a wall, table, chair, bed, etc. This point, as we saw in Chapter 1 – in connection with our (Kantian) objection to Hume's bundle theory of the self – is also evident when we recall that human consciousness is extended over time, and that we can be aware of succession in time. In order to hear several strokes of a bell as a succession of strokes, it will be recalled, it is essential that each stroke be retained in one and the same consciousness when its successor is heard.

Kant's transcendental deduction – or at least one key idea in one interpretation of his highly complex argument – turns on the relation between this fact of the unity of consciousness on the one hand, and the use of concepts of objects on the other. Notice first that unless we had unity of consciousness, we could not use concepts of objects. Consider a simple object like a chair. If each leg of the chair, the seat of the chair, and the back of the chair were always presented to different consciousnesses, then there could be no consciousness of a chair, and so no concept of a chair. Concisely put, consciousness of an object requires unity of consciousness; the parts of the object of which we must be aware in order to be aware of the object, be they few or many, must each be given to one and the same consciousness. Now the key idea in Kant's argument is both less obvious and more difficult; it is the converse of the claim just made: to wit, that unity of consciousness requires consciousness of an object.

To see why Kant thinks this is so, suppose that we ask: what unifies, or holds together in a single consciousness, a variety of experiences? This is not an easy question to answer, for there are at least four possible answers that must be eliminated:

1 It will not do to answer that a variety of experiences can be unified by introspectively spotting some relation that they all have to the self or conscious subject. This is because, as we saw in Chapter 1, Hume showed that we do not and cannot introspect the conscious subject – a point also made by Kant (1963: A107). It follows that we cannot introspect the self *in relation* to items of experience, since to be introspectively aware of a relation between X and Y we must be aware at least of both X and Y.

2 A variety of experiences cannot be unified by spotting some necessary connections between the experiences themselves. For, as we saw in Chapter 4, Hume showed that we never observe any necessary connections between different occurrences.

3 A variety of experiences cannot be unified by relations of association between them.[20] This is because, as the Kant scholar Robert Paul Wolff has shown (1963: 108–9), mere association is not sufficient for unity of consciousness. For, suppose that John and Mary's experiences have the following unusual relationship: whenever John smells bacon, Mary imagines eggs; and whenever Mary imagines eggs, John smells bacon. Then Mary's and John's experiences of smelling bacon and imagining eggs stand in a relation of association – one leads to the other and vice-versa – but they do not belong to one and the same consciousness. For it is not the case that when John smells bacon, *he* imagines eggs; or that when Mary imagines eggs, *she* smells bacon. To put it differently, the bacon-smelling and egg-imagining experiences are not in the same mind.

4 We cannot say that a diversity of experiences are unified in one consciousness because they are all in the head (see Wolff 1963: 115). For, even waiving objections to talking about heads in the context of trying to meet the sceptical challenge, as well as possible objections to talk of experiences being "in the head," this condition would not be sufficient: the experiences might be in different parts of the brain that did not communicate with each other.

If a diversity of experiences cannot be unified in any of the above four ways – by standing in an introspectional relation to the self, by exhibiting necessary connections between each other, by association, or by being all in the head – then what does unify them? The answer proposed by Kant is this: the experiences are unified by being related to an object, by being *of* an object. To grasp this idea better, notice that being related to an object is certainly one way to unify a diversity of experiences: the object serves, so to speak, as an anchor for them. Now Kant's idea is that, in light of the elimination of the other possibilities mentioned, this is the *only* way to unify a diversity of experiences in one consciousness (Wolff 1963: 116).

This idea is merely the nub of a lengthy argument that we shall not develop more fully here, since our purpose is merely to sketch the core of one reading of Kant's alternative response to an external-world sceptic.[21] Rather, let us test Kant's idea, by considering some possible objections to it.

One possible objection would be that Kant is wrong to think that relation to an object is required to unify a diversity of experience, because mere *co-presence* to one consciousness is sufficient to explain such unity. Kant could reply that this objection just begs the question; for "co-presence" is here merely another term for "unity of consciousness" – the very notion he is trying to explain. Further, co-presence may seem to provide the needed explanation, only because we can think schematically of a set of items that are all related to the same self by (the relation of) awareness. However, once we realize that we cannot spot any such self in introspection, we can see that co-presence offers no explanation of the difference between a set of experiences each of which exists for a different consciousness, and a set of experiences each of which exists for one and the same consciousness. Rather, it is only a label for the latter phenomenon, which is the one we are trying to understand.

A second possible objection goes as follows. What would Kant say about the experiences obtained in a hallucination? Does not his idea "prove too much," namely, that even hallucinatory experiences are experiences of objects? Kant could reply that even hallucinatory experiences *purport* to be of objects, they are conceptualized *as* experiences of objects. It is only because they do not cohere with other experiences, or with the broader context of our experience, that they are eventually classified as hallucinations.

This reply, however, leads to another, more basic, possible objection to Kant's approach: does not his idea show only that our experiences must be *conceptualized as* experiences of objects, while failing to show that they must really *be* experiences of objects? If so, then it would seem that Kant's approach completely fails to meet the sceptical challenge.

To see how Kant could answer this basic objection, we need to describe the question to which the constructive part of the *Critique* is addressed. This question can be put as follows: what can we know about what human experience (which is the only kind we can have) must be like, without prejudging or even addressing the question of whether that experience conforms to things as they are quite apart from our experience – indeed without even addressing the question of whether things as they are in themselves are the same things as or are different from the things we experience? For Kant, this question breaks down into two:

(1) What can we know about how anything must be *perceived* by us, without making any judgment on the question of whether this is the same or different from the way things are apart from the way we perceive them?

(2) What can we know about how we must *think* things are, or conceptualize them, without making any judgment on the question of whether the way we must conceptualize things conforms to things as they may be apart from such conceptualization?

To the first question, Kant answers, in the first constructive part of the *Critique*, called the "Transcendental Aesthetic," that things must be perceived by us as being in time and space. To the second question, he answers, in the second constructive part of the *Critique*, called the "Transcendental Analytic," that given just the fact of unity of consciousness as an incontrovertible datum, it follows that things must be conceptualized as physical objects (whose changes are, moreover, governed by causal laws).

We cannot explore in this work the deep and complex arguments by which Kant seeks to defend these answers to his questions. But let us try to say how his approach bears on the sceptical challenge. Notice that Kant's questions open up a kind of space in which we can talk about human experience without the worry of whether it conforms to things as they may be in themselves – things apart from our modes of experiencing them. Kant would say that this is in fact the proper domain of philosophy, and that both the non-sceptic and the sceptic make the same mistake. The non-sceptic claims that we can have knowledge of things as they are in themselves, quite apart from our ways of experiencing them. This, by Kant's lights, is a mistake; for we cannot possibly know what things are like apart from the ways in which we must perceive and think of them. As for the sceptic: it might, at first, be thought that Kant is himself a sceptic; for does not a sceptic hold precisely what Kant holds – that we cannot know what things are like in themselves? But there is a difference between Kant and the sceptic. A sceptic holds that we cannot know what things are like in themselves because our *evidence* or *justification* for any claim about such things is always insufficient or faulty, as in the case of the causal inference from impressions to objects, which, as we saw, Hume rejects. Kant, by contrast, regards as incoherent the very thought that there could be evidence as to what things are like completely apart from the ways in which we must perceive and conceptualize them. For that thought fails to recognize that in all human cognition, there is a contribution made by the knower: namely, the knower's ways of perceiving and conceptualizing things, the import of which for the content of our knowledge cannot be ignored or factored out.

The mistake made by sceptic and non-sceptic alike, then, is to assume that it makes sense to suppose that we could know what things are like "in themselves" – independently of the ways in which we must perceive and conceptualize them. In particular, the sceptic's supposition that all our experience might be produced by a Cartesian deceiver is precisely a supposition about what reality might be like totally apart from the ways we must perceive and think of it. So Kant presumably

193

would have to grant that we cannot know this supposition to be either true or false, for that would again be to know what things are like totally apart from our ways of perceiving and conceptualizing them. But he would maintain that we can at least know that we must perceive and conceptualize reality as a system of physical objects interacting causally in space and time. Whether this is a satisfactory reply to the sceptical challenge must here be left for the reader to ponder.[22]

NOTES

INTRODUCTION

1 As Hume scholars have shown, there were still other formative influences on Hume. Norman Kemp Smith especially, in his *The Philosophy of David Hume* (1941), has emphasized the influence of the British moralists Hutcheson, Shaftesbury, Mandeville, and Butler, especially Hutcheson.
2 This general account of Hume's basic program is indebted in part to D. G. C. MacNabb 1967: 75.

1 HUME'S THEORY OF MEANING AND ITS IMPLICATIONS

1 This summary of Descartes' presentation of the case for scepticism follows his *First Meditation*. See Descartes 1984: 12–15.
2 This topic will be discussed in more depth in Chapter 6.
3 Despite the advantages of the modern formulations, some contemporary scholars would resist the attempt to interpret Hume along these lines. For example, Garrett (1997: Chapter 2) argues that:
   (1) Hume did not regard the "copy principle" (as Garrett calls Hume's version of the principle of empiricism) as an a priori truth (p. 43); and
   (2) some of Hume's principles concerning the operations of the imagination offer him a way of explaining how one might have the idea of the missing shade of blue without having had the corresponding impression (pp. 51–2).
With regard to (1), it should be noted that Garrett's principal argument – that (a) impressions are *causes* of ideas and (b) for Hume causal claims are never a priori – is based exclusively on the *Treatise*. In the *Enquiry*, Hume does not insist or even say that impressions are causes of ideas. Given that Hume himself says in his prefatory "advertisement" to the *Enquiry* that it alone should be regarded as containing his "philosophical principles and sentiments," that he there also distances himself from the *Treatise* by calling it "that juvenile work" (E:2; S:xviii, F:52), and that one of the main differences between the two works is precisely that the *Enquiry* contains far less psychology, this difference between the accounts of impressions and ideas in the two works is not insignificant. With regard to (2), it should be noted that (as Garrett himself seems quite aware) explaining how one might, on Humean principles, arrive at the idea of the missing shade of blue is not tantamount to showing that there is no contradiction between the copy principle and Hume's admission that this idea need not be copied from any impression. Despite these reservations about Garrett's position, however, we need not deny that he may be right in claiming that his reading of Hume is historically accurate. For our claim is not that the modern formulations are *identical* with Hume's own views. Rather, it is that:

(1) the modern formulations are suggested by, and historically descended from, Hume's own views;

(2) they do not face the difficulties that afflict Hume's own views; and

(3) they can do the same critical work regarding "substance," "self," and "cause" that Hume's own principle of empiricism and test for meaning are supposed to do.

4 Since philosophers routinely distinguish between *properties* (e.g. redness, roundness), which are abstract or general and cannot be said to exist at one place and time rather than another, and property-*instances* (e.g. the redness and roundness of a particular apple) which are particular and can be said to exist or occur at a particular place and time, it would be more accurate to say that, according to the bundle theory, a thing is composed of coexisting property-instances (or coexisting instantiated properties, or co-instantiated properties), while according to the substance theory, it is composed of property-instances that belong to an underlying substance. But, for simplicity's sake, we shall continue to say that on the bundle theory a thing is composed of coexisting properties.

5 Descartes held that the basic or "primary" properties or qualities of matter are restricted to shape and size, which he calls "extension"; Locke argued that solidity must also be included, so as to distinguish matter from empty space. Both Descartes and Locke held that the so-called "secondary" qualities or properties – color, taste, smell, sound, and temperature – are merely capacities or dispositions that objects have, because of their primary properties/qualities, to produce certain experiences in perceivers.

6 It has been suggested to me that since substance is supposed to underlie a thing's properties rather than its surface, the appropriate thought-experiment here is that of trying to abstract or "think away" all of a thing's properties – an experiment that would lead us to realize that it is only through properties that a thing is perceptible, so that substance itself is not perceptible. Although this alternative way of making the point – that substance is unperceivable – is perfectly acceptable, it is also the case that substance is supposed to underlie a thing's property-*instances*, like the piece of wood's very own shape, size, and color (see note 4 above). Further, as shown by Berkeley's attack on the notion of substratum in his *Three Dialogues Between Hylas and Philonous*, it is hard to see how substance could underlie such instantiated properties unless it existed literally under a thing's surface (1993a: 187–9). But the thought-experiment described in the text shows that the actual removal of all such property-instances leaves nothing perceivable.

7 Berkeley, for reasons akin to Hume's, denies that we can have any *idea* of (even mental) substance. But, notoriously, he insists that we have what he calls a "notion" of mental (though not of material) substance.

8 For an excellent account of Hume's views on identity, and a trenchant, detailed critique of those views along the lines just indicated, see Penelhum 1955 and 1967. Some scholars, however, have tried to show that Hume is not really committed to the view that ordinary judgments of identity are mistaken: see for example Ashley and Stack 1974, and Noxon 1969. Penelhum 1975 replies to Ashley and Stack and to Noxon.

9 Two excellent sources to consult for an orientation to the issue of personal identity are Perry 1975 and Shoemaker and Swinburne 1984.

2 HUME'S THEORY OF KNOWLEDGE (I)

1 It may be objected that the use of the term "knowable" represents Hume as holding that there are two *kinds* of "*knowledge*," and that Hume restricts knowledge properly so-called to "relations of ideas," and refers to matters of fact as "probabilities." It is true that in the *Treatise*, Hume sometimes uses the term "knowledge" in a way that would restrict its application to what, in the *Enquiry*, he calls "relations of ideas" (see T:70, 82, 87, and 153). However, in the *Enquiry*, which Hume says, in his prefatory "advertisement" to that work,

represents his final views (should "alone be regarded as containing [my] philosophical sentiments and principles" – see E:2; S:xviii; F:52), he uses the term "knowledge" more broadly. In summing up his epistemology, he writes that reasoning concerning cause and effect (which, we will see, he holds to be our chief way of arriving at beliefs about matters of fact) "forms the greater part of human knowledge" (E:164; S:114; F:194). A little earlier, he says that the "abstract sciences of demonstration" (i.e. relations of ideas) are a "more perfect species of knowledge" (E:163; S:112; F:193). It is true that in the last sentence of the same paragraph, he adds that definitional and mathematical truths "may safely, I think, be pronounced the only objects of knowledge and demonstration." Here the words "and demonstration" are important: they signify that Hume's point is merely to deny that matters of fact are demonstrable, which is indeed what he goes on to say in the next paragraph's first sentence, which reads: "All other enquiries of men regard only matter of fact and existence, and these are evidently incapable of demonstration." There are many other places in the *Enquiry* where Hume applies the term "knowledge" or "know" to matters of fact and/or to the causal relation on which, he will argue, our beliefs in matters of fact chiefly rest (see e.g. E:27–9, 33, 35, 41, 45–6, 64; S:17–18, 21, 23, 27, 29–30, 42; F:73–4, 77, 80, 85, 89, 104). The fact is, then, that Hume sometimes (especially in the *Treatise*) uses the term "knowledge" in a narrow sense, to cover only (what turn out to be the *Enquiry*'s) "relations of ideas," and at other times (especially in the *Enquiry*) he uses it in a broader sense to cover both relations of ideas and matters of fact. In this work, I shall use it (or at least the cognate term "knowable proposition") in the broader sense. This terminological choice is largely a matter of convenience; it does not obviate the point that, for reasons that will be evident from the overall exposition of Hume's theory, knowledge of relations of ideas is for Hume indeed a "more perfect species of knowledge" than is knowledge of matters of fact.

2 The term "Fork" presumably stems from the way Hume's doctrine bifurcates knowable propositions into two types, and also from the aggressive use he makes of the doctrine in attacking Rationalist metaphysics.

3 The reason for the qualification "non-abstract" is the following. As Hume's examples show, his "relations of ideas" include mathematical propositions. Now some philosophers believe that mathematical propositions assert the existence of purely mathematical entities, such as numbers and geometrical figures. If we said simply that Hume's relations of ideas do not assert the existence of any entities, this would commit him to saying that these philosophers are mistaken. But although Hume would almost certainly have agreed that they are mistaken, nothing in his doctrine of the "Fork" commits him to a position on this controversial matter; this doctrine is neutral on the question of whether mathematical entities can be said really to exist. The purpose of the term "non-abstract" is to capture this neutrality. For if mathematical entities do exist, then they are abstract entities the existence of which does not depend on the existence of physical objects or mental objects or on the states of such objects, and of which it would be nonsensical to say that they had a beginning or an end in time. The number "2", for example, would not cease to exist if no pairs of things existed in the world, or if no one was thinking about that number; nor would there be only one "2" at a time when only one person was thinking of "2" and two "2s" when two persons were thinking of "2". By stipulating that relations of ideas do not assert the existence of any non-abstract entities, then, we leave open the question of whether they assert the existence of abstract ones such as numbers. We commit Hume only to the claim that relations of ideas do not assert the existence of non-abstract or "concrete" things like physical objects, minds, and such things' states.

4 Hume's use of "intuitively certain" in the *Enquiry* is thus different from Locke's notion of "intuitive knowledge" in his *Essay Concerning Human Understanding*. There Locke holds that the "agreement" or "disagreement" between some ideas is intuitive knowledge

(1975: 530–1); such relations between ideas would also be "intuitively certain" in Hume's sense. However, Locke also holds (1975: 537) that we have an intuitive knowledge that we have a given idea in our minds. As I indicated on p. 36, such introspective knowledge is not "intuitively certain" in Hume's sense.

5 So Hume's notion of "demonstratively certain" is the same as Locke's notion of demonstrative knowledge, namely: knowledge that is deduced from items of intuitive knowledge (Locke 1975: 531 and 533–4). But there remains the difference, mentioned in the previous note, between Locke's notion of those latter items and Hume's more restrictive notion.

6 This claim will be supported in part 5 of the present chapter and in parts 2 and 3 of Chapter 3.

7 More fundamentally, many philosophers would hold, following Kant, that no statement is knowable *just* by experience, because all knowledge requires conceptualization, which is a mode of thought that contrasts with the raw data of experience.

8 The *locus classicus* of Quine's attack on the analytic–synthetic distinction is his "Two Dogmas of Empiricism" (see Quine 1953: 20–46). One of the many responses to Quine is Grice and Strawson's "In Defense of a Dogma" (1956: 141–58). For a bibliography that lists many works relevant to this issue, see Moser 1987: 210–19.

9 Kant himself defined an analytic judgment as one such that the concept of the predicate is contained in the concept of the subject. Most contemporary philosophers, however, regard this definition as too restrictive, since it entails that only statements having a subject–predicate form ("S is P") can be analytic.

10 The standard example is actually "all bachelors are unmarried males." However, since, as the text goes on to indicate, the statement's analyticity is supposed to stem from its being a definition, and since neither male infants nor male non-humans are bachelors, we have altered the example a little.

11 Epistemologists generally accept the principle that "S knows that p" entails that p is true as an analytic truth turning on the meaning of "knows" – as a conceptual truth about knowledge. According to this "truth-condition" (as it is called) for knowledge, one cannot *know* things that are not so (e.g. that the earth is flat), though of course this does not mean that one cannot *believe* such things. Statements that seem to violate this principle – "Little Johnny just knows that there is a tiger under his bed" – are regarded either as simply false, or else as employing a non-standard or deviant sense of the term "knows."

12 I am indebted to Mr Adam Wilcox for first bringing this point to my attention, thereby setting into motion the train of thought in this part and the next.

13 The restriction of the range of "p" to consistent propositions is appropriate, because the argument attempts to demonstrate a conclusion about *knowable* propositions, and inconsistent propositions, being false, are not candidates for such knowability. But the argument could, for the sake of greater generality, be formulated without the restriction. It would have to be stipulated that "analytic" applies to analytically false as well as to analytically true propositions. Then premiss (1) could be formulated as "If p is not true or false solely in virtue of meanings, then p is true or false in virtue of some feature of reality;" and the phrase "true solely in virtue of meanings" could be replaced by "true or false solely in virtue of meanings" throughout the rest of the argument. Of course, the term "knowable," as it occurs in the argument, would have to be interpreted as "knowably true or knowably false," rather than as "knowably true."

14 For the benefit of readers who are familiar with symbolic logic, a formal proof of step 11 is given below.

Derivation of (11) from (7), (9), and (10):

1.	K ⊃ (R v E)	line (7)
2.	R ≡ A	line (9)
3.	K ⊃ (A v S)	line (10)
→4.	K	assumption for conditional proof
5.	R v E	1, 4, MP
6.	A v S	3, 4, MP
7.	R ⊃ A	2, Equiv.
8.	A ⊃ R	2, Equiv.
→9.	~(A & R)	assumption for conditional proof
10.	~A v ~R	9, DeM
→11.	~S	assumption for indirect proof
12.	A	6, 11, DS
13.	R	8, 12, MP
14.	~A	10, 13, DN, DS
15.	A & ~A	12, 14, Conj.
16.	S	11–15, Indirect Proof
→17.	~E	assumption for indirect proof
18.	R	5, 17, DS
19.	A	7, 18, MP
20.	~R	10, 19, DN, DS
21.	R & ~R	18, 20, Conj.
22.	E	17–21, Indirect Proof
23.	S & E	16, 22, Conj.
24.	~(A & R) ⊃ (S & E)	9–23, Conditional Proof
25.	(A & R) v (S & E)	24, Impl.
26.	K ⊃ [(A & R) v (S & E)]	4–25, Conditional Proof (= line (11))

Key: K: *p* is knowable; R: *p* is a priori; A: *p* is analytic; E: *p* is empirical; S: *p* is synthetic.

15 The fact that the predicate-term of MV is disjunctive (contains an "or") does not matter here. At the level of analysis relevant to the present context, "all crows are black" has the same logical form as "all crows are male or female."

16 The ontological argument for the existence of God, which was invented by St. Anselm (1033–1109), modernized by Descartes, and famously criticized by Kant, attempts to prove that God exists from the very definition of God as an unsurpassable or perfect being. Although the argument has some defenders even today, notably Charles Hartshorne and Alvin Plantinga, most contemporary philosophers regard it as an unsound argument.

17 As before, "Section IV" in this part refers to Section IV of Hume's *Enquiry Concerning Human Understanding*.

18 Passages where Hume gives noncontradictoriness of the denial as the reason why no matter of fact is demonstrable include: paragraphs 2 and 18 in Section IV of the *Enquiry* (E:25, 35; S:15, 22; F:71, 79); paragraph 5 of Section XII, part III of the *Enquiry* (E:164; S:113; F:193–4), the *Treatise* Book I, part iii, Section 3, paragraph 3 (p. 79); paragraph 11 of the *Abstract* (T:650; S:130; F:34); and *Dialogues Concerning Natural Religion*, Part X, paragraph 5. In only one of these five passages does Hume's wording unambiguously imply that noncontradictoriness of the denial is also the reason for a proposition's failing to be self-evident. This is the passage from the *Treatise*, where, in criticizing the causal maxim (the principle that every beginning of existence must have a cause of existence), Hume says: "But here is an argument, which proves at once that the foregoing proposition is neither intuitively nor demonstrably certain," and then goes on to give an

argument turning on the noncontradictoriness of the maxim's denial. However, in actually stating the argument, "intuitively certain" is not again mentioned, and the whole argument is cast so as to show only our inability to "demonstrate the necessity of a cause," or to "prove" or give a "demonstrative proof" of the causal maxim. Furthermore, Hume wrote the *Treatise* before fully formulating his distinction between relations of ideas and matters of fact in the *Enquiry,* and he explicitly asked that the *Enquiry* and not the *Treatise* be taken as representing his final position. For these reasons, the passage from the *Treatise* provides little if any support for the view that the non-contradictoriness of denials of matters of fact is Hume's considered reason for denying their self-evidence.

19 Here and below we abstract from the consideration that Hume would presumably include also empirical negative existential propositions in the class of matters of fact. Since Hume does not explicitly discuss such propositions, I shall for simplicity's sake continue to speak as if his matters of fact included only propositions that assert or imply existence.

20 If empirical negative existential statements are included among matters of fact, then the premises of the argument need to be revised by adding "or denies existence" to "*p* asserts or implies existence" in each. But it seems clear that this revision would not weaken the argument.

3 HUME'S THEORY OF KNOWLEDGE (II)

1 See for example Beauchamp and Rosenberg 1981: Chap. 2; Capaldi 1975; and Wilson 1983: 661–94; 1985: 52–68; and 1986: 611–28. The main inspiration for naturalistic readings of Hume's philosophy is Smith 1941.

2 See for example Fogelin 1985; Stove 1979: 203–25; and Penelhum 1992: 107–13.

3 For an excellent critique of the view that Hume's negative points about induction are intended only to discredit rationalist or "deductivist" views about knowledge, see Garrett 1997: 83–91. Among other telling reasons against such an interpretation, Garrett points out that it would render otiose Hume's famous point (to be discussed in the text below) that it is not possible to give even an inductive justification of induction.

4 In step (i), the full meaning I am giving to the term "inductively" is "by inductively correct reasoning from rationally acceptable premises," but for the purpose of making the present terminological point, the reference to the premises can be omitted.

5 Such an objection is made in Fogelin 1993: 97–8.

6 See part 5 of Chapter 2, where principle (P) was introduced and where the principle was shown to follow from Hume's definition of "demonstrable," together with the basic logical point that it is always a contradiction to affirm the premises and deny the conclusion of a valid argument.

7 For the argument showing that no matter of fact of either type is self-evident, see Chapter 2 part 5; for the argument showing that no matter of fact that asserts existence is demonstrable, see part 2 of the present chapter.

8 Here and below, it should be remembered that "inductive" is being used to mean "inductively correct."

9 It is possible to use the term "inductively correct" in such a way that it also applies to deductively valid arguments, because deductively valid arguments can be said to confer a probability of 1 on their conclusions. In discussing Hume's problem of induction, however, it is appropriate to use the terms "deductively valid" and "inductively correct" as mutually exclusive ones, as we are doing here, since the problem Hume raises about induction pertains only to arguments that are not deductively valid.

10 Alternatively, step (b) could be put as: "if *p* follows from some self-evident statements, then affirming those statements while denying *p* entails a contradiction."

11 The reasoning from (a) and (b) to principle (P) was presented in part 5 of Chapter 2.

12 Several different treatments of the problem of induction, and a bibliography, can be found in Swinburne 1974. Several recent discussions of the problem, addressed directly to Hume's treatment of it, can be found in Tweyman 1995.

13 Those who read Hume as holding that induction is irrational sometimes suggest that Hume simply assumes that an inductive argument is illegitimate unless it can be converted into a deductively valid form – that he is a "deductive chauvinist" who thinks that the only legitimate kind of reasoning is deduction. Inductive scepticism is then supposed to follow quite easily from this assumption plus the point that induction cannot be converted into deduction. Even if we granted for the sake of the argument that Hume holds that induction is irrational, such an analysis of his position would be deeply flawed; for it renders otiose his entire demonstration that an inductive justification of induction would be circular: if deduction is assumed from the outset to be the only legitimate type of reasoning, then what need is there to *argue* that an inductive attempt to justify induction cannot work? To show that Hume's position leads to inductive scepticism, one need make only the weaker assumption that induction stands in need of *some* justification. That this justification must be deductive in nature then follows as a corollary, because it would be circular to give an inductive justification of induction.

14 This illustration is based loosely on a strategy that the Cambridge philosopher G. E. Moore (1873–1958) used in order to respond to arguments for the unreality of time advanced around the turn of the century by Idealist philosophers such as F. H. Bradley (1846–1924). See Moore 1970: 209–10.

15 Perhaps, indeed, this point should be put in a more positive way: we can gratefully accept Hume's profound demonstration that induction cannot be justified, without having to swallow the sceptical moral that is sometimes drawn from it.

16 Our account of Hume's achievement may be usefully compared and contrasted with the account given by Garrett 1997. Garrett writes (pp. 91–5):

> Hume should be interpreted quite literally, as making a specific claim, within cognitive psychology, about the relation between our tendency to make inductive inferences and our inferential/argumentative faculty: he is arguing that we do not adopt induction on the basis of recognizing an *argument* for its reliability, for the utterly sufficient reason that there *is* no argument ("reasoning" or "process of the understanding") that could have this effect . . . . His point is that [inductive inferences] are reasonings that are not themselves produced by any piece of higher level reasoning: there is no argument that could lead us to accept the conclusion that inductive reasoning will be reliable if we did not *already* accept that conclusion in practice . . . . This interpretation of Hume's conclusion [is that it is] a claim that we are not caused to engage in induction by grasping an independent argument supporting its reliability, because there is no such argument available . . . . He is denying only that we come to engage in this species of reasoning as a result of any piece of reasoning *about* it . . . . Hume's famous argument . . . is one of the most persuasive arguments for a true and fundamental thesis in cognitive psychology.

As the passages compacted into this extract indicate, Garrett does not attribute to Hume the view that induction is in any way unreasonable or irrational. On the contrary, he explicitly rejects such an interpretation of Hume. For he says (p. 92):

> This absence of a determining argument for the practice of induction is, Hume implies, initially surprising. He is well aware that it leaves room for us to raise a theoretical question about the legitimacy of inductive inference.

But it does not entail that induction must be without evidentiary value, and Hume does not ever write as though he thinks that it does . . . . [H]e concludes only that we are not led to make inductive inferences by grasping a supporting argument, on the quite sufficient grounds that there is no such argument that could move us unless we were *already* inductive thinkers. Whether and in what sense induction is "reasonable" or provides "evidence" or increases "probability" in spite of this lack remains, at the close of the famous argument, an as-yet-unanswered question.

According to the position we have taken, Garrett's claim – Hume's argument leaves open the question of whether induction is reasonable – is exactly right, since we have argued that T3 does not imply inductive scepticism. However, Garrett also studiously declines to attribute to Hume *any* conclusion of a normative kind pertaining to the justification of induction; he regards Hume's conclusion as being only "a true and fundamental thesis in cognitive psychology." As he also puts it: "Hume's conclusion, as stated, directly concerns the *causation* of inductive inferences – a question in cognitive psychology – rather than the *justification* of such inferences, which is a question in epistemology" (p. 94).

I see no convincing reason for construing Hume's conclusion so narrowly. If Garrett's point is only that Hume *states* or *expresses* his conclusion in psychological language, it is quite correct. But if his point is (as it seems to be) that Hume's psychological formulations may not legitimately be interpreted as making more than a claim in "cognitive psychology," then I disagree. Garrett goes on to add (p. 94):

> Nevertheless, Hume's argument also provides good reason to conclude that no argument can show the reliability of induction by argument without *presupposing* that reliability. The failure of subsequent attempts to "justify" induction without begging the question, and thereby to solve "Hume's problem of induction", is convincing testimony to the strength of Hume's position.

How is this different from saying that Hume's argument shows that induction cannot be rationally justified? Garrett's point seems to be that the argument does indeed establish this normative epistemological conclusion, but that this conclusion is no part of, or that it goes beyond, what Hume intended his own argument to establish. This implies either (a) that Hume believed that his argument had no bearing on the possibility of justifying induction, or (b) that he was blind to the epistemological bearing of his argument, or (c) that he was aware of it but did not want his readers to believe that he was aware of it. But (a), (b), and (c) are simply not credible. Alternatively, Garrett might claim (d) that Hume expected or wished his readers to draw the obvious epistemological conclusion for themselves – just as we have done. But this would be to concede that Hume *did* intend to establish this conclusion after all (even if he did not use the twentieth-century epistemological language of "justification" to express it). Finally, when Garrett concludes his discussion by saying that "Hume's famous argument . . . is one of the most persuasive arguments for a true and fundamental thesis in cognitive psychology," does it not understate Hume's achievement to decline from saying that it is also one of the most persuasive arguments for a true and fundamental thesis in epistemology?

4 HUME'S THEORY OF CAUSALITY

1 The proponents of the "New Hume" include: Craig (1987); Livingstone (1984); Strawson (1989); and Wright (1983). A more complete bibliography is given by Winkler 1991: 578–9.
2 This is strongly maintained by Strawson, Wright, and Livingston in the works cited in the previous note.

3 In fairness to proponents of the New Hume, it should be noted that they are aware of this problem, and try to deal with it. Their attempts to to do so, however, are criticized effectively by Blackburn 1990: 239–41, 245–7, by Botterill 1990: 204–5 and by Winkler 1991: 552–61.

4 Winkler uses "Causation" rather than "necessary connection between events," but by "Causation" (with a capital "C") he means causal powers in objects or necessary connections between events.

5 Hume himself believed, with many of his contempories, that causes which seem to act at a distance are in fact linked by a chain of as-yet-undiscovered contiguous links (T:75). The question of whether action at a distance occurs is too technical to take up here, though it is worthy of note that according to one philosopher of science, certain aspects of quantum mechanics pose a difficulty for those who deny action at a distance (see Sklar 1995: 5).

6 It seems better to speak of observing events as *not violating* clause 2 of D1 than to speak of observing events as *satisfying* that clause, since, of course, we cannot observe that *all* events of one kind are followed by events of another kind.

7 This example is modeled on one given in Broad 1962: 455–6. Broad's example involves factory whistles blowing in Manchester being regularly followed by workers leaving for work in London.

8 In (M″), the clause "all strikings of D-decorated matches that might have existed would be followed by ignition" does not imply "all logically possible strikings of D-decorated matches are followed by ignition" or "in every possible world, striking a D-decorated match is followed by ignition." Such a construal would turn (M″) into the claim that it is logically necessary that striking a D-decorated match is followed by ignition of the match. Rather, the clause implies "for any event e, if it is logically possible that e occurs and e is of the kind: striking a D-decorated match, then if e does occur, then e is followed by an event of the kind: ignition of a D-decorated match." Here the modal operator "logically possible" governs only "e occurs." An equivalent formulation is "for any event e, if e occurs in some possible world and e is of the kind: striking a D-decorated match, then if e occurs in the actual world, then e is followed by an event of the kind: ignition of a D-decorated match." Thus the clause allows that in other possible worlds, such events are not followed by ignition. I am indebted to Kenneth G. Lucey and to Richard Taylor for vigorous discussion of this point (though I do not claim that they would accept my position).

9 The question of the truth-conditions of counterfactual conditionals is an unsolved one in philosophy, and I am certainly not claiming to solve it here. My point is simply that it does not appear that the type of counterfactual conditional involved in a law of nature can be understood only as importing the notion of necessity that the regularity theory eschews.

10 It should also be noted that in a section of the *Treatise* entitled "Rules by which to Judge of Causes and Effects," Hume stresses that not only does "the same cause always produce the same effect," but also "the same effect never arises but from the same cause . . . [so that] where several different objects produce the same effect, it must be by means of some quality which we discover to be common amongst them" (T:174–5). This implies that causes are necessary as well as sufficient conditions.

11 It has been suggested to me that, although the principle that if E_1 is a necessary and sufficient condition for E_2 then E_2 is a necessary and sufficient condition for E_1 holds for what logic calls material implication, it may not hold when E_1 is a causally necessary and sufficient condition for E_2. But it would seem that the principle does hold true in such cases. For example, suppose that striking the middle-C key on a particular piano is a (causally) necessary and sufficient condition for that piano to make the sound middle-C. Then that piano's making the sound middle-C is a necessary and sufficient condition for

the middle-C key to be struck, and the type of conditionality involved is causal (although, of course, given the asymmetry of the causal relation that generates the very problem under discussion, the piano's making the sound middle-C does not cause the middle-C key to be struck; rather, the middle-C key's being struck causes the piano to make the sound middle-C).

5 HUME'S CRITIQUE OF THE CAUSAL PRINCIPLE

1 The term "intuitively or demonstratively certain," and my paraphrase "self-evident or demonstrable," are explained in Chapter 2 part 2.

2 See Chapter 2 part 5, and Chapter 3 part 3.

3 This argument is given by Locke in his *Essay Concerning Human Understanding*, Book IV, Chapter 10.

4 Stroud makes this point, with maximum precision, by noting that "there is a husband who lacks a wife" is not obviously of the form "$\exists x(Fx \& \sim Fx)$;" rather, it seems to be of the form "$\exists x(Fx \& \sim Gx)$".

5 More precisely, "there is a man who has a wife and does not have a wife" is of the form "$\exists x(Fx \& \sim Fx)$," which is a contradiction since the expression within the parentheses has the form "$p \& \sim p$."

6 Here those who interpret Hume as an inductive sceptic would substitute "belief" for "knowledge" and "believe" for "know." This substitution would not affect the logic of Beck's analysis of Kant's position.

7 More accurately, *H* is a proposition that Hume accepts when he puts to one side his scepticism about perception (discussed in Chapter 6), as he invariably does when discussing causality and induction.

8 By "the manifold of empirical intuition," Kant means basically the things that are perceived (seen) as the observer views the scene.

9 Strawson calls reversibility "order-indifference." Thus his way of making the present point is to say that for Kant, "Lack or possession of order-indifference on the part of our perceptions is . . . our criterion . . . of objective succession or co-existence" (1966: 134).

10 For an influential defense of claim (a), see Grice 1976: 438–72 (especially 460–5).

11 Referring to Guyer's analysis in her Introduction to a recent English translation of Kant's *Critique of Pure Reason* (1996: 1*n*8), the Kant scholar Patricia Kitcher writes that "although [the argument of the second analogy] has been a very difficult argument to interpret, many current scholars believe that Paul Guyer has recently produced a definitive analysis."

12 In a fuller statement of this argument, incorporating elements of Kant's philosophy that we have not touched upon but that may be familiar to some readers of this book, this premiss might be expanded by adding to it: "or by knowing that these perceptions are of successive states of things-in-themselves, or by knowing that A precedes B by reference to absolute time."

13 Kant himself, as he is usually interpreted, would hold that the world we inhabit *must* conform to our ways of perceiving it, because it is partly *constructed* by our minds. This "transcendental idealism" is a complex and controversial position, from which I have abstracted in this discussion.

6 THE BELIEF IN THE EXISTENCE OF BODY

1 Here it would be very useful to review the discussion of scepticism in Chapter 1, part 1.

2 Descartes' version of the inference can be found in his *Sixth Meditation;* Locke's, in Book IV, Chapter 11 of his *Essay Concerning Human Understanding.*

3 For an informed and sensitive discussion of these issues, see Penelhum 1992: 107–13.

4 It might be asked whether Hume is here illegitimately equating existence "distinct" from ourselves with existence *spatially exterior* to ourselves. In Hume's defense, we may cite a point that Henry E. Allison ascribes to Immanuel Kant; namely, that the only way we can understand a thing's existing distinct from ourselves is to understand it as existing spatially outside ourselves. See Allison 1983: 83–6.

5 Here the term "impressions *of*" must not be taken to mean that the impressions must be caused by – or must in some way actually correspond to – the things "of" which they are impressions; it signifies only that an impression of X is a perceptual experience in which what we *seem* to perceive is (an) X.

6 This is not the only place where Hume is prepared to argue that since a given belief is *false*, it cannot be based on reason. Later in the same section, he argues that " 'tis a false opinion that any of our objects, or perceptions, are identically the same after an interruption; and consequently the opinion of their identity can never arise from reason, but must arise from the imagination" (T:209).

7 There are good bibliographies (as well as reading selections) on this topic in the following anthologies: Hirst 1965; Moser 1986; Swartz 1976. One of the most influential works criticizing the sense-datum theory is Austin's *Sense and Sensibilia* (1962). Finally, several of the arguments for the sense-datum theory are discussed critically in Dicker's *Perceptual Knowledge: An Analytical and Historical Study* (1980).

8 The point of the parenthetical qualification "(in one sense of 'seems')," is that "seems" has a number of different meanings, on at least one of which the object does not even seem to change: if "seems to change" means "is *judged* to change," then it is usually false that an object seen from different angles and distances "seems" to change. But if "seems" is taken in a more descriptive or phenomenological sense, where it describes how the object looks from different perspectives, then (1a) is true.

9 Here "unsound" is being used in accordance with the standard definition of a "sound" argument as one that (a) is logically valid and (b) has all true premisses: since premiss (1) is false, the version of the argument that contains that premiss fails to meet condition (b) and is accordingly unsound.

10 The first example is adapted from one in Chisholm 1978: 27; the second is adapted from Chisholm 1966: 95. Chisholm gives similar examples in many of his writings.

11 Chisholm 1957:151–2. This twentieth-century classic contains Chisholm's first exposure of the sense-datum fallacy. Other lucid accounts of it can be found, among other places, in Chisholm 1966: 94–5 and 1976: 47–52. Chisholm's account in *Person and Object* (1976) is peerless for its lucidity and wit.

12 See H. H. Price's *Perception* (1932: 32), and A. J. Ayer's *The Foundations of Empirical Knowledge* (1940: 8–9). These two works are classic defenses of the sense-datum theory.

13 This way of looking at the sense-datum theory – as an attempt to secure an epistemological objective that can be secured just as well without introducing such special objects of perception as sense-data – receives an in-depth defense in Dicker 1980.

14 Indeed, if the points made at the end of part 6 are right, then the epistemological problems of perception *do* arise independently of the sense-datum theory, and that theory is an attempt to deal with them. See Dicker 1980.

15 This passage is from the "Editor's Introduction" in Berkeley 1979: xxii; the quotation is from Descartes 1979: 15.

16 As the opening clause in this passage shows, throughout his discussion Bennett sees Hume as *not* realizing that a commitment to independent objects implies a commitment to continuously existing objects; Bennett's discussion is thus cast partly as a criticism of Hume for having failed to see this vital link. Indeed, in one place (p. 315) Bennett even says that "in the central mistake of the whole section, [Hume] apparently tries to keep independence upright while allowing continuity to collapse". Although my exposition of Hume in the previous parts of this chapter does not bear out this criticism (because it

presents Hume as offering continuity as the only basis for independence), I shall here remain neutral on whether Hume is really guilty of such a mistake. The important point for present purposes is Bennett's substantive, constructive claim that there is a link between object-independence and object-continuity – a claim that seems to be both correct and illuminating.

17 ". . . [my present perception]" is not an interpolation, but Bennett's own text (1971: 325).

18 There is a large philosophical literature on this sceptical challenge. I have discussed the issue in Dicker 1980. A bibliography can be found in that work (pp. 216–19) and also, among other places, in Moser 1986: 271–84 (especially pp. 271–3 and 283–4).

19 This interpretation is based on Wolff (1963: 105–17). The Kantian text on which Wolff's key point is based is Kant 1963: A105–A108.

20 Hume attempts to account for the unity of consciousness in terms of association in Book I, part iv, Section 6 of the *Treatise*, entitled "Of Personal Identity." But in the Appendix to the *Treatise* (T:635–6), where he recants the view of the self proposed in that section, he seems to realize that such an account cannot work: "All my hopes vanish, when I come to explain the principles, that unite our successive perceptions in our thought or consciousness."

21 According to Wolff, this idea is operative in a preliminary version of Kant's argument, but is superseded in the improved final version by the more powerful notion of "synthesis (basically, reproduction of past experiences) according to a rule". As Dieter Henrich (1994: 236) points out, however, Wolff does not really show that synthesis according to a rule is required for unity of consciousness. It is interesting that, in explicating the final version of Kant's argument, Wolff himself at one point reverts to the idea that what unifies experiences is relation to an object (Wolff 1963: 244–5). My suggestion, which cannot be developed here, would be that a fuller version of Kant's argument does indeed require synthesis (partly because of Kant's analysis of the concept of an object as a concept the application of which requires rule-governed relations of experiences to each other and partly because of the temporality of consciousness), but that synthesis enriches rather than replaces the notion of reference to an object, by implying that the experiences must be conceptualized as being of objects that have rule-governed time-relations different from the time-relations of the experiences themselves.

22 The secondary literature on Kant is immense. A useful bibliography can be found in Guyer 1992. Two introductory treatments of Kant's philosophy are Höffe 1994 and Kemp 1995.

BIBLIOGRAPHY

The secondary literature on Hume is immense. The list of works given below includes only the sources cited in this book. Among the items listed, two contain especially helpful bibliographies: the work edited by David Fate Norton (1993) and the book by Terence Penelhum (1992).

Allison, H. E. (1983) *Kant's Transcendental Idealism: An Interpretation and Defense*, New Haven, CT, and London: Yale University Press.

Ashley, L. and Stack, M. (1974) "Hume's Theory of the Self and its Identity," *Dialogue* 13: 239–54.

Austin, J. L. (1962) *Sense and Sensibilia*, London: Oxford University Press.

Ayer, A. J. (1940) *The Foundations of Empirical Knowledge*, London: Macmillan.

Beauchamp, T. and Rosenberg, A. (1981) *Hume and the Problem of Causation*, New York: Oxford University Press.

Beck, L. W. (1978) "Once More Unto the Breach: Kant's Answer to Hume, Again," in L. W. Beck *Essays on Kant and Hume*, New Haven, CT: Yale University Press.

Bennett, J. (1971) *Locke, Berkeley, Hume: Central Themes*, Oxford: Oxford University Press.

Berkeley, G. (1979) *Three Dialogues Between Hylas and Philonous*, ed. R. M. Adams, Indianapolis, IN: Hackett Publishing Company.

—— (1993a) *Three Dialogues between Hylas and Philonous*, in M. R. Ayers (ed.) *Philosophical Works Including the Works on Vision*, London: J. M. Dent, and Vermont, VT: Charles E. Tuttle.

—— (1993b) *A Treatise Concerning the Principles of Human Knowledge*, in M. R. Ayers (ed.) *Philosophical Works Including the Works on Vision*, London: J. M. Dent and Vermont, VT: Charles E. Tuttle.

Berofsky, B. (1983) "Review of Tom Beauchamp and Alexander Rosenberg, *Hume and the Problem of Causation*," *The Journal of Philosophy*, 80 (8): 478–92.

Blackburn, S. (1990) "Hume and Thick Connexions," *Philosophy and Phenomenological Research*, Fall, supplement vol. 50: 237–50.

Botterill, G. (1990) "Review of Galen Strawson's *The Secret Connexion*," *Philosophical Books* 31 (4): 203–5.

Brenner, W. H. (1989) *Elements of Modern Philosophy: Descartes through Kant*, Englewood Cliffs, NJ: Prentice-Hall.

Broad, C. D. (1962) *The Mind and its Place in Nature*, London: Routledge & Kegan Paul.

Campbell, C. A. (1962) "Self-Consciousness, Self-Identity and Personal Identity," in R. T. De George (ed.) *Classical and Contemporary Metaphysics*, New York: Holt, Rhinehart & Winston, pp. 224–35; originally appeared as Lecture V in Campbell, C. A. (1957) *On Selfhood and Godhood*, London: George Allen & Unwin, and New York: Macmillan.

Capaldi, N. (1975) *David Hume: The Newtonian Philosopher*, Boston, MA: Twayne.

Chisolm, R. M. (1957) *Perceiving: A Philosophical Study*, Ithaca, NY: Cornell University Press.

—— (1966) *Theory of Knowledge*, Englewood Cliffs, NJ: Prentice-Hall, 1st edn.

—— (1976) *Person and Object: A Metaphysical Study*, London: George Allen & Unwin.

—— (1978) "Is There a Mind-Body Problem?", *Philosophic Exchange*, 2(4): 25–34.

Craig, E. (1987) *The Mind of God and the Works of Man*, Oxford: Oxford University Press.

Descartes, R. (1979) *Meditations on First Philosophy*, trans. D. Cress, Indianapolis, IN: Hackett Publishing Company.

—— (1984) *The Philosophical Writings of Descartes*, ed. and trans. J. Cottingham, R. Stoothoff, and D. Murdoch, Cambridge: Cambridge University Press, vol. 2.

Dicker, G. (1980) *Perceptual Knowledge: An Analytical and Historical Study*, Boston, London, and Dordrecht: Reidel.

—— (1991) "Hume's Fork Revisited," *History of Philosophy Quarterly* 8(4): 327–42.

Fogelin, R. J. (1985) *Hume's Skepticism in the* Treatise of Human Nature, London: Routledge and Kegan Paul.

—— (1993) "Hume's Scepticism," in D. F. Norton (ed.) *The Cambridge Companion to Hume*, Cambridge: Cambridge University Press.

Garrett, D. (1997) *Cognition and Commitment in Hume's Philosophy*, Oxford: Oxford University Press.

Greig, J. Y. T. (1932) *The Letters of David Hume*, Oxford: Oxford University Press, vol. I.

Grice, H. P. (1976) "The Causal Theory of Perception," in R. J. Swartz (ed.) *Perceiving, Sensing, and Knowing*, Berkeley, CA: University of California Press.

Grice, H. P. and Strawson, P. F. (1956) "In Defense of a Dogma," *The Philosophical Review* 65(2): 141–58.

Guyer, P. (1987) *Kant and the Claims of Knowledge*, Cambridge: Cambridge University Press.

—— (ed.) (1992) *The Cambridge Companion to Kant*, Cambridge: Cambridge University Press.

Henrich, D. (1994) *The Unity of Reason: Essays on Kant's Philosophy*, Cambridge, MA: Harvard University Press.

Hirst, R. J. (ed.) (1965) *Perception and the External World*, New York: Macmillan.

Höffe, O. (1994) *Immanuel Kant*, trans. M. Ferrier, Albany, NY: State University of New York Press.

Hume, D. (1947) *Dialogues Concerning Natural Religion*, ed. N. K. Smith, London: Thomas Nelson & Sons, 2nd edn.

—— (1975) *Enquiries Concerning Human Understanding and Concerning the Principles of Morals*, ed. L. A. Selby-Bigge and P. H. Nidditch, Oxford: Oxford University Press, 3rd edn.

—— (1978) *An Abstract of a Book lately Published, Entituled, A Treatise of Human Nature, &c*, in L. A. Selby-Bigge and P. H. Nidditch (eds), *A Treatise of Human Nature*, Oxford: Oxford University Press, 2nd edn.

—— (1978) *A Treatise of Human Nature*, ed. L. A. Selby-Bigge and P. H. Nidditch, Oxford: Oxford University Press, 2nd edn.

—— (1988) *An Enquiry Concerning Human Understanding*, ed. A. Flew, Chicago and LaSalle, IL: Open Court Publishing Company.

—— (1993) *An Enquiry Concerning Human Understanding*, ed. E. Steinberg, Indianapolis, IN, and Cambridge, MA: Hackett Publishing Company, 2nd edn.

—— (1993) "My own Life," in D. F. Norton (ed.) *The Cambridge Companion to Hume*, Cambridge: Cambridge University Press.

Kant, I. (1963) *Critique of Pure Reason*, trans. N. K. Smith, London: Macmillan.

—— (1996) *Critique of Pure Reason*, trans. W. S. Pluhar, Indianapolis, IN, and Cambridge, MA: Hackett Publishing Company.

Kemp, J. (1995) *The Philosophy of Kant*, Bristol: Thoemmes Press.

Livingston, D. W. (1984) *Hume's Philosophy of Common Life*, Chicago, IL: University of Chicago Press.

Locke, J. (1975) *An Essay Concerning Human Understanding*, ed. P. H. Nidditch, Oxford: Oxford University Press.

Lovejoy, A. O. (1962) "The Meanings of 'Emergence' and its Modes," in R. T. De George (ed.) *Classical and Contemporary Metaphysics*, New York: Holt, Rhinehart & Winston.

Mackie, J. L. (1974) *The Cement of the Universe: A Study of Causation*, Oxford: Oxford University Press.

MacNabb, D. G. C. (1967) "Hume, David," in P. Edwards (ed.) *The Encyclopedia of Philosophy*, New York: Macmillan, vol. 4: 74–90.

Mill, J. S. (1973) *System of Logic*, Books I–III, in *The Collected Works of J. S. Mill*, ed. J. M. Robson, Toronto: University of Toronto Press, and London: Routledge & Kegan Paul, vol. VII.

Millican, P. J. R. (1995) "Hume's Arguments Concerning Induction: Structure and Interpretation," in S. Tweyman (ed.) *David Hume: Critical Assessments*, London and New York: Routledge, vol. 2: 99–144.

Moore, G. E. (1970) *Philosophical Studies*, London: Routledge & Kegan Paul.

Moser, P. K. (ed.) (1986) *Empirical Knowledge: Readings in Contemporary Epistemology*, Totowa, NJ: Rowman & Littlefield.

—— (ed.) (1987) *A Priori Knowledge*, Oxford: Oxford University Press.

Norton, D. F. (ed.) (1993) *The Cambridge Companion to Hume*, Cambridge: Cambridge University Press.

Noxon, J. (1969) "Senses of Identity in Hume's *Treatise*," *Dialogue* 8: 367–84.

Penelhum, T. (1955) "Hume on Personal Identity," *The Philosophical Review* 64 (4), October: 571–89; reprinted in A. Sesonske and N. Fleming (eds.) *Human Understanding: Studies in the Philosophy of David Hume*, Belmont: Wadsworth Publishing Company, 1965: reprinted also in V. C. Chappell (ed.) *Hume: A Collection of Critical Essays*, New York: Doubleday, 1966, and Notre Dame, IN: University of Notre Dame Press, 1968.

—— (1967) "Personal Identity," in P. Edwards (ed.) *The Encyclopedia of Philosophy*, New York: Macmillan, vol. 6: 95–107.

—— (1975) "Hume's Theory of the Self Revisited," *Dialogue* 16 (3), September: 389–409.

—— (1992) *David Hume: An Introduction to His Philosophical System*, West Lafayette, IN: Purdue University Press.

Perry, J. (ed.) (1975) *Personal Identity*, Berkeley, CA: University of California Press.

Price, H. H. (1932) *Perception*, London: Methuen.

—— (1965) "The Permanent Significance of Hume's Philosophy," in A. Sesonske and N. Fleming (eds) *Human Understanding: Studies in the Philosophy of David Hume*, Belmont, CA: Wadsworth Publishing Company; originally published in *Philosophy* 15: 10–36, 1940.

Quine, W. V. O. (1953) *From a Logical Point of View; 9 Logico-Philosophical Essays*, Cambridge, MA: Harvard University Press.

Robinson, J. A. (1962) "Hume's Two Definitions of 'Cause'," *The Philosophical Quarterly* 12 (April): 162–71; reprinted in V. C. Chappell (ed.) *Hume: A Collection of Critical Essays*, Garden City, NY: Doubleday, 1966, pp. 129–47.

Russell, B. (1912) *The Problems of Philosophy*, Oxford: Oxford University Press.

Shoemaker, S. and Swinburne, R. (1984) *Personal Identity*, Oxford: Blackwell.

Sklar, L. (1995) "Action at a Distance," in T. Honderich (ed.) *The Oxford Companion to Philosophy*, Oxford: Oxford University Press, p. 5.

Smith, N. K. (1941) *The Philosophy of David Hume*, London: Macmillan.

Spinoza, B. (1985) *Ethics Demonstrated in Geometrical Order*, in *The Collected Works of Spinoza*, vol. 1, ed. and trans. E. M. Curley, Princeton, NJ: Princeton University Press.

Stove, D. C. (1979) "The Nature of Hume's Skepticism," in D. F. Norton, N. Capaldi and W. L. Robison (eds) *McGill Hume Studies*, San Diego, CA: Austin Hill Press.

Strawson, G. (1989) *The Secret Connexion: Causation, Realism, and David Hume*, Oxford: Oxford University Press.

Strawson, P. F. (1952) *Introduction to Logical Theory*, London: Methuen.

—— (1966) *The Bounds of Sense: An Essay on Kant's* Critique of Pure Reason, London: Methuen.

Stroud, B. (1977) *Hume*, London: Routledge & Kegan Paul.

Swartz, R. J. (ed.) (1976) *Perceiving, Sensing, and Knowing: A Book of Readings from Twentieth-Century Sources in the Philosophy of Perception*, Berkeley, CA: University of California Press.

Swinburne, R. (ed.) (1974) *The Justification of Induction*, Oxford: Oxford University Press.

Taylor, R. (1967) "Causation," in P. Edwards (ed.) *The Encyclopedia of Philosophy*, New York: Macmillan, vol. 2: 56–66.

—— (1992) *Metaphysics*, Englewood Cliffs, NJ: Prentice-Hall, 4th edn.

Tweyman, S. (ed.) (1995) *David Hume: Critical Assessments*, vol. II, London and New York: Routledge.

Wilson, F. (1983) "Hume's Defence of Causal Inference," *Dialogue* 22(4), December: 661–94.

—— (1985) "Hume's Cognitive Stoicism," *Hume Studies*, tenth anniversary issue (supplement): 52–68.

—— (1986) "Hume's Defence of Science," *Dialogue* 25(4), Winter: 611–28.

Winkler, K. P. (1991) "The New Hume," *The Philosophical Review* 100(4): 541–79.

Wolff, R. P. (1963) *Kant's Theory of Mental Activity: A Commentary on the Transcendental Analytic of the* Critique of Pure Reason, Cambridge, MN: Harvard University Press.

Wright, J. P. (1983) *The Sceptical Realism of David Hume*, Minneapolis, MN: University of Minnesota Press.

INDEX

a posteriori: analytic 45; a priori distinction 11, 41–3; synthetic 45, 52–5
a priori: analytic 45–6, 50–2, 54–5; causal principle 133; induction problem 73; a posteriori distinction 11, 41–3; synthetic 46–9, 52–5
accidental generalizations, causal laws distinction 120–5
accidents 17
action: induction 90–1; will relationship 101–2
Adams, R.M. 183–4
analytic: a posteriori 45; a priori 45–6, 50–2, 54–5; synthetic distinction 41–2, 43–4
anti-Rationalist argument, modernized Hume's Fork 49–50
anticipation, necessary connection 107–8, 115–16
argumentation, inductive/deductive distinction 80
association: psychological 89–90; unity of consciousness 191
asymmetry, of causal relations 126–7, 129
Austin, J.L. 182
awareness: personal identity 32–4; transcendental deduction 190–2

background conditions, causality 127–9
Beck, L.W. 145, 146
belief, definition of 173–4
Bennett, J. 6, 154, 184–9, 205–6
Berkeley, G. 8, 19, 155, 156, 158–9, 160–1
Berofsky, B. 130–1
bodily movement, will relationship 101–2
body: belief in the existence of 154–94; contemporary perspective 183–9;

Kantian response to scepticism 190–4; nature and origin of belief in 163–74; psychological explanation of belief in 161–3; three assumptions 154–61; "vulgar" vs "philosophical" systems 174–8; see also objects
Brenner, W.H. 145, 153
bridging propositions 38–9, 58–60, 83–4
Broad, C.D. 203
bundle theory: of a thing 15, 19, 30, 31; of the self 21, 31–4

Campbell, C.A. 32
causal laws 120–5
causal reasoning: critique of 62–89; custom 75, 89–91, 107; induction problem 73–89; summary 87–9; see also causality
"causal theory of perception" 158–60, 175–8
causality 99–132; anti-sceptical assumptions 8–9; bridging propositions 58; critique of causal principle 133–53; definitions 110–16; existence 38–9; Kantian transcendental argument 143–53; necessary connection 100–10; non-demonstrability 134–40; Rationalist conception of 66–73; regularity theory 116–32; Stroud counter-critique 140–3; see also causal laws; causal reasoning
certainty 36–7, 40–1, 135; see also demonstrability; self-evidence
change: argument from 15–17, 21–3, 30; identity through 23–31
chaos, induction 96
Chisholm, R.M. 180–1
circularity, inductive inference 79, 84–6
Clarke, S. 138
classes, similarity theory 118–19

co-presence 192
coherence 169–71, 184–6
coincidences *see* accidental generalizations
collateral effects 130–2
conceivability, causal principle 142–3
conceptualization 192–4
conditionals, counterfactual 121–2
conditions, sufficient/necessary distinction 125–30
conjunction, constant 107–8, 114, 115
connection, necessary 68, 70–1, 99–110, 115–16, 120–1, 124
connectives, logical 43–4
consciousness: introspection 21; unity of 190–2; *see also* awareness
constancy 169–73, 184
constant conjunction 107–8, 114, 115
"containment" view of causality 67–8, 69–70
contiguity, spatial 112–13
continuity: spatiotemporal 24–31; of unperceived objects *see* object-continuity
contradiction: analyticity 44; causal principle 137, 141–3; induction problem 82–4; matters of fact 56, 58–60; object-continuity 185–6
contrary-to-fact conditionals *see* counterfactual conditionals
counterfactual conditionals 121–2
custom: induction problem 75, 89–91; necessary connection 107–8

"deceiver argument", Cartesian scepticism 7–8, 183–4, 188–9
deduction: causality 68–9, 71–2; induction distinction 80; justification of induction 92–3; necessary connection 103–4; Rationalist method 1–2
demonstrability: causality 71–2, 133–4, 135–40, 143; induction 82–4, 88; matters of fact 40–1, 58–60; a posteriori propositions 64–5; relations of ideas 36–7; *see also* demonstrative reasoning; self-evidence
demonstration *see* demonstrability
demonstrative reasoning 78–82, 88; *see also* demonstrability
Descartes, R.: causality 67; demonstration 40; dualism 1; scepticism 7–8, 183–4; substance theory 15, 17, 196; synthetic a priori propositions 47
determinable properties 16–17

determinate properties 16–17
double existence of perceptions and objects 167, 175–7
dualism, Cartesian 1, 15

effects: collateral 130–2; present in the cause 66–8, 69–70
Empiricist view of meaning 13–14, 34; *see also* "meaning-empiricism"
Empiricists: Hume's Fork 41, 52–3; Rationalist agreement with 45–6; Rationalist conflict with 46–9; *see also* Empiricist view of meaning; "meaning-empiricism"; "principle of empiricism"
enduring states of affairs, events distinction 145–8
events: enduring states of affairs distinction 145–8; objects relationship 111–12
evidence, inductive justification 93–4
existence: causality 63, 134, 135–8, 140–2; matters of fact 38–9; a posteriori propositions 64–5; relation of ideas 37; self-evidence 57; syntheticity 53–4
expectation *see* anticipation
experience: a priori/a posteriori distinction 42; as source of ideas 5; causal reasoning 64–6; conscious states 2; inference from see induction; transcendental argument for the causal principle 143–53; transcendental deduction 190–4; will/thought relationship 103; *see also* Empiricists; sense experiences
experimental method, Newtonian 2–3
external world *see* body

fact: matters of 35–41; causal reasoning 61, 62–3; non-demonstrability of 58–60, 82–4; self-evidence 55–8, 83–4; synthetic a posteriori comparison 53–5
falsifiability 11; synthetic a posteriori propositions 52–3
force *see* power

Garrett, D. 114, 195, 201–2
generalizations, accidental/causal distinction 120–5
God: anti-scepticism 8; causality 67–9, 105–6; ontological argument for the existence of 199
Goldbach's Conjecture 142

Guyer, P. 151–3

habit *see* custom hallucinations 6, 7, 157, 192
Hobbes, T. 137–8
human nature: belief in external world 161–3; custom 75, 89–91; science of 3
Hume's Fork 35–60; matters of fact 35–6, 38–41, 53–60; modernized version 41–55; relations of ideas 35–7, 46, 53–5

ideas: definition of 5; immaterialism 160–1; impressions distinction 6, 8; impressions relationship 9–10, 11–12, 13–14; innate 2; of memory 173–4; mental causation 102–3; necessary connection 100, 104–5; perception of 155–61, 178–83; self 19–21; substance 18–19; *see also* relations of ideas; "Way of Ideas"
identity: constancy 171–3; spatiotemporal continuity 24–31; through change 15–17, 23–31; *see also* personal identity
illusion, argument from 156–7, 181–2
imagination, object-continuity 169, 172–3, 176–7
immaterialism 8, 158–9; Hume's rejection of 160–1
impressions: causal inference to bodies 158–60; constancy/coherence of 170–1, 172–4; definition of 5; ideas distinction 6, 8; ideas relationship 9–10, 11–12, 13–14; necessary connection 100–1, 104, 106–7; object-continuity 166–7; object-independence 164–5; perception of 155–61, 178–83; self 19–21; substance 18–19; "vulgar" vs "philosophical" systems 174–8; *see also* sense-datum theory; sense experiences
independence, of unperceived objects *see* object-independence
induction: deduction distinction 80; deductive reasoning 92, 201; inference of bodies from impressions 160; justification of 91–8; Kantian transcendental argument 145; principle of 39; problem of 61, 64, 73–89, 112; psychological explanation of 89–91, 162; *see also* inductive reasoning; inference
inductive reasoning 78–82, 84–6, 88; psychological explanation of 89–91, 107
inference: bridging propositions 38–9;

causal relations 71, 107; counterfactual conditionals 121; from experience *see* induction; from impressions to bodies 158–60
innate ideas, Lockean denial of 2
instinct: belief in external world 161–2; inductive reasoning 90–1
introspectible experiences 5
introspection 2–3; inductive reasoning 82; mental substance 19–21; necessary connection 101; unity of consciousness 191
"inward" sensations 5
irregularity, induction 96
"irreversibility" argument, Kantian 147–51

justification, of induction 75–6, 91–8

Kant, I.: argument from the awareness of succession in time 32, 34; causal laws 123; a priori/a posteriori distinction 41–2; synthetic a priori judgements 48–9; transcendental argument for causal principle 143–53; transcendental deduction 190–4
Kemp Smith, N. 195
knowledge 35–98; causal reasoning 61–98; Hume's Fork 35–60; Hume's uses of term 197–8; via perception 183; transcendental deduction 192–4

language, natural/logical variations 141
law, analogy with induction 95
laws of nature 39; causality 113, 116; generality of 122; induction 78; regularity theory 116–17; *see also* causal laws
Leibniz, G.W. 1
Locke, J. 2, 8, 67–8, 139, 197–8, 204
logic: causal relations 68–9, 71–2; contradiction 58–60, 141
logical connectives 43–4
logical necessity, natural necessity comparison 116
Logical Positivists 46, 49
Lovejoy, A.O. 67

Mackie, J.L. 120
Malebranche, Hume's critique of 105–6
material things *see* body
matters of fact 35–41; causal reasoning 61, 62–3; non-demonstrability of 58–60,

82–4; self-evidence 55–8, 83–4;
synthetic a posteriori comparison 53–5
meaning 5–34; impressions and ideas
5–14; self 19–21, 31–4; substance
15–31; test for 12–14, 18–19, 21, 100,
109–10; verifiability criterion of 49; *see
also* "meaning-empiricism"; nominalism
"meaning-empiricism" 13–14, 19, 21
memory 62, 173–4
mental causation 102–3
mental substance *see* mind
method: Newtonian 2–3; scientific 123–4
Mill, J.S. 127–8
mind: bundle theory of 21, 31–4;
introspection 2–3, 19–21; perception
155; substance theory 15, 17
mind-body problem, necessary connection
101–2
movement, bodily 101–2

natural necessity 116–17, 121, 124–5,
149–50; *see also* necessary connection
naturalism, psychology of human nature
161–3
nature: laws of 39, 113, 116, 116–17, 122;
principle of the uniformity of *see*
induction; *see also* natural necessity
necessary conditions, causality 125–30
necessary connection: causality 68, 70–1,
99–110, 115–16; regularity theory
120–1, 124; unity of consciousness 191;
see also natural necessity
necessity: Kantian irreversibility argument
149–50; regularity theory 116–17, 121,
124–5; *see also* logical necessity;
necessary conditions; necessary
connection
New Hume interpretation 108–9
Newton, I. 2
nominalism 119–20
non-being 139–40
nothingness *see* non-being

object-continuity 163, 166–74, 174–8,
185–6, 187–9
object-independence 163–6, 175, 186–7,
188–9
objectivity, as criterion for impressions 6
objectivity-concepts 184, 187–9
objects: events relationship 111–12;
perception of 156, 157–8, 179–83;

transcendental deduction 190–4; *see also*
object-continuity; object-independence
observation: of causal events 100–1, 115;
transcendental argument 144
Occasionalism, critique of 105–6
ordinary language philosophy, inductive
justification 95–6
"outward" sensations 5

particularity, accidental generalizations
121–2
perception: "argument from causal facts"
156, 181; "argument from illusion"
156–7, 181–2; "argument from
perceptual relativity" 156, 179–81;
bundle theory of mind 32; causal
(representational) theory of 158–60,
175–8; definition of 5; double existence
theory 167, 175–7; epistemological
arguments 157–8, 182–3; of ideas
155–61, 178–83; immaterialism 160–1;
knowledge 62; object-continuity 163,
166–74, 185–6, 187–9; object-
independence 163–6, 175, 186–7,
188–9; scepticism 7–8, 183–4; of
substance 17–19; transcendental
argument for the causal principle 144,
145–6, 147–53; transcendental
deduction 190–4; "vulgar" vs
"philosophical" systems 174–8; *see also*
sense experiences
personal identity 19–21, 31–4;
psychological explanation of 162–3
"philosophical" system of sense-perception
174–8
physics, experimental method 2
Plato 156
Positivism *see* Logical Positivists
power, causal 77, 104–5, 108–9
prediction: causal relations 66; perception
186–7
Price, H.H. 13
"principle of empiricism" 9–13, 99–100
principle of the uniformity of nature *see*
induction
probability, inductive reasoning 78–9
probable reasoning *see* inductive reasoning
properties: accidental 17; argument from
change 15–17, 21–3; bundle theory 15,
19, 30, 31; determinate/determinable
distinction 16–17; identity through
change 25–6; nominalism 119–20

psychology: of human nature 75, 162–3; inductive reasoning 89–91

qualities, inference 76–7
Quine, W.V.O. 43, 142, 198

Rationalists: causality 66–73, 144; Empiricist agreement with 45–6; Empiricist conflict with 46–9; Hume's Fork 40–1, 49–50; Hume's reaction against 1
rationality: of induction 91–8; naturalistic alternative 161–3
realism, scientific 22, 26
reality, synthetic propositions 51–2
reason, perception of objects 165–6, 168–9
reasoning: causal 62–89, 73–89, 75, 89–91, 107, 159–60, see also causality; demonstrative 78–82, 88; inductive 78–82, 84–6, 88, 89–91, 107
reflection, impressions of 5, 18–19
regular succession see regularity theory
regularity theory 115–16, 116–32; causal laws vs accidental generalizations 120–25; collateral effects 130–2; similarity problem 117–20; sufficient/necessary conditions 125–30
relations of ideas 35–7, 46; analytic a priori comparison 53–5
"representational theory of perception" 158–60, 175–8
resemblance 39, 172–4; see also similarity
reversibility, of perceptions 147–51
Russell, B. 85–6

scepticism: Cartesian 6–8, 183–4, 188–9; inductive 92–3, 113; Kantian response to 190–4; of the material world 161, 178
"science of man" 75, 89, 162
scientific method 123–4
scientific realism 22, 26
"secret powers" 76–7, 108–9
self: bundle theory 21, 31–4; as mental substance 19–21
self-evidence: causal principle 133–5; induction 81, 83, 88; matters of fact 40–1, 55–8; relations of ideas 36–7; see also demonstrability
sensation, impressions of see impressions; sense experiences

sensations, "outward"/"inward" distinction 5
Sense Datum Fallacy 181
sense-datum theory 156, 179
sense experiences 5–6, 8, 18–19, 155, 183–4, 185–9
sense-perception see perception
sense-receptors see senses
senses: "argument from causal facts of perception" 156, 181; defective 10–12, 14; object-continuity 168; object-independence 164; reliability of 7–8
sentiments, "outward"/"inward" distinction 5
similarity, problem of 117–20
spatial contiguity 112–13
spatiotemporal continuity 24–31
Spinoza, B. de 1, 68–9
Strawson, P.F. 91, 93–7, 146, 148–50, 204
Stroud, B. 114, 115, 118, 140–3, 204
substance 15–31; argument from change 15–17, 21–3; bundle theory 15, 19, 31; identity through change 23–31; mental 19–21; Rationalist conception of 1; substance theory 15–21, 30, 196; test for meaning 18–19; unperceivability of 17–19
succession in time, argument from the awareness of 32–4
sufficient conditions, causality 125–30
synthetic: analytic distinction 41–2, 43, 44; a posteriori 45, 52–5; a priori 46–9, 52–5

Taylor, R. 117–19, 122–5, 203
temporality: causal relations 112–13, 126; object-continuity 167–8; see also time
time: argument from the awareness of succession in 32–4; see also temporality
"Transcendental Aesthetic" 193
"Transcendental Analytic" 193
transcendental argument, for the causal principle 143–53
transcendental deduction 190–4

uniformity of nature, principle of the see induction
unity of consciousness 190–2
universality, causal theory 112–13

verifiability criterion of meaning, logical positivism 49

vivacity, as criterion for impressions 6, 8

"vulgar" system of sense-perception 174–8

"Way of Ideas" 2, 82

will, necessary connection 101–3

Winkler, K. 108, 110

Wolff, R.P. 191, 206

'This book for b ...
Government refu...
like this is gold-dust. Clear, informative, straig...
wonderful touches of respectful humour. Helping staff and their refugee clients
overcome barriers and restart interrupted careers and lives.'

– Sheila Heard, Managing Director, Transitions London CIC,
Employment Services for Refugee Engineers and Business Services professionals

'Sarah Crowther has dedicated her life so far to making it easy for refugees in
West London to get help, to access services, and to integrate into society. This
wonderful book makes it easy for readers to understand why refugees come to
Britain and the issues they face, and to know what to do to help a refugee in
front of them.'

– Ezechias Ngendahayo, MInstF (Dip), Projects and
Training Coordinator, Development Team, Refugee Council

'This book will certainly help you to get a clearer, more realistic picture of the
present-day challenges refugees face in the UK and worldwide, and it will also
increase your understanding of the complexity of the lives of people in exile.

Reading this will inform you about all the relevant issues. More importantly,
using this book will prepare you to become better at what you do whenever
you help refugees and asylum seekers – regardless of your society, community,
profession or ethnicity, as it provides a wealth of practical knowledge that you
can use to develop a positive, proactive and progressive approach to your work
and the work your organisation does.'

– Oleg Pasichnyi, Ex-Refugee, Member of REAP,
Professional Interpreter / Translator, Social Policy Researcher

'This book transformed my thinking by releasing refugees and asylum seeker
from those static labels into becoming agents of their own lives; by creating a
role for any of us to assist each refugee engage with the access points for public
services. I liked the conversational style, supported with experience and resources.'

– John Murphy, London Churches Refugee Fund and Network

'The kind of book that can be read from any page and deserves a centre space
of a home library.'

– Ayman Uweida, Member of REAP, Professional Interpreter and Refugee

'This book fully appreciates the struggles that refugees and asylum seekers face, such as: identity, health, language barriers, living conditions and education. It tackles these deep and complex issues with an honest and sensitive approach which is important if we aim to have an inclusive, supportive and productive society.'

— Khalida Obeid, Afghan Women's Support Group Coordinator

'With specialist support for refugees dwindling, this book argues we can all expand our roles and expertise to support refugees more effectively. The book offers helpful practical advice, but also successfully navigates complex policy and ethical terrain, providing a valuable snapshot of the state of refugee support in the UK.'

— Asif Afridi, Deputy CEO, brap (UK-based equality and human rights charity)

Working with Asylum Seekers and Refugees

of related interest

A Practical Guide to Therapeutic Work with Asylum Seekers and Refugees
Angelina Jalonen and Paul Cilia La Corte
Foreword by Jerry Clore
ISBN 978 1 78592 073 8
eISBN 978 1 78450 334 5

Safeguarding Children from Abroad
Refugee, Asylum Seeking and Trafficked Children in the UK
Edited by Emma Kelly and Farhat Bokhari
Part of the Best Practice in Working with Children series
ISBN 978 1 84905 157 6
eISBN 978 0 85700 559 5

Art-Making with Refugees and Survivors
Creative and Transformative Responses to Trauma After
Natural Disasters, War and Other Crises
Sally Adnams Jones, PhD
ISBN 978 1 78592 238 1
eISBN 978 1 78450 518 9

Working with Asylum Seekers and Refugees

What to Do, What Not to Do, and How to Help

SARAH CROWTHER

Foreword by Debora Singer MBE

Jessica Kingsley *Publishers*
London and Philadelphia

All materials used or referenced from or via REAP have been
reproduced with kind permission from REAP

First published in 2019
by Jessica Kingsley Publishers
73 Collier Street
London N1 9BE, UK
and
400 Market Street, Suite 400
Philadelphia, PA 19106, USA

www.jkp.com

Library of Congress Cataloging in Publication Data
A CIP catalog record for this book is available from the Library of Congress

British Library Cataloguing in Publication Data
A CIP catalogue record for this book is available from the British Library

ISBN 978 1 78592 317 3
eISBN 978 1 78450 630 8

Printed and bound in Great Britain

MIX
Paper from
responsible sources
FSC® C013604

Contents

Foreword by Debora Singer MBE 12

Acknowledgements 13

1. Introduction 15
What do we expect? 15
Why this book and who is it for? 16
Why this book now – has something changed? 17
Ordinary, unique, active 21
Learning from refugees and this book 25

2. Why It Matters 27
Introduction 27
Question 1: Does it matter whether or not hands-on staff support
    refugees? 27
Doubts and concerns about whether to support refugees. 29
Question 2: Does it matter whether the people I am supporting are
    refugees or not refugees? 33
Summary and conclusion. 39

3. Defining 'Refugee' and Practical Entitlements – on a 'Need
    to Know' Basis 41
Introduction 41
A subjective definition of 'refugee' – based on people's experiences 42
Home Office definitions of 'refugee' – based on future likelihood 44
Popular and political definitions and confusion 55
Entitlements to publicly funded support and services 57
Summary and conclusion. 61

4. Refugees in All Their Diversity – Equality, Discrimination
    and Positive Action 64
Introduction 64
Protecting refugees from discrimination after they arrive in the UK 66
What you mustn't do. 69
What you can do to improve equality 73
The Public Sector Equality Duty (PSED) – what they (and you) must do . 77
Summary and conclusion. 80

5. Engaging with Refugees 82
   Introduction 82
   Access 83
   Motives, means and opportunities – reflect and boost 88
   How to engage – initiating a relationship 95
   Face-to-face engagement 97
   Longer-term relationships 100
   Summary and conclusion. 105

**6. Communicating in English – Plain English, Interpreters and
   Learning English** 107
   Introduction 107
   Narrow the gap 107
   Bridge the gap 109
   Learning English to close the gap 111
   A 'grass roots' model for volunteer-led English group sessions 111

7. Other Organisations, Networking and Advocating for Refugees . . 115
   Introduction 115
   The importance of networking 115
   Referral and the 'One plus One' principle 119
   Tackling third parties for your refugee clients – advocacy, complaints
      and influence 120
   Summary 129

   Introduction to Practical Chapters 8, 9, 10 and 11. 130

8. Roof, Food, Money and Essential Goods 134
   Introduction 134
   Outline of support 135
   Shelter and housing 136
   Money to live, food, clothing and other goods. 144
   Providing money and goods to refugees 148
   Summary and conclusion. 153

9. Health, Mental Health and Disability 155
   Introduction 155
   Physical ill health and wellness 157
   Mental and emotional health and wellbeing 164
   Disability 168
   What can you do? 174
   Conclusion 177

10. Learning English, Training, Employability and into Work 178
   Introduction 178
   Daily English and other non-formal learning 182
   Formal English, ESOL, training, formal education and qualifications . . . 185
   Employability, volunteering and into employment 192
   Conclusion. 206

11. Refugee Children and Young People – With and Without Families   207
    Introduction   207
    Children seeking asylum in the UK and their care   214
    Necessities for daily life – roof, food, money and essential resources
        for life   220
    Health, mental and emotional health and disability   223
    Learning English, education, training   226
    Conclusion   234

12. In Need of Refuge   235
    Introduction   235
    What is refuge?   236
    Who is a refugee?   239
    I don't want to be a refugee   241

    Acronyms   243

    Glossary.   244

    Appendix A   249

    Appendix B   261

    References   264

    Index   265

List of Boxes

CHAPTER 1

Box 1.1: 'We don't do refugees' 20
Box 1.2: Objectives 21
Box 1.3: Monitoring your own learning 26

CHAPTER 2

Box 2.1: There, but for the grace of God, goes John Bradford 28
Box 2.2: Aware of current dangers 34
Box 2.3: A discussion tool: I am a refugee 'by experience' 35
Box 2.4: Similarities between refugees and migrants 36
Box 2.5: Differentiating between refugees and migrants 37

CHAPTER 3

Box 3.1: 'A workshop on "How to stop refugees duping us"?' 42
Box 3.2: Credibility – showing you are honest and telling the truth 47
Long Box 3.3: Solicitors, Legal Aid, OISC and what you can do. 48
Box 3.4: Refugee defined in the International Refugee Convention 1951 and
Protocols 1956 51
Box 3.5: A sample of countries and numbers claiming asylum, and outcome of
decisions. 52
Box 3.6: Becoming British – what they need to do and ways you could help . . . 53
Box 3.7: The politics of language 55
Box 3.8: A fishing trip 56
Box 3.9: Persecution should not be confused with prosecution! 57
Box 3.10: Outline of entitlements for asylum seekers and refugees with Leave. . . 60
Box 3.11: Summary of definitions used in this book 61

CHAPTER 4

Box 4.1: Does the Equality Act 2010 apply to my organisation? 65
Box 4.2: Protection from persecution – what happens when you don't have
equality laws. 66
Box 4.3: Women and other 'particular social groups'. 67
Box 4.4: Nine protected characteristics in the Equality Act 2010 67

Box 4.5: How laws override each other, but nothing overrides human rights . . . 69

Box 4.6: Direct discrimination from local life – Case Studies A and B 70

Box 4.7: Forms and examples of illegal direct discrimination, including 'positive discrimination'. 71

Box 4.8: When not understanding leads to discrimination – Case Studies C–E . . 72

Box 4.9: When confusion leads to discrimination – Case Study F 72

Box 4.10: Hostility and discrimination within 'communities' 74

Box 4.11: Equality characteristic monitoring (ECM) and looking for refugees . . . 76

Box 4.12: What are public authorities? Does this affect my organisation? 77

Box 4.13: Further sources on anti-discrimination and equality. 80

CHAPTER 5

Box 5.1: Challenges to access with examples. 84

Long Box 5.2: Different ways organisations handle access, good and bad – Case Studies A–I. 86

Box 5.3: Understanding refugees' motives and improving engagement – some ideas 89

Box 5.4: The debate about charging for services 90

Box 5.5: Communication in English 91

Box 5.6: Tolerating intolerance? 92

Box 5.7: Food as a gift of love 92

Box 5.8: Understanding refugees' means and improving engagement – some ideas 93

Box 5.9: Snow or 'what seems impossible for one person is nothing at all to another'. 94

Box 5.10: Creating the possibility of a relationship – Case Studies J and K 96

Box 5.11: Protecting confidentiality and anonymity 98

Box 5.12: More about making the most of fixed-term activities 103

Box 5.13: Enabling refugees to engage – summary. 105

CHAPTER 7

Box 7.1: Appreciate and reciprocate 116

Box 7.2: Ideas for where to network 116

Box 7.3: Methods to facilitate networking 117

Box 7.4: The 'One plus One' principle 120

Box 7.5: Letters of support and references – credible and effective. 121

Box 7.6: 'Nudge, poke, slap' – some tactics for practice and policy changes 124

Box 7.7: 'Bang on the desk' tactics. 126

Box 7.8: Ideas for adjustments and positive/mitigating activities to request 128

INTRODUCTION TO PRACTICAL CHAPTERS 8, 9, 10 AND 11

Box 1: Summary – some consequences of having to leave and seek refuge 130

Box 2: Means and 'assets' refugees need to engage with formal organisations . . . 132

Chapter 8

Box 8.1: Network, build and change structures – Case Studies A–C 137
Box 8.2: Should we let them sleep in our side room tonight? 138
Box 8.3: If they are being dispersed, or moved out of your area 139
Box 8.4: Entitlements to shelter and accommodation for people with different immigration status 143
Box 8.5: Examples of support for refugees' resources, access to and control of accommodation – Case Studies D–I 144
Box 8.6: Dealing with debt 145
Box 8.7: Aspen cards for asylum seekers' NASS subsistence (living costs) support . 147
Box 8.8: Entitlements to subsistence and money for people with different immigration status 148
Box 8.9: Cash contributions to individuals or a small cash fund 148
Box 8.10: Know your donors and everyone will be happier 150
Box 8.11: Hints on handling donations 151
Box 8.12: Examples of projects and services relating to money, food and goods for refugees: Case Studies J–M 153
Long Box 8.13: How to apply to National Asylum Support Service (NASS) for subsistence and accommodation 154

Chapter 9

Long Box 9.1: Seeking refuge and refugees' health, mental health and disabilities 156
Box 9.2: Entitlements to health care for people with different immigration status . 159
Long Box 9.3: Entitlements to health and mental health care of refused asylum seekers in England 163
Box 9.4: Entitlements to NHS mental health care and treatment for people with different immigration status 166
Box 9.5: Wellbeing in the Care Act 2014 170
Box 9.6: HEAR briefing – transport for disabled asylum seekers and refugees . . . 171
Box 9.7: Entitlements to services and support for disabled people with different immigration status 173
Box 9.8: 'Deaf', 'deaf' and deafened refugees 173
Box 9.9: Challenging authorities on issues known to be important to refugee access to health 177

Chapter 10

Box 10.1: Refugees making their own choices about progress to work – Case Studies A–D 180
Box 10.2: Gender and the single-sex dilemma 182
Box 10.3: People get stuck outside formal learning 183
Box 10.4: Refugees mixing formal and non-formal learning – Case Studies E and F 184
Box 10.5: Examples of volunteers, activists and organisations offering non-formal learning for English – Case Studies G–K 185

Box 10.6: ESOL levels and how well someone can communicate in English 187

Box 10.7: UK NARIC (National Academic Recognition Information Centre) . . . 191

Box 10.8: People have very different skills– Case Studies L and M. 193

Box 10.9: A reference for a refugee 194

Box 10.10: Joining professional bodies 195

Box 10.11: Necessary policies for volunteering and employment 198

Box 10.12: Examples of refugee service/employer collaboration –
Case Studies N and O 200

Box 10.13: Making person specifications more refugee-friendly 202

Box 10.14: Refugees and dealing with the new pressures of finding decent jobs –
Case Studies P–S 205

Chapter 11

Box 11.1: Being aware that children might be from refugee families, even if
born here 207

Box 11.2: The child was hungry. 208

Box 11.3: Countries from which children are fleeing to the UK because of
persecution, conflict and harm 209

Box 11.4: Attacks on asylum-seeking youths. 210

Box 11.5: Private fostering. 211

Box 11.6: Reuniting families 214

Box 11.7: Age disputes 216

Box 11.8: Channelling goods to families and children – Case Studies A–C 222

Box 11.9: Children's mental health –expertise and resources in the voluntary
sector 224

Box 11.10: Examples of projects for wellbeing and emotional health for young
people/refugees – Case Studies D–H 225

Foreword

Anyone could be a refugee.

Each of my parents spent their childhood within a comfortable middle-class family life, assimilated within their country. By their early teens, they had been uprooted by the war in Europe and were living across borders, learning a new language, a new culture, a new school curriculum. They were helped to adapt to their new lives by many British people, the kindness of strangers.

This book provides a brilliant pointer as to how best to provide such help to refugees arriving on these shores three-quarters of a century later.

Refugees are ordinary people fleeing extraordinary circumstances. Whether a man fleeing political oppression, a woman fleeing domestic violence, a gay man fleeing a forced marriage or a woman refusing to wear religious dress, refugees are fleeing some form of persecution. The definition of a refugee is complex, but the warmth radiating out of Sarah Crowther's book reflects a simple empathy that will benefit refugees however you define them.

Having worked with asylum seekers for 14 years, I am all too aware of the complexity of their situation. This can lead to a sense of helplessness. A sense of 'I don't know what I can offer' or, in many cases, 'there is nothing that I can offer'. This book provides a practical, no-nonsense response to this sense of helplessness. It will be welcomed by professionals and volunteers alike, whether in community work, health and social care, education, employment and many other disciplines.

I have known Sarah professionally for many years now and I have always had great respect for her work. I am honoured to write the foreword for this book. It reflects its author's long experience and sound expertise. Its wide-ranging and comprehensive nature will support those who are keen to engage with and support refugees in their midst but would like some advice as to how to go about this.

With this book in hand, the only thing a reader needs is willingness.

Debora Singer MBE
Senior Policy Adviser
Asylum Aid

Acknowledgements

This work exists because of the people I have met over the last 20 and more years; refugees, migrants, practitioners and activists, wise women and men, children.

I started a project management job with Refugees in Effective and Active Partnership (REAP) in 2002 on a two-year contract and have never left, despite other work here and there. I owe a huge debt of thanks to the members, staff and trustees of REAP. I especially want to thank Valey Arya, who started everything, and colleagues over the years: Anab Abdalla, Ayo Olaogun, Emina Cokic, Olesya Khromeychuk, Patrick Wright, Poornima Karunacadacharan, Rachaporn Slater, Renu Bhimbat, Stephanie Yorath. In particular, Ayo who taught me to pause and try to see the world as others see it, and Rachaporn for all her humour, tolerance and support since I started writing this book. Thank you to Stan, for patience.

Members – some now trustees – have opened windows and doors and given me innumerable insights: Oleg Pasichnyi and Ameem Bint Amir, Christopher Geake, Earl Phillip, Ezechias Ngendahayo, Fariha Bhatti, Janpal Basran, Khalida Obeid, Maria de Lourdes Pale, Peter Jones, Santiago Aristizabal. Thank you to the current trustees for permission to use REAP materials in this book. I can only mention a few of many wonderful earlier trustees: Anab Abdallah, Kiran Seth, Sala Salih, Samuel Nersisyan, Seble Ephrem, Yuusuf Guuled. Some individuals are thanked within the text, in relation to specific lessons and ideas for action.

It could also not have been written without the lessons I have learned and people I learned them from, through HEAR – London's Human Rights and Equality Network of voluntary and community organisations. Many years of thanks to Christine Goodall, Tim Brogden and Geraldine O'Halloran and to Mhairi McGhee, to Lisa and Andy, and the many hugely committed people involved in the network.

I have been lucky to meet many extraordinary professional peers and guides who have informed, encouraged and advised me over the years: some are acknowledged below. I would like to highlight Ceri Baldwin, Freda, Tina Wallace, Misak Ohanian, Judith Kramer – much missed. Special thanks to Sheila Heard who suggested I write the book and made it possible. Also to Debora Singer for her wonderful foreword. I am very grateful to Elen Griffiths and her team at Jessica Kingsley Publishers.

And to John Campbell for his expertise; to him and Alex, Eleanor and Nina, who, with Judith Foster and Nicky Crowther, have genuinely helped with their patience and belief in this project and hardly grumbled at all.

Individual chapters have been made possible by the knowledge and personal contributions over years from great numbers of people, including those above and to name just a few:

Accommodation: Ian Scott, Steve Hedley and Team.

English, education and employment: Marcin Lewandowski, Giles Strachan, Nafisa Rahman, Azar Sheibani.

Health, mental and emotional health: Diana Garanito, Helen Pool.

Refugee children: Sharon Long, Rabbi Aaron Goldstein.

Any mistakes, errors or omissions are all mine.

Introduction

*When You Find Yourself Working with
Asylum Seekers and Refugees*

What do we expect?

Most of us expect to decide what kind of life we want to live. It might not be
easy but we can choose what to study and where to live and whether to have a
baby and how to work towards the kind of livelihood and lifestyle that suits us.
We develop our own sense of identity and grow connections with friends and
community networks. We make a home our own, and take care of our families,
raise our children as we see best. We might detour on the way and we all make
mistakes, but these are the choices we make.

Some people face day-to-day realities that remove all those choices: they
face unreasonable and unjustifiable constraints, hostility and discrimination,
humiliation, aggression and violence; they are impoverished and disempowered.
Many ordinary people suffer abuse by powerful players in social or political
systems where other people or the state or the legal system should be protecting
everyone, but they fail to do so. Although many people stand up against such
abuse, when abuse of a few becomes acceptable to the community, and those
who have the power to protect society fail to do so, your only choice is to keep
yourself and your loved ones safe. You change how you dress and act, change
where you shop, change job. When that isn't enough, you have to look for a
place where you and yours will be all right:

A wife leaves the house and moves ten miles away to a women's refuge.

A young man migrates south to London.

A father kisses his wife and children goodbye and gives the driver $500 to take
them over the border.

To escape the harm done by inequality and unbridled discrimination, people like
us leave behind their livelihoods and careers, and walk away from most of their
family and all of their friends, and most of what they have owned and worked
for. They leave the places where they learned everything they know, where they
speak the language, understand 'the System', have contacts. These people end

up in unfamiliar places, not knowing what their future will be, knowing their family is scattered across continents, and that they must start from scratch.

Why this book and who is it for?

Few of us escaped the heart-breaking image of a dead toddler, Alan Kurdi, washed up on a Mediterranean beach on 2 September 2015. For thousands of people across the UK, the immediate impact of meeting a refugee or refugee family for the first time has become a fairly regular, very personal experience. The family that has just walked through your office door is an ordinary family who couldn't carry on living where they lived. Now they are coping with the consequences of everything they have been through. They have to rebuild their lives in an unfamiliar society. Perhaps they will cope fine without your help, but they will probably cope better and rebuild a decent life faster with an extra hand.

In this chapter I am using 'refugees' to mean people who have the experience of coming to the UK to seek safety. In your work, and in later chapters in this book, different terms and definitions are sometimes needed, including those defined in immigration law and others, and I'll clarify those as we get to them.

You might specialise in health, mental health, education, English, youth work, social work, advice, housing, employment. Your field might be sports, arts, food, or engagement, campaigning and fundraising. You might already have extensive experience supporting vulnerable people, or focussing on women, or children with learning disabilities, or older people, for example. This book is for people who work in community, faith, voluntary or statutory organisations. It is also for activists, freelancers, trainers, trustees and volunteers. If you are part of any kind of group or organisation, or just have a new family move in next door and find yourself helping refugees, it is for you. Whatever your role, in most parts of urban Britain today, if you work 'hands on' and face to face in primary, community or local services of any kind, you will find yourself working with refugees.

> If you are a 'hands-on' practitioner or work closely with practitioners, and you find yourself working with refugees, then this book is for you.

Whether planned or not, you will find that with confidence and willingness to adapt, you already have most of the skills and experience you need. You will need a certain amount of new knowledge about refugee issues, entitlements and support, and ideas for adapting your existing activities to see your work through to your satisfaction. Your time and resources are no doubt already stretched, but hopefully you have team and management support and your other service users are sympathetic. But with or without team backup, the **first intention** behind

this book is *to broaden awareness and provide information, sources of expertise and ideas to help you respond effectively to the person in front of you.*

Why this book now – has something changed?

Why this book now? Refugees have always come to Britain. Have the 'flood-gates' opened? Is this book necessary because our systems can no longer cope? In fact, no.

Visibility

With the coverage in the press, it appears that huge numbers of refugees are arriving in Britain, but this is simply not the case. Refugees have always come to the UK, and the asylum system is tightly controlled by the Home Office. Although there are short-term peaks and troughs in 'flow', the annual number of claims for asylum in the UK is little different now to the year 2000 as persecution and war persist around the globe. The number of people being given 'refugee status' has actually dropped (although the definition of 'refugee' needs proper attention and is discussed in Chapter 3).

What has changed is the *political visibility* of refugee flows. Our media revels in dramatic footage of desperate people (almost all of whom are still in other countries), and the news and electoral agenda in Britain swirl around attitudes to foreigners and migration of all sorts as migrant flows and net migration rise and fall. Since the global credit crash and before, 'austerity' policies and changing UK demographics have stretched services and housing in the UK. The public has become sharply aware of who gets what, and refugees are part of that discussion.

Visibility is a double-edged sword. Syrians have been in the news for several years and are met by both compassion and panic. People ring charities because they really want to do something; they offer Syrians a sincere welcome, food, clothing, a bed, money, kindness. But how many British residents are aware that similar numbers of desperate Sudanese are asking for asylum, and how many British people have even heard of Eritrea? As well as the swelling of sympathy, there is the reaction: a news commentator compared them to cockroaches; would-be politicians scream that we are at breaking point.

Apart from numbers arriving to seek asylum now, we don't really know how many refugees are in Britain. History shows that when a country becomes safe again, large numbers of people leave their place of refuge and return home to look for their lost sister, care for their mother, reclaim their land, rebuild their homes. The Home Office has no system for recording how many people who have sought refuge leave of their own will.

You might want to know how many refugees live in your area and where they are from. Such facts would help services prepare and plan. But those numbers don't exist either. We know the larger cities have substantial refugee

populations, especially in more deprived areas where there is cheaper housing and there are larger migrant populations already. More asylum seekers are housed in the cheaper accommodation of the North West than anywhere else in Britain. Many young unaccompanied asylum seekers are in the care of the local authorities that cover the 'ports of entry' such as Heathrow (Hillingdon), Dover (Kent) and in Croydon, where the Home Office handles new claims. But in terms of readying yourself or your organisation, your awareness is what lets you see what isn't easily visible to others.

So this book is not written in reaction to a sudden increase in refugee numbers. Sadly, there will always be another Syria, or Sri Lanka, Srebrenica, Rwanda, Third Reich, Armenia, Tudor Reformation. Where will people flee from in the next ten years (North Korea? Iran?), and will we notice?

Organisations

Refugees have been among our service users for years. Practitioners have been supporting them as part of their daily work, addressing people's vulnerability, complex needs, inclusion and 'reaching the hard to reach'. But as individuals and British society have become more alert to refugees, refugees have appeared on the agenda of organisations that deliver services and support as a *distinctive category* of service user. 'Refugee support' has become a visible, legitimate and urgent concern for practitioners and finance directors alike. It is increasingly written into job descriptions, workplans and budgets.

There are two sides to any organisation. There is the textbook idea that organisations are structured and planned arrangements of people playing different roles, working together to achieve objectives that move towards an agreed goal. And there is the daily lived experience of individual staff and members with personal motivations and dynamic relationships with colleagues. They work within more or less helpful rules and targets, and have to justify their actions to others in the organisation, who in turn report to funders, commissioners and politicians outside the organisation who have different priorities. Senior staff, funders, commissioners and politicians have the power to cut off the resources staff need, in particular their salaries. Outsiders have the power to cut off the resources the organisation needs to exist. There never are enough resources, especially time.

Organisations that serve and support real people are always having to change and react to the complex, unpredictable and even chaotic lives of the people they serve. Unpredictable needs can disrupt organisational activities and processes in ways external judges might not understand. In this context, people within organisations often dread uncertainty and disruption because these create extra demands and could threaten their future.

Refugees' lives often introduce exactly that uncertainty and disruption to the organisations they approach. The people themselves may move through a series of crises, which are unpredictable and hard to manage resources around.

Refugees may be vulnerable on many fronts, and have interwoven needs all happening at the same time – some of which will probably be new to you and your colleagues. They often have few means to draw on as they work towards real-life goals: they don't have a car, or a bank account, or broadband. They aren't familiar with NHS and mental health service workings, nor the school system, local authority housing, tax, benefits, employment law, zebra crossings or other British institutions, systems, culture and manners. They don't have contacts and can be isolated (do *not* assume they have a supportive 'refugee community' to turn to). Some might have postgraduate degrees, but others might not be literate even in their own language. Like any migrant, they may not speak or understand or read and write English.

When you find yourself working with refugees, you will almost always find you are working beyond your job description: adapting plans, relationships, rules, priorities. You and your organisation find yourselves having to invest time and effort to learn new things, which is costly and might only help one person or family. There isn't even a guaranteed return on that investment, because the refugee may be rehoused, deported or may just move tomorrow. Later, when someone new arrives, she or he will be completely different and need different things. In the midst of these unfamiliar demands, you and your colleagues at all levels also have to look after yourselves and protect the organisation.

The **second intention** of this book is *to give practical assistance to your work with refugees, within the real-life world of the organisation.*

Nowhere else to turn

So refugees are more visible, and organisations are now paying them direct attention. The other thing that has changed is specialist support relating to refugees that you might have drawn on in the past. There never was enough, and shifting resources and ideologies in the past decade mean a lot of what was there has gone. Few local statutory or voluntary sectors have refugee services. There is less expertise available and a fraction of the communication links there were in the recent past.

As a consequence, refugees have fewer places they can turn to for help or that you can refer them to, and as a 'client-facing' practitioner there are not many places you can turn for advice/guidance or backup.

Take note, though: even when there were specialist services, there was a tendency across the social and community sector to refer a refugee away to 'a refugee organisation' or 'a refugee community group' because…

'We don't do refugees.'

This often appears to have been because practitioners assumed refugees are somehow different to 'us' – *other* people who needed *other* services, not the people *we* are responsible for helping. Or perhaps this tendency came from

the sense that ordinary people like us cannot help them, we can't cope, we don't know enough, only 'refugee specialists' can help. This is not so. When a refugee has toothache, she or he needs to go to a dentist, not to a refugee organisation. When a woman refugee is isolated, she wants to meet other people, perhaps other women – it doesn't really matter if they are refugees or not, and it might be better if they aren't (see Box 1.1).

Box 1.1 **'We don't do refugees'**

A woman approached us who had a disabled child. She had financial and practical support in place but was lonely and finding it hard to stay positive. We found there was an organisation near where she lived that existed to bring together families and carers with disabled children to break down isolation and create opportunities to socialise and make friends. I was delighted; she was an isolated mother of a disabled child – exactly who they had set up to support.

We rang them and asked for details so she could join their activities. Their reply was: 'We don't do refugees.' All they heard was 'refugee' and they rejected her.

Ironically perhaps, the fact there are so few refugee specialist services left means this 'referring away' can't really happen any more, which might not always be a bad thing. The current situation is that organisations with a specialism in one field – be it children, emotional wellbeing or sport – are finding they must adapt and deepen that specialism to include refugees. This is not new, nor is it only refugees who are affected. Specialists in one field are always adding new expertise to existing expertise. Primary schools built expertise to integrate children with special needs. Disability organisations developed their services to support carers. Women's groups are debating responses to transgender equality.

In other words, there is a new role for hands-on staff who find themselves working with refugees now. Your role is no longer to find out who to refer to. But you don't need to learn a whole new specialism either. You just have to expand the specialist knowledge and experience you already have so you can relate it to refugees. The task will connect your expertise with a broad range of issues and other specialist fields. There is advice and guidance out there to back you up, but the services that produce and provide such resources can't take on the role of giving direct support to your participant, member or client.

So the **third intention** behind this book is *to help you deal directly with what you might previously have been able to refer onwards.* You need to expand your role and expertise, because there is no one else to do the job.

You and integration – What is 'refuge'?
Finally, when you find yourself working with refugees, you also find yourself a potential agent for integration and social change.

When you ring a women's centre and ask them to help you support a refugee ('No, thank you, I don't want you to Google a refugee women's group for me; the person I am supporting would like to come to *your* centre'), you change how they see their role towards refugees too.

When you challenge a doctor's receptionist ('Yes, they are entitled to register with a GP; no, they don't need to have proof of address; yes, I am sure about that. Would you like a copy of the NHS leaflet that explains it?'), you are improving access for other refugees (and other people) at the same time.

When you look someone in the eyes and treat them as an equal, normal human being, you create a slightly healthier, stronger society.

So my **final intention** through this book is *to do my bit so we all make this society a more meaningful place of refuge for people who have lost so much* (Box 1.2).

Box 1.2 **Objectives**

- To broaden awareness and to provide information, sources of expertise and ideas to help you respond effectively to the person in front of you.

- To give practical assistance to your work with refugees, within the real-life world of the organisation.

- To help you deal directly with what you might previously have been able to refer onwards.

- To make this society a more meaningful place of refuge for people who have lost so much.

Ordinary, unique, active

Throughout the book I am going to keep coming back to three central concepts about people who are refugees:

Refugees are ordinary.

Each refugee is unique.

Refugees are active agents of their own futures.

Refugees are ordinary

People are people. They worry about their mother, get cross with their kids, don't mind working but don't want to have to work all the time, like a nice meal, enjoy a good film, have happy and sad memories from childhood, have ideas for the future.

People who have had to escape persecution are still only people, only human, ordinary. They still worry about their mother. Through no fault of their

own, they have been through extraordinary and often traumatic circumstances, and that might make them extraordinary to some extent. However, they are only extraordinary in the way any of us would become a bit extraordinary if we lived through extraordinary times and experiences. No miracles, no exceptional toughness or talent for survival. Not people who are 'better than us at handling death' or who are more used to oppression and loss and therefore don't feel it as much as we would.

> What does she do in those circumstances? What any of us would do, she depresses. It's an ordinary response, no one should be surprised about it. (Paraphrase from health visitor)

They are ordinary: persecution is not. To say refugees are ordinary is not to say it is ordinary to be a refugee. It is not ordinary to be subjected to discrimination, persecution, state-sponsored or state-tolerated aggression, abuse, injustice and violence. That is an entirely different matter. That is never ordinary. It must never become ordinary.

It is easy for you to feel a bit overwhelmed. You feel that if you faced what they have gone through, you would go under: I am just an ordinary person – how could any ordinary person cope with what he has been through? Mostly, like any ordinary person, this man you are talking to has just somehow managed to keep going despite everything. Maybe in similar circumstances I would just about manage to keep going, just about survive – maybe I would become a little extraordinary too? I hope I never find out.

If refugees are ordinary, what are they not?

Ordinary but not hopeless. People might have had experiences that crushed them. You will meet some people who are in the darkest places, but they do not stay there for ever. The seasons come and go, children learn to walk, new friends share delicious food. The past may have been appalling, the present may be tough, and there may be crises, flashbacks and delayed reactions for the rest of their days, but most of the time things are better than they were, and the future should be better than this.

Ordinary and not without standards. Refugees are trying to rebuild their lives and restore their dignity and a sense of pride and positive identity. They have standards and mostly they would like to raise those standards. Charities I have worked for have received 'donated' bin liners of old clothes that donors were probably sorting out to throw away, including stretched bikinis, worn-out and stained trousers, handbags with broken handles. Whether desperate or not, no one wants to be treated as if they are worthless. That is demeaning when really support should be enabling.

Ordinary and not in our debt. No person deserves to be a refugee, no person asks to be a refugee, so where a refugee is given help, it is a necessity, it is about decency – it isn't a loan. It does not mean they are in our debt.

There are lists of 'what refugees have done for us' that keenly proclaim how much more refugees put more into politics, society and the economy than they cost the country in the first few years. But this shouldn't be necessary. What is more, they don't have to earn the right to refuge – it is an essential element of a civilised country that it provides refuge to those who need it; as it is 'in our gift', so we give it. Refugees shouldn't even have to feel grateful. 'Grateful' implies supporters are doing something beyond the call of duty and deserve special recognition. It is fair that any person appreciates the effort another goes to for them, but 'grateful' implies that it would be acceptable not to help them.[1] However, as anyone who has worked with refugees will tell you, the gratitude and reciprocal generosity you sometimes receive can almost be embarrassing.

Ordinary and not angels. In the British population there are British people who are angelically kind and honest, people who are somewhere in the middle (most of us) and people who are genuinely hard to like. So it is with refugees. I am not talking about the crooks who cynically attempt to cheat the asylum system. I just mean average ordinary people, who have escaped danger to find safety, and happen to be truly lovely or actually not very nice. You might be bowled over by the warmth and sincerity of one refugee, only to find the next refugee grumpy, dismissive or a bit manipulative. You might be stunned by how frank and open one person is, while someone else is giving you highly selective information, dressing up the picture they present to you. You may be caught out by one person's liberalism in contrast to the lack of sympathy and sexism shown by another. Generally unpleasant behaviour might be a personal trait, but bear in mind that most of us ordinary people don't behave very well when we are miserable, short on resources, frustrated by endless bureaucracy and constantly anxious.

Ordinary and equal. Refugee does not mean more important or less important. It doesn't mean more entitled or less entitled. It doesn't mean better or worse. Ordinary means equal. People have a right to be treated as equals, with dignity and respect, neither better nor worse than anyone else, regardless of their sex, race and country of origin, religion, sexual identity, age, disability, marital status, whether pregnant or transgender. When we base our work and interactions on everyone being equal and with a right to equal treatment, we have a sound footing to go forwards on.

Ordinary and not 'other people'. The problem of people seeing refugees as 'other' people, 'them' and somehow different to 'us' will no doubt float up in your work, and it surfaces several times in this book.

---

1   Not always grateful. There is a wonderful article by Dina Nayeri called 'The Ungrateful Refugee' (*Guardian*, 4 April 2017), www.theguardian.com/world/2017/apr/04/dina-nayeri-ungrateful-refugee.

Each refugee is unique

Each person who has come here for refuge is unique. (Just as every ordinary person is unique.)

Each person's experiences are unique.

Each person's response to their experiences is unique.

Therefore, their response to their current situation (and their relationship to you) is unique. One person might cry all day, another might stand for election.

There is a huge range of variables (and unique combinations) in each refugee's life: their sex, age, nationality, education, current family situation and so forth. What they went through individually (and with their family) will be completely different to the person from the same town who stands next to them. Their journey though Britain's asylum system will be different to their sister's (Chapter 2).

You will find patterns, though – probabilities and likelihoods. Their entitlements and access to support are fixed by a combination of their asylum or refugee status and other cross-cutting legislation around health and social care, equality, human rights, children's rights and more (Chapter 3). Refugee populations face multiple disadvantages linked with equality characteristics, such as mental health disabilities that make individuals vulnerable to discrimination and compound poverty and disempowerment over time (Chapter 4). Many people will struggle with access processes and have limited means and language to engage with you (Chapter 5). They often need your help to negotiate with other organisations (Chapter 7). But these general patterns don't tell the whole picture, and, above all, do not tell you about the person you are talking to today.

To summarise, start from the knowledge that nothing is certain; there is no typical experience or normal refugee. You might see similarities, but look for differences. You can't simply learn a set of facts and reactions to a standard set of 'refugee problems', so your preparation has to be about your readiness to learn, to listen and build trust from the first contact, and your ability to find and make new contacts and resources to help you in your work.

Refugees are active agents

Refugees are active agents of their escape and adaptation. They are survivors, not victims. They are coping, recovering and working to rebuild their lives, which includes not only practical necessities for themselves and their dependants, but less visible priorities such as caring about distant family members or a sense of who they will be in the future.

As they build, they will pursue their own priorities and that means preserving and using their assets in the way they think best. They will shop around, might

test the boundaries now and then and perhaps accept a little more than they should at times. You might not always approve of their choices, but be careful before you judge. What they choose to do now is a tactic in a longer-term strategy, not their end goal, and most people want to get on with it.

You are a witness to their efforts; your actions facilitate theirs. You bring an essential toolkit of knowledge and skills. But they are not waiting for you to solve their problems. You, of course, are one of the assets they are juggling, so don't be surprised if things don't always go the way you thought they should. No matter what your skills or what you can offer, you are not in control of this relationship.

Learning from refugees and this book

This book exists because of refugees' own voices; it has grown from what I have learned when meeting and listening to individual refugees and families over more than 15 years. The testimonies, quotations and sometimes anecdotes are meant to give insight and ground what you are reading in the humanity and complex daily realities of a hugely diverse range of real people. Where I include direct quotations, they are anonymised, although I give what background I can where relevant, and please note the Acknowledgements which mention key individuals to whom I owe a lot. I also include real-life examples from my observations; some of the boxes are composites of several stories I have heard directly from people and gathered from primary sources over the years.

The book also combines expertise from many practitioners I have met or worked with over 25 years, many of them refugees. Their valuable knowledge, advice and expertise run through all chapters. Several have given their wisdom and knowledge freely and generously for this book, including input on accuracy and completeness, but any errors are mine alone.

The content and approach of this book have been shaped and tested by more than 15 years of giving direct support to primary and community practitioners who are *not* specialists in refugee issues but have found themselves working with refugees. I have learned from people on site, in meetings, in training and interactive workshops and by responding daily to practitioners' questions.

In this book I aim to answer practitioners' key questions:

What matters most?

What do I need to know?

What can I do?

I offer pragmatic ideas, working definitions and plain English rather than legal, clinical or pedagogical terms, although I make it clear where it is important to use specific terms in a more precise way. The way it is structured and presented,

including the Table of Contents, Index and Appendices, is designed to help the reader make good progress through the book, or to pick and mix over a cup of tea, but still be able to flick through the book while you are on the phone and quickly find what you need. You are welcome to quote in letters, reporting and bids if you think it will help: please do acknowledge the source.

The book falls broadly into two sections, Chapters 1–7 discuss experience and knowledge, definitions and information, diversity and approach, with, from Chapter 5, a growing focus on action. Chapters 8–10 are practical chapters by theme, addressing what you can do about the issues that refugees are likely to face, starting from most basic needs around surviving destitution and homelessness (Chapter 8), then health, mental health and disability (Chapter 9), and learning English, training and employment (Chapter 10). Chapter 11 is an overview of issues faced by refugee children and young people and options for supporting them. Chapter 12 draws some final conclusions about deeper meanings of 'refuge' and 'refugee'.

In some chapters there are 'Long Boxes' with more detail on specific topics. There are a great many organisations and resources you can find online, but be careful that the site is not out of date as things change fast. Appendix A lists all organisations mentioned in the book, including the considerable number mentioned in practical chapters from Chapter 8 to Chapter 11. If you ring organisations for advice, please respect their time.

Box 1.3   Monitoring your own learning

Put a mark on the lines below to record where you think your knowledge is, and add a date. Revisit now and then.

I have a good overview of refugees' experiences and issues they might face.

0% ————————————————————————— 100%

I have an adequate working knowledge of refugees' entitlements for my job.

0% ————————————————————————— 100%

I am confident my current activities and practices give effective support to refugees.

0% ————————————————————————— 100%

I know where to find expertise or how to go about finding it when I need it.

0% ————————————————————————— 100%

I have clear priorities for what I want to know next, to help me support refugees.

0% ————————————————————————— 100%

Why It Matters

Introduction

I have spent many rather cross hours arguing the big ethical, policy questions about the UK giving refuge to people who need it, and about why and how it matters to the UK and society as a whole. There are ethical *and* rational arguments in favour of welcoming and supporting refugees. This is a practical book, however, and even though the big national and international policy questions are gripping and often emotive, they probably aren't why you are reading it. Even so, for practical work you have to start by asking yourself: 'Why does it matter?' You need to be clear in your own reasoning because your views will affect what you do when you meet a refugee.

Our individual views and histories affect how most of us feel about helping refugees: maybe you have personal experience of violence or loss and rebuilding a new life; or your grandmother came to Britain as a refugee; or you feel the person whom you helped last year might have been taking advantage of you. You might be undecided or somewhat sceptical. It might not surprise you to learn that I think it matters a great deal whether or not we support refugees, and that we do so properly. Compassion and justice matter. Mutual respect and recognition matter. Preparedness and sensible resource allocation matter.

This book is for readers who are involved in supporting people who are recovering and rebuilding lives in the UK having escaped persecution and danger in other countries. Even if this is not your primary role at work, it is important to get this support right. To do that, you need to be clear what *your* answer is to the following two questions:

Question 1: Does it matter whether or not hands-on workers support refugees?

Question 2: Does it matter whether the people I am supporting are refugees or not refugees?

Question 1: Does it matter whether or not hands-on staff support refugees?

Polarised yelling matches aren't usually helpful, and the amount of yelling in Britain in the past few years has made people nervous about expressing their views and asking questions. There are several arguments for why hands-on staff

need to support refugee individuals or families, and several points where people have genuine doubts and concerns. You, the reader, might be uncertain how to explain your position in the face of opposition. It is good to look at the range of reasoning.

Many people make the ideological case that support for refugees is a matter of compassion and respect for human life, about common humanity and the collective and individual duty of a decent, civilised society. Then there is the argument that if you are in a line of work that supports people who are struggling, you cannot legitimately ignore the vulnerability and struggles that are a daily reality for so many ordinary people who have sought refuge here. You will have your own views on these arguments already.

One of the more abstract points of view can be expressed as 'There, but for the grace of God, go I' (Box 2.1). Are you someone who could be (or has been) discriminated against? A woman? A man? A religious believer? An atheist? Could it get worse rather than better?

Discrimination and persecution do happen in the UK, whether one looks at contemporary hate-crime and wage discrimination, the treatment of Irish people in the 1950s, the Reformation (c. 1520–1550) or the massacre of the Jews in York (1190). Discrimination is an underlying reality in any society – it's really only a matter of scale. So it could be you; it could happen here.

| Box 2.1 | There, but for the grace of God, goes John Bradford |

John Bradford was an English religious reformer – a Protestant Christian. The phrase 'There, but for the grace of God, go I' comes from him. He was imprisoned in London for his religious beliefs and campaigning. From his prison window he would watch people being led out to execution. He was burned at the stake in 1555.

Many other Protestants like him became refugees, fleeing to other countries in Europe to escape persecution, indefinite imprisonment, torture and execution by the royal family and the state in Britain.

Where would you go if the situation turned nasty here? Without an EU passport, you can't just hop over the North Sea or the Channel. Perhaps you can cross into the Republic of Ireland, but can you stay? Will America let you in? Will Iraq welcome you? Will a family in Eritrea give you a room in their house? One conclusion from such reasoning is that we had better support other people seeking refuge, because we never know if one day we might need them to return the favour.

The simplest argument to make within formal organisations is that we must support refugees effectively because the law says we must and there are consequences if we don't. Under equality law we must ensure that all the people we support receive the same standards of support, working towards the same good outcomes, and this includes asylum seekers and refugees (see Chapter 4).

There are other obligations under other laws. You might not think the law is reasonable, and you have probably met several people who believe various laws and rights should be done away with. Nonetheless, this is how the law stands at present, and we must comply or face the consequences.

Finally, pragmatically, getting it right first time saves resources and builds trust that makes future working relationships more productive.

Doubts and concerns about whether to support refugees

Many people have genuine concerns about whether supporting refugees is a risk to Britain in the long run. *Hostile reporting* that plays to people's fears also scares people who dread the rise of intolerance. *Sympathetic reporting* tends to dwell on moral imperatives and the scale of need, which scares people who are concerned about consequences and who are upset about being labelled inhumane and racist.

Ideally, different views about our roles – and possible consequences of giving refuge – would be a source of creative debate and critical reflection, not least about practice. But at present different views are a source of damaging conflict, simplistic contradiction and rejection. It is important to think through doubts and concerns for ourselves and ensure that our own views are well informed from many sources. Then we can act with confidence, knowing our actions are justified, and we can keep learning and engaging with others – including those who have different views.

Doubts and concerns can be loosely grouped into three: Why us? Is it fair? Can we afford to care?

Why us? There are many who recognise that refugees have a legitimate need but have questions such as: Why us? Why do they all come to us? Aren't there other countries, other towns, or other organisations who should support them? Are we soft? Shouldn't they help themselves?

Higher visibility has given a distorted view of how many refugees there are in the UK. Very many countries are, of course, supporting refugees, many of them in far higher numbers and with fewer resources than Europe. The United Nations High Commission for Refugees (UNHCR), for example, estimates that Ethiopia hosts nearly six times as many refugees as the UK, and Pakistan 13 times as many (Refugee Council 2016).

Asylum seekers and refugees are not evenly distributed across the UK. Those asylum seekers who are housed by government are housed in economically depressed urban areas, where there is cheaper housing and multiple occupancy. Refugees settle where they can, which tends to be cities, starting in the poorer wards. These two factors have concentrated asylum seekers visibly in areas where there is usually already serious deprivation. It is interesting to note that the more ethnically diverse areas seem to be the least worried about this. This doesn't appear to be because earlier migrants and refugees are more sympathetic

– in fact, the opposite might even be true, but perhaps with more familiarity there is less concern about impact.

In some fields your organisation might be *wrong* to try to help – for example, immigration case work or counselling for post-traumatic stress that you aren't qualified to do. In terms of other organisations, there may be bodies who *should* be supporting the refugees who are coming to you. (Perhaps their response is 'We don't do refugees'.) It is important to ask around. In this case your organisation should not step in to fill the gap another organisation should fill, but you will probably find your role becomes helping your refugee client or member get past misinformation and climb through the necessary hoops to access the services they are entitled to.

But when you ask around, you could be surprised how little is there. Since cuts already noted in Chapter 1, there is often no 'other organisation' or 'other service' to help. Social Services are only obliged to support asylum seekers or refugees if they are assessed to be 'children in need' or disabled or on a few other grounds. Many local authorities have set up Syrian Resettlement services for selected Syrians, but don't support other refugees – even Iraqis or Syrians who came here overland all fleeing the same conflict. Refugees' own organisations and refugee specialist services in the voluntary sector have largely gone or are cut so thin you can see through them. Where they remain, they can connect expertise and perhaps run some restricted projects, but they rarely have capacity for the kind of holistic work they once did. Chapter 1 introduced the view that refugees have few places to turn, meaning specialists in all fields now need to work inclusively, broadening their expertise to include refugees, as they can no longer refer refugees elsewhere.

Regarding helping themselves, refugees are active agents of their own regrowth, and are constantly striving to improve their own situation. Sometimes that's enough and they don't need you. Sometimes their best efforts aren't enough, and they need an extra hand to move on and up. If people don't present to you as refugees in need of help, you may not notice they exist – you only meet those who come to you for help.

Is it fair? A second area of doubt revolves around whether it is fair that we pay for refugees from our taxes. Are they coming over here just to get our benefits, NHS and education for free? Our jobs? We paid tax – they haven't! Are they cheats? Are they crooks? Are they terrorists?

Within any system there are people who rip it off, but that doesn't mean the system isn't needed or is necessarily failing. Think of politicians' expenses: some Members of Parliament work flat out for 25 years for their constituents and claim exactly what they need or less; one person buys a duck house.

To some extent these 'Is it fair?' questions rotate around whether our asylum decision-making system works. Yes, there are people who try to exploit the asylum system, but it is not easy to get away with it. The British system is tough.

Some would say too tough, to the point of risking injustice. Broadly speaking, the British government is looking for ways to keep people out or refuse their claims. So if the Home Office or the Courts decide the person in front of you is a legitimate refugee, you can be pretty sure they are. There are plenty of other people who have suffered and asked for refuge, and are refused.

About benefits: people need to eat. Our 'benefits' system stops refugees (and other British subjects and eligible women and men) living under flyovers and suffering long-term (expensive) health problems related to malnutrition. Homelessness is not an option. Sofa-surfing is unsafe and unsustainable. Night shelters are an expensive emergency patch. The average lifespan of someone sleeping on the streets in the UK is apparently three years. Flight from war and persecution is often a matter of life and death; benefits and services can be about life and death too.

People want to earn a decent living instead of relying on sub-poverty-line benefits, and as soon as they have the permission and opportunity to work and pay for themselves, they will. Our staff time spent on education and health is not wasted on refugees. It is as much an investment in them as in any member of society – it enables them to contribute to society, as ordinary members of society, in the future. Not paying back a 'debt' – just enabling them to contribute skills and productivity, look after themselves and their family, and pay normal taxes.

Do criminals and terrorists try to get into the UK through the asylum process? Yes, they probably do try this route, and many others. That is, if they aren't born here and living here already with British family. If people are determined to do British people harm, they will use what means they can. The asylum system makes us neither more nor less vulnerable to attack. Other factors are at play.

Can we afford to care? or **What about my mum?** Concern is often connected with the feeling that supporting refugees means British people will lose out. We know we are a rich country. Everyone knows we can afford to support some refugees, but how many is too many and have we reached the tipping point? Will our living standards change? Will our culture change? Will change be for the worse? What about my mum's hip replacement?

Britain changes all the time and always has. So no doubt the refugees and migrants arriving now will change the country as so many other things in the past have changed this country. Eritrean culture might be new to Britain, but refugees aren't, and nor is social change. Land enclosures, the slave trade, industrial revolution, colonialism, women's suffrage, world wars, cars, the pill, privatisation, broadband have all had a huge effect on Britain's economy, society and politics. Changes arising from the arrival of refugees are part of that picture. Taking the long view, most people would say the arrivals of Dutch Protestants under Elizabeth I or Jewish children escaping Nazi Germany changed many aspects of British society for the better, despite initial hostility and even violent conflict in some quarters. But it is slightly risky to argue that we can 'afford'

refugees because we gain from refugees, as it is a return to the view that refugees have to earn the right to be here.

Whether we can afford refugees is an area where issues about migration and about refuge get mixed up. We need to keep these issues separate. Even though refugees are one kind of immigrant, this book isn't addressing migration or immigration as a broader issue. Some of the points in later chapters about working with refugees will apply to any work you do with any migrant person (including students, tourists, workers and business people, EU nationals, family members joining spouses, undocumented migrants, etc.), but the experiences of refugees coming to the UK are completely different to those of other migrants and many of their needs are different too. The number of refugees compared with overall migration figures is small: about 30,000 people ask for asylum per year, although it varies year to year and 2016–2017 was higher. Roughly a quarter – about 8000 – are allowed to stay. Many go home when home becomes safe. By comparison, after the Brexit vote, overall net migration figures *dropped* to 230,000 in 2017 (www.ons.gov.uk).[1] Thirty thousand asylum seekers is a substantial number, but it isn't a flood. Looking only at the larger number of asylum seekers (rather than people given status and Leave to Remain), it works out to 46 people per Parliamentary constituency (650 constituencies) if spread evenly, although refugees tend to end up in deprived urban constituencies. An average constituency has 70,000 voters. The source of these figures, and the best quick reference source for anyone needing statistics, is the Refugee Council Quarterly Asylum Statistics; this data is from May 2018.

Successive decisions by Her Majesty's Governments about how to spend our tax money also get confused with issues about refuge. Political ideologies about the role and value of the welfare state, public services and public workers, and social housing shape decisions about how money is spent and what resources are available to the people of Britain – including my mum – now and in the future. Those are the decisions that fix who has to wait how long for what. But when someone's hip replacement operation is delayed, people tend to look for an immediate solution. We can't ignore the fact that some interests in the UK manipulate perceptions to promote certain agendas. Pictures of a thousand people at a border point stir fear of a future in which Britain will cease to exist as we know it, as poverty-stricken and desperate strangers pour in. If frustrated members of the public are pointed towards a visible group of 'other' people (who are not likely to stand up for themselves), they appear to have a simple solution for the problem: 'I'm worried public services will let me down: stop refugees and migrants and the problem will be solved.'

---

1   Net migration is calculated by the total number of people coming in per year minus the total number leaving per year – therefore, the overall increase or reduction in numbers of migrants in the UK.

Question 2: Does it matter whether the people I am supporting are refugees or not refugees?

Refugees' needs are different to other service users', participants', members' needs. But also the same. This second question comes down to how we treat refugees. Should we treat them differently to other people or not? Having picked up this book, this question is probably already in your mind. It is a great question to start off a training session or team discussion.

There are plenty of hands-on workers who will say with pride, 'We don't single people out', 'We don't agree with labelling people', 'We treat everyone the same', 'Everyone has equal opportunities here', 'We accept people as they are'. Some reply cautiously, 'We don't like to ask in case they feel stigmatised', or 'in case they think we won't help them'.

But I am less ambivalent about my bugbear, 'We don't do refugees' (see Box 1.1). Perhaps these organisations 'do' everyone? Or they really mean 'our' services aren't for 'them': refugees aren't like us. Perhaps like a respondent to a survey REAP did, who said, 'We do housing for gay men; we don't do refugees' as it hadn't occurred to him that gay men might be refugees, or that refugees might be gay men. Maybe 'don't do' comes from confusion about refugees, like the man who replied to the same survey, 'We do not encourage refugees to access our services as our funders would not be happy about us providing services to people who are not supposed to be here...' (see Box 4.8; REAP 2009). Refugees can appear as 'other' people – exotic, threatening, scary, extraordinary. In these cases it matters very much if the people who need support are refugees or not, because if they are, in that organisation's view, they can shove off.

I fully agree it is all wrong to label people, pick them out as 'different' and judge them for something that is outside their control. However, refugees have had extraordinary experiences and therefore some of their needs are likely to be out of the ordinary too. There are also legal constraints. If we don't recognise differences, including where there are extraordinary needs, we cannot support people in the ways they need supporting. 'Equal opps' is not treating everyone the same; it is treating everyone differently. You don't have to know for sure that someone is a refugee, or what their immigration status is or any detail about what they have been through, but you should be aware they might be a refugee, because you need to take that possibility into account as you work out the best way to support them. If treating everyone the same means responding to all individuals with respect, listening and learning, and taking responsibility for our decisions, then, absolutely, we should treat everyone the same.

> If treating everyone the same means responding to all individuals with respect, listening and learning, and taking responsibility for our decisions, then, absolutely, we should treat everyone the same.

Experiences

You need to be aware of what people *might* have been through (see Box 2.3). In current narratives about refugee experiences, we are very aware of war and violence and horrendous journeys across continents. But most people's experiences of persecution go back further and start with less dramatic experiences, with more subtle impact.

People may have experienced direct and indirect discrimination, social and economic losses, intimidation and invasions into their lives for years, even generations before they eventually leave their country. 'The community' and even their own family might have been the perpetrators or just did nothing to stop the attacks. The police and government turn a blind eye, 'fail to protect' and perpetrate or even promote persecution. People are disempowered and impoverished. Abusive social and political structures cut back their options and opportunities.

Perhaps they stand up and fight back, or perhaps they don't. They adapt to cope and survive, trying to look after themselves and their loved ones. There will be a series of losses and departures. If you were in this situation, you might change how you act, your livelihood and what you aspire to, how you dress, how you raise your children. People make little moves. Your daughter moves desks in her maths lesson so the kid next to her can't kick her any more. You move flat because the neighbour was aggressive, then say goodbye to your father and move the family to a bigger city where you can get on with life but be less visible. Your son goes to university over the border.

You start to run out of options. Hostility develops into theft, violence, imprisonment and torture (Box 2.2). You decide it would be best to leave the country. There may be triggers to departure: a new prime minister makes a speech, a bomb in the market place, your uncle is taken away. You and your children and your parents fly or drive or walk over the border, perhaps to stay with a cousin, perhaps to a camp, where you will stay for now; perhaps you will head for another country where you have contacts or you think you might be able to find peace and rebuild a home for your family to join you.

Box 2.2 **Aware of current dangers**

It is good to be informed about other countries so you realise what this person might have gone through or witnessed at first hand. Congo has a long history of torture. Iran hangs gay men. Bosnians witnessed neighbour turning on neighbour.

But make sure you have the historical context too: Syrians who came to the UK before the current war travelled from a liberal and prosperous country.

The journey is hard and you have to pay lots of people who take most of your money off you and tell you what you must do. You stay in crowded places,

suffer assaults, lose weight and get ill. You feel anxious all the time, you don't know what will happen next, you can't reach your family by phone, you live off rumours, you keep going.

You arrive in a country and ask to be allowed to stay – a claim for asylum. You have to explain your traumas and why you left over and over again to strangers via an interpreter who is also from your country. You don't quite trust him. You don't want to talk about the rape but you have to. You don't know who is on your side. You get a letter that says no, go home, you were not in danger, you will be safe enough there. Your solicitor writes more reports and fills in more forms for an appeal. Then you wait. You are in a hostel. It is with a lot of other asylum seekers; the people living in the area don't like you. People come and try to sell you drugs, documents and opportunities for cash-in-hand work. Everyone tells you what to do but they all tell you different things. There is a nice woman in a nearby community centre who gives out food and soap. She looks at you as if you matter.

You go into a court. You've never been in a court before. There is an interpreter and they ask you questions and the legal people talk. Then you go back to the hostel and wait.

A letter comes; it says you can stay. You have 28 days to find a place to live and apply for benefits before you have to leave your accommodation and they cut off your money. There are no interpreters at the benefits office. The nice woman helps you fill some forms and gives you food and a paracetamol. In the end you promise someone £20 per week to let you sleep on the floor, and after three weeks you manage to find a room and your first benefit money arrives. Your relief is overwhelming.

Box 2.3 A discussion tool: I am a refugee 'by experience'

I feel I am a refugee. I came here for safety.

I survived and adapted, coped with bullying and discrimination in my home country.

I had to leave because it was too dangerous. I left one place after another: moved college, moved town; finally, I left the country. A lot of people like me face crises, danger, violence, fear; some can leave with their families, some have to leave alone.

I travelled through other countries where I could not stay. I lost most or all the people I know and all my things, and I had to pay a lot of money to get people to help.

I arrived in one country where I think I can stay, and have asked to stay, or I might only be able to stay for a while. I don't know what will happen next.

They said yes, I can stay. I have refuge! I have asylum, safety, a chance to recover and rebuild. But I need to learn the language, new systems, new people; I don't know anyone and no one knows me.

They said 'no', I have to go. Now what?

Questions to ask the group

What impact might these experiences have on a person's ability, sense of identity and mental health? What impact might these experiences have on parents' ability to nurture their children? On their ability to engage with you and your organisation? On someone's ability to plan their future? On their financial situation?

Refugees are different to other migrants but also the same

Refugees are migrants, but not all migrants are refugees.

Refugees face the full range of issues that all migrants face, but not all migrants face the issues refugees face.

Chapter 3 looks in depth at definitions of 'refugee' and entitlements, and Chapter 5 at the issues refugees and other migrants face when trying to engage effectively with staff and structures in formal organisations. But there are points that need noting here in relation to whether we treat refugees differently to other people, which includes whether we treat them differently to other migrants.

Box 2.4   **Similarities between refugees and migrants**

Migrants with work, student, spouse or several other visas may be here a long time and put down roots here. They have made friends, made a home and started a business; they have a life here. Love affairs and divorces happen; children are born and start school; life gets complicated. The prospect of leaving can be traumatic.

On the surface, this person and a person seeking refuge are both suffering, facing the same dire anxieties about being forced to leave. They need letters of support, they are still struggling with English, they are extremely anxious about deportation. There is a human sitting in front of you who has done nothing wrong and is desperate to stay.

They present with such similar needs that they get mixed up. But they aren't really the same. The non-refugee person has not been through the same experiences of powerlessness, fear, loss, transit, insecurity and the asylum process. They can go back safely even if they really don't want to. They have the prospect of applying to return.

In my work I have repeatedly been asked how to help 'a refugee' but then found that the person is some other kind of migrant entirely – a Commonwealth national on a student visa perhaps, the spouse of a person here on a work permit, or even an EU national (see Boxes 2.4 and 2.5). We all do what we can. But the majority of migrants have different visa arrangements and entitlements to refugees, especially those still in the asylum process (see Chapter 3). More important than that, other migrants have different reasons for being here and different experiences of leaving their original home, in transit and since arriving in the UK. Which is not to say that other migrants don't have genuine needs, or that life is necessarily easy for them. But their situation is different. They were

safe, they chose to come, they can go back any time they want, and may be able to return to the UK after that (Box 2.4). These days there is often no right place for any migrant to go for advice, so any migrant might come to you. But the support refugees need starts from a completely different base to other migrants.

Box 2.5 **Differentiating between refugees and migrants**

Sometimes the fact someone is from a 'refugee exit' country such as Lebanon, Somalia or Syria leads supportive workers to assume they are refugees. Sometimes just being from abroad or having brown skin or being Muslim is the sole basis on which people make this assumption. One time a young British black man was referred to us – a refugee charity – for housing advice. We didn't offer housing advice. He wasn't a refugee. He wasn't a migrant. I assume this ridiculous decision was well intentioned, but we had to conclude that it was founded purely on his skin colour and it was actually racist.

All migrants face a big challenge with communication in English, especially with bureaucrats and professionals such as medics or solicitors. Any newcomer to any country will find the accents, manners and local terminology new at first. Those with little or no English may have to invest years in learning the language to be able to communicate effectively in the UK. Some never do, remaining poorly informed or dependent on others all their lives.[2] Even fluent arrivals lack the cultural familiarity and competence that helps smooth out interaction – for example, use of body language or how to interact with the opposite sex.

With or without good English, it takes all migrants time to cope with unfamiliar institutions in a new country, and to learn how to negotiate access and prove eligibility to organisations that control useful resources. Although some people will gain the essential knowledge, skills and contacts (and documents!) to function effectively in months, others might still struggle with basics years later. Refugees have to do more of this than other migrants. Most migrants will have their documents and necessary evidence. Refugees often don't.

At risk of repeating myself, the biggest difference between refugees and other migrants is that most migrants chose to leave their country and come to the UK – mostly for economic reasons or to develop their lives in other ways. People in most categories of migration can work from the minute they arrive, but not asylum seekers, who are still waiting for a decision on their application for refuge and will be heavily penalised if caught working (see Chapter 3). Refugees who are allowed to work often aren't ready to work, as they lack relevant skills, recognised qualifications, job contacts.

Add to this the fact that other migrants who are in the UK were given permission to enter usually before they travelled. They will have made

---

2   Children can be extraordinary at learning languages, but don't succumb to the temptation of using them as interpreters (see Chapter 5).

arrangements for the family they leave at home and will have prepared for life in Britain before leaving, reading about it, choosing what to pack – probably with a degree of excitement. They have a good sense of what will happen after they arrive. Family members may be allowed to visit or join them while they are here. Such 'voluntary' migrants are more stable, less vulnerable. They are likely to have higher levels of physical and mental health than refugees.

All migrants are likely to experience a degree of homesickness, changes in family and personal relationships, and especially pressures and concerns about distant family. Being in a new social context often includes isolation in some form and challenges to a person's sense of identity and direction. Refugees will feel all these things, but for refugees the homesickness might be for places and experiences that no longer exist. Their family may have changed for ever and they might not even know where some family members are or what has happened to them.

Certain migrants may not have originally fled persecution but nonetheless have similarly traumatic experiences to refugees and end up in similarly vulnerable situations. For example, people who were trafficked into the UK, male and female migrants being forced into marriage, escaping domestic abuse or at risk of abuse linked to culture. They may end up in the asylum process as they ask the UK for protection. They are also coping with what they have experienced as they wait to find out if they will be allowed to stay.

Consequences for them and for you

What refugees have experienced has consequences for them, and therefore for your work. Each person deals with what life has handed them in their own unique way, but there are patterns and probabilities to be aware of with refugees that are additional to those you might find in your work with other people – plus, of course, the practical issues of entitlements and eligibility.

Refugees are often wary when dealing with **authority** – for example, being visited at home by a health visitor, deciding whether to report a crime to the police, or just filling in a form. You are an authority figure. Their perception and ability to build a relationship of trust with you will be shaped by earlier experiences before and after leaving their original home, and having come through the British asylum system.

They are also sensitive about **stigma and hostility** from the public, whether that is a neighbour or fellow student or a stranger insulting them as they walk home. This extends to caution about letting staff and volunteers in organisations know they are refugees, particularly where they fear discrimination could prevent them accessing the help they want or need.

Refugees are often dealing with short-term horizons, instability, vague but critical deadlines, insecure housing, health and financial situations that can easily tip into crisis. It takes time and stability to build up resources and resilience,

and a 'shock' such as a car accident or losing a job, which you or I might overcome relatively quickly, can do long-term damage. Their impoverishment over time leaves them short of assets and forced to make difficult choices with their limited cash, time and energy. Their physical, mental and emotional health is often compromised, further challenging their confidence and scope for action, including what they aspire to in the future.

It all affects whether and how they engage with you and how easy it is to build an effective working relationship.

Summary and conclusion

So my answer to Question 1 is yes. I believe it matters that we support refugees. It matters that we support refugees because they have suffered and lost. They are struggling with British bureaucracy. They are recovering and actively rebuilding their lives, and if aware and informed people help them along the way, they will be able to build decent lives more quickly. The more effectively we do this, the better value we get from our scarce resources.

Likewise for Question 2, yes. It also matters that we know whether the people we are supporting are refugees or not because it has consequences for what we do.

1. You need to reflect on your own practice in light of who refugees are.

    They are ordinary and equal. Be professional, but connect as a real person too. Be aware that there may be serious issues at play. But don't poke. Find out what you need to know. But don't dig.

    Each refugee is unique. This means nothing is certain. Act with sensitivity. Don't assume the worst happened to the person in front of you, but don't assume it didn't either.

    Refugees are active, strategic agents of their own futures. Allow time and space. Let trust grow. Facilitate. Be flexible and prepared to respond to what emerges.

2. Refugees may have experienced powerlessness, fear, loss, transit, insecurity and struggles with the UK asylum system and bureaucratic processes. You need to be aware of what refugees might have been through and the possible consequences:

    •   mistrust of authority, a series of crises, difficulty negotiating access to British organisations and institutions, reluctance to engage (Chapters 6 and 7)

    •   poverty, homelessness, insecurity bordering on destitution (Chapter 8)

    •   impaired physical, mental and emotional health (Chapter 9)

- struggles with language, skills and accessing opportunities and work (Chapter 10 – see also Chapter 6)

- all the normal trials and tribulations of life – for example, growing up and growing older.

3. Practically, you have to be aware of different ways 'refugees' are defined in different contexts that relate to asylum seekers' and refugees' entitlements and constraints, which are introduced in the next chapter, with details on practical topics in Chapters 8–11.

To conclude: as I see it, whether or not we support refugees depends on what kind of society we want to live in. What do we want 'British Values' to be? Clearly we have the potential to make a difference. The alternative is to walk away and leave refugees struggling, or just leave them swimming in the Mediterranean. What impact does that have on us? What do we gain by walking away? What do we have to lose by helping?

What I don't think Britain can afford is people who could be self-sufficient, and who could even contribute to society, being made poor and incapable, their lives wasted and their children disadvantaged. It doesn't make sense to save £100 on English lessons now, and spend £1000 on unemployment benefits later.

When asked whether we should give special treatment to refugees (What about people escaping domestic abuse? What about kids with HIV? What about my mum?), my answer is no. Being a refugee doesn't make a person more important. Being ordinary makes them important, as important as anyone who has suffered, lost, struggled, has the chance to rebuild and who needs meaningful support at this moment in time. If we focus on the experiences these people have faced, their current vulnerability and the possible long-term consequences for their lives and families, then the fact they are refugees becomes less significant, and so does the way immigration law defines them. It becomes instead about responding to the actual needs of real people whom we are in a position to help. If your services are set up so you can respond effectively to people with real and diverse needs and constraints, then you can respond better to everyone, including my mum.

Defining 'Refugee' and Practical Entitlements – on a 'Need to Know' Basis

Introduction

This chapter makes the transition between *why* we help refugees in the opening chapters and *how*, which is the rest of the book.

You have to be able to define who *you* mean by 'a refugee'. Your definition will shape what you do.

You have many choices, ranging from legal definitions in international law right through to people's own descriptions of how they see themselves. Different bodies use different definitions for different reasons.

This book is meant to help you in the day-to-day world of working with real people. So this chapter looks at the practical implications of different bodies' definitions. It considers subjective definitions, a pragmatic summary of immigration, legal and governmental definitions, and some attention to popular uses of 'refugee'. Whoever *you* decide to consider a refugee, you still need a sound working knowledge of language from immigration law because government uses legal categories to set people's entitlements and to constrain certain people's actions and agency. Popular uses of 'refugee' are likely to come up in conversation with colleagues or volunteers and can have an impact on your freedom to support people as you think best. The right definition at the right time matters.

When you understand the language to use in different contexts, you can explain yourself clearly and confidently when you advise, reassure or even argue with your colleagues. This applies to trustees and even funders. Having the right words for the right moment means you get the correct information to and from other professionals, so you give accurate support to the individual, especially in matters of access, entitlements and benefits. Knowing the language means you can communicate and collaborate with other practitioners to improve processes and systems, especially when you need to prioritise scarce time and resources.

The Glossary lists the terms and various definitions given in this and other chapters. Appendix A lists all organisations mentioned. Appendix B is a collection of documentation and evidence referred to in the book.

WARNING! This chapter is not giving legal definitions or advice. The definitions discussed in this chapter are *not* for immigration-related case work or advice. If you aren't licensed to do immigration work, don't do it!

Box 3.1 **'A workshop on "How to stop refugees duping us"?'**

I was asked to run a workshop on how to stop support organisations being duped by refugees. I asked for further explanation. It emerged the enquirer didn't know the people's actual immigration status, but as they were males from Asia who had not been in the country long, it had been assumed they were refugees. One had been aggressive and manipulative towards staff and was probably involved in criminal activity and exploiting other migrants. Another had tried to defraud members of money and goods.

They assumed the problem was about refugees. I saw it as more about their own supervision and safeguarding procedures. They were not looking at what mattered, and by labelling them 'refugees' they merged criminal behaviour and refugees as if they were the same thing.

A subjective definition of 'refugee' – based on people's experiences

The previous chapter was about *why*. It concluded that the reason we should support 'refugees' is that they have suffered and lost and must rebuild their lives. On top of this they are often struggling with British systems and culture. It all centred on people's experiences.

It also set the scene for *how*. Chapter 2 concluded that practitioners need to be able to distinguish between refugees and other people, such as other migrants. This is necessary because refugees' experiences shape their situation at present, and what they are able to do about it. Therefore, people who have faced traumatic losses may now be struggling with mental health problems. People impoverished and disempowered by persecution and flight are probably facing an ongoing series of practical crises. People asking the UK government for refuge have their movements and activities limited and have fixed rights and entitlements. It all impacts on people's effectiveness and their willingness to engage with you. Chapter 2 noted that you need to be aware of these additional factors as you work out how to help.

This adds up to a strong argument for hands-on workers to have a core working definition of 'refugee' that starts from people's subjective realities.

A subjective definition of 'refugee'

So if we take 'a person who has fled persecution' and make it subjective, we can start from:

'a person who feels she or he has fled persecution'.

But often refugees flee from what has not yet happened, but that they fear will happen next. (A 'fear of persecution' is also embedded in international law – see Box 3.4). So adding this we get:

'a person who feels she or he has fled actual or potential persecution'.

So far this locates people's experiences in something that happened to them before arriving in the UK and is now done and over. But a meaningful definition needs to reflect the new reality too, so perhaps:

'a person who has found refuge in the UK, feeling she or he has fled actual or potential persecution'.

However, many people don't feel they have *found* refuge here – people who are scared of their neighbour, or are still in the asylum system and dread the post each morning. Which gives us:

'a person who feels she or he has sought refuge in the UK, from actual or potential persecution'.

A subjective definition like this is inclusive – it includes people who other observers might say are not refugees. For example, it could include someone still in the asylum process. It could even include someone that the government has refused to accept as a refugee, and I will return to this conflict of definitions later.

But this subjective definition can include other people too, unrelated to government categories. Some time ago I helped organise an event where I met two impressive women: Prossy and 'Lily', both lesbians. Prossy was gang-raped, tortured and abused by national police in her country of origin because of her sexuality. She struggled with negative decisions, deportations and appeals through the British asylum system for years, before she finally won the right to remain in the UK. Lily is from the United States of America. She and her British partner felt they would never be able to live freely in Lily's home town. So they moved to the UK where they could live openly as a couple.

You need to decide for yourself if this definition includes people fleeing war. Some say yes, war is appalling, there is great suffering and loss, and they are seeking safety so it is essentially the same as people fleeing persecution. Certainly, war usually involves persecution. Even if root causes are economic and political, violent conflict worsens or is worsened by national and ethnic and/or religious and political alignments. Aggression is often played out along lines of identity. The extreme 'macro' persecution of war is often brutally manifested at the micro level through abuse of selected individuals, families or whole villages.

People who have been trafficked, women being forced into marriage or people relying on spousal visas who have been abused by partners while in the UK have suffered and lost – and are allowed to ask for permission to stay in the UK in their own right, via the asylum system – and so fulfil part of the criteria of this definition.

Some who are concerned about suffering and loss might include people escaping natural disasters as 'refugees'. The most inclusively minded may include 'economic refugees'. They argue that history, powerful economies and leaders have caused such misery through exploitation and inescapable poverty and hopelessness that people have no choice but to flee.

Few would deny the suffering of these groups, or deny them sympathy. But some consider the aspect of persecution makes refugees' experiences fundamentally different. Not necessarily worse or more important, but still different.

A subjective and therefore inclusive definition leaves the practitioner having to make choices. We can't do everything, we can't help everyone.

We might decide to help anyone (any refugee) who comes to us, to the best of our ability, for as long as we can. It is a kind of 'non-decision' option. But it raises the question whether the people who need support most are the ones who get it – a question revisited in Chapter 5. I would argue that 'If you don't ask, you don't get' is not a good method for rationing services.

So with this subjective and inclusive definition, we are left still having to judge between Prossy and Lily. *Whom* do we prioritise and *how* will we help them?

So how do we judge? We haven't the information to judge objectively. We know barely anything about the person in front of us and it is unacceptable to dig. We can't start setting tests and making people compete for who has the worst trauma – although I have filled in a few funding applications that feel that way.

It ends up being a somewhat risky judgement call. We combine what people tell us, papers they show us, what we have learned about refugee issues over the years. We make good use of peer advice. Most of us also draw on a degree of instinct and trust and/or cynicism that goes a bit beyond accepting what we are told at face value. We start with a cautious approach. Over time, we shrink or expand the space within which they can engage us. We hope that we build mutual trust and respect and that the working relationship grows.

This book uses this subjective, inclusive definition as its 'default'. When the text simply says 'refugee', this is what it means:

> A person who feels she or he has sought refuge in the UK, from actual or potential persecution.

Home Office definitions of 'refugee' – based on future likelihood

This section goes through what 'refugee' and other important terms such as 'asylum seeker' mean in immigration law. It touches on processes the applicant goes through. (Entitlements are outlined later, towards the end of the chapter.)

The precise governmental department handling refuge (and other immigration) moves around every few years, but it remains the responsibility of the Home Office overall.

Several Immigration Acts have been passed by Parliament in the past 20 years and new Bills will almost certainly continue to arrive in Parliament. Although details and entitlements change a lot, essential definitions change little. This section aims to gives a pragmatic understanding of key terms and processes.

This section is *not* provided so you can give immigration advice or comment on whether someone is likely to succeed in their asylum claim. Even if you stay up to midnight searching the internet several nights in a row, you *will* get it wrong. You could jeopardise someone's whole claim. Leave it to the lawyers.

It is provided for practical reasons. You need working knowledge of Home Office definitions or you won't appreciate the impact they have on people seeking refuge. You need to understand something of what the refugee is experiencing as she or he goes through asylum and immigration processes. You will need to be familiar with essential legal and Home Office language to know how to help with practical needs, especially accommodation, money and work. Confusion on your part could mean a lot of wasted time and effort for you and, more importantly, for the refugee.

Home Office decisions about who does or doesn't fit the definition of 'refugee' are meant to be objective and based on evidence. But each case is unique. Situations change fast. There are a great many staff and other professionals involved in the decision-making system, with different knowledge and different interpretations of evidence, process and law. Home Office decisions are based on predicting the likelihood of certain things happening in the present and future, discussed below. With many uncertainties, and people's lives at stake, campaigners constantly scrutinise and challenge the system. Many thousand Home Office decisions on individual cases are challenged by those individuals and their solicitors each year.

'Asylum seeker' in immigration law

The law distinguishes between 'asylum seekers' and 'refugees' and gives them different rights and entitlements. The meaning of asylum seeker can be pragmatically summarised as:

> someone who has asked to stay in Britain on the grounds that if s/he goes 'home', s/he will be in danger; and is still waiting for a final answer.

They might still be waiting for an 'initial decision'. Or they have had their case refused and have appealed for the decision to be changed and are waiting for the result, in which case they are still considered an asylum seeker.

Initial claim for asylum. Starting the process of claiming asylum can be as simple as saying 'Asylum' to the right official. Most of the people you meet will

have applied for asylum when they arrived in Britain. A large proportion make their *initial claim* at the airport or docks, although some go to a Home Office building such as Lunar House in Croydon after arriving overland, possibly helped by smugglers. People who are already here on student or other visas can claim asylum if trouble has broken out in their country.

Initial screening. Having made the claim, the asylum seeker might be detained until initial screening (conducted without a lawyer), which should happen within a matter of days, usually in Croydon or Belfast. Home Office officials process the paperwork and 'screening' interviews. Most people are released after the screening interview.

Where previously they had 'temporary admission' while they waited for a decision, now they are technically on 'immigration bail'. They will receive an Application Registration Card (often called an 'ARC card' by users) with a photograph and Home Office number. You can see images of these and other documents mentioned on the internet (Appendix B has more details). They may need to comply with reporting and other requirements, including being prohibited from work.

Detention. They could be detained again during their time in the asylum process. Men who are considered likely to abscond might be detained in centres near Heathrow (Harmondsworth, Colnbrook) and throughout the UK; women are mostly detained in Yarl's Wood in the Midlands and Lanarkshire. Detention centres are officially not prisons, so people wear their own clothes and can move around within the buildings. They can have visitors and make phone calls.

Unless you are involved in visitors groups such as Yarl's Wood Befrienders, AVID (Association of Visitors to Immigration Detainees) or BID (Bail for Immigration Detainees), for example, you are only likely to meet people after they have come out of detention. You may find yourself dealing with some of the after effects of their detention. People who were imprisoned or tortured before fleeing their original country, or who are vulnerable for other reasons, can become seriously distressed by detention, with longer-term impacts. Freedom from Torture has a number of personal testimonies on its website (www.freedomfromtorture.org).

Reporting. People might be required to 'report' or 'sign on' weekly, monthly or six-monthly to a reporting centre which might be a Home Office base or a police station. These can be some distance from where the person is staying and travel can be a problem although people on National Asylum Support Service (NASS) get travel costs refunded. At any one of these reporting appointments they might be detained pending deportation. People often find reporting distressing. It is important they don't miss a date, as that increases the likelihood they'll be detained.

There is meant to be some flexibility for people with disabilities or women with babies, for example. You can help with phone calls and letters even if you aren't licensed for immigration advice, although it can be frustrating.

Building a case. After screening, they need to build and make a case. Roughly speaking, they must prove they will be in actual danger if they return to their original country now. They must argue the state there cannot or will not protect them, either as someone who is a member of a particular group of people or as an individual.

They also have to show they are 'credible' – that is, honest and telling the truth (Box 3.2).

Box 3.2 **Credibility – showing you are honest and telling the truth**

As well as building a case, the asylum seeker will need to show they are credible – in other words, honest and telling the truth. They need to prove their ethnicity, nationality, identity and age, and how long they were in the UK before making a claim. The Home Office may 'dispute' the person's age if they claim to be under 18 (see Box 11.7). A late claim or being caught working for cash, for example, can undermine someone's credibility.

Credibility is also judged by gaps and inconsistencies in people's cases, or evidence and details that are added later. Even the testimony of highly respected organisations such as Freedom from Torture and the Helen Bamber Foundation may be ignored if it is submitted later in the process. This is particularly controversial when asylum seekers have been traumatised by torture, deaths, rape or other experiences and are only able to articulate their experiences after or over a length of time.

They should document their case with help from a licensed and specialist solicitor. Not all solicitors are licensed and not all licensed solicitors are equally good (Long Box 3.3). You cannot advise them on their asylum case, but you can help in other ways such as reading and writing letters in English or ringing their solicitor to check progress.

Next is a face-to-face substantive interview with a Home Office 'case-owner' who will follow this person's case through to decision.

To check their credibility, the individual's story and evidence will be checked against what is known to have happened in the country they have left. For example:

- If someone claims to have been persecuted when living in a certain town, or imprisoned in a certain jail, they or their solicitor will need to provide evidence that this kind of event happened at that time and place.

- They may be asked for details such as the name of certain streets where they lived, as this can be checked to prove they really are familiar with the place.

- The solicitor may call on an expert witness – someone like an academic who knows the country and its politics in depth.

Long Box 3.3 Solicitors, Legal Aid, OISC and what you can do

Getting the right solicitor. If you are assisting someone who wants to claim asylum and does not have a solicitor, don't look in Yellow Pages. The asylum seeker might have been given a list of licensed solicitors by the Home Office, but it is best if you contact your nearest community law centre, the Office of the Immigration Services Commissioner (OISC), or the Law Society of England and Wales, Scotland or Northern Ireland, and ask for a recommendation. You can also ask the Refugee Council or Coram Children's Legal Centre. Asylum applicants sometimes instruct solicitors who are not approved immigration solicitors, perhaps because of a recommendation or because they speak the same language. Changing solicitor is complex and costly – try to get someone good first time.

Legal Aid and fees. It changes fast and often. At the time of writing, solicitors can take up someone's case on Legal Aid for the initial claim, preparing and submitting appeals, and a stay of deportation. They cannot get Legal Aid for representation at Appeals Tribunals, or submitting human rights cases against removal. Legal Aid can be used to pay for expert witness reports.

Free or 'pro bono' advice and even representation can sometimes be gained via law centres, and also law schools at universities might take up cases. If a young migrant's case might be useful to make case law or for practice, the Refugee Legal Fund might fund it. Local Citizens Advice bureaux and other formal advice agencies often have someone with OISC1 (see below) who can give free advice.

OISC/Getting licensed yourself. Anyone can study and apply for an OISC licence at Level 1. It is a one-day intensive course (costing around £500) plus study, but you will need to register with OISC and may have to pay a registration fee of up to £500, although some non-profit organisations are exempt, and be supervised after that by an approved body, such as a law centre. The supervising body might be registered already, saving you the registration fee. If you find a free course, grab it – you will be better informed and could collaborate with a local registered body to be able to give basic advice. In addition, Right to Remain (righttoremain.org.uk) has tutorials for general knowledge. They also have self-help tutorials in other languages.

Decision. The applicant will get a 'positive decision' or a 'negative decision'. Positive is yes, you can stay (though see variations under 'Refugee with Leave' below). Negative decisions might be appealed, in which case the person continues as an 'asylum seeker'.

At this point, one of the big differences between a subjective definition of refugee based on (past and present) experience and the Home Office objective process (present and future likelihoods) becomes very clear. The Home Office might agree the person is credible and there was genuine persecution. They might agree the person is genuinely fearful. But if the Home Office considers the danger to be over, or that the person could live safely in another part of the country ('relocate') and live 'discreetly', it will probably refuse the application for asylum. So if you meet someone who says they are a refugee

because of what has happened to them, but the Home Office says they are not a refugee and has refused them permission to stay, it doesn't mean the person is lying. It just means the Home Office is reasonably sure it won't happen again. In this situation, if your definition is similar to the subjective definition above, you would continue to work with them. If you are working in line with Home Office definitions, you might turn them away.

Appeal. When people are refused, they get a detailed letter explaining the reasons for their refusal. They have 14 days to put in an appeal, from the date of the written reasons for refusal, so if someone comes to you for help in this situation, you need to get them to contact their solicitor immediately. Immigration issues can crop up overnight, so keep your contacts up to date.

Asylum appeals will be considered on grounds that there was a failure in Home Office decision-making processes or reasons for refusal did not have enough evidence. The next step is First-tier Tribunal.

Of between 10,000 and 15,000 who appeal per year, about 36 per cent overall are successful (Refugee Council 2018). However, it is worth noting that a higher proportion of women's appeals are successful than men's. Asylum Aid (2017) argues this is an indication that those making the first decision may not fully understand issues about gendered forms of persecution.

Waiting. An initial decision should take three to six months, but can take years. An appeal might take months or years. There are backlogs and delays at all stages. During the wait, asylum seekers and their families are in limbo. If the decision is taking too long, you can help the person to make contact with their Member of Parliament. They can get an appointment at a constituency surgery session (ask your local library for dates). Or they can write (with your help) via the House of Commons, SW1A 0AA.

Refused asylum seekers

'Refused asylum seekers' are people who have asked for asylum and received a 'negative decision'. Their claim and any appeals have failed and they have been told the UK will not give them refuge. They might have been refused any further appeals ('Appeal Rights Exhausted'). You sometimes hear them called 'failed' asylum seekers.[1]

Fresh claims. If the situation in someone's original country significantly worsens, a refused applicant's lawyer might prepare a 'fresh' asylum claim delivered by the applicant in person to the 'Further Submissions Unit'

---

1   Although the government has said, based on future likelihoods, they are not refugees, you might consider a share of them to be refugees in the subjective sense, based on their past experiences. For that reason, the situation and entitlements of 'refused asylum seekers' are included in this book.

in Liverpool. If it meets certain standards, the asylum process starts over again, although a decision might be made faster.

Notice to depart. In their refusal letter, refused asylum seekers may get notice to depart, saying that they must take steps to leave the UK and return to their country of origin, that they may be 'subject to deportation'.

- Some will apply/appeal for a Stay of Deportation if their solicitor thinks they have grounds, for example, for a further appeal.

- They might make a case under the Human Rights Act 1998 – for example, if they are getting treatment for HIV or severe mental health problems which they will lose if they are deported (Article 3 'Freedom from cruel and inhuman treatment'), or because they have a family life here (Article 8 'Right to family life').

- Some leave.

- Some 'take steps to leave' – buying a ticket, for example. For a few people this might involve taking the option of Voluntary Assisted Return and Reintegration, when they receive a small amount of assistance to resettle on strict conditions.

- Some refused asylum seekers are detained pending deportation and might be put on a flight within a day of being detained.

- Not everyone can be deported, though. For example:

  – People under 18 can only be deported if there are suitable 'reception facilities' for children in their country of origin.

  – People can only be returned to their country of origin, but there are some countries that simply refuse to allow them back in, which would make them 'stateless'. It is prohibited under international law to make someone 'stateless', so the UK cannot deport them.

Some refused applicants will 'drop out of sight' and live 'off the radar' of the authorities. This might only be a short-term strategy. They might survive by trading and working cash in hand. They avoid coming into the vision of authorities. They may not even access the limited health care they are still entitled to (e.g. treatment for TB) because they are nervous about being reported to the Home Office. Other people who are 'off the radar' might include 'undocumented migrants' (which certain newspapers call 'illegal immigrants') or 'overstayers' (tourists or students whose visas have run out). Someone in this situation might contact you now and then. You do not need to report them. If you intend to help them in your professional role, check your organisation's funding restrictions (especially if using 'public funds') and policies (eligibility/safeguarding/confidentiality and data sharing?). At times it will be better to

consider what you are comfortable doing as an individual. You could get advice from a relevant outside body such as a community law centre, food bank or homelessness charity (see Appendix A).

Refugee with Leave – in international and UK immigration law

Although there is only one legal definition of 'refugee', several other legal categories have been defined which the hands-on worker can include under the name 'refugee'. The differences are usually quite minor for social, health, community and other local workers.

Most people assume 'refugee' means someone who has been given the right to stay under the International Refugee Convention 1951, making them an 'International Refugee'. The shorthand you'll hear most often, and which is used in this book, is a **'Convention refugee'**. For practitioners who support people in health, education and so forth, the most useful notion of refugee from the angle of immigration law is a bit wider than that. But let us start with Convention refugees (Box 3.4).

Box 3.4	Refugee defined in the International Refugee Convention 1951 and Protocols 1956

'…owing to a well-founded fear of being persecuted for reasons of race, religion, nationality, membership of a particular social group or political opinion, is outside the country of his nationality and is unable or, owing to such fear, is unwilling to avail himself of the protection of that country; or who, not having a nationality and being outside the country of his former habitual residence as a result of such events, is unable or, owing to such fear, is unwilling to return to it.' (www.unhcr.org)

When you meet Convention refugees in the UK, they either got their status within the international system, before arriving in the UK, or they got a 'positive decision' after applying 'in-country', within the UK. People who already have Convention status when they arrive have often been in refugee camps or in the care of the UNHCR.

This has been the case with people fleeing the war in Syria via camps in Lebanon and other neighbouring countries that are providing a home and some level of support to millions – that is, *millions* – of Syrians and Iraqis. David Cameron agreed Britain would take 20,000 Syrians with greater needs from those camps. But this is spread over five years. So, on average, that means 4000 per year, which works out to roughly seven Syrians per MP's constituency per year – perhaps two families. Some local authorities have refused to take any.

Going back to look at people who asked for asylum in the UK system, many who get positive decisions do not get Convention status but receive some

other form of 'Leave to Remain'. Having Leave to Remain is like having a visa or permission to stay here. Their experiences are very similar to Convention refugees who claimed in the UK:

- They went through the asylum process.

- The Home Office decided their case to stay was strong enough.

- They have very similar rights and entitlements to Convention refugees.

Very often you will need to know if someone has leave, or 'status'. It is the first question most other professionals will ask you when you are discussing someone's situation: 'Has s/he got status?' But if you don't work in immigration law, there will be only a very few instances when you need to know if they have Convention status or some other kind of leave. Because of this, when the discussion needs to distinguish people by their immigration status (rather than subjective experiences). I will use **'refugees with Leave'** to mean those who have come through the asylum system and got some form of 'Leave to Remain'. (I am including Convention refugees who received their status abroad.)

Box 3.5	A sample of countries and numbers claiming asylum, and outcome of decisions	
At the end of 2017 the largest number of new applications for asylum came from:	Number of applications	In the same quarter, refusal rates for applicants from those countries were:
Iraq	786	80%
Iran	674	56%
Pakistan	607	88%
Sudan	446	62%
Eritrea	412	21%
Bangladesh	383	95%
Afghanistan	362	65%

(Refugee Council 2018)

After a positive decision, the next most significant thing is whether people get **temporary** or **permanent** forms of Leave to Remain. Convention status used to mean protection for life, wherever you went in the world. But it may surprise some readers that the UK now gives Convention refugees protection for just five years at a time, although this is usually renewed for a further five years. Other temporary or 'fixed-term' forms of leave include 'Discretionary', 'Humanitarian Protection Status' (HPS – often for people fleeing war), 'Unaccompanied Asylum-Seeking Child Leave' (UASC-Leave), 'Leave outside Immigration Rules'

Defining 'Refugee' and Practical Entitlements – on a 'Need to Know' Basis 53

and others. (There are some older forms of leave such as 'Exceptional' or 'ELR' that no longer exist.) The refugee with temporary leave gets permission to stay for one, two, three or five years. For UASC-Leave, it is until they are 17.5 years old (Chapter 10).

The problem with **temporary leave** is that the refugee is still insecure. They have to apply for an extension before their leave runs out, but can't submit the application more than three months or, in some cases, one month in advance. Then they wait, again, not knowing what will happen or when. If their new decision is a refusal, the whole appeal/reporting/risk of deportation process starts again.

On a day-to-day basis, temporary leave shrinks refugees' options. You can't get credit. Universities won't let you start a three-year course – you'll probably do better to get a low-skilled job than go to college and get qualifications anyway. A pregnant woman might choose between having the baby and having an abortion. Mortgages and pensions are out of the question.

Permanent leave is much better. People who got Convention status before 2005, or who have 'Indefinite Leave to Remain' (almost always called just 'ILR') are secure. Convention refugees with five years initially seemed to get their five years extended to ten years without too much trouble, but the Home Office steadily tightens the rules, so most refugee specialists expect this to get tougher. With permanent leave, you can work towards applying for British nationality and a British passport. You can get on with building the rest of your life. After five, six or ten years, depending on status and 'legal residence', comes the possibility of applying for British citizenship or naturalisation.

Migrants of all sorts will take this step, but where refugees have little hope of ever being able to return to their country of origin, it sometimes has an extra resonance. No longer an exile? Perhaps no longer a refugee. No longer here for refuge, but belonging here, and your children and grandchildren belonging, and their children too.

Box 3.6 | **Becoming British – what they need to do and ways you could help**

To apply for citizenship or 'naturalise', they need to:

- Pass the 'Life in the UK' test. You could use questions in the test as themes for discussion in support groups, host a study group, do a quiz night fundraiser based on official 'Life in the UK' questions (available from HMSO.gov.uk).

- Pass an intermediate-level English test (about ESOL Level 2; see Box 10.6). You could help with English, find where they can do the exam, help people get on to proper ESOL courses (see Chapter 10).

- Have two referees.

- Give evidence of where they have been throughout the whole ten years, explaining any gaps or travels. You could (should) keep old attendance records in good order for at least 15 years! Make sure you keep up good data protection services.

- Add evidence that they are helpful members of society. You could write a letter, create or broker opportunities for people to volunteer (e.g. help them apply to volunteer at a food bank).

- Download a form, fill it all in and send it off to the Home Office with the better part of £1000. Reassure them they *don't* need to pay someone extra money to do this for them. You don't need an OISC licence to help with this.

- Attend an interview. You could rehearse with them.

- Take part in a Citizenship Ceremony. You could be part of the audience!

When is a refugee not a refugee?

There are times when there is something (in law) about a refugee that defines their legal rights and entitlements more powerfully than their immigration status.

Any person who is present in the UK:

- …is protected by the Equality Act 2010 from direct and indirect discrimination and through the Public Sector Equality Duty, although some exceptions are allowed under immigration law.

- …has all the human rights laid down in the Human Rights Act 1998 which protects them from a wide range of abuses, although there are qualifications and some articles are 'relative' – for example, around detention (Chapter 4).

- …who needs primary or emergency health care will receive it and other care too (Chapter 9).

Any disabled person has the same entitlements to additional care and support under the Care Act 2014 as any person who is 'ordinarily resident' in the UK, regardless of their immigration status, although many statutory and voluntary sector bodies are not aware of this (Chapter 9).

Any child, from birth to the day before their 18th birthday ('0–17') is first and foremost a child in British law. So any child in a family claiming asylum or with Leave, any 'unaccompanied' child, any children of a refused asylum seeker, any child born in the UK to refugee parents – they are *all children* in British law and their rights as children laid out in the Children's Act 1989 and other related legislation, including care and education, all of which override their immigration status (Chapter 10).

Popular and political definitions and confusion

You can't leave daily conversation out of the picture. Most people muddle through using 'migrant', 'asylum seeker' and 'refugee' interchangeably. But where people are uncertain about what the terms mean, there is a risk of wariness or tipping into being overcautious. That's when people start to say things like 'We don't do refugees' or 'You should go to a refugee organisation'. It results in turning people away whom they could and you might think should have helped.

Language has suffered in the polarised debates of our times. Meanings have been blurred and words are politicised (Box 3.7). Many commentators in the British Press and on both sides of debate in the local pub use 'refugee' to mean a whole mix of people. People with different views select different words to strengthen arguments for and against refuge. But value-laden usage adds to uncertainty, and feeds into the doubts and concerns acknowledged in Chapter 2 (see also Box 3.1). The clearer you are on meanings, the easier it will be for you to increase the level of reasoning in the discussion.

Box 3.7 **The politics of language**

Because the debates on asylum and refuge are so polarised, language has also become polarised. Language has real power to change the tone and direction of debate and perception. The problem comes when value judgements are then applied to the whole massed body. It is used as a tool (or weapon) by one party against others to change the nature of the debate and strengthen or deny the legitimacy of refugees to our support. For example:

Migrant **v** refugee

UASC (unaccompanied asylum-seeking child) **v** UCSA (unaccompanied child, seeking asylum)

illegal asylum seeker, illegal immigrant **v** overstayer, undocumented migrant

failed asylum seeker **v** refused asylum seeker

removal centre **v** detention centre, prison

So let me mention a couple of groups who are not refugees, but get called 'refugees' in ways that are unhelpful and bring very negative undertones to the debate.

There are a few people who are cynically abusing the asylum system by claiming asylum as a way to stay in the UK even though they know they have no legitimate claim (Box 3.8). They are not 'refugees' by any meaningful definition of the word, no matter which immigration channels they use and what documentation they obtain. What they are doing is unethical and dishonest, although they are not breaking the law and there is no crime of which they can be convicted. They may be a minority, but cynical, false asylum claims undermine political and social support for refuge. When observers and politicians don't trust the system, the system gets redesigned to focus on cheats

rather than on people who have suffered already. Cynical claimants waste our scarce time and resources. People who work with refugees day to day get angry about this.

Box 3.8 A fishing trip

One woman who had overstayed a student visa was referred to the refugee charity where I worked, for advice. She had just found a job and wanted to stay. She quite seriously asked me whether she should claim asylum. I was more cross with the organisation that referred her to us than with her. They had decided not to help her, so they sent her to a refugee charity! Did they think we would knowingly help someone abuse the asylum system?

People smugglers are not refugees. Many decent Germans risked (and lost) their lives smuggling Jews out of Germany in the 1940s. Refugees often need someone to get them out of a country and across borders in secret. They have to pay people with boats to get them over a stretch of sea. They need documents, so they buy what they can off people who have made it into a profitable business. They ask smugglers what they should say and do.

It is not illegal for the refugee to do any of these things, as it is recognised that refugees may have no other way to get away from danger to a place of safety. The fact that someone has paid a smuggler for help does not mean that person is a crook, coming here to abuse the system. It does mean they are desperate.

Many other migrants also turn to people smugglers, but that does not make them refugees.

The international community has not tackled the problem of providing safe passage to places of refuge. So 'commercial' smugglers continue to operate and make a lot of money. Some are dangerous. Smugglers are all mixed up in debates about refuge.

People traffickers are not refugees. Traffickers are the lowest of the low. Trafficking is a specific crime in international law and different to smuggling. Traffickers buy and sell people, they own people and move people around and across borders with or without their consent in order to exploit them for labour, sex, benefits fraud, body parts or 'modern slavery'. Some refugees are so desperate that they have little choice but to enter into such slavery, or they are tricked into thinking this person will smuggle them out of or into a country without knowing what is really going to happen to them.

People being deported after criminal sentences are not refugees. People who have been convicted of a crime and completed prison sentences of over a year can be deported if they are migrants or dual nationals (foreign national offenders). This can include people who are naturalised, even refugees. Post-prison deportees are often kept in the same removal centres as refused asylum seekers while appealing against or waiting for deportation. Please do not confuse deporting people at the end of a prison sentence with deporting

refused asylum seekers (also see Box 3.9). Refused asylum seekers are at the end of a legitimate process. They have not broken the law.

Box 3.9 **Persecution should not be confused with prosecution!**

People cannot get refuge to avoid legitimate prosecution in other countries for crimes they have committed. However, they might make the case that their 'prosecution' is actually 'persecution' – that is, they are being unjustly accused of wrongdoing by a government that wants to silence them. This latter case is what Julian Assange of WikiLeaks claimed when he sought asylum in the Embassy of Ecuador to avoid being extradited from the UK.

Entitlements to publicly funded support and services

If you can define categories of who is and who isn't and who can and who can't, you are very powerful. It is a great responsibility.

Whoever defines the category decides:

- who belongs to it – eligibility

- what they have to do to prove they belong in that category

- what evidence they must provide (see Appendix B).

They decide who decides.

Whoever defines the category also defines what rights and entitlements the people they put in that category have:

- how people are treated once it is decided they belong to that category

- what they can do and what they can't do

- what they have to do

- what services, money, opportunities and so forth they can get

- what they have to do to access their entitlements

- when and where the entitlements will be delivered and by whom.

Again, they decide who decides.

Formally or informally, all our organisations define people into categories and have rules on who is entitled to what. The 'rules' aren't always clear or written down, especially when the organisation finds itself facing something new, like refugees. Different people within an organisation might work to their own 'rules'.

This rest of this section looks at what the Home Office has decided asylum seekers, refused asylum seekers or refugees (i.e. refugees with Leave) can do and

the services and support they can receive from public funds – in other words, paid for with taxpayers' money. Other areas of law noted above – for example, concerning disability – override Home Office definitions.

Just because someone is entitled to support or a service does not mean they always get it when they need it. The problem with access is drawn out in Chapter 5 and is a theme running through all the practical chapters.

This is just an introduction. Box 3.10 gives a 'quick reference' outline of entitlements and refers you to Chapters 8–11 for fuller practical details.

Even this introductory outline comes with a warning: things change fast! You will need to research details to get the right information for each unique individual. Advice from specialists is always valuable where you can obtain it.

Asylum seekers

Accommodation and living costs. In outline, asylum seekers can apply to the National Asylum Support Service (NASS) for accommodation and subsistence/living costs. At its simplest, they fill in a form and send in evidence that they are destitute. The process is described in Long Box 8.15. If successful, they will be offered one option for 'dispersed' accommodation in a sub-contractor-run hostel, shared accommodation or flat/house somewhere around the UK, away from the ports of entry (Dover, Heathrow, etc.).

For living costs, the successful applicant will get about £38 per week. A family will get that amount per head with a few pounds extra for pregnant women and babies. The money is provided via an 'Aspen' card which can be used broadly as a debit or cash card (Box 8.9). Pregnant asylum seekers get a one-off maternity grant of £300. Costs are refunded for travel that is required by the Home Office – for example, for reporting.

Health, disability and social care. In summary, regarding health, mental health and disability, asylum seekers are fully entitled to most NHS services, although access can be a problem as GP practices are often unsure about entitlements. The local authority must assess the support and care needs of all disabled people, which includes disabled asylum seekers. It must provide necessary additional support as identified. This might mean free local transport, hearing aids and so on, although there are no fixed rules on this. It could even mean adapted accommodation if the assessor finds this is needed, but they do not go ahead of other people in the queue.

English-language training. The introduction of immigration bail conditions in 2018 potentially prohibits almost all adult asylum seekers, as well as undocumented migrants, from studying. Until then adult asylum seekers could study if they could afford fees or find places on free English-language or other training courses, although free places were in short supply. Asylum seekers can challenge immigration bail conditions set by the Home Office through their legal advisers, including prohibitions on study.

Employment. Asylum seekers *may not take paid work* (there are some very rare exceptions). They can volunteer with some restrictions.

Asylum-seeking children and young people. Asylum-seeking children, with or without families, have full access to education up to 18. Families with NASS support will get free school meals and might get other state help if the child is considered to have special educational needs, for example, depending on the individual school and local authority. Unaccompanied children seeking asylum will receive care as children in need and/or looked after children regardless of immigration status, with variations as they approach 17.5 years. There are also variations if the government or local authority disputes the age the child claims to be.

Refused asylum seekers

For refused asylum seekers, the situation is harder and more complicated. They start from having 'No Recourse to Public Funds' – usually called NRPF or 'No Recourse'. It means they get no financial support and cannot use any of the facilities, resources or services that are provided with public tax money. This group of people has minimal legal means of support beyond any savings or gifts of help from contacts or charities/religious bodies. The online NRPF Network is very useful, especially for local authority workers.

Accommodation and living costs. However, if refused asylum seekers agree to deportation, they can apply for continued support from NASS. They may be allowed to stay on in any previous NASS accommodation if their claim for Section 4 is handled quickly.

Health. People with NRPF are allowed GPs, public health, emergency and other NHS care and treatment for free, including crisis mental health care. In Scotland and Wales they can also have free urgent care and medicines. In England they will be given urgent treatment if needed, but will be invoiced for the full cost. Disability assessment and care as above.

Employment. Refused asylum seekers may not take paid work.

Children. Even if a family is NRPF, children must still go to school free because of children's law. If the family does not have NASS support, the children might not get free school lunches.

Refugees with Leave to Remain

Refugees with any form of Leave (except UASC-Leave – see Chapter 11) have much the same entitlements as each other. They have nearly the same entitlements as UK nationals.

Accommodation and living costs. There is a cliff-edge moment when asylum seekers get the letter informing them they have Leave. From the date of the letter with their positive decision, they have just 28 days before their asylum

support is cut off. If they are in NASS accommodation, in some cases they may be able to stay where they are, or they have to find new accommodation. The process is explained in Chapter 8. They have 28 days to access and start receiving mainstream benefits such as Universal Credit, Child Benefit, Housing Benefit – there is often a gap.

Health, training, employment. They have full access to NHS services and assessment/care relating to disabilities, as other resident UK nationals. They can access English-language and other courses, training, apprenticeships and other opportunities, and these are often free for refugees with Leave if they are also receiving benefits related to employment.

Refugees with Leave can take paid work.

Travel rights for refugees. People with Leave, other than Convention status, can travel on non-British national passports if they have them as long as they don't leave the UK too often for too long. Convention refugees have a 'travel document' which they can in theory use for travel anywhere in the world except to their country of origin, although actual processes, visa arrangements and inaccurate advice cause problems. All will face additional scrutiny on return.

They are likely to need evidence of their movements at some point – for example, if they apply for British nationality. So remind your refugee contacts to keep records of dates, flight numbers, itinerary reference numbers and details.

Family reunion for refugees. Adult refugees with Convention status and Humanitarian Protection status can apply for family reunion immediately, which would allow them to bring dependants, spouse and older parents to join them in the UK. If successful, the family members who join them automatically receive Convention status. It can get complicated in cases of divorce or domestic abuse and they/you will need to turn to licensed legal advice.

Box 3.10 | Outline of entitlements for asylum seekers and refugees with Leave

Accommodation

Asylum seekers can get NASS housing 'dispersed' across the country, and refugees with Leave can apply for Housing Benefit/Universal Credit and social housing on the same criteria as any UK person (Chapter 8).

Money

Asylum seekers can get some money to live from NASS; refused asylum seekers might get a little money (and housing) if they agree to leave the country. Refugees with Leave can apply for mainstream benefits including Universal Credit and Child Benefit (Chapter 8).

Health

Everyone is entitled to a GP free, even including 'off the radar' individuals. Everyone can get family planning, HIV, TB and other public health care, and emergency care including care for life-threatening mental health crises free. Everyone will be given urgent care, but in

England some refused asylum seekers and other migrants will then be charged. Some pay for prescriptions (Chapter 9).

Disability

Everyone can have their support needs assessed by the local authority where they are 'ordinarily resident'. The local authority provides for any specialist needs identified (Chapter 9).

Work

Asylum seekers and refused asylum seekers can't work; refugees with Leave can (Chapter 10).

Children

Every child gets the same state support, education and care as UK national children until they are 18, regardless of immigration status, with minor exceptions (Chapter 11).

School

All under-16s must go to school; under-18s can access education (Chapter 11).

Further reading/training

For organisations that provide detail and training on status and entitlements, see the relevant practical chapter and Appendix A for organisations.

Summary and conclusion

Box 3.11 Summary of definitions used in this book

To make best use of this book, check you can distinguish between the following:

- Refugee – a subjective definition, used throughout this book: 'Any person who feels she or he has sought refuge from persecution, in the UK.'

- Asylum seeker – legal term, summarised as: someone who has asked to stay in Britain on the grounds that if she or he goes 'home', she or he will be in danger, and who is still waiting for a final answer.

- Refused asylum seeker – legal term, summarised as: people who have asked for asylum and received a 'negative decision' – the UK will not give them refuge.

- Refugee with Leave – shorthand, used in this book especially in relation to entitlements: a person who has claimed asylum in the UK and been given some form of 'Leave to Remain'.

- Convention refugee – shorthand for people who have been given International Refugee Convention status (Box 3.4).

You might like to revisit Box 1.3 Monitoring your own learning. See also the Glossary.

Whom you support and *how* go together when you work with refugees. You have to have a proper way of deciding whom you help because you can't help everyone. Having clear but pragmatic definitions for your working relationships with refugees isn't about dumbing down, but about doing the job (Box 3.11).

You need to know where your definition might *clash* with others' definitions, both within the organisation and where there are obligations to funders and regulators such as Ofsted and the Care Quality Commission (CQC) who have their own categories and requirements. Members of the public may have their own views about who should get what. Be especially aware of potential clashes with Home Office definitions and rules. They can't be ignored.

Look out for immediate limits and constraints so you don't waste your time, energy and resources, or the refugee's. Be certain you are not encouraging someone to do something that could get them into trouble, such as taking paid work when they are still in the asylum system.

Other definitions and rules shape the *space* within which the refugee lives. Equally important, they shape their choices and potential to get on with rebuilding. At the same time, definitions you might not like but cannot ignore are framing the space you have for action in your role, although you have more flexibility than refugees.

You have *discretion*. Or you could call it wriggle room. Discretion is your ability to choose to do more or to do less to help someone.

You can *negotiate* the rules – not necessarily formally. You can stretch, interpret and argue, and at times choose to ignore rules.

You have *agency* – you can change things by engaging with others from a position of confidence and knowledge: change views, change definitions, change the rules.

But be careful. Without a good enough understanding of the whole picture, you can get it wrong.

With a subjective, inclusive definition of 'refugee', your *responsibility* is to make decisions; decide whom to support and decide on the best plan of action, even when you know you don't know enough. There are things you won't know – experiences that people are not ready to reveal, the things that desperate people are hiding. There are some people trying to get things they aren't entitled to. It is quite likely that at some point you will look back on a decision and wish you had or wish you hadn't.

There are four implications for you and your organisation:

1. Decisions over categories and entitlements are forms of power that restrict opportunities for whole groups of people. Hands-on workers need to look at each contact with a refugee with fresh eyes. You need to *keep on learning and sharing* your reflections on best practice.

2. As you and your team are making the best decisions you can on partial information and somewhat on principle, the organisation as a whole has to be willing to *share the responsibility* if it turns out you made a mistake. Talk to colleagues; keep them informed.

3. There are always risks when people interact, whether 'provider and client' or a mix of participants, members and service users. You still need *effective supervision and safeguarding procedures* in place.

4. Collaboration and good-quality referral to other services is important for the people you decide you can't help. Your *knowledge of other services* is an important part of your expertise.

Refugees in All Their Diversity – Equality, Discrimination and Positive Action

Introduction

Can anything demonstrate the importance of protection from discrimination and inequality more clearly than the arrival of people asking for asylum?

People from around the world are escaping from people who abuse their power and discriminate aggressively against those whom they see as different. The persecuted often face humiliation and abject impoverishment, as their intolerant societies strip away their goods, their identities and their futures. Their own governments fail to protect them (see Box 4.2)

The utter injustice is that the people who have been abused are the ones who give up everything. They may live in limbo for years, disempowered and their potential wasted.

They lose. Discrimination and abuse win.

According to British equality laws, everyone is equal, and people who come for refuge should be equal with everyone else and equally protected. Though, to quote an old friend of mine, 'Should?… Schmould!'

Discrimination exists in many ways in British society. Refugees are often on the receiving end of asylum-hate, but also more subtle forms of discrimination, when professionals create policies and processes that unintentionally leave people disadvantaged, and the decision-makers don't see the impact of what they have done.

Inequality is a real and current issue for refugees in the UK. They usually start with almost nothing in a society where people already have so much, but it is more than that.

First of all, take 1000 refugees and compare them with 1000 people drawn randomly from the UK population. More of the refugee group or 'population' will be struggling with disabilities, more will be religious believers, all are of ethnic minorities. These and other 'characteristics' are known to be linked to patterns of inequality and poverty in Britain.

Second, refugees often have poor English, few resources and little familiarity with British structures and culture. But such things don't need to disadvantage

people if the necessary services can be adapted and provided in an equitable way that responds to the needs of diverse individuals. It is often a matter of awareness and willingness.

Do you have to read this chapter? It is perfectly OK to skip over it – at first. Especially if you are looking for something to help someone who needs something done for them today.

But you should read it as part of your organisation's longer-term planning. Learning about equality law and relating it to your work is a bit like flossing your teeth. We all tend to put it off, but you'll feel better once you've done it and in the long run you'll be really glad you did.

Making use of the Equality Act 2010

This chapter makes use of the Equality Act 2010 ('the Act'). The legislation has been put in place to protect people from discrimination: the very protection refugees were lacking in their original countries. But this is not a briefing about the law (see the suggestions for finding out more in Box 4.13). It is about how you can use the ideas and principles spelled out in the Act to help make sure refugees – and other disadvantaged people in the UK – get a fair crack at things.

The Act is designed to make sure people and organisations – private, voluntary and statutory – avoid discrimination and try to improve equality. Of course, it is a tool for enforcement so there is an element of 'stick' to it. You can be challenged by users or outsiders if you don't comply (Box 4.1). It isn't optional.

Box 4.1 **Does the Equality Act 2010 apply to my organisation?**

Almost certainly. The Act applies to any organisation that provides services, regarding how it treats its service users, employees and volunteers. Your organisation is responsible for the actions of any staff member and, to some people's alarm, for the actions of any person or other body who is 'your agent' or 'carrying out your instructions'. This means your organisation is responsible for the behaviour and actions of your trainees and volunteers, and if you have other organisations working for you, you are also responsible for them as they are also your 'agent'.

As well as 'stick', however, there are potential 'carrots' in terms of relations with funders and statutory bodies, whether proving work is worth funding or your ability to lever changes in local statutory services. Changes in council or local NHS policy and services could benefit refugees well beyond the scope of anything most organisations could provide alone. This latter point is covered in Chapter 7.

The Act can be used in other practical ways.

- It spells out many useful concepts that can raise awareness about diversity among refugees – and any of your members or service users for that matter.

- It helps you scrutinise your organisational practices for any risk that what you are doing and the way you are doing it might accidentally make life harder for some of the people you aim to help (see Chapter 5).

- You can check you aren't doing certain things you mustn't do ('direct discrimination', 'indirect discrimination', 'positive discrimination').

- You can use the Act to justify taking 'positive action' if you think some special actions are needed specifically to help refugees, so they can catch up more quickly, although you still need to have evidence of the need.

The final reason equality law is valuable for practitioners who work with refugees goes back to the immigration definitions in Chapter 3. It is hard to use immigration law to help your work. It is imposed on you and is probably outside your original field of expertise. But equality law is already part of your working world and relates directly to everyone you support, not only refugees. Equality law is consistent with work responding to lived experience, unique individuals and subjective identities – where immigration law often clashes. Where immigration law controls and limits refugees, this chapter will show how equality law gives you tools to facilitate them.

Box 4.2	Protection from persecution – what happens when you don't have equality laws

Refugees are living evidence of what happens when you don't have equality laws and protection.

Different social, economic and political structures play out in different ways in different countries, but the protection in the UK's Equality Act 2010 is not provided in many countries across the world. In some countries, people of certain ethnic populations can only work in prescribed tasks. Disabled children are often secluded, refused education, even denied food. Girls are forced into marriage and sexual service; women are burned when they are disobedient. People in minority religions are moved into ghettos. Children work as unpaid labour. Gay men and lesbian women are beaten to death.

Protecting refugees from discrimination after they arrive in the UK

International refugee law specifies protection for 'race, religion, nationality, membership of a particular social group or political opinion' (see Box 3.4). Certain characteristics, such as sex, disability or sexuality, were not recognised initially, but have had to argue for protection as 'particular social groups' (Box 4.3).

Box 4.3 Women and other 'particular social groups'

Certain populations, such as women, were not initially recognised as being subject to persecution. Women refugees have had to argue for refugee protection for women as a 'particular social group' and this is now established in international practice. It also took a long time to get British decision-makers to see gendered and sexual acts inflicted on women as acts of persecution and not just general aggression to be expected in war. The battle is still not securely won.

Activism by equality campaigners in recent years seem to have created space in UK asylum debates for more thorough consideration of certain social groups, in particular around sexuality and disability. The work of the UK Lesbian and Gay Immigration Group (UKLGIG) and Micro Rainbow are good examples.

British equality law names 'protected characteristics', including race, religion, sex, disability, sexuality, transgender and others (Box 4.4). Anyone with any of these characteristics should be protected from discrimination and persecution while they are in the UK.

Box 4.4 Nine protected characteristics in the Equality Act 2010

- **Age.** A person who has a particular age in number of calendar years (e.g. 32-year-olds) or range of ages (e.g. 18–30-year-olds).

- **Disability.** A person has a disability if she or he has a physical or mental impairment which has a substantial and long-term adverse effect on that person's ability to carry out normal day-to-day activities.

- **Gender reassignment.** A person in the process of transitioning from one gender to another. (This also includes people who are intersex, transsexual or transgender.)

- **Race.** A group of people defined by their race, colour, nationality (including citizenship), ethnic or national origins.

- **Religion and belief.** Religion has the meaning usually given to it, but belief includes religious and philosophical beliefs including lack of belief (e.g. atheism). Sincerely held, observant, a belief that affects your life choices or the way you live.

- **Sex.** A male or female (man/woman girl/boy = gender/age).

- **Sexual orientation.** Whether a person's sexual attraction is towards their own sex, the opposite sex or to both sexes.

- **Marriage and civil partnership.** Civil partners must be treated the same as married couples on a wide range of legal matters.

- **Pregnancy and maternity.** Maternity, considered the first six months after birth.

So let's be clear what 'protected characteristic' means.
We all have 'characteristics'.

- I am right-handed. I am wearing jeans, etc.

Some of our characteristics are lifestyle choices which we can or could change:

- I can't become left-handed. I could change into a skirt.

Some we can't change, although they might change:

- I need stronger glasses each year.

We share many of our characteristics with other people.

- I am one of a couple of dozen people in my street who drives a car.

- The last census showed about 65 per cent of the people who live in my town are white English; about 95 per cent are British.

Some characteristics that we can't change and we share with a number of other people have been and are used by other people to disadvantage us:

- I am female. In some professions, employers tend to choose to employ men so I am at a disadvantage, through no fault of my own, if I want to go into that profession. The same applies to men being disadvantaged in other professions.

The Act protects everyone in the UK from discrimination on the grounds of any of the 'protected characteristics'. Therefore, any woman refugee has the same rights to equal treatment as any woman in the UK, and is also entitled to treatment that is as good as that shown to any man. Or any male refugee the same rights as any man; any child, young or older person; believer or non-believer, or any person residing in the UK has the same rights as anyone else in the UK with whom they share any of the nine 'protected characteristics', and also with those who don't share those characteristics. And your organisation has to treat them all equally, giving equal opportunities and perhaps equitable support – with an extra hand up here and there where people are behind.

Campaigners are challenging the Home Office and NASS to ensure they are fulfilling their duty to give equal opportunities and equitable treatment to people with diverse characteristics who are in the asylum process. The Women's Asylum Charter, for example, has challenged the Home Office regarding interview processes that disadvantage women and has had some real success (Asylum Aid 2018).

Refugees and race. Refugees are not specifically named as a protected group in the Act, but they are directly protected under the characteristic of 'race'. It is illegal to discriminate against people because of their colour, their nationality including citizenship, and their ethnicity or national origins.

Under 'race/nationality' the Act does not just ban discrimination against someone because she or he comes from a certain country, such as Afghanistan, but makes it illegal to discriminate against any person on the basis that she or he is not a British national. In other words, non-British people in the UK must be treated as well as people with UK nationality.

Exceptions affecting refugees. There can only be exceptions to the ban on discrimination if a law is passed by Parliament that makes it legal to discriminate in certain situations. Immigration laws passed in the past 15 years have made it legal to treat asylum seekers, refused asylum seekers and refugees with Leave differently, and less well than British nationals. But it isn't a general licence to discriminate. The different treatment allowed is only what is specified in the legislation. Against that, as noted in Chapter 3, are other areas of law such as children's, health and social care laws and mental health law that override immigration law. Ultimately, nothing can override the Human Rights Act 1998.

Box 4.5 | **How laws override each other, but nothing overrides human rights**

So it could go like this. A refused asylum seeker is in labour. The Equality Act 2010 says all people in the UK should receive equal health services. Immigration laws (in England) says refused asylum seekers are an exception, and can be charged or refused some care and treatments. The Human Rights Act 1998 Article 2 says public bodies such as hospitals cannot violate the right to life, and Article 3 enshrines freedom from inhumane and degrading treatment, so the hospital will take care of her during childbirth and give any further urgent treatment needed. But they send an invoice later.

For the hands-on worker, it is important not to look at a refugee and see only a refugee. People are complex and unique: queer or questioning, young and growing older. People persecuted them because they didn't like who they saw them to be. Now in the UK, they still have all their previous, complex characteristics, plus now that of being a refugee. Refugees are often categorised under race or 'BME' labels (Black and Minority Ethnic), or maybe 'BAMER' (Black, Asian, Minority Ethnic and Refugee). But if you want to avoid discrimination, you need to look at the whole person, with a whole mix of characteristics, all of which are significant in their lives and the support we offer them. (For an example, see Box 1.1.)

What you mustn't do

Now to you and your organisation. What mustn't you do?

Discrimination really does happen in the daily activities and life of many organisations. Staff may feel secure that colleagues or volunteers would not express direct hostility towards refugees. But there must always be concern

about people misusing wriggle room – their discretion to do more or to do less. There is also the risk that a policy that was meant to help everyone accidentally makes it worse for a certain population with a shared characteristic.

Direct discrimination

Direct discrimination is when a person is knowingly treated less favourably than another in the same or a similar situation. It might seem reasonable to segregate people by a certain characteristic, but unless there is an objective reason to do this, it is direct discrimination. Therefore, although the Home Office is allowed to treat non-nationals differently to British nationals, you aren't – except in the ways the Home Office tells you to, such as letting asylum seekers apply for a job vacancy.

Hostile and insulting behaviour on grounds of people's characteristics is direct discrimination. This includes voiced expressions of 'asylum-hate' such as telling a refugee to 'go home' or 'go back to where you came from' (Box 4.6). It also includes some actions that would probably never see you in court, but which get noticed by people who are on the receiving end.

One little cut that a lot of migrants feel is when people make no effort to pronounce their name correctly, or make it sound ridiculous, or anglicise it without permission, as if it is unreasonable that a person has a name from their original culture. These little 'micro-aggressions' belittle and downgrade the receiving person's humanity, and express implicit hostility and a sense that the person is not equal in the perpetrator's eyes.

Box 4.6 **Direct discrimination from local life – Case Studies A and B**

Case Studies are referred to in the text as 'CS/A', 'CS/B', and so on.

A A refugee member's young daughter was verbally insulted by an adult volunteer at her school, who told her she had no right to be here and made her cry. The situation was dealt with swiftly and emphatically by the school to the parent's satisfaction.

B A Tamil woman on her way to a workshop we were organising about equality and refugees was waiting to cross the road with her baby in a front-facing pushchair, when the passenger of a passing van yelled abuse at her and squirted water at the baby.

In most services, professional and hands-on staff have a great deal of discretion in whether and how they serve someone. If someone gives refugees lower-quality support than they give non-refugees, because of personal hostility or cynicism, that is direct discrimination. It might be as simple as deciding not to book an interpreter, even though they could. It can also be direct discrimination when people repeat the way they acted for one refugee for different refugee, because they assume 'they are the same' (see also Box 4.7).

| Box 4.7 | Forms and examples of illegal direct discrimination, including 'positive discrimination' |

- Discrimination 'by association' – for example, not sending someone who cares for a disabled person on a course that other staff go on, because you assume they will take time off.

- Discrimination 'by perception' – for example, someone who insults a woman because they think she is going out with an asylum seeker, even if she isn't.

- Deliberately causing disadvantage (by comparison) – for example, not letting a refugee volunteer with an older person's lunch group because the participants and other volunteers might not like it.

- Harassment, unwanted conduct – for example, deliberately telling jokes about gas chambers in front of a Jewish person (association and perception apply).

- Victimisation – picking on someone because they complained or protested about discrimination affecting them or anyone else.

- 'Positive' discrimination: favouring one person or group over another for no objective reason – for example, giving one of three equally good candidates a job because she is a refugee and you want to help refugees. Please note: this is illegal discrimination (but see 'positive action' below).

Indirect discrimination and 'We don't do refugees'

Indirect discrimination is when a practice, policy, set of eligibility criteria, and so on is set up and applied generally, but in a way that means a whole body of people with a shared characteristic is accidentally ruled out or unable to access the resources for no good reason. It might be a long time before people within the organisation notice a whole group of people are not using their services, so it is very useful to take a fresh look at patterns in take-up or get an outside view now and then.

For example, if a hospital gets all its interpreters through agencies that require interpreters to be self-employed, it makes it likely that a substantial block of migrants will be stranded in insecure employment with limited rights, career prospects, insurance and pensions. If there is a more mixed group of people within the hospital, with equivalent levels of skill and responsibility, have regular job contracts and full rights, the policy of sourcing interpreters through agencies may be indirectly discriminating against migrants, or, in other words, indirectly racist.

Box 4.8	**When not understanding leads to discrimination – Case Studies C–E**

C   During a survey of support organisations of and for lesbian and gay people in 2009, looking at awareness of lesbian and gay refugees, one organisation told us, 'We…are fighting AIDS; we don't have a service for refugees' (indirect discrimination).

D   A second said, 'We do housing for gay men; we don't do refugees' (indirect discrimination).

E   A third said, 'We do not encourage refugees to access our services as our funders would not be happy about us providing services to people who are not supposed to be here…' (direct discrimination).

A participant in the survey review workshop commented: 'Sometimes individuals, groups and organisations start to impose their own "migration law", by making it a condition which the law does not actually state.'

It can be difficult to avoid discriminating if you are unclear about immigration status and want to avoid getting your employer into trouble. Immigration law, exceptions, case law, judicial rulings, entitlements and documentation have been changing constantly for 20 years. The result is widespread confusion and misinformation about refugees' rights and entitlements. Few people outside refugee specialist bodies are confident about the definitions and differences between asylum seekers, Convention refugees and others.

With pressure from government not to employ, treat, serve, house or educate people who are not entitled, there is a risk that hands-on staff will err on the side of caution and refuse to serve a refugee, perhaps saying 'We don't do refugees' because they don't want to make a mistake. But this is how mistakes are made: refugees are disadvantaged without justification; refugees who *are* entitled and in need are wrongly turned away. This is discrimination (Boxes 4.8 and 4.9).

When social services incorrectly refuse to assess a disabled asylum seeker's needs because they think non-nationals are not entitled to local authority support, that is discrimination.

Box 4.9	**When confusion leads to discrimination – Case Study F**

F   When one of our members was refused accommodation by a landlord because he was an asylum seeker, the landlord apologised but explained he didn't want a fine for housing an illegal immigrant. A letter enclosing the government guidance with relevant passages highlighted reassured him and he happily let our member move in.

There are also times, especially under pressure to cut costs, that structures designed to improve efficiency disproportionately disadvantage refugees and other migrants. For example, cuts to child care at colleges particularly affect migrant women who cannot access English classes if they have children under school age, preventing them from even starting on the ladder to employment and integration. Even attempts to avoid discrimination might unintentionally discriminate – for example, a recruitment panel that wants to avoid personal assumptions might anonymise application forms in an effort to be fair to all, but set criteria such as minimum qualifications that candidates need to have to be considered. In doing so, they could accidentally exclude migrants and refugees who are qualified but whose qualifications are non-UK, without ever knowing, because their qualifications aren't on the approved list.

If you see something that seems discriminatory, or have it reported to you, there are some straightforward things you can do, starting with a gentle nudge. See Chapter 7 for details and what you can do next if a nudge doesn't work.

What you can do to improve equality

You can't treat people less favourably, or disadvantage them because of their protected characteristics, but you can treat them differently and do things especially for them.

You can differentiate. In fact, you must. There is no point giving a deaf person braille to read or a blind person sign language interpreters. It is not about splitting resources 50/50 for men and women. You can't avoid discrimination by calling everyone 'person' or 'friend' or 'community members'. You don't help refugees gain an equal footing and an equal stake in society by ignoring the fact they are refugees and 'treating everyone the same' (Chapter 2).

It is fully legitimate to differentiate refugees and argue that refugees are so disadvantaged that they must be treated as a high-priority equality group. Refugees have many difficult characteristics, often linked to disadvantages they have faced and unfair new challenges now. They need to be at high risk of discrimination and disadvantage alongside other high-priority groups. This is *not* a hierarchy, or competition for who is most disadvantaged; many people in British society are seriously disadvantaged and struggling with multiple disadvantages – refugee populations are one of those groups.

When you differentiate between people, you can then get proper information about their needs and provide the right support for them. Different treatment is fine as long as it is based on the person's actual situation at that point, and is *appropriate* and *proportionate*. You also need to differentiate within a population – for example, Iranians with mobility difficulties, Iranian teenagers, Iranian lesbians (Box 4.10). The key is the quality and detail in your organisation's data, your working relationship with the refugee/s and your own awareness and knowledge.

Box 4.10 **Hostility and discrimination within 'communities'**

'Community' as in 'refugee community' is not a helpful concept for hands-on workers.

The feel-good implications of 'community' gloss over 'refugee' problems such as the long-term impact of civil war, inter-family, inter-tribal, inter-regional, inter-ethnic or inter-faith conflict between people from the same country, ethnic group or religion.

So bear in mind that people within the same ethnic or national population, who 'share a characteristic', do not necessarily like each other or approve of each other. Discrimination and intolerance are not ruled out by having one or two things in common. A relatively small number of people with the shared characteristic may develop a shared, positive identity and build forms of social organisation on that, but that can raise issues about the loyalty and conformity required for people to 'belong', often denying diversity and cultural change.

It is especially important to be aware of this if you work to support 'a community', such as 'the Iranian community' or 'the gay community'. Some 'members of the community' might actively discriminate and exclude and even persecute others whom they see as different even if you see them as similar.

'Community' inverts the real absence of any kind of meaningful connection between people who happen to share a certain characteristic, and implies they all know and care for each other. Its ideological undertones assume a degree of solidarity, self-help and shared identity that are not usually realistic and tend to give a sense that if public authorities let people down, some kind of mutual self-help system will function in their absence.

'Community' overemphasises place, locality and proximity. It ignores stigma and fear of being made visible as 'a refugee'. Often outsiders treat the few who make themselves visible as 'community leaders' if they typify and/or represent and can communicate with the many.

You can make reasonable adjustments. All service providers and employers have a duty to make reasonable adjustments for someone with impairments, to ensure she or he is not disadvantaged by things that could be avoided. Where feasible, they should change practical activities and facilities or put in extra support, so an individual with an impairment can participate or benefit to the same level as someone without that impairment. Ideally, employers and service providers should also be looking ahead to what might be a barrier.

With refugees, this might include a policy of always using plain English or having a contact list of interpreters to hand if needed. Mental ill health is considered a disability and is a frequent challenge for refugees, so making waiting, treatment or working environments for service users less stressful is a very reasonable adjustment.

'Reasonable adjustment' is a good principle, one most people are familiar with, and difficult to argue against. It is a good tool to use in your organisation to improve opportunities and make your services more responsive and accessible. What is

good for one disadvantaged person is sometimes good for others: plain English and a less stressful working environment are usually a good thing all round.

Where budgets are tight, people might feel they have little room for adjustments, but thinking ahead might include arguing you need a budget line for reasonable adjustments in next year's budget or bid – funders are often supportive of a realistic budget for reasonable adjustments. It is after all about complying with a legal duty.

You can take positive action. Positive action is one of the great assets created by the Act. It gives service providers permission to do extra things for some people only, if those actions will help them catch up and avoid future disadvantages. It lets you put extra effort and resources into helping certain people; you can treat them *more* favourably than others, as long as you have evidence that there is a need. You can take positive action to:

- Overcome disadvantage (about the past): Your extra, targeted project, service or resources will help people get over the harm done by inequality and discrimination that held them back in the past, or if, as in the case of newly arrived refugees, their circumstances mean they are far behind people who are like them in other ways (age, ability, etc.). For example, free English lessons would be a positive action to help people who have arrived in Britain without English to learn more quickly. Another example could be a 'migrant immunisation catch-up' project.

- Facilitate participation (about the present): This is the extra things you can do to make sure particularly disadvantaged groups don't miss out on current opportunities, when they might have trouble accessing them without extra help. Your local research might show Tamil-speaking refugees are unaware of a certain course that would be particularly useful to them, or they can't afford your normal course fees, or can't get child care and so can't attend. You might do a Tamil-language publicity leaflet, offer some 'refugee bursaries', ask a Tamil-speaking crèche worker to provide play activities in the next room, even though non-Tamil speakers might also want help with child care.

- Meet their different needs (about the future): Where there is an aspect of people's lives that will probably continue to be a source of challenges, you can set up ongoing specialist services that are only of use to them and no one else, to stop these being disadvantages in future. This positive action relates only to those ongoing needs. An example could be a Pashtu-language counselling service for young Afghan refugees with post-traumatic stress disorder.

You have to have evidence that refugees need positive action before you can provide it. You need to gather data and evidence which you can present to

non-refugees who might challenge what you are doing as they might accuse you of discriminating against *them*. This can be direct from your organisation's monitoring and research with users, or from local and/or national sources (see Box 4.13 and Appendix A).

Your positive action has to be for people who are disadvantaged in comparison with the general population. You don't have to put on positive action for all the disadvantaged groups you identify, or even the most disadvantaged. And positive action has to be related to the particular disadvantages showing up in your evidence.

So if your evidence shows that recent Sudanese refugees arriving in your area are suffering from dental problems, you can put on something to help with their teeth. You can't take them all out for a day trip to the seaside and call it 'positive action', no matter how much everyone would enjoy it.

Remember to be careful that your 'positive action' is not 'positive discrimination' (see Box 4.7).

You can monitor equality characteristics. It is not only all right, but very important to monitor the diversity of who uses which of your services, who is and isn't satisfied with services, your applicants for volunteer or paid positions, diversity of staff, trustees and more. Characteristic monitoring will show you whether the people involved in and using your organisation are coming from all protected populations or just some. Then you can decide if that is a problem. It can even show you whether there are different patterns in use or different levels of satisfaction for people with certain combinations of characteristics too, such as African women or older Muslims.

Saying you can and should monitor for equality characteristics is not to say it is easy or popular. There are no one-size-fits-all equality characteristic monitoring forms or processes that will work for everyone. You need to design a process that will make refugees visible. Funders often have their own set forms, which usually renders the process meaningless for the organisation that has to get people to fill them in. See Box 4.11.

	Equality characteristic monitoring
Box 4.11	(ECM) and looking for refugees

- You want your ECM to make refugees visible, so that you can see if they are using your service. You will usually need to adapt your form and process.

- Don't use other people's categories. Start with the nine protected characteristics but decide what will make refugees visible within your respondents.

- Does 'Asian' give you meaningfully differentiated data? With refugees? No! Asian = Chinese, Russian, Afghan, Tamil, Turkish, Palestinian, Indonesian, Korean, Vietnamese, Myanmar, Bangladeshi, Pakistani, Iraqi, Iranian, Syrian, Yemeni, Indian, Nepalese, Japanese and more.

- You can invite people to describe their ethnicity, religion, and so on in their own words, which is more meaningful for them, although it will cause difficulty collating. You need to do your research to find out which of the ethnicities are likely to be refugees.

- Collect it, collate it, analyse it, discuss it, report on it, act on it. If you aren't going to use the data, don't ask people for it.

The Public Sector Equality Duty (PSED) – what they (and you) must do

It is worthwhile investing time in understanding the Public Sector Equality Duty (often just called 'the Equality Duty' or PSED). You can use it to help refugees when you are dealing with other organisations, and practical suggestions for advocacy and lobbying public sector bodies are given in Chapter 7. It has potential to help people with all characteristics, of course, but this section gives a simple overview, and highlights points that have particular relevance to refugees.

In Chapter 3, I noted how having the authority to define people gives a body great power over their lives and over the actions of those who support them. The body that can define categories decides what someone is and isn't, what they can do, what support and services they will get and how.

Many public or statutory bodies – councils, the NHS, colleges – also have scale. Where the decisions a small charity makes about its priorities might affect 30 people, or 300, a governmental body might make changes that affect 3000 or 3,000,000. A change of plan could help a great many people but, without any ill intention at all, mess things up for some smaller groups. Refugees are one of those groups.

The Act places the Equality Duty on all 'public authorities' – roughly, bodies using taxpayers' money – and their 'agents', which might include your organisation (Box 4.12). If they fund you, you should comply with the Equality Duty and the public authority might check you do.

Box 4.12	What are public authorities? Does this affect my organisation?

A public authority is, broadly, any state body that has powers given to it by law and/or which operates with taxpayers' money – so councils, police, the NHS, most schools, and so on are public authorities.

Other organisations doing work for these bodies also count as public authorities because they are directly or effectively operating on behalf of the state body. This can include your organisation, if it is using funds from a contract or grant from a public authority. The public authority must make sure you comply. Public authorities and their agents must comply with the whole Equality Act 2010, including the Public Sector Equality Duty (PSED).

The Equality Duty is meant to push public authorities to take far more care about indirect or what used to be called institutional discrimination. There is no doubt it has potential to bring about change for the better, both for refugees and my mum.

'Due regard...' Under the Act, public authorities must have 'due regard' to the equality needs of staff and services users. Due regard means the public authority has to be proactive in checking for inequality and always look for ways to improve the situation. It is not just about avoiding discrimination. It is about equality in a broader sense. If a group of people have substantially lower living conditions, education, health, etc., the public body has to address this. Refugees are very much in this category.

For example, many Afghan women have had no schooling and are illiterate and innumerate in any language. They often live in family structures with strict gender roles. They tend to have poor health, partly because they rarely take up preventative screening or treatment and often present to health professionals when illnesses are advanced. If a public authority is paying due regard to inequalities across its area, and has an Afghan population living within its boundaries, it should be aware of this. It must make sure the way it runs local services does not reinforce or worsen this inequality. Staff can take positive action – for example, health workers can target activities to improve Afghan women's take-up of preventative and primary health.

A service provider can't tackle all inequality in their area at once. So it is all right to support a health group for Afghan mothers, even if it means a public authority does not have enough resources to run an exercise group for men with diabetes – as long as the decision is based in sound evidence. However, the Equality Duty is an ongoing duty. Although organisations can prioritise, they cannot ignore other existing inequalities: the needs of the diabetic men must not be forgotten.

The Equality Duty says public authorities must work to:

- *'Eliminate discrimination, harassment, victimisation and other conduct that is prohibited by or under the Act.'* This means they must make sure no staff behave badly, that decisions are always properly made and their implications for people who might be disadvantaged are thought through, and that administration and organisational management, such as eligibility criteria, access routes and evidence noted in Chapter 3, have no bias.

- *'Advance equality of opportunity between people who share a protected characteristic and those who do not share that characteristic.'* This means reviewing and making changes and creating strategies, including positive action, so that both staff and volunteers in the organisation and diverse members of the public all have a fair chance of gaining equally good outcomes from what the organisation offers.

- *'Foster good relations between people who share a relevant protected characteristic and those who do not share that characteristic.'* Public authorities must encourage mutual knowledge and positive relationships between populations and among the mass of diverse individuals in its area. This includes tackling intolerance or hostility and preventing or dealing with hate-crime.

Equality Duty procedures. The PSED lays out certain documents and procedures that public authorities have to have in place, although they often go under different names. These procedures are designed to improve local data, ensure long- and better short-term planning, and stop people relying on guesswork. Where these processes are weak, refugees and many small disadvantaged populations will always be at risk of being passed over.

The various documents and procedures are an asset for practitioners and any member of the public who wants to feed into decision-making. You can use Equality Duty processes to get refugees on authorities' agendas, encourage better refugee-related data and heighten attention to refugees in design, planning and commissioning/funding, and reviews of how effective something has been. You can trigger positive actions that will benefit refugees – perhaps with you as a partner in the delivery.

Equality Evidence Review. The Equality Evidence Review should include local primary data from local statistics from the Census and Joint Strategic Needs Assessment and any reliable local source. There are few local statistics about refugees, and the Census doesn't record immigration status. Refugee populations change too fast for the Census to keep up. But detailed ethnic and language data in the Census can be useful, and schools and NHS also collect language and even interpreter data if you can access it.

The Evidence Review should also have qualitative data from consultations, case studies and local voices, which is where you can get refugees' voices heard. It should use evidence from respected sources and can include national bodies, including specialist bodies in the voluntary sector such as the King's Fund and the Refugee Council. The amount of good-quality national work on refugee needs and good practice can make up somewhat for the lack of local statistics (see Appendix A).

Equality Objectives. Every public authority must agree Equality Objectives for the organisation at the highest level and publish them so the public can see them. The choice of Objectives should come from the Evidence Review. Equality Objectives state what the public authority's priority populations will be for the next few years, and what changes it aims to bring about for those populations. Equality Objectives should then, in theory, be included in plans (including plans for positive action) and monitoring across all activities. It doesn't usually work quite that well.

Equality Objectives create space for action. If you can get refugees, or Afghan women, for example, named in the Equality Objectives, it gives the authority's staff more freedom to do something about the disadvantages they face. You could well see some big local improvements for them in the years ahead.

Annual Equality Duty Review. Every January the public authority should publish a review of updated evidence, and the progress they have made towards their Equality Objectives.

Equality Impact Assessment (EIA) and mitigating actions. Every time there is a substantial change in policy, new, changing or decommissioning (ending) of services, the public authority must assess what impact the change will have on the 'equality' populations in their area. The purpose is to spot any damage to certain groups 'in the community' before it happens, so staff can put in mitigating actions to avoid the harm. Any shock-prone group with high needs and low means, such as refugees, is vulnerable in times of change where information and rules change, especially as new teams set up new access structures which usually start off as one-size-fits-all.

EIAs use the data in the Evidence Review and should also gather fresh local participatory data and relevant national research in relation to the proposed change. The EIA can be used to trigger 'mitigating actions'. Where positive action is about making things better, mitigating actions try to stop things getting any worse than they have to.

Equality characteristic monitoring. This has been mentioned already. If done correctly, especially if integrated throughout feedback and evaluation, equality monitoring provides stronger data for the Evidence Review and future Objectives and EIAs. Get your refugee participants to fill in the forms – they will probably need reassurance and your help to understand.

Summary and conclusion

Box 4.13 **Further sources on anti-discrimination and equality**

There is a great deal of high-quality training and writing to draw on, face to face and online. Look for Equality and Human Rights Commission, Equality and Diversity Forum, National Equality Partnership reports (NEP has ended), Open University, British Institute of Human Rights, HEAR and brap and other regional networks that have managed to keep going. Also, Race on the Agenda (RoTA), Women's Resource Centre, Age Concern, Disability Law Service, Stonewall.

Regarding refugees with protected characteristics, see Asylum Aid (women), Forward (women and girls/female genital mutilation – FGM), UKLGIG and Micro Rainbow (sexual orientation), JCORE, Children's organisations in Chapter 11.

The Equality Act 2010 gives you a structure that you must comply with but also a range of concepts, opportunities and tools of real use. You might use it to advance the interests of refugees and protect them from harm. But any step towards better access and equality is good for all your vulnerable clients. Equality law is there for all of us.

Already wary of authorities, refugees are unlikely to stand up against discrimination and for equal treatment. They often rely on the bodies they should sometimes be challenging. Stretched thin as they are, they are more likely to suffer a long-term impact from discrimination – or from poor policy and planning. 'They are particularly vulnerable to discrimination as [unlike other migrants] they do not have the choice to leave the UK and go back to their countries of origin' (EDF and REAP 2011, p.2). Refugees, like everyone, care about having a reasonable chance to get on with life. No country can afford to ignore discrimination if it wants a healthy society in which people can fulfil their potential. Inequality makes it harder to design your own future, and more likely that a person's or a group's potential will be wasted. They don't usually articulate their frustration in terms of inequality. 'As long as we are human beings we face challenges,' one workshop participant said.

If people who have left behind discrimination and persecution find themselves limited to an underclass existence here, we can hardly claim to have given them refuge. Sadly, refugees often accept discrimination as normal.

But you don't have to.

Engaging with Refugees

Introduction

I could have called this chapter 'Working with Refugees', or 'Dialogue and Inter-action with Refugees' or 'Participation, Agency, Empowerment and Integration', 'Responding to...' or 'Creating spaces for...'. But 'Engaging' gets across a sense of urgency, of *negotiating a creative relationship*. As a friend of mine said about his daughter who had been struggling with mental health and drug issues, 'She's engaging with us, and that's good enough for me.'

'*With* Refugees' emphasises that this is not about getting *them* to do something, but about *mutual influence and communication*. This is communication in its full sense, as dialogue between diverse parties that builds new knowledge and helps all parties grow and develop. Fluent English language is helpful, but there is more to it than that.

It is crucial to see what you and your organisation do *as refugees might see it*. As any detective film says, you have to figure out their motives, means and opportunities. Then reflect that in your practice. What motivates someone who has to rebuild a life? Given the hoops refugees have to jump through, do they have the skills and assets they need to make that leap? Are there timely, local openings they can take advantage of and use in their strategies?

> You have to figure out their motives, means and opportunities.

Refugees are just ordinary people, all different and doing the best they can. They will shop around – engage where and when they believe they can get the best out of their scarce resources. Don't see this as cynicism. Nor is it some kind of failure in the relationship. They are making their own decisions, taking responsibility for their own lives. What comes out of it might not be quite what you expected. Can you adjust?

Chapter 2 highlighted how refugees' experiences and current pressures might affect their willingness and ability to form good working relationships with people like you, especially if they see you as an authority figure. Then there are the broader issues all migrants face, such as working in an unfamiliar language and culture. Some stability lets the relationship grow. You will need to be clear, adaptable, build mutual knowledge and trust to gain a degree of collaboration.

This chapter is about practical action. About *how*. It starts with understanding issues about access that everyone needs to recognise, and then seeing the view from where refugees stand. The ideas come from many lessons and voices over the past 15 years: from refugees, practitioners and my own experiences and observations. But it isn't a 'How to...' manual. It isn't a ready-to-eat cake or even a 'results guaranteed' packet mix. Please think of it as a cupboard of ingredients to pick from as you mix and flavour for your needs.

Access

The first step in any work to engage people is understanding 'access'. Whether or not the resources refugees need exist is certainly a big issue. Whether they are entitled is another. But when something out there could be useful for them, the most significant issue is: can they access it? Have they got the knowledge, documents, skills to negotiate access, and is it worth the effort? Britain may have some of the best justice, education, medicine and arts in the world, but what good is that to refugees if they can't access them?

You can start with the well-established idea of three 'access stages' that people have to work their way through to use formal services. Think of a job application. First, you submit an application form and they look at two or three key points to check you meet the minimum requirements – a work permit, an appropriate qualification, etc. If you don't, your form goes in the recycle bin. If you do, you are through 'the gate' and they will consider your application. They read the whole form carefully and compare it with all the other applicants' forms, while you wait to hear if you are shortlisted for interview. That is 'the queue'. The interview is a face-to-face 'encounter', where people see you, hear you and judge you on the spot.

In other cases, encounters are the moments of direct interaction when the staff or the organisation negotiate exactly what they will offer you, which might include them making some reasonable adjustments and the decision-maker using a degree of discretion. Some services may also be provided directly through encounters – you get your injection, you sit and learn English, or you talk with a therapist.

One refugee I discussed access with said that for him what he called the 'pre-gate' was even more important. He needs a wheelchair to get around, but for his first two years in Britain he didn't know he could get help to get a wheelchair, he didn't know buses had ramps and he had never heard of independent living centres. 'I just sat in the four walls of my room.' He says many refugees (and people in all walks of life) don't even know there is something useful out there. Or even when someone knows something is possible in the UK – for example, you can get a wheelchair – they don't know how to find the service, or how to tell if it is the right one for them or good quality, or even whether the provider might rip them off. They never get as far as the gate. (See Box 5.1.)

In asylum, assuming people know what to do (pre-gate), the initial asylum claim and screening interview (gate) usually includes face-to-face interaction with officials (encounter). Then knowing how to find a decent solicitor (pre-gate) and get to an appointment (gate) to brief them on your case (encounter). Then gathering evidence and documents to build that case while you wait (queue) for your substantive interview (encounter). Then you wait and chase people for news (queue). Asylum seekers can write to or contact their MP at constituency surgeries (gate/encounter) to ask for help to speed thing up (queue), but few asylum seekers know this (pre-gate). During this waiting period you find the number (pre-gate) to ring the subcontractor (encounter) who screens your eligibility for NASS support (gate); then you submit your application for support (gate) and wait (queue), possibly with no money, nowhere to stay and no food (pre-gate-foodbank). If you get Leave to Remain (gate) you go to a Jobcentre Plus…and so it goes on. There is a kind of sequence but it is more loops. You are judged by anonymous strangers on paperwork and in face-to-face encounters throughout.

Box 5.1 Challenges to access with examples

Challenges to access		Examples
'Pre-gate'	When people are not even aware that a service exists or that they might be entitled to it, or how to find it or how to choose between different options.	Never having heard of an independent living centre. Not knowing you need to register with a GP (or how) to get free health care. Not knowing that as you have impairments you can ask your council for a community care assessment. Having a list of solicitors (or child care, or college courses) but having no idea how to choose.
Gate	The point a person first comes into contact with an agency and has to persuade 'gatekeepers' that she or he is eligible for the resources and services that the organisation provides or controls.	Asking a GP receptionist to register you with the GP. Asking your GP to refer you for specialist counselling. Filling and posting an application for NASS support (subsistence funds/accommodation; see Chapter 3). Going into a bank with ID papers to try to open a bank account. Open the door of a café and walk in.

| Queue | Submit and wait for your request or claim to be dealt with, as it is assessed for completeness, credibility, entitlements and priority compared with need and with others; waiting for an appointment, a decision. Might request special treatment, a quick decision, priority over others. | Waiting in the Accident and Emergency department of a hospital before and after triage. Sending extra letters and documents to strengthen your claim for NASS support, answering further questions, ringing for news, getting an advocate to ring for you. Waiting to hear about your asylum appeal. Asking your solicitor or MP to support you. In a café, you catch the waitress's eye. |
| Encounter | Face-to-face or other direct interaction with a decision-maker and/or person providing the service, who tells you what they will provide for you, with some discussion/negotiation. Depending on the service, it might be provided in this or another encounter. 'Encounters' are often also 'gates'. | Triage nurse examines you. A duty nurse treats you. A family support worker spends an hour with you helping you fill a form. You meet the bank manager to discuss a loan for a college course. The waitress brings your food. |

'Access stages' is rather a neutral term. Each stage is an anxiety-provoking hurdle, another mini-crisis that refugees have to get through as they try to sort out their lives. Whether you run a little local play group or a 980-bed hospital, to engage effectively with refugees your organisation needs to make sure that what happens day to day in all four different access settings is equitable and easy for a refugee to deal with. Long Box 5.2 has several examples of ways – good and bad – that organisations arrange access to their services.

Even if an own-language leaflet improves things pre-gate, and empathetic staff are wonderful at making encounters productive, neither means anything if a reception volunteer (gate) turns the asylum seeker away, saying you can't help. I have an alert word when looking at access: 'just'. As in 'they just need to…' I instantly know there is going to be a problem.

> I have an alert word: 'just': As in 'they just need to…' I instantly know there is going to be a problem.

Long Box 5.2	Different ways organisations handle access, good and bad – Case Studies A–I

Pre-gate

A This organisation established its professionalism with local social services and staff are permitted to work directly in a hostel for young refugees. They spend quite a lot of time there each week, and because they go to where refugees are, they make contact and support people who have just arrived, even though they could be moved to other regions soon.

B Several organisations created a shared list of groups to be distributed. But the list only reaches refugees who are already connected with services such as primary school or other groups. The majority of new group participants still come because of word of mouth.

C This organisation runs services in an area with a substantial refugee population. It serves hundreds of people. When asked how many refugees use their services, a staff member answered, 'We don't want to stigmatise by asking, but at a guess, one or two.' Because they do not monitor, they can't find out if they have refugee users or not. They have no way of knowing whether they should be putting special effort to avoid indirectly discriminating against refugees by leaving them outside the gate.

Gate

D A local advice service gave out appointments by a first come, first served queuing system where people waited from 8am to get an appointment. Ironically, when cuts bit hard it improved the access, as the service linked up with two others to set up a single freephone number which people ring and most now get initial advice by phone. Face-to-face appointments are only given if absolutely necessary.

E An adult learning team offered a four-session 'Boost Your English' course funded by a Government source which needed ten people to go ahead. About 18 people arrived the first week, several of whom spoke almost no English and struggled to understand instructions. As well as proof of identity and address, they were unexpectedly asked to prove they were refugees and prove how long they had been in the UK. Women who had refugee status through their husbands were told to come back with evidence of their husbands' refugee status plus their marriage certificates. The 'Boost Your English' team didn't have a photocopier so they told people to bring their own photocopies the next week. There was no time for any English. The course was cancelled before the second week.

F Freedom from Torture's reception area in Birmingham has warm soft colours, open windows, sofas and chairs with cushions, attractive art works done by clients, tissues, fresh fruit; a low-level desk which the calm and experienced volunteer receptionist sits behind, with a vase of flowers, a photograph board showing good-sized photos of staff,

their names and roles; a clean toilet with tampons and condoms available for anyone to take; one neat short list in large print of key advice services and no other notices or signs, except a couple on the back of the toilet door about confidential domestic violence or sexual health services.

Queue

G A social housing bidding system sends emails to people when a property comes up. Registered individuals bid online, and viewings are allocated on a first come, first served basis. One of our members had to go to the library just to read her emails, causing such delays that she had no realistic chance of a successful bid and gave up. The IT system that worked very well for some people meant she had no chance of getting off the bottom of the queue.

Encounter

H A session with free food was held at a local church hall. Volunteers say a blessing before distributing the food to their diverse applicants. 'Mostly people don't mind,' one said.

I Regular participants at an English group had very little English but were familiar with signing in, a regular circle exercise for greeting everyone, role plays and how to work the tea urn. They made sure new people know what to do and took part in what was going on.

So far this view on access does not do justice to the critical *relationship* between a hands-on worker and a service user. That relationship is not a fifth 'stage'. It is fundamental to all the challenges that access presents to refugees and, ultimately, to whether they get what they need.

A relationship can exist without trust, but it is more productive with, and there is a mutual need for honesty and appreciation to get the best outcomes. Much of what refugees have been through makes trust all the more precious. They might hold back while they observe you and decide if they can trust you. Make sure they know what you are doing and why, and what is being written on forms and on computers. Trust is about your credibility and earning their respect, not about getting them to like you. Friendly? Yes. But not friends.

> Trust is about your credibility and earning their respect... Friendly? Yes. But not friends.

Don't ever risk your credibility by being vague. Be honest about what you don't know. Be upfront and clear about your role and limits. And only ever promise what you are certain you can deliver.

The end reality is that you – the staff member – hold all the control cards. Power here is very one-sided whether you like that fact or not. In many cases the only way a refugee can take control is to walk away.

However, in any interaction, and especially in face-to-face encounters, there is an element of influence in both directions as you ask them questions and their answers change your awareness and knowledge. They appeal to your discretion and you consider your potential to change wider systems. Make space for refugees' influence and the relationship can become more creative and productive.

Motives, means and opportunities – reflect and boost

The chapter opened with the need to look at your own work as refugees might see it, figuring out the motives, means and opportunities refugees have when they engage with you. Then you have to adapt your work so it reflects their motives and means and creates opportunities that work for them, rather than necessarily for you.

At times you don't know enough; so try things out and do it better next time. At times adapting everything around their perceptions and priorities just isn't possible. But think through the issues, and do what you can. And make sure you talk to people who *don't* come as well as those who do.

Motive to engage with you

Refugees are active agents of their own development. They are motivated to act. But to what end? What would you or I care about if we had been through what they have been through? Are we offering refugees what they feel they need?

> Question from workshop trainer: 'Any methods you have tried that did not work?'

> Answer from participating professional: 'Anything, when they don't wish to communicate.'

People are motivated to pursue their subjective interests. These are by no means selfish interests but a drive to improve the things and usually benefit the people we care about. Personal standards and principles also matter.

Many of us are familiar with Maslow's hierarchy of the needs which motivate people to act. It is a good place to start. We go from rudimentary human needs for 'survival' – safety and welfare, food, shelter, warmth, physical safety. Then the needs around 'security' – personal and family stability and independence, current and future livelihoods. Then the need for 'self-actualisation' – dignity, status among peers, an ability to express oneself. In reality, they co-exist.

I recently heard Journalist Yasmin Alibhai-Brown tell an anecdote about a refugee she had known for years who got her first job. She rushed up to Alibhai-Brown shortly after starting and waved a handbag at her. 'Look! I bought it myself! I bought my own handbag.'

As people pursue their interests, they may be interested in getting *resources* such as money or food, but usually their actions are about *access* – getting a job, or obtaining a voucher for the food bank. Some may be motivated by the wish to be *more in control* of their lives, more independent, less at the mercy of other people or the vagaries of institutions. For example, they might take a job that pays only the same as Universal Credit but frees them from the Benefits Agency.

People may have an element of calculation in what they do, of balancing different priorities and weighing up a choice of actions with different costs and possible benefits. But they rarely act only for rational reasons. Nothing is certain; refugees' lives change fast, and priorities shift: 'Sorry, teacher, my solicitor needs to see me.' Unpredictability is a feature of refugee life.

As a support worker, you may have a sense of a refugee's motives, but you can't say what individual priorities are. Plus each refugee is unique. So your engagement work and your activities need to relate to several possible interests at once, which might motivate people to engage with you for more than one reason. You absolutely cannot work on a one-size-fits-all, 'typical' refugee (Box 5.3).

Box 5.3 | **Understanding refugees' motives and improving engagement – some ideas**

- Find out more about people's motives. For example, do a 'school gate' survey and find time to talk to parents picking up primary-age children over several days.

- Address common motivations. What do most of us care about? Our parents, our children, money, a home, a decent job, enjoying some sociable time? For example, offer training in employable skills such as interpreting or food hygiene. Build from there.

- Address multiple motivations at once. For example, English groups relate to future employment, the ability to interact and look after your own interests in Britain, making social contacts within the group, a sense of personal progress and better self-esteem, access to other activities and services provided by group leaders/host organisations.

- Include 'self-actualisation' and social interests – socialising but also status such as recognition ceremonies, framed certificates for people who have completed a course or 50 hours' volunteering, a written acknowledgement that can be used as a reference.

- Work in a little rational cost–benefit calculation. For example, 'This workshop will help you save money because…'

Means to engage with you

The *means* to engage are skills and assets such as financial or practical resources, a sense of energy and agency, and contacts. They are the tools we need to get things done, including jumping through hoops that other people set us (see Box 5.8).

Migrants generally have fewer practical assets and less knowledge to draw on than life-long UK residents. Refugees have even less. Do our practices ask too much of their current resources? Can we adapt our practices so they demand less of refugees' means?

Money and time. Refugees are usually low on money, whether that means no cash, irregular income or no access to banks and reasonable credit (see Chapter 7). They make careful choices (Box 5.4). Financial poverty results in people having to use a lot of their time on daily practicalities, shopping around, waiting for off-peak buses or walking home. It leaves them short of time for other activities and limits their mobility and freedom of choice.

Box 5.4 **The debate about charging for services**

I was involved in offering a full Level 3 interpreting qualification course for free. People on the course didn't value it and completely wasted the opportunity. When we charged, attendance was 100% and all participants submitted all assignments.

The English groups where I worked were free for years, then we started to ask for £1, although we waived it if people had no money. Attendance stabilised and people came on time and participated better. But two people certainly stopped coming because of this, and we never were sure about the decision.

Means to keep in touch – phones, post and IT. Keeping in touch nowadays requires phones and IT. The post can work but be aware of misspelled addresses and the lack of security in blocks of flats, shared houses or bed-and-breakfast accommodation. For convenience and security, most refugees see a mobile phone as a top priority, mostly using top-up cards so they can keep in touch cheaply by text and various free apps, even internationally. They may have no other access to IT or printing and copying. The 'digital divide', where parts of the population zoom along online and other parts are completely sidelined, is very significant for refugees who frequently lack both access and skills (see Long Box 5.2, CS/G).

Documents. For refugees, documents and evidence are critical (Long Box 5.2, CS/E). Documents have already been mentioned in Chapter 3 and Appendix B includes details. Refugees and especially asylum seekers often don't have all the evidence they need, because they are at the Home Office or solicitors, or people didn't have them in the first place (e.g. birth certificates) or can't get them (e.g. National Insurance number).

English language, literacy and confidence to speak. One of the most immediate and obvious means for successful engagement – or challenges to it – is how well refugees can communicate in English. It isn't usually about how good their vocabulary and grammar is – although, of course, that is a factor. It is a great deal to do with confidence. People often understand better than they speak, but with confidence they will look you in the eyes and have a go (Box 5.5). They'll use smart phones and dictionaries and get by. Those who don't have the confidence to try or to say they don't understand are more likely to miss out (see Chapter 6).

Box 5.5 **Communication in English**

I recommended a man for a Level 3 interpreting course once. I thought he was fluent in English, but he failed the language assessment by a mile. He was so good at communicating that I simply never realised his level of English was far too low for interpreting.

A few years before that I had turned down a fully qualified interpreter for a job because, despite his accurate grammar and technical vocabulary, he spoke so fast with such a strong accent that I couldn't understand half of what he said.

Knowledge, skills. Knowledge of rights and services is an important 'pre-gate' asset. Skills with IT, language and office practices are valuable, particularly for handling the gate and the queue.

Cultural competence. Social skills and understanding of social context and interaction and culture in Britain are probably more important in a successful encounter than they really should be. Body language, for example, is highly cultural. One person will use space, their eyes, face, hands, touch, and their whole body position to encourage (or discourage) someone else, but the other person can't interpret these physical displays. Choice of words (even when both are fluent in English), turn taking and knowing how to interrupt, and understanding whether/how people ask/answer questions and agree/disagree are all cultural.

Many refugees and migrants with limited experience of British culture act or behave in the way they would expect to act or behave if still in their home country, which might be out of place or misinterpreted here. People have assumptions about hierarchies by gender, age, race, disability, faith, education, profession and combinations of these. They read different messages and have different responses to how we express ourselves, whether I am wearing a Mulberry scarf or tongue and eyebrow piercings. Behaviour is shaped by different experiences of the client/professional, supplicant/patron, customer/salesman, master/servant relationship. If they act on earlier rules that don't fit their new cultural context, they might waste good advice and ignore instructions, or cause offence and lose support (see Box 5.6).

Box 5.6 Tolerating intolerance?

When you live within an established culture, and you find yourself working with people who are facing new social concepts and beliefs, you will inevitably get clashes of idea and opinion about gender, sexuality, race, values, power and much more. It takes time for new arrivals to recognise the differences, learn what it all means and work out their own position. They have to learn new skills for agreeing and disagreeing to avoid causing offence.

Nobody has to tolerate hostility or discrimination; whoever you are working with, there are still boundaries. But we need flexibility (and support) to learn and engage with people whose views and behaviour might sometimes be challenging to us personally and ideologically.

On the other hand, if you are a teacher or medical clinician reading this book, you might have been taken aback by the degree of respect and deference you have been shown. (It can be a pleasant relief, but also alarming as you feel the weight of someone's dependency falling on your shoulders.) It is particularly disconcerting when gifts of some value appear on your desk, and it is useful to cite an 'organisational policy' of not accepting gifts, so you can politely refuse, with grace and gratitude (see Box 5.7).

Box 5.7 Food as a gift of love

I love it when people bring in food they have cooked. It tastes great. It is an expression of pride and skill and positive identity. There is no monetary value to cause embarrassment. It means I have really done something right. As one of our earliest members said, 'Food is love'.

Although some people learn and absorb and adapt quickly, others – especially older people – may never gain the bi-cultural fluency that would make their lives so much easier. It is probably hardest for those who don't get into work – asylum seekers, parents, carers, older people and people without necessary skills.

Contacts and networks. In juggling their scarce resources, refugees probably depend more on peers than on workers within formal organisations. Reciprocity and collaboration among peers, including sharing knowledge, helps people cope with life. The down side is that people will often accept friendly but inaccurate advice (and pressure) from peers rather than listen to you. People compare and choose, and your credibility is critical in whether they follow your advice or their friend's.

Very many asylum seekers and refugees don't have local peer networks because of multiple moves, social or mental health issues, lack of opportunity to meet and consolidate acquaintances, all leaving them increasingly isolated. Or they might have a limited view because language leaves them relying on peers from similar ethnic and cultural backgrounds. Do *not* believe the romantic

notions about a 'refugee community' where people are just waiting to look after each other (see Box 4.10 for a critical view on 'community').

A sense of agency. Over the years I have come to the conclusion that a sense of agency – a firm belief in one's own ability to bring about changes – is the most important means for refugees to engage effectively with formal organisations. It requires self-belief and energy to keep going through the hassle of dealing with multiple institutions. A sense of agency makes people strategic and helps them get over knockbacks. It might not get a person everything she or he wants, but it helps a lot.

> **Box 5.8** Understanding refugees' means and improving engagement – some ideas

- Money: Pay travel expenses, give top-up cards as thank-you gifts instead of flowers.

- Time and mobility: Bus routes matter, free parking less so. Piggy-back activities – for example, book the benefits adviser to come directly after an English group session, not the next day.

- Means to keep in touch: Set up group texting from your computer. Have group apps on an organisational mobile. Hint: Don't leave voicemail messages on mobiles – recipients have to pay to listen to them.

- Making the post work: When people hand-write addresses, check you can read it before they leave. Look out for 1 and 7, 2 and 3, 0 and 6.

- Documents: Provide proof of address. Post a formal letter to them showing charity/company number and an original signature to their current address. Include their full name, date of birth and immigration/NASS reference numbers (see Appendix B).

- Communication in English/confidence to speak – see Chapter 6.

- Knowledge and skills: Training, volunteering, experience, of course, but consider peer-building approaches – for example, 'Connectors'.

- Cultural competence: Don't be shy to tell people 'You should shake hands now', 'You must be on time'. We all want to get it right. Be assertive: 'Now it is my turn to speak'. Be consistent from day one: 'Thank you kindly but I can't take gifts'.

- Peers and contacts: Plan plenty of time in sessions for introductions. Hint: Social events often reinforce isolation so manage them carefully to ensure a positive experience for all individuals.

Opportunity to engage with you

Opportunity is a simpler idea. Motive is like asking 'Will they (try to) be there?' Means is like asking 'If they come, how effective are they likely to be when they are there?' Opportunity is simply 'Can they be there at all?'

Compared with reflecting people's motives or means, it is relatively simple to keep improving the opportunities we create, although you will rarely get things exactly as you want them. Talk to refugees. Ask them about the various demands they are juggling and what works for them (Box 5.9). Monitor take-up – note sudden drops or increases. Follow up to find out why people didn't come. You probably can't find solutions that suit all individuals, but the more carefully you look at it, the better it will get.

Box 5.9 | **Snow or 'what seems impossible for one person is nothing at all to another'**

We organised a workshop and woke up to snow. None of the participants from hotter countries showed up. The Brits were wrapped up to the eyebrows in hats and scarves and walking boots. The Afghans, Poles and Ukrainians who strolled in wearing trainers thought it was really funny.

Timing. People with limited means have limited opportunities – if you have 15 minutes to get somewhere, you could make it by car, but you don't have a car so you end up not going. For some people, timing means working round school hours; for others, it is working round shift patterns or observing Ramadan. You have your own timing restrictions: part-time staff hours or the organisation's end-of-quarter reporting deadline. But fixed 'office hours' don't work – you will be wise to allow time in your plans each day for people dropping in.

Location. Within reach? Already familiar or easy to find? Accessible on public transport? How many buses? Is it seen to be a safe journey? You might need to choose convenience and familiarity for your refugee users over quality, especially as refugees often live in deprived areas. Ask primary schools. Ask a supportive local restaurant if you can use its dining space some mornings.

Venue. Does the venue seem welcoming when you arrive? Is there good physical access such as ramps or a lift? Is the building strongly associated with an ethnic or religious group? Is it a women-only space? Do they need ID or someone to sign them in?

Your awareness and space for refugees to make their own opportunities. Keep slack in the system so you can be opportunistic and make use of refugees' own approaches and initiatives. Leave space in your day or your session plan to respond to what refugees bring to you. Always plan time to stay on after a group or session for half an hour to see what happens. Make sure your team and volunteers have space to share and discuss issues they have learned about from refugees.

Initial opening/consolidating. Refugees need an opportunity to start engaging, something to create the possibility of a relationship. Then they need ways so they can take it forward; not because you want them to, but because they want to and they can. The rest of the chapter concentrates on this.

How to engage – initiating a relationship

So far this chapter has focussed on constraints that affect how likely refugees are to engage effectively with you. This section and the following two are about different aspects of what you can do about those constraints, and how you make engagement happen:

first, initiating a relationship

second, face-to-face engagement

third, developing a longer-term relationship and a deeper collaboration for your organisation's and refugees' mutual benefit.

A lot will be quite familiar as good practice to any hands-on practitioner, but it is about adapting to 'refugee' factors such as trust issues.

Information and publicity

If part of your role is publicity and outreach or recruitment, you have to think about getting information and publicity out that will overcome the risk of refugees being stuck in 'pre-gate' limbo, not even knowing you exist. Whether it is for ongoing services or one-off events, you need information where refugees will find it even when they aren't looking.

- ☑ It has to be where people will come across it.
- ☑ It has to be noticeable and understandable by the people you want to notice it and understand it.
- ☑ It has to leave them with the feeling that they want to get in touch with this activity or organisation.
- ☑ It has to be up to date.

Scrutinise your *hard-copy* leaflets, posters and letters, and *online* information and social media. Are they right for refugees? Are they clear with plain English or good translations? Are they something people can identify with, including photos or pictures of people they find familiar that will reassure them they are welcome? Are the dates (include the year somewhere), venue and postcode accurate?

The best way to get information out there is by getting out yourself and making direct contact, because it starts the possibility of a relationship with people who are stuck outside the gate (see Box 5.10). Humans are social animals. One face-to-face meeting outweighs a hundred fliers.

If you are trying to reach refugees from scratch, start by asking *where refugees live*. Usually where accommodation is cheaper. *Where do they go?* They shop for food, and might use shops where the shopkeeper speaks their language. Get the shopkeeper's support. They probably see the GP – ask the practice manager to tell the practice team. They take kids to primary school. Some attend faith services but many don't. Those who work have many jobs, but agencies, taxi companies and social care agencies are often where people get started.

Box 5.10 — **Creating the possibility of a relationship – Case Studies J and K**

J A lawyer and mental health nurse go out with a central London soup run. They are taking 'the gate' to the people, giving initial information and then setting up referrals for anyone who needs more support.

K In my home area, diabetes awareness workers occasionally do on-the-spot pin-prick blood tests at the Muslim centre after Friday prayers.

Making contact via a credible third party

If you are in touch with a *credible third party*, they can use their direct and personal contact with refugees on your behalf. Distributing information via others works well if:

☑ they actually have direct contact with refugees

☑ they are keen on what you are doing

☑ they remember you are doing it, and

☑ they have the information to hand when they need it.

Send your third-party contacts updates by a mix of methods: post, text, email, phone. If your contacts use Facebook and Twitter, so should you. Best of all, drop in, go and see them face to face at their desk, not just at committee meetings. If you can, back it all up with links to a website which can be easily found online.

As well as refugee specialists and own-language organisations, many other hands-on workers in your area are probably finding themselves working with refugees – English as an Additional Language (EAL) coordinators in schools, community midwives, police community support officers. *Think broadly.* They might be grateful for a source to refer to and many people value networking

(see Chapter 7). They might have events you could piggy-back on – fêtes and festivals, advice sessions.

One-off events

Your aim might be to engage refugees who are already part of your larger user-group, such as parents of children in a school, or heart patients, library-users or people living within a mile. One-off events or time-limited activities, such as a short course, can be very effective. They require a burst of effort rather than ongoing energy.

But it is pointless attracting people to a one-off event if that is where it ends – plan what you want to happen after the event as a way to the goals and framework for planning the event itself. We want women to get independent income through decent jobs? Let's put on a women's 'feel-good' day to recruit to a five-week self-esteem course linked to volunteering and work experience with a local employer.

There is no guaranteed topic that will always work, and it is important the event doesn't put migrants and refugees at a disadvantage. They might not know the rules of bingo or have cash to spend at fundraising events such as fêtes. Events are a risk. See them as experimental, evaluate afterwards and you will get better results over time.

Face-to-face engagement

Now that you have created the opportunity to engage, the refugee's first experience when contacting your organisation is crucial. It will be greatly affected by what happens in their first face-to-face encounter. If that encounter does not work, you are unlikely to see them again.

Points have been raised already about trust, clarity and practical issues such as cultural competence and having time for the unexpected. These are principles that underlie successful, productive encounters.

Safe and confidential encounters

SENSITIVITY

You will often need to know details about someone's life to be able to help them – regarding entitlements, for example. Don't be shy to ask for the information you need to know; just make sure they know why. Stop asking questions as soon as possible. You are talking to a fellow adult, and it is important to balance asking with listening. You want to build a positive relationship – not one that reminds them of their Home Office interview. But if people decide to tell you more than you asked, be ready to listen.

PRESENTING

It is likely someone will start to talk to you about something you didn't know – they 'present' a new problem or something that is really worrying. Similar principles apply whether someone starts to talk about trafficking, domestic abuse or past traumas. Stay calm and listen without encouraging or challenging. Explain about confidentiality. Ask them if they want you to do anything about it. Are they willing to report it to the police? Find out if there is counselling or other support available. You cannot act without their permission. Don't make promises you can't keep.

CONFIDENTIALITY

Remember how important confidentiality is in building trust, as well as being good practice. Confidentiality is not the same as secrecy. Remind the person you will keep what they say and their personal details ('identifiable' data) confidential, and make sure they know what 'confidential' means, in 'plain English'. Even native English speakers often think confidential means secret and you won't tell anyone. Anonymity might also be important to people.

Box 5.11 | **Protecting confidentiality and anonymity**

'You can feel confident and happy I will only talk to people who must know, not to my friends or other people here, or anyone who knows you. I will talk to my manager or an expert to ask them for professional advice. They only talk to the right professional people too.'

- Revisit your organisation's data protection and confidentiality policies and make sure the whole team is familiar with them.

- Generally, volunteers should not be able to access databases/files with personal data, but reliable volunteers could sign a confidentiality agreement.

- Only take notes if you must and don't recycle! Shred.

- Only take copies of personal documents, especially Home Office, identity, health records and passports, if you know you must, and ensure copies are kept securely and then shredded. It is better to note key numbers and dates and sign a written, dated note of what you have seen.

- People must give permission before you discuss their situation or refer their case to anyone outside the organisation. (Safeguarding may be an exception – follow your policy.) You can ask for advice if you are careful to keep the person anonymous.

- Always ask permission before taking photos (including group photos at socials), and also ask before publishing in print or online, even if you do not include people's names. Many refugees refuse to have their names or photographs online.

SAFEGUARDING

Safeguarding procedures must also be properly in place and there is a section about safeguarding in Chapter 11. As a minimum:

- You should know your organisation's safeguarding policy and procedures, and have had training.

- If someone does present to you with a safeguarding issue, or you are concerned about someone, stay calm.

- Remind them you will keep it confidential but not a secret.

- Confirm and clarify without encouraging further detail.

- As soon as you can, write down everything they said in their own words. Date and sign it.

- Report it to the correct person in your organisation, as given in the policy.

SAFETY

You need to be conscious of general safety, of course, and no doubt you have health and safety policies in place – check them. But also look at personal safety in any interaction and especially where participants or services users might be frustrated, unhappy, desperate. Think of your own vulnerability to harm, and that of the refugee, other staff, volunteers, service users and, at times, members of the public. Do assert your own views and keep colleagues informed if you are not happy with how an interaction is going – do not allow compassion to override your instincts or training. You might need an organisational line on giving lifts in cars, use of personal mobiles to ring 'clients', 'lone working' and certainly on home visits.

Do not allow compassion to override your instincts or training.

Expanding engagement

In case work, engagement is more limited and your encounters are probably very focussed, but mutual trust is still just as important. If you are going to expand the number of people or parties involved in their case, they should understand why, should feel they can trust the new players and should have the chance to say no. To discuss their case with others, you need their permission, preferably in writing. If others will take over their case, consider whether and how you want to keep your working relationship with the refugee going, or build up new areas of engagement around other interests. There is discussion of referral in Chapter 7.

Where not dealing with confidential matters, it works well to start up engagement between a refugee and an individual at first but actively involve more people as you go along. To broaden that engagement, you need to find ways to increase how often you have contact, and different kinds of interaction that might serve other interests for the refugee. There are ideas in the rest of the chapter. As you become more familiar with each other, a wider range of issues will come into your exchanges, but remember: you are friendly, not friends.

A couple of hints:

- Keep in touch in small ways too – even a quick text is appreciated.

- You need to be quite organised if you are in touch with a lot of people, so that you don't get names mixed up and you remember their husband was ill.

- If you are making more regular contact, make sure you don't appear to be favouring anyone.

- Don't be slow to ask refugees to help – it shows you value them and that you see they have potential to do more than they are limited to at present.

Communication in English

Communication and language will usually be an issue in face-to-face engagement. Language has come up several times already, and also confidence to have a go, and use of language and the need for new conversational skills. A lack of English does not mean a refugee cannot engage with you, or you with them.

Before you think about *their* English, how is *your* English? Is it plain and clear? Can you slow down and use simpler vocabulary and shorter sentences? It is easier to communicate face to face than by phone, as you can both use so many visual cues, and it is easier to check people have understood. So face-to-face encounters are very important to refugees who aren't fluent.

Where you can't get the English to work well enough, and you both need to have a sound understanding, you need interpreters to bridge the gap. Not online translation, not someone's husband, but a trained and capable interpreter. Many practitioners don't make good use of them or think they will be too expensive. Communication in English and good practice are considered further in Chapter 6.

Longer-term relationships

In the longer term, the best engagement develops to the point at which individual users, and participants as a body, become influential forces in the

organisation. You can strengthen relationships over time, evolving activities and reflecting wider interests, while refugees get better at accessing and making the most of opportunities.

Regular activities

If you can draw refugees into regular interaction, you have a real asset and so do they. You want people to come repeatedly over time, but this is often difficult for refugees. Coming often can be a drain on limited energy, cash and time – for example, finding £2 for buses not once, but every week. At £6/day to live off, this will be too much for some asylum seekers. Bear in mind also that set days, locations and times help some people set up a routine, but always rule some other people out.

The inescapable issue with regular activities is retaining participation – getting people to keep on coming and engaging. A great turnout in the first two weeks is wonderful, but you still want a good turnout eight weeks later and perhaps still a year later. Many people will give something new a go, but they are assessing and judging, comparing with other demands, coping with difficult, even chaotic lives. The 'law' of diminishing returns mean they will get more immediate benefit from the first few sessions than they get at each later session. To retain them you must make sure activities serve their interests and motivation. This means:

- ☑ Regular activities have to be high quality, delivering actual benefits so the refugee feels it is valuable to attend each and every session.

- ☑ Rewards are not just about enjoyment – friendship and pleasure might mean people want to come, but they won't be enough when other pressures arise, and refugees often have chaotic lives.

- ☑ If they have family demands and pressures, it is best if the family also sees their involvement as a good thing, so they will encourage and support your participant to come.

- ☑ Activities have to be reliable from your end, come snow or train strike.

- ☑ Participants' attendance is tracked, contact is followed up and they are reminded to keep coming, and know they matter as individuals.

- ☑ Activities stay fresh. There are easy re-entry points (e.g. a party, new term) for people who have stopped coming.

Any community development text book will also warn about group dynamics: pressures on individuals to conform and the risk of intolerance towards diversity. Many people are also wary or outright hostile to people who are

not familiar or not similar, including, for example, people with mental health or behavioural difficulties or just body odour. Group activities often involve tensions over dominance, how to behave and group decisions. So a last addition to the list:

☑ You have to manage group dynamics *proactively*.

There are a couple of models with slightly different implications for your work.

Regular 'roll on, roll off' or drop in when it suits them – for example, conversation café, women's wellbeing drop-in coffee morning, Somali mothers' own-language toddler playgroup, free hot meal once a month. Many faith activities including times of worship fit this model.

It is flexible, so if people miss a few, they still feel they can come back. But it is hard work to retain numbers and you will constantly be recruiting and introducing new participants. New arrivals can find it hard to come in/fit in with people who already know each other. There is less of the helpful social glue that can build up in steady membership, and bad weather, festivals and holidays can leave you with more volunteers in the room than participants. (Few funders really understand this.)

On the other hand, you can't predict when you will go over numbers, which is a real problem with small rooms, handouts/equipment and if children are involved. If your numbers are limited and too many people turn up, you have a problem. It is hard to make waiting lists work with people who don't use IT or post, and have low language skills, confidence and little trust in authority – I generally assume that if I turn a refugee away, I won't ever see them again. Have a 'what if?' in place already to avoid turning people away if you possibly can. Have a standing agreement that you can use an overflow room if you need it, a 'stand-by volunteer' who lives nearby or an 'on-call' colleague who can run and join you; ask parents to take 15-minute turns helping in the crèche to keep ratios safe; ring for pizza to supplement the lunch.

Finite or fixed-term activities – for example, a men's talking therapy group for six weeks, or a one-term English course. This might involve buying in skilled input from outsiders (e.g. the therapist) and supervision costs. The sense of having only a limited time can intensify engagement and peer-building (Box 5.12).

Track participation closely – ring or text the same day if someone misses a session. It is nice to have some kind of recognition at the end – an extra hour for a shared meal, a group thank-you card to volunteers, group photo, certificates of attendance or special effort. Think in advance about how you will keep the relationship going when the current activities are complete, which might mean trying to keep the peer connections going too. Maybe a celebration later when results or qualifications arrive, or ask your first participants to support the new group members next time the course runs.

| Box 5.12 | **More about making the most of fixed-term activities** |

Plan some lead-in time and 'lead-up' sessions, by which I mean sessions in the same place and time slot before the real work/course gets going. You could call them Orientation, Enrolment, a Taster Session. They are a way to get people coming in, publicise and get some word of mouth going, help refugees check if it is really going to be useful to them, get paperwork out of the way, and lay groundwork for the real thing by introducing vocabulary, principles, resources, and giving them time to prepare (e.g. realising they need to bring money, pen and paper, working out the route in advance and trying out child care). This lead-in should mean better value for everyone from the start, and fewer people dropping out.

Regular ongoing sessions with an element of progress or development – for example, English, children's health group for Afghan mothers, food bank with advice – that build up a group of repeat attendees or members who really should attend every week. Regular activities, especially where they build a group atmosphere (e.g. a choir), have a different mood and benefits. Habit and social glue can help retention. But motivation wavers, so quality and freshness really matter. It can help if people can see they are building towards longer-term achievable goals or markers along the way, such as a trip, a test, a performance, a qualification. Get participants taking responsibility for as much as possible – setting up, cleaning up, collecting money or attendance sheets, planning for social elements or how they want to thank volunteers, evaluation and steering or planning group.

Hosting another organisation's services

'Hosted' activities may be regular and group-based (e.g. health visitors), or for individuals (e.g. legal advice sessions), or one-off events that might happen a few times a year (e.g. public authority consultations). Make sure they are of *real* interest to the refugees you wish to engage, as many large bodies find refugees, ethnic minorities and other disadvantaged populations 'hard to reach' (although it can be seen as being the other way round). Some will see your organisation as a miracle cure without any sense of how much work it is to build up good engagement.[1] The wrong kind of event or garnering people to come to an event they find to be a waste of their time damages *your* credibility – not the outside organisation's.

People often start with dates, publicity, catering but stop there! Before you agree to anything, clarify with the representative right from the start…

☑ topic, content, their purpose, follow-up.

---

1   When this is highly paid consultancy firms, I get really cross – write and complain to the authority that has contracted them.

If you are satisfied that this will be of interest and value to your refugee contacts, and only if you are satisfied, go on to clarify...

☑ eligible participants and the evidence they require to prove eligibility, *in detail.*

If and only if you are satisfied, go on to clarify...

☑ who is responsible for publicity, costs of publicity, recruitment, 'did not attends', evaluation, data, participant expenses.

If and only if you are satisfied, go on to clarify...

☑ whether they will pay you, how much they will pay you and what they will pay for your overhead, volunteer and staff costs.

If and only if you are satisfied, go on to clarify...

☑ insurance/safety/safeguarding during their sessions.

If and only if you are satisfied, go on to clarify...

☑ a date to review the arrangements and who is the responsible decision-maker.

After all this is clear, *then* start talking about dates, details for fliers, rooms, refreshments, etc. (and can they do some free training for your volunteers, donate a box of paper and let you do a raffle on the day?).

Involving other individuals – involving refugees

It can work well if you choose to involve a few of your service users in the role of 'links', 'bridges', 'connectors', 'befrienders', 'core' group and steering group 'representatives', 'champions'. Their relationship with you is a kind of volunteer who is an informal part of your team (see Chapter 10 on volunteering).

'Connectors' or core members help the organisation to spread information and credibility outwards by word of mouth, to reach more people who are stuck pre-gate. They can encourage people to make contact – for example, accompanying someone the first time she or he comes in and helping with language. They offer people on the outside a familiar face who is not an authority figure, but who can answer questions about the organisation and reassure. They may also have knowledge and insight to contribute to your planning. It would be good if today's new refugee client was playing this role in a year or two. In the best case, they make the organisation something better than it was.

The downside is that newer contacts don't necessarily trust other migrants or refugees just because they are from the same country, ethnicity, language or religion. They may even trust them *less*. A 'connector' who has a strong relationship with a member of staff is in a position of power, and might be

selective or unreliable; there is a risk to confidentiality, a risk of gossip or judgement, or they may just be unpopular. They may be seen as your favourites. Don't fall into the habit of relying on the views of a few helpful individuals or assuming that because you have agreed something with them, everyone feels the same. Nor that having told them something they will pass it on to everyone else in full or at all.

Summary and conclusion

Box 5.13 summarises the points in this chapter.

Box 5.13	Enabling refugees to engage – summary
Stages of access	'pre-gate', gate, queue, encounter (Box 5.1)
Motive	resources, access, control
Means	money, time, to keep in touch, documents, English, knowledge, contacts, sense of agency
Opportunity	timing, location, venue, new space, your awareness
English	theirs, yours, checking understanding, plain English, bridge the gap, learning, interpreters
Regular activities	roll on, roll off/drop in, fixed-term, ongoing with progression, hosting others', individual 'connectors'

Seeing the refugee's view of your work is crucial. Without it you will waste a lot of time and effort.

Be strategic. Be clear on your aims and reasons for wanting to engage refugees. Try things out, and work towards a longer plan formed around learning from relationships.

Create ways refugees can gain and learn from positive experiences so they become more effective when engaging with organisations and in their new culture.

Create space for refugees to bring in their own issues and agendas. Those new ideas might not fit with projects and objectives put in writing at an earlier date. The spaces you create are opportunities for communication in the fuller sense, which will also change your work and your organisation. You are also a party in this dialogue, this praxis.

One last note: the message about the importance of relationships and responsiveness in this chapter is out of kilter with the dominant model of objective support, rule-bound, fragmented service provision via fixed-term, fixed-objective projects approved in advance by financial controllers sitting a long way away.

But engagement works with refugees when it is based on relationships of trust. So it also becomes the job of hands-on practitioners to interpret,

mediate and advocate for refugees as they try to negotiate formal organisations and institutions, built on the objective model. After a short chapter about communicating in English, Chapter 7 will work through this challenge and some of the options and tools hands-on workers can use when advocating with and for refugees.

Communicating in English – Plain English, Interpreters and Learning English

Introduction

When you find yourself working with refugees, you usually find yourself working with people who have little or no English, or if they speak English, they are still unfamiliar with the usage and communication habits they come across in their new country.

It is an issue shared by most migrants, and also an equality issue, because when communication and therefore knowledge and negotiation are constrained, it is harder to resist discrimination and make sure you have the same opportunities as other people (Chapter 3). The ability to communicate in English affects how effectively people engage (Chapter 5) and in some cases puts the hands-on worker in the role of mediator and advocate in relation to other formal organisations (Chapter 7) such as housing or health services providers, where someone able to communicate freely would be more independent.

You have a few paths you can take to cross the gap in skill. In summary, you can narrow it by adapting your use of language, bridge it with interpreters, enable refugees to learn by providing activities or facilitating their access to college. A number of non-formal and formal avenues for learning English are considered in Chapter 10 as well as an example of one approach included below.

Narrow the gap

Try to find out how good their English really is.

- Can they understand you OK, even if they don't have the skill or confidence or practice to reply?

- Can they read? Can they write English? Can they read and write in their first language?

- Can they use numbers in English? Is it the same script they know?

- Have they had their English assessed (most colleges will do this for free at various points in the year), or have they taken English/English as a Second Language/ESOL courses? Ask them what level they are (see Box 10.6).

- To get an initial idea, ask them to write their name, their address, their postcode and phone number. Give them a simple leaflet and ask them to read it to you.

Don't see these checks as an imposition; you need to know so you can adjust the way you communicate. Even without training, you can tell fairly quickly whether you'll have problems communicating, either face to face or at distance. If nothing else, you will know you can't rely on leaflets and letters but will have to arrange face-to-face meetings.

Don't confuse lack of English with lack of intelligence. People who can barely speak a word in English were teachers, business owners, musicians, civil servants before they had to leave.

What about *your* English? Is your English accurate, plain and clear? Do you finish your sentences? Do you use simple short sentences, take your time? You should pause between sentences for them to run through what you said and check they know what it means before you go on. Do you have a clear and reasonably loud voice and sound all your vowels and consonants?

Do you limit your vocabulary – avoid jargon, long words, complex tenses, double negatives, acronyms? You might need to compromise on precision to get the core part of a message across. 'I am the safeguarding officer' becomes 'I am the person who wants to know children are OK. If you have a problem, talk to me.'

> You might need to compromise on precision to get the core part of a message across.

If you are writing or printing anything, keep it short and aim for *plain English*. You could use standards set out by Plain English Campaign (plainenglish. co.uk). You could use 'Easy Read' standards and methods designed to improve communication with people who have learning difficulties. Some people find this patronising; I find it pragmatic and it works all right.

Check they understand. If you ask, 'Do you know what I mean?' you will get the reply, 'Yes.' Instead, ask them to summarise what you told them – if they didn't understand, start again from scratch. After checking they understand, write down the main points (can they read your handwriting?). They can take your summary with them and read it to check they understand, look up words and remember. It will help them explain to other staff elsewhere what you are doing for them. A leaflet doesn't achieve the same thing.

Bridge the gap

Bridge the gap (a bit). You may be able to bridge the language gap a bit if you find you have a mutual language such as French, German, Russian, Urdu, possibly Arabic.

As long as you start with plain English, smart phones and online translation packages can help for a few non-technical words or a very rough or 'gist' translation. Some digital translation is unintelligible and worryingly inaccurate, so don't rely on it.

Bridge the gap with interpreters. When their English isn't good enough or full understanding is especially important, *use an interpreter*.

Staff often start off by asking people to bring a family member. This is a bad idea. Obviously, school children should be doing other things. Adult children are also unhappy about it. I have a bilingual friend who had to tell her own mother she had cancer. It messes up family relationships – inverting care and authority structures, compromising confidentiality, preventing disclosure of family difficulties or control issues such as money problems, depression, violence. Husbands, sisters, friends rarely 'interpret' – they filter, summarise, reword, advocate and argue. It puts them in a strengthened and informed position, and your client in a weakened and ill-informed one.

There is the option to get training for staff from your organisation, or trained volunteers from your own contacts, or perhaps from a nearby ethnicity-based organisation or church/mosque. This can work when:

- it is not a highly confidential situation

- they are strangers to your client and there are no gender complications

- they understand and stick to fundamental principles and good practice

- their language skills are adequate in both languages (note that second-generation speakers, whose parents migrated here, don't usually speak their parents' language well enough)

- they are available and willing.

Or *use a professional interpreter*. In health, social, education, housing and advice work, you would usually use a 'community interpreter'. At first sight this might appear costly. If you have direct contact with self-employed, qualified, experienced professionals whom you can contact and book directly, this may be about £20–25/hour. An agency will charge £50 plus, of which the interpreter gets about £17. In theory, agencies have insurance, quality assurance, minimum standards for qualifications, DBS checks all in place, but in reality very few do this consistently. Charity- or local authority-based professional interpreting services probably have the best consistency and quality control.

Although £25/hour seems a lot, think about the potential cost to both the refugee and you of any misunderstandings. With a capable, professional interpreter in place, one meeting will be worth five meetings without interpreters. If you are a 'worthy cause', you might find even professional interpreters will waive their fee once or twice, but they do have to eat, so please don't ask too much of them.

Essential principles and good practice for community interpreters

The most important relationship in community interpreting is between the service provider and the service user – the 'community' interpreter's role is to facilitate communication and understanding between them.

There are fundamental principles community interpreters have to follow:

- Confidential – not secret.

- Always neutral, never take sides, never give advice, make no comment, have no influence.

- Be accurate, but interpret the meaning of what they say, not only the words.

- If in doubt, or the speaker is vague, ask for clarification. If they say things you don't understand, ask for explanation. If they speak too quietly, in unfinished sentences or for too long, interrupt politely and ask for clarity and time to interpret. If you have to interrupt or ask one party a question, make sure the other knows what you are doing.

- Be very clear about your role; clarify your role and principles to both parties before you start.

Normal practice consists of:

- Consecutive interpreting: The speaker stops after each sentence for the interpreter to interpret. Best in face-to-face encounters.

- Simultaneous interpreting: Interpreting into the other language at the same time as the first person speaks, without a break. Like TV voiceovers.

Interpreting qualifications. Profession community interpreters should have at least a Level 3 interpreting qualification (equivalent to A-Level standard but not an A Level). Ideally, they should have 30–50+ hours' experience and a DBS check.

Thank you to Oleg, Khalida, Ayo, Renu, Ayman.

Learning English to close the gap

Confidence to have a go

You can do a lot to help people gain the confidence to speak and improve their communication in English. There is the hope your refugee clients will gain confidence from their engagement with you. Most kinds of interaction with English speakers will help, so social, art and sports events where only English is spoken, visiting other organisations, participating in meetings or volunteering opportunities of almost any kind are all valuable.

Regular English groups

Chapter 5 talked about how to make regular group activities, such as English groups, work. Chapter 10 also looks at non-formal learning opportunities. Community or 'grass roots' English groups, conversation cafés, 'Speaking with Confidence' sessions add up to an informal approach that is neither coffee morning nor college course, but a ladder between them. They help many people gain confidence in their ability to speak and learn, as long as the group leaders take the role seriously and prepare well.

Community or 'grass roots' English emphasises people feeling more confident to speak English in daily life. They aren't usually formally structured or like an assessed or college ESOL course, and most groups strongly emphasise speaking over writing. They often have a social element, and might be flexible around babies and children, although that doesn't suit people who want to push on fast.

They can also help with more peripheral but important skills of punctuality, study skills, group and pair work, using IT. If the refugee is to go on to success in formal English courses and classes – at college, for example – they will need all this.

The model that follows is just one of dozens of community English models and approaches.

A 'grass roots' model for volunteer-led English group sessions

Thank you to REAP for permission to include the GREG model (REAP.org.uk).

This model, called Grass Roots English Groups, or 'GREG', works well for group leaders who are volunteers, backed up by a more formal organisation supporting them. It is designed to help people who have little experience of planning and teaching to deliver sessions that refugees (and other migrants) find valuable. It is only a suggested starting point to help you get going and very quickly you will develop your own approach and content to fit your group and resources.

The GREG model emphasises speaking and confidence to speak through a mix of activities including plenty of interaction. A good session should also include some work on:

- reading and writing

- numbers in English – for example, writing 1 and 7 in English format, saying 3.15pm and 3.50pm clearly

- local orientation, news, opportunities, contacts and visits

- practical vocabulary that adults will use in daily life (clinic and appointment, rather than zoo and zebra)

- helping people to 'progress' to future formal English courses at college.

It is best to design group activities on the basis of a full 10–13-week term in line with schools, including:

- weekly sessions

- two-hour sessions which can have a break

- 9.30–11.30 or 1.00–3.00 slots, which are often good times to fit around school hours

- adults with basic and beginner English (pre-entry, Entry 1–3), usually very mixed.

A basic term plan of 10–13 weeks includes:

- Group and session leader volunteers meeting to plan the term, what to include, who will do what and when. Start preparing a term plan and all session plans for the term, and handouts in group folders.

- 1–2 welcome and introduction sessions: new arrivals, welcomes, getting to know people and their standards, with time to help people who are too advanced to find something right for them. Perhaps 'Bring a Friend'.

- 6–8 sessions with lots of speaking and listening, and some reading/ writing and other knowledge and skills, mixed in with…

- 1–2 sessions with visits, speakers, special themes (e.g. Eid, winter health).

- A session break at school half-term – although it is good to avoid this if possible.

- 1–2 outside events not in group time when people arrange to meet up somewhere local (e.g. college open day, visit to Citizens Advice office, a visit to another group).

- 1 final session with some kind of performance or party – invite guests! Give certificates.

To get started, try one term of two-hour sessions, each based on these sections:

1. Hello (20 minutes). Sign in, name badges, paperwork, homework, welcome/introduction phrases, ice-breakers, news.

2. Drills and Chains* (20 minutes). Check understanding, practise (mostly verbs and tenses) in full sentences as whole group then pair work and feedback.

3. Vocabulary work* and/or number work (10 minutes). They build up a glossary over time.

4. Three Quick Things (5 minutes) – for example, write out five postcodes, practice 'rrrr', find Hull on a map.

5. Practical English for Daily Life* (40 minutes). Ideally one theme with three to four activities – for example, Q&A phrases, role play, writing letters, reading, numbers, etc.

6. Poems and Songs* (10 minutes). Accent, flow, stress and love of English. Perform at end of term.

7. Finish and Farewell Recap. Homework – five words from the session. Praise, targets. Farewell phrase.

* Repeat and develop each theme and activities over two to three weeks.

Allow at least half an hour afterwards for individuals and holistic/case work.

Hints for groups with very basic beginners

- Don't leave very basic learners out. They might not even be able to say hello or write their name, but exposure to English, especially through interaction, will help them. Just make sure they feel welcome and that they matter. Make sure every session has lots of repeats and practice – good for everyone.

- Concentrate on getting basic beginners to speak, even if it's just words or half sentences. Social interaction (1. Hello and 7. Finish and Farewell) is good for this and quickly builds confidence to have a go. Also 6. Poems and Songs, which involves learning poems by heart and performing in front of an audience.

- Even if basic beginners don't understand the meaning of a sentence, encourage them to say the whole sentence loudly and clearly, then work on understanding again. This means 2. Drills and Chains and 3. Vocabulary can still work very well for basics even if the others in the group are more advanced.

- If you have several very basic beginners, try to have extra helpers or volunteers to work directly with them. For 5. Practical English it might be best to have simpler activities and material for them on the same theme, in a side group if you have enough volunteers to do this.

- Basic beginners often hardly write or write very slowly. Put 90% of your effort into speaking; writing can come later. For the glossary, you might need to write the words for them to take home.

Hints during the session

- Always do your speaking and listening first and don't start writing until later on. If you write things down too soon, people concentrate on copying and not on speaking and learning.

- Everyone needs lots and lots of practice – better one thing ten times than ten things once each, but put it in context and check understanding.

- Your participants are *not* children – use useful words, examples and themes (e.g. money, family, appointments), not things designed for children (e.g. discos and zoo animals). Give them responsibilities – they can collect money, do the attendance sheet, etc. (see Long Box 5.2, CS/5).

- Make sure everyone is involved and learning or they won't come back next week. Treat everyone as your equal. Don't let anyone dominate or talk over other participants, including volunteers.

Thank you to Ayo, Chhinder, Fatme, Ivone, Jamila, Jasmin, Kashmira, Marcin, Mari, Marimar, Poornima, Priya, Rachaporn, Rekha, Renu, Sharon, Stacey.

Other Organisations, Networking and Advocating for Refugees

Introduction

The following chapters (8–11) will be centred around the entitlements and organisations that refugees *should* be able to access for support. 'Should' is not the same as 'can'. Being entitled is one thing; accessing what you are entitled to is another. Where Chapter 5 was about refugees engaging with organisations generally, and your organisation in particular, this chapter is about *you* having to engage with *other* organisations in order to support refugees properly.

Part of the reason this book exists is because so many refugee specialist bodies, resources and structures have been lost over the past decade that people who are specialists in their own, non-refugee fields are having to expand their specialisms and work with refugees directly. You need to be fairly aware and well informed to do the right thing by refugees.[1] But you probably can't know everything you need to know. Your best strategy is to know who knows already and where to find out what you need to know, when you need to know it.

> Know who knows already and where to find out what you need to know, when you need to know it.

The importance of networking

The key is networking – *forming direct contacts and getting to know people*. Google and directories simply don't give you what direct contact gives you. Good-quality networking means you get access to a wide range of good-quality information, advice and sources of help that other people don't know exists. You will do well if you can build connections by phone, email and social media, and sometimes this is the only option.

---

1 Remember, no matter how well informed you are, if you aren't licensed to give immigration advice, you must not do so – see Box 3.3).

But it is often direct, face-to-face interaction with people in the know that builds the most meaningful connections, even if subsequent contact is all done at distance. Nothing can compare with personal interaction if you want to find out what is really going on in your local area or region. Who are the 'friends within the system'? Whom do you trust and who should you not waste your breath on? This feels quite sociable, but it is work: people need to remember you too, trust you and respect you – or they won't return your phone calls. Mutual trust and respect can evolve into reciprocal support and real collaboration (Box 7.1).

Box 7.1 Appreciate and reciprocate

Please consider how a specialist refugee organisation feels when lots of different people who need advice and favours keep ringing up and demanding help, and then ring off – surely it has happened to you too. Check online and especially their website first and see what you can find out for yourself. Consider their capacity, what they invested to get that information, how they value their contacts and don't want you to mess them up. Appreciate the individual's time and consideration; they may have three people standing behind their shoulder waiting to talk to them while they talk to you. Don't ring at 5pm. Ask the person's name.

Give them a chance to gain something – for example, to tell you about an event they have coming up. Offer to send out their leaflets to your mailing list. Reciprocate: 'If I can ever offer ideas about children's health…' Send a thank-you. Send a nice quote they can use in a funders' report: 'It really helped and I was able to change what we do because of your advice. PS. You can quote me.'

Invest some time. Your time at any event or meeting is an investment – think of your time costing your organisation about £200/day (even if you aren't paid half that!). Don't just turn up and take part; double your winnings by actively seeking new contacts who have real potential to help you. Check the attendance list when you arrive, and make sure you are in time to hear the initial introductions so you can identify four to five people you want to talk to. Make sure you talk to them directly, not just in a group; check their role, check their attitude; discuss an issue of mutual concern (not the quality of the lunch). Get *their* contact card/leaflet with a direct email address (they will lose yours) (see Box 7.2 for where to start).

Box 7.2 Ideas for where to network

- Events: Go to Refugee Week/multicultural events, the AGM of any local refugee organisation or refugee project; International Women's Day or Holocaust Memorial events; BME Health Forum; White Ribbon Day events. Look out for what's on in the next town or city.

- Other people's meetings: If there are no meetings specifically about refugees, ask other meetings to add 'refugee mapping' as an item to the agenda and ask to share contacts to help your support to refugees. Try inter-faith groups, homelessness networks, advice networks and food bank meetings; join local mental health networks (e.g. Thrive), or ask to visit a health visitors' forum. More controversial are meetings around the 'Prevent Agenda' and offshoots. Go to local authority meetings such as Stronger Communities, Women in the Community. There are still BME, women's, disability, older age and other equality fora in some regions (e.g. West Midlands).

- Or you could set something up especially (see Box 7.3 for methods to help facilitate networking). Your AGM could take 'refuge' as a theme.

Follow up with an email within two days while you are still 'Sarah from...' and before you become 'you know, the one who...' – 'It was good to meet you. Here's that link I mentioned and please send me that report you wrote.' Be organised – add them to your database and circulation lists. Two good new contacts (about £50 each) isn't a bad afternoon's work.

Your networking doesn't only mean finding out where the refugee specialists are. You will find it necessary to connect with a combination of specialists in other fields (e.g. mental health, family law) even if you haven't done so before. You might find you are the one to bring people together (Box 7.3).

Box 7.3 **Methods to facilitate networking**

If you run an event with a refugee or migrant and refugee theme, there are certain participatory methods that will help. Ask for information about organisation/project/role and involvement with refugees as part of the process for registration; collate and make available on the day. Give out a full attendance list showing people's organisation to every participant and have name badges that clearly show their organisation. Use an arrival questionnaire for people to fill in while they wait for the event to start, asking questions like 'What organisations would you like to meet?', 'Can you recommend any organisations?', etc. Always have enough time for names and introductions, ideally with a question – for example, 'How many refugees contacted you last year?' Use methods like 'Find someone who...' and other ice-breakers, line-up, wheel activities and 'speed dating' methods where everyone talks to everyone for two minutes – very noisy!

Who is out there? If you are new in post or are feeling under pressure to develop your networks because you unexpectedly find yourself working with refugees, there are certain bodies or groups of bodies where you should be able to find useful contacts. This quick list gives an overview and more details are in Appendix A.

Local statutory and democratic bodies

- Local authority/council teams: housing and homelessness; social work – vulnerable adults, looked after children (LAC), domestic violence/violence against women and girls (VAWG); public health; other council teams –stronger/safer/cohesive communities, integration.

- Council services: libraries, children's and Sure Start centres, primary schools.

- NHS bodies: Clinical Commissioning Group (CCG); engagement and equality team; mental health; CSE (Child Sexual Exploitation/FGM/safeguarding nursing lead. Providers: community health – midwifery, health visitors, immunisation.

- Local MP, Assembly members, metropolitan authorities/mayor's teams for integration, equality, hate-crime, VAWG. Local councillors, district councillors.

In local areas: voluntary/community/faith

- Refugees' own community organisations (RCOs), Refugee Support, Refugees Welcome, City of Sanctuary, Student STAR, food banks.

- Citizens Advice (CAB), community law centres, advice services.

- Colleges: English and ESOL; employment teams.

- Equality bodies: women's centres, disability groups, mental health (e.g. local Mind), faith and inter-faith networks.

- Council/association/alliances of voluntary services where they still exist.

- Activist bodies: unions, campaign groups such as Amnesty International.

- Local businesses.

Regional and national specialists

- Refugee specialists: Refugee Council, Refugee Action, Freedom from Torture, Asylum Support Appeals Project (ASAP).

- Related: JCORE, British Institute of Human Rights (BIHR), Maternity Alliance.

- Federations: Law Centres Federation, Citizens Advice, Mind, Age UK, Children's Society.

- Smaller organisations with national significance: Bail for Immigration Detainees (BIDS), Yarl's Wood Befrienders, etc.

- Online networks: ASAN, Frontline, Refugee Support. Email for an invitation to join.

- Think tanks, policy organisations and universities: Runnymede, Rowntree, British Futures, Universities of Manchester, Birmingham, Oxford (Queen Elizabeth House), South Bank.

Referral and the 'One plus One' principle

The advantages of good referral are that you are brokering an arrangement that gives the refugee expert support and a range of inputs and options that is broader than you could offer. They gain experience of different organisations and a wider knowledge of what is available which boosts their means to engage in future.

You could just signpost someone by handing them a list or a name and wish them luck on their way. Or you might pass over all future responsibility for their support to another person or organisation. But the *best* referral respects your existing relationship with a refugee and all the work they have put into engaging with you, while expanding that relationship to include other useful parties.

When you refer someone to another organisation, you put them into a new relationship with a new organisation, and they have to make a success of it. To be sure you are taking the right approach, you need to have a realistic awareness of the refugee's own motives, means and agency at that moment to be sure they can make the most of the expertise and service you are connecting them to. You might consider accompanying your member or client initially, or facilitating access at the gate, queue, encounter in other ways. You can try to keep in touch with the refugee and/or the other professional to see how it's going, bearing in mind that confidentiality might limit what they can tell you.

A *bad referral* can do real damage, not least to your own relationship with the person you have been trying to support. Referral multiplies the cooks who are stirring the broth, and the number of faces and forms, competing suggestions and stakeholders. It can easily get confusing. Your refugee referee will be expending time and energy coping with multiple relationships. It might even be that the other organisation lets them down. Or maybe their expectations are too high. Disappointment can dampen people's enthusiasm to engage with formal organisations, not least yours.

It is about finding the *right body*. Your sense of the real quality and capacity of the organisation and even the individual professional you are referring them to is one issue. Simply finding the right expertise is another. Look at the issue they are facing first, and the fact they are a refugee second, if at all – remember, someone with toothache just needs a dentist.

It is not acceptable to deflect someone to a 'refugee' body simply because the person presenting is a refugee (see Box 1.1). Good referral adopts the 'One plus One' principle (WRC/REAP 2011) – in which any referral to a specialist refugee organisation or service is matched by at least one other referral to a service that has other relevant expertise but no special knowledge about refugees (Box 7.4).

For example, you would refer a female Iranian refugee who needs advice on housing to a housing advice service. You might also put her in touch with an Iranian women's association, but if so, you should make the extra effort to help her access another women's support organisation that has no refugee or ethnic focus.

A refugee male with a disability who wants to get some training for work may gain from being referred to a refugee community organisation that runs training, at the same time as a disability rights group that can explain his employment rights as a disabled person. But what he really wants is to be done with all those extra gates and queues and just get on to a good course from a high-quality training body that will respond to his needs as a unique individual, so that he can get on with building his future. If there isn't one, then the refugee organisation and the rights group might just have to do for now.

Box 7.4 **The 'One plus One' principle**

Each time you refer a refugee to a refugee specialist, project or group, you also refer her/him to at least one other non-refugee specialist, project or group.

Tackling third parties for your refugee clients – advocacy, complaints and influence

When your member or refugee client – let's call her Burtilla – is struggling with access to a service, you may be able to help the relationship along by helping *both* parties. Perhaps she has been turned away incorrectly at the gate or she is getting slow and poor service. The other organisation or individual staff member might be supportive but working within constraints. Or Burtilla may be meeting misinformation, denial and hostility. Start softly, with a gentle but firm 'nudge', although you might need to progress to a 'poke' and even a 'slap' (Box 7.6).

Advocacy

Don't take over. This isn't your problem; it's hers. Burtilla might not be keen on you getting involved and you must respect her wishes (although some people would prefer it if you did take over). You want her relationship with that organisation to work; you don't want to make it your relationship. Think of

your role as improving the space within which this person is engaging the other body. Your aim is to clear away confusion and help to clarify what is expected of both parties. If you do this, your refugee client has a better chance of sorting out the relationship herself or himself.

To advocate in this situation, you must make sure the case is clear-cut. Check Burtilla's actual needs and what she hopes to achieve and whether she is realistic. Check entitlements carefully from authoritative sources (Appendix A). Get credible backup materials – for example, Freedom from Torture or ASAP briefings. Check she has the right evidence and documentation. Provide a credible, summary letter clearly laying out the facts and your sources (Box 7.5).

Ensure your client knows what the minimum is that the organisation has to comply with, and do not give optimistic reassurance that she will get more than that. Then Burtilla can try again.

Box 7.5 **Letters of support and references – credible and effective**

You will be asked or will decide to write many letters on behalf of refugees – supportive letters, informative and advocacy letters, personal and job references. Your credibility is as important as the message you are trying to get across.

- Look professional. Reply quickly, use letterhead, formal layout and correct grammar – also in emails and include an email 'signature'. Include a few words about your organisation and, if a charity, include the registration number. Include direct phone and email. Keep to one side of A4.

- Clarify your role and profession, qualifications; indicate your experience and expertise.

- Include relevant reference numbers and personal details from the refugee, which might include their Home Office asylum number, for example, but only include the details that are needed. Add how long you have known them and in what capacity and that you have their permission to write.

- Deal with one issue in one letter.

- Problem? State the situation, state what is wrong, what it should be, back up with evidence and preferably quotes from their organisation's own documentation on standards. State what you want them to do to put it right, by when.

- Reference? Think about what they want to know, be accurate on what you actually know, give reassurance rather than sales talk, don't emphasise friendship or friendliness – it might make you look less trustworthy.

- Don't plead.

- Follow up.

If Burtilla is still not successful, your next tactic is probably to accompany her to a face-to-face encounter, or ring, email or write on her behalf. Some organisations will want to see written and signed consent to speak on someone's behalf. (Interpreters might also need signed consent from the client.) Even though you are now acting directly and you are there to protect your refugee client's interests, your objective is still simply to facilitate the relationship between the two parties, by bringing clarity and perhaps some reassurance.

Make sure you fully understand the organisation's position and how staff are justifying that position – it may be logical or consistent with the information they have, but you have *better* information. Identify the points where there are inconsistencies (e.g. in their guidance regarding immigration status or suitable identity documents) or there are commitments or obligations outside normal practice that they aren't aware of (e.g. to register a patient even if they don't have proof of address). Show them the authoritative information you have gathered.

You may need assertiveness methods. You may need to involve a manager who has a broader overview and greater discretion to overrule the staff handbook.

Complaints

If this level of facilitative advocacy does not succeed, you need to change mode. Go from working alongside both parties to standing beside your client as you face the organisation together. In other words, you take this up a level, and now move to a potentially confrontational position to support your client.

This change in the nature of the relationship can easily provoke defensiveness, a closing of ranks and a search for ways in which you or your refugee client can be shown to be at fault. Make it clear that although you are taking her side, you are looking for resolution, not escalation. So it is usually best to start off calm, positive and polite – but calmly and positively and politely determined – rather than to bluster and demand.

Your next tactic is probably to let staff know that if there isn't a satisfactory resolution, you might, with regret, make a formal complaint.

- Assume it will go well. Act quickly, but only if you and your client both feel calm and have all the material you need.

- Keep a record of all communications with all relevant parties (date, name, role, notes of discussion, decisions, deadlines). Keep copies of everything, in one place, in order.

- Closely read the organisation's own policies such as a customer service charter, equality policy or complaints policy.

- If you have a 'friend within' the organisation, ask them *off the record* (phone or face to face, not by email!) if there is any context you need

to know. Or you can contact someone more senior by phone or email to 'ask for advice'.

- Following their complaints policy, inform them, whether in writing, phone or face to face, that you are not satisfied and your concerns mean you are considering making a complaint. Explain what you hope will happen and by when. Provide copies of the materials from your authoritative source, having highlighted the key points.

- If this still doesn't work, help your refugee client to put in a written complaint following the organisation's complaints procedure to the letter. It should be in her/his own words. Add a letter which explains your role and your concerns as advocate. Keep copies.

- Follow up within a couple of days, to ask when you might hear something. If their eventual response is still not satisfactory, their complaints process should include details on how to appeal, and is likely to have a time limit.

At some point Burtilla and you have to decide whether to take it up a level or to give up. Your client will probably ask your view on this. If they don't want to go further, you must respect that. You are not obliged to help them take it further if you don't consider it reasonable. Either way, talk it through thoroughly to reduce the risk that it will damage your working relationship.

Formal complaint. If your refugee client isn't satisfied, follow the formal complaints process to the next step, which is probably an appeal to the next level up. You can write to the chief executive or even directors/governing board members/trustees. You may be able to write a 'Question from the Public' to a board meeting (e.g. CCGs/statutory bodies).

Third parties. When you get stuck, third parties might advise or advocate for your refugee client. Local advice bodies, CAB and law centres can advise. For NHS bodies, try PALS and Healthwatch, but especially Doctors of the World for asylum seekers, refused asylum seekers and refugees (see Chapter 9). Nationally, the Public Law Project might be interested in cases, especially if there is potential to make case law.

Newspapers. Local newspapers often like a personal story especially with a nice photo. But think carefully. What if they turn the story round? How sympathetic are most newspapers, especially local papers, to refugees?

Freedom of Information. If it is a state/statutory body and you need information about how it runs, budgets, waiting lists, guidance on prioritising and so on for your case, you can put in a Freedom of Information request. (For practical details, visit www.gov.uk.) To get the results you want, get some advice first; ACAS also has guidance.

Regulators. If you have a genuine concern about a failure of a legal duty such as safeguarding, misuse of data, or about misuse of public resources, institutional

discrimination, etc., you can contact the relevant ombudsman (e.g. Ofsted, Care Quality Commission, Charity Commission), but get advice first. This is a big step – not the way to tackle a complaint about service delivery or a poorly thought-through policy.

Note that there are time limits on many complaints, appeals and judicial review processes – sometimes a matter of days. First try to resolve the problem, but quickly, and if you think it needs higher-level action, act quickly.

Box 7.6 | 'Nudge, poke, slap' – some tactics for practice and policy changes

Nudge

- 'We would love you to talk to our steering group/give an interview for our newsletter about refugees' entitlements and access to your services. Can you come next month?'

- 'Here you are, I've brought you a flier from the EHRC about rights and eligibility. I hope it's helpful.'

- 'I always find working with your team very productive, but I have to have a bit of a grumble…'

Poke

- 'When I asked Doctors of the World about this yesterday…'

- 'Dear Head of Services, cc. Chair, I would appreciate your view on…'

- 'Sadly, I don't feel this is satisfactory and I am considering putting in a formal complaint.'

Slap

- 'Dear… With regret, my client wishes to make a formal complaint.'

- 'As, unfortunately, we have not been able to resolve this issue, if I have not had a more satisfactory response by the end of the day on Friday, I will be contacting the ombudsman, Ofsted, etc.'

Influencing practice and policy

In the long run, better opportunities and better access for refugees come from better policies and practice. You *can* influence other organisations, although it isn't guaranteed.

Changing the views of an individual staff member is probably more effective than filling in any number of surveys, as one person can be a strong influence on others in their organisation. There is an element of 'reflexivity' in

any interaction – in other words, any new experience changes all the parties involved. Anyone who meets face to face with a woman or a man who has come all the way to the UK to escape danger and persecution will tend to become more aware of refugees. Maybe you can set up an opportunity for face-to-face interaction outside the staff member's normal working environment – an invitation to present certificates at a training day, for example. Heightened awareness now often means a person rethinking and changing what they do further down the line. Could this person become one of your good networking links? Even a 'friend within'?

Organisations often set up channels and activities exactly for your input, including input to policy and planning reviews. You can use feedback and suggestion boxes, of course, answer evaluation questionnaires, surveys, needs assessments, attend focus groups and consultations. Whether this makes any actual difference is outside your control. But most organisations do struggle to get decent input to evaluations and consultations; a concerted input by you and ideally also from refugees whom you are supporting could work.

If you feel there is a good chance of bringing about change, make a definite decision about whether to go for it or not. If you decide to lobby, select your issue wisely and invest real commitment and energy in it. A quick response dashed off between phone calls gives their consultation credibility but probably won't lever the changes you want.

Build a good case and provide credible evidence and solutions that they could almost 'copy and paste' directly into their policy and planning documentation. Whether you are replying to a survey, attending a public event or putting in an independent submission:

- establish your/your organisation's credibility – local expertise, history and track record, refugee involvement, number of refugee and other clients, quality and achievements (quantified if possible – otherwise, cases)

- it helps if you have respectable funders, good governance and a positive relationship with the body you are lobbying

- provide one or more detailed, relevant case study from actual work (anonymised)

- add data, views and quotes you have collected from refugee members or clients specifically for this case

- give a selection of solid, relevant statistics backed up with links to national research

- where possible, link your request for change to the organisation's constitution and strategic plans/mission statement, and also make the links to relevant legislation clear, which they can quote.

Decisions are often made by committees. If you can't manage the time to attend the right meetings, see if you can find a supportive voice who is there already and is sympathetic to the changes you want, and provide her/him with the data, case studies and so forth.

Sometimes, when reason and due process aren't working, you have to have a row (Box 7.7)

Box 7.7 **'Bang on the desk' tactics**

You might be the kind of person who is comfortable with good old 'bang on the desk' tactics, whether simply to ask, 'What about refugees?' or to lobby for a specific change: For example:

- Harass – turn up for everything, ideally accompanying a refugee member/client.

- Bombard – write letters (better than emails) to different layers in the organisation, asking for a response; get individual refugees and/or other members to write.

- 'Chain yourself to the railings' – simply don't take no for an answer; ask repeatedly for the same thing, asking what action has been taken since the last time you turned up.

- 'Bring in the cavalry' – your Chair writes to their Chair; involve your local councillors, MP, AM, MEP.

- Build alliances – try to persuade other local organisations round to your point of view so they will send the same message.

- 'Bus people in' – make sure several sympathetic members or friends of your organisation attend any open or public meetings; brief them first.

- But don't bluff – it is likely you will meet a counter-offensive and be invited to meet or asked to provide written recommendations, data and evidence, recruit people to respond to consultations, attend focus groups, sit on committees and other contributions that will demand your time – be ready to go and make a constructive input.

The great opportunity – the Public Sector Equality Duty

The Public Sector Equality Duty (PSED) really is too good to waste. It is discussed in some detail in Chapter 4, as an asset for the hands-on worker. Chapter 4 describes concepts and principles, protected characteristics, scope for positive action, and documents and processes that public authorities must fulfil under the PSED. It is designed to stop groups such as refugees getting pushed further and further behind in society. The PSED is there to make sure public authority staff think about disadvantaged groups such as refugees when they

make decisions, design, deliver or commission other organisations to deliver services and activities.

This section revisits the documents and processes of the PSED and how they give you a chance to advocate for special attention to refugees in your area. These processes give you leverage.[2]

Public authorities must review the documents on this list at regular points. There should be an element of public consultation and public scrutiny, meaning there can be several opportunities to ask questions throughout a year, and to present evidence and arguments. Feed in questions and voices from refugees, send local data and add relevant reports from the Refugee Council, Women's Asylum Charter, King's Fund, Maternity Alliance. Hint: Resend the team doing the review a full range of evidence each time a review is done, as it is never exactly the same team and they will not remember or know about what you sent last time.

The relevant PSED documents should be in the public domain – they are normally on organisations' websites. Read them closely with a critical eye. You can quote them and refer to them when you argue for certain projects or challenge decisions.

There are strong opportunities where the Equality Evidence Review is the starting point and justification for Equality Objectives, annual Evidence Reviews or Reports and Equality Impact Assessments (each one is described in Chapter 4).

For greatest success, you will probably have to challenge the authority to increase the detail in its data, so that it makes refugees visible. It won't be enough if they look at the nine protected characteristics one by one (Box 4.4). You need them to identify sub-groups within protected groups – for example, within race, recognise certain nationalities that are likely to be refugees (e.g. Afghan):

e.g. race = ethnic minority – Asian – Afghan

…or identified a sub-group by national status:

e.g. race = not British/migrant – refugee.

Equality Objectives (based on Equality Evidence) are the five or ten priority areas public authorities have committed to tackling over two to three years. They create space and a framework for decisions and actions. Try to get refugees listed. But if you can't get refugees listed as a distinct group, make the case that they face multiple disadvantages as a sub-group of a group that is listed in the Objectives.

For example, if there is an objective to improve support to people with mental health difficulties, refugees have very high rates of mental health disability.

---

2   The Equality and Diversity Forum (EDF), which is a national network, Race on the Agenda (RoTA), a national race equality organisation, and also the Equality and Human Rights Commission (EHRC) have guidance, toolkits and training to support PSED lobbying.

If young mothers are a priority group and a special service is being commissioned to support them, many young refugee mothers will have additional needs, related to their experiences of flight and refuge.

e.g. sex = woman + age = young + maternity = with baby under six months

+ race = ethnic minority – Asian – Afghan + migrant (refugee)

+ disability = mental health

Equality Objectives create the space for action, but you will still need to push staff a bit to remember refugees when they design and fund services.

Equality Impact Assessments (EIA) with this kind of detail are of real value. Where the assessment shows some groups might not get the same full benefit (language 'barrier') or have additional needs (mental health and post-traumatic stress disorder), the EIA should trigger mitigating actions. Afghan mothers might need interpreters and specialist attention to mental health.

If you can feed into an EIA consultation and get your comments recorded, you can come back in a year and ask the authority what impact the service had on refugee mothers compared with other mothers. Did their mitigating actions work? Were there equal outcomes? Is their equality characteristic monitoring up to scratch? Does it make refugees visible? (See Box 4.11.) And if you have real-life real-time evidence from refugees that a new or changed service isn't working for them, the fact that you raise a flag at the original EIA gives you a strong footing to push for improvements.

Box 7.8 | **Ideas for adjustments and positive/ mitigating activities to request**

For example, you might lobby for:

- budget and proper standards for interpreters, letters in plain English, translated letters and information

- additional time in appointments to explain processes and give full information

- staff to have permission and resources to provide more holistic casework-style support

- training staff properly about refugees' documentation and entitlements so they don't discriminate, especially at the gate

- the organisation and staff to form links and communicate/collaborate with refugee support networks and have access to/be able to buy in relevant expertise

- scope for child care, transport costs, fee waivers and other cash-savers for refugee service users

- staff to run a special focus group with refugees as part of an Equality Impact Assessment review

- waiving a requirement – for example, two years' 'ordinary residence' – to be eligible for a service

- access to post-traumatic stress disorder (PTSD) counselling, even if it involves paying travel costs

- placement opportunities for young refugees who have no experience of British organisational culture.

Summary

Advocacy and lobbying is not only for refugee specialists. It is about children specialists with an expanding professional knowledge lobbying for refugee children as one of the special groups within their remit, disability groups to voice and argue for attention to disabled refugees, and so forth.

The practical focus of this book means we brush past wider issues about lobbying on British or international policy. It doesn't cover British democratic institutions, where helping refugees to understanding party politics, voting or standing for election would help them have a voice.[3]

And there is, regretfully, no space for the influential power of the arts, and, of course, comedy and satire in public awareness-raising. But that doesn't stop you enjoying yourself on YouTube/iPlayer with Alexi Sayle, Omid Djalili, Shappi Khorsandi; or satirists in print such as Steve Bell, the late great Ronald Searle, even Michael Bond and Paddington. There are more ideas in the footnotes.[4]

After this point Chapters 8 to 11 are about practical services and support that refugees and families should be able to depend on as they tackle daily life. You will be needed.

---

3   Operation Black Vote and parliamentary schemes exist to improve ethnic minority engagement in democratic processes.

4   The arts and creative expression are part of full and fulfilling lives. If you are interested in engaging refugees in art for art's sake – for creative expression and performance or aesthetic reasons rather than just functional wellbeing – look up groups such as Writers in Exile and engagement work by the British Museum. There are many highly skilled performers and teachers among refugees, whom you can meet performing at festivals and often contributing to Refugee Week events. No doubt they would be pleased to be offered a performance fee to add some zing to your AGM.

Spirituality is not my field, but St Ethelburga's in London does some very interesting work, and who could ignore the humanity of the late Rabbi Lionel Blue in the Radio 4 backlists?

If you are looking for sources for awareness-raising, there are powerful collections and archives held by the Imperial War Museum and Jewish Museum, some of which are available online. For school-age citizens, look up Benjamin Zephaniah's *Refugee Boy*, and Mary Hoffman's *The Colour of Home*.

Introduction to Practical
Chapters 8, 9, 10 and 11

Chapters 8 to 11 look at what you can do practically, by theme. Broadly speaking, these practical chapters go from supporting people to survive and recover to helping them build a future:

- Chapter 8: basic needs such as shelter, food and goods, money for essentials

- Chapter 9: physical and mental and emotional health and wellbeing and disability

- Chapter 10: learning English, education, training and employment

- Chapter 11: refugee children and young people, including unaccompanied children.

It is likely that, at some point, someone you find yourself working with will hit a bad patch. It could escalate into crisis. They/you will need to act fast to avoid disaster. Most of the time, though, you will meet people who are coping with a situation that is generally poor – never enough money, stuck in overcrowded housing, vulnerable to sudden changes and so forth. They might also be in touch with you because you are a resource for their longer-term strategies to build a decent future.

The **first aim** of these chapters is to *alert you to issues* that come up regularly when you find yourself giving practical support to refugees (Box 1). Introductions outline why and how certain issues are more likely to affect refugees and some of the kinds of tangle that people are likely to ask you to help them get through.

	Summary – some consequences of having to
Box 1	leave and seek refuge (see Chapter 2)

Many factors that are related to people's need to escape persecution and search for refuge have consequences that complicate refugees' potential to manage with the resources they have and access the resources and services they need:

- mistrust of authority, reluctance to engage

- difficulty negotiating access to British organisations and institutions (see also Chapter 5)

- poverty, insecurity, vulnerability and crises

- impaired physical, mental or emotional health

- struggles with language, skills and accessing opportunities and work.

The **second aim** is helping people to *identify entitlements*. Each chapter gives information about rights and state entitlements. You will need an adequate understanding of different kinds of immigration status relating to refugees, and when and how immigration status matters, as outlined in Chapter 3. Throughout these chapters, 'refugee' continues to be used in the subjective, inclusive sense, and 'asylum seeker', 'Convention refugee', 'refugee with Leave' and so forth are used only when necessary to differentiate between people with different immigration status and therefore entitlements defined by the Home Office. You can refresh your memory of the differences via Box 3.11 and the Glossary.

Refugees' entitlements may not vary as much from British citizens' entitlements as you expect, and each chapter explains what kind of mainstream state benefits and services – housing, health services, education – refugees are entitled to on the same footing as any British person. Where information on mainstream benefits is the same as for any British person and widely available, this book simply gives pointers to where you can find that information.

Be clear and confident in your knowledge about rights and entitlements. This is valuable when staff in other organisations are unsure about what they should do, but you can insist with visible confidence that refugees *are* entitled to their services. You don't need – and realistically probably could not gain – all the expertise it would take to answer every question or help in every unique situation. Just be realistic about gaps in your knowledge and know when to look for more expertise.

The **third aim** is to help you find *relevant services and sources of expertise and support*. There are sections in Appendix A giving important sources of specialist backup – statutory and voluntary – relating to the subjects in these chapters. Key organisations relevant throughout the practical chapters include:

- Scottish, Welsh and London-based Refugee Council, British Red Cross, Asylum Support Appeals Project (ASAP)

- local Citizens Advice and remaining community law centres, libraries.

Specialist help is not always easy to source, especially locally. Remember the 'One plus One' principle (Box 7.4) and start with the person's needs; their immigration status comes second. People are often very well served by bodies outside the refugee sector and any organisation offering support to people in need should be equally effective in supporting refugees.

The specialist services noted are also sources you can turn to yourself for expert advice as you build up your own knowledge and professional networks. Do make the most of your chances to network, and network well beyond the refugee sector.

The **fourth aim** is to suggest *ways you can help refugees cope with and improve their situation.* You or your organisation might be in a position to provide resources directly. Or you might end up diverting a lot of your energy into advocating for people just so they can access what they should be getting anyway. Alternatively, you might feel your most valuable role is to help individuals take more control of their own situation, by helping them strengthen assets such as knowledge, skills and their own contacts (Box 2). Chapter 5 described approaches you can use to facilitate refugees' engagement with your own organisation. Chapter 7 suggested strategies and tactics for advocacy in relation to other organisations. The following chapters build on ideas and recommendations in those chapters and add examples on each theme.

Box 2 | **Means and 'assets' refugees need to engage with formal organisations (see Chapter 5)**

- money and time

- the means to stay in touch

- documents

- English language literacy and confidence to speak

- knowledge skills and cultural competence

- contacts and networks

- a sense of agency.

Refugees are active agents of their own survival, but a part of this picture is 'the kindness of strangers', the generous responses of individuals when they meet face to face with a refugee in need, offering shelter, essentials and humanity.[1] Such kindness, however, is essentially random and no refugee can rely on it. You – in your hybrid role that is part stranger and part professional – are a critical asset for a refugee who is trying to find meaningful reliable support.

Do familiarise yourself with the content and layout of these four practical chapters. Any of the practical issues outlined might arrive with the refugee who walks through your door on Monday. Boxes contain additional details on

---

1	The kindness of strangers was the theme for Holocaust Memorial Day in 2013 when people across the world recognised the individuals who hid and smuggled Jews out of Germany and gave them refuge, sometimes being murdered by the persecutors in revenge.

subjects you might need in specific situations. The Table of Contents and List of Boxes at the start of the book give you an overview and the Index in the back of the book is your best tool for searching out specific topics.

All facts and details are accurate going into 2018, but be aware that some things change fast; remember to check, compare and record the date of any facts or figures you find in your research, especially if you have found things on the internet.

Roof, Food, Money and Essential Goods

Introduction

It could be me.

Any one of us can end up destitute and struggling to find the basic essentials for life – shelter, warmth, food, clothing, money, social interaction. Perhaps things were OK, but a set of problems has turned into a crisis because a housemate stole your money or you got bad advice. Something like losing a job or the end of a relationship can turn anybody's life into chaos.

There are many ways a refugee in Britain can end up on the edge of destitution. Many exiles are already impoverished and dependent on others, with compromised health and restrictions on their movements and actions. There are difficulties with the official support systems. They might be caught between stages in asylum or immigration processes, bounced between multiple agencies with no progress or stuck on waiting lists. Mental ill health is often a contributing factor when people lose the means for a secure, decent life.

Asylum seekers can get some state support, but there are gaps and cracks. This person might still be waiting for a first asylum support payment. That one didn't comply with her NASS contract and the support was cut off. Refused asylum seekers may have to survive without any government support.

Even refugees with Leave are vulnerable to destitution. When they first get their Leave to Remain, refugees are caught by the '28 day' rule – 28 days after getting Leave to Remain all NASS support stops. By this time the refugee is meant to have obtained a National Insurance (NI) number, found new accommodation and have successfully registered for and be receiving mainstream benefits. If a refugee fails to achieve this, they can end up with no support at all coming in until the paperwork is sorted out. There are active campaigns challenging this and maybe by the time you read this it has changed (Refugee Council 2014).

Destitution is not just about money.

First, it is a *chronic insecurity* about the basic necessities in life such as personal safety, a secure, warm place to sleep and live, decent food and clothing, positive social interaction.

Second, it is a *lack of control* and *inability to access* structures and institutions – the food is there, the work is there, but you can't get to it. You are dependent on what others decide to do. A life on the edge of destitution is chaotic, and people are unable to manage, predict, plan, invest for the future.

Third, it is a *lived experience*, a struggle to ensure physical safety and dreading theft, abuse and violence. This is constant anxiety about yourself and others you care about, not just now but into the future. Destitution is an experience of failure and rejection or blame by authoritative bodies. There is deteriorating health, resources, loneliness, negative self-identity, lost aspiration. Such feelings and experiences are bad for anyone, and for refugees they could echo earlier experiences.

Fourth, it is has *consequences*. How deep is the impact of destitution? How long will it be before someone overcomes the damage to their financial situation or mental and emotional wellbeing? Some of the more dangerous strategies people adopt to survive have consequences too – borrowing, begging, stealing, trading sex and other commodities. Even the fear of destitution can have a long shadow.

This chapter starts with supporting people to survive. But 'refuge' is about more than surviving. It is surely about facilitating people to re-establish a *decent* life for themselves and their families. However, at present, you may have to sort out daily essentials before you can start discussing the future.

This chapter focusses first on shelter and housing, then food, clothes and basic goods and consumables, including the money to get them. Some necessary terms, defined earlier in the book, are in the Glossary. Useful organisations and all sources of expert advice and support mentioned are given in Appendix A. As well as Refugee Council, Red Cross, Citizens Advice and law centres mentioned in the introduction to these practical chapters, ASAP and the NRPF Network are important sources of advice relating to all of this chapter.

Outline of support

Although you give advice on immigration cases if you aren't licensed, you can work with someone on their claim or appeals for support. You just need sufficient knowledge or online access to information and advice, plus determination. If it is about state support, you will probably do better if you coordinate with their solicitor. Individual and family cases for support can get very complicated, so at times both you and your 'client' must get expert backup. There can be tight timescales and they/you might need to move fast.

There is limited **government or state support** from public funds for refugees via the National Asylum Support Service (NASS) or mainstream benefits. It includes accommodation and money for some asylum seekers via NASS, and for refugees with Leave to Remain via mainstream state welfare benefits.

Refused asylum seekers might have No Recourse to Public Funds (NRPF), although if they are taking 'all reasonable steps to leave the country' or the Home Office agrees they can't leave, NASS may continue to provide accommodation and money. Don't forget the different support and entitlements flagged up in Chapter 3, for disabled people (details in Chapter 9) and children (Chapter 11).

Voluntary, community and faith organisations also provide basic essentials. A lot of what asylum seekers and refugees draw on is what exists to protect any homeless, destitute or near-destitute person – for example, winter night shelters and food banks. There are often shortages and other restrictions and conditions, especially when services rely on governmental funds (e.g. Housing Benefit, European Social Fund), but sometimes because of the organisation's own policies. Check *before* you refer – a person who is on the edge cannot afford to waste time and energy.

Shelter and housing

What scale are we talking about here? With approximately 26,500 new asylum seekers in 2017–2018, NASS accommodated a total of 39,000 people (including dependants) dispersed across the UK (Refugee Council 2018). They are often housed in economically depressed areas, with the largest numbers going to the North West, Yorkshire and the Humber and the West Midlands, where there is vacant and 'hard-to-let' housing. The asylum seekers who are not accommodated by NASS find their own housing.

Others are in temporary hostel-style accommodation referred to as 'initial accommodation' while they wait to be allocated housing. People may share same-sex rooms in a mixed-sex unit. Families stay together unless adults are detained.

Because it is rare for hands-on workers to meet them or help them directly while in detention, detention is not covered in any depth in this book. If you are interested in visiting and supporting people in detention and want to know more about detention, see Association of Visitors to Immigration Detainees (AVID) and Bail for Immigration Detainees (BID); also Yarl's Wood Befrienders, working with the women's removal centre in the Midlands.

Once people are granted Leave to Remain or refused asylum, they mostly leave NASS accommodation. We have no statistics on the housing people find when they get Leave to Remain, whether sharing, renting privately, council, social housing or even buying property. But a substantial proportion of the approximately 25,000 people per year who get Leave are probably moving into the private rental or social housing market.[1]

---

1   In Chapter 2 I commented on debates about whether refugees are reducing the amount of social or other housing for British nationals.

At least initially, people looking for their own housing will find it in poorer urban areas. Many will be staying with existing contacts, with shared facilities, whether with extended family or others. They are possibly involved in some domestic or economic arrangement such as housekeeping, child care or other labour or exchange. They may be sharing space or a 'home in multiple occupancy' (where a single property is broken up into units or has rooms added) or even so-called 'beds in shed'.

Entitlements are summarised in Box 8.4 and some examples of support with resources, access to and control of accommodation are in Box 8.5. Prime contacts on any accommodation matter are community law centres, Homeless Link and the Shelter Helpline for advice. Networking is essential in preventing homelessness and supporting accommodation (Box 8.1). Your local authority will have a housing department with homelessness teams who may have or give information or referral, but they are very limited in what they can do.

Box 8.1 **Network, build and change structures – Case Studies A–C**

A REAP runs an annual 'Refugees – Home and Homelessness' half-day event with a format designed so that practitioners and managers who work with refugees and asylum seekers can do some intensive networking, share knowledge and make useful contacts. There are no speakers, but different methods are used to optimise networking – for example, 'spotlights' by participants, peer-led discussion workshops, a detailed list of participants with project information and follow-up email listings.

B Frontline Workers Network is a highly accessible free, national peer-network of hands-on practitioners in housing and homelessness and related fields such as mental health and substance use. It facilitates workers to share experiences, information and questions.

C NRPF Network serves local authority and non-local authority staff and provides guidance particularly relating to people with care needs who have NRPF.

To find and access accommodation – now, soon, later

So what issues might people bring to you for your help?

(A) I NEED ACCOMMODATION TONIGHT

Rarely, but sometimes, an individual or even a family will ask for your help because they need to *find accommodation tonight* (see Box 8.2). Individuals might be sleeping on the streets already, or a parent and child could be on the point of physical eviction, or leaving a dangerous situation. They haven't been sitting around passively up to this point – they will have been actively seeking out solutions, so find out if they already have contact with homelessness bodies.

They might be seeking your view as an alternative to other views they have already gathered, in the hope that you can give them better news. However, unless you can provide them directly with accommodation, they will probably do better at this critical moment to be listening to specialists who know the exact local options available to avoid sleeping on the streets.

Start by ringing the local authority as soon as possible for advice. You will need to know the person's immigration status. Even if the local authority cannot or will not help, they may have suggestions or contacts you can follow up.

You might find there is a local homelessness organisation that has access to a 'clearing'-type system to find the nearest shelter with space that night. Many overnight shelters are only open in midwinter. Many shelters and also women's refuges are funded via Housing Benefit and may not be able to accommodate asylum seekers and people with NRPF.

The person you are assisting will be expected to take up any options they still have – staying on in their previous accommodation, paying for a hotel – before any state or homelessness charity will house them. If they are running away from violence, it is in their interests to contact the police.

The local authority might give a person with Leave to Remain an appointment as soon as the next day to assess their case, but this might only mean they get a list of contacts. If the person has Leave to Remain, their situation is similar to any British resident. Broadly, single males are unlikely to get immediate help from most local authorities, although pregnant women or women escaping violence should get some help which might mean bed-and-breakfast or help to get space in a refuge if anything is available. The local authority has a legal duty to safeguard and protect children if the family is homeless (Chapter 10).

Some voluntary hosting organisations exist where people give asylum seekers or refugees a home in their own house for the night or for longer (e.g. Refugees at Home, Housing Justice). Most are set up for short- to mid-term stays. There are usually some screening processes such as any criminal record or references. If asked for a reference, you need to consider carefully if you really are in a position to give assurances to the potential host.

Box 8.2 **Should we let them sleep in our side room tonight?**

Giving a roof, even for a night, is, of course, of real, immediate value to someone who has nowhere. But be clear on what you expect of them and what they should expect of you.

How long can they stay? What about food and washing? Fire and hygiene? Smoking and rubbish? What about obligations to other users, safeguarding, security within the building, security from the outside? Who will be cleaning up if there is a mess?

What is your legal position? Will this be a problem with your current insurance, licence or landlord? Will you need extra insurance?

Prepare yourself for someone who is having a hard time. Be 'friendly but not a friend'. Consider what giving (and then possibly later refusing) direct support does to the nature of

your and your organisation's relationship with the person involved. No one can stay living as a 'guest' for long.

What if others hear and ask for accommodation too? Can you help with a longer-term solution?

(B) I NEED ACCOMMODATION TOMORROW OR VERY SOON:
ASYLUM SEEKERS AND REFUSED ASYLUM SEEKERS

If an asylum seeker asks for your assistance, they might not need accommodation tonight, but ask you to support them to find somewhere new or better to stay very soon.

This might be because they had their own accommodation but can't stay any longer because of poverty, worsening relationships or a risk such as violence. It may have been a temporary arrangement anyway, sofa-surfing or subletting from contacts. If they can no longer stay where they are, and can show they are destitute, they can apply (or reapply) for NASS accommodation, but there will be a wait.

Or they:

- are in NASS accommodation but their asylum application or appeal has been rejected, and they have 21 days to leave the property. They can ask to stay there if:

  - their solicitor is going to submit a new claim for asylum

  - they can show they are taking 'all reasonable steps' to leave the UK or

  - they can't return to their country of origin (see Chapter 3 and ASAP Factsheets)

- are being evicted from NASS accommodation because they are accused of being absent for extended periods, or subletting, or there are complaints about violence towards staff or other residents

- are finding the conditions utterly intolerable perhaps because of their own mental ill health, and have a strong case to move (e.g. rape survivors requiring single-sex accommodation, ground-floor accommodation for someone who has impaired mobility)

- or they are being placed in other accommodation but want to stay where they are (Box 8.3).

In many circumstances, they and you need to act fast. They get 21 or 28 days' notice to leave and then the landlord or landlord's agents can removed them, backed up by police. This is *different* to standard eviction processes for private tenants which you may be more familiar with and which can take months.

Box 8.3 **If they are being dispersed, or moved out of your area**

To resist the move, write to NASS immediately. Get other letters of support. Write to the refugee's MP.

If the move is unavoidable, you might be able to help them prepare for the move.

Talk about the new town; look at pictures and maps together. Search online for local organisations (sports, arts, cooking, refugee support or mental health groups – remember the 'One plus One' principle).

Ring around until you find a group that seems interested and friendly. Explain the situation, and pass the phone to your client so she or he can speak direct to someone in the new organisation and start to establish new contacts before getting there.

If they are learning English or studying, help them contact a college in the new area and try to arrange a transfer, instead of them having to start again. You may need to ring as an advocate to sort out an application.

Find out what the cheapest fare is from that place back to your area, and how long it takes, so they can see they won't be completely cut off.

(c) I need accommodation tomorrow or very
soon: refugees with Leave to Remain

Refugees with Leave could be asking for help with accommodation because they:

- have just received Leave to Remain and are now several days into the 28-day period and must leave NASS accommodation

- had their own accommodation but can't afford it for similar reasons to asylum seekers or

  - have rent arrears because their past and current circumstances mean they are in debt and have irregular income

  - face delays in benefit payments resulting in a risk of or notice of eviction

- are looking for something cheaper, better or more convenient

- hope to get social housing.

People with Leave to Remain in some dispersal areas might be able to stay in their NASS housing by arrangement with the local authority, paid for with Housing Benefit/Universal Credit. They can apply to the local authority for housing. They must show they are homeless, but not intentionally homeless, and that they have a 'local connection' – that they have been resident in the area and/or have important contacts and attachments there. The area where NASS housed them will usually be seen as their local connection. If they had a choice of staying in previous accommodation but left, they might be considered intentionally homeless.

However, people often have unrealistic hopes and waste a lot of time because they believe rumours and misinformation about being given social housing. They might wait months or years before they realise a better option is to find a private landlord who will accept them as a tenant. If they aren't earning enough, they need to find a landlord who will accept benefits.

Finding private accommodation can be harder for refugees (and other migrants) as landlords may be wary of housing refugees even if they have Leave because of 'Right to Rent' requirements from 2016, obliging landlords to check people are in the country legally.[2] Most landlords have no idea what different documentation means and may wrongly reject asylum seekers and refugees with Leave.

You could write a letter for the refugee to carry with them, explaining the law and documentation and reassuring potential landlords that the person you are supporting is eligible and that the landlord will not be fined or get into trouble. You may be asked to write a reference or to act as a guarantor. Consider carefully what you and your organisation will do if it goes wrong.

There are a few other possibilities for refugees who need housing soon:

- Longer-term hosting arrangements – for examples, Refugees at Home (Box 8.5, CS/D).

- Charities and churches that have registered schemes or registered as social landlords in order to provide accommodation, which often has a specialist or therapeutic element such as Birmingham Hope (also CS/E).

- Deposit loan schemes (CS/F).

- Case workers in some organisations help individuals find and manage accommodation – for example, at Freedom from Torture, Room to Heal (also CS/G).

- If someone does get Housing Association housing, there is usually a support worker or team who helps new tenants learn how to manage a property, so they don't lose the tenancy (also CS/I).

- Activist members of voluntary networks such as the range of Refugees Welcome groups that have grown across the country will sometimes take up individual cases.

---

2   Search www.gov.uk for 'Right to Rent' for official guidance leaflets that refugees can give landlords.

I need to improve on my existing accommodation

Refugees and asylum seekers might be in touch with you to help them improve their current accommodation. Whether they are in NASS, social or private accommodation, refugees may be finding it hard to maintain a decent standard of living and sense of wellbeing in crowded, shared facilities or poorly maintained properties. They might be concerned about safety, cleanliness, space, heating, facilities and bills. Some people have co-residents who are also in distress, with difficult behaviour or coping strategies, or who may be aggressive or discriminatory.

A tenant who wants improvements in their accommodation should check (or ask you to check) their contract first. Residents should record dates and details of conditions and incidents. Then contact the manager or landlord. If you are going to contact the manager or landlord for the tenant, you need to have permission, preferably in writing. They should keep records of contact or attempts to contact managers/landlords, keep photos and copies of correspondence/texts.

If they are in NASS hostels or housing, they will have a named accommodation manager who is usually non-resident. There is talk of expanding the manager's role, but their role at present is more to run the property rather than promote asylum seekers' welfare. Some are more helpful than others. NASS housing is run by commercial companies on behalf of the Home Office. They have sub-contracts with private landlords. If the NASS landlord or direct accommodation manager does not help, you contact the commercial contractor. You might need to involve the local authority – environmental or public health – to pressure the NASS contractor, or other landlords, into action.

There are cases of criminals targeting asylum accommodation or housing because they know vulnerable people are staying there, attempting fraud or trying to involve people in activities such as illegal forms of trade and working, false papers, loan-sharking, or because of other kinds of intimidation or acts of asylum-hate. If your contact fears for their safety, it is best also to contact the police, but it is quite possible asylum seekers or refugees will not want to involve the police. Residents should keep the manager/landlord informed. Landlords might be able to fit CCTV, alarms, panic buttons or new locks, or contact the police themselves if they are also concerned.

There are also obligations on tenants to maintain the property and not compromise safety (e.g. not smoking indoors). Being new to the UK, there might be unfamiliar problems, such as condensation and damp, drains, gardening, fire alarm systems. Tenants usually risk eviction if they sublet.

Box 8.4	Entitlements to shelter and accommodation for people with different immigration status		
	State/social accommodation	Shelters/hostels, refuges	Private rental
Asylum seeker	If NASS approves their application for support, they are likely to be dispersed outside London/major areas; may be moved several times. Single or joint (same-sex) room, often in shared accommodation. Prime contractors sub-contract to smaller organisations and landlords. Accommodation manager visits. Contract includes not being absent for long periods, not subletting. NASS will not pay for accommodation they find themselves. Family or parents with children – see Chapter 10.	A few hostels, charitable organisations, etc. will accommodate asylum seekers but not hostels that are contracted by local authority or other government-sourced funding. May accommodate from one night to longer e.g. three to six months. Also see voluntary 'hosting' schemes e.g. Housing Justice.	Allowed. No financial support. Landlords are required to check immigration status for 'Right to Rent', and might be wary but asylum seekers are allowed to rent. Might need deposit, references. Often via extended family networks, sublets. Often rent directly from contacts without a tenancy agreement. Might include exchange of labour or other exchanges.
Refused asylum seeker/ NRPF	Only if agree to leave or can't leave and successful application, in which case NASS accommodation as above.	As asylum seeker.	As asylum seeker.
Refugees with Leave to Remain	They can apply for social housing on grounds of homelessness when first granted, or for other needs. They need to show a 'local connection' which includes having been accommodated there by NASS. They might be able to remain in the same accommodation. Local connection might also be close family or a new job. Financial support via Universal Credit (previously Housing Benefit) or pay rent themselves if earning. Temporary accommodation still paid via Housing Benefit.	As for British national. Shelters/hostels/ refuges mostly rely on being able to claim costs from Housing Benefit (Universal Credit has been problematic). There may be waiting lists, eligibility questions e.g. normal residence in a local authority area. Only 'verified rough' sleepers' with a 'CHAIN' number access some services, and might get additional services.	As for British national. Allowed. Financial support through Universal Credit (previously Housing Benefit) with UC rates and process and Council Tax relief as for a British national. Ownership, also as for British national.
For organisations offering specialist advice, see Appendix A.			

| Box 8.5 | Examples of support for refugees' resources, access to and control of accommodation – Case Studies D–I |

Providing resources:

D   Refugees at Home, Room for Refugees, Housing Justice: hosting schemes. They coordinate and support people to give room in their own houses to asylum seekers and refugees.

E   Micro Rainbow: an International human rights charity that supports lesbians and gay men who are being persecuted around the world. It set up its first 'safe space' hostel for lesbian and gay asylum seekers in London in 2017.

Assisting refugees to access accommodation:

F   Wycombe Refugee Partnership finds a property for a refugee family with Leave, and pays the deposit from donations. Universal Credit/Housing Benefit pays the rent. If or when the refugee can pay it back, the deposit is used to secure another refugee family's home.

G   Glasgow Housing Association has a migrant support worker who helps new refugees negotiate access routes into social housing in Glasgow.

H   ASAN (Asylum Support Appeals Network) is run by ASAP. It is a highly active national network of support and appeals advice workers taking on NASS cases where something isn't right. Members can email out a question about the specific issue they are tackling that day, and almost instantly get expert responses from other members.

Refugees take control:

I   Crisis 'Skylight' is more than a training programme, with 'turn up and start' options from ESOL and 'ready to rent' classes, to employment and wellbeing activities open to anyone who has been homeless recently or is at risk.

Money to live, food, clothing and other goods

This section looks at essentials such as food, clothes, basic consumables and the money to get them. Employment in order to earn a living is covered in Chapter 10. Entitlements are summarised in Box 8.8.

People need certain resources to meet the *basic functions of life*: food to eat, money to pay rent and electricity bills. Health and medicines are mostly free; details are in Chapter 9. Your interaction with a refugee might start by getting enough food or money to buy food for the next few days. It might be for 'private' goods such as underwear, paracetamol and tampons that aren't available from donations or charity shops. Some money is required to manage your asylum claims – photocopying, post, special delivery, travel to interviews and solicitors, and larger expenses such as £500 to instruct a new solicitor.

Money to live a *decent* life – rather than just surviving – means accessing and managing a wider range and quality of food, suitable clothing for all weathers, glasses so you can read, bus fares to see your counsellor. Some assets increase a person's agency and ability to manage things efficiently for themselves: a charging cable, a smart phone. There are longer-term needs such as saucepans, a vacuum cleaner, home broadband. Many courses are not free and student fees can be in the hundreds. At some point the person who has nothing today might need clothes for a job interview or a wedding.

People's needs go beyond the immediately functional – they also need to relax, get exercise, to socialise and keep in touch with distant family. Don't underestimate how important it is to have enough money to give birthday presents or feel good about yourself in the presence of peers, whether that is about putting on deodorant or lipstick.

People get into problems. *Urgent cash problems* happen for many reasons, some already noted above. Suddenly, your asylum-seeking volunteer needs £18.60 for travel to a Home Office interview – a travel voucher is due but has not arrived so they must pay up front and apply for a refund. With very low cash flow, it is not easy to budget or save for unexpected costs like a breakage or a theft or a £25 fine for dropping litter that will double if it isn't paid by Friday.

Refugees rarely have any capital, struggle to get bank accounts, have no safe source of credit, especially in their first years in the UK. Many of us are so used to managing our money with a bit of capital, bank accounts or credit that we hardly notice. I have course fees due? Put it on the credit card. Dentist wants proof of address? Show them a bank statement. We don't realise how critical (or convenient) banking is to our lives.

Refugees get into debt. When people are just coping, they can start to slip; borrowing £5 this week but paying back £3 before the money runs out again. Many people in the UK are struggling with debt, and refugees are especially vulnerable because they have low and erratic incomes that they can't improve (unless allowed to work), and no ways to spread costs. If you need £500 to instruct a new solicitor, you have to get it some way. There can also be problems with repaying smugglers and traffickers. See Box 8.6.

Box 8.6 Dealing with debt

Debt – often hidden debt – is a big problem for refugees. Once someone is in trouble with debt, the first evidence to hands-on workers is often problems with utility bills and rent, where people have prioritised other demands on their money over bills, although the actual debt problem may be bigger and more complex than household bills.

Rent, tax or 'pay-day' lenders with extreme interest rates should be prioritised. If someone comes to you with a final demand on rent, tax or utilities, you can contact the creditor and ask for time, or a repayment plan.

> Contact National Debt Line for one-to-one advice by phone that can help people over several months. They may not have interpreters, so you might make the initial call. Their video tutorials do have language options. The Debt Line is linked with Citizens Advice where the refugee can get face-to-face advice and they might book interpreters if you ask in advance.

Many people send or 'remit' money back home to parents even if it leaves them short.

Some people make bad decisions. Some people drink.

The Joseph Rowntree Foundation talks about a 'poverty premium': the poorer you are, the higher the prices you are probably paying for heat, food and so forth (JRF 2014). Should we talk about refugees paying a 'non-resident' premium? Besides bank accounts, many asylum seekers or refused applicants can't get a local authority residents' card, for example, which gives other people free access to libraries, discounts for leisure centres, adult education, etc. And also a 'new resident' premium —when they are new to the country, with a low level of English and little familiarity with British bureaucracy and commerce, it is easy to misunderstand costs, deadlines and penalties. When people are new to your area, they won't know about the library, travel passes and cheap shops, and won't have peers with whom they can buy rice in bulk, or to help smooth out shortages (see Box 8.12, CS/M).

What money can refugees get?

People may have left their home country with savings, and even had some still when they arrived in the UK. Distant family can sometimes send money. After this has all run out and they are destitute, asylum seekers can apply for NASS (Box 8.13).

Between 2012 and 2017 the numbers receiving asylum support roughly doubled: by the end of April 2018 more than 42,000 asylum seekers (including dependants) were receiving NASS money for subsistence. They receive under £38 per head per week – less than £6 per day. They receive the money via an 'Aspen' payment card (Box 8.7). All members of a family get the same allowance, just less than £6/day, although children may get free school lunches (worth about £2 a day) in term time. If you are an asylum seeker, you can request NASS subsistence without requesting accommodation. ASAP Factsheets are your first stop as details change often.

Pregnant women or babies under three get £3–5 per week extra. Parents can apply for a one-off Maternity Payment of £300 or £250 if they have been refused asylum. Maternity Action are the experts here.

> **Box 8.7** **Aspen cards for asylum seekers' NASS subsistence (living costs) support**
>
> An asylum seeker or refused asylum seeker receiving NASS subsistence support has an Aspen card which is charged weekly with their asylum support money. It can be used as a payment or debit card in shops. Asylum seekers (not refused) can draw cash from it at bank machines (not the ones in shops which might debit the card but not give the money!).
>
> Some individuals have made a direct arrangement with refused asylum seekers who have Aspen cards and can't get cash. They go shopping together. The supporter chooses items they need at shops that take the Aspen card. The refused asylum seeker pays for them with the card. The supporter pays them back in cash.

On receiving Leave to Remain, refugees can legally start paid work.

In the 28 days after getting Leave, the Job Centre/Jobcentre Plus is the main focus of activity in order to get the mainstream benefits they are entitled to:

- Their National Insurance (NI) number should arrive in the post, but if it doesn't their benefits might be delayed too. They should ask staff at the Job Centre to sort out problems with NI numbers, or you can ring the NI application line for them.

- They should go and start the process of applying for Universal Credit or other mainstream benefits straight away, taking all evidence, documentation and Home Office letters with them.

- The Job Centre might help them find a job or get on employment-related training.

- They will need a 'basic bank account' which payments can go into and from which they can withdraw the money, but will have no overdraft or cheque facility. This can be difficult to open as banks require proof of identity and address, which is difficult if refugees are in the middle of leaving NASS accommodation. (You might be able to write a letter to help – see Box 7.5.) A 'Change Account' (thechangeaccount.com) might be an alternative although they need an email and residential address.

- While they wait for their advance or first payment, handouts and food banks might be their only safety net.

Box 8.8	Entitlements to subsistence and money for people with different immigration status	

	State support/benefits/relief	Private income
Asylum seeker	NASS (main source for asylum seekers) c. £37–38/head via Aspen card which acts as a cash card (banks only) and debit card. Pregnant women or women with a baby under three get £3–5/week extra. Once-only maternity grant £300 or £600 with twins.	Not permitted to work for money
Refused	No Recourse to Public Funds (NRPF). Or, if approved for NASS, c. £36–37/head via Aspen card acting as debit card only, but not cash. Maternity grant £250.	Not permitted to work for money
Refugee with Leave to Remain	As British national, Universal Credit (previously JSA, IS, ESA, Housing Benefit and Council Tax, Family Tax Credit). Child Benefit, maternity grant, etc. as British national.	[AQ] Not permitted to work for money

Providing money and goods to refugees

So what can you do? (See Box 8.12.)

Can I give them cash?

Most people reading this book probably don't feel comfortable giving out cash. If a stranger arrives in your centre asking for money, the response is usually no. When there is already familiarity and mutual trust, you may feel more inclined to go to your treasurer or even get out your own purse. Do you make it a gift? A loan? What if they tell others who then turn up asking for money? (See Box 8.9.)

Box 8.9	Cash contributions to individuals or a small cash fund

It seems nice for people to pass the hat around or even sub someone from their own pocket. Staff or other members might pay someone to fix a computer or to clean. But consider how this looks to outside observers. Your board could authorise you to set up a small cash fund that you can use to support people in crisis. You can make it up from a special appeal, skimmed from income or reserves.

To be fair, and to avoid unmanageable expectations, you must set clear criteria on eligibility, deciding who and why and how much to give them, and who decides and how you will report to your donors, if any, or to the public.

Rather than giving cash, you could pay the fare or purchase the necessary item directly. Some local refugee partnerships or welcome groups pay money for house deposits directly to the landlord.

Even small organisations can set up emergency grants or loans. You must set rules which you stick to and be able to justify your decisions if challenged. Your trustees are accountable. Make sure everyone in the organisation understands and accepts the responsibility and the risks. If you give loans, make sure it won't cause a problem if they can't or don't pay it back.

It might seem a wonderful solution simply to give money to a refugee who has been especially helpful during an event or assisted with office work, but it would be seen badly by the Home Office and NASS, not to mention the Inland Revenue, Charity Commission and your employer's public liability insurance provider. A gift? Yes. A prize? Yes. A reward for contributions to...? Best not. You also need to be careful about expenses, which should clearly be only *actual expenses* in return for *original* receipts. Some possibilities you can consider for offering paid work are presented in Chapter 10.

Giving or lending money changes a relationship; it confirms how unequal your positions are and introduces new tensions

Cash from other bodies. There are small grants available for 'relief of poverty' or 'prevention of destitution' – for example, the Vicar's Relief Fund handled by the Frontline Network. Many larger organisations such as colleges have small funds to help members or students. These funds often pay for something specific and practical, like a fridge or a part of course fees. There may not be anything official, or publicised, but it is always worth ringing up to ask in a crisis.

Ask local libraries, local councillors, the local council and inter-faith networks whether they know of anything in the area. There are grant-search packages by NCVO 'Funding Central' and Directory of Social Change 'GrantsforIndividuals' which you pay subscriptions to use directly, but local voluntary sector support bodies and even councils and libraries may have subscriptions to these search packages, and will often help you search.

You might consider making links with a credit union where people can save via your organisation and borrow against what they have saved. Credit unions are not used by large numbers of British people, especially the majority of us who have access to credit. But many cultures across the world have forms of savings societies where people put in money regularly and all pay towards any one member's major costs – whether it is a house, an operation or a funeral. So the concept of a credit union (if not the language) will often be more familiar to your refugee contact than it is to you (www.findyourcreditunion.co.uk).

Can I collect donations of goods for refugees?

Perhaps your organisation already runs a food bank satellite, or you take part in a regular community lunch, or you know someone who volunteers in a charity shop. These are important access routes for refugees to source food and items they need – hot meals, groceries and goods, clothes, books, bedding. And don't forget the value of what you take for granted in your office every day – photocopying, broadband, electricity or surplus stationery – just check with the boss first!

If you and your organisation are inclined to collect donations of cash or goods, *start small* and learn as you go along.

Whether cash or items of any value, *keep proper records*. The good news is that with proper records you can claim Gift Aid on cash donations, though not on goods (unless you run a charity shop). Be honest and clear: if you say to donors that the donation is for 'refugee children', then you can't legally use it for adults or any other migrant children (Box 8.10).

Think whom to ask. Your members, suppliers and local businesses or strangers?

Box 8.10 **Know your donors and everyone will be happier**

Are they…

- regular supporters or members who might not have much, but who will help over and over again in small ways, including giving their time?

- reasonably well informed, and will want to know about your organisation and whether you will use their contributions intelligently?

- strangers attracted by the idea of doing something nice for someone, and don't much mind what as long as it isn't too inconvenient?

- other local organisations like the school or Muslim centre, who can use their networks to channel goods to you, probably as part of a longer-term exchange of information and ideas?

Acknowledge with thanks and appreciation, get permission to keep contact details, protect people's data, maintain relationships.

Make sure you get good items that people need (Box 8.11). It works well if you:

- mobilise supporters, donors and volunteers to build up to a date or event that acts as a deadline (Refugee Week? Eid? Your AGM?). Most people prefer a finite commitment.

- ask for specific things – such as winter coats – not 'clothes' or you will get bin liners full of stretched bikinis.

- only appeal when someone has a specific need – we were asked if we could provide a second-hand baby buggy. We put the word out, and a few days later one of our members brought one in from a friend of hers.

Don't underestimate how easy it can be to get donated goods and clothes, nor how difficult it can be to manage, store and distribute them properly. I worked in a small two-desk office at one point and had to talk someone out of bringing in a double bed they wanted to donate, without appearing ungrateful.

Who gets what and how will you get it to them? You can give donations out 'first come, first served', which is simple and fairly quick. But first-comers will not necessarily be the people in most need. Alternatively, set priorities and criteria. Only people who use the services already? Only asylum seekers? Or will you judge by some level of need? This puts you in the position of judging between people – a responsibility you must face up to, including the risk of getting it wrong.

Can you reach out to other organisations for referrals? Or pass what you can't distribute to other charities?[3] One way out of complications with quality, storage and distribution is to collect donations on behalf of other organisations – for example, asking for food to pass to a food bank. We were once asked to collect winter coats for detainees in an Immigration Removal Centre – we had the networks to collect from; they had the people in need to distribute to. It was very satisfactory.

Success is not measured by how much you collect but whether you get the things people need and get them to the people who need them, when they need them.

Box 8.11 Hints on handling donations

- Don't ask for more than you can handle. Donations need handling and might need cleaning. Are you going to wash those eight bags of clothes that just arrived?

- If you receive food, you need to consider hygiene, refrigeration, vermin and the sheer bulk that demands space and transport. Even tinned food goes out of date.

- If you can't pass donations on straight away, they have to be logged and labelled and stored. If you end up not knowing what is in those boxes in the cellar, you might as well throw the whole lot away.

- Staff time is expensive, so do you have volunteers you can rely on to label and organise efficiently without supervision?

---

3 I persuaded the bed-donor to kindly dismantle the bed and take it to a community furniture store which we used to refer refugees to if they needed furniture, so we were all happy in the end.

Help refugees access other services that have goods and resources

You can multiply refugees' access to resources by finding out and forming connections with other activities and organisations in advance. Look for:

- Weekly or monthly refugee or homelessness drop-ins where there may be food, clothes, nappies, toiletries, as well as haircuts, health care, advice, friendly company and central heating. There may be showers (Box 8.12, CS/J).

- Gurdhwaras (Sikh temples) and Salvation Army halls often provide free hot foot. Mosques and Muslim centres may have donations to give during Ramadan and Eid celebrations.

- Permanent services that have been mentioned already, such as libraries and children's centres.

In addition to the usual benefits of networking, you can make direct links with other organisations. For example:

- Food banks partner – where you refer refugees in need to collect a week's worth of food and perhaps have a hot meal and advice check at the same time. One model is the Trussell Trust approach, and you can search for food banks across the UK on their website (CS/K).

- Get a wholesaler trade card (e.g. Costco) for your organisation and let groups of people shop together (there is often a minimum spend and only named people can use the card).

You might assist refugees to learn ways to manage in the UK:

- Volunteering opportunities can give refugees access to practical resources as well as other benefits.

- Opportunities for building local peer contacts so they can swap news and information and lend/borrow/pool/share resources and knowledge.

You might channel services or relevant training from other organisations:

- Training and advice from a local 'financial capability' network, where different organisations can provide training and information on managing money, credit, household savings and benefits (CS/L).

- You can find opportunities to gain life skills for a tight budget such as healthy cooking classes, riding bikes, allotment projects:

    - search for 'community furniture' projects (try British Heart Foundation, YMCA shops, Sue Ryder), including environmental 'upcycling' charities and projects; also municipal dump or 'reuse' shops, where you probably need transport but can get household goods and

furniture and even sports gear, electronic goods, gardening equipment for virtually nothing – just a bit of luck on the day

- free or bargain make-up, hairdressing, meals, even fitness coaching from colleges and gyms that need practice opportunities for their students

- in big cities there may be dentistry schools which need practical opportunities for students to do work that would costs hundreds of pounds otherwise.

Box 8.12 | **Examples of projects and services relating to money, food and goods for refugees: Case Studies J–M**

J The New North London Synagogue has made running volunteer-based drop-ins for asylum seekers into an art form, with themed collections, drop-off deadlines and a rota for volunteers to prepare items before the day.

K A Foodbank Voucher Partner – the director can sign a voucher for a refugee in need, who takes it on the right day to the nearest satellite distribution point that hosts a 'touring' food bank. You can contact the food bank administrator in advance if there are special dietary needs.

L Energy Best Deal Scheme (now ended) provided speakers to groups, including English-learning and migrant groups, to give a one-hour talk about saving money on fuel bills.

M All-languages women's welcome groups were put on by a women's centre to draw attention from a mix of women – those who wanted to learn English, those who wanted to support refugee and migrant women. The women's centre's idea was to bring women from all walks of life together to form friendships and mutual solidarity as a valuable commodity for many aspects of life.

Summary and conclusion

There is no doubt that refugees' anxiety and distress is worsened by experiences of negotiating the NASS system. (Some of the impact of this is picked up by health services which are the subject of the next chapter.) Destitution is a reality for refugees in Britain, and some would say the government is deliberately using impoverishment as a tool (weapon?) to create a 'hostile environment' for 'illegal immigrants' as a way to reduce 'demand' for asylum.

Even within Parliament there is widespread criticism of the way immigration support is run.

One must also surely be concerned about what this all means in the long term for British society, as people who could easily have started contributing to society, not to mention to the economy, take years to recover from the hardship and distress that living on the edge of destitution has caused them.

As a practitioner, you may have already been a little surprised to find yourself working with refugees. Many people who never expected to become knowledgeable about homelessness or poverty are finding they have to become specialists in these as well.

People don't only need a room or a house. They need a home, where they can have some kind of life that isn't just survival.

Long Box 8.13	How to apply to National Asylum Support Service (NASS) for subsistence and accommodation

- Ring the Refugee Council or Migrant Helpline to find out whom to ring. Migrant Helpline has multilingual advisers and you dial a different direct number for different languages. The applicant may have to wait a long time. If the number is 0800, this is a free call – it is only a question of how long their battery will hold out. But it can be expensive if someone is not on a contract, so let them use your landline if possible.

- NASS will ask for Home Office reference numbers and specific questions about existing support to check if the claim is eligible. They will tell the applicant how to prove they are destitute.

- They will send application forms and information about what the asylum seeker needs to do. The applicant will need to explain how they supported themselves to that point – for example, they were helped by friends. They must give details of all bank accounts here and in other countries, any savings or assets, and bank statements showing there is no money left.

- Then the applicant needs to explain why that is no longer possible – perhaps their friends can't afford it any more or the relationship has broken down. They will need a letter from the friends to confirm this is true.

- Copy everything.

- Post the documents as soon as you have everything together. It is best to get at least proof of postage.

- They are likely to request further evidence and confirmation on certain points.

- Expect to wait a month or more. Act fast if refused – the asylum seeker may have only days to notify their intention to appeal.

- Note: It is easy to get confused about addresses and reference numbers so be very careful. If letters are handwritten, check for legibility, especially numbers as 1 and 7 are often confused in handwriting.

- Problems? Contact Citizens Advice or the local law centre.

Health, Mental Health and Disability

Introduction

Physical, mental and emotional ill health and disabilities are big issues for refugees and anyone who works with them – more so than for the main UK population at random. Refugees are ordinary people but some have been through extraordinary and damaging experiences. They have faced loss and prolonged stress. Even after arrival, poor living conditions, poverty and stress can further compromise health and wellbeing and compound disabilities.

Long Box 9.1 at the end of this introductory section looks at refugees' experiences in more depth, and possible consequences for health.

It is important that we think about refugees' health in terms that go beyond illness and medical treatment. We shouldn't pathologise depression as if it is a failure of some bodily or mental system, when it is a normal response to what someone has been through. We mustn't perceive disability as a problem inherent to that person; it is a contemporary situation in which current social and bureaucratic norms make life harder than it should be. Refugees are actively pursuing their and their families' health, wellbeing and ability to shape life ahead.

Resources are stretched, but they exist, and refugees are entitled to care and support. In outline:

- Asylum seekers, refugees with Leave and to some extent refused asylum seekers get free health and mental health treatment and care on the NHS. (This is not the case for all migrants.)

- All disabled people can ask their local authorities for support to address care and wellbeing needs related to their disability, regardless of immigration status, although they need to be 'ordinarily resident' in the area.

- Some charities have specialist support for refugees, especially relating to mental health.

But do refugees engage effectively with health, mental health and social work professionals? Refugees, as with all migrants, have to learn about the NHS and

local authority social services – what exists, their rights and entitlements, who does what, where to go first and how to take things up a level.

Language is an issue. Even if they speak some English, they may not understand the vocabulary of health and social care services, let alone the flow of acronyms: A&E, UCC, UTC, MIU and so on.[1] They might lack details or ways to express physical feelings or pain.

Some find it hard to trust clinicians and social workers. They may worry about confidentiality. They may fear Home Office surveillance (unfortunately, in 2016–2018 NHS Digital provided the Home Office with data on patients' name, date of birth, GP and last known address, although even within Parliament criticism was fierce). They may find treatment approaches unfamiliar.

There are without doubt failures and errors in the overstretched system and people share stories about poor treatment or perceived rudeness.

This chapter looks at issues, entitlements, sources of support and ideas for action when you find yourself working with refugees around health, mental health and disability. The information on entitlements as always comes with a 'health warning' that laws and policies change. If you are dealing with a complex or critical matter, or if you are moving from 'poke' towards 'slap', you need to get up-to-date advice from expert sources (see Appendix A).

Refugees might come to you directly with health questions, but their initial contact is more likely to be about training or some such interest (unless you are a health professional, of course). Health issues tend to emerge while you are discussing other things. They might ask you for reassurance about processes or what to expect before, during or after an encounter with a health or social care professional, to help them judge the value of what the professionals told them.

This chapter is not about you stepping into the shoes of a clinician or therapist (unless you are one!). Please don't attempt to therapise if you are not qualified to do so. Our health system is stretched, and long waiting lists for counselling and other treatments are frustrating. Even so, the best support you can give a refugee is to smooth out access to the clinical and professional support that is right for her or him, and offer wider opportunities for self-help and a healthy, enabled life.

Long Box 9.1	Seeking refuge and refugees' health, mental health and disabilities

Being discriminated against over a number of years, possibly including exclusion from services, could have affected people's long-term nutrition and resulted in inadequate treatment of conditions, including lack of preventative care such as immunisations. Across the world, people with a diverse range of physical, learning, mental health and other

---

1   Accident and Emergency, Urgent Care Centre, Urgent Treatment Centre, Minor Injuries Unit.

disabilities are neglected, abused and persecuted in many ways. Poor living conditions means higher levels of infection and disease with long-term impact.

Abuse, violence and torture or the effects of war on military or civilian populations will cause physical injury, including head, back and joint injuries, and long-term harm which might still need treatment. Or it can result in mental and emotional trauma and other disabilities such as impaired movement and mobility, sensory damage such as hearing loss, or chronic pain, disfigurement and other health issues. Abuse and its physical and emotional consequences are often gendered; both males and females may have been sexually assaulted and raped, resulting in sexual and reproductive complications.

Transit from town to town and country to country in poor conditions, with little access to hygiene or health care, will often mean higher levels of infection, disease and illness, compromised immune systems, under-diagnosis and under-treatment with longer-term consequences and worsening impairments. Illnesses such as HIV, TB and other infections spread fast in camps and crowded conditions. People get problems with teeth and feet.

Once in the UK, pressures within the asylum process create and heighten mental distress, increasing both physical and mental ill health, and contribute to refugees becoming disabled in the longer term. Poor housing, food, unhealthy coping strategies (e.g. drugs, alcohol) and unregulated employment continue to be factors in nutrition, infection and injuries through accidents or violence.

Migrants generally have a low take-up of preventative and screening services, so there is a problem of people presenting late with cancer and heart disease, making treatment harder and often less effective, or simply, for example, not knowing they have diabetes until it has already done them permanent harm that could have been avoided.

On a lighter note, younger couples and families quite often have babies in the first few years after they first arrive.

Physical ill health and wellness

Some of the physical impact of past experiences is described in the Long Box 9.1.

For refugees, the NHS system is not always easy to understand. The General Practitioner (GP) system is unusual and will not be familiar to people from most countries in the world. People often have certain expectations of treatment, formed in their original country, where health care might have been private or hospital-based, or methods such as injections or X-rays used routinely. They may doubt the competence of UK clinicians who follow different pathways.

Their health and best chance of full recovery depend on getting to the right service via the shortest route, first time. People who are used to getting health care at hospitals and don't understand the system, or for whom the system isn't working well, are more like to go to A&E when a GP would have served them better.

There are many positive reasons for the hands-on worker to put in some effort to help them get this right. It improves their care and speeds up any recovery. It saves them time, effort and anxiety. It also saves the NHS and the taxpayer money, and none of us can afford to watch NHS resources being wasted.[2]

Entitlements and access

Advocacy is again often necessary, but entitlements are simple at first sight. Project London, part of Doctors of the World, has up-to-the-minute guidance.

Asylum seekers, refused asylum seekers and refugees with Leave have access to all primary, community and acute/emergency services for free.

In Wales and Scotland, they all have free urgent and secondary care.

In England, asylum seekers and refugees with Leave get free urgent and secondary care

In England, refused asylum seekers do not get free urgent and secondary care, unless they are still receiving NASS support because they are taking steps to leave or because the Home Office has recognised they cannot leave or be deported at present. The situation of refused asylum seekers in England is described more fully in Box 9.3.

Entitlements are summarised in Box 9.2 below.

What does this mean in practice? As a starting point...

- ☑ Everyone can (and should) register with a GP who will see them for free. You can help a great deal just by encouraging and helping people to get registered as soon as possible.

- ☑ Everyone will be treated free in a life-threatening emergency.

- ☑ Anyone can ring 111 free across the UK, for health advice and clarification.

- ☑ Anyone can attend walk-in family planning and sexual health clinics, including HIV testing and treatment and termination of pregnancies.

> Everyone can (and should) register with a GP who will see them for free...
> Everyone will be treated free in a life-threatening emergency.

This is what should happen when someone arrives in the UK:

- • A person who has claimed asylum registers with a GP wherever they are staying and gets an NHS number and an initial health check. It might include being checked for tuberculosis and giving a medical history

---

2   The NHS Right Care, Right Place public education campaign has some very useful, plain-English resources that are also helpful for handouts in English groups.

including immunisations. The GP will use an interpreter – probably by phone – if needed.

- The GP treats them or refers them for secondary, specialist treatment for any existing conditions. They fill in an HC1 form (this has lots of pages – they might need help) and should get an HC2 certificate that they show to the pharmacist for free prescriptions, free dental treatment, optician appointment and more. They get an appointment to see the GP for any new condition they want attention to and so on.

- They register with an NHS dentist and have a new patient dental check and the dentist starts any work that needs doing.

- If they move or are moved by NASS, they register with a new GP, but they don't need a new health check each time as their records should be transferred. If and when their status changes, and even if they become homeless, they can still always register and be seen by a GP for free. Even if their claim is rejected and they lose part of their entitlements, they will continue and complete any course of treatment that has already started.

- They can take up screening opportunities, smoking cessation, diabetes testing and self-care training.

Box 9.2	Entitlements to health care for people with different immigration status			
	Primary care (planned)	**Community care (also see Box 9.3 (planned)**	**Secondary care (planned)**	**Emergency/ urgent (unplanned)**
All	GP temporary or permanent registration, family planning, sexual health, immunisation, TB, HIV. NHS 111, NHS Choices (online). Free prescriptions if they have a means-tested HC2 certificate.	Clinical care for home-based nursing care, child development, podiatry, speech and language therapy, health visiting (families with babies under five), occupational therapy, diabetes, dentistry, optometry, community pharmacy.	Public health e.g. support and education on healthy eating, smoking cessation.	Free A&E, ambulance in emergency, emergency treatment for life-threatening condition, plus continuing treatment resulting from the life-threatening emergency treatment. Acute mental health.

cont.

	Primary care (planned)	Community care (also see Box 9.3 (planned)	Secondary care (planned)	Emergency/ urgent (unplanned)
Asylum seekers and Refugees with Leave to Remain	Same as resident British nationals.	Same as resident British nationals.	Same as resident British nationals.	Same as resident British nationals.
Refused asylum seeker NRPF	Yes, free England NRPF must pay full price for prescriptions. Scotland and Wales free prescriptions.	Yes, check if a service 'in the community' is considered secondary, e.g. hospital providing clinic.	Wales and Scotland secondary treatment and care free. In England, a course of treatment that has started will be completed free. Can access secondary care but not free. See Exceptions.	If an ambulance is used but it is not an emergency, NRPF may be charged. Urgent/immediate treatment and care including treatment to protect human rights will be given immediately but may be charged later. See Exceptions.

*Exceptions on secondary care. Refused asylum seekers who were trafficked, those receiving NASS (if making efforts to return/cannot be returned) and disabled people receiving care from their local authority have same entitlements as asylum seekers and refugees with Leave. Trafficked people who are NRPF will be treated for urgent conditions resulting from their trafficking, but not other conditions.

Sources: HEAREquality.org.uk; Public Health England 'NHS entitlements: migrant health guide'; Doctors of the World; NHS England leaflet 'How to Register with a GP – asylum seekers and refugees'.

There are some other opportunities for free access to health care and alternatives for some free treatment and care easily available to all.

- 111 is a free telephone service staffed by teams including nurses and doctors, giving advice on treatment and the correct service for your condition. Interpreters are available.

- NHS Choices website has information about a wide range of conditions, prevention and self-help treatment, and local services. There are online apps and ways of asking GPs for advice using smart phones.

- Pharmacists in the UK are highly qualified. They are largely private businesses although they handle NHS services as well as prescriptions. They give high-quality advice and can treat a wide range of conditions including giving some medicines that GPs might also prescribe. They will advise whether or not to see the GP or get more urgent care.

- In London, Doctors of the World run walk-in clinics that don't require any identity or immigration papers, with qualified paid and unpaid medics. Project London will also advocate strongly and effectively at distance to get individuals access to free NHS services, including secondary care.

- Faith organisations and homelessness bodies may run weekly or monthly 'drop-ins' and also street outreach with medics.

- Fairs, shopping centres, even supermarkets host NHS screening services. Patients will probably need NHS numbers and/or proof of name and address, but not always.

- Health visitors (specialist nurses) run sessions and groups at children's centres where mothers can get health care for themselves as well as for their babies, but they might need paperwork.

- Health charities provide advice and help with lifestyle and healthy living around specific conditions, both small local charities (e.g. community cancer centre), and branches of national charities (e.g. British Heart Foundation) and therapeutic support and expertise like Maggie's Centres.

Some alternative routes are less reliable and may be dangerous to the person's health:

- buying antibiotics, medicines, etc. from abroad via family or on the internet from people who aren't licensed in the UK, or being given partial packs from friends who haven't finished medicines they got on prescription

- seeing unregistered clinicians such as doctors from the person's home country who are practising in the UK without a licence

- using homeopathic or folk and cultural or popular remedies, including faith healing

- discharging themselves, refusing treatment or delaying looking for treatment because of money.

The most basic access issue for health care is *registering with a GP*. You might think the GP practice would be the expert in access entitlements but you would be wrong. Many asylum seekers and refugees with Leave are turned away at

'the gate'. This is despite NHS guidance and sometimes even after the local Healthwatch[3] or even Doctors of the World has tried to help right the situation. GP receptionists do not always have sufficient or accurate training on this. The most common reasons given seem to be that they think the person is not entitled to register, or that they don't have proof that they are 'ordinarily' resident in the area, or proof of address.

- They are entitled. Everyone is entitled.

- Although the practice can ask for proof of residence or address and photo identity, they cannot insist on them, and cannot refuse to register someone who can't provide them. (They *can* refuse to register someone if their lists are full.)

- They have to give you the reason for refusing to register you in writing. Insisting on this usually improves the situation as staff will check before committing themselves on paper.

In England, there is an NHS England leaflet, 'How to Register with a GP – asylum seekers and refugees', that you can give the refugee. And add a letter from your organisation to the practice, offering your help to clarify. Or accompany the refugee as she or he speaks to the receptionist or practice manager directly (glance through Chapter 7 for hints on effective communication). You will be most useful in this situation if you are confident in your knowledge. People usually want to do the right thing; they don't want a fight.

If it doesn't work, you can complain, or talk to Healthwatch, the local NHS Clinical Commissioning Group (CCG), NHS England, your councillor, your MP and campaigning groups such as Doctors of the World. Realistically, though, most refugees prefer to walk away and try another practice.

Perhaps the second most immediate issue is having *adequate interpreting at appointments*. Interpreting is an essential aid to communication in English (see Chapter 6). Having appropriate interpreting counts as 'ensuring equal opportunity' and 'positive action' under the Public Sector Equality Duty (Chapter 4). If someone doesn't have good English, they should make sure the receptionist writes down that they need interpreters in appointments and put it on their computerised patient record. They might get telephone interpreting using a conference call or hands-free or Skype-style system. But face-to-face interpreters are better for longer appointments such as initial health checks, health visitors on home visits, physiotherapy, complex or sensitive situations such as abortions. Many non-English-speakers find 'tele' interpreting alienating where a good face-to-face interpreter can be reassuring.

---

3   Healthwatch is an independent statutory body that exists in every local authority area, backed up by National Healthwatch, that has powers to acts as an independent 'champion' or watchdog for local people, checking on health and social care commissioning and providers.

The third most common thing people ask for help with is understanding letters about appointments, especially being confused and worried by cancellation letters when their appointment is moved. Confusion often leads to them not turning up or turning up at the wrong time or place, wasting everyone's resources.

Long Box 9.3	Entitlements to health and mental health care of refused asylum seekers in England

Refused asylum seekers who have NRPF still get free primary, community and emergency treatment and care, including emergency mental health care. Several services are available free to everyone, such as family planning.

But in England refused asylum seekers do not get free urgent and secondary care, unless:

1. they are supported by the local authority in relation to disabilities

2. they are still receiving NASS support

3. they started treatment before receiving their refusal (they complete the treatment free)

4. they were trafficked, in which case they may continue getting free secondary care relating to their experiences and treatment during trafficking, including secondary mental health care, but not for other needs or mental health issues if they are not related to the trafficking or abuse.

If they are receiving NASS, it is probably because they have proved they are taking steps to leave the UK, or the Home Office recognises they cannot be deported at present. They may have made a successful human rights case to stay, which could be on the grounds that they are receiving ongoing treatment for a serious health condition, or care relating to a disability, and stopping the care would amount to degrading and inhumane treatment.

If they need secondary (elective) or urgent (immediate, unplanned) care, it will not be refused but they will probably be sent a bill for payment, for example:

- for antenatal care, delivery and postnatal care, if it is not a matter of life and death

- if they attend for emergency services but it is considered their need is not an emergency and they are diverted to urgent care

- they pay for medicines.

Take a few minutes to consider if you are clear on the differences between primary, NHS community, emergency care (999, A&E) and secondary care and immediate care. Confusion could result in a *large* bill.

- Generally speaking, *secondary* care is elective, more specialist or advanced diagnosis or treatment. It is often delivered in a hospital, but this is no longer always the case as the NHS moves secondary services into the community. People can agree a payment plan in advance.

- *Urgent* care is something to address an immediate problem, such as stitching a flesh wound, which has to be done now but is not life-threatening.

To be sure, ring 111 or ask Healthwatch or the doctor or nurse. They might not know straight away – they aren't accountants. But they are in the best position to find out. Receptionists may not be clear on details.

If they can't pay, they might be able to challenge the decision to charge them or the amount charged. The NHS might pursue the debt, although they don't tend to be aggressive. The NHS can arrange a payment plan as low as £5 per week or write it off. If people leave the UK without paying, it will probably reduce the chance of getting permission to return to the UK in the future.

Pregnancy and birth – Selna's birth-plan

Refused asylum-seeking women in England, like the fictional Selna, have to pay for at least some of their care around childbirth.

- Family planning is free to everyone.

- Antenatal care – care, screening and monitoring and education during pregnancy, before the baby comes – is secondary care, so Selna can arrange a payment plan in advance to pay the costs of between £1500 and £4000. If she had already started antenatal care before her claim was refused, treatment is free.

- Emergency care: if Selna has to go to emergency services (A&E) because the situation has become life-threatening, emergency care is free but she may have to pay for follow-up treatment later on.

- Delivery is immediate care and immediate care will always be given, but she will be billed for at least £2000.

- Postnatal/health visiting is community care and Selna will be invoiced depending on the amount of care she requires (upwards from £300).

See Maternity Alliance.

Mental and emotional health and wellbeing

Without being clinically trained in any sense, anyone who comes into contact with refugees can hardly avoid being concerned about their mental and emotional health and wellbeing. Any ordinary person who has been discriminated against to the point of persecution because of their sex, gender, ethnicity, sexuality, beliefs, etc., and any person who has gone through experiences of violence, departure and transit and losses, will probably end up dealing with painful memories and complex, difficult emotions. Such difficult feelings are not the same as mental illnesses, but it is reasonable to expect that a substantial proportion of the refugees with whom you come

into contact will struggle with mental ill health at some point, or repeatedly over time.

You may also meet refugees who:

- had to seek refuge in the first place because they had mental health issues and would have been discriminated against, degraded and persecuted

- had pre-existing conditions that were triggered or worsened by their flight for safety

- are traumatised by their experiences of detention in the UK, while in the asylum process

- are refused but allowed to remain temporarily because their mental health is so poor that to remove them would amount to degrading treatment or torture

- are caring for a family member or others who have more or less severe mental illnesses

- are facing mental health difficulties for other reasons (e.g. postnatal depression).

Feeling sad and unhappy, or grieving because of bereavements and losses, or suffering loneliness and homesickness are not the same as mental illness. No matter how intense and painful these feelings are, they are normal responses to what people have gone through. These feelings are part of a bigger picture of mental and emotional health. Depression or PTSD, however, are treated as mental illnesses. Some might call it mental ill health, mental health issues or challenges – people use different language according to their view of what is appropriate and useful. A high proportion of refugees must deal with PTSD, but the proportion of British soldiers returning from active duty, or people involved in serious accidents or incidents are similar.

What indicators might you see that someone is struggling? It might be one of your refugee volunteers, a group member or a parent of one of your students. They probably aren't going to approach you for help with their mental health.

You might notice someone demonstrating or expressing difficult feelings through their actions or how they dress and behave in relationships. You might see signs of self-harm or dangerous coping strategies. A person might constantly suffer from physical aches, pains, headaches or sleeplessness. People receiving treatment might be taking medicine which affects their concentration and memory or ability to express themselves.

Feelings and symptoms come and go. If you aren't a qualified clinician, don't try to diagnose, don't prod or try to treat. If you are concerned, look up the website of Mind and NHS Choices. For better understanding, consider taking 'Mental Health First Aid' courses (mhfaengland.org) and become your organisation's 'mental health first aider'.

What is the *scale* of mental health issues among asylum seekers and refugees? Estimates range as high as 50 per cent of asylum seekers having mental health needs at any one time. Even people who get through the asylum process reasonably well may have a serious mental health crisis some time later, even after years.

The consequences can be far-reaching. Not only do people often suffer when they are mentally ill, but their illness can have an impact on their future as people find it harder to take back control of their lives and rebuild a fulfilling life. People may neglect their health, family needs and relationships, threatening any job they have or their accommodation, bringing them nearer to homelessness and destitution. Carers and families are also affected.

There are all the usual difficulties 'pre-gate' before people access support for mental health difficulties, such as doubts about authority, lack of knowledge, etc. With mental health, there are other questions. Do people believe their feelings or illness can be relieved or treated? Do they have to and can they accept the label 'mentally ill'? How will peers treat them if they find out?

But most people recover or learn to manage their mental health. Experiences and memories don't go away, but with support and access to good care, the personal and wider impact can be reduced.

Entitlements and access

Everyone gets mental health services and emergency services free (with the exception in England of refused asylum seekers, covered in Long Box 9.3).

Box 9.4	Entitlements to NHS mental health care and treatment for people with different immigration status			
	Primary	Community	Secondary	Acute plus 'emergency' (A&E)
Asylum seeker	Yes, mostly via GP Also voluntary sector commissioned by CCG/LA	Yes, including community teams	Yes	Yes
Refused			Restricted and conditional in England, as Box 9.2	
Refugee with Leave to Remain			Yes	

Services available to refugees from the NHS

The NHS concentrates resources on patients with fairly intense needs, although this varies by area. Concerns about scale, availability and quality of resources for adult mental health generally have been in the news for years. There are

few specialist refugee services in the NHS, although there are specialist mental health teams, for example, in community health, PTSD and acute specialisms who might find themselves working with refugees as part of their case load. Capacity is a real problem and the majority of refugees will need to access general NHS mental health services.

NHS Choices and 111 have information, with some translation and interpreting available. Otherwise, the first point of access is the GP, who can provide some treatments directly such as medication, and is the key to referral to NHS counselling services and to approved charities and private counsellors providing talking therapies, which people might be asked to pay for. Parents with children under five can also start the process of getting help through family health visitors. As an alternative to GP and health visitor routes, other professionals, including you, can contact the local community mental health team directly (ring 111). In some areas there is now a 'Single Point of Access' (SPA) system that connects enquirers, including professionals in other fields, with the right service for them or their clients. The refugee will usually be offered an assessment, although they may have to wait many months, then wait again for the treatment. If they do not attend their appointment, it could delay getting treatment by weeks – so make sure they go!

Treatments are outlined usefully on the NHS Choices website. They are often provided in the community, and can include group therapy, talking therapies including cognitive behaviour therapy (CBT), and inpatient/residential treatments, although these are rare.

If a person gets to a crisis point, and especially if they are a danger to themselves or others, the routes are a little different, although they can still start by visiting their GP. If they are actively suicidal, they can go/you can take them/you can call the police/the police might take them to A&E. This might involve restraint if they are a danger to themselves or others.

They will be assessed at A&E – sometimes in a separate unit designed both for security and to provide a better environment for the person in crisis. They may be detained or 'sectioned' for hours, days or months. An independent mental health advocate should be available to the person in need at this point (contact your local Healthwatch). When people come out of residential or sectioned care, they should receive support to remain stable or recover, such as regular contact from a community psychiatric nurse. Mental ill health is considered a disability, and the local authority can be requested to do a community care assessment with a mental health advocate involved, which might give the refugee a level of ongoing support; this is discussed in the next section.

The NHS does not provide much treatment for mild to moderate mental health needs. Lower-level support is often provided by or via the voluntary and community sector (VCS), sometimes having been commissioned by the local NHS Clinical Commissioning Group or local authority, but often relying on

grants or public fundraising and therefore not bound by immigration rules in the same way that physical health care is.

Highly specialist regional and national charities such as the Helen Bamber Foundation and Freedom from Torture[4] care specifically for refugees with mental and emotional health difficulties. Your local Mind, Rethink and some disability and carers' organisations, bereavement support organisations, arts or gardening therapy projects and similar can often provide services with few restrictions.

Other specialist bodies and some smaller local organisations provide holistic, 'wrap round' and therapeutic case work for refugees that combine care at many levels, sometimes tackling case work such as housing and money at the same time. One example worth noting is the Baobab Centre for Young Survivors in Exile – very small, but expert.

Disability

One way to define disability is the way it is described in the Equality Act 2010: 'a physical or mental impairment' that has 'a substantial and long-term adverse effect' on your ability 'to carry out normal day-to-day activities'.

Definitions aside, what the hands-on worker needs to focus on at this point is whether and how and why a person finds it harder to take the best care of her or his daily needs and interests, including communication and learning. If getting on with the normal business of life is harder for one person than it is for someone else, who has different physical, visual, learning capabilities or better mental health, then as a decent society we should try to change the way we do things so the person or people who are finding life harder can find it less hard. Disability is not about medical problems; it is about self-determination.

Many people look at disability as society's problem, a 'social model', believing lives are being wasted, and unnecessary and avoidable difficulties are being caused by ignorance and poorly thought-through attitudes and policies. They argue that unhelpful assumptions throughout political, economic, educational and social systems in Britain underpin decisions that fail to reflect the fact that everyone has different needs. If you support this view, one implication is that we all need to put our houses in order.

(As an aside, although this argument about 'the social model' is led by disability rights campaigners, it can also be applied to age, gender, sexuality, for example, and also to the way refugees are rendered less capable by attitudes and policies in the UK.)

In places across the world, people with physical, learning, mental health and other disabilities are neglected, abused and persecuted in many ways. People's

---

4   Previously known as the Medical Foundation for the Care of Victims of Torture or just 'the Medical Foundation'.

physical or other impairments may be caused or worsened by persecution or in war or transit, or in the continuing struggle for survival once in the UK.

It is difficult to get a sense of scale regarding disabled refugees. Neither Home Office nor local authorities nor NASS keep relevant statistics. The way 'disability' is defined varies across different sectors in the UK, so any statistics that do exist are hard to compare (see, for example, Box 9.8). But the average proportion of disabled people in the general British working-age population, given in government census data from 2011, is 16 per cent. You will come across a high proportion of refugees with learning, physical, sight or hearing impairments, facial disfigurements or other disabilities. When you factor in levels of mental ill health noted among refuges, in the region of half the refugees you meet are disabled, using the definition above.

Disabled asylum seekers need reasonable adjustments to be able to manage their lives even on a par with other asylum seekers. If data is not gathered, their needs will not be identified, recognised or addressed under the PSED, either individually or as a group.

Entitlements and access

Disability, social care and equality laws protecting disabled people are more significant in shaping their entitlements than immigration status. Entitlements are summarised in Box 9.7.

- Disabled people who are supported by a local authority are entitled to free secondary care even if they have NRPF.

- The NHS has a duty to provide accessible information and communication, primarily to make sure the NHS communicates effectively with people who have learning difficulties, but this is relevant also to refugees.

- NASS, like any public authority, must make reasonable adjustments. Therefore, they might reasonably allocate someone a ground-floor room if they have mobility problems, or case workers can argue for a single room if someone's mental health difficulties make this reasonable.

- The Equality Act 2010 protects all disabled people in Britain from discrimination. The PSED requires authorities to ensure that disabled people have equal opportunities to those who are not disabled.

Community care assessments. It is the responsibility of the local authority where someone is 'ordinarily' resident to assess adults' needs for (non-medical) special care if asked to do so, or if they appear to require care and support (Care Act 2014). The person requesting an assessment may be asked to show they have a 'local connection' (See Chapter 8). The local authority where NASS houses an asylum seeker is where they are 'ordinarily' resident; or if a refugee

has found their own accommodation, it is the area where they are living now, even if they are in temporary accommodation such as shelters or sofa-surfing.

Local authorities differ. The person whose needs are being assessed can and should have an independent advocate present, and if their disability is related to mental health, an independent mental health advocate. If the assessment concludes that the disabled refugee needs support and care, the local authority has an obligation to provide or fund appropriate support. There is no set minimum for this support and it should include not only health and hygiene but wellbeing (Box 9.5). It might include:

- counselling

- support to deal with bureaucracy and entitlements, information and advocacy

- equipment and aids (e.g. hearing aids, mobility aids such as wheelchairs, household aids for independence)

- a Freedom Pass or free local travel

- adapted housing, including residential accommodation

- a carer/personal assistant should also be assessed on need, even if they are NRPF, under the Care Act, although they are not entitled to Carer's Allowance.

Box 9.5 Wellbeing in the Care Act 2014

The Care Act 2014 (www.legislation.gov.uk) introduced a 'general duty' on local authorities to promote an individual's 'wellbeing' when making decisions about them or planning services. Wellbeing can relate to:

- personal dignity (including treatment of the individual with respect)

- physical and mental health and emotional wellbeing

- protection from abuse and neglect

- control by the individual over day-to-day life (including care and support)

- participation in work, education, training or recreation

- social and economic wellbeing

- domestic, family and personal relationships

- suitability of living accommodation

- the individual's contribution to society.

Although care may be arranged, it is means-tested and will *not* necessarily be free.

A copy of the assessment and decision should be given to the individual in writing. A refugee may need your help to understand this document and any actions arising from it, or to correspond with the authority if there are errors or they disagree with any aspect and want to appeal.

There are a number of reasons why what should happen does not always happen. These include:

- Some local authorities have introduced 'pre-assessment' or forms of screening and on that basis may refuse to do a care assessment.

- Staff think asylum seekers or people with NRPF aren't eligible for care assessments, or imagine that the assessment is done by the Home Office or NASS or sub-contractors.

- The work is poorly done.

Several organisations across the UK have now successfully appealed on behalf of clients against 'pre-assessment screenings' that led to refusing a 'full' assessment. Staff of one organisation I spoke to felt that having been successful with one appeal had made it far easier to insist on proper care assessments ever since. They felt it had been well worth the frustrations and effort involved.

Do not confuse NHS 'community care' which is free (including nursing care at home and 'nursing homes') with 'social care' at home such as washing and dressing, or 'home care' or care in a 'care home' which are not NHS services and are not free. The latter are provided by the local authority and are usually means-tested.

There are some other useful entitlements. UK nationals and permanent residents can ask to register as disabled with their local authority often without needing to request a community care assessment. This gives them access to various additional services such as community transport, free public transport (Box 9.6) or free adult learning classes which might include English or British Sign Language.

Refugees with Leave can access mainstream benefits including the benefits available to disabled people who are British nationals, such as Carer's Allowance and Access to Work funds when in employment. Once they have registered with the Job Centre, this process should move along routinely, but they will be subject to the same further assessment process regarding potential employment and benefits as other disabled people in the UK, with the same controversies and inadequacies.

Box 9.6   **HEAR briefing – transport for disabled asylum seekers and refugees**

'Disabled and older people are also entitled to free and concessionary travel from their Local Authorities and public transport providers. Every local authority has different eligibility (some include mental health service users and others) but concessionary transport must be provided to all people with sensory impairments, mobility issues and learning difficulties regardless of immigration status under the Transport Act.' (HEAR.org.uk)

Besides local authority services, alternative sources of support include:

- Colleges of further education, which provide the majority of ESOL for adults in the UK, have welfare teams and often include a specialist support worker for disabled learners.

- Trades unions support workers' rights and often have peer-based sub-sections for disabled workers, who will advise people to some extent even if they aren't in the union, although they will get full support if they join.

- Deaf and disabled people's organisations (DDPO) are 'user-led' and 'expert by experience' groups run by and for people and carers who have direct experience of being disabled and struggles with bureaucracy. They are often local, but good at networking, and there are many 'user-led' networks that connect groups such as the National Survivor User Network. DDPOs sometimes include all disabled people, sometimes only people with specific characteristics, such as HIV.

- Older people's organisations often have expertise on disability.

- Organisations supporting people with all disabilities can often be found working within one or a few local authority areas, partly because of funds from local authorities' commissioning advice services and social care. There are also larger-scale (e.g. Scope) and national specialists (e.g. Terrence Higgins Trust). Some, such as Freedom from Torture and the Helen Bamber Foundation, have been mentioned already.

There is a definite problem in the arena of disability rights and support. Although many refugee and many disability organisations claim to have a 'we help everyone equally' approach, they don't consider it necessary to have the knowledge to 'do' disabled refugees:

People and organisations who 'do refugees' often 'don't do disability'.

People and organisations that 'do disability' often 'don't do refugees'.

Many disability bodies assume asylum seekers and refugees are not entitled to the support British nationals can get, and I have heard more than my fair share of activists express doubts that refugees should be entitled to the same. If you are looking to refer someone, check carefully first.

Given the scale of disability among refugees, this is a worrying problem. HEAR (HEAR 2018) has a Googlegroup trying to connect people who work with disabled refugees, to build up a collaborative network of people, with enough members to improve the situation.

| Box 9.7 | Entitlements to services and support for disabled people with different immigration status |

Disabled	NHS	Local authority	NASS and mainstream benefits system
All disabled people in UK, regardless of immigration	All 'public authorities' have duties of care for safeguarding and health and safety, and are bound by the Human Rights Act 1998 and Public Sector Equality Duty under the Equality Act 2010 to make reasonable adjustments to ensure that disabled people are not further disadvantaged by the planning and delivery of their services and design of their physical facilities.		
Asylum seeker	Yes.	The Care Act 2014 requires a community care assessment on request for anyone 'ordinarily resident' to determine the person's needs, which the local authority must then provide. For mental health, an independent mental health advocate should be involved. If they are found necessary, this can include additional financial support and adapted accommodation. Also Freedom Pass, equipment, personal assistant, etc.	Standard NASS financial support. No additional amounts from NASS. NASS accommodation with 'reasonable adjustments'.
Refused asylum seeker/ NRPF	As Box 9.2 (health care) and Box 9.4 (mental health care) except people who have had a care assessment and were found to have care needs which are being provided by the local authority and who are entitled to free secondary care.		
Refugee with Leave to Remain	As Box 9.4 (health care) and 9.6 (mental health care).		As British national/ permanent resident. Includes, potentially, Disability Living Allowance (DLA), Carer's Allowance, Personal Independence Payments (PIP) and Employment Support Allowance (ESA) (also Universal Credit). DWP Access to Work funding via employer.

Box 9.8 'Deaf', 'deaf' and deafened refugees

It seems hearing impairments and hearing loss are more common with refugees than the general population, especially for younger people, particularly where refugees have been caught in military conflicts, but also through long-term under-treated infections.

In Britain the body of people who use British Sign Language (BSL) as a shared language, often from birth or early childhood, often identify as Deaf and part of a 'Deaf Community'. People who are deaf or hearing-impaired but do not speak BSL – whether they did not grow up in the UK or were deafened at some later point in their life – are not generally considered to be part of the 'Deaf Community' in the sense that there is no shared language. People from other countries may speak national versions of sign language (e.g. Lebanese Sign Language) or a simpler international sign language.

In many countries, people who are deaf from birth have not had access to any form of education and language – spoken or sign – and if they arrive in the UK as adults, language acquisition of any kind is more difficult. They may always struggle to master more advanced forms of language, beyond vocabulary. People who were deafened but did first speak a language need to learn English as well as BSL, but do at least have a base of language to work from.

What can you do?

When asking people what I should put in this book the answer that came back to me most often was:

'Don't poke.'

You can't and *mustn't* take over the clinician or psychologist's role and seek to diagnose and treat from your good will and general knowledge. But there is a lot you *can* do to facilitate refugees as they try to manage their own health, mental health and disabilities. This section picks up from points from Chapters 5 and 7.

Engaging – a resource for refugees' health and wellbeing strategies

You want refugees to engage with you as a resource for their own health and wellbeing strategies. You don't want to add unhealthy or disabling pressures, so check your own house is in order. Refugees may be just outside your metaphorical 'gate', but if they have health and mental health difficulties and are already coping with disabling environments and rules on various fronts, they might not come through.

For people to trust you, they need to feel it is a safe space – where they won't be judged for their condition and will meet only acceptance and thoughtfulness. We don't know if the man drinking tea in our office has decided life isn't worth living, or the woman who rather annoyingly keeps missing appointments is only able to cope because of medication. Does your job allow you flexibility

to adapt around people who are not functioning quickly and efficiently? If not, you might need to raise this with managers.

> A safe space – where they won't be judged for their condition and will meet only acceptance and thoughtfulness.

You have your own limits too: supporting someone as she or he copes with traumatic experiences could bring you or colleagues close to your own tipping point. Know the boundaries and keep to them.

Build trust, listen and acknowledge their experiences of injury, illness or mental difficulties – some might call it witnessing. Whatever you do, don't tell people to 'go home and have a nice cup of tea and try to think positively'. You are denying their experiences, you are rejecting their attempt to engage with you, you are belittling and criticising their efforts to cope with their difficulty. They will agree, smile and leave.

Quite modest practical activities can become an asset for refugees' health and wellbeing strategies and be an alternative to other structures that disable them. Without doubt, any work you do that lessens someone's housing or financial problems will help take off the pressure and free them up to work on their health and agency. Helping to register with a GP and understand letters from the hospital protects their practical access. You might put on activities that people use for their health and mental health benefits directly, but avoid the stigma that would result from labelling them as 'refugee' or 'mental health'. For example:

- Put on free exercise classes, yoga or 'family wellbeing' days.

- Work with local faith bodies to lobby for a women-only swimming session.

- Give out screening kits for bowel cancer.

Chapter 5 described the potential of hosting professionals from other services. Also, for example:

- Many organisations arrange 'drop-in' opportunities at a lunch or a summer fete, when NHS community health staff give advice, check blood pressure, etc.

- Offer free space to an outreach counselling service.

- Fix a fortnightly slot for a job advice service run for people with disabilities.

- Invite a speaker from the local carers' wellbeing charity to your English group (you might have to find someone to interpret what she or he says).

Without necessarily being health-focussed, any activities that break down isolation and enable people to interact with peers are positive for wellbeing: writing courses, team sports, a monthly 'bring your own' lunch. The Refugee Council runs a bread-making group called 'Just Bread' for just this purpose – people find kneading bread soothing and rewarding.

Opportunities for self-expression in a safe space are good: read about Freedom from Torture's 'Write to Life' groups. I have known of dance, drama, writing groups, gardening, a scrapbook project, even flower arranging for refugees, but you have to have backup structures in place. Schemes like mentoring and befriending are valuable, but you must know what you are doing. British Red Cross and many local Minds have experience here and collaboration may be your best route.

Networking and advocacy – a mesh of support

Finding and networking with contacts, good referral and advocacy, and tackling failures in services were the themes of Chapter 7. Some people need more specialist health, mental health or disability services than you can provide. Normal good practice on referrals and 'One plus One' apply (Box 7.4).

You could look at ways to help refugees step it up, to start engaging with practice and policy-makers directly. For example, encourage them to:

- take up opportunities to train in health improvement so they can play the role of Health Champions, Health Connectors and other voluntary and potentially paid positions for the local NHS, or as interpreters

- become members of Healthwatch, where they can get involved in getting patients' voices heard, train to do 'Enter and View' visits and perhaps join the Healthwatch board in future

- train in health or mental health advocacy.

I noted under difficulties with GP registration that you can escalate from service provider to manager and upwards. There are multiple feedback mechanisms, starting with evaluation and feedback forms and complaints processes in each and every statutory service. You can talk to PALs services in the NHS, approach Healthwatch or the relatively new GP Patient Participation Groups. Contact campaigning groups such as Doctors of the World or Disability Law Service; or go direct to the CCG or local authority, perhaps putting in 'written questions from the public' (see Box 9.9), or to NHS England/Local Government and Social Care Ombudsman/Care Quality Commission. There is your local councillor and your MP if you want to raise a case to illustrate a wider issue.

Remember, as well as needing to meet – and be seen to meet – their PSED/ equality duty, the NHS wants asylum seekers and refugees to get the right treatment at the right place, which gives you a positive lever for suggestions that would improve communication and access for them.

Box 9.9	Challenging authorities on issues known to be important to refugee access to health

Where there are gaps in health services, you may consider using consultation opportunities and the PSED channels mentioned in Chapter 7 to ask questions on specific topics known to be frequent problems for refugees in access to health, such as:

- Do you have performance data on GP registration of newly arrived asylum seekers?

- How many PTSD-trained counsellors are there in the borough?

- What services have you commissioned to support survivors of torture?

- What is your policy on using interpreters?

- How many disabled refugees use your service?

Conclusion

Refugees' health, mental health issues and disabilities are interconnected. They affect what refugees can do as they try to get by. Helping them access treatment and care is part of the picture, but should end at some point. What we should aim to be supporting instead is their good health, wellbeing and ability to get on with life.

Each of us can only do so much, but we can see our role alongside clinical, social work and legal professionals as filling some of the gaps so that refugees can gain strength and support in the context of a much larger mesh of wide-ranging services.

Learning English, Training, Employability and into Work

Introduction

Acquiring decent English, learning new skills and obtaining useful qualifications are necessary and positive steps for a person as she or he takes back control, and starts to build a new life in the UK. Refugees who lost careers when they went into exile have mixed emotions about starting from scratch, but the sooner a refugee can function in British society, the sooner she or he becomes employable. Perhaps after a couple of courses and 'transition' jobs, your contact will get into a decent job with a reasonable salary and be able to re-establish a career. This chapter is all about the future.

There are risks in taking on the challenges of study and work: investing time and money but failing the final exam; extra pressures on fragile mental health; bad advice, bad courses, bad employers; unrealistic expectations. Some people struggle to bend to unfamiliar educational, economic and authority structures as well as the social dynamics within them. These things can set people back. But in the daily hubbub of finding the right room or lending someone a pen, people gain confidence and new skills to act and interact within this diverse society. As they progress through and beyond 'English for Speakers of Other Languages' (ESOL) and casual contracts, people broaden their experience, knowledge, support networks and contacts, and some find a new British identity.

There are a few points to bear in mind as you support refugees along this road.

Respond to individual diversity. What people are capable of doing will change with time. There are many factors:

- the consequences of the past, present realities and how they are coping

- their current 'motive, means and opportunity' (see Chapter 5) which influence how effectively people 'engage' in education or the job market – their sense of agency will be significant

- their existing means, knowledge and skills, and also, regarding employment, English, level of previous education, qualifications, working experience, training, volunteering, working in the UK to date

- other 'equality' characteristics including age, gender pressures, undiagnosed learning disabilities such as dyslexia, cultural expectations about teachers or bosses

- immigration status – people face different restrictions, described below.

Explore possibilities. There are hundreds of options.

Be aware that training providers/employers can be flexible. Unlike asylum support or acute mental health services, training providers and even employers have a good deal of flexibility if they choose to respond to an individual refugee. Managers can often use discretion and squeeze in a few extra students who don't fit the funders' criteria, or find room for a placement. Teaching especially is highly vocational and teachers don't like turning people away if they want to learn, although admissions staff might be less sympathetic.

Think strategically towards realistic goals. You and the person you are supporting will do well to think and talk about longer-term life and career goals before setting things in motion. People have to have money to live, and many schemes are designed to get people a job. Being employed is a good thing. It improves income and stability and has other advantages such as learning to handle pay slips and the tax system, or feeling part of a team.

But some jobs are dead ends. For example, work as a security guard has few opportunities for promotion; social care can lead into caring professions such as nursing, but can also drain people's physical and emotional resources; changing shift patterns make it hard to follow a course; bad jobs undermine confidence. To quote a discussion I was party to: 'The risk is that they will get somewhere but be going nowhere.'

> The risk is that they will get somewhere but be going nowhere.

Goals motivate a person and give a sense of identity. Some people still need to hold on to dreams to get through today. But there is a risk that an individual will waste time, even years, turning down opportunities while they wait for the perfect break. They may burn up energy proactively applying for courses, degrees and jobs that they stand no chance of getting. The price can be humiliation and cynicism, even debt (Box 10.1, CS/A).

Reasonable goals help people make strategic choices about how to invest their time and energy today. When someone has a clear and reasonable goal, they can see a low-skilled job as a step towards what they really want, and accepting the job offer becomes a positive tactic rather than a negative compromise (CS/B and CS/C). Being strategic helps people face setbacks with determination and might help mental and emotional resilience (CS/D).

Do remember you are not the architect of their strategies, but one of their strategic assets. Refugees have to do what they feel is best for them and

their families. They value your knowledge, your help and advocacy, your encouragement and advice in bad patches. They may fully appreciate the effort you put in to finding them a good course, but if it doesn't fit *their* priorities, they will probably walk away (Box 10.1).

Box 10.1 | **Refugees making their own choices about progress to work – Case Studies A–D**

A was a secondary school teacher in the Middle East who took a one-year postgraduate course to teach in the UK. However, he could not make the cultural shift to cope with student behaviour in British schools. He left one and then another teaching job, then turned his back on teaching and got work in a food factory. He had to quit because he couldn't cope with the physically demanding work. The last time we spoke he was still unemployed.

B was a plumber before he came to the UK. He started training as an interpreter, but quit as he didn't feel comfortable or believe it would provide a full-time income. Despite being in his late 50s, he joined a utilities company at a junior grade, rapidly got accreditation and promotion through their internal scheme, and became a Corgi-registered gas engineer, making a good, reliable living in his own trade.

C was a refugee doctor who spent more than five years unemployed while he repeatedly failed the English tests needed to start requalifying as a doctor in the UK. After five years, under pressure from the Job Centre, he took a job as a porter in the NHS. Within a month he had been trained and moved to phlebotomy (bloods); within three months the NHS made him an offer of a funded place on a full-time degree in a therapeutic field, which he took.

D had been stopped from working as a nurse because of discrimination against his religion. Now in the UK as an asylum seeker, he is not allowed to work or requalify unless he can pay private fees, which he can't. So he goes on every free first aid course, health and safety course, health improvement course we can find him, plus every free English group he can get to, so he is ready to restart his career should he ever get Leave to Remain.

Know about entitlements and eligibility. There are a few common restrictions that affect education, volunteering and employment opportunities (restrictions that relate only to non-formal or formal training are described in the training sections):

- Immigration status (for a reminder of definitions, see Box 3.11 or the Glossary): asylum seekers, refused asylum seekers and people who have No Recourse to Public Funds (NRPF) can't legally work. Therefore, they have limited access to free or subsidised training funded by government,

most of which is related to employment, from ESOL to professional qualifications. Some support is further restricted to Convention refugees.

- At present if an asylum seeker has been in the asylum process for more than six months, they can access slightly more ESOL, but changes to immigration bail in 2018 mean an asylum seeker can be prevented from studying any course that could lead to a qualification, including English-language ESOL courses.

- Asylum/NRPF status restricts volunteering that might be seen as 'unpaid work' – for example, a former teacher offering to teach for free.

- The time remaining on visas and permits: even refugees with Leave to Remain may not be able to get places on longer-term schemes or employment opportunities (e.g. three-year courses, apprenticeships or permanent contracts).

- Voluntary sector projects and programmes may have eligibility restrictions if they are funded from governmental sources, plus the constant confusion over entitlements and 'we don't do refugees' attitudes mentioned in several chapters are still an issue.

- Clumsy criteria for shortlisting: staff recruiting for courses and jobs often have a set list of qualifications, experience, continuity of employment, residency, which disadvantage refugees – for example, requiring a GCSE in English or a reference from your most recent employer.

- Evidence: whether people have credible evidence of status, ID, address, qualifications and proof of address (Appendix B).

Do look out for public authorities using the PSED to justify 'positive action' schemes that give extra help to people who are recovering from mental ill health or who are disabled, carers, young people, women, Tamils or Bangladeshis and many more ethnic groups, plus combinations (e.g. Bangladeshi women). It is not common to find one specifically aimed at refugees, but it does happen.

Put these points together and your role starts to emerge. Refugees are diverse, and are active agents of their own futures – you need to respond to the individual. Be aware but make no assumptions. Network and be informed – you can help with accurate knowledge and up-to-date information. Listen and create space for people to think and act – where they can articulate their goals and analyse their chances. You can talk strategy and tactics, work out alternative routes and help them to negotiate access.

This chapter covers issues and entitlements, opportunities and ideas for action in your work with refugees. It does not look at teaching methods and resources, or at practical advice such as how to do a job interview or access 'in work' benefits, as that information is widely available. Chapter 11 will look at

education and training for children/young people. Appendix A has sources of further advice and expertise.

Daily English and other non-formal learning

Building on what has already been said in Chapter 5, and with reference to the 'GREG' model in Chapter 6, this section looks at 'non-formal' learning opportunities set up outside formal settings (some say 'community', 'grass roots', 'informal' learning).

These are activities that are not usually matched to fixed standards such as ESOL levels or exam board assessments. They tend to focus on daily life. English is what most people put on for refugees, although the focus of activities might be job seeking, better parenting, managing money, health, learning to cook or how to do beauty treatments, or many others, often with a wellbeing element. Don't forget that through your organisation, refugee 'volunteers' can access a wide range of free non-formal training put on by and for the voluntary sector, from first aid to Freedom of Information. All of these – plus activities that go alongside such as summer picnics and helping with publicity – help people to learn, to gain British experiences and look to the future.

Non-formal learning activities tend to be led by volunteers and local activists, identity-based groups such as an Iraqi association or women's group, or by/ supported by charities and faith bodies (see also Box 10.2). Schools, mental health bodies, the NHS, local authority or the police might give a 'community outreach' brief to staff to run non-formal sessions, courses or groups as a way to establish a bridge with the wider public. Often there are no eligibility criteria, but when activities are funded or aim for a specific result, eligibility may still be restricted to certain social groups – for example, families with children under five (most children's centres) – or by postcode.

Box 10.2 **Gender and the single-sex dilemma**

You might be asked to segregate males and females, on the grounds that:

1. You will get a higher turnout from people who avoid mixed-sex groups, in particular when families disapprove or where women have faced sexual assault or domestic abuse.

2. Some people learn better in single-sex groups, although the opposite is also true.

3. Men often dominate discussion in mixed-sex groups.

Before you decide, remember that a good facilitator mediates group dynamics; that this is an integrated country and women and men need to learn to interact as equals for a healthy society; and that exposure to new experiences builds confidence to tackle similar situations in future.

If you set up single-sex activities, ensure the quality and benefits to men and women are equivalent, or you risk consolidating inequality.

Non-formal does not mean unimportant. Someone who has means and assets has plenty of choices and will probably see non-formal learning as a form of leisure. But this kind of 'community' opportunity may be the only structured learning available to asylum seekers and people with NRPF, and even people with Leave to Remain who have other constraints or disadvantages.

Those who need non-formal learning need to guard their resources carefully. They can't afford the costs or risks or demands of more formal options. In the best non-formal learning, they gain skills, knowledge, experience and confidence, social interaction and perhaps a shared identity, acceptance and holistic backup. But even in relatively low-cost, low-risk, non-formal learning, if they feel their investment is not helping them get where they want to go, they will cut their losses and stop coming. Socialising is not enough. Quality and relevance matter; without them, you'll have no participants.

> In the best non-formal learning, they gain skills, knowledge, experience and confidence, social interaction and perhaps a shared identity, acceptance and holistic backup... Quality and relevance matter.

You usually find some people who are stuck in non-formal groups (Box 10.3). They would prefer to be elsewhere – in college, for example, or working – and they are capable of more demanding activities. But college arrangements, immigration status, money, caring roles, family pressure and health mean they have nowhere else they can go. Their only 'investment option' is the non-formal group, even if they feel it gives a 'poor return'. They can be frustrated and even disruptive as they try to gain what they need rather than what you intend the group to provide.

Box 10.3 People get stuck outside formal learning

Although some choose non-formal learning over formal, a distinct group of people are stuck in non-formal activities but would rather be moving faster in their lives. Perhaps…

- Courses are full. There are no courses at their level. They have been excluded for poor attendance or inadequate progress. They are newly arrived or have just moved to the area, or their circumstances have recently changed. Courses often start once a year and they just have to wait.

- Their immigration status restricts them. They don't have the necessary evidence. Accommodation is temporary or insecure and means they aren't eligible for courses. They can't get free places and they can't afford to pay.

- They care for children or others, are pregnant or just gave birth, or have demanding families. There is no suitable or affordable transport from their accommodation, taking into account disabilities or other constraints on time such as school pick-up. Paid work prevents formal learning.

- They are avoiding people who go to the college who might be a danger to them.

Non-formal learning is not better or worse than formal learning – it is different. Refugees might be making use of non-formal opportunities before, during or after other, formal training (Box 10.4). As with wellbeing-focussed activities considered at the end of Chapter 9, the best non-formal learning complements the formal. If you are creating non-formal opportunities, you will be most effective when you work alongside formal providers to create a good mesh of services and support so that individuals can step across the gaps (Box 10.4, CS/E and CS/F).

Box 10.4	Refugees mixing formal and non-formal learning – Case Studies E and F

E   has attended informal English groups for some years. She also attends formal college two days per week under an employability programme, a regular women's group that runs a range of learning and mental wellbeing activities, and NHS physiotherapy sessions teaching and encouraging self-care for chronic back pain.

F   attends two colleges which both offer him part-time study for free, plus a 'grass roots' English group that also runs social lunches, and one-to-one mentoring by a specialist refugee charity.

In current social policy, non-formal learning is largely invisible. You might also come across some qualified teachers who are inclined to dismiss 'community' English and 'barefoot' teachers. (None of this addresses the fact that formal education excludes many of these learners.) Non-formal learning is seen as fuzzy and unproductive, and this can be true. It tends to gets little serious attention and sporadic, small-grant funding if any. It has become part of the 'new role' for hands-on workers who are not refugee specialists. Longevity and effectiveness usually hinge on the commitment of key individuals acting on their own initiative. They may have limited training or backup, but a sharp eye for what can disable people and a knowledge of possibilities (Box 10.5).

	Examples of volunteers, activists and organisations offering non-formal learning for English – Case Studies G–K
Box 10.5	

G   is a qualified, unpaid English teacher who runs her own 'English with Confidence' class in a community centre, and offers one-to-one lessons to women with babies in their own homes.

H   is a charity that supports young adults who are mostly full-time at college. A volunteer runs several study sessions per week where refugee students do homework together, with his help.

I   and her friends run an own-language-based group with support from a children's centre. Each week their three-hour session combines a two-hour crèche with an hour of English run by her next-door neighbour, a one-hour slot for topics such as parenting or weaning delivered by professionals over three to five weeks, and an hour of everyone sharing food and socialising.

J   is a school that asks Somali-speaking bilingual parents to interpret so that other Somali parents can attend sessions where they learn about their children's school work, phonics, maths methods, homework and school trips.

K   could not manage the demand for English, so set up a listing service for other English groups and volunteers, plus numeracy and conversation-related activities within a five-mile radius, to help people find groups across the area.

See also the example of a model for 'Grass Roots English' in Chapter 6.

Formal English, ESOL, training, formal education and qualifications

Formal learning is education and training with set standards, learner assessment and qualifications, usually with outside scrutiny and run by a mix of non-profit and profit-making bodies as well as statutory providers. Learners are in classes separated by topic, level of skill and knowledge, and by the qualification they are aiming for. For refugees, formal education often includes support to get a job or move closer to the job market by becoming more 'employable'.

A good-sized college may have cheap food, warm rooms, free IT and sports facilities, even 'access' funds, plus supportive staff, welfare and advice teams, tutoring, mentoring, even counselling. There might be celebrations, clubs or volunteering schemes. There should be help for disabled refugees and somewhere to turn to in crisis.

Access to formal learning is likely to be restricted by funders' requirements. In addition to restrictions noted in the introduction, you will often find refugees are limited by:

- How long they have been in the country (e.g. less than six months, at least three years).

- Where they live or are 'ordinarily resident': usually based on local authority areas, although some institutions might defined catchment areas based on postcodes or distance.

- For refugees with Leave, whether they are 'economically active' (available for work, actively seeking work) and/or on employment-related benefits (e.g. Jobseeker's Allowance or Universal Credit). Some courses are aimed at groups who are 'economically *inactive*' to try to move them 'nearer to work'.

- Nationality: asylum seekers and recent refugees are mostly 'non-EU', although some will have British or EU passports gained in recent years, but this may all change with Brexit.

- Evidence: for example, someone who is the spouse or dependant of a refugee may need evidence to prove the relationship, such as marriage and birth certificates (see Appendix B).

Refugees depend a lot on personal recommendation when it comes to choosing courses and colleges. If someone asks your opinion, they have several decisions to make.

SUBJECT

There is an incredible array of subjects, courses and facilities, especially with the current phenomenon of colleges merging. Refugees who are keen to get on might look at the following.

Topics to function in daily life:

- ESOL and other English (e.g. literacy). You might find English as an Additional Language (EAL), as a Foreign Language (EFL) (e.g. Teaching EFL or TEFL)

- other functional and 'skills for life' (e.g. numeracy)

- wider relevance (e.g. driving theory, first aid, life in the United Kingdom)

- wellbeing and resilience (e.g. positive thinking, arts, health).

Related to getting into a job:

- courses that link ESOL and job skills (e.g. ESOL and beauty, entry-level health and social care)

- entry-level 'into work' training (e.g. Level 1 and 2 health and social care, lifting, chemicals handling, security, forklift driving, food hygiene, catering, hospitality, safeguarding)

- functional skills for employability and getting into work (e.g. basic IT, job interviews)

- the above combined with later 'on the job' study (e.g. apprenticeships, structured study with assessed work experience element).

Looking strategically towards a career or profession:

- into work but also creating routes to higher qualifications and careers (e.g. Level 2 and 3 health and social care, child development, interpreting, teaching assistant, catering and nutrition, advice work, book-keeping, IT skills, business studies, self-employment)

- occupational/professional (e.g. nursing, accountancy, law, IT)

- requalification (e.g. engineering, teaching, medical, nursing, including IELTS (see next paragraph)

- academic (e.g. GCSE or A-level English, maths, history, psychology, 'access to university' courses).

LEVEL (BOX 10.6)

There are regulated scales for assessments and qualifications across the UK that almost all British education and exam boards can be mapped to. In ESOL, new English learners will be at one of the 'Entry' levels, from 'Pre-entry' (no English at all) to 'Entry 3' which was once described to me as 'good enough for a job in an all-night garage'. There are also international testing levels that refugees might have or want to get:

- IELTS – International English Language Testing System (people say 'I-Yelts') ranging from 1 to 9, where 5+ would be needed for entrance to a British university and 7.5 for refugee doctors and dentists wanting to requalify and practise in the UK.

- TOEFL – Test of English as a Foreign Language, scored out of 120, where 90–100 would be adequate for a place at most universities.

- SELT – the Secure English Language Test, taken at approved centres only and the candidate must prove their identity. It is required for visa applications.

Box 10.6	ESOL levels and how well someone can communicate in English
Pre-entry	Not even hello
Entry 1	Personal information, name
Entry 2	Simple questions and answers
Entry 3	Basic functional, sufficient for 'a job in an all-night garage'

Level 1	Conversation
Level 2	Conversation: GCSE pass
Level 3	Discussion and debate, sufficient to start training as a community interpreter: A Level, International Baccalaureate, Scottish Highers
Level 4	Teaching English to migrant adults: approximately second-year undergraduate
Level 5	Fully fluent: honours degree
Level 6	Sufficient for international interpreting, and teaching English language and literature in schools: Master's

DURATION AND FORMAT

There are many options that people new to Britain might not know about. The right choice will probably mean a better result.

- **Duration.** From one week to three years. To avoid losing everything if you have to drop out and for flexibility, learners often study a combination of separate units or modules to earn credits for a full qualification.

- **Part-time.** Part-time might be certain days only, or evenings and weekends. Learners lose some of the benefits of peer support that can build up with daily interaction. It can be hard to keep up momentum over a long period with gaps. Part-time courses spread the costs although they are often more expensive over their full term than full-time courses, and some learners can sign on for benefits or work while studying.

- **Full-time.** The learner is expected to spend at least 35 hours per week on study, although this includes placements and private study time. Learners on full-time courses can focus more intensively on the subject, and some prefer to struggle financially for a short time but make progress fast. Full-time courses are not usually possible for people who rely on benefits.

- **Online courses.** Many courses can be found online but learners need to check the site is real and their qualification will be recognised. Some courses combine online study and assignments with webinars and face-to-face time with tutors or seminar sessions. It can be hard to keep going on an online course over time, especially with no peer support. People expect online courses to be cheap but they usually are about the same as 'classroom-based' training, although there are fewer travel costs. Subsidised online courses at lower levels are increasingly available through the voluntary sector.

- **Start dates.** Most courses (not online) are still usually based on three terms per year, and by far the largest choice of full-time courses and others will be those starting in September, with the second largest choice

starting in January. Shorter and part-time courses and apprenticeships can start around the year, and even practical degree programmes such as nursing sometimes start at other times of the year.

PROVIDERS
The nature and size of different providers means they can and do offer different things. The refugee, with your support, needs to check quality. Try the Ofsted website and use your local contacts but make sure they/you are up to date. For example, where some bodies will provide placements, less good providers might leave the student to find their own.

- 'Adult learning' is run by the local council, usually aimed at local residents, with a scale of fees including subsidised places for people on benefits who are ordinarily resident in the area, but not usually people who have NRPF.

- Colleges of Further Education (FE) are independent non-profit bodies, with funding from multiple governmental sources and various related restrictions on eligibility and fees. Academic and vocational courses mingle in FE, usually with considerable emphasis on employability and often links with local employers.

- Private training companies might be linked to national or international corporations, providing, for example, Secure English Language Tests (SELTs)/International English Language Testing System (IELTS) and 'Life in the UK' tests, and handling contracts for the Job Centre. Many have a strong public ethos; others are profit-driven. Some are very good and some are not. Some providers push eligible learners on to unsuitable courses in order to meet quotas for the Job Centre. Some courses are only internally assessed, leaving students without a recognised qualification. Some providers are more focussed on getting migrants to take out loans for fees than on the quality of teaching. Unfortunately, refugees and migrants are targeted by companies that sell qualifications.

COST
Money matters, but the cheapest course is not always the best investment.

- Fee structures can be confusing and may be negotiable. Don't rely on brochures and websites – talk to someone. Encourage the refugee to start finding out about fees at the very beginning and well before the course starts.

- Add on travel costs. (Can they walk? Cycle? Bike locks and safety gear?)

- Allow for extras such as Student Union subscriptions, cost of identity cards and replacements if lost, exam fees, decent IT access, photocopying

and printing tokens, books and equipment, placement costs, extra costs for trips and opportunities outside their course.

- Compare the total with net income over this period, and then compare it with likely increased income after the course.

- Can they pay in instalments? (They might not be allowed to have their final results if they haven't paid by then.) Can they get benefits or work at the same time? Is a grant or access funding possible? (Hint: They should get an offer of a place *before* they apply for grants.) What about a career or student loan (also ask the college)?

Once your refugee contact has made these decisions and come up with a shortlist of their best options, there is still the process of applying. I have known people miss out for a whole year because they didn't start this process in time. For a full-time course, ideally start to apply six months before – popular courses will be full well before the term starts. Apply now. You can always turn the place down later.

Inevitably, there are forms to fill and they can be surprisingly difficult, even for ESOL courses. Most are online and people often need help. A few hints:

- At open days, perhaps with your help, people can check the course is right for them, confirm they are eligible and show evidence, get an on-the-spot assessment of their English if necessary, and usually apply there and then, saving months as well as the risk of wasting time and effort.

- When filling in the application, make sure the refugee includes:

  - qualifications or experience from *before* the UK – many people don't realise it all counts. Help them include the British equivalent if possible (see Box 10.7)

  - a list of non-formal training in the UK (easier if they have attendance certificates)

  - a recommendation letter from you – it might encourage the provider to take a risk on a borderline candidate

  - your phone number and direct email in case the provider has trouble communicating with them.

- Keep in touch and make sure they are following up their application:

  - Have they heard anything? Should they ring to check?

  - Do they have an interview? Do they have the right date and place? Do they need to rearrange?

- Have they accepted any offer in writing?

- If they have a conditional offer, do they understand what they need to do next?

- If they are on a waiting list, they will probably still get on the course as a lot of people drop out. Have they rung up to show they are still keen?

- Do they know they must attend an enrolment day before the course starts, and do they have the right date and place? Do they have everything they need – photos, evidence, cash, etc.?

• Help with the mini-crisis of getting started: your council has a list of childcare providers, get a recycled computer from a green project, a bike from a bike project…perhaps you can donate pens and paper.

Box 10.7	**UK NARIC (National Academic Recognition Information Centre)**

NARIC uses an extensive database to provide an informed opinion of the equivalence of British and overseas qualifications. They provide an equivalent national qualification name but don't compare specific institutions or provide an equivalent grade. Most universities pay for access to the NARIC database in order to assess overseas qualifications. A growing number of employers know about it.

With thanks to Sheila Heard, Transitions.

People often drop out in the first few weeks when time, financial, physical and emotional demands are higher than expected and the reality of classroom life including peer dynamics becomes clear. You can continue to help your contacts after they start. Poor study skills or time management can mean missed deadlines and disappointing results, even when people have worked hard. Poor punctuality or attendance under 85% can result in being excluded. Ring and encourage them, organise a study group for the first half-term, book in a couple of one-to-one sessions. The provider will usually be working hard to keep people's attendance, behaviour and progress up to scratch. Encourage the refugee to make use of help within the system:

• teachers and tutors for subject and content

• staff such as 'learning mentors' for study skills, including time management

• less formal 'buddy' and peer-support systems or welfare and disability support services, pastoral staff, counselling service and more specialist referral to outside services

- financial support which might be available mid-course if it is a question of helping a good student stay on a course – teaching and welfare staff will bend over backwards to help students who are doing their best.

Employability, volunteering and into employment

Earning a living can mean so many things – plaiting hair or building nuclear reactors. No one doubts the significance of starting employment and gaining control over your income, being active, interaction, experience. Getting into work is one problem; poor employment and poor employers, under-employment, drudgery and low pay are others.

Entitlement to work is fairly simple as already described: asylum seekers can't work, nor can refused asylum seekers. Adult refugees with Leave to Remain can. There are a very few exceptions where asylum seekers who are highly skilled in IT and 'shortage' professions are permitted work, and there has been campaign after campaign since asylum seekers were banned from paid work in 2002 to reverse the ban – so far all unsuccessful.

This final section is about how you can help refugees' strategies to get decent work.

Helping refugees make themselves more attractive to employers

Employers are all different: statutory bureaucracies must recruit staff who will reliably help them work towards set standards; private businesses are driven by profit calculations; agencies want people who will turn up where and when needed and send in timesheets on time. To get employed, you have to persuade an employer to employ you. Employers only look for staff when they need a job done, so they only want someone who will do that job. Refugees need to see themselves through employers' eyes.

> Refugees need to see themselves through employers' eyes.

Refugees will almost always need to adapt, if not requalify. Some skills that refugees bring are more immediately transferable and useful to UK employers than others (Box 10.8, CS/L). Work in catering, retail, music, many building skills or academic research, for example, are fairly global and easy to adapt. Engineering, medicine and agricultural practice have core principles, although practical application will differ in the UK.

Other professions such as teaching, journalism, public relations or law might not transfer as easily as you'd expect, because they are more cultural (see Box 10.1, CS/A). Lawyers need to 'convert' their knowledge to English/ Welsh or Scottish law, and might start with a law 'conversion' course if they

can fund it, or work upwards by entering advice work – for example, getting an OISC licence (Box 3.3) to start working their way in through immigration law.

Computing and IT skills are transferable but change very fast, and people who were stuck in transit or asylum fall behind. Even if refugees have something similar on paper, it is from another country and possibly some years out of date.

Box 10.8 **People have very different skills – Case Studies L and M**

L was a veterinary specialist in his 60s who couldn't get a job in Britain. His special field was camels. Eventually, he found a small charity with a London office that raised funds for rural projects in his region of Africa and became an expert adviser, although up until we lost contact, I don't think he ever got paid work.

M was a young man I interviewed for a job. He promised that no matter what, we would always be laughing if we employed him. With some regret, I gave the job to the more boring and experienced candidate, thinking that we would probably get more work done that way.

Employers also want people who can line-manage, think ahead, make decisions, understand money, monitor standards and engage well with the public. They value organisational skills such as planning, logistics, handling data and IT. These are skills that many people bring from work in earlier countries, and from real-life experiences, including parenthood, and don't necessarily rely on training. Employers are also looking for a new colleague – a person they will have to spend days and months with. But they are not looking for a friend – they want someone who will add to the effectiveness of the team and who will make their working life a bit easier, not harder (Box 10.8, CS/M).

Legitimate employers need evidence. They need formal and paper-based evidence of entitlement to work. They might need your advice or reassurance on what immigration paperwork means.[1] They want proof of identity, address, NI numbers and bank accounts as evidence the person is legitimate.

They might want original certificates for formal qualifications. You could ask someone independent, whom you trust, to read the refugee's own-language certificates and letters, or ask someone credible, such as a teacher, to do an informal assessment and give their written feedback which you quote on your letterhead.

They also want evidence in the sense of being able to see that someone is genuinely capable. A reference is a powerful tool for this, especially where it is clearly from a credible person and organisation (see Box 7.5 and Box 10.9). When other evidence is missing, you can help by offering your own assessment, but acknowledge this is informal and state its limitations.

---

1   The Refugee Council's Guidance for Employers, *Employing Refugees* (2014), is good and due an update as this book goes to press.

Box 10.9 **A reference for a refugee**

Box 7.5 on writing letters for refugees spells out how important your credibility is. Regarding job references, there are further points:

- In references, the employer or course convener is looking for reassurance, not a sales pitch.

- Give dates and details: when you first met them, dates of trainings or volunteering tasks, responsibilities and duration.

- Think about what the employer wants to read, not about all the things you could say.

- Help them see that the person has the skills and aptitude they want. Ask for the job description and person specification and go through these carefully, giving examples of something the refugee has done with your organisation that demonstrates the right skills. Remember other organisational assets: she is a fast learner, team player, thinks ahead, has good judgement. If you would employ them, say so.

Employability

Supporting a refugee's 'employability' includes helping them access training – largely covered in the sections above. Non-formal learning also plays its part, which includes helping with cultural competence. You can also help people access specialist schemes.

REQUALIFICATION SCHEMES

- Requalification schemes are for people who have already worked in skilled professions before coming to the UK (e.g. medicine, engineering) – see Box 10.10. These tend to be focussed on refugees, because other skilled migrants had to sort out accreditation before they got a visa. Most schemes were decimated by short-sighted funding cuts from 2010 onwards, and requalification can take several years, so those schemes that remain are nearly overwhelmed by demand.

- Examples of providers: Refugee Council, Transitions, Refugee Assessment and Guidance Unit (RAGU), BMA Refugee Doctors Initiative.

- Eligibility: refugees might need Leave to Remain or be 'permitted to work' and there might be restrictions based on length of time in the UK. Some schemes have a minimum English requirement, because they are designed to finish off the process of requalification that may have started some years earlier.

- Support provided: includes one-to-one and group and career guidance, study groups and seminars, applications for grants to help study or pay exam fees, work experience and searching opportunities for supervised placements, support during placements and help with job search, application, interview and sustaining employment for the first six months.

Box 10.10 **Joining professional bodies**

Another way to give UK employers confidence in overseas qualification is to join a UK Professional Body as a graduate member. Professional bodies will often use NARIC (Box 10.7) as part of that process. Graduate membership is seen by employers as an evaluation of graduate-level professional knowledge and skills.

With thanks to Sheila Heard, Transitions.

EMPLOYABILITY SCHEMES

- Employability schemes are open to a wider public, although a few might have funders that guarantee places for refugees, possibly for Convention refugees, or positive action schemes – for example, increasing the chance for Somali women to enter the labour market.

- Examples of providers: Jobcentre Plus (Department of Work and Pensions, DWP) includes Job Coaches and referral to providers. Also colleges of FE, non-profit bodies including social enterprises.

- Eligibility: as above, except English as ESOL might be provided.

- Support provided: usually short-term or up to 18 months, classroom and online, practical IT, book-keeping, office practice and skills, mentoring, job search, CVs, applications and interview skills in the context of equal opportunities. Might include preparing people for self-employment and setting up small businesses. Some bodies have direct links with local employers who can give workshops, work experience placements and guaranteed interviews. Some schemes follow up after someone gets into paid work to help them manage the practical, financial and emotional pressures of transition into work, and might mediate if there are difficulties between the employer and employee.

SELF-EMPLOYMENT SCHEMES

- Self-employment schemes prepare people, including refugees, to set up their own businesses. Many 'mid-life' refugees have run businesses but need help converting their experience to the British context with its strict financial, tax/NI/pension, employment, health and safety regulations.

- Eligibility: as above, though excluding ESOL.

- Examples of providers: Tern, Chaigaram.

- Support provided: goal-setting, business planning, book-keeping, support on regulations and finding help with resources and premises, credit and subsidies.

SCHEMES THAT SUPPORT DISABLED PEOPLE/REFUGEES INTO WORK

- These include people with mental health issues or recovering from mental ill health.

- Examples of providers: voluntary sector, DWP funding through 'Access to Work'.

- Eligibility: varies but may include postcode.

- Support provided: DWP will assess an individual's needs such as IT equipment, and pay up to 100 per cent of what is required for them to be able to maintain their job. Other schemes include personal planning, volunteering, one-to-one support, phased start to work, ongoing support in employment.

RELEVANT NETWORKS AND SOURCES OF PEER
SUPPORT AND EXPERTISE AND CAMPAIGNING

- For refugees: Council for At-Risk Academics (CARA).

- For career and other advisers: RCAN in London, Refugee Employment Network, Career Development Institute, Women's Resource Centre, Age Concern.

Volunteering and helping refugees towards work

Helping people make themselves more employable especially means finding them opportunities for work-related experience. It is essential that asylum seekers are not seen to be doing 'unpaid work' and that the Job Centre knows people with Leave to Remain are still 'available for work'. Volunteering such as befriending or gardening don't look like work and might not seem to provide work skills directly, but they do provide a chance for team work, receiving and giving instructions, time management and so forth.

Volunteering might be just helping out here and there, or a particular task over time, or in some cases a formal arrangement including job description, interviews and volunteer 'contract', often for more than six months. This is generally considered good practice, but for asylum seekers it could look like

'unpaid work'. It probably isn't the style best suited to refugees with demanding lives, who are treading several paths at once towards paid work.

Try contacting other organisations that use volunteers:

- Volunteer bureaux: there are still some bodies, associations of voluntary services and local authorities that run agency-style brokerage that matches would-be volunteers to organisations that need them. Other brokerage points include libraries, local authority magazines, online sources such as *The Guardian* voluntary work and volunteer support jobs.

- Direct contact to organisations that use a lot of volunteers and unpaid time. For example:

  - A range of one-off activities, usually unstructured: Women's Institute, churches, parents at schools, even local campaigning groups such as Amnesty International or 38 Degrees.

  - Can someone shadow you for a day? Attend a public event for you? Be your representative at a regular meeting?

  - Ongoing but less formal, although there should still be an orientation at least: food banks, English groups, charity shops, sometimes libraries.

  - Formal with training and a commitment of at least six months: hospitals, Age Concern visitors, Age Concern advisers, Citizens Advice (one year+), Scouts and Guides with a 'career'-type ladder of increasing responsibility. Some have application processes and might require evidence.

  - Persuading organisations such as a community centre to create a volunteering or 'work experience' opportunity specifically to give a refugee a chance. There are commercial organisations that do this for schools.

You can set up volunteering opportunities. But don't rush into it. It is not as simple as you might think. Discuss and plan before you start. Like many things, when volunteering works well, it's great. But both sides lose if you don't manage it well. Be clear in your own mind whether you are doing this because you want to help the refugee or because you need extra help to manage your own workload. You have little control over volunteers, who have demanding lives and can't always be reliable. At the same time, they can't make decisions without you. So when volunteers are doing something, you usually need to be there, which could make you less productive in other ways.

Get the blessing of more and less senior staff, as they will feel the effect if a volunteer has problems or if you do. Remember other service users. Will group

members be happy with the volunteer's style of leadership? You are responsible and liable for volunteers' behaviour, wellbeing and safety. You have a duty of care to keep the organisation and all its staff and members safe. DBS checks are essential if anyone in contact with your organisation is vulnerable.

If you are setting something up from scratch, an agreement on a task-by-task basis within a well-organised environment (Box 10.11) is a more manageable approach for you at first, and for refugees as it allows for their daily realities and gives you and the refugee clarity on what is expected and what to expect, plus a chance to do it differently next time. Remember to keep a record of what they do over time, including training and responsibilities, so you can write meaningful references in the future.

Box 10.11 **Necessary policies for volunteering and employment**

Make them aware of your existing policies and procedures, and make sure you comply with them yourself. Key policies are likely to be:

- safeguarding including DBS checks, confidentiality, data protection, health and safety including daily and more irregular safety procedures, fire drills and security

- expenses

- equality and diversity

- supervision, discipline and grievance, bullying and harassment, whistleblowing

- IT and financial security

- task description, code of conduct, complaints for the volunteer's own reference.

If you can invest a little time up front, you improve their experience and opportunities to learn, and reduce the risk of disruption later.

- Allow a proper training and orientation (also Box 10.11). Be realistic in what you ask volunteers to do with or without training; even photocopying confuses people who aren't used to doing it.

- If your system relies on volunteers (e.g. asking them to lead regular activities), build in time for ongoing recruiting. Have routine backup plans in place for when someone rings in ill.

- Make your volunteer expenses policy clear and stick to it consistently. And note: expenses can really add up, just £4 per day two to three times a week is £250+ over six months, so give a monthly deadline for claiming expenses and avoid nasty surprises.

- Be sure that thank-you gifts can't be interpreted as a substitute for payment – by the Home Office or the Tax Man (or by the refugee).

Even gift cards could be problematic, but a nicely presented bag of stationery or a basket of food treats is usually appreciated.

And check your insurance – it will only cover a certain number of people per year.

Going up a notch from volunteering, you may consider something more substantial such as offering refugees **structured work experience, a part-time placement, career-oriented internships or apprenticeships**. You might recruit from your own contacts and participants, but it is a very good idea to host trainees from requalification or employability schemes that specialise in supporting refugees. A good scheme will usually support you to set up something appropriate including selection, task and supervision structures, and will provide ongoing external supervision and support. There is an initial cost implication in staff time and possible insurance, IT and so forth, but most schemes will pay people's travel expenses at least, and some degree-level schemes give a small fee to organisations that host placements.

A placement that is set up properly in advance can be an asset to your work, and after the first placement it will be less work to set up each time, but the benefit to refugee trainees remains extremely high. Be honest and thorough in your feedback – trainees are there to learn.

For increasingly direct access to employment, you can try to build links with local employers (look out for guidance from the Refugee Employment Network). Remember: few organisations will employ someone just to help that person out, or to do you a favour. But employers do have discretion. It helps if they know and trust you. If you want to encourage a local employer to facilitate refugees into work, you will need to make a commitment yourself, and be organised and efficient.

- Maybe you can find a 'friend within' the company (ideally at executive level). Some managers or bosses have experienced migration or refuge themselves, although that doesn't necessarily make them sympathetic.

- Make sure employers are confident that refugees are allowed to work and that they are familiar with the paperwork that proves someone can work.

- Ask employers if their staff can provide coaching, mock interviews or hands-on 'work tasters' or introductory training (Box 10.12, CS/N); or work together to design and manage work experience or work placements (CS/O).

- Offer to help advertise their vacancies and send to all the refugee contacts you have built up. Then invite people to the office to work on applications and interview skills.

- Discuss how they shortlist. Can they avoid requiring UK qualifications and UK experience that rule out very capable refugees? They can choose

to interview all refugees who apply, but they have to be careful not to discriminate either against or in favour of refugees when they appoint.

Box 10.12 Examples of refugee service/employer collaboration – Case Studies N and O

N   In 2017 a major chain linked up with the Refugee Council to provide four days of training and one-to-one job coaching, plus guaranteed interviews to refugees. Over half the refugees who completed the first set of courses were offered jobs by the chain.

O   Transitions is a non-profit social enterprise in the model of a commercial recruitment agency, which works with large employers to set up placement schemes for suitably skilled and qualified refugees in engineering, IT and other fields. The aim is to 'convert' the placement to full employment if the refugee adapts and progresses well.

To give themselves the best chance of a decent job sooner rather than later, refugees need to understand British recruitment approaches. Whether you use group discussion or mock interviews where refugees play the employer, find ways to help people understand that they should:

☑ not apply for jobs they stand no chance of getting

☑ recognise this *is* a competition

☑ take up strategic opportunities of all sorts to make themselves more attractive to employers

☑ show off their full range of experience, including UK/elsewhere, paid/unpaid, plus community and family life

☑ present themselves in a way that the employer sees what she or he is looking for

☑ make the equal opportunities system work for them:

– answer the specific questions fresh each time

– make sure they score something for every single part of the person specification, including drawing on family or voluntary experience

☑ review their expectations of working relationships with bosses and colleagues

☑ not see a refusal letter as a measure of their worth

☑ hope for just a little bit of luck.

Employing a refugee

Can you employ a refugee?

A small warning before you start. If you give one person a job, remember how other members might feel. People who have been committed to the organisation for a long time often feel that they deserved something back. It is worse if they applied but weren't appointed. To avoid losing them, you need to tackle this head on: talk to each individual directly about how they will feel if they aren't successful. In addition, have outside involvement in decisions, and inform the whole organisation and membership about all processes and decisions. You could involve members in the selection and interview panels. People passed over still won't be happy but it *will* be worse if you ignore the problem.

If you already recruit and employ staff, a few adaptations might be enough to make it more likely that a refugee can successfully apply for your next vacancy. Recruiting and employing a refugee is like recruiting and employing anyone. You are still bound by the laws against discrimination which forbid 'positive discrimination', so you can't employ someone just because she or he is a refugee, or Syrian or Sudanese, for example, as that would be race discrimination. But you can take positive action to encourage refugees to apply: you can state in adverts that your organisation is keen to encourage refugees to apply, you can send job adverts to refugee charities and employability projects, and you can guarantee interviews to all refugees who apply. But when you appoint, you have to do so on the basis of equal opportunities, for reasons based on merit, not on race, disability or other personal characteristics.

You might need to adapt your selection processes.

- Edit your person specification (Box 10.13) and application form so it is really clear and explains the equal opportunities process, including how people's answers will be scored for shortlisting.

- Under 'Employment History' make it clear people should include time and skills from other countries, volunteering, community activities and skills they have gained in other contexts.

- Rather than a blank 'Personal Statement' section, lay out a series of questions that echo the person specification.

- Do not judge the application by the handwriting or quality of the grammar and presentation (unless writing and presentation are relevant to the job and in the person specification).

- Their interview skills will not be honed for British culture, so include a series of practical tasks related to the job. You could ask them to teach you something, complete a spreadsheet, write one page about a 'what would you do if' scenario. Tasks reveal skills and abilities that people might not know how to express in English.

Box 10.13 Making person specifications more refugee-friendly

Standard person specification	Refugee-friendly person specification
GCSE English	Or the equivalent of Level 3 (GCSE standard) English
Safeguarding training at Level 2	Or willing to complete Level 2 safeguarding training within the probation period
Knowledge of local authority structures and opportunities for influencing the commissioning cycle	Or understanding of bureaucratic organisations, and keen to learn about local authority structures and identify opportunities to influence commissioning

Make good use of probation, because it lets you take a risk on someone. It gives the person time to prove their potential. Make it clear from the start that you will *only* confirm them in post at the end of probation if they meet reasonable goals and conditions which you have laid out clearly. It is likely to be about training or skilling up so they can clearly do the full job properly by the end of probation. You might even make the job offer *conditional* on passing a certain qualification or English test, for example. You should have substantial additional supervision to support them to develop as quickly as possible, achieving the understanding, skills and performance you need from them.[2] Be in constant communication about what is working and what isn't working. If it doesn't work, say goodbye, and start a new recruitment.

Look at it from a step further back. You might consider *adapting existing or potential opportunities* in the organisation to be more accessible and suitable for refugees. One possibility is to revisit job descriptions and pay scales and therefore the person specification. If they are currently based on people already having skills when they come into post, you can review them so that someone with potential who is short on experience and qualifications can apply. This might mean slightly lower salary costs, but will also mean a greater commitment on the organisation's part to good-quality, effective supervision and access to training. It might be worth exploring apprenticeships – information is widely available.

You have a number of options regarding job structure and contracts:

- **Temporary contracts.** If the job on offer is for less than one year, you can appoint anyone, without full equal opportunities recruitment (although check the conditions from your funders), but you can't extend the contract over one year. If you decide to continue the job over one year, you have to start a proper equal opportunities recruitment from scratch, and at that point the post holder has to apply for the job in open and fair competition.

---

2   Usually, when people reach the end of probation having met any conditions and so can take on their full responsibilities, they should have a proportionate pay increase to reflect their greater value to the organisation.

- **Part-time contracts for set hours or variable hours**, usually with a maximum or minimum. You might take a full-time job and split it into two or more jobs. Coordinating roles and work can be an issue. Part-time hours might allow people to continue studying.

- **Casual or 'zero hours' contracts.** These have been controversial in the 'gig economy' because they are open to misuse, but, when used well, they are flexible and effective for both employer and worker. If there is no work one week, you don't have to offer the person work. If you offer work, they don't have to take it. But if they do, the casual contract defines the terms and conditions. The employer pays the worker's tax and NI. Casual workers still have annual leave and other rights. If the work becomes regular, it should change to a normal employment contract.

  Another advantage of casual contracts is that you can split one job and give three or four people an opportunity for some work experience. But beware of management costs, and the risk that it clashes with benefits rules, or that the little income might be eaten up by commuting costs. If this is primarily about giving experience, make it time-limited and be sure people know that and keep looking elsewhere. After six months, give another four people a chance.

- **Self-employed.** 'Gig economy' employers have been in the courts to determine whether their drivers, cleaners, plumbers, etc. are 'self-employed', especially because self-employment means people have fewer rights than employed workers. Arrangements with self-employed refugees can work well, perhaps as interpreters or caterers. But be sure they really have self-employed status with Inland Revenue. If not, you might be accused of avoiding tax or NI. They must invoice you for payment. Although you are not obliged to check, for their sake make sure they understand that they still have to pay tax, but they pay it themselves and must keep paperwork and do tax returns. Self-employment messes up benefits and makes it harder to get loans or a mortgage. If people aren't self-employed already, I would advise caution and obtaining outside advice.

You might also consider making a job flexible to allow for the pressures some refugees are under with mental health difficulties and multiple pressures from the other demands of rebuilding a life. Remember that you are required to make reasonable adjustments by law so as not to discriminate against disabled people, and mental health is a disability. Phasing in from part-time to full-time might help people make the adjustment. Every job should have a probation period, and if you are employing someone who is recovering from mental ill health, you should have sufficient supervision to support them as they develop their confidence and resilience.

Even if you are taking positive action to employ refugees, you are still bound by normal regulations on terms and conditions. Trying to do a decent thing does not mean you can downgrade terms and conditions, even if that would tip the balance towards making something financially viable. So bear in mind that part-time or temporary employees cannot be treated less well than full-time or permanent staff, so you still need to include annual leave and, in due course, statutory maternity and parental leave, pension contributions and potentially redundancy pay.[3]

Once a person is in post, they are (and you treat them as) just another colleague, even if they are getting additional training and support. As described in Chapter 1, refugees are just normal people, not angels. There is no guarantee they are nice or that you will like them. Nor will they necessarily be grateful, even if you have gone to considerable lengths to create this opportunity. You never know if anyone you recruit – refugee or not – will turn out to be the right choice. They might turn out not to have the potential you thought, or to be unable to do the job for other reasons. You should already have suitable probation and employment/employee policies in place so just apply them consistently and make sure all colleagues – refugee or not – are treated fairly and equally.

To help protect refugees once they are in work

Other than jobs via friends and family, when refugees first get paid work, it is often through agencies, such as catering and waiting, warehouse and security, health and social care, cleaning plus 'self-employed' options in the gig economy such as driving taxis, food delivery and interpreting. Many get work through peers in small businesses which might be cash in hand. Also there are entry points into direct employment in schools, supermarkets, shops and the NHS (www.jobs.nhs.uk, for example, as porters – see Box 10.1, CS/C – and healthcare assistants).

When they start, you might need to give a little extra support. There's a lot to adjust to and crises that refugees are prone to, such as ill health, caring responsibilities and time to see their lawyer, might compromise their value to the employer.

Refugees might find it difficult to cope with the new pressures of employment: travel, timings, urgency to learn and perform, physical demands, life outside their 'comfort zone' and not necessarily in a 'safe space' (Box 10.14). They will have intense interaction with new people who may have no idea about – or empathy with – their life experiences. People's aspirations and hopes shift as daily working realities blur longer-term goals (Box 10.14, CS/P).

---

3   Information on employment rights is widely available and not specific to refugees; see, for example, www.gov.uk, ACAS or Citizens Advice. See also www.redundancycalculator. gov.uk.

Refugees are vulnerable to poor treatment at work: they have little knowledge of norms and rights, and may not communicate well in English. As their whole family might depend on their wage, they may not be able to walk away from an opportunity to earn. For those working outside the law, the cash their employer puts in their hand is the only food and roof they have.

Not all poor treatment is cynical exploitation. Often employers or managers just don't pay enough attention to their staff's rights and needs (CS/P). Employees who don't know what good practice is, or are nervous about asking questions, are likely to lose out. But there are employers who deliberately underpay, pay late or don't pay at all (CS/Q), or who ignore safety and welfare, or bully and intimidate staff, pushing them into dangerous situations (CS/S).

Box 10.14	Refugees and dealing with the new pressures of finding decent jobs – Case Studies P–S

P was one of three refugees who all trialled for a job. One calculated the travel was too expensive for the pay. One worked during the pilot stage but found the long shifts exhausting. P stuck in the job for ten months but ultimately left because she found the stress level and tensions between staff in the department intolerable.

Q another interpreter, lost in the region of £500 pounds she was owed when the agency she worked for went into liquidation.

R is an interpreter who served the NHS and courts. He had a casual contract with his agency, but a new agency was appointed and interpreters were required to be self-employed to continue working through the new provider, which also does not pay travel time or expenses or insurance, as self-employed workers are obliged to cover those costs themselves. R is working in a group that is mounting a legal challenge to the decision to end their casual contracts, with union support.

S was offered car mechanical work. He was driven a long way to the site to find they were breaking cars that had probably been stolen. He refused the work and was harassed for over a year by the contact. He didn't report it to the police.

You *are* familiar with British employment. Your ability to listen and take a strategic view is valuable. You can offer 'coaching' sessions or mediate when a refugee has difficulties at work. Having a neutral third party to help communication can reassure both refugee and employer, but be aware of the demand on your time and patience. Or you may move into an advocacy role, supporting the refugee to 'nudge' employers into remembering good practice, or 'poke' them with a potential or actual grievance (scrupulously following their procedures). If necessary, you might need to back the refugee to use 'slap' tactics, which could mean bringing in legal advice or even action from a trade union such as Unite,

a community law centre or employment solicitors. In some very serious cases, the refugee might be well advised to involve the police.

Conclusion

Maybe one day your refugee member or client will retire on a handsome pension and look back over their career and remember you. Refuge is more than having permission to stay somewhere. It is about the people around you, having space and opportunities to build and create your own future. So that even if your old life is no longer possible, you still have a life you made yourself – just not the one you grew up expecting.

Refugee Children and Young People – With and Without Families

Introduction

Even if your job doesn't centre around children, you may well find yourself supporting refugee children or young people at some point (Box 11.1). They may be with parents or members of their extended family or living with other adults. They might be on their own, as 'unaccompanied minors', in which case they are probably 'looked after children' in the care of the local authority.

If they arrived young or were born here, they might have no memory of life outside the UK, but their lives are fundamentally shaped by what their family has been through before and since arriving in the UK. Their experiences in the next few years could affect their whole lives.

	Being aware that children might be from
Box 11.1	**refugee families, even if born here**

Waiting in a primary school playground with the head teacher, watching the children say goodbye to parents at the start of a school day, I asked him how many refugee or asylum-seeking children there were in his school. 'We had one a couple of years ago,' he said. I was astonished. The playground was full of people from Afghanistan, Iraq, Sri Lanka, Somalia and other countries that people have been fleeing for years. I had expected him to say about a third of the school. He didn't see them as refugees.

Until someone reaches the end of their 17th year, up to their 18th birthday, they are still legally a child. Their rights and statutory entitlements in the UK are set by children's law which for statutory bodies is more important than immigration law or immigration status. Voluntary and community bodies and some health, mental health and youth services such as careers are more flexible around age, and young people's or youth services go up to 25 (Box 11.2).

This chapter looks at the issues you might meet if you find yourself working with refugee children (and sometimes their parent or parents). This chapter

doesn't go into detail on 'mainstream' children's rights, services and good practice as that expertise is easily available elsewhere.

It looks at supporting children who have refugee status or other Leave to Remain, asylum-seeking children and those who have been refused asylum or have Unaccompanied Asylum-Seeking Child Leave (UASC-Leave) (revisit Box 3.11 and Glossary for a reminder of definitions).

Many of the definitions and issues were laid out in earlier chapters regarding definitions and entitlements (Chapter 3), daily necessities (Chapter 8), health/ mental health and disability (Chapter 9), and education (Chapter 10), and this chapter is best read in combination with those. Organisations and sources of expertise are listed in Appendix A.

Box 11.2 **The child was hungry**

A young man came into our office. An age ruling had found him to be over 18 and he was en route to dispersal accommodation. As he talked, he demolished a tin of biscuits, a whole bag of satsumas and 12 stale fairy cakes left over from a volunteers' meeting. I asked him if he'd had breakfast – yes, but no dinner last night or money for lunch today because the paperwork hadn't reached his temporary accommodation. I don't know how old he was, but he was still very young – fresh-faced and spotty. If an adult, then barely so. And he was hungry.

Persecution and experiences before reaching the UK

Some forms of persecution and abuse inflicted on children are different to those inflicted on adults. Children are conscripted into fighting forces and bullied and intimidated and brutalised into soldiers and 'camp followers'. Children are forced into marriage, sexually exploited, mutilated. They are exploited for their labour, and trafficked for labour and sexual exploitation. Abuse often takes different forms (and has different consequences) with children: not only physical violence, but emotional manipulation, neglect and denial. Everything is gendered.

It is difficult to keep up to date with all the news from around the world, but being aware of recent conflicts and persecution affecting children will heighten your sensitivity to what *might* have happened to the young refugee in front of you (Box 11.3). Maybe nothing too bad has happened – her mother or father got her to safety before anything serious happened to her, or maybe they didn't. And the children live every day thinking about people they have left behind.

Box 11.3	Countries from which children are fleeing to the UK because of persecution, conflict and harm	
Country of origin	Forms of persecution and danger that children have fled from	Children with family or unaccompanied (UC) (UC mostly 10+)
Afghanistan	Violence, militias and forced conscription of boys and young men	Family and UC; UC mostly male; babies born here
Albania	Localised conflict appearing to target sons, trafficking of young men, economic migration	UC mostly male; most are refused
China	Targeting families of political and human rights activists, trafficking for labour, also impoverishment linked to ethnicity Arrivals increasing from 2017	Both
Eritrea	Forced conscription, slave labour and maltreatment of boys and girls, young women and men, ethnic persecution, female genital mutilation (FGM) practised on girls	Mostly UC male and female, mostly from early teens; earlier arrivals now settled
Iran	Persecution and murder of gay men, persecution of Christians, non-conformism, also conflict between religious groups, persecution of political activists affecting families	Family but increasing UC; UC mostly male
Iraq	Young men forced into militias, religious and ethnic persecution of families	Family and UC; UC mostly male
Nigeria	Religious persecution, forced marriage, persecution of gay and lesbian young people	UC mostly male; most are refused
Pakistan	Forced marriage, persecution of disabled people, persecution for political activity	UC forced marriage female; others mostly male
Somalia	Ethnic conflict over many decades, FGM practised on girls in a wide age range	Families, babies born here
Sri Lanka	Ethnic and political conflict and widespread violence, at height in 2009	Families of all ages; babies born since 2009
Sudan	South Sudan, persecution, violence and destruction, by ethnicity and religion in civil war. On and off for many decades, but increasing since 2017	15% of UC applicants in 2017*

cont.

Country of origin	Forms of persecution and danger that children have fled from	Children with family or unaccompanied (UC) (UC mostly 10+)
Syria	Widespread ethnic and religious violence in civil war, by government and non-government forces. Families and UC arriving in the EU/UK overland and across the Mediterranean. Also small number of families in the UNHCR resettlement scheme	Families and UC; UC includes families through the international resettlement schemes
Uganda	Persecution, murder and rape of young gay men and lesbians. Child soldiers	UC young people, female and male
Vietnam	Trafficked and escaping trafficking, increasing since 2017	12% of UC applicants in 2017*
Refugee children who do not reach the UK: children from Cameroon, Central African Republic, Chad, Democratic Republic of Congo, Myanmar, Niger, Northern Nigeria, Yemen	Huge numbers are displaced and in refuge outside their country of origin, but do not come to Europe/the UK	All ages including babies born in exile

* Refugee Council Quarterly Statistics, 2018

Refugee children, abuse, protection and safeguarding

After arriving in the UK, young people still need to be protected from further traumas, including sexual, financial and other forms of exploitation and abuse. Some people will target refugee children with racist and hate-filled actions (Box 11.4). Others might just seek to fool or manipulate. Traffickers can reconnect. Their own families might harm, neglect or exploit them. New peers, friends, girlfriends and boyfriends can wield a lot of power over a refugee child or young person, especially if the child or young person is relying on them for emotional support, social networks and peer identity. There is also the spectre of gangs and of radicalisation.

Box 11.4 **Attacks on asylum-seeking youths**

In 2017, in Croydon, three teenagers were found guilty of beating up an asylum seeker in a suspected hate-crime.

In 2017 a group that had been harassing a young asylum-seeking man for some days followed him when he got off a bus, and when he ran into a refugee charity's office block for help, they followed him into the reception area and beat him up.

In addition, we can't ignore the frightening possibility that people in professional or responsible positions, including staff, contractors, volunteers, members and participants *in your own organisation*, could end up in situations and relationships where they could abuse the young refugees you help.

There are some conditions that make refugee children particularly vulnerable to abuse. Any person who is isolated and can't communicate easily or anyone who doesn't know – or trust – the people who could protect them is vulnerable to abuse (see, for example, Box 11.5). Any child refugee (or any adult refugee, or any child anywhere) could be in this situation. Add to this the extraordinary experiences refugee children have gone through already, and growing up between conflicting cultural backgrounds, it is not unusual for young refugees to be unsure about what is and what is not OK for people to do. They are normal children in abnormal circumstances that make them unusually vulnerable.

Box 11.5 **Private fostering**

Private foster carers are adults who have privately arranged to care for someone else's child, under the age of 16, for more than 28 days. They should tell the local authority. Private foster carers are in a very powerful position, especially if no outside body or other person is aware the child is living with them. Although a lot of private fostering is perfectly fine, it can be a front for trafficking, and the potential harm these adults could do is almost without limit. You may remember the death of Victoria Climbié in 2000. She was an eight-year-old child from the Ivory Coast who was privately fostered with an aunt who tortured her and eventually killed her (vcf-uk.org). If you become aware that a child is privately fostered, you must tell the local authority, who will make contact with the carer and child and ensure that the child's care, education, safety and other needs are properly dealt with. See Coram Children's Legal Centre and the British Association of Adoption and Fostering.

Whatever your role is, it includes protecting children and young people from abuse. If you have any concerns, you must act. You might feel a child is acting strangely, has changed in some way, or they might say something that worries you. You cannot raise your concerns directly with the child, but you can create a safe space and a trusting relationship.

If a child – or parent, for that matter – does 'present' to you with their experiences and fears, stay calm. Remind them you will keep it confidential, but it is not a secret – make sure they know what 'confidential' means. Confirm and clarify what they have said to you without encouraging further detail. If there is an interpreter present, check that they understand safeguarding procedures too. As soon as you can, preferably within minutes of them leaving, write down everything the child said in the words they used, date and sign it, and contact your safeguarding officer as quickly as possible.

Safeguarding: Calm. Confidential. Confirm and Clarify. Record. Report.

There are no special safeguarding or protection procedures for refugee children – you just follow good safeguarding practice:

- You and your organisation's safeguarding knowledge should be sound.

- Policies and processes must be effective, clear and well known to all staff, volunteers and trustees, especially what an individual should do if they are concerned about a child.

- Make good use of the collected safeguarding resources on the NSPCC website (www.nspcc.org.uk), including checklists and free training.

- Sign up for local safeguarding networks or bulletins (if there are any) from the local Safeguarding Children Board so you know whom to contact if a concern arises, and so you can access advice and training which might include some free training.

- Safeguarding is more than protection from abuse; it is also about concerns to do with children's health and safety, their care and their development as they become young adults. If you feel there is a risk that a child will be harmed or be held back, it is a safeguarding matter. In addition, the ideas, actions, services and structures you create to give them positive support and experiences are also 'safeguarding'.

To avoid any doubt, the Home Office, National Asylum Support Service (NASS) and NASS landlords are also bound by obligations to safeguard and promote children's welfare.

Recovering and going forwards

Children and young people have a life ahead of them. Although refugee children are normal kids, they have been through extraordinary experiences and they have the potential to become extraordinary adults. The faster they can function and connect with others in their new context, making the best of their own strengths and opportunities, the sooner they will take control of their own futures.

Any list of the things young people might have to overcome must give us pause.

- Dealing with the consequences of some of the violence and persecution already mentioned above.

- Regaining health after poor nutrition or malnutrition, missed immunisations, illnesses and physical injuries, including living with impairments.

- Coping with loss, separation and bereavement.

- Their lives might not have had much relaxation, social interaction, happiness and play.

- They probably have a broken education and might have to start from scratch.

Within families, children still live with poverty and insecurity even if protected by a parent's tenacity, determination and long-term aspirations. But family structures can buckle under the pressure, break up or become less functional. Parents might become less able to nurture their children because of their own struggles. Parent-and-child relationships might not follow their expectations – or yours. You often find power and role reversals when even young children care for parents, act as interpreters and manage communication with formal organisations.

Now in day-to-day life there are new challenges:

- Identity is a big issue from teens onwards. Most avoid being identified as an asylum seeker or refugee (Box 11.10, CS/E), and some struggle to balance feelings of family and national identity with the fluidity and diversity of urban British identities.

- They have to form and re-form relationships, sorting out their relationships with ever-changing peers, including sexual relationships, and managing long-distance family relationships including expectations, but also where family might be lost or in danger.

- They depend on negotiating successfully with multiple staff in different support bodies simultaneously, and so often shop around a bit to find people and places they can trust, especially where they must relate to authority.

    – Many value trust and personal relationships over specialist knowledge.

    – Accessibility is very important, especially as young refugees' lives can be chaotic and – as for adults – lurch into crisis.

- At the same time they are sorting out a lot of practical realities – learning to manage money, making a room into a home, their changing physical life, health and emotions, exam pressures and life aspirations.

- Whenever someone is moved, they have to start all over again.

They are unlikely to see their situation the same way you do.

How do children end up alone in the UK?

In times of danger, families split up. Families get separated by detention and death. Children are sent ahead with relatives or friends. People get lost in the

chaos of flight or because of the demands of smugglers or traffickers' lies (see Box 11.6 on reuniting families). And there are also children who flee their own families for many reasons – including homophobia or to avoid being forced into marriage.

Box 11.6 **Reuniting families**
In 2017 the British Red Cross (redcross.org.uk) helped more than 2000 families reunite in the UK. Not all cases involved children under 18, but many did. Once someone has Convention refugee status, they have a right to family reunion – bringing their spouse or children under 18 to join them, although children cannot bring parents to join them. When a family member knows where other family members are, this is an arduous, expensive and even dangerous process. But when they don't, the Red Cross has a Family Tracing Service where a person appeals for their (free) help. They gather as much background detail as possible from that person, then connect with colleagues in the Red Cross and Red Crescent movement in the relevant countries to find out if there are camp or detention records or other ways to identify missing family members. There is no guarantee of success. The Red Cross needs volunteers to help this process.

Sometimes parents will make strategic choices and send their children away. It is traumatic for the child and often dangerous. But as with London's 1.5 million child evacuees in 1939 or the Kindertransport trains that brought 10,000 unaccompanied Jewish children to Britain from 1938 onwards, parents are trying to do the best thing. Get them away from the Taliban. Get them away from forced indefinite conscription into the Eritrean army.

Lack of hope also drives some parents' decision to send children alone across the world, and the children themselves are sometimes part of that decision. Families see that the national or local situation means their children will not get a decent education or a decent future and they look for somewhere they will stand a better chance.

Children seeking asylum in the UK and their care

How many children? Numbers rise and fall with crises around the world. For example, only six Iraqi children arrived alone in 2013, but 324 arrived alone in 2016.[1] Young Afghans and Eritreans (males and females) have been arriving on their own for more than 15 years, but their numbers also fall and rise in

---

1   The Refugee Council produces useful quarterly statistics from Home Office data on 'Children in the Asylum System' which are excellent for a quick picture for your own knowledge, very useful in training, policy-making and funding bids. These figures are from the report in November 2017.

close connection to events in their homelands. In the years leading up to 2015, up to (but usually fewer than) 2000 unaccompanied children claimed asylum in the UK each year. This rose to well over 3000 in both 2015 and 2016 with the crisis in Syria and Iraq, before falling back towards 2000 in 2017 and 2018. Unaccompanied children are predominantly males, and more than 60 per cent are 16 or older; fewer than 10 per cent are 13 or younger.

Although patterns in Home Office decision-making vary from year to year, generally a quarter to a third of unaccompanied children get Refugee Convention status or one of the other forms of Leave to Remain that will let them stay in the UK after they reach the age of 18. In 2017 more than half the children from Eritrea, Syria and Vietnam were given refugee status. Iranian and Iraqi children had many positive decisions, though under half. Only two of 228 children from Albania were given refugee status. Children's asylum processes are considered in more depth below.

About 4000 children arrived with families each year until the start of the Syrian and Middle East crisis when the number rose as high as 6000. The largest majority of those dependent children, about three-quarters, are under the age of ten. Families have babies born in the UK. If their parents are still in the asylum process, babies become asylum seekers at birth, but don't show up clearly in published statistics on asylum.

How likely are you to meet these children, with or without their families? It depends very much where you live and what you do. Wherever an unaccompanied child or young person comes to the notice of (or 'presents' to) authorities for the first time, they become the responsibility of the local authority for that area, regardless of immigration status. Highest numbers present to authorities that are responsible for the 'ports of entry':

- Kent (Port of Dover) registered 930 children in 2015 (although not all stayed in Kent).

- Hillingdon (Heathrow Airport) handles 800+ arrivals per year and looks after around 300.

- Croydon (where the Home Office's Lunar House processes up to 80 per cent of initial claims for asylum for much of the UK) looks after around 400.

- As context, about 60 unaccompanied asylum-seeking children present in Scotland in a whole year.

You might meet unaccompanied children if you work near one of these, or any busy airport such as Manchester or Edinburgh, if they are fostered by their authority in your area, or if they are one of the few transferred to the care of children's services in new areas to spread the load. Overall, the children are

concentrated in the South, South East and London. Asylum-seeking families with NASS accommodation will be mostly in the main dispersal areas of the North West, West Midlands, Yorkshire and the Humber. Many families who do not have NASS housing and those who get Leave to Remain return to London or cities where they have existing contacts, despite the cost of housing.

Children and the asylum processes

This section is about being aware of the processes children go through in the asylum decision-making process (the care system is considered in the next sub-section). This section summarises the main processes for an overview, and is not intended for case work. When you work with a child who is still waiting for an asylum decision, don't forget that you cannot do immigration case work if you are not licensed to do so. It is important to be generally aware of asylum processes and more important to know who to talk to in a hurry, especially as a child approaches 18. The main specialists in this field are Coram Children's Legal Centre (known as Coram or CCLC) and the Refugee Council's Panel of Advisers, usually called the Children's Panel, which gives direct support and advice to individual children seeking asylum, and carers and professionals who work with them (also see Appendix A).

The Home Office might think someone is lying about their age in their screening interview. This happens in up to a quarter of older unaccompanied children's cases. If they believe the person's appearance 'very strongly suggests' that person is significantly over 18, that person will simply be treated as an adult thereafter.

If the Home Office doubts their age but cannot be sure, the benefit of the doubt must go to the young person. They will be referred to the local social services, which will take care of the young person until social workers have done a full age assessment. An age assessment must follow the 'Merton' principles: be done by qualified social workers, with the young person fully informed at each stage, and told the reasons behind the decision on their age – which they can respond to. The final decision and reasons will be shared in full with the Home Office (Box 11.7).

You can be asked to give an opinion on someone's age – school and college teachers, including ESOL teachers, even vicars sometimes get requests from social workers, but there is no obligation. If you don't have relevant training or expertise, you could give an opinion, making your level of contact with the child and background expertise or lack of it clear, but unless you are very confident your opinion is sound, you should probably refuse. There are many controversies and judicial reviews or even determinations in the High Court regarding age disputes.

Box 11.7 Age disputes

If the Home Office rejects someone's claim to be a child, they might be detained in adult removal centres. But sometimes a child looks physically aged by a harrowing journey, by sleeping rough and eating badly, and maybe substance misuse. The Refugee Council has a quick-response Age Dispute team which visits the person in detention and makes its own age assessment. If the team is convinced the person is under 18, they contact the local authority to take them into care.

Wrist and dental X-rays are not usually accepted as evidence of age, as they have a five-year margin of error (depending on nutrition, for example); some people also raise ethical questions about unnecessary medical interventions.

Children who arrive with or without family go through different processes for their asylum claim.

Children in families are usually included in the mother's or father's asylum claim. If a child is born to the parents after they arrive in the UK, that does *not* give either the child or their parents a right to residency or British nationality, and hasn't done so for more than 30 years.

Unaccompanied children (and some older children in families) submit a claim in their own name or it can be submitted on their behalf. Among other things, their social worker ensures the child has a solicitor who will handle the case on Legal Aid, and should make sure necessary steps in the process are followed properly, such as case reviews and filling in 'statement of evidence forms', and assisting the child to engage with the process.

Children aged 12 and over will have an initial screening, a welfare interview and a 'substantive' interview. Children under 12 can be interviewed if the child is willing and considered mature enough by his or her carers. Children can only be interviewed with a responsible adult present who is not connected with the Home Office – usually a parent, guardian or their social worker – in addition to their solicitor.

For the substantive interview, the unaccompanied child will need to provide evidence to support their asylum claim. A young gay man might be asked to give evidence of homosexual relationships or other activities such as attending a youth club for gay youth. A person claiming religious persecution will be expected to provide evidence that they are actively following their religion. The solicitor or child might also be looking for evidence to support their stated age. They might want evidence to strengthen their credibility, showing the young person is of good character, a good student, a good influence on their peers or playing an active role in the community. They might ask you for a letter that details their activities, or to confirm your opinion that they are gay or Christian or under 18, or a character reference. If you have any relevant expertise or experience in the matter in hand, or are a pillar of the community yourself, make this clear to strengthen the credibility of your statement (see Box 7.5).

If the family gets Leave to Remain, the whole family, including children under 18, are included in the parent's status, as is any child who turned 18 while they were waiting for the decision. If the family has a fixed-term Leave and the child is still under 18 when it is time for renewal, the child continues on the parent's claim. There is a substantial charge of around £1000 per head for extensions and more than £2000 for Indefinite Leave, so family applications can be very costly.

If a child is born in the UK and lives here continuously until their tenth birthday and is of 'good character', she or he can apply to register as British. If children do not register before they are 18, it becomes harder to apply. Many children, families, carers and even social workers are not aware that registration or nationality might be a problem when children reach 18, which is why there is an active campaign called Project for the Registration of Children as British Citizens.

If the family gets refused – if a parent is refused, sometimes the children might make their own claims, especially if approaching 18. If not, or their claim is refused, the family becomes subject to deportation. Since scandals in 2011 that shocked many, families with children are very rarely detained, but the father might be. Families are allowed to visit a relative detained in a 'removal centre' any day at set times, sometimes by appointment, as long as they can manage the travel. Any attempt to deport one member of a family – the father alone, for example – could be challenged on the basis of the right to family life enshrined in the Human Rights Act 1998.

If the unaccompanied child gets Leave to Remain when under 18 (except UASC-Leave), they will stay in the UK with the rights and entitlements of an adult with Leave to Remain, plus the continuing rights and support that any British 'care-leaver' has (see below).

If the unaccompanied child gets refused – about a fifth of unaccompanied children's asylum claims are refused outright – they can be deported, but only if the Home Office rules they can return to family support in their country of origin, or if there are 'suitable reception facilities' for children, which is not the case in most countries.

Those whom the Home Office rejects but accepts cannot be deported before they are 18 are given UASC-Leave. It lasts for 30 months, or up to the age of 17½ (often written 17.5), whichever is sooner. They might be detained 'in suitable facilities' from 17½ which usually means a separate section of an adult removal centre. On reaching 18, whether or not they have an appeal outstanding, they can be deported.

Asylum and refugee children in care and children's law

Children's law trumps immigration law and the Children's Act 1989 is fundamental. As someone is first and foremost a child until they turn 18, their rights and the support they receive are the same as a British child would get.

Practical details on accommodation, money, health and education will be covered in the following sections.

A **'child in need'** under **'Section 17'** of the 1989 Act (also called 's17') is any child – British or refugee, unaccompanied or with family – who is unlikely to be or stay healthy and develop well if they do not get support, and any disabled child. The local authority must safeguard and promote their welfare and should take the child's wishes and feelings into account.

The local authority assesses the child's needs and should make a 'child in need' plan. Needs of asylum-seeking children include ensuring they have solicitors accompanying them to Home Office interviews. It could also mean maintaining contact with the Children's Panel and providing other help such as starting to trace their families and applications for British nationality. The local authority might need to provide support including accommodation and cash and/or identify a range and level of other special support – anything from mental health, disability or education bodies to sports clubs and art projects. These needs might put the social work team in touch with you. You can make sure your local social services are aware of your activities and services. Remember, though, that they will need to be assured you have top-notch safeguarding in place.

A **'looked after child'** under **'Section 20'** ('s20') is accommodated by the local authority when the child would not be safe, or her or his welfare would suffer if she or he was not accommodated. There should be a care plan including immediate and longer-term health, education, emotional wellbeing, social relationships and self-care. Social services can apply for a court 'Care Order' ('Section 31') which gives the local authority as a body 'parental responsibility' for the child, formalising requirements that clarify duties such as the need to follow through on the asylum case and promote the child's longer-term welfare. Some argue this would be in the interests of refugee children. However, Care Orders are more often used for children of British families when adults may object to sharing care and decisions with the local authority.

Care-leavers. With actions starting from their 15th year, the looked after child (if she or he arrived more than three months before turning 18) will get 'leaving care' support for a smooth transition to adult rights and services, and to address their ongoing needs. For unaccompanied asylum/refugee children, this usually means financial support and accommodation up to their 21st birthday, plus advice and assistance with education, training and employment through a 'pathway plan'.[2] Support will be continued to their 25th birthday if they stay in full-time education or have a disability. Failed asylum seekers (including UASC-Leave) lose this support if they refuse to comply with 'removal directions' or deportation after they turn 18.

---

2   The Immigration Act 2016 includes scope to reduce the support for some migrant care-leavers.

Necessities for daily life – roof, food, money and essential resources for life

Regarding children's access to other necessities for survival – accommodation, food and money for daily life and necessities such as clothes – Chapter 8 has relevant background information.

Children with families

(A) A ROOF

Families in the asylum process make a single-family application to NASS. Families with disabled children who have care needs will usually be housed by NASS until a care assessment is done by the local authority where they are housed, if it is done at all. If you are aware of a disabled child, find out if they have had an assessment; if not, assist them to request one. As with disabled adults, if a disabled child needs a higher level of adjustment or special support than NASS can 'reasonably' provide, it becomes the local authority's responsibility to provide suitable support and possibly adapted accommodation.

If refused asylum with no claim or appeals outstanding, NRPF families usually get 21 days' notice to quit their NASS accommodation as NASS will no longer support them. If the local authority finds there is no reason the family cannot exit the country, they can also refuse 'child in need' support, even when a family is homeless, on the grounds that the family has a reasonable alternative – that is, to return to their country of origin. If a family is taking steps to return, they can reapply to NASS or the local authority. But it is all very complicated and often does not work smoothly or quickly. A family stuck like this needs specialist advice, and you do too – you can start with Coram Fact Sheets but you should help them access community law centres, Coram, ASAP or Shelter. The latter three have helplines; details are on their websites.

Families with Leave to Remain have the same entitlements to housing as families with British nationality. The 28-day period after first receiving Leave to Remain, where they have to access mainstream benefits including Housing Benefit or Universal Credit, may be even harder for a family as family accommodation is hard to obtain. A family without housing at this point can apply to the homeless team of the local authority where NASS had housed them, as that is their 'local connection'. The children might be considered 'in need', even if not destitute, so families may be considered 'priority need' for housing or get temporary support, such as a bed-and-breakfast room. The Refugee Council and local charities' hosting and deposit schemes mentioned in Chapter 8 are invaluable.

(B) MONEY FOR FOOD AND ESSENTIAL RESOURCES

For asylum seekers, the weekly NASS rate for children and babies is the same as for adults at under £38 per person, so a family of one adult and two children will receive 3 x £38 = £114 per week. For babies, there is an extra £5/week until they are one year old, then £3/week extra until they turn three to cover milk, nappies and so forth, and during pregnancy women can claim £3/week extra. Parents who receive the one-time-only maternity grant of £300 are expected to use that for expensive items such as prams (see Maternity Action, also their advice line). When a family is refused asylum, if there were children under 18 when the decision was made, they might continue receiving NASS support (see NRPF Network).

All children get free school meals and fruit in reception, Year 1 and Year 2 (and to Year 3 in Scotland). Some schools, including secondary schools, have free breakfast clubs. Parents and carers apply for free school lunches from Year 3, although a fact that surprises a lot of people is that asylum-seeking families who are not receiving NASS support might not get free lunches for their children. Many people feel this is at odds with safeguarding principles and policies. Some schools and local authorities choose to be flexible.

Families that have Leave to Remain follow the same processes and rules as British nationals to claim the full range of housing and financial support that British nationals can claim, including crisis loans, Child Benefit and means-tested benefits such as free school meals.

In addition to those services and resources already mentioned in Chapter 8, bodies that support children or struggling families with food, clothes and other daily essentials, include the following.

Daily essentials for babies and children under five:

- Health professionals – for example, health visitors, in addition to their health role, often find goods and services for mothers with few resources. GPs might prescribe baby milk, supplements, shampoos, and skin creams.

- Mostly run by local authorities, children's and family centres, family information services, Sure Start in Northern Ireland and Cymorth in Wales run health, educational, childcare, advice and other free activities such as toy libraries, and might receive donated goods. They often provide milk, fruit and snacks in play sessions.

- Food banks and homeless organisations or drop-ins might have nappies, milk powder, etc. in addition to food, plus advice workers. Children's charities/charity shops gather children's goods (Box 11.8, CS/A, CS/B), and have very cheap baby clothes (CS/C). There might be local charitable trusts and grants (see Box 11.8).

Daily essentials for school-age children, up to 18:

- Primary schools often have Family Support Workers who respond to practical needs. Secondary schools have welfare staff. Schools will often provide clothes, coats, shoes, uniform and other kit from lost property and might have uniform grants. You could contact schools on behalf of the family if they want to remain anonymous.

- Holiday play and lunch schemes in some areas, especially Scotland, provide food, activities and sometimes advice at times when access via schools isn't available.

- Some areas have free school travel, and even outside school hours, usually with conditions, although local bus companies usually require evidence or a pass with age or address. A letter from you might help.

Box 11.8 | **Channelling goods to families and children – Case Studies A–C**

A   collects donations of toiletries and treats specifically for refugee children, from a network of churches before Christmas, boxes and wraps them and gives them as gifts.

B   is contacted informally, when necessary, by local community health staff and will seek out donations such as baby buggies or cots and blankets on request – this is not limited to asylum seekers or refugees, but is for anyone facing homelessness.

C   is a regular drop-in for asylum seekers run by volunteers and relying on donations. It appeals specifically for donations of disposable nappies.

Unaccompanied children – roof, food, money and goods

In addition to the above, the support that is specific to looked after children and care-leavers includes:

- Foster carers in their own home.

- Children's homes – houses for two to eight children, staffed by paid workers. They mostly house older children or children with complex needs.

- From 16+ the local authority has to continue to provide or help the young person find housing. It provides money for food and essentials and to facilitate education (see below). Local authorities cannot refer asylum-seeking care-leavers into the NASS system.

- Supported living for any young care-leaver (refugee, asylum, refused or UK national), such as:

- 'staying put' with their existing foster care family

- assisted access to social housing

- lodging with an approved supportive carer for up to two years

- foyer schemes which provide independent accommodation with life skills and other training

- 'move on' and 'floating support' services to young people in private or social rented property

- in emergencies, Nightstop/Crashpad schemes for short- or medium-term accommodation with a 'supported accommodation' family – usually voluntary; also hostels, night shelters (see Homeless Link).

The local authority is responsible for care and maintenance for unaccompanied young women and men with Leave to Remain (except UASC-Leave), so the individual cannot access Housing Benefit, Income Support or Jobseeker's Allowance. They can access some mainstream benefits such as Child Benefit for a baby, or disability allowances. There are funds such as a 'home allowance' or 'leaving care grant' for essentials.

Health, mental and emotional health and disability

Regarding health, mental and emotional health and disability, there is relevant information in Chapter 9, although in mental health in particular there are specialist children's services.

Children get all health care and treatment free, whether primary, secondary or emergency care and prescriptions, including dentistry, speech and language, and mental health care and treatment. Safeguarding duties for any organisation must take into account children's health and physical safety, wellbeing and future health and development outcomes, including any long-term health conditions and disabilities.

Young refugees and physical health

Some of the risks to children's physical health have been touched on already, such as trauma from conflict, forms of persecution of children such as female genital mutilation, lacks and gaps in nutrition and immunisations or adult care. Where families don't engage with health services for any reason – ignorance, suspicion, beliefs or just not being able to read letters sent home from school – children still might not benefit from the screening, prevention and treatments available to them.

There are certain health services set up for or more likely to be useful to children – such as health visiting, child development, speech and language

therapy, different paediatric specialisms, separate emergency streaming and processes. The GP, A&E, minor injuries/urgent treatment sections and 111 (which has interpreters) are still the initial contact and access point for almost everything. Babies, children and young people have routes into health care via children's centres, health visiting services, referral via schools and social services, and increasingly any body or professional such as you.

You can start by ringing 111 while the child or parent is there. The 111 service has interpreters, and you can hand over the phone. With this simple action, you can start off a chain of accurate advice, referral, even basic assessment and a direct appointment with the correct service for them, speeding up the whole referral process. Children should always be registered with a nearby GP; if you realise they aren't, help the family to register as covered in Chapter 9.

Young refugees and mental and emotional health

Young refugees are coping with huge changes and stresses. They may be coping with earlier traumas. Some children have difficulty forming trusting relationships or emotional bonds. They may feel disconnected and isolated even from immediate family, from peers and from support workers.

Certain mental health services focus on children (Box 11.9). All NHS areas have Child and Adolescent Mental Health Services (CAMHS, pronounced 'Cams') for children and young people, but waiting times even for a needs assessment can be terrible and many CAMHS services have no specialist trauma counsellors. In many places, secondary schools now have their own counselling services and can access bereavement counsellors, but school counsellors may not have training in trauma counselling.

	Children's mental health – expertise and
Box 11.9	**resources in the voluntary sector**

Freedom from Torture (Birmingham, Glasgow, London, Manchester and Newcastle) works with children and families, and therapeutic bodies such as the Baobab Centre in London and the Haven Project in Hull develop ideas, models, evidence and lessons from working with young refugees.

They pass this expertise on through training, conferences and publications found on their websites.

If you are not a trained counsellor, be cautious – don't encourage young refugees to open up to you. It is possible that you could speed up referral and waiting times by getting on the phone and writing letters arguing that their need is urgent. Remember, young people can also talk to their GP while they wait for counselling. If it is a crisis, get them to A&E – call 999 for the police and an ambulance if necessary.

Where young people need ongoing mental and emotional support, but are not at the level to need or get NHS interventions, or are waiting, other local organisations sometimes have young groups or activities (Box 11.10). Ask your local Mind/Support in Mind, Inspire (Northern Ireland), carers' organisations, disability groups and also youth bodies such as YMCA. Perhaps you can set up or find activities that include interaction and prevent isolation (Box 11.10, CS/D, CS/E) or could help build life skills (CS/F, CS/G) and a positive self-image through music, drama, exercise, relaxation or sports (CS/H). Remember, if someone wants to talk about how they are feeling, listen, witness and accept what they say, but you may need to alert someone in the safeguarding chain, so *don't* promise to keep what they say *secret*.

| **Box 11.10** | **Examples of projects for wellbeing and emotional health for young people/refugees – Case Studies D–H** |

D   Mosaic is a centre for young lesbian, gay, bisexual and transgender people where people from any background can socialise and also access other support.

E   Diversity was a partnership between two local youth organisations to expand refugee teenagers' social networks, building more links with young Britons. They named it 'Diversity' to avoid any link to 'refugee' or 'asylum' because of earlier experiences where young people avoided anything that might identify them as refugees or asylum seekers. The funding ended but the organisations still collaborate on other work.

F   Chrysalis is a life-skills course that helps young refugees up to age 25. It combines learning and other opportunities with social interaction, over two to three months.

G   STAR is Student Action for Refugees – more than 40 self-run groups of higher education students who campaign and volunteer with local refugee projects in their area, including schools, youth clubs, homework clubs and sports.

H   DOST was a small all-round refugee youth charity which had to close in 2017 due to lack of funding. They organised talks, walks, sports, tea, networking, safe space, gardening, sailing and campaigning. They never turned anyone away. They were hoping to reopen as an independent charity – search on the internet and see if they made it.

Young refugees and disability

Disabled children and their carers (including parents, other adults and siblings) have the same rights to support whether they are UK nationals or refugees or asylum seekers.

They are protected by laws on equality, disability, safeguarding, children in need and caring.

They are entitled to assessment and support by the local authority and an integrated approach involving other services which might include your own:

- The Early Help Assessment (EHA, replacing the Common Assessment Framework or CAF) which is a shared document which coordinates support for a child, to be overseen by a lead professional. Many different children's professionals can complete one. If there doesn't seem to be one for the disabled child you are supporting, and you aren't the right person to do it, ask the local children's centre, child's school or health professionals such as health visitors if they can help, or contact the local authority.

- The more detailed 'Children's Act assessment' by asking the local authority's disabled children's team directly. It should happen in less than 45 days although urgent care should start immediately, so if a refugee child with urgent care needs has just arrived in your area, they should be supported straight away, before the full assessment is completed and without waiting for medical diagnosis.

- Assessment by an educational psychologist, usually coordinated by the child's school, but parents/carers can request the school to arrange an assessment.

- Carer's needs assessment.

- Local authorities must also assess and plan for a smooth transition from child to adult services between 16 and 18 (Care Act 2014).

- Education, health and care plan up to age 25 for some children with special needs.

They should be able to access the normal resources that any disabled child should get:

- Information that the local authority must make available called the 'Local Offer' or 'SEND Local Offer' which should be in accessible forms including different languages. You search online using the local authority's name plus 'Local Offer' and you will usually get a directory or something similar.

- GP practices, nurseries, schools, children's services, etc.

- Local generalist disability services and rights groups or networks, some of which might be branches of national bodies (e.g. Carers UK, SCOPE) or national.

- Local or national condition-specific organisations (e.g. for blind children).

Learning English, education, training

Please read this section alongside Chapter 10, especially the education and training section. This section uses 'refugee children' as a general term, unless there is a reason to specify a child's immigration status.

All children in the UK must be in full-time education until at least 16. The local authority has a duty to provide places, regardless of the child's immigration status. In England, after 16 children can move into apprenticeships, traineeships or at least 20 hours a week working or volunteering, while in part-time education or training.

Education carries the promise of a good future. Refugee children can make remarkable progress, especially where their life experiences have given them skills and attitudes that support determination.

To start off with, refugee children might still have fresh memories of trouble and transit. It may also be a long time since they were last in school. Education in their original country may have been based on very different ideas about learning methods, content, examinations and goals. Or they may have moved schools several times during dispersal by NASS and after Leave to Remain.

Refugee children join at any stage in the school system, and often mid-year. They may have little or no English and their numeracy skills might be low, or just low in English. They might be behind or fall behind other children their age, but it is extraordinary how fast some children adapt and learn.

Refugee and migrant parents are sometimes surprised by the different relationships and responsibilities of child, teachers and parents – for example, by the use of play – or by poor behaviour in the classroom. They might not help their children to engage effectively in education. Unfortunately, some children develop behavioural problems, and suspensions and exclusions occur.

This section is not about educational methods or therapies to re-enable learning – that is for the specialists. It is focussed on how hands-on workers can help refugee children and families make the best use of education opportunities. Fortunately, the current ethos of formal education in Britain is to engage and nurture every child, and most schools are excellent at this.

Education for refugee children

Schools have much more than classes and exams. There is fun and interaction with other children and with kind and supportive though still authoritative adults. They are warm, safe, bright and friendly, positive places and spaces, with varied activities in secure routines (Monday to Friday, start time, play time, home time) and welfare such as food, drink, health checks and safeguarding included. These conditions are designed to engage children and make them feel enabled and confident, to nurture children and support their development.

At the same time schools give access to services that can provide urgent and longer-term specialist assessment, support and therapy for children with learning difficulties or trauma, for example, and some will support individual parents or families too.

The first thing you might help with is getting a school place. It can be disappointingly difficult.

- Children in initial accommodation cannot apply for a school and some wait months before NASS contractors house them.

- Parents need to choose a school but might not know it's useful to look at special educational needs (SEN) support, English as an Additional Language (EAL), 'inclusion' staff or welfare support. It is not only about exam results and Ofsted/Education Scotland/ETI NI/Estyn ratings.

- There might be confusion over multiple processes for different schools in the same area, and 'in-year' admissions.

- Poor spoken or written English and limited IT cause parents difficulties with phone calls, visits, brochures, forms.

- Parents can be asked for evidence such as council tax bills, utility bills, birth certificates that they might not have.

- If schools are full, children will be allocated a place at a school the parent/carer does not like or that is too far away, so hard-up parents and children have to make expensive bus journeys.

- Parents can appeal and apply to move the child. Moving school is often disruptive and difficult for children.

- There are many reports of older children waiting months for a place, even until the new school year, especially 15/16-years-olds at the top age for compulsory education.

Issues for refugee children, and opportunities, by age

(A) PRE-SCHOOL AND EARLY YEARS (0–5)

The pre-school and early years are increasingly seen as crucial to a child's development, and an important time to identify children who need 'early help', some of which is truly useful to refugee children. NHS health visitor home visits, clinics, weaning and parenting groups start from virtually the first week of birth and children's or family centres, commissioned or run by local authorities, mostly offer services for 0–5, from 'stay and play' baby and toddler groups or crèches open to all, to individual support and more specialist services by referral only. If the mother you are supporting is not making use of these already, strongly encourage her to do so. You can explain that they are free and safe, and

help her read and understand the timetable of activities. It can be a great help if you go with her the first time she visits.

In some cases – for example, a parent sent on a training scheme by the Job Centre – child care will be paid for, but only if the childminder or nursery is Ofsted-approved. It is the parents' responsibility to choose and register for child care – difficult in an unfamiliar system and with poor English. You could form links with a couple of good local childminders you are happy to recommend, and help refugee parents get through the paper-heavy registration processes with them.

There are free nurseries attached to some primary schools that take children as young as two for a few hours per week, if the parents are on certain mainstream benefits – excluding asylum seekers and NRPF – although there might also be a postcode catchment area. There can be waiting lists and parents should apply early.

(B) PRIMARY (4–11)

At five years old, full-time education becomes compulsory and children often start from four or four and a half. Schools have extra support for children who are behind, or need intensive help to learn English. There might be a deputy head responsible for inclusion, a SEN coordinator or 'SENCo' (England) or teacher who oversees English as an Additional Language (EAL). Throughout the UK there are school systems to plan extra support for individual pupils. This can be anything from an extra 15 minutes per week to referral for assessment by an educational psychiatrist.

Some schools may employ a family support worker giving extra help to parents and carers to understand and communicate with the school, and may help with practical necessities such as reading letters and filling forms, or accessing health or benefits advice. School lunches and uniform have been mentioned above. Refugee children will get support for extra activities like educational trips, based mostly on means testing. Some outside activities such as learning musical instruments must be paid for, although schools can often use discretion.

Collect a small fund to contribute to extra activities, build communication with inclusion and SEN staff, welfare or family support staff, write to governors. The individual who brings you into contact may be one of several refugee children at that school.

(C) SECONDARY (11–16)

Moving to secondary school is another big change for refugee children. Peer networks and identity are issues for all refugees, and children at this age are also hitting puberty, so identity and relationships outside the family are a big feature of secondary school life – adding new tensions inside the family unit. Many refugee children avoid any 'refugee' or 'asylum seeker' labels (Box 11.10, CS/E). Secondary schools can be huge, and children get less individual attention

from teachers and must take more responsibility for their own progress. Help is available, but they may have to ask for it. There is a strong link between parents and carers being engaged and the effectiveness of extra support to help the child progress.

Unaccompanied children are more likely to arrive at secondary school age than primary. The school staff will be aware if they are looked after, though not necessarily that they are refugee children. Education is included in their care plan and they get guaranteed support such as priority for school places, coordination between school and social workers (involves foster parents too), and necessary funds for activities and trips.

The school puts children in the school year the child claims (or is ruled) to be and provides extra interventions to help children catch up. Schools with substantial numbers of migrant children often have specialist inclusion/EAL teams and quiet 'safe' spaces and support for children struggling with anxiety and mental/emotional health difficulties. There are activities within and outside the curriculum to prepare children for adult life, which can also help children from other nations and cultures learn about life in the UK: citizenship, life skills, physical, social, health education (PSHE), employability and career guidance.

Schools have activities and authoritative structures to tackle anti-social attitudes and behaviour where refugee children might be victims, but might also victimise – for example, bullying, harassment, discrimination such as racism, homophobia – and radicalisation. Schools provide easy access to certain health services, such as screening and immunisations. They safeguard and protect.

(D) FURTHER EDUCATION (17–19+) AND HIGHER EDUCATION (HE)

Chapter 10 discussed many formal English, education and training opportunities that are available to adults from 17 onwards, whether starting from scratch or moving from school.

Getting a place:

- Eligibility is based on qualifications to date, although interviews may give some young people the chance to impress admissions staff, who can waive normal requirements.

- As well as A Levels/Highers, if young people have the International Baccalaureate (also called 'IB'), this counts for HE/university admission.

- University access courses or schemes might enable a person without A Levels/Highers to get to university.

- The HE body will want assurance that the young person can stay in the UK for the full length of the course, as the institution is penalised when people drop out.

- Explore HE/university-level courses with modules or with distance learning elements, or work placements.

Fees are a problem. Looked after children/care-leavers will continue ESOL and other full-time education fee-free to 21 or longer, whether at school or college. But for children in families, if they are still in asylum when they reach 18, there could be fees, even for ESOL. The situation keeps changing, but fees can reach £7000 a year even at A Level and more in HE. An asylum seeker or person with discretionary leave, for example, might be assessed as due to pay overseas student fees up to £18,000/year for HE courses.

- There are schemes to continue free education and support for young people who are otherwise 'NEET' or 'not in employment, education or training' and young people can sometimes join schemes for refugees, ethnic minorities, etc., mentioned in Chapter 10.

- Student loans for fees and maintenance are available from government for approved Level 3 or HE/Level 4, 5 or 6 courses. Young refugees with Refugee Convention, Humanitarian or Indefinite Leave can apply if they will be over 19 when they start. Student loans for courses to access university might be written off when you finish your degree.

- 'Long residency' in the UK may mean people on limited leave can still pay home fees and access student loans if they have lived here for a 'substantial' part of their lives. See the 'Let Us Learn' campaign.

- Fees can be reduced through internal bursaries at the discretion of the establishment. Several HE bodies have asylum and refugee scholarship/bursary schemes, but the student must almost always have a firm offer of a place on the course *before* applying. They must check the details or they will waste time and might miss a deadline on something more relevant. STAR (Box 11.10, CS/G) lists more than 50 HE bodies with refugee bursaries.

- Some trusts can fund studies. See Educational Trusts' Forum or contact Refugee Support Network for advice on refugee access to HE.

Living and eating while studying (looked after children – see above):

- There is the possibility of around £1000–£1200 per year for living costs for those with Leave to Remain and in a low-income household, as a '16–19 bursary' in England or the Education Maintenance Allowance (EMA) in the rest of the UK, as long as attendance and progress are good.

- Under certain conditions, young people with Leave to Remain can claim Jobseeker's Allowance while they study.

- Colleges continue to provide free meals up to age 19 (not if NRPF). Some cities give students free bus travel.

(E) TRAINING AND EMPLOYMENT

In addition to material in Chapter 10 regarding trades and employability, it is worth looking at apprenticeships. Young people with Leave to Remain can do apprenticeships. It counts as paid work, so people in the asylum process, with UASC-Leave, refused or with NRPF cannot start apprenticeships. Those with Leave to Remain can start apprenticeships from 16 years, and can go as far as getting a degree-level qualification, without incurring any of the fees they might be charged for further or higher education. From age 16 to 18 the minimum apprenticeship wage is about half the adult 'living wage' for the UK, and from 19 years it is the UK minimum wage, but it increases as the person learns.

Those who can't do apprenticeships might still be able to get work experience during other studies (14+) or through volunteering, and there are many young persons' and youth volunteering schemes such as the Duke of Edinburgh's Award (14+; may be fees), National Citizenship Service/The Challenge (15+) and local schemes.

Putting on non-formal learning and education opportunities

Alongside formal education, there is always the non-formal. Chapters 5 and 10 are relevant. Talk to Children in Need for their advice, guidance and possible funding support, and check your insurance, safety and safeguarding.

You don't necessarily have to put something on yourselves, but can help young refugees make full use of the range of informal opportunities that others are already putting on for young people. What is there out there for young refugees?

- Libraries offering information and putting on activities directly, providing access to IT, books and materials, displays and exhibitions.

- Local authorities running or commissioning/funding organised activities in parks and public venues, plus sports and team games, sports and schemes at leisure centres and sports facilities.

- Children's, youth and specialist play associations, churches and other faith bodies run or host playgroups, youth clubs, Beavers, Cubs, Brownies, Guides and Scouts, plus alternatives like Woodcraft Folk, Girls' Brigade, Boys' Brigade, armed forces cadet groups (there may be 'subs', or subscriptions but these are usually low and might even be negotiable). Half an hour visiting and browsing noticeboards in a community centre or church hall normally gives better results than searching online.

- Some young people's bodies arrange camps and trips away which might be the only chance some children have for a holiday or time in the countryside, although parents might need reassuring.

- Private lessons and activities that adults or young people pay for: maths, English and homework 'cramming' schools; supplementary schools where children might learn their parents' language or religious teachings; dance lessons, sports teams, music and drama classes and choirs. Private or supplementary schools should be registered and inspected by Ofsted. If you suspect one isn't, you should contact Ofsted.

For older children:

- Consider if young people could visit or study your work or organisation. First Give is a scheme where young people research a charity and present what they learn to an audience; they might even win a prize for you.

- Offer work experience placements.

- Offer volunteering opportunities so young refugees can complete award schemes for citizenship or other skills, such as National Citizen Service/ The Challenge or the Duke of Edinburgh's Award.

- Run longer-term sports, music or homework activities, or offer sessions or training to other young people's organisations – a 'cook on a budget' night or 'fix a motorbike' day or 'make a film' course at a youth centre, children's home or if there is foyer accommodation for young people near you.

- Organise mentoring or coaching training for some of your staff/members who can then support a school or college's older students.

- And when you hear a child who you are supporting is in a play or getting an award, try to go.

For families – if you don't work directly with children or prefer not to, you could provide:

- Family activities: events, outings, advice sessions and case work, or concentrate on supporting just one family – for example, if there is a support scheme run by your local authority for families arriving through the Syrian Vulnerable Persons' Resettlement Scheme.

- Help for parents to engage effectively with schools – for example, in English classes you can include vocabulary and role plays to practise talking to teachers.

You might work with school, college or youth workers rather than directly with refugee children.

- You can provide information or promote events to raise awareness and help people develop their own resources to work with refugee children.

- You can offer to find volunteers, training, advisers, speakers (LGBT History Month? Human Rights Day? Holocaust Remembrance Day? Self-esteem for girls?) for them to draw on.

- Use your connections to fundraise or donate equipment they can use for children or pass on to families.

- Combine your networks, and exchange contacts as well as making sure you know what they offer, so you can refer refugee children and families to their services.

- Keep open good channels of communication in case you need to raise a concern. Bear in mind that you can contact senior staff, the local authority or regulators if you have a serious concern.

Conclusion

What I raised in Chapter 1 as the 'new role' for hands-on staff is strikingly clear when looking at support for child refugees. The many local specialist and referral services that once existed have largely gone. The expertise still remains but there is very limited capacity to provide services any more. Regular children's and young people's services and education have expanded their expertise and built strong networks for collaboration and coordination, so they can respond to refugee children's needs. To support refugee children effectively, you need to be part of those networks.

CHAPTER 12

In Need of Refuge

This chapter is dedicated to Judith Kramer, who brought people together.

Introduction

I set out to answer three questions, laid out in Chapter 1:

What matters most?

What do I need to know?

What can I do?

There is so much more than can be covered in one book. You can go much further, starting with sources in the Boxes and Appendices. Doing things is the best way to learn about them. Please share what you learn.

The book starts from the point that when you find yourself working with refugees, you are working with ordinary people. They couldn't carry on living where they lived because of how they were treated. They left, leaving their former lives behind.

Now you are meeting them in the UK. As you get to know them, they are still dealing with their past. They are managing with very little. As someone supporting refugees directly, any response you make to them must take their real, very diverse life experiences into account.

Refugees are usually impoverished and incapacitated to some extent by their experiences, but they are still doing what they can to rebuild their lives. They do so in a context shaped by dependency on many other parties, and their success, to some extent, relies on their ability to negotiate those relationships.

There are numerous formal organisations that control resources and 'the rules of engagement'.

There's you and your team, volunteers and activists like you. There are lots of other local and hands-on, practical staff and your peers and 'friends' within other organisations.

There's the social context: popular views and ignorance, other service users, your members or participants. There are people with doubts, and there are donors of food and clothes.

You provide a service to refugees. You arrange activities, interpret systems, advocate to other bodies. You create ideas and space. Maybe it's just doing your job and you are expanding your existing expertise to reflect these new relationships as you absorb the knowledge you need to support refugees properly. Just a normal part of professional development. Or maybe it's more than a job to you, and you are becoming a hybrid between professional and 'kind stranger'. But your focus might be growing wider.

You *and* the refugee have agency and can bring about change. It might be that you consciously try to change hearts, minds and paperwork. But simply by doing what you can to make things work, you also challenge other parties to be more aware, accurate and adaptable. And by making services work better for refugees, you make them work better for everyone – including me and my mum (thank you).

It's time to look back at a couple of fundamental issues about 'refuge' and 'refugees'. These queries have come from the discussions about giving practical support and go a bit beyond practice.

What is refuge?

What is 'refuge'? This question has emerged at several points in the book, wherever there has been a choice about the level of support for refugees, or the standards to aim for, which depend on what we are trying to achieve. What can we conclude?

Refuge is safety

Whether it is international refuge from persecution or a women's refuge in the next town, refuge starts from being safe now.

But refuge also means being safe tomorrow, and many asylum seekers, refugees with Leave and, of course, refused asylum seekers aren't safe, as they might still be sent back – if not tomorrow, perhaps in two or three or five years' time.

You aren't safe if you are scared to walk down the street because thugs are attacking asylum seekers in your area. You aren't safe if you can be identified and preyed on by traffickers or fraudsters, or if compatriots continue to persecute you in the UK. You aren't safe if you are vulnerable to discrimination or exploitation which others can inflict on you because you are so impoverished and dependent that you can't walk away. The state has a duty to protect refugees from such dangers, just as it must try to protect British nationals.

Someone who is giving good-quality, direct support to a refugee is also keeping them safe. If your organisation has proper safeguarding for anyone who might be vulnerable, you are quite literally keeping people safe. By being trustworthy, listening and treating what they say in confidence without letting it

become a secret, you give people a safe connection to communicate fears, actual threats and harm. Then something can be done about it. When others might refer someone with a 'refugee' problem away, you take it on board and take action: you give refugees security.

Refuge is a decent life

Refuge must surely be more than survival. Living in the UK must be better than living in a temporary camp on the border between two countries at war.

A decent life means a certain standard of services and resources and practical goods and help. Practically, it means a decent roof over your head. It means being able to eat nutritious and even pleasant food. It means enough money, health care and a fair chance of getting a decent job.

It isn't only services, though. A decent life means leisure, social and peer connections. Not just a roof but a home. It isn't only about being able to see a doctor but about being healthy, both physically and mentally; it's about emotional wellbeing. Perhaps it also means being able to look in the mirror and know who you are.

In ordinary life all these practical things link together. If you have a home where you feel comfortable, you can invite friends over and cook them a good meal. Afterwards, you can clean everything up, bath the kids and still feel able to revise for half an hour before you go to bed.

Refugees have a lot to deal with before they can start building a decent life for themselves and their families. The UK's asylum system creates its own challenges, as people waiting for a decision and living on NASS rations know very well. Some difficulties, such as mental health problems or lack of capital, take time to overcome. So refuge isn't only about arriving and scraping together the means to live. It's longer term.

Refugees will often need support on and off over time and through a series of crises. Staff or activists who stay working in the same area might find themselves looking back on decade-long relationships. Building a new life is a long-term project for a refugee. I hope this book has shown how much a competent and willing practitioner can help along the road.

Refuge is respect and equality

In 2017 I had the privilege of asking a mix of over 100 refugees and supportive workers the question 'What is "refuge"?' The answers from the British and the professionals in the room had a strong theme of 'welcome'. So then I had to ask, 'What is "welcome"?'

There is warm welcome to a guest or a visitor, friendly, even enthusiastic and kind. Strangers making a special effort to help people get sorted out – creating a first impression that will never be forgotten.

There is also the kind of welcome given to a new member of staff. Equally enthusiastic and helpful, but with an eye to a longer-term relationship. You don't only help them out because they need help, but because they will have a role to play and you need them to play it well, as soon as possible. After orientation briefings and a 'honeymoon' period, everyone settles back into 'business as usual'. The no-longer-new employee becomes part of ordinary interaction between people getting things done with a degree of mutual interdependence.

The welcome to a refugee is not the welcome given to a guest, but to a new member of UK society. Refugees are ordinary people. Look them in the eye and connect, not as a friend (although friendly is nice and friendship might come), but as a fellow citizen worth arguing with. This is the origin of respect and equality.

Refuge is being able to take control of your future

Most of us expect to decide what kind of life we want to live. We don't expect it to be easy, and we will make mistakes, but they are ours to make. Refugees lost most of their power to make decisions about their lives when they had to leave their homes, or even before that.

Now in the UK, refugees are often disabled by attitudes and processes, whether it is 'We don't do refugees' from some organisations (see Chapter 2), constraints from the Home Office (Chapter 3), direct (Chapter 4) or indirect discrimination in access channels (Chapter 5), or the 28-day cliff edge after getting Leave to Remain (Chapter 8). They might be disabled by the side effect of cuts and scarce resources – for example, when free education only goes to the level that makes you employable in low-paid work. Unnecessary barriers make it harder for refugees to make decisions about their own lives. Sometimes it feels as if they are being set up to fail.

Where systems disable, to some extent you can re-enable. You help people obtain the means – English, for example – to tackle relationships for themselves. When you facilitate someone practically in their struggle for the daily necessities of life, and help them access services that will be useful to them, you free up their energy and resources to work on longer-term strategies.

When you build up your own contacts and networks, it makes you part of providing refuge because of your role as a safe connection. You provide refugees with a mesh of support from different people and organisations that they can navigate for a range of needs. You are also putting in place things they can grab hold of when they are at risk of falling.

Most of what you do is not about helping refugees (although a hand up now and then might be good) but about finding and creating more space for them to help themselves. They are active agents. If they are not held back, they'll get on with doing what they think is the best thing to do, even if it isn't what you think they should do. That is their choice.

Perhaps 'refuge' only exists when you can start to make your own decisions again, and take control of your future. If you are in a situation where you are prevented from doing that, perhaps the people who make it possible again are creating refuge.

Then you can get on with building a new life, beyond refuge.

Refuge is whatever a refugee thinks it is

What is refuge? It's only refuge if it feels like refuge to the person who needs it. In an English group I ran for interpreters, an older man told me he used to write poetry before he was an exile. Now that England was his home, he wanted to write poetry again, in English. Perhaps that is refuge, being able to do the thing that makes you feel like you, as a normal part of your new life.

Or perhaps you just need to go and talk to refugees and ask them yourself.

Who is a refugee?

We need to return to the question of defining 'refugee' one final time.

The definitions in Chapter 3 were chosen to let us distinguish between who is and who is not refugee for practical actions and therefore how we support people. This book has argued for defining a 'refugee' pragmatically by the experiences a person has had, as experience is the most important factor in working out how best to support them, and shapes how effective they are in engaging with us and the support we can offer.

Now I want to revisit the question of 'Who is a "refugee"?', still on the basis of experience, but putting aside the practical element for now. I want to unpick experiences until we get to an essential core of what 'refugee' means.

The refugees we have been talking about throughout this book are the people we find ourselves helping in the UK. The experiences related to being in a new country, or in the UK, are very significant for them. But a great deal of what they experience here is shared with other migrants. Besides, asylum could be very different in another country. Their experiences after arriving in the UK are often problematic, but they are not essential to what 'refugee' means.

They are people who have crossed an international border, leaving their country of origin behind. Is this crossing an essential element of being a refugee? Leaving your country of origin behind, where you have nationality, entitlements, rights, culture and language?

The rules change as you cross the border. People crossing no longer have certain access to services or a voice, which, as taxpayers and voters in their original country, they might have expected. Language, ethnicity and culture often change across borders too, and refugees are rendered inarticulate, maybe illiterate, by the new language. Their identities, arts and history are largely unknown to their new hosts.

People migrate across borders every day. Usually, they have fairly clear plans to return – but so do refugees, although it might not come to pass. What makes refugees essentially different?

To observers, refugees crossing an international border looks like a very big step. The government of the new territory they are in becomes aware of them for the first time, as their arrival has implications for rights and resources, and might create social and political unease. By crossing the border, the refugees become visible for the first time in the realm of international law.

But in terms of what refugees themselves are experiencing at the border, it might not feel like such a big deal. Refugees often lose their rights, culture and normal life a long time before they reach the border. State protection failed them well before they got there. Human rights to family life, freedom from degrading treatment and so forth have frequently been compromised, if not worse. Some may never have had a vote. And the culture and society they are leaving behind very possibly tolerated and even encouraged their persecution and tried to destroy their identity.

Ordinary life changed in substantial ways a while earlier, when people had to start being careful what they said in public, or the child first moved desk to stop the boy next to her kicking her. If there is a moment when you become a refugee, it is some time before that moment at the border. The border is one more set of changes in a long series of moves and changes.

It could be that moment of the first move that defines a refugee. Not the act of moving itself, but the reason for the move.

A move because if you don't move, you will be harmed – physically or in other ways. You have to move because you have to get out of danger and out of the reach of people abusing their power.

You have to move when there is nothing you can do to avoid the abuse, nothing you or a whole group of people like you can do to prevent or resist or stop them. They have the keys and the weapons, and people will let them get away with it. They have the power and they are in control, doing what they want to do. No one and nothing is going to protect you or can be trusted to stop the harm. The only power you have remaining is to walk away. You lose a lot by leaving, but you might lose more if you stay.

Therefore, the move is not just for safety. It is to regain at least some control in your life. Even though someone in search of refuge starts off with very limited control over what happens next.

But what if you are unable to walk away? They have too much power over you, or you would lose too much – your children perhaps, everything you know and have lived and worked for. Maybe you can't walk away because you have nowhere to go or the alternatives seem as bad as staying. Perhaps you are working on a plan, saving money, trying to contact friends, but are still stuck for now, powerless and without protection.

Which means the critical point is not when you leave, but when you *need* to leave.

That is when you become 'a refugee'.

Because you need refuge even if you haven't gone looking for it. You *need* to go somewhere else if you are to take back control of your life, from people who are abusing their power. You could be a refugee when you are still running your own business or cooking in your own kitchen.

Risk is a factor, too. Not just actual harm, but well-founded fear of harm from abuse. Any time there is nowhere to go. Any time protection is lacking. Maybe everything is fine for now, but getting worse. Or it could get worse and you wouldn't be able to stop it. If you could get away now, you would avoid the worst that might happen.

I don't think any of us can be completely sure this will never happen to us.

I don't want to be a refugee

I don't want to be a refugee. Ever.

I never want to be powerless, with no control over my life and my family's safety and wellbeing.

I live in a country where, for now, things are pretty much OK (for me) and I am in control of my life. If there was a problem, I would know where to turn. UK systems are far from perfect, and British society has some nasty streaks. On the other hand, there are strong movements of people who believe in inclusion and we have checks and balances on the powerful.

So I'm OK for now.

I am OK because I benefit from generations of people who have fought, sometimes literally, for the rights and protections I have. Over centuries, committed political and social activists and reformers have managed to build democratic and legal systems in the face of great opposition. These campaigners have pushed into place protections for the public, working people, women and men in all their diversity. The Human Rights Act 1998, the Equality Act 2010 and the fact that we are signatories to the Refugee Convention are because of them. And don't underestimate the achievement of laws protecting children, disabled people, people needing health and mental health care.

The great-great-grandchildren of their opponents are still part of UK society. We have constant reverses; exceptions are written into law that undermine equality, and other provisions have been downgraded. There are endless attempts to undermine human rights. Legal Aid has been stripped away. Ill-thought-through policies ignore diversity and cause injustice. Many people living in the UK would remove our rights to protection tomorrow.

At the local level, hands-on workers and activists inherit and develop knowledge, practice, structures and spaces that offer people security. It isn't only

community law centres, housing associations or specialist refugee networks. Protection comes in the form of coffee mornings, work experience placements, an open door. Hands-on workers are not peripheral to a safe society: they are the protectors. We are an integral part of effective checks and balances on government in this country.

Interaction at the local level is where real life is lived and mass attitudes are formed. Organisations don't grow knowledge and change perceptions – you do. At present, inclusive social attitudes and informed debate in the UK are stronger than the nasty streaks. Diverse voices can just about be heard.

But it isn't only the malicious who are dangerous. Those people and organisations who 'don't do...' deny real needs and reject diversity. They close down space. They take away your power to choose and decide for yourself. This is also agency, but not for a safer society.

What we certainly don't have is some kind of magic force field that will just always be there, one that means it could never happen here. State-sanctioned persecution, civil wars, slavery and abuse of power have happened throughout Britain's history. Britain is a diverse nation and some people are stronger and better protected than others. Discrimination and inequality are part of daily life for many UK residents. And no one is 100 per cent safe.

We must always be afraid that abuse and persecution will happen again. We all have a part in preventing it, including the newest members of British society. Refugees must also use their voices and agency for a safe society, and be part of our democracy. We must learn from their experiences in a creative process that will make us all safer.

A little paranoia doesn't hurt.

Acronyms

Acronyms that are the names of organisations are in Appendix A.

Acronyms are not included if the full expression is used throughout the text, even if the acronym is given once for reference because it is likely the reader will come across it elsewhere in their working life.

A&E	Accident and Emergency Department (NHS)
ARC	Application Registration Card – given to asylum seekers as an identity card
CCG	Clinical Commissioning Group – local decision-making body contracting NHS services
EAL	English as an Additional Language (children)
ECM	Equality characteristic monitoring
EIA	Equality Impact Assessment
ESOL	English for Speakers of Other Languages (adults)
GCSE	General Certificate of Secondary Education – examination taken at age 16
GP	General practitioner – also known as a family doctor (NHS)
HE	Higher Education
NASS	National Asylum Support Service – see Appendix A
NHS	National Health Service
NRPF	No Recourse to Public Funds – also referred to as 'No Recourse'
PSED	Public Sector Equality Duty – in the Equality Act 2010
PTSD	Post-traumatic stress disorder
s17	Section 17 of the Children's Act 1989 – refers to care for children in need (Chapter 11)
s20	Section 20 of the Children's Act 1989 – refers to looked after children (Chapter 11)
s4	'Section 4', refers to NASS accommodation and subsistence support to some refused asylum seekers
UASC-Leave	Unaccompanied Asylum-Seeking Child Leave to Remain
UCSA	Unaccompanied child, seeking asylum
UK	United Kingdom of Great Britain and Northern Ireland

Glossary

This glossary includes words, terms and 'shorthands' that are used in more than one chapter and are not in widespread use outside refugee support work.

'Shorthands' are words or short expressions used in a specific way for this book. Although these expressions are used by some practitioners in direct discussions, they are not technical terms and might not be in widespread use. They should not be used in correspondence or formal exchanges.

This is not a legal book, and many terms are defined in pragmatic ways suitable for local, hands-on practitioners, activists and volunteers who are supporting refugees in welfare, social, health, wellbeing, learning and development. These definitions are not suitable for legal, immigration cases or detailed case work such as housing appeals. You must not give immigration advice if you are not licensed to do so (see Box 3.3).

If you want further explanation, you can find fuller discussions in the main text, using the Index.

Access	Routes and methods people have to follow to get or use resources and services, involving the notions of: pre-gate – before people know a service exists; gate – proving eligibility to be considered; queue – waiting and putting a case for the kind of resources and services needed; encounter – face-to-face or other direct interaction between the person seeking resources and the people who control them (Box 5.1).
Asylum seeker	Legal term, summarised as someone who has asked to stay in Britain on the grounds that if she or he goes 'home', she or he will be in danger, and who is still waiting for a final answer (Box 3.11).
Characteristics	Features of a person or their life, such as being right-handed. Nine characteristics that cannot be changed by the person (e.g. sexual orientation) and are known to be used as an excuse for discriminatory treatment (e.g. insults or refusing a service) are listed as 'protected characteristics' by the Equality Act 2010, making it illegal to discriminate against people because of any of these nine characteristics (Box 4.4).
Children's centre	A place where multiple services are provided in a pleasant and informal environment to babies and children under five and their families.

Convention refugee   Shorthand used in this book for a person who has status under the International Convention on the Rights of Refugees 1951 (Boxes 3.4, 3.11).

Country of origin   The country where a person was ordinarily living and where they had rights as a national, usually from birth, but left because of danger or persecution.

Detention   Held or detained in secure premises, for new arrivals, asylum seekers and refused asylum seekers, especially if they are due to be deported. It is officially not prison, so detainees are allowed phone calls, their own clothes, etc.

Direct discrimination   See *Discrimination*

Discretion   The ability to choose to do more or to do less.

Discretionary Leave to Remain   See *Refugee with Leave*

Discrimination   Treating people less favourably or in a way that disadvantages them, because of a characteristic they share with a group of other people (e.g. their ethnicity, sex or sexual orientation) where there is no objective or justifiable reason for doing so. Discrimination can be direct (roughly speaking, deliberate), indirect (incidental – e.g. a side effect of a decision); 'positive' (but illegal) aiming to boost a group that is seen as disadvantaged; or take other forms (Box 4.7).

Eligibility   Being legitimately entitled to a resource or service according to criteria and policies set by others – usually requires evidence.

Encounter   See *Access*

Equality   Having the same rights and being treated equally well, with equally good outcomes, regardless of a person or group/ population of people's different or shared characteristics.

Equality characteristic monitoring (ECM)   See *Public Sector Equality Duty*

Equality Duty   See *Public Sector Equality Duty*

Equality Evidence Review   See *Public Sector Equality Duty*

Equality Impact Assessment (EIA)   See *Public Sector Equality Duty*

Equality Objectives   See *Public Sector Equality Duty*

Failed asylum seeker   See *Refused asylum seeker*

Gate   See *Access*

Health visitor   Specialist nurse providing holistic support to individuals and families, including clinical and social work elements, usually 'in the community' and involving outreach and home visits.

Home country   See *Country of origin*

Home Office   Government department responsible for managing immigration into the UK.

Human rights	Individual protections for a safe and decent life, laid out in the Human Rights Act 1998, includes Article 2 Right to life, Article 3 Freedom from inhuman and degrading treatment/torture, Article 8 Right to family life
Humanitarian Protection Status	See *Refugee with Leave*
Immigration Bail	Conditions that asylum seekers must comply with or be detained, includes restrictions on activities, affects final and other support.
Indefinite Leave to Remain	See *Refugee with Leave*
Indirect discrimination	See *Discrimination*
Leave	Shorthand used in this book for Leave to Remain, a catch-all for several forms of permission to stay in the UK granted by the Home Office.
Local connection	Having attachments and investments in a local area that justifies having support from the local authority, using local taxpayers' money, usually based on residency, family, employment.
Migrant	Any person who has moved from one country to another; includes refugees, but also tourists, students, people with work permits, spousal visas, etc.
Mitigating action	See *Positive action*
National Asylum Support Service (NASS)	Service that handles accommodation and money for subsistence for asylum seekers and refused asylum seekers, part of the Home Office but working via prime and sub-contractors.
Naturalisation	Process of a person becoming a British national.
Negative decision	Refusal of a request for asylum. See *Refused asylum seeker*
No Recourse to Public Funds (NRPF)	Having NRPF means not being allowed to make use of resources or services that originate from tax money. A person with NRPF can still use several state-funded services if and only if it is specified that they can or if the services, such as parks, are open access and anyone can use them without evidence of being entitled.
'One plus One' principle	'Each time you refer a refugee to a refugee specialist, project or group, you also refer her or him to at least one other non-refugee specialist, project or group.'
Ordinarily resident	Someone who has lived in an area for a length of time, or who has just arrived but will be living there for the foreseeable future.
Overstayer	Migrant whose permission to be in the UK has run out but she or he is still here.

Positive action	Additional support, activities, resources or services for a group of people who are disadvantaged compared with the wider population, perhaps because of earlier discrimination, or other circumstances, justified from sound, objective evidence. *Mitigating action* is similar but taken to prevent disadvantages being caused in future by changes or decisions being made today.
Positive decision	A grant of Leave to Remain in the UK having requested asylum; may be permanent or fixed-term.
Positive discrimination	See *Discrimination*
Post-traumatic stress disorder (PTSD)	A condition of mental ill health, where someone who has suffered or witnessed trauma, such as injury, extreme fear, near death or witnessed death, is caused ongoing severe distress which may have a range of symptoms and affects their ability to function in everyday life.
Pre-gate	See *Access*
Protected characteristics	See *Characteristics*
Public authority	Broadly speaking, any state body that has powers given to it by law and/or operates with taxpayers' money – so councils, police, NHS, most schools, etc. are public authorities. Also agents of that body that work to deliver services and resources on its behalf, which includes contractors and charities with grants or commission to deliver services (see Box 4.12).
Public Sector Equality Duty (PSED)	All public authorities are bound by the duty, that they must pay 'due regard' to equality in all their work, and proactively work to eliminate discrimination, advance equality of opportunity, foster good relations. They have a number of procedures to follow and documents they must produce and make public, which they may call by different names but include: Equality Evidence Review, Equality Objectives, Equality Impact Assessments, Annual Report on the Equality Duty, Equality Characteristic Monitoring. See Chapters 4 and 7.
Queue	See *Access*
Reasonable adjustment	Obligation to take sensible and manageable steps to enable people to live, act and work equally with others.
Reflexivity	Change in behaviours and action, including how other bodies or people are seen and treated, simply through having a new experience that expands awareness.
Refugee	Shorthand, a subjective definition used throughout this book based on people's past and present experiences: 'Any person who feels she or he has sought refuge from persecution, in the UK' (Box 3.11).

Refugee with Leave   Shorthand used in this book especially in relation to
                          entitlements; a person who has claimed asylum in the UK and
                          been given some form of 'Leave to Remain', meaning permission
                          to stay in the country that gives similar rights to resident British
                          nationals (Box 3.11).

Refused asylum seeker Legal term, summarised as 'people who have asked for asylum
                          and received a negative decision'; broadly, the UK government
                          will not give them refuge and expects them to leave the country.

Removal centre   See *Detention*

Slavery   See *Trafficking*

Smuggling   Also called people smuggling – moving people who want help
                          to cross border; often secret, illegal, profit-making. But smugglers
                          are also at times individuals helping people escape real danger, at
                          serious risk to themselves.

Status   A person's immigration situation; how they are defined by the
                          Home Office.

Sure Start centre   See *Children's centre*

Trafficking   Trafficking is a specific crime in international law (and different
                          to smuggling). Traffickers control people; they buy and sell and
                          own them. They move people within countries and also across
                          borders to exploit them for labour, sex, benefits fraud, body parts
                          or 'modern slavery'.

Unaccompanied   Here, used in relation to a child, meaning without any adult who
                          is responsible for their welfare, safeguarding and development.
                          Unaccompanied children are usually 'looked after' by the local
                          authority (Chapter 11).

Unaccompanied   Permission for a young person under 18 who has been refused
Asylum-Seeking Child asylum to remain in the UK until they are 18. It ends when they
Leave (UASC-Leave)   are 17.5 years old and they may be detained pending removal.

Undocumented   Someone who does not have papers that show they are legally
                          entitled to remain in the UK. It doesn't mean they are necessarily
                          illegally here.

Voluntary Assisted   Governmental scheme to remove people with their consent,
Return   providing them with a limited amount of support for the journey
                          and reintegration to their country of origin only.

Appendix A

Organisations and Sources – By Theme

This list provides sources of expertise for support, knowledge and networking. It is not intended to be a complete list but to give you a starting point when you are looking for advice or projects. It includes large and smaller specialists and other relevant organisations, plus examples of the kinds of local organisations you would expect to find when you network in your region. Organisations supporting or serving children are grouped together at the end of the Appendix.

An online search will give you up-to-date contacts, projects and details of eligibility. Please remember how busy people are, and do your own research before you ring!

Local level organisations and networks
Statutory and democratic bodies
COUNCIL TEAMS AND SERVICES:
Social work departments rarely have a specialist asylum/refugee team but will probably have:

Vulnerable adults teams – disabled asylum seekers and refugees including those with mental health difficulties.

Looked after children (LAC)/LAC Transition teams – unaccompanied asylum-seeking children.

Domestic violence/violence against women and girls (VAWG) teams – including trafficking, forced marriage.

Housing and homelessness –may include Syrian Vulnerable Persons Resettlement support teams.

Public Health is usually responsible for the Joint Strategic Needs Analysis and has statistical data. They work on relevant issues such as TB and HIV, and often manage Health Visiting teams. Environmental Health will investigate housing and employment including asylum accommodation contracted by NASS.

Other council teams: Ask if you have a Stronger/ Safer/ Cohesive Communities, Integration team or carers' support teams. A few local authorities have in-house interpreting services where there can be a reservoir of expertise.

Council services across your area: Key points –libraries, children's, Sure Start, Cymorth Centres, primary schools.

DEMOCRATIC STRUCTURES:
The local Members of Parliament (MPs) (www.parliament.uk/mps-lords-and-offices/mps) and Assembly Members (AMs), nearby MPs/ AMs who have taken up refugee causes in the past; individual local councillors and Party groups (eg. Labour group, Liberal Democrat group, Conservative group); metropolitan authorities/Mayor's teams tackling integration/diversity, migration, equality and anti-hate-crime, health equality, homelessness, women and girls.

Voluntary, community and faith organisations
Refugees' (and other migrants') own community organisations (RCO or MRCO).

Local refugee support groups e.g. Refugee Support, Refugees Welcome (often set up where there is a Syrian Vulnerable Persons Resettlement scheme), City of Sanctuary/Places of Sanctuary, Student Action for Refugees (STAR). Thanks to REAP (West London) for supporting this book.

Citizens Advice/Citizens Advice Bureau (CAB), Community Law Centres and other community-based advice services, sometime hosted or run by the local authority.

Equality/identity-based bodies: women's centres, disability groups and Independent Living Centres, mental health e.g. local Mind/Support in Mind/ Inspire (NI).

Faith and inter-faith networks, local Age UK/Age Concern, carers support organisations, LGBT networks, a very few equality/race equality centres survive.

Council/Association/Alliances of Voluntary Services and/or Community Empowerment Networks or similar, where they still exist.

Activist bodies, e.g. Amnesty International, 38 Degrees, United Nations groups, groups focussed on a specific country for cultural reasons or to provide support, e.g. Syrian support groups. Local Union branches, e.g. Unison.

Local businesses that serve specific ethnic populations, e.g. food, clothing, cafés.

Churches, mosques, gurdhwaras, synagogues and other local faith bodies.

National organisations and networks
Refugee specialists
NATIONAL SPECIALISTS:
Refugee Council, Scottish Refugee Council, Welsh Refugee Council, Refugee Action. Others include Freedom from Torture (Manchester, Birmingham,

Newcastle, London, Glasgow), Right to Remain, STAR-Network, Refugee Support Network, Jewish Council for Racial Equality (JCORE). Also Home Office (NB Asylum Screening Unit, Lunar House, Croydon, and Further Submissions Unit, Liverpool).

SMALLER ORGANISATIONS WITH NATIONAL SIGNIFICANCE:
Bail for Immigration Detainees (BID), Yarl's Wood Befrienders, City of Sanctuary, Refugee Week, Migrant Help (including Trafficking – see also Anti-Slavery Commissioner), St Ethelburga's Centre for Reconciliation and Peace, UK Lesbian and Gay Immigration Group (UKLGIG), Holocaust Memorial Day Trust, Writers in Exile, British Museum, The Imperial War Museum and Jewish Museum.

SEEKING IMMIGRATION/ LEGAL ADVICE/ IMMIGRATION SOLICITORS:
Immigration Law Practitioners' Association (ILPA), Office of the Immigration Services Commissioner (OISC), Refugee Legal Fund, or the Law Society of England and Wales, Scotland or Northern Ireland.

REFUGEE-FOCUSSED 'THINK TANKS', POLICY AND ACADEMIC BODIES:
Queen Elizabeth House (known as QEH) Oxford. Many universities have small departments or teams specialising in refugee issues, e.g. London South Bank University, University of Sussex (Law) SOGICA and University of Aberdeen. Individual academics may have specialist research interests. See also All-Party Parliamentary Groups (APPGs).

Democratic engagement: Operation Black Vote and Parliamentary schemes.

ONLINE NETWORKS:
You usually need to contact the host or organisers (shown in brackets) to be invited to join more specialist networks.

ASAN (Asylum Seeker Appeals Network): Regarding case work around entitlements and support for asylum seekers (Asylum Support Appeals Project).

Disabled Refugees: Rights and Campaigns (HEAR Equality and Human Rights Network).

Frontline Network: Mostly homelessness but wider issues.

Homeless Link: Destitution, homelessness.

NRPF Network (No Recourse to Public Funds) mostly local authority but open to all.

Refugee Support: Projects (London-centric), (Refugee Council).

Women's Asylum Charter: Campaigning for gender-aware recognition of asylum-seeking women's realities (Asylum Aid).

Directly related organisations (not specific to refugees)
ADVICE AND LEGAL:
Citizens Advice, Law Centres Federation (LCF), Public Law Project, Charity Commission.

EQUALITY, ANTI-DISCRIMINATION AND IDENTIFY-BASED GROUPS:
Equality Policy: Equality and Human Rights Commission (EHRC), Equality and Diversity Forum, National Equality Partnership reports (NEP has ended). Also The Kings Fund, Runnymede Trust, Joseph Rowntree Foundation, British Future, Council of Midwives, brap (Birmingham), Race on the Agenda (RoTA), Women's Resource Centre, Age UK, Stonewall.

Regional and national inter-faith networks: Faith Forum, Council of Christians and Jews,

Unions, e.g. Unison and especially Union officials can be well connected in relevant fields.

OTHER RELATED SPECIALISTS:
(See further contacts by theme below.) British Institute of Human Rights (BIHR), Amnesty International.

Housing, homelessness, money, food and essential goods
Accommodation
NATIONAL SPECIALISTS:
Homeless and at risk of or already street sleeping:
Access to practical support: Homeless Link, Shelter Helpline, Combined Homelessness and Information Network (CHAIN), also Streetlink service.

Expertise: Frontline Network, NRPF Network, Housing Associations' Charitable Trust (HACT).

Housing entitlements, rights, advice and access for asylum seekers:Asylum Support Appeals Project (ASAP), Refugee Action plus CAB, LCF. National Asylum Support Service (NASS) – Home Office/ Government, accessed via Migrant Helpline.

Detention:
BID, Free Movement, also expertise from Association of Visitors to Immigration Detainees (AVID), Set Her Free Campaign (Women for Refugee Women).

Training for staff:
ASAP (also Factsheets), Shelter.

LOCAL HOUSING AND SUPPORT PROVIDERS:
Some advice and assistance from local authority homelessness teams but note there will be local variations in waiting lists, priorities, criteria, etc.

Housing Associations, e.g. ARHAG, YMCA, often regional or local, e.g. Birmingham HOPE. Night shelters: see Shelter. There may be very small specialist refugee housing agencies, e.g. Micro Rainbow (LGBT – two properties in London).

Local Home Office/NASS accommodation for asylum seekers is sub-contracted to agencies who often sub-contract further to private landlords. To find your local provider agency, ask directly at the accommodation or contact ASAP.

EXAMPLES OF OTHER VCS ORGANISATIONS AND PROJECTS:
Voluntary Hosting Schemes: Refugees at Home, Housing Justice, Rooms for Refugees (Refugee Council), Room for Refugees (Glasgow).

Rent Deposit/Bond Schemes e.g. Refugee Council, Wycombe Refugee Partnership, various Refugee Welcomes.

Holistic case-workers connected with specialist organisations: Freedom from Torture, Refugee Council's Therapeutic Case Work Team.

ADVOCACY:
Advice for Renters, CAB, Shelter, Crisis.

CAMPAIGNS:
28 Days Campaign (Refugee Council), Participation and Practice of Rights Project (Belfast). Also No Second Night Out.

Money and essentials

NATIONAL SPECIALISTS:
Advice on Entitlements and Rights: CAB, LCF, NASS/Migrant Helpline, Refugee Action, Refugee Council, ASAP, Frontline Network, NRPF Network, Joseph Rowntree Foundation, on poverty.

Money and debt: National Debtline (Citizens Advice), Money Advice Service. Also Credit Unions (see Association of British Credit Unions).

LOCAL SUBSISTENCE AND ESSENTIAL PROVISIONS
(OFTEN NOT REFUGEE SPECIALISTS):
Food: Foodbanks/free food, find via The Trussell Trust. Ask Gurdwaras, churches at Harvest Festival (late September) and Christmas, Mosques during Ramadan/Eid. Drop-ins, e.g. New North London Synagogue Asylum Drop In. Soup runs/soup kitchens by homeless and night shelter bodies and Gurdwaras, Salvation Army, some local YMCAs.

Clothing banks/charity shops, toy libraries, furniture-, bicycle-, IT-recycling projects. Municipal dump 'reuse' shops. Try British Heart Foundation, YMCA shops, Sue Ryder, local 'upcycling' projects.

Libraries, Children's Centres, Women's Centres.

CAMPAIGNS:
Still Human – Still Here, Asylum Matters (City of Sanctuary).

FUNDERS:
Vicars' Relief Fund, NCVO- 'Funding Central' for small organisations, 'GrantsforIndividuals' (both by subscription).

Physical, mental and emotional health and disability
Physical health
NATIONAL SPECIALISTS:
Health policy, rights and entitlements: NHS England, NHS Scotland, NHS Wales, NHS NI, Public Health England, Healthwatch England (access and patient rights and voice), National Institute for Health and Care Excellence (previously 'Clinical' Excellence; NICE), Kings Fund (social policy and health), Doctors of the World (access and rights), NRPF Network, ASAP, NHS Choices (online), NHS 111, Maternity Action, Royal College of Midwives, British Medical Association (BMA), Forward (Anti-FGM).

LOCAL HEALTH SERVICES AND PROVIDERS:
Available across the UK (www.nhs.uk): As above plus:

GP (General Practitioner)/Family Doctor Practices/Surgeries – anyone can register. It is very important to register. Community pharmacies, Health Visiting, community midwives; immunisation, safeguarding, TB teams. Primary care in clinics and delivered through schools. NHS dentists, Healthwatch in each local authority area.

NHS Minor Injuries Units, Urgent Treatment Centres, Accident and Emergency (A&E).

NHS Clinical Commissioning Groups (CCGs) – the body that commissions and oversees quality of health services delivered by hospitals, GPs and other providers. NHS England Customer Contact Centre.

Basic clinical assessment and referral is sometimes provided through (non-medical) drop-in sessions (see Food), street/homelessness outreach projects, also e.g. (medical) Doctors of the World/Project London walk-in clinic (see -also Praxis).

EXAMPLES OF OTHER VCS ORGANISATIONS AND PROJECTS:
Advocacy:

Nudge: GP Practice Manager > Lead GP > the local Healthwatch. Poke: Patient Advice and Liaison Services (PALS) > local CCG > Doctors of the World. Slap: complaints processes > NHSEngland > Care Quality Commission > local MP.

Campaigns:

Project London (Doctors of the World), Docs not Cops, Maternity Alliance, BMA is also active.

Local CCG or 'providers' may commission or sub-contract activities and services through smaller, e.g. non-clinical, local charities and community groups running engagement or communication/self-care/health education activities/active living sessions or projects.

Try contacting the Engagement and Equality team, Commissioners for Mental Health and/or Young People Safeguarding Nursing lead (also Sexual Exploitation, FGM).

Maternity Action, Age UK.

Mental health

NATIONAL SPECIALISTS:

As Physical Health, plus: information from NHS Choices, Mind online, NICE (offers clinical guidance on PTSD). Rethink, for anyone affected by mental ill health.

Survivors of violence, abuse, torture and sexual violence: Freedom from Torture, Helen Bamber Foundation. Expertise and training: Freedom from Torture; Bristol University.

Bereavement: Bereavement Trust, Cruse Bereavement Care, Mind.

Counselling, befriending, talking: British Association for Counselling and Psychotherapy and sister website itsgoodtotalk.org.uk for local practitioners. Samaritans, Refugee Council Therapeutic Services.

Available across the UK locally, mental health services and providers: NHS mental health care and treatment: GP practices, Community Mental Health Teams, A&E if actively life-threatening.

EXAMPLES OF OTHER VCS ORGANISATIONS AND PROJECTS:

Refugee specialist: (Examples in South East) Room to Heal, Manor Gardens Centre, Refugee Resource Therapeutic Services Oxford. Also small self-help, self-run groups. Support services offered within housing associations or the women's refuge movement, e.g. Ashiana.

(National) Richmond Fellowship, Richmond Fellowship Scotland.

CAMPAIGNS:
HEAR, Mental Health Foundation Scotland, Asylum Aid/ Women's Asylum Charter group.

Disabled refugees

NATIONAL SPECIALISTS:
Freedom from Torture: physical and mental health disabilities resulting from torture.

Rights and Entitlements: Terrence Higgins Trust (HIV/ AIDS), Scope, National Survivor User Network, Disability Law Service: Right to Community Care Assessments/ Care Act 2014 – Disability Law Service, CAB, HEAR and contact individual local authorities; Displaced People in Action (Wales). Also Department for Work and Pensions (DWP) support for disabled people in work/ employers through 'Access to Work'.

Information/ campaigns: Refugee Action, Asylum Aid, EHRC, earlier work by Joseph Rowntree Foundation.

Deaf refugees/ deafness/ Deaf rights: City Lit (London) – Centre for Deaf Education;Manchester University – Social Research with Deaf People team; Deaf Plus; British Deaf Association; Age UK for older people becoming deaf.

LOCAL SERVICES AND PROVIDERS:
Available across the UK: Refugees' own community organisations and deaf and disabled people's organisations in some cases; local independent living centres where they remain; carers' charities.

Learning, employability and employment
Non-formal learning

NATIONAL SPECIALISTS:
Non-formal English programmes and approaches: Faith Action/ Creative English, Speaking English with Confidence, Talk English Together, BBC Learning English team.

Online Resources: BBC online and many others – choose carefully.

LOCAL OPPORTUNITIES (THERE MAY BE ELIGIBILITY CONDITIONS):
Library activities: e.g. literacy activities, classes, writers groups, even children's story time for parents too. Online access – librarians will assist people to access courses and resources: provide local and authority-wide information about groups, classes, courses and activities.

Children's centres, including child development and health, e.g. weaning, parenting courses, English, health education, Job Clubs. Primary schools for

parents, e.g. Stay and Play, school activities like events, parent information evenings, there might be 'community' activities for parents, even English groups.

Charities, faith bodies, equality and identity and refugee self-help groups, e.g. Tamil community groups; Women's Centre, e.g. self-esteem courses, arts and crafts, English. Community centres and church halls are a venue for many activities, though they don't necessarily run them directly – check the notice boards rather than online.

Outreach, e.g. Health Improvement; talks from health outreach staff, NHS Right Care Right Place, cancer screening, diabetes, etc.; Citizens Advice outreach trainings – usually delivered to existing groups (e.g. saving money, consumer rights); Volunteer bureaux might offer e.g. safeguarding, equality and diversity, book-keeping; housing associations often provide training and employability as part of their support packages, e.g. Crisis Skylight, Glasgow Housing Association.

Women's Institute, Women's Guild, University of the Third Age (U3A), Workers Educational Association, The Citizens Trust, Groundwork.

Teacher training centres and colleges often need opportunities for teachers to gain experience; they might provide free classes taught by trainees.

FUNDERS:
The People's Health Trust, Post Code Lottery, Awards for All (Big Lottery), local authority small grant schemes and councillors discretionary funds, Local Wellbeing structures. European Social Fund has been a significant funder of refugee employability up to 2019.

Formal learning including employability and employment (for children and young people see next section)

NATIONAL:
The Open University has free introductory to advance modules available online.

'Life in the UK' Government reference resources and commercial and some voluntary sector courses.

Professional Bodies' 'continuing professional development'; also may support requalifying, e.g. midwifery, engineering.

Evidence of qualifications and skills: UK National Recognition Information Centre (NARIC). Evidence of level of English: contact local colleges.

Supporting refugees into and in employment, including requalification: Refugee Council/Refugees into Jobs/Scottish Refugee Council, The Council for At-Risk Academics (CARA), General Medical Council (doctors), Transitions (engineering), The Entrepreneurial Refugee Network (TERN) (see also Chaigaram, StarBucks). Refugee Career Advisers Network (RCAN), contact via ELATT.org.uk, Refugee Advice and Guidance Unit RAGU at London Metropolitan University – London-based), Refugee Employment Network.

LOCAL OPPORTUNITIES (THERE MAY BE ELIGIBILITY CONDITIONS):
Education: Colleges of Further Education (FE); Colleges of Higher Education and education and employability programmes including placements and apprenticeships, student volunteering programmes. Increasing numbers of universities are offering scholarships (see STAR website for partial list).

Employment: Job Centre Plus including 'Job Coaches', NHSJobs.nhs.net, children's centres sometimes run job clubs. Apprenticeships can be accessed via colleges and some commercial brokers or directly through the potential employer if they are already committed to apprenticeships.

Volunteering: Volunteer Bureaux – ask libraries for contacts. Local authorities may run brokerage schemes. Schools can provide opportunities to parents and carers. Hospitals and CAB usually require a one- to two-year commitment. Ask at Food Banks directly.

ADVOCACY:
Education – poke: contact College Director. Slap: Ofsted, Education Scotland, ETI NI, Estyn Wales.

Employment and case work – CAB, Unions, LCF members may have employment specialists. Clarity on rights from Advisory, Conciliation and Arbitration Service (ACAS).

CAMPAIGNS:
Education – Action for ESOL, National Literacy Trust, Plain English Campaign. Right to Work – Refugee Council, Trades Union Congress, Movement of Asylum Seekers Ireland. Wage poverty – Living Wage Foundation, Joseph Rowntree Foundation.

Children and young people (CYP) asylum seekers and refugees (ASR)

In addition to services mentioned above:

NATIONAL:
Children's Panel Advisory Committee/Service, c/o Refugee Council; Scottish Guardianship Service; Refugee and Migrants' Children's Consortium (previously RCC) – a collaboration of several British charities and other organisations; Every Child Protected Against Trafficking (ECPAT).

CYP specialists supporting ASR: Children England, Barnado's, The Children's Society, Save the Children Fund, Aberlour Child Care Trust, Child Poverty Action Group (CPAG), Action for Children, Children in Need.

Legal support and lobbying for CYP: British Red Cross, International Organisation for Migration, Coram Children's Law Centre (CCLC), Just for Kidz Law.

Age Assessment: ADCS Association of Directors of Children's Services.

Family reunion: (International) Red Cross/ Red Crescent, Children and Families across Borders (CFAB), UNHCR.

Safeguarding: Safe Network, Children England, NSPCC, ChildLine, CASPAR (free weekly Safeguarding Bulletin). Also e.g. Victoria Climbie Foundation 'vcf.uk'.

Housing and accommodation: Foyers, Housing Associations, local authority responsibilities, e.g. P3, YMCA, Stonham, Centrepoint. See also Accommodation.

Fostering and Care: CoramBAAF (Adoption and Fostering Academy), Chrysalis (Sheffield). Local authorities' own connections.

Money for essentials: advice/case work ASAP/ASAN, CCLC, Educational Trusts' Forum (care-leavers).

Health, emotional and mental health (EMH) and disability: Baobab Centre for Young Survivors in Exile (London); Young Minds.

ADVOCACY:
Strategic Legal Fund (fund test cases), Local Safeguarding Children Board, Ofsted. Authors – Jill Rutter, Angelina Jalonen and Paul Cilia La Corte (JKP).

CAMPAIGNS:
Project for the Registration of Children as British Citizens; campaigns for family reunion (Refugee Action, UNICEF); Campaign for Equal Access (to university) (STAR/National Union of Students); Let Us Learn (c/o Just for Kidz Law).

Local opportunities (may have eligibility criteria):
As above, plus: Family Information Services, 'SEN offer' for your local authority.

Safeguarding: Local Safeguarding Children Board – local authority with NHS/CCG.

Housing, money and essentials: e.g. Haven (Hull).

Physical health, EMH, disability: children's centres, sports and youth clubs and centres.

Learning and Employability: children's centres/Sure Start centres, schools, colleges of FE and HE (especially ESOL departments), universities, apprenticeships.

CYP LGBT support groups: e.g. Mosaic.

Voluntary and community: sports, arts, National Citizen Service, Duke of Edinburgh, Princes Trust, Youth groups (e.g. Beavers, Cubs, Brownies, Scouts, Guides, Explorers, Woodcraft), other leagues including Armed forces cadets.

Examples of small organisations or projects: Young Roots, Salusbury World.

FUNDERS:

Children in Need, Reaching Communities, Tudor Trust, Paul Hamlyn Foundation, Jack Petchey Foundation. Look into 'First Give'. There are often local schemes for children or youth welfare and activities, including looked after children and care-leavers: ask your council, library or council/association of voluntary organisations.

Appendix B

Evidence and Documents Relevant
When Supporting Refugees

You might find it useful to look up images online.
See the Index for explanations and discussion about use.
Remember:

- Only ask to see documents if you need to.

- Don't keep copies unless you have to and then only with permission; keep them safe and shred when no longer needed.

- It is better to make a written and signed note that you have seen the documents and note key numbers and dates, and then only if you must.

- If you are returning documents, check the safest way with the refugee.

Refugees find it helpful if you can make them copies, and might ask you to verify that the copy you give them is of a genuine original. You must be certain the original is genuine before you agree to do this, but for bank statements, course certificates, etc. there is a fairly low risk. If they need certified copies of birth certificates, identity papers, etc., refer them to a solicitor.

If you are satisfied, mark the copy with a company stamp, sign and date it, and state that in your opinion it is a true copy. Add your full name, job title and contact details on the copy itself.

Former national and earlier personal documents

National passport	With their status stamp in it.
Birth certificates	This confirms name, date of birth, etc. and states details such as whether they have Leave to Remain and what kind, whether work is permitted, No Recourse, etc. The spouse of a refugee counts as a refugee, but it might not say so in their passport.
Marriage certificate	For self and children.
Spouse's documents	Passport, immigration status.

Immigration-related documents

ARC | Application Registration Card (often called 'ARC card' by users): photographic ID with status.

Aspen card | Debit and/or cash card that is charged with money from NASS. Very difficult to replace. Do not lose them.

BAIL 201 | Letter from the Home Office to an asylum seeker specifying conditions (e.g. no study, or regular reporting) that they must comply with to avoid being detained.

Decision letters | From the Home Office: give the person's actual status and date from which it comes into force, and sometimes detailed instructions on what they need to do next. They should read it carefully and keep it safe. They might want to make spare copies for safety.

Evidence of movements | Keep tickets and itineraries, especially for overseas travel, but any travel over a few days. They might be necessary for NASS and also in the long run for naturalisation as a UK national as the applicant must prove they have not travelled out of the country for too long a period or too often, and might need to give continuous proof of their location – for example, all addresses without gaps for several years if applying for certain jobs with security implications. Keep your own records of attendance for a decade or more.

Home Office number | Found on ARC and on letters from the Home Office.

NASS contract | Many people don't read the contract which is not in simple English, but it has important information in it such as what they should do if they need to be away from the accommodation for a period of time. If they break the contract, they will probably lose their financial support and accommodation.

NASS letters | NASS number, which is different to Home Office/asylum application numbers.

Refugee Travel Document | With their status stamp in it: an internationally recognised document they can use for international travel. It confirms name, date of birth, etc.

UK documentation

Bank account | See Chapter 8 on getting a bank account. Cards and statement can be used as ID for various uses. It is worth the trouble to get a bank account as soon as possible, as any bank account will probably prove useful in its own right or to help get credit ratings, etc. in future.

DBS certificate | Difficult to obtain for newer arrivals, but necessary if people volunteer or work with children or vulnerable adults. Refugees can get DBS checks from a couple of years after arriving in the UK, though they might not be accepted by the organisation/agency/employer if the checks are for a period under five years. DBS takes much longer if people have moved several times. They are free to do while someone is a volunteer. It is not good practice to keep copies of DBS papers, but you can note the name, date of birth, DBS number and dates if you need records to show your safeguarding is up to scratch or to complete a reference.

Disability	May be able to register with the local authority as disabled without examination or medical certification. Any medical letters or certificates from country of origin, Red Cross or UNHCR medics from transit, or from the UK might be useful for requesting care or reasonable adjustments. Some clinicians may charge for letters. A printed copy of a community care assessment is strong evidence.
NHS number/ GP registration/ HC2 cards	They do *not* need proof of address to register with a GP, but it helps. GP registration papers/letters and ARC/NASS together will be enough for them to get a HC1/HC2 certificate for free prescriptions.
NI number and card	Will only be issued when they receive Leave to Remain. If it does not arrive by post, chase via the Job Centre/Jobcentre Plus.

Other evidence and documentation

Evidence of address	If they don't have NASS accommodation, they might find it hard to get evidence of address as they don't have bills in their name, leases, mobiles are usually pay-as-you-go, etc. If their name is not on a lease, they can still ask landlords for a letter confirming they have the landlord's permission to stay there, but most landlords are reluctant.
	You can write and post a letter to the person on formal letterhead with your charity, company or other registration numbers so they have something. You can issue a membership card or volunteer identity card, and if yours is a charity, include the full name and Charity Commission registration number. Ideally, print with a photo, sign, laminate and provide with a lanyard with the organisation's name on. It might even help them get discounts, memberships, etc.
Library card	Gives access to free IT and numerous courses, and can be used as local ID and proof of living locally (e.g. at a sports centre). Usually needs proof of address. A letter from you to the library vouching that the person lives locally might be sufficient.
Ordinarily resident	They should try to get a local authority residents' card which brings many benefits; varies according to area.
Qualifications	National or British. As well as formal qualifications, refugees need and appreciate certificates of attendance at workshops and courses even if there was no qualification.
	Level of English will be required for some courses and jobs. As well as formal qualifications, informal evidence can sometimes be given by colleges or teachers through admissions procedures or for a small fee. A retired teacher might be willing to write a letter stating their assessment of a person's English.
Recognition/ references	Present a 'Notice of Special Effort', 'Recognition of Progress', 'Certificate of Volunteering', etc. to show appreciation and build up someone's portfolio to show course administrators or future employers. Write personal references and references describing participation and/or voluntary involvement in activities (see Box 10.9, Box 7.5).

DISCARD

References

Asylum Aid (2017) *Through Her Eyes: Enabling women's best evidence in UK asylum appeals.* Women's Asylum Appeals Project. Accessed on 05/07/2018 at www.asylumaid.org.uk/womens-project/throughhereyes

Asylum Aid (2018) *Women's Asylum Charter.* Accessed on 05/07/2018 at www.asylumaid.org.uk/womens-asylum-charter

EDF and REAP (2011) *Refugees, Migrants and the Equality Act 2010: A briefing for refugee and migrant community organisations.* Accessed on 05/07/2018 at www.edf.org.uk/wp-content/uploads/2011/06/EDF-Briefing_Community-Organisations_Web_draft-3.pdf

HEAR (2018) *A guide to the right to free and concessionary transport for disabled asylum seekers, refugees and reused applicants in the UK.* Accessed on 05/07/2018 at https://hearnetwork.files.wordpress.com/2016/10/rights-and-entitlements-of-disabled-asylum-seekers-refugees-and-refused-applicants.pdf

Joseph Rowntree Foundation (JRF) (2014) *Poverty and the cost of living.* Accessed on 05/07/2018 at www.jrf.org.uk/report/poverty-and-cost-living

REAP (2009) *We Don't Do Refugees – Refugees for Equalities Report.* Hard copy available from reap.org.uk

Refugee Council with Lisa Doyle (2014) *28 days later: Experiences of new refugees in the UK.* Accessed on 05/07/2018 at www.refugeecouncil.org.uk/assets/0003/1769/28_days_later.pdf

Refugee Council (2016) *The UKs role in the international refugee protection system.* Accessed on 05/07/2018 at www.refugeecouncil.org.uk/stats

Refugee Council (2017) *Children in the Asylum System – November 2017.* Accessed on 05/07/2018 at refugeecouncil.org.uk/stats

Refugee Council (2018) *Quarterly Asylum Statistics – May 2018.* Accessed on 22/07/2018 at www.refugeecouncil.org.uk/stats

Nayeri, D. (2017) 'The ungrateful refugee: "We have no debt to repay".' *The Guardian*, 4 April 2017. Accessed on 05/07/2018 at www.theguardian.com/world/2017/apr/04/dina-nayeri-ungrateful-refugee

WRC/REAP (2011) *One plus One: Supporting frontline organisations to work effectively with refugees.* Women's Resource Centre and National Equality Partnership; hard copies from reap.org.uk

Index

accessing support
  challenges to 84–5
  overview 83–4
  stages of 84–7
accommodation
  after Leave granted 136, 140–1, 143
  applying to NASS 154
  asylum seekers 139–40, 143
  children with families 220
  entitlements overview 58, 59, 59–60,
      136–7, 143
  homelessness 137
  immediate need for 137–9
  improving existing 142
  NRPF 136, 143
  private landlords 141
active agency 24–5, 93, 238–9
activities 101–4, 175
address, proof of 93
advocacy 120–2
'affording' refugees 32
Afghanistan 209
age disputes 216–7
agency, active 24–5, 93, 238–9
Albania 209
anonymity/confidentiality 98, 211
appeals 49
apprenticeships 199, 232
ARC card 46
Aspen cards 147
Asylum Aid 49, 68
asylum seekers
  appeals 49
  building a case 47
  children 216–8
  credibility 47
  decision made 48
  definition 45

detention 46, 136
entitlement to support 58–9
false asylum claims 55–6
fresh claims 49–50
initial claim 45–6
initial screening 46
licensed solicitors 47–8
notice to depart 50–1
'off the radar' 50–1
refused asylum seekers 49–51, 59
reporting 46
timescale 49

bail 58
bank accounts 147
benefits 31, 171
Bradford, John 28
building a case (asylum seekers) 47

Care Act (2014) 54, 169, 170
children
  accommodation 220
  age disputes 216–7
  asylum process for 216–8
  in care 218–9
  disabled 225–6
  education (overview) 227–8
  entitlement to support 59
  experiences before reaching UK 208–10
  financial rates for 221–2
  health services 221, 223–4
  mental health support 224–5
  new challenges for 213
  private fostering of 211
  rights under Children's Act (1989) 54,
      218–9
  safeguarding 210–2

children *cont.*
  statistics 214–6
  unaccompanied 213–4, 217, 218,
    222–3
  youth groups 232–3
  see also education; school
Children's Act (1989) 54, 218–9
China 209
citizenship application 53–4
comedy/satire 129
'community', making assumptions about 74
community care assessments 169–71
complaints, making 122–4
confidentiality 98, 211
'connectors' 104–5
Convention status 51–2, 60
credibility 47
culture
  changes due to refugees 31–2
  competence in British 91–2
cutbacks in refugee services 19–20, 30

DBS checks 198
deafness/hearing impairment 174
debt 145–6
decision letters 48–9
definitions of refugee
  asylum seekers 45
  experiences before reaching UK 34–6
  Home Office 44–54
  overview of 41–2, 61–2
  popular 55–7
  refugee with Leave to Remain 51–4,
    59–61
  subjective 42–4, 48–9
  used in book 16, 44
deportation, post-prison 56
destitution 134–5
detention 46, 136
direct discrimination 70–1
disability
  accessing mainstream benefits 171
  asylum seekers 173
  children 225–6
  community care assessments 169–71
  confusion around entitlement 173
  employment 196
  entitlements/access 169–73
  Equality Act definition 168

  hearing impairment 174
  Leave to Remain 173
  NRPF 173
  registering 171
  social model of 168
  sources of support 172
  statistical data 169
  travel/transport 172
discrimination
  direct 70–1
  in history 28
  indirect 71–2
  micro-aggressions 70
  see also Equality Act (2010)
dispersal 140
documents
  ARC card 46
  HC2 card 159
  importance of 90
  passport/travel 53, 60, 98, 186
  proof of address 93
donations of goods 150–1

EDF and REAP 81
education
  further/higher 230–1
  NARIC (National Academic Recognition
    Information Centre) 191
  overview 227–8
  pre-school/early years 228–9
  primary 229
  range of courses available 186–8
  secondary 229–30
  single-sex groups in 182–3
  training 179, 180–1, 232
  see also English (learning); school
employment
  apprenticeships 199, 232
  disabled people 196
  employability schemes 195
  employing a refugee 201–4
  evidence of entitlement to work 193
  joining professional bodies 195
  part-time contracts 203
  probation period 202
  reasonable goals for 179–80
  recruitment practices 200
  references for 194
  requalification schemes 194–5

self-employment 195–6, 203
supporting once in work 204–5
supporting refugees to gain 192–4,
    196–200
temporary contracts 202
work experience 199–200
zero hours contracts 203
engagement with refugees 88–9, 174–6
English (learning)
applying for courses 190–1
assessing level 107–8, 187–8
clarity of own English 108
cost of 189–90
course providers 189
duration of courses 188
eligibility for 180–1
formal 185–92
Grass Roots English Groups ('GREG')
    111–3
IELTS 187
non-formal 182–5, 232–4
ongoing support for 192
online courses 188
qualifications 187–8
range of courses available 186–8
SELT 187
TOEFL 187
see also education; school
entitlement decisions 57–8, 60–1
equality
differentiating between people 73–4
equality characteristic monitoring (ECM)
    76–7
improving 73–7
positive action 75–6
Public Sector Equality Duty (PSED)
    77–80, 126–7
reasonable adjustments 74–5
right to 23
Equality Act (2010)
on disability 168, 169
overview of 65–6
protected characteristics 67–9
Equality Impact Assessments (EIA) 128–9
Equality Objectives 127–8
Eritrea 209
ESOL see English (learning)
events/publicity 95–7

fairness, questions around 30–1
false asylum claims 55–6
family reunion 60, 214
financial issues
'affording' refugees 32
charging for services 90
poverty 90
see also money
food banks 152, 153, 221
fostering, private 211
free school meals 221
Freedom of Information request 123
fresh asylum claim 49–50

gifts 92
GP, registering with 158–9, 161–2
grants 149
Grass Roots English Groups ('GREG')
    111–3
gratitude, no need for 22–3
group dynamics 101–2

HC2 card 159
health
asylum seekers 160
categories of care 163–4
children's services 221, 223–4
entitlements/access to care 58, 60,
    158–64
interpreting at appointments 162
Leave to Remain 160
NRPF 160
overview of situation 155–7
physical impact of past experiences
    156–7
pregnancy/birth 164
process on arrival in UK 158–9
refused asylum seekers 160
registering with GP 158–9, 161–2
see also mental health care
Healthwatch (statutory body) 161
HEAR 172, 173
hearing impairment 174
Home Office number 46
homelessness 137
Human Rights Act (1998) 54, 69

IELTS (International English Language
    Testing System) 187
immigration bail 58
immigration status
    Leave to Remain 51–4, 59–61, 140–1,
        218
    NRPF 59, 136
    refused asylum seekers 49–51, 59
    see also asylum seekers
indirect discrimination 71–2
interpreters 109–10, 162
Iran 209
Iraq 209
IT, access to 90

Joseph Rowntree Foundation (JRF) 146

language
    politics of 55
    see also definitions of refugee; English
        (learning)
learning see education; English (learning)
Leave to Remain 51–4, 59–61, 140–1, 218
Legal Aid 48
letters of support 121
licensed solicitors 47–8
location/venue of meetings 94

mental health care
    access to 163
    children 224–5
    entitlements to 166
    NHS services 166–8
    overview of issues 164–6
micro-aggressions 70
migration 32, 36–8
mobile phones 90
money
    Aspen cards 147
    bank accounts 147
    cash contributions 148–9
    debt 145–6
    entitlements 146, 148
    grants 149
    NASS rate (children and babies) 221–2
    overview of situation 144–6
motivation to engage 88–9

Nayeri, D. 23
NARIC (National Academic Recognition
        Information Centre) 191
National Insurance (NI) number 147
needs, hierarchy of 88
networking
    by refugees 92–3
    community organisations 118
    importance of 115–7
    local authority 118
    specialists 118–9
NHS number 158
Nigeria 209
non-formal learning 182–5, 232–4
notice to depart 50–1

'off the radar' asylum seekers 50–1
OISC licence 48
'One plus One' principle 120
online English courses 188
ordinary people, refugees are 21–3
organisations, effects of refugees on 18–9

Pakistan 209
passports/travel documents 53, 60, 98, 186
people smugglers 56
people traffickers 56
permanent leave 53
persecution 57
personal safety 99
phones, mobile 90
policy
    constant changes to 241–2
    influencing 124–6
positive action 75–6
post-prison deportation 56
pre-assessment screenings 171
pregnancy/birth 164
private fostering 211
private landlords 141
professional bodies, joining 195
protected characteristics 67–9
public authorities (definition) 77
Public Sector Equality Duty (PSED) 77–80,
        126–7
publicity/events 95–7

qualifications (English language) 187–8

REAP 111, 33
reasonable adjustments 74–5
references 121, 138, 194
referral 119–20
refuge, components of 236–9
Refugee Council 134, 136, 193, 210, 214,
    29, 32, 49, 52
refugees
    experiences before reaching UK 34–6
    see also definitions of refugee
refused asylum seekers 49–51, 59
regulators, public 123–4
relationships
    initiating 95–7
    longer-term 100–3
    trust in 87
reporting 46
requalification schemes 194–5
resources
    access to 152–3
    see also money
respect 238
reuniting families 60, 214

safeguarding
    children 210–2
    procedures 99
safety
    personal 99
    refuge as 236
satire/comedy 129
school
    free school meals 221
    support from 222
    see also education
self-employment
    issues around 203
    schemes to help with 195–6
SELT (Secure English Language Test) 187

single-sex groups 182–3
smugglers, people 56
solicitors, licensed 47–8
Somalia 209
Sri Lanka 209
statistical data 32, 214–6
status, Convention 51–2, 60
Sudan 209
Syria 210

temporary leave 52–3
timing of meetings 94
TOEFL (Test of English as a Foreign
    Language) 187
traffickers 56
training 179, 180–1, 232
    see also education
travel
    for disabled people 172
    rights 60

Uganda 210
unaccompanied children 213–4, 217, 218,
    222–3
uniqueness of each refugee 24, 89

venue/location of meetings 94
Vietnam 210
visibility, increase in 17–8
volunteering 196–9

wellbeing (in Care Act 2014) 170
women, as 'particular social group' 67
women's refuges 138
WRC/REAP 120

youth groups 232–3